THE RESTORED CHURCH

The Prophet Joseph Smith

The
RESTORED
CHURCH

By WILLIAM E. BERRETT

A Brief History of the Growth and Doctrines of
The Church of Jesus Christ of Latter-day Saints

Fifteenth Edition
Published by
DESERET BOOK COMPANY
1973

Tenth Edition, Revised and Enlarged
1961

Fourteenth Edition — 1969

Fifteenth Edition, Revised and Enlarged

1973

Lithographed by

DESERET PRESS

in the United States of America

ACKNOWLEDGMENTS

This brief history of the Church was first written in a shorter form in 1936 as a text to be used in the Seminaries and schools of the Church.

In 1944 the original book was combined with materials from another book, *Doctrines of the Restored Church*, by the same author. With various corrections and additions it has been published in nine different editions.

This edition is a drastic change from previous editions, the work being enlarged and enhanced with many illustrations and other materials.

The entire manuscript, both in the original and revised forms, has been carefully read and approved by the Church Reading Committee. Appreciation is herein expressed for their many helpful suggestions. Special appreciation must be expressed for the help of the late members of the Quorum of the Twelve, Joseph Fielding Smith, Charles A. Callis and Joseph F. Merrill who carefully read the first four editions, some years ago, and gave numerous helpful criticisms. Appreciation is extended to the many individuals who have contributed to this new edition.

Table of Contents

Unit I

CHRIST RE-ESTABLISHES HIS CHURCH UPON THE EARTH

Unit II

THE GOSPEL OF JESUS CHRIST LEADS MEN TO CONQUER THE GREAT AMERICAN DESERT

INTRODUCTION

Nineteen centuries ago John the Baptist called upon the Jews who had gathered about him on the banks of the Jordan River in Palestine to "repent" for the Kingdom of God was at hand. The Kingdom was indeed at their very doors, for the Son of God was coming with authority to accept into His Kingdom all who would prepare their hearts for that entrance. To those who had faith in God, and sought to enter into the Kingdom, John announced:

"I indeed baptize you with water unto repentance: but he that cometh after me is mightier than I, * * * he shall baptize you with the Holy Ghost and with fire."[1]

So Jesus when He came established the Kingdom of God upon the earth, that all who would, might enter and partake of the Spirit of God with Him. To officiate in the Kingdom upon the earth Jesus ordained twelve men as Apostles and gave them power and authority to preach the gospel and administer in all of its ordinances. They were instructed to carry the Gospel first of all to the children of Israel. Later Christ chose Seventy and commissioned them likewise to preach the Gospel unto the people.

After the death and resurrection of the Savior this nucleus of Church officers, acting according to the Authority which they possessed, perfected the organization. The vacancy in the quorum of the Twelve Apostles, caused by the death of Judas Iscariot, was filled by the calling and ordination of one Matthias to that office. The offices of priest, teacher, deacon, evangelist, and bishop were added.

Of the people living in western Asia and in Europe at that day the Israelites alone were prepared by training and tradition for the high standard of religion set forth by Christ. The moral laws of the Hebrews and the teachings of their Prophets should have prepared that people for the Gospel of Jesus Christ. So it was that the Savior commanded His disciples to carry the Gospel first to the House of Israel, and then to the Gentiles. By the Gentiles here we refer to those "heathens" or "pagans" who had never accepted, or perhaps heard of, the God of Abraham, Isaac, and Jacob, but were believers in gods of nature to whom they built graven images and offered sacrifices.

A church can, after all, be no better than its people, and the immorality and licentiousness of the heathen peoples of that day were notorious. Those Jews who, with their background of Hebrew training and history, accepted the teachings of the Master, became genuine followers of Him and were indeed worthy of membership in His Kingdom. But because the Jews as a nation had also drifted into immoral practices and had become subjected to a rigid priestly interpretation of their religious laws, the nation as a whole rejected the Gospel of Jesus Christ.

It was with great disappointment that Jesus perceived the hardheartedness of His own people. One gets a glimpse into His great soul as, pausing with His disciples on the brow of the Mount of Olives on one occasion, and gazing upon His beloved City of Jerusalem below them, He burst into tears, exclaiming,

"Jerusalem, Jerusalem, * * * how often would I have gathered thy children together, even as a hen gathereth her chickens under her wings, and ye would not!"[2]

---

[1]*Matthew* 3:11.

[2]*Matthew* 23:37.

As it became apparent to the Savior that the Gospel would be rejected by those who should have been, by tradition and training, prepared for it, and must be taken to the heathen who were not prepared for its high moral requirements, He warned His few faithful followers of what the result would be:

"And then shall many be offended, and shall betray one another, and shall hate one another. And many false prophets shall arise, and shall deceive many. And because iniquity shall abound, the love of many shall wax cold. But he that shall endure unto the end, the same shall be saved."[3]

Speaking of the period of apostasy and persecution which was to come the Savior added:

"Then shall they deliver you up to be afflicted, and shall kill you: and ye shall be hated of all nations for my name's sake."[4]

"Then if any man shall say unto you, Lo, here is Christ, or there, believe it not. For there shall arise false Christs, and false prophets, and shall shew great signs and wonders; insomuch that if it were possible, they shall deceive the very elect. Behold, I have told you before. Wherefore, if they shall say unto you, Behold, he is in the desert; go not forth; behold, he is in the secret chambers; believe it not."[5]

The World into Which the Gospel Was Taken

It could hardly be hoped that the Gospel would survive in purity among the heathen peoples of the Mediterranean world of that day. For the church can be no better than its members and the people of the Mediterranean world had at that day sunk into the depths of wickedness. This is evident from any extended study of the social conditions of the times. The heathen gods worshipped by these peoples were, with rare exceptions, reputedly immoral, given to excesses and indulgences; full of jealousy; motivated often by hate and seldom by love.

In the great Greek and Roman cities sex relationships had reached a stage of license where marriage became a temporary convenience and immorality a virtue. Indeed, on certain festive occasions immoral relations were demanded as a part of public worship. Even the Jews had been affected by the lax conditions prevailing in the Greek and Roman world and all sorts of fictions were devised to avoid the more rigid Jewish laws of marriage and divorce.

It was into this maelstrom of licentiousness that the intrepid Apostle Paul and others carried the Gospel of Jesus Christ, determined to save sinking humanity. The fire and enthusiasm of these great Hebrew leaders, together with the manifestations of the power and authority they possessed caused the Gospel to spread like a conflagration throughout the Mediterranean world whose mystic religions were on the verge of dissolution and decay. But while multitudes of the Greeks and, later, of the Romans were baptized members of the Church of Christ, they did not always change their manner of living or follow the high standard set by the Master. Some did so, and of these Justin Martyr, who lived in the second century, said:

"We, who were once slaves of lust, now have delight only in purity of morals; we, who once practiced arts of magic, have consecrated ourselves to the Eternal and Good God; we, who once prized gain above all things, give even what we have to the common use, and share it with such as are in need; we, who once hated and murdered one another, who on account of differences of customs would have no common hearth with strangers, do now, since the appearance of Christ, live together with them; we pray for our enemies; we seek to convince those that hate us without cause, so that they may

[3]*Matthew* 24:10-13.
[4]*Matthew* 24:9.
[5]*Matthew* 24:23-26.

order their lives according to Christ's glorious doctrine and attain to the joyful hope of receiving like blessings with us from God, the Lord of all."[6]

The immoralities which the majority of the newly-baptized members continued, despite their membership in the church, caused Paul great concern. With almost superhuman effort he combatted by letter and by his visits these evils which were destroying the spirit of the Church. Repeatedly, he admonished the churches for their immoralities. An example of this is shown in his first letter to the Saints at Corinth:

"It is reported commonly that there is fornication among you, and such fornication as is not so much as named among the Gentiles." * * *
"And ye are puffed up, and have not rather mourned, that he that hath done this deed might be taken away from among you."[7]

Paul was aware that the continued existence of the Church depended upon the members so living that the Holy Ghost would be their companion and comforter. Unless they lived lives of purity the blessings of the Holy Ghost could not be had. Without the Holy Ghost there could not be that burning testimony of the Christ which Paul himself possessed and the possession of which caused men to devote their lives to God's Kingdom. He warned the Corinthian Saints: "No man can say that Jesus is the Lord but by the Holy Ghost."[8]

Peter likewise admonished the Saints to live lives of righteousness that they might receive the Holy Ghost as an instructor in the study of the Scriptures, "Knowing this first, that no prophecy of the scripture is of any private interpretation. For the prophecy came not in old time by the will of man: but holy men of God spake as they were moved by the Holy Ghost."[9]

With the branches of the Church so widely scattered and with little written scriptures other than the Jewish Testament, the Church could not be kept in unity without the guidance of the Spirit. Especially was this true in the face of Greek philosophies which were strongly entrenched in the minds of converts to Christianity.

Dr. Philip Smith says of the period:

"The sad truth is that as soon as Christianity was generally diffused, it began to absorb corruption from all the lands in which it was planted, and to reflect the complexion of all their systems of religion and philosophy."[10]

Paul Anticipates Apostasy

Even while Paul lived some of the churches he had established in Asia Minor turned from his leadership and the doctrines of the Church.

Paul predicted that an apostasy from the true Gospel would certainly occur. In speaking for the last time to the Saints of Ephesus he said:

"For I know this, that after my departing shall grievous wolves enter in among you, not sparing the flock. Also of your own selves shall men arise, speaking perverse things, to draw away disciples after them."[11]

Again, in a letter written from Laodicea to his beloved follower, Timothy, he said:

"Now the Spirit speaketh expressly, that in the latter times some shall depart from the faith, giving heed to seducing spirits, and doctrines of devils; speaking lies in hypocrisy; having their conscience seared with a hot iron; forbidding to marry, and commanding to abstain from meats, which God hath created to be received with thanksgiving of them which believe and know the truth."[12]

[6]Neander, *Church History*, Volume 1, p. 250.
[7]*I Corinthians*, 5:1-2.
[8]*I Corinthians* 12:3.
[9]*II Peter* 1:20-21.
[10]Philip Smith, *Students' Ecclesiastical History*, Volume 1, p. 49.
[11]*Acts* 20:29-30.
[12]*I Timothy* 4:1-3.

In a later letter he added:

"For the time will come when they will not endure sound doctrine; but after their own lusts shall they reap to themselves teachers, having itching ears; and they shall turn away their ears from the truth, and shall be turned unto fables."[13]

It was the leadership of great Jews, men like Peter, James, John, and Paul, who, during the first century, by sheer weight of personality, and the fervor of their testimony, held the churches in some semblance of order. When these great Jewish leaders were silenced by death there were none to replace them. The Jewish nation had rejected the Gospel, and the Greek and Roman converts though often exceedingly brilliant and capable, nevertheless lacked the fundamental foundations in tradition and training to comprehend the spiritual Kingdom established by Jesus Christ.

Immorality crept into all sections of the Church until the historian who lived in that period wrote:

"By reason of excessive liberty, we sunk into negligence and sloth, one envying and reviling another in different ways, and we were almost, as it were, upon the point of taking up arms against each other with words as with darts and spears, prelates inveighing against prelates, and people rising up against people; * * * some indeed like atheists, regarding our situation as unheeded and unobserved by a Providence; we added one wickedness and misery to another. But some that appeared to be our pastors deserting the law of piety, were inflamed against each other with mutual strifes, only accumulating quarrels and threats, rivalships, hostility and hatred to each other, only anxious to assert the government as a kind of sovereignty for themselves."[14]

Changes Made in the Ordinances

Under those conditions of unrighteousness the Holy Ghost could not oper-ate, and men were left to quarrel over private interpretations of the scriptures and doctrines.

Further, the gifts of the Holy Ghost, so evident in the period of the Apostles, ceased to be manifest. As the gospel continued to spread among the heathen people it began to partake more and more of the nature of heathen practices. In the Institutes of Mosheim we read:

"Many rites were added, without necessity, to both public and private religious worship, to the great offense of good men; and principally because of the perversity of mankind who are more delighted with the pomp and splendor of external forms and pageantry than with the true devotion of the heart. There is good reason to believe that the Christian bishops purposely multiplied sacred rites for the sake of rendering the Jews and pagans more friendly to them. For both these classes had always been accustomed to numerous and splendid ceremonies, and believed them an essential part of religion. * * * To add further to the dignity of the Christian religion, the churches of the east feigned mysteries similar to those of the pagan religions; and, as with the pagans, the holy rites of the mysteries were concealed from the vulgar: 'And they not only applied the terms used in pagan mysteries to the Christian institution, particularly baptism and the Lord's supper, but they gradually introduced also the rites which were designated by those terms.' "[15]

It must not be supposed that all of these changes in ordinances and doctrines came about in a short period of time. Several generations were involved in some of these changes. Nor did the changes occur uniformly throughout Christendom. Rather, until the fourth century, there existed widely divergent practices in the ordinances of the Church, often two forms of baptism, for example, being allowed in the same church.

Persecutions and Their Effects

During this period of the Church

---

[13]II Timothy 4:3-4. See also II Thess. 2:1-12; II Peter 2:1-3; Jude 17, 18.
[14]Eusebius, Ecclesiastical History, Book VIII, Chapter 1.

[15]Institutes, Volume 1, Century II, Chapter IV.

there were frequent persecutions which brought about the death of the Christian leaders and thereby weakened the resistance to pagan philosophies. The earliest persecutions were by the Jews who had rejected the Gospel. To them Christianity was a Jewish Heresy whose very success seemed to strike at the foundation of Judaism. In 64 A.D. the Roman Government under Nero took cognizance of the growing Christian Church and commenced a bitter persecution against the sect. Later persecutions also occurred at intervals until the time of Constantine, who professed Christianity and constituted it a State Religion. These persecutions were caused by two things:

"They dared to ridicule the absurdities of the pagan superstition, and they were ardent and assiduous in gaining proselytes to the truth. Nor did they only attack the religion of Rome, but also all the different shapes and forms under which superstition appeared in their ministry. From this the Romans concluded, that the Christian sect was not only insupportably daring and arrogant, but, moreover, an enemy to the public tranquility, and every way proper to excite civil wars and commotions in the empire. It is probably on this account that Tacitus reproaches them with the odious character of 'haters of mankind,' and styles the religion of Jesus as 'destructive superstition'; and that Suetonius speaks of the Christians, and their doctrine in terms of the same kind."[16]

However, while the persecutions drove a number from the Church, they did not seriously retard its growth, and may in fact have contributed to it. It was rather the internal weakness which caused a departure from the Gospel of Jesus Christ.

Summary of Changes

It is not our purpose here to follow through, step by step, the growth of paganism in the rituals and ordinances of the Church, and the loss of priesthood which occurred. Reliable historians have done so with considerable skill. Nor can we here delve into the problem of determining when the apostasy was complete. Suffice it to say, when we glimpse Christianity several hundred years after the Christian era began we see few of the original ordinances established by Christ. The gifts of the Holy Ghost are no longer manifest and the organization of the Church is changed.

Of this change, the first editor of Gibbon's famous work on the fall of the Roman Empire, Henry Hart Milman, writes:

"If, after all, the view of the early progress of Christianity be melancholy and humilating, we must beware lest we charge the whole of this on the infidelity of the historian. It is idle, it is disingenuous to deny or to dissemble the early deprivations of Christianity, its gradual but rapid departure from its primitive simplicity and purity, still more from its spirit of universal love. It may be no unsalutary lesson to the Christian world, that this silent, this unavoidable perhaps, *yet fatal change* shall have been drawn by an impartial, or even an hostile hand."[17]

The changes which had occurred in the Christian Church might be summarized briefly as follows:

First, the ordinance of baptism, originally performed by immersion of the candidate beneath the waters[18] was changed to the sprinkling of holy water by the priest upon the head of the convert. A multitude of added ceremonies also changed its original simplicity. Baptism of infants also commenced.[19]

Second, the ordinance of the sacrament of the Lord's supper was changed.

---

[16]Mosheim, *Ecclesiastical History*, Century I, Part I, Chapter 5:6-7.

[17]Gibbon, *The History of the Decline and Fall of the Roman Empire* (1845 edition), Vol. 1, Preface by Dean Milman [Henry Hart Milman], p. 15.

[18]See *Matthew* 3:13-17; *Acts* 8:26-39. Talmage, *The Great Apostasy*, note pp. 93-95. Talmage, *Articles of Faith*, Chapter 6, pp. 123-134; Chapter 7.

[19]Talmage, *Articles of Faith*, Chapter 6. Milner, *Church History*, Century III, Chapter 13.

The original simplicity of partaking of the bread and wine in remembrance of the Savior gave way to an elaborate ceremony of pomp and mystery. The doctrine of *Transubstantiation* became an essential doctrine of the Roman Church. This doctrine is to the effect that the bread and the wine used in the sacrament lose their character as bread and wine and become literally the flesh and blood of the crucified Christ. The change is assumed to occur mysteriously in a way beyond the power of mortals to perceive. These consecrated emblems then came to be worshiped of themselves and led to a pernicious practice of idolatry.

The celebration of the "Mass," as the ordinance came to be called, was conducted at greater and greater intervals. Later the custom of administering only the bread was introduced, the assertion being that in some mystical way both the body and blood were present in the one emblem.[20]

Third, unauthorized changes occurred in Church organization and government. The officers found in the Primitive Church, namely, apostles, pastors, high priests, seventies, elders, bishops, priests, teachers, and deacons, had largely disappeared. Further, the general membership of the Church was not permitted to hold the priesthood but a special class known as the "clergy" segregated themselves from the common people and professed to hold the authority of the priesthood.

The office of "bishop" had been retained, but unlike the order that prevailed in the Primitive Church the bishops were not considered of equal rank. The Bishop at Rome, under the protection and sanction of the Roman Government, had assumed jurisdiction over all other bishops, and had acquired the name of Pope, or "Papa Bishop." Mosheim says that the popes "carried their insolent pretentions so far as to give themselves out for lords of the universe, arbiters of the fate of kingdoms and empires, and supreme rulers over the kings and princes of the earth."[21]

Fourth, the gifts of the Holy Ghost were no longer evident in the Church. Indeed, it was declared that these gifts had been given during the period of the Apostles for the purpose of aiding in the establishing of the Church and that after that establishment the gifts were withdrawn from the earth as being no longer necessary. Hence revelation, prophecy, the gift of tongues, and the interpretation of tongues, healings, the gift of discernment, etc., had wholly disappeared from the Church.

Fifth, the Church had assumed the right to punish those who had broken Church rules by giving them civil penalties. Further, the Church assumed the power to forgive men their sins upon evidence of repentance. This led to the shocking practice of selling *indulgences,* or pardons for money, which was one of the outstanding causes of the later rebellion of Martin Luther against the Church.[22]

Growth of Christian Ideals

But the Gospel of Jesus Christ was not defeated nor was the mission of the Savior to mankind a failure. Christ came at a period when the spiritual life of the world was at low ebb. Immorality, selfishness, hatred, love of money,

---

[20]See Talmage, *The Great Apostasy*, pp. 94-95. Roberts, *Outlines of Ecclesiastical History*, p. 133.

[21]Mosheim, *Ecclesiastical History*, Century XI, Part II, Chapter 2:2.
[22]See Talmage, *The Great Apostasy*, p. 105. For an account of the terrible condition into which the Papacy sank, see Talmage, *The Great Apostasy*, pp. 105-108.

cruelty, and slavery abounded. Into this sick soil He planted the seeds of the gospel, not with the idea that the whole world would immediately become righteous, but with the assurance that, like the leaven kneaded into the bread, a little leaven would enlighten the whole lump and eventually produce a better world in which to live.   To His Apostles he said:

"The kingdom of heaven is like unto leaven, which a woman took, and hid in three measures of meal, till the whole was leavened."[23]

While the priesthood of Christ disappeared among men and the Church ordinances and doctrines became corrupted, the leaven of the gospel survived through the Bible, which was preserved in the monasteries and convents during those trying times.   The example which Christ set in his life and the beauty of His teachings continued to touch the hearts of many people and to change their lives for good. Gradually mankind was being prepared for the restoration of the Gospel in its fulness.

The effects of that leaven upon mankind is evident throughout the centuries of Christian history and attest the great love of God for all mankind and His hope that they would prepare for the great restoration of His Kingdom. When one reads many of the dark pages of Christian history one wonders if the leaven of Christ's words has not been wholly lost. For many individuals that was true, and at times the spirit of the Master was at low ebb among all peoples. Gradually, however, the leaven of righteousness began its work.

In order to understand the victory of Jesus Christ over the dark forces of sin and despair it is necessary to keep in mind the condition of the world into which Jesus came. The Jewish Historian, Josephus, says of the Jews who lived in Jerusalem shortly after the death of Jesus "that a more wicked generation of men" had not been upon the earth since the days of Noah.[24]

In the great Greek city of Athens, at the time of Christ, three-fifths of the population were slaves and a similar condition existed over the Mediterranean world.   Individuals convicted of crime were executed in the most brutal fashion, often being hung on crosses along public roads and in the market places as examples to others. Fear was the chief restraining influence upon men. In parts of the Roman Empire the sick and aged were left upon mountain sides to perish. Starvation of the poor was commonplace. The natural affections for blood kin seemed woefully lacking. Brothers murdered brothers for gain; wives poisoned their husbands, and husbands destroyed their wives. Even the great Constantine ordered his wife and one of his sons killed, without arousing much comment among a people depraved by sin.

There were, during this period, many righteous people, but they were comparatively few in number and their very righteousness had become a reproach to them. The Greek writer, Xenophanes, in depicting in one of his novels his ideal man, said of him:

"No man ever did more good to his friends or more harm to his enemies."

It was a long step from this time of hatred to the high ideal of manhood portrayed by Tennyson in his character of King Arthur, who does not become the perfect knight until, realizing his Queen Guinevere has deeply wronged him, he generously forgives her. It was

---

[23]*Matthew* 13:33.

[24]*The Genuine Works of Flavius Josephus*, seven books on the Jewish War.

likewise a long step from the sick and aged dying on the mountains of Greece to the modern program of civilized nations for the social security of the sick and aged. It is likewise a long step from the time when victims of Roman Justice were writhing upon the Cross in the sight of women and children, to the modern view of some criminologists that the criminal is spiritually and socially maladjusted and must be treated sympathetically and understandingly.

It was a slow process of development for the masses of mankind. Its success is first manifest in the great reformations which began in the 14th century— a great desire to receive and understand more of the Gospel — which moved individuals like John Wycliffe, Martin Luther, John Calvin, John Knox, and others, to rebel against restrictions on the Gospel. While immorality has continued in many quarters during all the Christian ages, the exponents of righteousness have become more and more numerous. The little leaven has at least leavened a portion of mankind.

During the ages of Christian history priesthood disappeared from the earth. It could neither function nor be perpetuated in unrighteousness. The best evidence of its absence is the total lack of those gifts which have accompanied priesthood in all ages of the world.

Revelation, prophecy, speaking in tongues, healings, and other gifts of the Holy Ghost were not found among men. Without the Holy Ghost to guide men in the reading of scripture, diverse opinions and interpretations sprang up. Following the rebellion of Martin Luther against the Catholic Church, sects sprang up on every hand until they numbered more than four hundred. All of these professed to have the true understanding of the Gospel and assumed power and authority to officiate in the ordinances of the Master. The Christian world became a world of confusion.

Nevertheless, beneath this confusion were many fine Christian virtues. Men as a group were conforming more and more to those qualities exemplified by the Master. It was a long period of preparation, but the time came when God had fully prepared the way for His authority to be again established upon the earth and for the Gospel to be taught again in its fulness. The words of John the Revelator were ready to be fulfilled.

"And I saw another angel fly in the midst of heaven, having the everlasting gospel to preach unto them that dwell on the earth, and to every nation, and kindred, and tongue, and people."[25]

---

[25]*Revelation* 14:6.

PREVIEW OF UNIT I

CHRIST RE-ESTABLISHES HIS CHURCH UPON THE EARTH

In this division of the book we shall witness the restoration of the Gospel of Jesus Christ to the earth, the organization of his Church, and the unfolding of the great plan of salvation unto God's children.

This period of restoration is contemporaneous with the life of Joseph Smith, the Prophet, an instrument in the hands of the Lord in the accomplishment of His great purposes.

In a reading of these chapters we shall see Joseph Smith as a great man, and witness the growth of personality which was necessary to that greatness.

We shall witness prayer, revelation, and priesthood at work as vital realities. We will follow the Church from its organization in Fayette, New York, to the city of Nauvoo, a city beloved of the Prophet and his people. We will get a brief insight into the origin and importance of the *Book of Mormon* and witness its effect upon the lives of men. Above all we will come to understand that the Church is of God and not of men and that the principles on which it is founded are eternal truths.

THE RESTORED CHURCH

CHAPTER 1

A VITAL FAITH

A Visit to a Remarkable City

In the early summer of 1843 an English traveler stepped from the gang plank of a Mississippi River steame and set foot for the first time in America's most remarkable city. It was not the largest city in America, nor the oldest, but from the moment he had come within sight of it he had been amazed.

The very first view had been a pleasant surprise. The river vessel fighting its way north through the mighty Father of Waters had rounded a bend and brought into full view a magnificent city which had until that moment been entirely hidden. Situated on the east bank the river swept round it on three sides and from the water's edge the land rose gently toward a central eminence a mile or so away. The whole was covered with human habitations interspersed with trees and gardens.

The noted traveler, deeply moved, had involuntarily breathed its very name—"The City Beautiful." Could he have but known that three years earlier the region lay almost wholly empty of human life, relatively worthless, a mosquito-infested swamp—that Nauvoo, "The City Beautiful," was then but a fertile dream in the mind of a penniless and persecuted man — he would have marveled indeed at the dream so quickly come true.

Now as he stood firmly upon the new soil, with the fresh river breeze rustling the tails of his long coat, and the scent of roses beckoning him on, it seemed as if he stood in a new world, a haven of peace and happiness.

Before him a street, eight rods in width, ran straight as an arrow into the heart of the city, paralleled and intersected at regular intervals by other streets equally wide and equally straight. A simple thing this matter of streets—and yet in all his wanderings on two continents nothing of this kind had been encountered. The streets of Boston, New York, and Philadelphia were notoriously haphazard, narrow and crooked. Further, these streets were clean—free from the refuse which found its way at that time even into the thoroughfares of great cities.

Rows of small trees, apparently well cared for, lined the avenues, the bright green of the new leaves reflecting the vigor of the inhabitants. Upon either side of these wide roadways beautiful houses, newly erected, adorned the landscape. Built largely of stone or brick, of a type commonly found at that date in the better residential districts of the Atlantic seaboard, they seemed strange indeed on this western fringe of civilization. Two-story buildings of the colonial type predominated. Set well back from the street, in an even row, and fronted by well kept lawns and flower beds, they bespoke volumes in industry and civic pride.

Artist's sketch of Nauvoo, looking across the Mississippi River from the Iowa side, as it appeared in the days of the Prophet Joseph Smith.   Used by permission, Utah State Historical Society

As the stranger wandered idly from street to street, oblivious to time, his amazement deepened. The industrial and manufacturing centers, the stores and shops, the public buildings, and the residences of the people appeared to be in separate areas or zones designated for that particular use, and the sophisticated[1] traveler who had slept in the best hotels of the great cities of the world, with the sound of factory wheels in his ear, and the odors of the markets in his nostrils, furrowed his brow in thought.

What a strange thing in an intemperate world! There were no saloons. A city of twenty thousand inhabitants and no dispensers of liquor — and no drunkenness. One might search the

proud annals of history in vain for such a parallel.

And strangest of all, the jail was empty, its strong iron doors flung open, their hinges already rusty from disuse. Boston, New York and Philadelphia constructing new jails, bigger jails, their old ones filled to overflowing— and the city of Nauvoo, on the borders of civilization, without a single condemned man!

Small wonder that the eyes of the traveler fixed themselves time and again on the great imposing structure rearing its unfinished head against the sky, at the corner of Mulholland and Wells Streets, and felt that the grey stone walls, nearly white in the fading sunlight, were a monument to a new social order.

[1]Sophisticated—knowing or worldly-wise.

A million dollar structure at the edge of a wilderness—a structure so imposing that it might have caused the proud inhabitants of famed cities a sense of pardonable pride. A structure the like of which no state west of the Allegheny Mountains could boast. From its top the traveler might have gazed far to the West across the mighty Father of Waters into the unsettled domain of the savage and the voyageur,[2] or to the east over miles of regular and well-tilled fields. Or one might ponder over the city lying at one's feet, embracing features in city building nearly a century before their time—a city thrice the size of Chicago of that day—a city embracing the largest center of industry and manufacture in the West—a city of so remarkable fame that men were crossing half a continent merely to visit and to marvel.

And this city was but three years old. As late as the close of 1839 the site had been considered unhealthy and relatively of little value, so that even its founder wrote in his journal, ". . . the place was literally a wilderness. The land was mostly covered with trees and bushes, and much of it was so wet that it was with the utmost difficulty that a footman could get through, and totally impossible for teams. Commerce [as the place was then called] was so unhealthful very few could live there; but believing that it might become a healthful place by the blessing of heaven to the Saints, and no more eligible place presenting itself, I considered it wisdom to make an attempt to build up a city."[3]

As the traveler approached the great grey structure, which he had observed so frequently from a distance, he read on its massive doors these words, "Holi-

ness to the Lord." The Temple of Solomon had once been a Mecca for a whole nation. What more fitting than a new shrine in this marvelous metropolis?

A Remarkable People

What people had transformed this bog into a paradise? From what races and creeds and cities had they come?

In traversing the city the visitor had encountered many people and had conversed with a few. Although largely of New England stock, many were from his own native England, some from Canada, a few from nearly every state of the Union. The faces of the men were strong faces, and the eyes which met his so frankly were keen and intelligent. The majority appeared to be in the full flush of their manhood, with few of the old among them. Their dress was ordinarily plain, typical of the farm rather than the city. Their greetings were open and cordial; all were addressed as "Brother" or "Sister." All were full of optimism and good will. They seemed indeed a people buoyed up with a new hope.

Clearly, here was a new brotherhood of man; a new way of behavior; a new social order.

No idlers sat upon the street corners, no beggars had accosted him for alms, no loud profane voices had attracted his attention. Yet the city was full of people, each going about his task with cheerful countenance, each busy, each apparently happy.

In all the city he had not encountered a policeman, and yet the dwellings seemed unfitted with locks, and the stores and warehouses were ordinarily unbarred. There seemed indeed to be an innate trust in one's neighbor, an

---

[2]Voyageur—Any boatsman or trapper of those regions.

[3]*History of the Church*, Period I, Vol. III, p. 375.

innate good fellowship, which seemed to say, "There can be no theft, for all that I have is thine."

Groups of children too young for labor in the fields or in the stores and factories, played along the streets or on the lawns, happy, boisterous, and full already of a certain confidence of their elders.

From open windows came broken snatches of song, as the busy housewives plied their several tasks, and as the day waned, savory odors occasionally found the outside air.

The power of unity—the strength of cooperation—the energy of hope—were everywhere present. Farmer, carpenter, mason, musician, artisans of a dozen sorts, all found a happy niche in the new society.

And these were largely the people who, three years before, had huddled, cold and miserable, and utterly poor, in their tents and dugouts on the banks of the Mississippi River. Driven from their Missouri homes in the dead of winter, their property lost or confiscated,[4] a prey to famine and disease, their leaders imprisoned.

What loyalty had held them together? What zeal had driven them on? What motives had guided them? What hopes and understandings were at the base of their abounding optimism?

Here, with the land scarcely cleared, a people were erecting a Temple to their God. Here, with the terrific struggle for bread about them, a people were establishing a University for higher learning. A city so new that geographers had failed to notice it, possessing a Legion of Soldiers, one of the finest trained militias in America.

---

[4]Confiscated—To seize, without due process of law.

The visitor seated on the steps of the great Temple, from which all the workmen had departed, arose and looked once more over the remarkable city with its remarkable inhabitants, and felt an inner thrill such as he had never known before.

A Remarkable Man

Traversing the city in a southerly direction along Durphey Street for nearly a mile, the visitor came to Water Street. Turning west on Water Street for a distance of three blocks, he came to the newly erected Nauvoo Mansion. Here, he had been informed, lodging might be had. He was now in the extreme southern part of Nauvoo, some two miles from the spot where he had entered the city earlier in the day.

The two-story frame building before him bore a double interest. It was already noted on the upper Mississippi for its fine accommodations and its good foods. It was also the home of the city's founder, the leader of this unusual people. The building, in the shape of the letter L, stood well back from the street, facing Main Street on the west and Water Street on the south. A white picket fence enclosed the grounds. When our traveler entered the door of the inn he found himself in a sort of waiting room, or what in other cities might have been termed a bar-room. This room was for the time-being deserted, the individual who had admitted him having gone to announce his presence.

Through an open doorway the visitor could see a group of people seated about a long table, evidently for the evening meal. From the brief glimpse he perceived them somewhat shabbily dressed and rather oddly out of place in a frontier tavern. They were, as he was later to learn, immigrants from his own native England, converts to this vital faith, who had crossed an ocean and half a continent in the firm belief that this man, whom he was out of curiosity about to meet, was a Prophet of the Living God.

What expectations our visitor may have had as to the appearance of the Latter-day Prophet we do not know. Suffice it to say that if he expected the type of Prophet depicted by the artist as associated with Bible times, severe of countenance, pale, emaciated, given to fiery denunciations and dark prophecies, he was to be greatly disappointed.

The man now introduced to him as Joseph Smith was tall in stature and splendidly proportioned. His whole being radiated strength and energy. But it was the eyes which instantly captivated the observer and held him with an intentness which rather prevented closer scrutiny of his person. Those eyes were blue, with a rare clearness. The glance from them was easily capable of reading the human heart or gazing into the secrets of eternity. His face was without a beard, smooth shaven, with an unusually clear complexion. The lips were thin and firm, his nose Roman in type.

From his rather prominent eyes a high forehead sloped back to wavy brown hair. The whole countenance was mild, affable, friendly; a face in which intelligence and kindness were admirably blended. A woman might have described him as "handsome;" a man, as "striking."

His cordial greeting carried with it a feeling of genuineness, a rare magnetism which emanates from great personalities, and draws people to them.

Here was the man to whom thirty thousand people turned for leadership, believing him to have seen visions and to have received the word of God. Here was the man whose literary works alone would fill many volumes, who had published a book which had become a center of world controversy, whose name was already known for good or evil in many lands. Here was the man who, without opportunity for scholastic training, had challenged the world of astronomy, astonished the archaeologist and the historian, and threatened the economic foundations of a nation. Here was America's foremost religious pioneer—the advocate of a new way of life—a vital faith.

Not that this man was without faults. The Englishman, during the weeks which were to follow, would find many of them. But they were the faults of the man—not of his teachings. The vitality of this new movement, in which he had played such a vital part, was bigger than men, greater than books, stronger than governments. That this man was to go to a martyr's death at the early age of thirty-eight may not in itself be important to the world. But that there is in the world a faith so vital that men and women are willing to devote their lives to it, to die if necessary for it, is quite another matter. One is reminded of the fire of early Christianity which swept from heart to heart until no power on earth could quench it. One hears again the voice of the Galilean, "He that believeth on me, the works that I do he shall do also; and greater works than these shall he do; because I go unto my Father."[5]

Whence Comes This Vital Religion?

We cannot follow the conversation

---

[5]John 14:12.

between the English traveler and the Mormon Prophet. Suffice it to say that the visit to Nauvoo lengthened into days and weeks; that when the visit was over an interesting letter from the noted traveler describing the adventure found its way into nearly all the newspapers of the United States.[6] During the remaining few months of the Prophet's life many people of note visited the Mormon leader at the height of his greatness—all went away puzzled, charmed by the man and his people, but frankly disturbed by his teachings. All asked themselves, "Whence came this peculiar faith?" "What loyalty prompted these converts to gather to this western frontier?" "What knowledge led them to count faith above home or comforts?" "What high sense of love or duty sent them forth into the world to teach and convert others?"

―――――――
[6]Part of this letter is reprinted by George Q. Cannon in *The Life of Joseph Smith*, p. 333.

"Where did this Prophet come from? Who were his ancestors? How did it all begin? What experiences, visions and revelations did he lay claim to? What strange circumstances brought this movement to Nauvoo?"

The story is a long one, but an intensely interesting one—a challenge to thinking men and women. It is a story of the frontier, the physical and religious frontier of America, part of a great epic in American history.

Supplementary Readings

Between 1841 and 1844 many notable people visited Nauvoo and the Mormon Prophet. In the following you will find their intensely interesting views recorded:

1. George Q. Cannon, *Life of Joseph Smith*, pp. 321-343.

2. Roberts, *Comprehensive History of the Church*, Vol. 2, pages 189-190.

3. Evans, *Joseph Smith, an American Prophet*, Chap. I.

4. Josiah Quincy, *Figures of the Past*, Chapter on "Joseph Smith."

Nauvoo, Illinois, from a painting by Francis R. Magleby. This painting hangs in the Relief Society Building, Salt Lake City, Utah.

CHAPTER 2

HOW IT ALL BEGAN

Joseph Smith Relates His Own Story

The time is early spring in the year 1820. The place—a backwoods farm in western New York. A young boy of perhaps fourteen has just left the log farmhouse. He goes down the lane to the west across the small brook, and finally into a grove of trees. An hour later, or is it two, he emerges and returns slowly to his home.

What has happened to him? What is different? For there is a difference. Perhaps his very bearing, his apparent concentration in thought, his disregard of things about him, are the outward evidences that the boy had been left in the grove and a man had emerged. And his mother, noticing the change as he re-entered the home and leaned against the mantel, asked what was wrong. The boy, evidently recalling the church she had recently joined replied, "Never mind, all is well—I am well enough off. I have learned for myself that Presbyterianism is not true."

That evening a young man by the name of Joseph Smith thrilled his family with the recounting of his unusual experience. This story was to be retold many times in future years. Let us follow the story as it was written for all the world to read.[1]

[1](Note) The following account is taken from the Journal of Joseph Smith, now published as the *History of the Church*—Period I, in six volumes, with an introduction and notes by B. H. Roberts. This writing was commenced by the Prophet in 1838, eight years after the organization of the Church and was published to the world in 1842, commencing in Vol. 3, No. 10, of *The Times and Seasons*, a Mormon newspaper of Nauvoo. A briefer history was written by Joseph Smith in a document called the "Wentworth Letter," which was written to Mr.

"I was born in the year of our Lord one thousand eight hundred and five, on the twenty-third day of December, in the town of Sharon, Windsor County, state of Vermont. My father, Joseph Smith, was born July 12, 1771, in Topsfield, Essex County, Massachusetts; his father, Asael Smith, was born March 7, 1744, in Topsfield, Massachusetts; his father, Samuel Smith, was born January 26, 1666, in Topsfield, Massachusetts; his father, Robert Smith, came from England. My father, Joseph Smith, Senior, left the state of Vermont and moved to Palmyra, Ontario (now Wayne) County, in the state of New York, when I was in my tenth year, or thereabouts. In about four years after my father's arrival in Palmyra he moved with his family into Manchester, in the same county of Ontario, his family consisting of eleven souls, namely, my father, Joseph Smith, my mother, Lucy Smith (whose name previous to her marriage was Mack, daughter of Solomon Mack) my brothers, Alvin (who died November 19th, 1824, in the 27th year of his age), Hyrum, myself, Samuel Harrison, William, Don Carlos, and my sisters, Sophronia, Catherine and Lucy.

"Some time in the second year after our removal to Manchester, there was in the place where we lived an unusual excitement on the subject of religion. It commenced with the Methodists, but soon became general among all sects in that region of country. Indeed the whole district of country seemed affected by it, and great multitudes united themselves to the different religious parties, which created no small stir and division amongst the people, some crying, "Lo, here!" and others, "Lo, there!" Some were contending for the Methodist faith, some for the Presbyterian, and some for the Baptist. For, notwithstanding the great love which the converts to these different faiths expressed at the time of their conversion, and the great zeal manifested by the respective clergy, who were active in getting up and promoting this extraordinary scene of religious feeling, in order to have everybody converted, as they were pleased to call it, let them join what

John Wentworth, Editor and Proprietor of the *Chicago Democrat*. This remarkable document was published to the world in the *Times and Seasons*, Vol. 3, No. 9, March 1, 1842.

The Joseph Smith Memorial Monument erected by the Church of Jesus Christ of Latter-day Saints near the site of the Prophet's birthplace in Sharon, Windsor County, Vermont and dedicated on December 23, 1905, the one hundredth anniversary of his birth.

Used by permission, Church of Jesus Christ of Latter-day Saints Information Service.

sect they pleased; yet when the converts began to file off, some to one party and some to another, it was seen that the seemingly good feelings of both the priests and the converts were more pretended than real; for a scene of great confusion and bad feeling ensued—priest contending against priest, and convert against convert; so that all their good feelings one for another, if they ever had any, were entirely lost in a strife of words and a contest about opinions.

"I was at this time in my fifteenth year. My father's family was proselyted to the Presbyterian faith, and four of them joined that church, namely, my mother Lucy; my brothers Hyrum and Samuel Harrison; and my sister Sophronia. During this time of great excitement, my mind was called up to serious reflection and great uneasiness; but though my feelings were deep and often poignant, still I kept myself aloof from all these parties, though I attended their several meetings as often as occasion would permit. In process of time my mind became somewhat partial to the Methodist sect, and I felt

some desire to be united with them; but so great were the confusion and strife among the different denominations, that it was impossible for a person young as I was, and so unacquainted with men and things, to come to any certain conclusion who was right and who was wrong. My mind at times was greatly excited, the cry and tumult were so great and incessant. The Presbyterians were most decided against the Baptists and Methodists, and used all the powers of both reason and sophistry to prove their errors, or, at least, to make the people think they were in error. On the other hand the Baptists and Methodists in their turn were equally zealous in endeavoring to establish their own tenets and disprove all others.

"In the midst of this war of words and tumult of opinions, I often said to myself: What is to be done? Who of all these parties are right, or, are they all wrong together? If any of them be right, which is it, and how shall I know it? While I was laboring under the extreme difficulties caused by the contests of these parties of religionists, I was one day reading the Epistle of James, first chapter and fifth verse, which reads:

"'If any of you lack wisdom, let him ask of God, that giveth to all men liberally, and upbraideth not; and it shall be given him.'

"Never did any passage of scripture come with more power to the heart of man than this did at this time to mine. It seemed to enter with great force into every feeling of my heart. I reflected on it again and again, knowing that if any person needed wisdom from God, I did; for how to act I did not know and unless I could get more wisdom than I then had, I would never know; for the teachers of religion of the different sects understood the same passage of scripture so differently as to destroy all confidence in settling the question by an appeal to the Bible. At length I came to the conclusion that I must either remain in darkness and confusion, or else I must do as James directs, that is, ask of God. I at length came to the determination to "ask of God," concluding that if he gave wisdom to them that lacked wisdom, and would give it liberally, and not upbraid, I might venture. So, in accordance with this, my determination to ask of God, I retired to the woods to make the attempt. It was on the morning of a beautiful, clear day, early in the spring of eighteen hundred

The Sacred Grove, where appeared the Father and the Son to Joseph Smith in the Spring of 1820.

and twenty. It was the first time in my life that I had made such an attempt, for amidst all my anxieties I had never as yet made the attempt to pray vocally.

"After I had retired to the place where I had previously designed to go, having looked around me, and finding myself alone, I kneeled down and began to offer up the desires of my heart to God. I had scarcely done so, when immediately I was seized upon by some power which entirely overcame me, and had such an astonishing influence over me as to bind my tongue so that I could not speak. Thick darkness gathered around me, and it seemed to me for a time as if I were doomed to sudden destruction. But, exerting all my powers to call upon God to deliver me out of the power of this enemy which had seized upon me, and at the very moment when I was ready to sink into despair and abandon myself to destruction—not to an imaginary ruin, but to the power of some actual being from the unseen world, who had such marvelous power as I had never before felt in any being—just at this moment of great alarm, I saw a pillar of light exactly over my head, above the brightness of the sun, which descended gradually until it fell upon me.

"It no sooner appeared than I found myself delivered from the enemy which held me bound. When the light rested upon me, I saw two Personages, whose brightness and glory defy all description, standing above me in the air. One of them spake unto me, calling me by name, and said, pointing to the other—

"*'This is my beloved Son. Hear him!'*

"My object in going to inquire of the Lord was to know which of all the sects was right, that I might know which to join. No sooner, therefore, did I get possession of myself, so as to be able to speak, than I asked the Personages who stood above me in the light, which of all the sects was right—and which I should join. I was answered that I must join none of them, for they were all wrong, and the personage who addressed me said that all their creeds were an abomination in his sight; that those professors were all corrupt; that 'they draw near to me with their lips, but their hearts are far from me; they teach for doctrines the commandments of men; having a form of godliness, but they deny the power thereof.' He again forbade me to join with any of them: and many other things did He say unto me, which I cannot write at this time. When I came to myself again, I found myself lying on my back, looking up into heaven. When the light had departed, I had no strength; but soon recovering in some degree, I went home."[2]

Reflections on the Experience

It would seem at first glance that we must depend upon the testimony of one man (or boy) as to what occurred in that grove of trees on that beautiful spring morning, 1820. No one accompanied him. No one saw him enter the grove and likely no one observed his leaving.

It must be evident, however, to the biographer or the historian that something unusual had occurred. Three facts are of interest. First, whatever had happened in the grove changed Joseph's outward bearing—he had suddenly become less the boy and more the man. His mother was the first to notice it, but to many others it was equally evident.[3] Secondly, Joseph came out of the grove with a set of definite ideas, ideas which he did not possess when he entered, indeed, ideas not to be found among the people with whom he associated or in the few books he had read. True, his ideas were not new. This idea, or that, might be found among the writings of his contemporaries. They were taught by the Christ eighteen hundred years before—but it seems plain that so far as Joseph Smith is concerned, those ideas were received in the grove in upper New York State on that spring morning, 1820. He had not possessed them before—he did not acquire them later. To the first person he met—his mother—he began to pronounce them. Within a week those ideas were known over an entire community.

In the third place, he had received a testimony. Where before he had wavered as to where to place his allegiance—now the picture of a future church to embrace the Gospel in its fullness, was so real, and the existence of God so certain, that he would not deny it. To read again from his journal:[4]

"It caused me serious reflection then, and often has since, how very strange it was that an obscure boy, of a little over fourteen years of age, and one, too, who was doomed to th necessity of obtaining a scanty maintenanc

[2]*History of the Church*, Period I, Vol. I, pp. 2-6.

[3](Note) Joseph's father, the Methodist Ministe of the village, and the boy's playmates noticed the change.
[4]*History of the Church, Joseph Smith*, Period I, Vol. I, pp.7-8.

by his daily labor, should be thought a character of sufficient importance to attract the attention of the great ones of the most popular sects of the day, and in a manner to create in them a spirit of the most bitter persecution and reviling. But strange or not, so it was, and it was often the cause of great sorrow to myself. However, it was nevertheless a fact that I had beheld a vision. I have thought since, that I felt much like Paul, when he made his defense before King Agrippa, and related the account of the vision he had when he saw a light, and heard a voice; but still there were but few who believed him; some said he was dishonest, others said he was mad; and he was ridiculed and reviled. But all this did not destroy the reality of his vision. He had seen a vision, he knew he had, and all the persecution under heaven could not make it otherwise; and though they should persecute him unto death, yet he knew, and would know to the last breath, that he had both seen a light, and heard a voice speaking unto him, and all the world could not make him think or believe otherwise. So it was with me. I had actually seen a light, and in the midst of that light I saw two Personages, and they did in reality speak to me, and though I was hated and persecuted for saying that I had seen a vision, yet it was true; and while they were persecuting me, reviling me and speaking all manner of evil against me falsely for so saying, I was led to say in my heart: Why persecute me for telling the truth? I have actually seen a vision; and who am I that I can withstand God, or why does the world think to make me deny what I have actually seen? For I had seen a vision; I knew it, and I knew that God knew it, and I could not deny it, neither dared I do it, at least I knew that by so doing I would offend God, and come under condemnation."

It is not our purpose at this time to delve into a discussion with the critics of Joseph's story. The truth of the first vision is deeper than a mere discussion of a boy's truthfulness. The true test of his story is a test of a principle involved—a spiritual principle—Can one pray to God and receive an answer? Can a man go into a grove, or into his bedroom, and through prayer receive new ideas which he did not before possess, new knowledge, which to him if not to the whole world, was before hid-

den? Is revelation and inspiration from God a reality? Can you or I have such an experience? Is the experience of the boy Joseph Smith an eternal verity that can be reproduced today and tomorrow? If we "lack knowledge" is there a channel which, with the requisite faith, we can open to God? If the answer is yes, God becomes suddenly, as to the boy Joseph Smith, a vital reality in our lives.

The answer is written in the hearts of thousands of men and women. The boy Joseph's testimony does not stand alone. In the years which were to follow thousands, stirred to their depths by Joseph's story, sought knowledge and testimony through the channel of prayer and were converted. Converted to what? To a belief that Joseph Smith was an honest man? To the belief that he had seen what he claimed to have seen? No. At least that is not the vital thing. The conversion was to the eternal truth that one might receive an answer to prayer—a testimony that God lives—that he speaks unto men. And this type of conversion was as strong as the conversion of Joseph Smith, or of Paul the Apostle, or of Peter—the recipients were willing to die for it as Paul and Peter died for theirs, and as Joseph Smith was to die for his. Because the testimony arose in the same way, the result of the same type of experience, an outgrowth of obedience to the same law.

When Joseph came out of that grove and announced his experience to the world—Peter, Paul, and the prophets of all ages really stood at his side to vouch for his story—for all had testified to similar experiences.

Supplementary Readings

Interesting stories concerning Joseph

Smith's ancestors and his own early life may be found in the following:

1. Evans, *Joseph Smith, an American Prophet*, pp. 20-32. (Joseph Smith's Forebears.)

2. Evans, *Joseph Smith, an American Prophet*, pp. 33-37. (Early Life of the Prophet.)

3. George Q. Cannon, *Life of Joseph Smith*, pp. 1-4. (Joseph's Ancestry.)

4. Widtsoe, *The Restoration of the Gospel*, pp. 1-12. (A Religious Revival.)

5. Smith, *Essentials in Church History*, pp. 27-29. (Advice and Predictions of Joseph's Grandfather—Asael Smith.)

6. Smith, *Essentials in Church History*, pp. 33-38. (Joseph's Mother Tells of His Early Courage.)

7. Ibid. pp. 25-28. (Joseph Smith's Genealogy.)

8. Roberts, *Comprehensive History of the Church*, Vol. I, pp. 60-68. (An Explanation of the Words Joseph Received.)

"Joseph Smith's First Vision," a sculpture by Avard Fairbanks.

THE HILL CUMORAH, historic shrine of the Church, as it is today.

Used by permission,
Hill Cumorah Bureau of Information

JOSEPH SMITH RECEIVES THE PLATES FROM THE ANGEL MORONI, photograph of oil painting by Lewis A. Ramsey.

Used by permission,
DESERET NEWS PRESS

ANGEL MORONI MONUMENT atop the Hill Cumorah near Palmyra, New York.

Used by permission,
Hill Cumorah Bureau of Information

RESTORATION OF THE AARONIC PRIESTHOOD,
monument near Harmony, Pennsylvania erected under
the direction of the Presiding Bishopric.

THE SUSQUEHANNA RIVER, view near where Joseph Smith and Oliver Cowdery
baptized each other.

CHAPTER 3

THE RELIGIOUS FRONTIER
OF AMERICA

The Spirit of the Frontier
Frees the Minds of Men

It is difficult for us to get a mental image of the boy, Joseph Smith, to realize the circumstances which surrounded him, and the physical conditions of the country at the time he went into the woods to pray. We see America today as a vast nation stretching from sea to sea and embracing within the fifty states more than 200 million people. We live in, or near, great cities with their high office buildings and fine brick dwellings.

It taxes the imagination to vision the boy, Joseph, living with his parents, brothers, and sisters, in a log dwelling set in a clearing of a great forest—and that forest which was then the frontier, situated in the western part of New York State. Today we can go in any direction over the face of the land and encounter people of our own race dwelling in large numbers—but in that America, one need travel west from New York State but a short distance to find a wilderness, largely uninhabited. We climb into our automobiles and speed from place to place, fifty or sixty miles in an hour, while the finest carriage of Joseph's period covered less than half that distance in a day. We traverse wide, hard-surfaced roads stretching straight as arrows in a great network over the country—but at that time the few roads the region boasted were narrow, crooked, and unsurfaced; veritable bog holes in the spring of the year after heavy rains. At times travel ceased altogether.

Our products are transported by steam railroads or giant trucks, amazing distances in a comparatively short time—but then, the steam railway was an untried idea[1] and freight was carried by pack horse, wagon, or boat over weary and tedious miles, and at great expense. We awaken often at night to hear the drone of a mail plane overhead and realize that the letter we have written but a few hours before will have been carried across a continent by morning. In 1820, weeks were required to deliver a letter from New York City to an outlying settlement on the Ohio River.

If we would understand even the conditions of the home in which Joseph lived as a boy, we must in imagination remove the brick from the walls of our own homes and put rough logs in their stead. We must take out the electric lights and substitute a lighted cotton-wick set in a vessel of tallow. The electric sweeper must give way to a broom; the electric washer to a crude washboard; the smooth polished floors to rough planks covered with hand-woven rugs; the overstuffed set to old wooden rocking chairs. Our hot and cold water system would have to be set aside for a great wooden bucket and dipper, and a steaming kettle over an open hearth fire. A score of modern conveniences, like the electric refrigerator, electric and gas ranges, and porcelain bathtubs, were luxuries unknown.

---

[1](Note) The first successful steam railroad was in Stockton and Darlington, England, in the year 1825. The first attempt in the United States to use locomotive engines, otherwise than for mere experiment, was made on the railway from Carbondale to Homesdale, Pennsylvania, sixteen miles, built by the Delaware and Hudson Canal Co. The Stourbridge Lion, as the engine was called, was built in England, and placed upon the road in August, 1829. While predictions that machines would some day fly through the air had been made before 1820, the idea was generally thought to be an idle dream.

The Smith Family Home near Palmyra, New York.

The tremendous change from that period to our own has been brought about in a little over a hundred years. In that relatively short space of time mighty migrations of people have swept ever to the westward in great waves which have carried with them the restless, the turbulent, the discontented, and the radical, until the eastern and western frontiers finally met and the waves subsided.

The boy, Joseph, lived on the frontier. The frontier spirit was in the very air he breathed. It was a mighty force which was to transform the boy into a man and sweep him with it to the West a thousand miles, to immortal fame as a great American.

The physical frontier of America is gone—but the story of the frontier is a great epic which will never die.

Religious Leaders

Entwined with that constantly shifting physical frontier has gone the religious frontier of America, so interlaced that a study of the one is impossible without the other. The boy Joseph was destined to play an important role in both, and to wield an influence on the frontiers of America that has been felt and will yet be felt for many generations. From the first hardy English Pilgrims facing starvation on a bleak New England coast, even to the present day, the mass of immigrants pouring into America, have been the discontented people of the earth. This discontent has arisen out of the economic, political, social, or religious conditions of the old world.

The new world offered a new freedom —not because men and women transplanted to a new world suddenly became different and more tolerant, but because the American continent offered room to move away from one's neighbors when conflicts of opinion became oppressive. So new ideas survived in American soil.

The story of the American frontier is a story of adventurous people; people seeking a change, fostering new and radical plans, throwing old ideas overboard.

In the matter of religion the frontier played a vital part. In the Old World of settled ideas the religious liberal recanted[2] or was killed—in America when

[2]Recanted — Disavowal of a belief or opinion previously held.

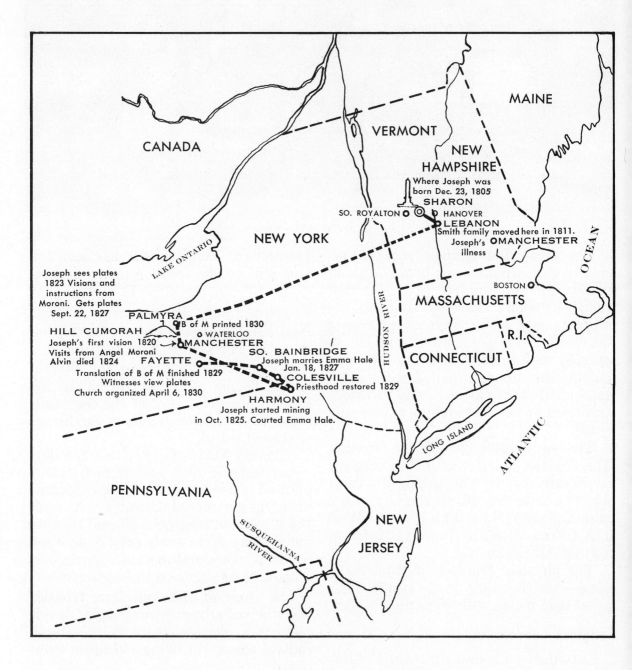

CANADA

VERMONT

MAINE

NEW
HAMPSHIRE

Where Joseph was
born Dec. 23, 1805
SHARON

NEW YORK

SO. ROYALTON   HANOVER
                LEBANON
Smith family moved here in 1811.
Joseph's   MANCHESTER
illness

LAKE ONTARIO

BOSTON

MASSACHUSETTS

HUDSON RIVER

R.I.

Joseph sees plates
1823 Visions and
instructions from
Moroni. Gets plates
Sept. 22, 1827

PALMYRA
           B of M printed 1830
HILL CUMORAH   WATERLOO
Joseph's first vision 1820   MANCHESTER
Visits from Angel Moroni   SO. BAINBRIDGE
Alvin died 1824   Joseph marries Emma Hale
FAYETTE   Jan. 18, 1827
Translation of B of M finished 1829
Witnesses view plates   COLESVILLE
Church organized April 6, 1830 Priesthood restored 1829
                HARMONY
                Joseph started mining
                in Oct. 1825. Courted Emma Hale.

CONNECTICUT

LONG ISLAND

ATLANTIC

PENNSYLVANIA

NEW

JERSEY

SUSQUEHANNA
RIVER

the pressure became too great he moved. Because the west was practically virgin land, the movement was always in the one direction. The vast empty west encouraged the liberal thinker. It offered him safety and exile, if need be. Only if he refused its invitation need he be martyred for his beliefs. So the story of the frontier is a story of new religious ideas—vital, challenging ideas, which often declared war on all existing creeds.

In Canada, the Huguenot[3] immigrant, driven from France, defied the power of Catholicism, and took refuge with his liberal ideas from the arm of the law.

In New England, Roger Williams had saved his radical religious views, and incidentally his life, by fleeing west to found the colony of Rhode Island.

The Reverend Thomas Hooker, having incurred the wrath of the Boston Puritans, pushed west with his followers and the first "covered wagons" in America, to found the colony of Connecticut.

Always the liberal aroused persecution by his war on existing creeds and institutions—and always his safety lay in the west. The frontier was a constantly shifting fringe of civilization—poor in the comforts of home, and rich in independence of thought.

No religious system was free of men and women too radical for it. The history of religion in America in the first half of the nineteenth century shows a constant spirit of rebellion from old creeds, resulting in the splitting of many churches and the establishment of some thirty new ones.[4]

Eleven years before Joseph Smith went into the grove to pray, one Alexander Campbell, having come to the conclusion that primitive Christianity was lost, "broke with mighty struggles the bonds of all creeds and made war upon them, whether they were true or false, with all the vigor of his giant mind."[5] His followers, known as "Disciples" or "Campbellites," although later regarded as Baptists, were independent thinkers of the frontier. From them Joseph Smith was to receive later a multitude of converts.

The early part of the nineteenth century witnessed a great revival in religious interests in America. In the first thirty years of the century most religious denominations doubled their membership, while the number of converts to new religions increased rapidly.

A Few of the Religious Pioneers

Among those people along the religious frontier of America, the Smith family played a prominent part. Joseph's grandfather had been discontented with existing creeds and forms of religious worship. This dissatisfaction with the New England religions, coupled with a toleration toward all religious beliefs, brought him under suspicion of the orthodox Puritans. When he went so far as to shelter a despised and persecuted Quaker in his home, he so aroused the displeasure of the community of Topsfield, Massachusetts, where he then lived, that he resolved to sell his home and move to a more congenial society to the westward.[6]

The same freedom of religious

---

[3]Hu-gue-not, hu-genot—A French Protestant of the 16th and 17th Centuries. The Huguenots suffered bloody persecutions during the religious wars of the time.

[4]The reader is referred to William Warren Sweet, *The Story of Religions in America*, published by Harpers, 1950.

[5]D. B. Ray, *Textbook on Campbellism*, p. 29. Southwestern Publishing House, Memphis, Tennessee, 1867.

[6]See Brigham H. Roberts, *Comprehensive History of the Church*, Vol. I, p. 5.

thought is evident in the life of Asael Smith's son, Joseph Smith, Sr., father of the Prophet. He was vitally interested in religion and a firm believer in dreams.[7] His dissatisfaction with existing creeds prevented his joining any of them. His wife, Lucy Mack Smith, says of him, "About this time [March, 1811] my husband's mind became excited upon the subject of religion; yet he would not subscribe to any particular system of faith, but contended for the ancient order, as established by our Lord and Savior, Jesus Christ, and his apostles."[8]

Joseph's mother also shows the independence of religious thinking along the frontier. She early showed a discontent with the creeds of her time. An investigator in many religions, none seemed to satisfy. She says of one occasion:

"I heard that a very devout man was to preach the next Sabbath in the Presbyterian Church; I therefore went to meeting, in the full expectation of hearing that which my soul desired—the Word of Life.

"When the minister commenced speaking, I fixed my mind with deep attention upon the spirit and matter of his discourse; but after hearing him through, I returned home, convinced that he neither understood nor appreciated the subject upon which he spoke, and I said in my heart that there was not then upon the earth the religion which I sought."[9]

That the boy Joseph Smith should be disturbed in his mind as regards the religions of his time could well be expected. That at the age of fourteen he had joined none of them shows that he early shared the religious independence of thought which characterized his father and mother. He had been born indeed on the religious frontier of America.

[7]*History of Joseph Smith by His Mother Lucy Mack Smith*, With Notes and Comments by Preston Nibley (1958), Chapter 13, pp. 46-50.

[8]*Ibid.*, Chapter 13, p. 46.
[9]*Ibid.*, Chapter 10, pp. 35-36.

The boy's announcement, "They are all wrong," is typical of the religious frontier. As previously mentioned, Alexander Campbell had openly declared war on all creeds a few years before. But, whereas the usual free thinker often broke with the old church, he seldom had a new system to substitute. He rather left the old fold because of the perplexities and uncertainties in his own mind—and those perplexities continued to follow him into new creeds and religious organizations.

Joseph's break with the religions of his day was different. He came from the grove with definite, fixed ideas— ideas which were never changed in his subsequent life. He suddenly had something to offer the world, and those religionists who hated the usual liberals in thought were aroused to more than hatred against a boy who attempted to correct their established views of God.

It might be well at this time to mention other names along the religious frontier with which we are later to become familiar. We find them, like the Smiths, dissatisfied with existing religious creeds and all looking and hoping for a religion to meet their need. We must constantly keep the picture of the frontier in mind and realize that the step which these people later took into Mormonism was at times a very small one indeed. Before the Prophet Joseph Smith had been heard of, these people were believing many of the doctrines he was later to advance.

In the state of New York, at Mendon, forty miles from Joseph Smith's home, three families were looking for a new religion. These were the Youngs, Greenes, and Kimballs, some of whom were later prominent in the Church. All were dissatisfied with existing creeds.

An artist's sketch of Lucy Mack Smith, mother of the Prophet Joseph Smith.
Used by permission, Church Historian's Office

Although some of the Kimballs joined the Baptists, and some of the Youngs and Greenes the Reformed Methodists for a short time, the dissatisfaction only became the greater. In the journal of Heber C. Kimball we read:

"From the time I was twelve years old I had many serious thoughts and strong desires to obtain a knowledge of salvation, but not finding anyone who could teach me the things of God, I did not embrace any principles of doctrine, but endeavored to live a moral life. The priests would tell me to believe in the Lord Jesus Christ, but never would tell me what to do to be saved, and thus left me almost in despair.[10]

In Hartford, Connecticut, the Woodruff family was displaying the same unrest. We read in the journal of Wilford Woodruff:

[10]Orson J. Whitney, *Life of Heber C. Kimball,* 1967 edition, p. 14.

"At an early age my mind began to be exercised upon religious subjects, but I never made a profession of religion until 1830, when I was twenty-three years of age. I did not then join any church for the reason that I could not find a body of people, denomination, or church that had for its doctrine, faith, and practices those principles, ordinances, and gifts which constituted the gospel of Jesus Christ, as taught by Him and His apostles. Neither did I find anywhere the manifestations of the Holy Ghost with its attendant gifts and graces."[11]

In Burlington, Otsego County, New York, the Pratts showed a similar inclination. Parley P. Pratt writes in his autobiography concerning his father:

"He taught us to venerate our Father in Heaven, Jesus Christ, His prophets and Apostles, as well as the Scriptures written by them; while at the same time he belonged to no religious sect, and was careful to preserve his children free from all prejudice into which the so-called Christian world was then unhappily divided."[12]

The dissatisfaction of Parley led him to the West, where he joined with a branch of the Campbellites under Sidney Rigdon, at Kirtland, Ohio. Of the Campbellites and their opposition to all existing creeds we have spoken earlier.

The Snow family has a similar history of dissatisfaction with religions of that day. In the *Biography of Lorenzo Snow,* written by his sister, Eliza R. Snow, we read:

"In their religious faith our parents were by profession Baptists, but not of the rigid, iron bedstead order; their house was a resort for the good and intelligent of all denominations."[13]

Concerning her brother, Lorenzo Snow, she writes:

"Although religiously trained from infancy, up to this time (1830) my brother had devoted little or no attention to the subject

[11]Matthias F. Cowley, *Wilford Woodruff,* 1965 edition, from his journal, pp. 14-16.
[12]*Autobiography of Parley P. Pratt,* 1965 edition, Chapter 1, p. 19.
[13]Eliza R. Snow, *Biography and Family Record of Lorenzo Snow,* p. 2.

of religion, at least not sufficient to decide in preference of any particular sect."[14]

In Toronto, upper Canada, one John Taylor (later to become the third president of the LDS Church), had become so dissatisfied with the Methodist Church, of which he was a minister, that, together with some of his congregation, he was expelled from office and condemned for his views. He and his followers firmly believed that the various religious sects of their day were wrong.

"They believed that men should be called of God as in former days and ordained by proper authority; and that in the Church there should be apostles and prophets, evangelists and pastors, teachers and deacons; in short, that the primitive organization of the Church of Christ should be perpetuated.

"They believed that men who accepted the gospel should have bestowed upon them the Holy Ghost; that it should lead them into all truth, and show them things to come. They believed also in the gift of tongues, the gift of healing, miracles, prophecy, faith, discerning of spirits and all the powers, graces and blessings as experienced in the Christian Church of former days."[15]

This condition was typical of the entire frontier. Great numbers had either broken away from existing denominations or were retaining their membership only in despair of finding something better, when the announcements by Joseph Smith began to spread from settlement to settlement.

Practically all who were later to become prominent in the organization Joseph Smith established had broken with old faiths, before encountering "Mormonism." Not a few of them were preaching from the pulpit many of the beliefs which Joseph was later to advance. These independent religious thinkers included four men who were to follow Joseph Smith successively as President of the Church, and practically all those who were chosen as the first quorum of twelve apostles.

Thus the field was ripe for the harvest. Joseph Smith, despite all the antagonism of the older churches, was to find a fertile soil in which to plant the Gospel of Jesus Christ. Men and women were eager for the doctrine he was to advance. All this had not come about in a day. It was a gradual growth in religious thinking that had its roots in the Old World and had flourished and blossomed in the free air of the American frontier. It was as if the mighty Director of human events had for centuries been preparing the stage for the principal actor to enter.

The Effect of the First Vision

We must not get the impression that the first vision of Joseph Smith in the grove near Palmyra had at that time any vital effect along the religious frontier. On the contrary, aside from the Smith family and the small community surrounding them, the incident was to remain relatively unknown for a number of years. Newspaper reporters did not flock to the village, nor was the experience heralded on the headlines of even the local papers. Distorted accounts, growing out of second-hand information, and written in a jocular vein, did find their way into several eastern newspapers, but created no particular stir. This was largely due to the fact that claims to visions, revelations, and dreams were common at that time. In the distorted fashion in which Joseph Smith's experience reached the majority of people along the frontier it sounded very much like the experiences claimed by others.[16]

Further, the announcement of what happened in the grove was not followed

---

[14]Snow, *Biography and Family Record . . .*, p. 3.
[15]Brigham H. Roberts, *Life of John Taylor*, 1963 edition, pp. 31-32.

[16]The reader is referred to Daryl Chase, *Doctor's Thesis*—University of Chicago, 1936.

immediately by any action on the part of the young man.

The local ministers had become irritated by the boy's announcement to them and those who believed their words, that they were "all wrong," and that their creeds were an "abomination" in the sight of the Lord. In their irritation they turned from the boy and advised their people against him—so that he became ostracised[17] in the community. This result was not strange. No learned man enjoys being told by a boy that he is "all wrong." Joseph's declaration made him a very lonely young man.

But although Joseph had declared the falseness of existing creeds, he did nothing further. He went about the usual pursuits of a young man of the frontier. He continued to labor on his father's farm, outwardly no different, except as to a sudden maturity which seemed to sober him. Later, in writing his journal, he says of this period:

"I was left to all kinds of temptations; and mingling with all kinds of society, I frequently fell into many foolish errors, and displayed the weakness of youth, and the foibles of human nature; which I am sorry to say, led me into diverse temptations, offensive in the sight of God. In making this confession, no one need suppose me guilty of any great or malignant[18] sins. A disposition to commit such was never in my nature. But I was guilty of levity,[19] and sometimes associated with jovial company, etc., not consistent with that character which ought to be maintained by one who was called of God as I had been. But this will not seem very strange to anyone who recollects my youth, and is acquainted with my native cheery temperament."[20]

It is quite evident from the writings of Joseph Smith and Lucy Mack Smith, that his mother, father, brothers, and sisters believed in his related experience, although it is not evident that it particularly changed their lives or the manner of their living during the next few years. It was not, in fact, until seven years after the first vision that the frontier began to pay attention to the young man in northern New York— and then it was in connection with something very tangible—a book which he was preparing for publication, translated from gold plates, and containing in clearness the Gospel for which the reformers of the frontier had been waiting. This book, published in 1830, was suddenly to elevate the Prophet to mighty leadership on the religious frontier of America. But in the meantime the Prophet had enjoyed other visions and visitations quite as vital as that in the grove near Palmyra, and now it will be necessary to go back and gather the thread of his story.

Supplementary Readings

In the journals written by men who became leaders in the Church we get an insight into their independent religious nature.

1. Brigham H. Roberts, *Life of John Taylor*, 1963 edition, pp. 29-34.

2. Matthias F. Cowley, *Wilford Woodruff*, 1965 edition, Chapter 1.

3. Eliza R. Snow, *Biography and Family Record of Lorenzo Snow*, Chapter 1.

4. *Autobiography of Parley P. Pratt*, 1964 edition, pp. 24-26.

5. *Ibid.*, pp. 35-40.

6. William Warren Sweet, *The Story of Religions in America*, 1950 edition, pp. 283-284.

7. *Ibid.*, pp. 249-251.

8. *History of Joseph Smith by His Mother Lucy Mack Smith*, With Notes and Comments by Preston Nibley (1958), pp. 35-50.

---

[17]Ostracised—Excluded from public or private favor.

[18]Malignant—Evil in nature, or tending to do great harm.

[19]Levity—Frivolity; light-mindedness.

[20]*History of the Church*, Period I, Vol. I, pp. 9-10. For a similar statement, letter of Joseph Smith to Oliver Cowdery, contained in the above reference, p. 10, is noteworthy.

CHAPTER 4

THE ORIGIN OF THE
BOOK OF MORMON

A Voice Speaks From the Dust

Three and one-half years elapsed after Joseph's vision in the grove at Palmyra before he again had a like experience—a like experience in that it came in the same manner, by obedience to the same spiritual law—the law of prayer. Often the boy wondered why the heavens had remained silent for so long, why the Lord had not made clear His purpose in regard to him. Now, on the evening of the twenty-first of September, 1823, Joseph came to the realization that the reason for that silence was within himself. The Savior, while living in the flesh upon the earth, had instructed his followers: "Ask, and it shall be given you; seek, and ye shall find; knock, and it shall be opened unto you: For everyone that asketh receiveth; and he that seeketh findeth; and to him that knocketh, it shall be opened."[1] For three and one-half years he had failed to properly knock at the door of God. He had done so once and the promise had not failed—he would do so again. To quote his own story:

"After I had retired to my bed for the night, I betook myself to prayer and supplication to Almighty God for forgiveness of all my sins and follies, and also for a manifestation to me, that I might know of my state and standing before Him; for I had full confidence in obtaining a divine manifestation, as I had previously done. While I was in the act of calling upon God, I discovered a light appearing in my room, which continued to increase until the room was lighter than at noonday, when immediately a personage appeared at my bedside, stand-

ing in the air, for his feet did not touch the floor. He had on a loose robe of most exquisite whiteness. It was a whiteness beyond anything earthly I had ever seen; nor do I believe that any earthly thing could be made to appear so exceedingly white and brilliant. His hands were naked, and his arms also, a little above the wrist; so, also were his feet naked, as were his legs a little above the ankles. His head and neck were also bare. I could discover that he had no other clothing on but this robe, as it was open, so that I could see into his bosom. Not only was his robe exceedingly white, but his whole person was glorious beyond description, and his countenance truely like lightning. The room was exceedingly light, but not so very bright as immediately around his person.

"When I first looked upon him, I was afraid; but the fear soon left me. He called me by name, and said unto me that he was a messenger sent from the presence of God to me and that his name was Moroni; that God had a work for me to do; and that my name should be had for good and evil among all nations, kindreds, and tongues, or that it should be both good and evil spoken of among all people. He said there was a book deposited, written upon gold plates, giving an account of the former inhabitants of this continent, and the sources from which they sprang. He also said that the fulness of the everlasting Gospel was contained in it, as delivered by the Savior to the ancient inhabitants; also that there were two stones in silver bows—and these stones, fastened to a breastplate, constituted what is called the Urim and Thummim—deposited with the plates; and the possession and use of these stones were what constituted 'Seers' in ancient or former times; and that God had prepared them for the purpose of translating the book.

"After telling me these things he commenced quoting the prophecies of the Old Testament. He first quoted part of the third chapter of Malachi, and he quoted the fourth or last chapter of the same prophecy, though with a little variation from the way it reads in our Bibles. Instead of quoting the first verse as it reads in our books he quoted it

[1] Matthew 7:7-8.

thus: 'For behold the day cometh that shall burn as an oven, and all the proud, yea, and all that do wickedly shall burn as stubble; for they that come shall burn them, saith the Lord of Hosts, that it shall leave them neither root nor branch.'

"And again, he quoted the fifth verse thus: 'Behold, I will reveal unto you the Priesthood, by the hand of Elijah the prophet, before the coming of the great and dreadful day of the Lord.'

"He also quoted the next verse differently: 'And he shall plant in the hearts of the children the promises made to the fathers, and the hearts of the children shall turn to their fathers; if it were not so, the whole earth would be utterly wasted at his coming.'

"In addition to these, he quoted the eleventh chapter of Isaiah, saying that it was about to be fulfilled. He quoted also the third chapter of Acts, twenty-second and twenty-third verses, precisely as they stand in our New Testament. He said that that Prophet was Christ; but the day had not yet come when 'they who would not hear his voice should be cut off from among the people,' but soon would come. He also quoted the second chapter of Joel, from the twenty-eighth verse to the last. He also said that this was not yet fulfilled, but was soon to be. And he further stated that the fulness of the Gentiles was soon to come in. He quoted many other passages of scripture, and offered many explanations which cannot be mentioned here.

"Again, he told me, that when I got those plates of which he had spoken—for the time that they should be obtained was not yet fulfilled—I should not show them to any person; neither the breastplate with the Urim and Thummim; only to those to whom I should be commanded to show them; if I did I should be destroyed. While he was conversing with me about the plates the vision was opened to my mind that I could see the place where the plates were deposited, and that so clearly and distinctly that I knew the place again when I visited it.

"After this communication, I saw the light in the room began to gather immediately around the person of him who had been speaking to me, and it continued to do so, until the room was again left dark, except just around me, when instantly I saw, as it were, a conduit open right up into heaven, and he ascended until he entirely disappeared and the room was left as it had been before this heavenly light had made its appearance. I lay musing on the singularity of the scene and marveling greatly at what had been

told to me by this extraordinary messenger; when, in the midst of my meditation, I suddenly discovered that my room was again beginning to get lighted, and in an instant, as it were, the same heavenly messenger was again by my bedside. He commenced, and again related the very same things which he had done at the first visit, without the least variation; which having done, he informed me of great judgments which were coming upon the earth, with great desolations by famine, sword, and pestilence; and that these grievous judgments would come on the earth in this generation. Having related these things he again ascended as he had done before.

"By this time, so deep were the impressions made on my mind, that sleep had fled from my eyes, and I lay overwhelmed in astonishment at what I had both seen and heard. But what was my surprise when again I beheld the same messenger at my bedside, and heard him rehearse or repeat over again to me the same things as before; and added a caution to me, telling me that Satan would try to tempt me (in consequence of the indigent[2] circumstances of my father's family) to get the plates for the purpose of getting rich. This he forbade me, saying that I must have no other object in view in getting the plates but to glorify God, and must not be influenced by any other motive than that of building his kingdom; otherwise I could not get them. After this third visit, he ascended into heaven as before, and I was again left to ponder on the strangeness of what I had just experienced; when almost immediately after the heavenly messenger had ascended from me the third time, the cock crowed, and I found that day was approaching, so that our interviews must have occupied the whole of that night.

"I shortly after arose from my bed and, as usual went to the necessary labors of the day; but in attempting to work as at other times, I found my strength so exhausted as to render me entirely unable. My father, who was laboring along with me, discovered something to be wrong with me, and told me to go home. I started with the intention of going to the house; but, in attempting to cross the fence out of the field where we were, my strength entirely failed me, and I fell helpless on the ground, and for a time was quite unconscious of anything. The first thing that I can recollect was a voice speaking unto me, calling me by name. I looked up, and beheld the same messenger

---

[2]Indigent—Destitute of property: poor.

standing over my head, surrounded by light as before. He then again related to me all that he had related to me the previous night, and commanded me to go to my father and tell him of the vision and commandments which I had received. I obeyed; and returned to my father in the field, and rehearsed the whole matter to him. He replied to me that it was of God, and told me to go and do as commanded by the messenger. I left the field, and went to the place where the messenger had told me the plates were deposited; and owing to the distinctness of the vision which I had had concerning it, I knew the place the instant that I arrived there."[3]

The Hill Cumorah

If one travels today on New York State Highway 21, from Palmyra south toward Manchester, he will pass directly by the most impressive monument in the northern part of that state. If the journey be made at night, the sight is doubly impressive—for then one sees from a distance a veritable pillar of light ascending from the open plain. On closer approach the phenomenon becomes an illuminated monument on the very apex of a hill that rises some hundred fifty feet above the surrounding country. Surmounting the huge granite shaft is a representation of the Angel Moroni. Six great flood lights play upon the unusual work of art. The hill at the base of the beautiful monument lies to the east of the highway, its north end rising abruptly from the surrounding plain, and sloping gradually to the level terrain on the south. This is the hill Cumorah, known locally as "Mormon Hill."

This hill, like the smaller ones in the same region, is a glacial deposit of the last ice-age, and this line of peculiar elevations across New York State marks the southernmost advance of the great ice cap which once covered the northern part of America.

---

[3]*History of the Church*, Period I, Vol. I, pp. 11-15.

Extending for nearly the length of the hill, near its summit, skillful gardeners have written its name in living shrubs. The face of the hill is planted with young pine and spruce trees, which, when mature, will give it the appearance of a century ago.[4] At the edge of the highway is a huge signboard which never fails to catch the eye of the motorist. In large letters one reads, "The Hill Cumorah." Underneath is a brief history of the connection of the hill with the *Book of Mormon*, and superimposed upon the sign is a huge representation of the book, with the name, "The Book of Mormon," and a brief statement of its mission. Hundreds of thousands of people visit this shrine annually. When the young man, Joseph Smith, ascended this very hill over a century ago, somewhat excited and stirred by his expectations, he little dreamed of the multitudes who would some day follow in his path, or of the tremendous consequences of his visit. The hill then lay as it had lain for centuries, untouched by human gardeners. Its very name buried within it—its great secrets locked from the minds of men. Through faith and prayer a young man had received a key to hidden centuries. A voice from the dust would soon stir the religious frontier of America and eventually the whole world.

Joseph's Visit to the Hill

Ascending the hill on its western side, nearly to the top, Joseph walked directly to the spot shown in his vision. Even with the ground surrounding it was the rounded upper surface of a large stone,

---

[4](Note) This historic site is now owned by the Church of Jesus Christ of Latter-day Saints. The monument was dedicated in the summer of 1935. The remarkable sculpture work is that of a Salt Lake man, Torlief Knaphus, a Norwegian convert to the Mormon faith.

its outer edges covered with soil and grass. Removing these, Joseph was able by the use of a pole as a lever, to raise the stone, which he found had a flat undersurface. Beneath the stone, which outwardly appeared much like other stones strewn over the hillside, was a box or container. Joseph writes of this occasion:

"I looked in, and there indeed did I behold the plates, the Urim and Thummim, and the breastplate, as stated by the messenger. The box in which they lay was formed by laying stones together in some kind of cement. In the bottom of the box were laid two stones crosswise of the box, and on these stones lay the plates and the other things with them."[5]

When the young man, in his eagerness to handle the treasure, reached into the cavity to remove the contents, a shock like that produced by electricity rendered his arm powerless and caused him to withdraw it. Three times he made the attempt with like failure, only each time the shock seemed harder than before. Joseph cried aloud in his anguish, "Why cannot I obtain this book?" A voice by his side replied, "Because you have not kept the commandments of the Lord."

The Angel Moroni stood by him and his presence reminded Joseph of the injunction of the night before, "Have no other object in view in getting the plates but to glorify God." In that journey to the hillside, wild dreams of wealth, ease, and fame, had flashed through the young man's mind. A desire for a share of what wealth could offer, for a moment overpowered him—it all lay within reach—but he was powerless to touch it. Now he knelt, humbled and repentant, before the heavenly instructor. In his humility and sincere repentance the power of his soul again

awakened: ". . . the heavens were opened and the glory of the Lord shone round about, and rested upon him. While thus he stood gazing and admiring, the angel said, 'Look!' and as he thus spake Joseph beheld the 'Prince of darkness,' surrounded by his innumerable train of associates. All this passed before him, and the heavenly messenger said,

'All this is shown, the good and the evil, the holy and impure, the glory of God and the power of darkness, that you may know hereafter the two powers and never be influenced or overcome by that wicked one. Behold, whatever entices and leads to good and to do good is of God; but whatever does not is of that wicked one; it is he that fills the hearts of men with evil to walk in darkness and to blaspheme God; and you may learn from henceforth, that his ways are to destruction, but the way of holiness is peace and rest. You now see why you could not obtain this record; that the commandment was strict, and that if ever these sacred things are obtained they must be [obtained] by prayer and faithfulness in obeying the Lord. They are not deposited here for the sake of accumulating gain and wealth for the glory of this world: they were sealed by the prayer of faith, and because of the knowledge which they contain they are of no worth among the children of men, only for their knowledge. On them is contained the fulness of the Gospel of Jesus Christ, as it was given to his people on this land [America], and when it shall be brought forth by the power of God it shall be carried to the Gentiles, of whom many will receive it, and after will the seed of Israel be brought into the fold of their Redeemer by obeying it also. Those who kept the commandments of the Lord on this land, through the prayer of faith obtained the promise, that if their descendants should transgress and fall away, a record should be kept and in the last days come to their children. These things are sacred, and must be kept so, for the promise of the Lord concerning them must be fulfilled. No man can obtain them if his heart is impure, because they contain that which is sacred; and besides, should they be intrusted into unholy hands the knowledge could not come to the world, because they cannot be interpreted by the learning of this generation: consequently, they would be considered of no worth, only as precious metal. There-

---

[5] *History of the Church*, Period I, Vol. I, p. 16.

fore, remember, that they are to be translated by the gift and power of God. By them will the Lord work a great and marvelous work: the wisdom of the wise shall become as naught, and the understanding of the prudent shall be hid, and because the power of God shall be displayed those who profess to know the truth but walk in deceit, shall tremble with anger; but with signs and with wonders, with gifts, and with healings, with the manifestations of the power of God, and with the Holy Ghost, shall the hearts of the faithful be comforted. You have now beheld the power of God manifested and the power of Satan: and you see that there is nothing that is desirable in the works of darkness; that they cannot bring happiness: that those who are overcome therewith are miserable, while on the other hand the righteous are blessed with a place in the kingdom of God where joy unspeakable surrounds them. . . . I give unto you another sign, and when it comes to pass then know that the Lord is God and that he will fulfill his purposes, and that the knowledge which this record contains will go to every nation, and kindred, and tongue, and people under the whole heaven. This is the sign: When these things begin to be known, that is, when it is known that the Lord has shown you these things, the workers of iniquity will seek your overthrow: they will circulate falsehoods to destroy your reputation, and also will seek to take your life: but remember this, if you are faithful, and shall hereafter continue to keep the commandments of the Lord, you shall be preserved to bring these things forth; for in due time he will again give you a commandment to come and take them. . . . Your name shall be known among the nations, for the work which the Lord will perform by your hands shall cause the righteous to rejoice and the wicked to rage: with one it shall be had in honor, and with the other in reproach; yet, with these it shall be a terror because of the great and marvelous work which shall follow the coming forth of this fulness of the Gospel.' "⁶

One must be prepared in order to do

the work of God. Mere willingness is not enough. The angel made this perfectly clear to the young man. Four years must be spent in preparation, years of hard study, of living the commandments of God, of receiving instruction from the glorious personage before him, who would meet him annually at this same spot.

"Accordingly," says the Prophet, "as I had been commanded, I went at the end of each year, and at each time I found the same messenger there, and received instruction and intelligence from him at each of our interviews, respecting what the Lord was going to do, and how, and in what manner, His kingdom was to be conducted in the last days."⁷

When Joseph first climbed this peculiar elevation of ground it was to him a mere hill, one of many in the vicinity; but his return was from "Cumorah," a sacred shrine, which held the secrets of a once great people and the glorious message of Christ to all the world.

Supplementary Readings

For a description of the Hill Cumorah see:

1. Roberts, *Comprehensive History of the Church*, Vol. I, pp. 75-76.

For a modern description of the Cumorah Shrine see:

2. *Improvement Era*, September, 1935, p. 542.

3. *Church Section—Deseret News*, July 13, 1935, July 20, 1935, and January 18, 1936.

---

⁶(Note) For the feelings and thoughts of the Prophet during this encounter, and for the words of the angel to him we are indebted to Oliver Cowdery, whose written account of these matters appeared in

a series of eight letters to W. W. Phelps, published first in the *Latter-day Saints' Messenger and Advocate*, Kirtland, Ohio, 1834-5, Vols. I and II. The letters have been reproduced several times in LDS publications, the latest being in the *Improvement Era*, Vol. II, 1899. Since Joseph Smith was the editor and this edition of the *Messenger and Advocate* bore his approval, it can be considered authentic, as if coming from his own pen.

⁷*History of the Church*, Period I, Vol. I, p. 16.

CHAPTER 5

THE TRANSLATION AND PUBLICATION OF THE BOOK OF MORMON

A Brief Glance at a Young Prophet's Life

A prophet is, after all, a human being like any one of us. He must eat and sleep, seek warmth, and shelter, and that often means long hours of physical toil. He is subject to the same laws, susceptible to the same pains, and governed by the same passions. His fitness to be an instrument in God's hands is not a gift from the eternal, but a growth from within.

If one would converse with God or learn his will one must conform to the law by which that communication may come and without such conformity there is no prophet. Nor is a prophet, so-called, always a prophet. The conformity to that law by which the will of the Heavens may be known is a rare accomplishment, and the attainment of it may be at more or less infrequent intervals. Relatively few people in history have obtained this conformity at all, and none for any sustained period of time. And this is true because the requirements seem to involve a purity of soul and an accumulation of faith rarely attained in this drab world of selfishness and dissension. A mere breath of air on the delicate weighing instruments of the skilled chemist defeats his experiment. The mechanism of the soul seems equally sensitive. The slightest doubt or impure thought disturbs its balance, and the would-be-prophet sinks to the level of common humanity. But on those rare occasions when men's souls have communed with the Most High, mankind has received its greatest enlightenment.

During the period from September 22, 1823, until the same day four years later, Joseph Smith lived the life of perhaps any other young man of the frontier whose parents were poor, and to whom there was little opportunity for education or travel. He continued to labor on his father's farm near Palmyra. Occasionally he was employed by his neighbors at various tasks requiring manual labor. He was fast growing into manhood and seemed imbued with the same desires and tendencies as any other normal young man.

We have very little direct account of those years. There is no doubt that his thoughts were more serious than otherwise, and contemplation of the task ahead sobered him and prevented his doing many of the foolish things or making the serious mistakes common among young men of his period.

Each year he revisited the Hill Cumorah and received instructions from the Angel Moroni. We have no record of the nature of these instructions, although it is evident that they had to do with the work ahead of translating the plates and organizing a church.

Joseph's Courtship

During these years in which he kept very silent in regard to his newly acquired knowledge he found time for an interesting courtship. When he appeared suddenly at his father's home in Manchester with a beautiful dark-eyed girl leaning on his arm, and introduced her as Mrs. Joseph Smith, Jr., tongues began to wag throughout the community. Especially did the gossip become rife when it was learned that the two young people, thwarted in their desires for a parental blessing, had eloped.

Emma Hale Smith who married Joseph on January 18, 1827.

Emma Hale, the beautiful and highly intelligent young bride, had not hesitated to leave her father's dwelling against her father's will, to follow the man of her choice. That same loyalty was to bind her fast to her unusual husband in a devotion undimmed by all the subsequent wanderings and hardships.

Joseph at this time was twenty-one years of age and his bride two years older. Emma of course did not need her father's consent, but both had desired it.

Joseph had been boarding at the Hale home in Harmony, Pennsylvania, while in the employ of one Josiah Stoal. To the elder Hale he was comparatively a stranger. The town was full of gossip of the visionary young man and the hardened old pioneer cannot be blamed for his attitude. He was not long, however, in getting reconciled to affairs and was soon inviting the young couple to live at his home.

Several months were to pass before obtaining the gold plates. It was a year of quiet happiness for the two young people. It proved to be but the calm before the storm—the prelude to years of persecution.

It was the morning of the twenty-second day of September, 1827, when the storm broke—for on that morning the Hill Cumorah gave up its secret. The "gold book"—the first tangible evidence of "Mormonism"—was delivered into the Prophet's hands.

The Ancient Records Come into the Possession of Joseph Smith

For the fifth time Joseph knelt before the stone receptacle in which the ancient records had lain hidden for fourteen centuries—but now that receptacle was empty. The sacred treasure was in his arms and he heard the angel beside him say:

"Now you have got the Record into your own hands, and you are but a man, therefore you will have to be watchful and faithful to your trust, or you will be overpowered by wicked men; for they will lay every plan and scheme that is possible to get it away from you, and if you do not take heed continually, they will succeed. While it was in my hands, I could keep it, and no man had power to take it away! but now I give it up to you. Beware, and look well to your ways, and you shall have power to retain it, until the time for it to be translated."[1]

The angel left him and the young Prophet was alone on the hillside, surrounded by forests and scattered settlements. From his elevation he could see evidences of a civilization which was spreading over the great American continent. He held in his hands the records of other peoples who long, long before had witnessed their civilization cover the land for centuries and then pass away.

The importance of the record, the seriousness of his calling, the realization of his own weaknesses, and of the trials which awaited, must have humbled him indeed, as he made his way down from a hill which had been hallowed for fourteen hundred years.

If his mind contemplated for a time that remarkable past, the feel of the plates beneath his outer coat must have brought him constantly into a sharp reality of the present—and there was his wife, Emma, at the foot of the hill—and there the horse and buggy of Joseph Knight, which had been borrowed for the occasion.

When Joseph and Emma returned to the Smith residence at Manchester, they were without the gold plates. These, wrapped in Joseph's outer cloak, or farmer's smock, had been taken from the buggy and carefully concealed within in a fallen birch log in the woods some two miles away.

Joseph did not take anyone, not even his wife, into his confidence concerning the plates or their hiding place. His friends knew, however, that he had received the records, and that knowledge

through some source was soon known over the entire settlement.

The effect upon the community is interesting. Whereas the story of the first vision had aroused a resentment wherever Joseph went which had isolated him from the society of some people, no active antagonism had been asserted. When the news spread that Joseph had in his possession a book with gold leaves, however, all manner of violence and strategy was used to wrest it from him. What motives prompted these attempts, other than man's greed for wealth, is a matter of mere conjecture. Joseph has left us little in writing concerning it. He says, "As soon as the news of this discovery was made known, false reports, misrepresentations, and slander flew as on the wings of the wind in every direction; the house was frequently beset by mobs and evil designing persons. Several times I was shot at, and very narrowly escaped, and every device was made use of to get the plates away from me."[2]

During the ensuing months the records found many curious hiding places—an excavation beneath the Smith hearthstone, the loft of a workshop, a barrel of beans, etc. All efforts to get them from Joseph met with failure.[3]

The Nature of the Ancient Records

In a few hundred years time, if it is not otherwise destroyed, this book in your hands will have utterly decayed despite any attempts to preserve it. In a very short period much of our writings become dim and faded. The record in Joseph's keeping had lain

[1]History of Joseph Smith by His Mother Lucy Mack Smith, With Notes and Comments by Preston Nibley (1958), Chapter 22, p. 10.

[2]Account of the famous Wentworth Letter. See footnote, p. 7. Also see a reprint of the letter in History of the Church, Period I, Vol. IV, p. 537.

[3]The details of these experiences, the successive hiding places of the plates, and the various attempts of the mob to obtain them are found only in one account, History of Joseph Smith by His Mother Lucy Mack Smith.

buried in the earth for fourteen hundred years, yet the characters were plain and decipherable. What manner of record was this? What materials had the writers used that could withstand the elements for so long? The best answer is the written statement of the Prophet.

"These records were engraven on plates which had the appearance of gold; each plate was six inches wide, and eight inches long, and not quite so thick as common tin. They were filled with engraving, in Egyptian characters, and bound together in a volume as the leaves of a book, with three rings running through the whole. The volume was something near six inches in thickness, a part of which was sealed. The characters on the unsealed part were small, and beautifully engraved. The whole book exhibited many marks of antiquity in its construction, and much skill in the art of engraving. With the records was found a curious instrument, which the ancients called 'Urim and Thummim,' which consisted of two transparent stones set in the rim of a bow fastened to a breast plate. Through the medium of the Urim and Thummim, I translated the record by the gift and power of God."[4]

The secret of the preservation of the record lay in the fact that ordinary writing materials were not used. There was no ink to fade—but the letters had been cut or engraved in the thin leaves of a metal which would not corrode or alter its appearance with the passing of time. A gold alloy had been used for this purpose.

It is impossible at this date to accurately estimate the weight of such a set of gold leaves or plates. Neither the Prophet, nor those witnesses who were privileged to handle the plates, have left written testimony as to the weight of the volume.

While the book had the "appearance of gold" we read in its contents that the plates were made of ore[5] and hence

would be an alloy rather than pure gold. The weight cannot now be determined. Elder J. M. Sjodahl, after an exhaustive study of the subject, came to the conclusion, "The entire volume could not have weighed fifty pounds."[6]

The language in which the major part of the record was written does not correspond to any known ancient system.[7] The writers called it a reformed Egyptian, that is, a variation of one of the Egyptian forms of writing. Perhaps the nearest known language is the ancient Phoenician, which likewise developed from the Egyptian. Hieroglyphic symbols were used rather than the common written language of the people, which was akin to the Hebrew, because it occupied less space. If we wrote on gold plates today we could indeed afford to waste few words. It was also engraved in "fine characters," Hence a few plates would suffice for what now occupies a book of some 522 pages in the English tongue. In the facsimile on the following page is shown fourteen and three-quarters pages of the *Book of Mormon* written in Hebrew. The language used in the record occupied still less space. Elder Sjodahl estimates that less than forty-five plates, engraved on both sides, would be necessary for the entire record translated, including that portion for which the translation was lost.[8]

With the plates was an ancient breastplate to which, when the Prophet first obtained it, the Urim and Thummim were attached. Lucy Smith, his

---

[4]Wentworth Letter, see footnote p. 7.
[5]I Nephi 19:1; Mormon 8:5.

[6]J. M. Sjodahl—*An Introduction to the Study of the Book of Mormon*, p. 44. See "Supplementary Readings" at the end of Chapter 6.

[7]Note: The small plates of Nephi were written in one of the Egyptian forms of that period, and would be now a known system of writing.

[8]Sjodahl—*Introduction of the Study of the Book of Mormon*, p. 42.

[Hebrew text — 2 Nephi, Chapters 5:20 to 11:3]

Hebrew translation of 2 Nephi, Chapters 5:20 to 11:3 inclusive (about 14 and ¾ pages of the English version).

Used by permission. J. M. Sjodahl

mother, who claims to have been shown this breastplate by her son, says of it:

"It was wrapped in a thin muslin handkerchief, so thin that I could feel its proportions without any difficulty. It was concave on one side and convex on the other, and extended from the neck downwards, as far as the center of the stomach of a man of extraordinary size. It had four straps of the same material, for the purpose of fastening it to the breast, two of which ran back to go over the shoulders, and the other two were designed to fasten to the hips. They were first the width of two of my fingers (for I measured them), and they had holes in the end of them, to be convenient in fastening. After I had examined it, Joseph placed it in the chest with the Urim and Thummim."[9]

It is not known what part, if any, the

[9]*History of Joseph Smith by His Mother Lucy Mack Smith*, With Notes and Comments by Preston Nibley (1958), Chapter 23, pp. 111-112.

breastplate played in the subsequent translation of the book.

The Translation of the Record

The attempts on the part of various persons to get possession of the plates proved unsuccessful, but prevented Joseph immediately beginning the important work of translation.

Arriving in Harmony with his wife, Joseph made an agreement to purchase a small house and some farm land belonging to members of the Hale family. It was here that he began to make a real study of the ancient records.

Between December, 1827, and February of the following year, the Prophet

Joseph Smith Home (center section) near Harmony, Pennsylvania where major part of the Book of Mormon was translated.
Used by permission. Church Historian's Office

In December, 1827, Joseph received an invitation to the home of his father-in-law, Isaac Hale, in Harmony, Pennsylvania. Desiring a place where he could find the necessary peace and quiet for his work, he accepted the invitation.

Joseph was without means to make the journey and commence the translation, but at this time a prosperous farmer of Palmyra proved a friend indeed. Martin Harris had heard and believed the account of Joseph's visions and was especially interested in the "gold book." As Joseph was preparing to depart for Harmony he came to the Smith home and presented fifty dollars as a gift for "the work of the Lord."

made a manuscript of some of the characters on the plates (see the facsimile on the following page) and translated some of them "by means of the Urim and Thummim."[10]

Some time in February Martin Harris arrived in Harmony and, securing a transcription of the characters which Joseph had made, took them to New York—evidently determined to check on the story of Joseph Smith concerning them.

It is evident from various accounts and documents[11] that Professors Anthon

---

[10]*History of the Church*—Period I, Vol. I, p. 19.
[11]Roberts, *Comprehensive History of the Church*, Vol. I, Chapter IX.

Facsimile of characters made from the Plates of the Book of Mormon by Joseph Smith and given to Martin Harris and by him submitted to Professors Charles Anthon and Samuel I. Mitchell.

Used by permission, Church Historian's Office

and Mitchell of New York viewed the two papers Harris had, one a transcript of characters without a translation and the other containing both characters and translation. According to the story told by Martin Harris, Professor Anthon gave him a writing certifying that the characters shown him were genuine and that the translation of the part was fairly accurate. Upon hearing from Harris that the ancient records had been obtained from an angel, the professor asked for the certificate and tore it into shreds. The reason for this is quite obvious. Neither Professor Anthon nor any other man could read the characters. Even at the date of this writing the language of the plates remains a hidden secret. The characters were in a language which, as Moroni informs us in Mormon 9:32, had developed from the Egyptian. Even had they been in close harmony with ordinary Egyptian hieroglyphics it is improbable that Professor Anthon could have read them, as that language was then little known and no single American was as yet skilled in its reading.[12]

Bearing these facts in mind we must arrive at the following: Professor Anthon knew nothing as to the correctness of the translation or the genuineness of the characters, and was either scheming to get possession of the plates or was not willing to confess his ignorance of the ancient language. Hence he fabricated the certificate. After finding the nature of the ancient records and what might happen to his certificate he was wise indeed to destroy it before his pretended knowledge made him the laughing stock of other learned men. If Professor Mitchell, to whom Martin Harris also showed his copies, agreed as to the genuineness of the characters, he at least was wise enough to refrain from writing that which he could not possibly have known.

Suffice it to say that the two learned men were visibly impressed by the characters and the translation. Returning from his encounters, Martin Harris was ready to devote much time to the work, as well as to borrow money to pay for the publication of the translation.

This incident fulfilled the following words of the *Book of Mormon*:

"And it shall come to pass that the Lord God shall bring forth unto you the words of a book, and they shall be the words of them

[12](Note) Champollion's work on Egyptian grammar did not appear until 1836 and it is the basis, along with his other works, for all study on Egyptology.

which have slumbered. And behold the book shall be sealed. * * * Wherefore, because of the things which are sealed up, the things which are sealed shall not be delivered in the day of the wickedness and abominations of the people. Wherefore the book shall be kept from them. But the book shall be delivered unto a man, and he shall deliver the words of the book, which are the words of those who have slumbered in the dust, and he shall deliver these words unto another; But the words which are sealed he shall not deliver, neither shall he deliver the book. * * * But behold, it shall come to pass that the Lord God shall say unto him to whom he shall deliver the book: Take these words which are not sealed and deliver them to another, that he may show them unto the learned, saying: Read this, I pray thee. And the learned shall say: Bring hither the book, and I will read them. And now, because of the glory of the world and to get gain will they say this, and not for the glory of God. And the man shall say: I cannot bring the book, for it is sealed. Then shall the learned say: I cannot read it. Wherefore it shall come to pass, that the Lord God will deliver again the book and the words thereof to him that is not learned; and the man that is not learned shall say: I am not learned. Then shall the Lord God say unto him: The learned shall not read them, for they have rejected them, and I am able to do mine own work; wherefore thou shalt read the words which I shall give unto thee."[13]

The prophecy was the primary factor which led Joseph Smith to prepare the transcript of characters which he gave to Martin Harris, and its fulfillment accordingly had a great effect upon the latter.

Martin Harris as Scribe

Martin Harris arranged for a long stay from his farm and repaired to Harmony about April 12th. Here he acted as scribe for Joseph Smith until June 14, during which time he had written 116 pages upon foolscap. The writing had been interrupted many times, business often causing Martin to return to his home for many days.

Some time after beginning his work

as scribe, Martin Harris began to importune Joseph Smith for the privilege of carrying home the writings he had made, in order to convince his wife and skeptical friends of the nature of the work in which he was engaged. Joseph inquired of the Lord and received an answer that he should not do so. A second inquiry produced a like answer. Martin Harris continued his pleading with Joseph, and Joseph continued his inquiries to the Lord, until he felt that the Lord had acceded to his request.

On June 14, 1828, Martin Harris left Harmony with 116 pages, on foolscap, of the translation of the *Book of Mormon*. It was the last the Prophet saw of it. Martin Harris broke his solemn promise to Joseph to show it to none other than a designated few, with the result that the manuscript was stolen or destroyed.

The consequences of the incident were that the Angel Moroni took from Joseph the Urim and Thummim and the ancient records. These were returned only after he had humbled himself before the Lord. Martin Harris was denied the privilege of further acting as scribe, despite his repentance for what had occurred.

The rebuke of the Lord to Joseph Smith at this time contains a message for all mankind: "Although a man may have many revelations, and have power to do many mighty works, yet if he boasts in his own strength, and sets at naught the counsels of God, and follows after the dictates of his own will and carnal desires, he must fall and incur the vengeance of a just God upon him."[14]

Joseph did not immediately resume his work of translating. He was with-

---

[13]*Book of Mormon*, II Nephi 27:6-20. Compare with Book of Isaiah, 29:10-13.

[14]*Doctrine and Covenants*, Sec. 3:4.

out a scribe and, further, was under the necessity of working on the small farm he had purchased in order to earn a livelihood for his family.

In the midst of these momentous occurrences a deep sorrow came to the Prophet's home. In July, 1828, a son was born to Emma, which soon died. The mother was also very near death's door. The care of his wife and the labor on his farm prevented further work on the ancient records. As the months passed and Emma began to convalesce she would often take up the work of scribe while her young husband, after a hard day's labor, would devote further hours to the slow task of translation. Often the Prophet prayed that circumstances might again allow him to devote full time to his mission.

Oliver Cowdery Enters the Scene

It was on a Sabbath evening, April 5, 1829, that Oliver Cowdery, a young schoolteacher, knocked on the Prophet's door in Harmony, Pennsylvania. Joseph accepted the young man as an answer to his prayers, and two days later the work of translation continued with the young convert as scribe.

In the autumn of the preceding year Oliver Cowdery had filled a teaching appointment in the township of Manchester, upper New York. He heard of the young Prophet, his visions, and his alleged receipt of sacred records. The accounts took serious hold of his mind. Were they true? He took his problem to the Lord and came from his prayer with a firm conviction that Joseph was engaged in the work of God. So firm was that conviction that he obtained a release from all his teaching labors, journeyed to the home of the Prophet, whom he had never before seen, and

volunteered his entire time and service.

There was no hope of monetary reward. The job paid no salary. There were to be no royalties. The task brought the ridicule and hatred of the world upon him.

But there are rewards greater than gold or silver, and one of these is an association with a Prophet of God. Oliver later wrote of this period:

"These were days never to be forgotten— to sit under the sound of a voice dictated by the inspiration of heaven, awakened the utmost gratitude of this bosom. Day after day I continued, uninterrupted, to write from his mouth, as he translated with the Urim and Thummim, or, as the Nephites would have said, 'Interpreters,' the history or record called the Book of Mormon."[15]

During the period of translation, Oliver, in company with Joseph, sought through prayer and received answers to many perplexing problems. Of these unique experiences we will speak further in a later chapter.

Oliver Cowdery came from these experiences with a testimony concerning the work in which he was engaged and the mission of Joseph Smith which was never shaken.

(*Photo by George Albert Smith*)

German E. Ellsworth and Mrs. George Albert Smith are standing upon the spot where stood the old home of Peter Whitmer, Fayette, Seneca County, N.Y., where the Church was organized, April 6, 1830.

[15]B. H. Roberts, *Comprehensive History of the Church*, Vol. I, p. 122.

The work of translation went forward rapidly, but opposition in Harmony gradually gathered and only the determined stand of Isaac Hale that law and order should prevail prevented open mob violence. Oliver had been writing for some time to his friend, David Whitmer, and had acquainted him with the work of the Prophet.

Of this period the Prophet writes:

"Shortly after commencing to translate, I became acquainted with Mr. Peter Whitmer, of Fayette, Seneca County, New York, and also with some of his family. In the beginning of the month of June, his son, David Whitmer, came to the place where we were residing, and brought with him a two-horse wagon for the purpose of having us accompany him to his father's place and there remain until we should finish the work. It was arranged that we should have our board free of charge, and the assistance of one of his brothers to write for me, and also his own assistance when convenient. Having much need of such timely aid in an undertaking so arduous, and being informed that the people in the neighborhood of the Whitmers were anxiously awaiting the opportunity to inquire into these things, we accepted the invitation, and accompanied Mr. Whitmer to his father's house, and there resided until the translation was finished and the copyright secured. Upon our arrival, we found Mr. Whitmer's family very anxious concerning the work and very friendly toward ourselves. They continued so, boarded and lodged us according to arrangements; and John Whitmer, in particular, assisted us very much in writing during the remainder of the work."[16]

The work was rapidly completed, David Whitmer and Emma, the Prophet's wife, at times relieving Oliver Cowdery in his task as scribe. The great task was brought to a close some time in July or August, 1829.

Having learned the folly of trusting to a single manuscript, Joseph instructed Oliver to make a copy of the entire translation, which he did. It was this copy from which the *Book of Mormon* was finally published.[17]

The Method of Translation

As previously mentioned, the ancient records were written in a language entirely unknown in modern times. Had Joseph been schooled by the greatest tutors of his time, had he been the peer of all the modern readers of ancient languages, the records before him would have remained a blank page so far as his own human ability to decipher them was concerned. Had all the learned linguists of the world been called into conference and the ancient records of the Nephites placed before them, they would have been unable to read one single sentence.[18]

How, then, was the translation effected? The prophet was emphatic in his claim to divine aid. This divine aid was received by means of an instrument which he called "Urim and Thummim." A brief description of the breastplate which held this peculiar instrument has been previously given.[19]

The exact method by which the strange device was used is not known.

[16]*History of the Church*—Period I, Vol. I, pp. 48-49.

[17]Footnote—The original manuscript was in the handwriting of several persons who had acted as scribes, although the greater part was by Oliver Cowdery. The later statement of Oliver Cowdery that he had written the entire *Book of Mormon* manuscript, save a few pages, with his own hand could only have referred to the copy of the original, which he retained. The original manuscript remained in the hands of Joseph Smith and was later buried in the cornerstone of the Nauvoo Temple. Later a portion of this manuscript came into the hands of the late President Joseph F. Smith (see article by Joseph F. Smith in the *Deseret News,* December 23, 1899.) The copy from which the *Book of Mormon* was published remained the prized possession of Oliver Cowdery. At the time of his death in 1850 the manuscript came into the possession of David Whitmer and is now owned by the Reorganized LDS Church.

[18]J. M. Sjodahl, author of *Introduction to the Study of the Book of Mormon*, once sent the seven lines of characters which are generally considered a genuine copy of Nephite characters from the plates (see p. 33) to the most learned linguists of the world. Although the characters were declared genuine, none could read them.

[19]See pp. 30-31.

Joseph Smith has left us little or nothing in regard to it. Aids to the senses are common in our own day. The telephone and the radio are mechanical aids to the human ear. The microscope, sensitized films, and television instruments are aids to the human eye. The "Urim and Thummim" seems to have been an instrument designed to aid the senses and enable prophets to communicate readily with divine powers. This device has been used in both ancient and modern times. The Prophets of Israel possessed a "Urim and Thummim" by which the will of the Lord could be obtained.[20] The particular one used by Joseph Smith was found deposited with the plates, and according to the translated record was first given by the Lord to an ancient prophet called in the account, "The brother of Jared."[21] In Ether 3:23-24 we read,

"And behold, these two stones will I give unto thee, and ye shall seal them up also with the things which ye shall write. For behold, the language which ye shall write I have confounded; wherefore I will cause in my own due time that these stones shall magnify to the eyes of men these things which ye shall write."

It is quite evident that the translation of the record, even with the use of the mechanical device, was not a simple accomplishment. It evidently required great thought. At times, when Joseph's mind was in a turmoil over family disagreements or other matters, he was unable to translate at all. Faith in God and purity of soul seemed, as in the case of any communication with God, to be the prime requisites.

A key to the problem of translation is found in Section 9 of the book of *Doctrine and Covenants*. It appears that the wish of Oliver Cowdery to do some

translating had been granted and that the Urim and Thummim, together with an ancient writing, had been placed in his hands. His attempt was an utter failure, and the Lord, through the Prophet Joseph Smith, said to him:

"You have not understood; you have supposed that I would give it unto you, when you took no thought save it was to ask me.

"But, behold, I say unto you, that you must study it out in your mind; then you must ask me if it be right, and if it is right I will cause that your bosom shall burn within you; therefore, you shall feel that it is right.

"But if it be not right you shall have no such feelings, but you shall have a stupor of thought that shall cause you to forget the thing which is wrong; therefore, you cannot write that which is sacred, save it be given you from me."[22]

Thus the Lord set forth the method of translation which certainly applied to Joseph Smith or any other translator as well as to Oliver Cowdery. The Prophet, from his study of the characters which were "magnified" before him, "thought it out in his mind." and when he had the assurance that the thought was right, spoke the thought in his own words and language to the scribe, from whom he was separated during the process of translation by a curtain. The translation was thus subject to the imperfections of language and grammar which characterized the early writings of the Prophet, and the mistakes in spelling to which the scribe was addicted.[23]

There is no doubt that, as the Prophet progressed with translation, he became familiar with the ancient manner of writing and with the interpretation of

---

[20]See Exodus 28:30; Lev. 8:8; Num. 27:21; Deut. 33:8; I Sam. 28:6; Ezra 2:63; Neh. 7:65.
[21]*Book of Mormon*—Ether 1:34.

[22]*Doctrine and Covenants* 9:7-9.
[23]Most of the mistakes in grammar and spelling were corrected by Joseph Smith in the second edition of the *Book of Mormon*. The style of expression and the meaning of the sentences has, however, remained unaltered. Orson Pratt, a member of the Quorum of the Twelve, divided the book in chapters and verses in 1879.

the symbols, so that he need not always resort to the Urim and Thummim, but could immediately state the meaning previously found for the same characters. As in ancient languages a single character might have many shades of meaning according to the particular use, some of the beauty of the original must have been lost in the translation.

Further, as all who have made translations know, there are often no equivalents in the translated language for the expression or shade of meaning in the original. These are regrettable and unavoidable factors in translation.

It is also evident that the Prophet had his Bible by his side during the translation. Where he found the ancient writers quoting from the Hebrew scriptures, a copy of which they possessed,[24] he undoubtedly called the King James' version of the Bible to his aid in fashioning the thoughts into the English tongue. Such a use of the Bible was a recognition of his own lack of literary ability and of the beauty of expression in that early English translation. He did not hesitate, however, to correct the English translation when the meaning failed to agree in any vital way with his interpretation of the quotations on the plates before him.

The exact amount of time occupied in the translating will perhaps never be known. The Prophet spent many, many hours with the records when scribes were not present. In the first two months of intensive study—December, 1827, to February, 1828—very little was set forth in the English tongue, indicating something of the tremendous work involved. If the work of translation appears to be rapid later, when Oliver Cowdery was the scribe, it must

be remembered that the foundations for the final work were being laid by many months of previous labor.

The Publication of the Book of Mormon.

The Prophet's difficulties were not over when the translation was complete and the sacred record had been returned once more to the keeping of the Angel Moroni. The publication of the book presented many a problem. Joseph Smith was without funds for its publication, and so great was the feeling against the unseen volume, that publishers hesitated to undertake the task.

Martin Harris, the one-time scribe of the Prophet, now came to the rescue. Borrowing money on his farm he induced Mr. Egbert B. Grandin and Company, of Palmyra, to print 5,000 copies of the *Book of Mormon* at a price of $3,000. The contract was signed on the twenty-fifth day of August, 1829.

Extreme caution was taken by the Prophet to protect the publication. The original manuscript was kept by the Prophet and only the copy made by Oliver Cowdery, a few pages at a time, was entrusted to the printer. Oliver Cowdery, in going to and from the printing establishment with a portion of the translation was always accompanied by a guard. The house where the manuscript was kept was also under guard day and night.[25]

Notwithstanding these precautions, a garbled account of the *Book of Mormon* story very nearly reached publication before the *Book of Mormon* itself. One Squire Cole was found to have access to Grandin's printing office for the

---

[24]See I Nephi 5:10-16.

[25]*History of Joseph Smith by His Mother Lucy Mack Smith*, (1958), pp. 99-101. See also Gregg—*The Prophet of Palmyra*, pp. 34-36.

View of Palmyra, New York where the Book of Mormon was printed by Mr. Egbert B. Grandin and Company.

publication of a weekly periodical called, "Dogberry Paper on Winter Hill." He was found by Hyrum Smith and Oliver Cowdery to be about to publish mutilated extracts of the *Book of Mormon* obtained from the printer's copy. Only threat of ·suit for the infringement of the copyright law caused him to desist.

The first copies of the publication issued from the press March 18-25, 1830, with the effect along the frontier previously alluded to.

Supplementary Readings

There are many interesting accounts connected with the events of this chapter which could not be included in the text. The following are especially worth while:

1. *History of Joseph Smith by His Mother Lucy Mack Smith* (1958), pp. 99-101. (Joseph is chastised by the Angel Moroni for his lack of diligence.)
2. *Ibid.*, pp. 102-110. (Joseph gets the plates but has a hard task to keep them from the hands of wicked men.)
3. *Ibid.*, pp. 114-123. (Martin Harris offers his services and his wife objects.)
4. *Ibid.*, pp. 143-146. (A judge rebukes Joseph's enemies.)
5. Roberts, *Comprehensive History of the Church*, Vol. I, pp. 120-122. (Oliver Cowdery prays to God for a testimony concerning the work.)
6. *Ibid.*, pp. 123-124. (The power of a Seer is illustrated.)
7. *Ibid.*, pp. 125-127. (Superhuman events in connection with the coming forth of the *Book of Mormon*.)

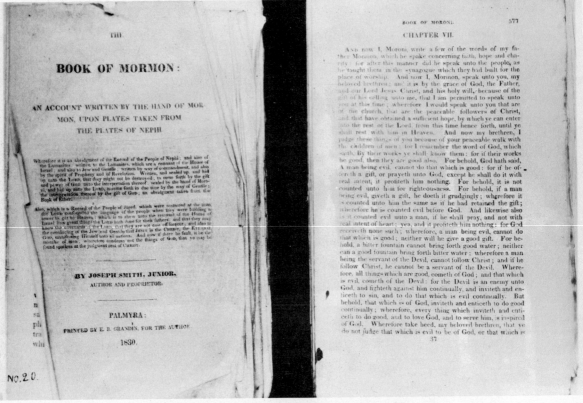

Pages from the original copy of the Book of Mormon.

CHAPTER 6

A NEW BOOK CHALLENGES THE WORLD—THE BOOK OF MORMON

A New Book Stirs the Frontier

In April, 1830, ten years after the experience of Joseph Smith in the grove, the religious frontier was startled by the appearance of a strange book. The title on the cover was the "Book of Mormon," but everywhere people were speaking of it as the "Golden Bible."

Five thousand copies found their way from Palmyra, New York, into nearly all the hamlets and settlements of the frontier. It was a religious bombshell which threatened to shake the very foundations of the religious creeds.

In the ten years following the first vision of 1820, the name of Joseph Smith was scarcely known outside a few small villages. Brigham Young, living only forty miles away, and later to become his trusted lieutenant, had not as yet heard of him. Within a year after his strange book appeared, his name was known for good or evil along the entire frontier, as far north as Canada, as far south as New Orleans, and a thousand miles to the west, at the trading post of Independence, Missouri. "The Golden Bible" was a lively topic of conversation.

Newspapers took a sudden interest in the "Prophet of Palmyra." Comments and criticisms of the new volume found voice in their columns. The contract for the printing of the translated record was made with E. B. Grandin and Company of Palmyra on August 25, 1829. The earliest press notice appeared six days later.

In their issue of August 31, 1829, the *Rochester Daily Advertiser and Telegraph*, published the following account:

"The Palmyra Freeman says—'The greatest piece of superstition that has ever come within our knowledge, now occupies the

THE BOOK OF MORMON:

AN account written by the hand of Mormon, upon plates, taken from the plates of Nephi.

Wherefore it is an abridgment of the Record of the People of Nephi, and also of the Lamanites; written to the Lamanites, which are a remnant of the House of Israel; and also to Jew and Gentile; written by way of commandment, and also by the spirit of Prophecy and of Revelation. Written, and sealed up, and hid up unto the Lord, that they might not be destroyed; to come forth by the gift and power of God unto the interpretation thereof; sealed by the hand of Moroni, and hid up unto the Lord, to come forth in due time by the way of Gentile; the interpretation thereof by the gift of God; an abridgment taken from the Book of Ether.

Also, which is a Record of the People of Jared, which were scattered at the time the Lord confounded the language of the people when they were building a tower to get to Heaven: Which is to shew unto the remnant of the House of Israel how great things the Lord hath done for their fathers: and that they may know the covenants of the Lord, that they are not cast off forever; and also to the convincing of the Jew and Gentile that Jesus is the Christ, the Eternal God, manifesting Himself unto all nations. And now if there be fault, it be the mistake of men; wherefore condemn not the things of God, that ye may be found spotless at the judgement seat of Christ.

* * *

The above work, containing about 600 pages, large Duodecimo, is now for sale, wholesale and retail, at the Palmyra Bookstore, by

HOWARD & GRANDIN.

Palmyra, March 26, 1830.   339

Advertisement in the *Wayne Sentinel* on March 26, 1830 announcing the publication of the Book of Mormon.

attention of a few individuals of this quarter. It is generally known and spoken of as the 'Golden Bible.' Its proselytes give the following account of it."[1]

There followed a garbled account of the discovery of the plates and their translation. Other newspapers, such as the *Rochester Gem*,[2] also gave accounts of the "Golden Bible," while it was yet in the hands of the printer. These articles, despite their contempt for the unseen volume, aroused considerable curiosity as to the book, and undoubtedly hastened its sales when it appeared.

The Book proved to be a unique missionary. Religious pioneers of the frontier on reading it, found it convincing and sought the man who had produced it. Among those thus converted to the new Prophet were such future leaders as Parley P. Pratt, Orson Pratt, Brigham Young, Heber C. Kimball and Sidney Rigdon.

Within the year the nucleus of a great organization had come into being and the "Prophet of Palmyra" had suddenly emerged as the most vital figure on the religious frontier of America.

Many, on reading the book for the first time, declared it to be the revealed word of God, and accepted the truth of the record. The majority treated the volume with contempt and heaped ridicule upon its author. Everywhere it divided men into two camps, and its effect upon both is remarkable.

Those who believed were ready to give up their homes, change their occupations, endure privation, sacrifice their lives, if necessary, rather than relinquish that new-found belief. Those who condemned the volume did so with all the scorn and contempt of which they

were capable. Men spent time and money to combat it, and those of a literary tendency began to write new volumes, trying to expose it as a fraud and a hoax. Preachers from the pulpit made it the subject of vigorous attacks and warned their audiences against it as "an instrument of the devil."

An Invitation to Read the Book of Mormon

What is the *Book of Mormon*? What does it contain which so disturbed the religious world of 1830? What message from within its pages caused Jo-

Copy of the original edition of the Book of Mormon printed by E. B. Grandin.

[1](Note) This account is printed through the courtesy of Dr. Francis Kirkham who has collected much valuable material concerning the origin of the *Book of Mormon*.
[2]Issue of September 5, 1829.

seph Smith to loom suddenly as a great religious leader?

Let us examine a *Book of Mormon* today as thousands of people in the world are doing and as so many did when the book first appeared in 1830. The content of the volume is of prime importance. If its message is true, the book will live, regardless of its origin. If the book has no merit—the origin loses its interest or importance.

If we open the volume as Parley P. Pratt and others did in 1830, we will find on the title page a most interesting preface (see the facsimile on p. 44) containing a brief summary of the content and purpose of the book.

Four items are outstanding:

First, this volume claims to be an abridgment of sacred records, some of them dating from the tower of Babel.

What an amazing claim! What lover of history, after reading that announcement, could lay the book aside until he had thoughtfully perused its contents? Such a document, if genuine, would be most priceless. The British Museum in 1933 paid the Russian government $500,000 for a single document, the Codex Sinaiticus, which is a 4th or 5th century copy in the Greek language of New Testament books. That ancient manuscript was copied at approximately the time when the *Book of Mormon* was sealed and hidden up by Moroni. But many other copies of the early Hebrew and Christian scriptures are in existence, which tend to lower the value of any single one of them, while the *Book of Mormon* is the only known record of the people concerned and is a translation from the original abridgement.

In the second place, the title page declares that this volume has been preserved and "brought forth by the gift and power of God" and "the interpretation thereof by the gift of God," through the instrumentality of Joseph Smith.

This, too, is an amazing assertion, superior to the claim of any book in the entire world. Many books of the Bible might claim preservation by the power of God, but no translator of the Bible has ever claimed that his translation was made possible solely through the instrumentality of God. If this claim is true, the message of the volume must be God's message to the world, and who among men is not interested in the voice of the Creator?

Thirdly, this volume is addressed especially to the "remnant of the House of Israel," the Lamanites, and "also to Jew and Gentile."

This announcement is important in view of the fact that, aside from the Jews, the remnant of the house of Israel is lost, as far as the world is concerned. Who are the Lamanites? The answer can easily be found. The book shows that this "remnant of Israel" is none other than the American Indian.

Lastly, this peculiar preface declares that the book contains a message which will convince the world that "JESUS is the CHRIST, the ETERNAL GOD, manifesting himself unto all nations."

Historians have contended from time to time that a single authentic account of Jesus and his teachings, other than that of the New Testament, would be priceless; and here we have before us an entire volume dedicated to the purpose of convincing the world of the reality of Jesus' mission as the Messiah.

What could the ancient inhabitants of this continent know of Jesus of Nazareth? What possible proof could they have that Jesus was literally the Son of God? In an age when much of the Bible

THE

BOOK OF MORMON:

AN ACCOUNT WRITTEN BY THE HAND OF MORMON, UPON PLATES TAKEN FROM THE PLATES OF NEPHI.

Wherefore it is an abridgment of the Record of the People of Nephi; and also of the Lamanites; written to the Lamanites, which are a remnant of the House of Israel; and also to Jew and Gentile; written by way of commandment, and also by the spirit of Prophesy and of Revelation. Written, and sealed up, and hid up unto the LORD, that they might not be destroyed; to come forth by the gift and power of GOD; unto the interpretation thereof; sealed by the hand of Moroni, and hid up unto the LORD, to come forth in due time by the way of Gentile; the interpretation thereof by the gift of GOD; an abridgment taken from the Book of Ether.

Also, which is a Record of the People of Jared, which were scattered at the time the LORD confounded the language of the people when they were building a tower to get to Heaven: which is to shew unto the remnant of the House of Israel how great things the LORD hath done for their fathers; and that they may know the covenants of the LORD, that they are not cast off forever; and also to the convincing of the Jew and Gentile that JESUS is the CHRIST, the ETERNAL GOD, manifesting Himself unto all nations. And now if there be fault, it be the mistake of men; wherefore condemn not the things of GOD, that ye may be found spotless at the judgment seat of CHRIST.

BY JOSEPH SMITH, JUNIOR,

AUTHOR AND PROPRIETOR.

PALMYRA:

PRINTED BY E. B. GRANDIN, FOR THE AUTHOR.

1830.

Title Page from the first edition of the Book of Mormon.

is under the fire of critics, this New Witness for Christ should be of intense interest.[3]

Early Views Concerning the Aborigines of America

If we read the contents of this unusual book we find it to contain, interwoven with its greater message, the brief account of two peoples, the aborigines of America, who came to this continent at widely separated periods, and whose descendants are now found among the American Indians.

When the first Europeans set foot upon this western hemisphere, some four and a half centuries ago, they found both North and South America inhabited by copper-colored people. In the belief that he had reached an outer fringe of islands in the East Indies, Columbus called these natives "Indians."

Judged by the standards of the Spaniards, the Indians were largely uncivilized, save for a few centers in Mexico and Peru, where a degree of culture flourished. Even this culture was stamped out by the European invaders in their ruthless quest for gold. Unfortunately, the few Indian libraries also met a universal destruction, and with this destruction the hope of solving the enigma[4] of the Indian seemed gone. Despite the attempts of many learned men to unravel the story of these dark races, the early history of America remained a blank page.

When the Europeans came in contact with them, the Indians were not using the type of writing with which we are now familiar. There were no written equivalents for the spoken word. The Mexican Indian conveyed his message in the form of a pictograph. The Indians of Peru used both pictures and a complicated system of conveying ideas by the tying of knots in a multitude of strings. Although some of the pictographs have been read with some success, they throw little or no light upon the history of the people earlier than the past few hundred years, and only fragments concerning this later period.

The Europeans found, however, upon the walls of ancient buildings, many writings in characters resembling Egyptian hieroglyphics. The Indians living in the very buildings knew nothing of their meaning and they have baffled all efforts of scientific men to decipher them. Their presence on the walls indicates an earlier and higher civilization than that found by the Spaniards. Who built those great buildings, which are now the wonder of the world? What story would the reading of the inscriptions reveal? These questions remain unanswered.

The early Spanish priests who followed Columbus to America wondered at certain forms of worship found among the Indians. Some were so closely akin to Christian ceremonies that the good Bishop Las Casas wrote to his superior in Spain, that the Devil had beaten him to America and had implanted in the hearts of the natives a religion so akin to Christianity that

---

[3] Following the preface, we read in our late editions "Translated by Joseph Smith, Jun.," but in the book Parley P. Pratt and others opened it read "By Joseph Smith, Junior, Author and Proprietor." Enemies of the Prophet, in their ignorance, often made much of this statement as refuting Joseph's claim that it was a translation. To Parley P. Pratt and countless others it means nothing at all, inasmuch as they were aware that the copyright laws required just such a statement before a copyright could issue. At that time a mere translation could not be copyrighted.

[4] Enigma—puzzle: mystery.

they would not listen to the Christian Fathers.[5]

One tribe in Central America had an unusual ceremony akin to the ordinance of the Sacrament or the Catholic Mass. Ground corn and other ingredients were molded into the form of a man, raised on a pole, and then taken down and eaten by the people. Nearly all the tribes conducted religious ceremonies of immersing newly-born babies in water. Many anointed the head with oil in times of sickness.

Theories concerning the origin of the Indian almost immediately began to be published, but no harmony of opinion has been reached. Some writers on the subject advanced the idea that the Indians were all a related people with a more or less common origin. While the majority of writers were agreed thus far, when the attempt was made to say what that origin was, there were as many views as writers.

Garcia, a Spanish author, thought them the lost tribes of Israel and cited evidences of Hebrew culture and belief.[6] Johannes de Laet advanced the theory of an origin in Eastern Asia, probably Mongolian.[7]

Lord Kingsborough, in a nine volume treatise published in 1830-1848, went to great length to establish the Indians as descendants of the Israelites, giving a multitude of facts and observations to back his contention.[8] His conclusions,

however, failed to meet general scientific approval, nor has any writer since met with better success.

It is extremely improbable that Joseph Smith had access to any of the writings of the above-mentioned men. It is certain that none but Lord Kingsborough's works would have been of any value to him, for the contention of the *Book of Mormon* is greatly at variance with all of the earlier works, and Lord Kingsborough's volumes were not in print at the time the *Book of Mormon* was being prepared. This much has been here set forth to make clear to the student of American History, that the message of the *Book of Mormon* is unique in itself, and not a borrowed compilation of existing views.

The View Set Forth by The Book of Mormon

Briefly, the *Book of Mormon* story is as follows:

About 600 years before Christ, a small group of Israelites warned of an impending destruction of their native city, Jerusalem, left their homeland and journeyed southward. Eventually they crossed the ocean in a ship of their own construction and landed somewhere on the American continent. Here they proceeded to develop a civilization, but soon divided into two groups. The most advanced group were white of skin and were firm believers in the God of Israel, and the Hebrew Scriptures, a copy of which had been carried to America. The group was called, "Nephites," after their leader. The less advanced group, called after their first leader, "Lamanites," became darker skinned, due to a curse of God upon them for their rebellious spirit. The two people were often at war with each other, the Nephites being at times forced to abandon their homes and seek new ones.

---

[5](Note) The Story of Bartolome de Las Casas 1474-1566), who is called the "Apostle of the Indies," may be read in any standard encyclopedia. His book, *Historia de las Indias* (published 1875-1876), throws great light upon the early treatment of the Indians by the Spaniards. Las Casas was the first man to contend that the Indians were the lost tribes of Israel.

[6]*Origin de los indios de el neuvo mundo* (Valencia, P. P. Mey, 1607), by Gregorio Garcia. Garcia (1560-1627) spent 12 years in America as a missionary.

[7]The theory of Johannes de Laet (1593-1649), set forth in 1643 is often referred to as the Dutch Theory of Indian origin.

[8]*Antiquities of Mexico* (London, A. Aglio, publisher), nine volumes, by Edward King, Viscount of Kingsborough (1795-1837), was published in London, 1830-1848.

Some four hundred years after the arrival in America, the Nephites, in seeking a new place for settlement, encountered another people, the Mulekites, who, like themselves, were Israelites who had left Jerusalem because of the political disturbances at the time of King Zedekiah (about 587 B. C.). The two people united under the Nephite ruler, King Mosiah.

During the reign of this king, an exploring expedition encountered extensive ruins of an earlier civilization and discovered a writing in very ancient characters upon 24 gold plates. These were read by aid of the power of God, and found to contain a history of a race called Jaredites, who had formerly occupied the land as a numerous people. These former inhabitants, according to the account, had left the vicinity of the Tower of Babel at the time of the Confusion of Tongues, and finally crossed the ocean in eight peculiar barges, to America. Here their civilization had flourished for better than two thousand years, finally destroying itself by internal wars.

The warfare between the dark-skinned Lamanites and the now enlarged group of Nephites continued, with some long periods of peace, during which trade and commerce flourished between the nations. A rather remarkable civilization was developed, which involved the mining, smelting and casting of metals, the weaving of fine cloths and fabrics, the use of coins, the domestication of animals, the building of ships, and the erection of great cities of stone, and cement.

The Nephites developed two forms of written language, a revised Hebrew and a reformed or revised Egyptian. Art reached a high stage, even the exteriors of buildings being highly decorated with artistic designs. The sciences of astronomy and mathematics were unsurpassed in their day, and the accomplishments of their engineers incite the wonder of the present world.

These people became especially advanced in their religious concepts. Temples were erected to God, comparable to the Temple of Solomon. They had prophets who communed with the Most High and taught their people a wholesome philosophy of life. These prophets labored without salary, performed miracles like unto those of the prophets of Israel, and kept sacred records of their people. Great personalities were developed. Nephi, the first of that name, is one of the finest characters of all time. King Benjamin, one of the most beloved monarchs, and Moroni, one of the most skilled commanders of men.

Christ Appears in the Western Continent

The Nephites firmly believed in a Messiah who was to come to Jerusalem and, through signs which had been given by their prophets, knew the day of his birth on the old continent, and of his subsequent death.

At the time of the crucifixion a terrible storm broke over the cities of the Nephites and Lamanites. This, with disturbances of the earth and volcanic eruptions, destroyed a large part of the population, and buried many of their cities.

Following His resurrection, Christ appeared to the remnant of the Nephites on the American continent, preached great sermons to them, and ministered unto them. Having chosen twelve disciples among them and provided for the organization of His

Ruins of early American cultures as seen today. Top: Ruin at Chichen-Itza in Yucatan. Bottom: Steps to Temple Zaculea in Guatemala.

JOSEPH SMITH PREACHING TO THE INDIANS, photograph of oil painting by William Armitage which hangs in the Salt Lake Temple.

Used by permission, First Presidency, Church of Jesus Christ of Latter-day Saints

Church, with the proper ordinances, He departed from them into the heavens.

So great was the effect of the destruction and the visitation, that all wars ceased between peoples and a Golden Era of prosperity began. There were no rich or poor, but all lived in a happy brotherhood. This era lasted nearly two hundred years before dissension broke out again. A series of wars followed. In the last of these, the victorious Lamanites annihilated the Nephites as a separate people. Prior to this great destruction, Mormon, a great Nephite general and prophet, compiled the records of his people, and made an abridgment of them. His son, Moroni, survived the greater part of the destructions and prior to his death hid the completed records (about 420 A. D.). It is the abridgment by Mormon, and some of the writings of his son Moroni, which came into Joseph Smith's hands. The translation thereof constitutes the *Book of Mormon*.

The Real Message of the Book

Startling as are the claims of the *Book of Mormon* as to the white, Israelitish origin of the American Indian, and the existence of early civilizations upon this continent—the real worth of the volume lies in other things. The early writers of the Nephite records have made no attempt to relate an exhaustive history, or to acquaint future readers with the details of their civilization, or the geography of their land. Rather, the object has been to preserve a religious philosophy of life, to convince the reader as to the reality of God, and to establish the certainty that Jesus is the Christ. The reader who searches for these things will find them in rich abundance. The volume abounds with striking examples of the rewards of righteous-

ness or unrighteousness, especially as it affects the life and prosperity of a whole nation. A world in turmoil could learn much from its pages.

But deeper even than the effect of the belief in Christ upon nations, is its fundamental philosophy of the development of human personality. Out of this volume has come the basic philosophy of Mormonism which has made development of personality the important goal of life.

The beauty of this religious philosophy which breathes from its pages cannot be over-emphasized. Its harmony and balance defy the severest critic. Its message touches the human heart—it points the way to happiness. None can read its pages without a mellowing of the soul.

It is its deep message which converts its readers. Those who read the volume in 1830 cared little for history or archaeology, but the philosophy answered their inner needs. The great pity is that so many become too lost in debate over the origin of the book to see clearly its message.

While the various books of the New Testament were written to accomplish distinct objectives none of the gospels or letters was written to preserve the gospel in its fulness and plainness in the event that the Church should be destroyed or become corrupted. It must have seemed to the New Testament writers that the early Church would continue forever, and that neither its doctrines nor its ordinances were in grave danger of change or oblivion. Indeed, while they wrote in a time of stress, it was the stress occasioned by growth, and the prospects of the church looked bright when the last gospel and epistle were penned. The *Book of Mormon*, on the other hand, had been written in a day of doom for Christ's Church in America and for the ostensible* purpose of restoring at some future and happier day the gospel which was then being distorted.

Unlike the Apostle Paul who wrote his epistle to solve the immediate perplexing problems of the newly founded Greek and Roman churches, the American prophet, Mormon, was not attempting to solve the immediate problems of his day. That he had made a heroic effort to revive the gospel in the hearts of his people is apparent from his narration of disappointing missionary efforts. The record which he set himself to make, however, was to be addressed to a generation then unborn, a generation to be chosen as the recipients** of his book by the Lord God. And for that generation he gathered and selected his material for one great purpose—to bring them to an understanding of the Gospel of Jesus Christ in its simplicity and purity and to convince all the honest in heart "that JESUS is the CHRIST, the ETERNAL GOD, manifesting himself unto all nations."[9]

The Source Materials

In carrying out his purpose Mormon had at his disposal a vast collection of church records and personal journals. Only a small part of the total could be used for his purpose. But among the records were many accounts of God's dealings with His people which cast light upon His attributes and the nature of His commandments unto men. Various Nephite Prophets had manifested remarkable faith, so much so that the will of God and the nature of

the Gospel principles had been revealed unto them. Further, following His crucifixion and subsequent resurrection at Jerusalem, Christ had appeared on the American continent. Here He had organized His Church, commanded a continuance of His ordinances, and instructed the Nephites in the way of abundant life. The recorded words of Christ among the records at the disposal of Mormon must have been voluminous, for he informs us:

"And now there cannot be written in this book even a hundredth part of the things which Jesus did truly teach unto the people.

"And these things have I written, which are a lesser part of the things which he taught the people. . . .

"Behold, I was about to write them, all which were engraven upon the plates of Nephi, but the Lord forbade it, saying: I will try the faith of my people."[10]

Truth Concerning Baptism

The fullness of the Gospel as revealed by the *Book of Mormon* is best studied from the *Book of Mormon* itself. A few examples, however, will illustrate the part played by this ancient American record in the restoration. As previously pointed out, the Bible is an insufficient guide on the matter of baptism, being entirely silent on many vital issues. Concerning baptism the *Book of Mormon* contains many direct words of the Savior. Consider the clarity and value of the following:

"And the Lord said unto him: I give unto you power that ye shall baptize this people when I am again ascended into heaven.

"And again the Lord called others, and said unto them likewise; and he gave unto them power to baptize. And he said unto them: On this wise shall ye baptize; and there shall be no disputations among you.

"Verily I say unto you, that whoso repenteth of his sins through your words and

*ostensible—plainly to be seen.
**recipient—one upon whom an honor, gift, or favor is bestowed.
[9]See *Book of Mormon*, title page.
[10]3 Nephi 26:6, 8, 11.

desireth to be baptized in my name, on this wise shall ye baptize them—Behold, ye shall go down and stand in the water, and in my name shall ye baptize them.

"And now behold, these are the words which ye shall say, calling them by name, saying:

"Having authority given me of Jesus Christ, I baptize you in the name of the Father, and of the Son, and of the Holy Ghost. Amen.

"And then shall ye immerse them in the water, and come forth again out of the water.

"And after this manner shall ye baptize in my name; for behold, verily, I say unto you, that the Father, and the Son, and the Holy Ghost are one; and I am in the Father, and the Father in me, and the Father and I are one.

"And according as I have commanded you thus shall ye baptize. And there shall be no disputations among you, as there have hitherto been; neither shall there be disputations among you concerning the points of my doctrine, as there have hitherto been."[11]

Upon the subject of infant baptism the Nephite prophet, Mormon, is exceedingly plain:

"For, if I have learned the truth, there have been disputations among you concerning the baptism of your little children.

"And now, my son, I desire that ye should labor diligently, that this gross error should be removed from among you; for, for this intent I have written this epistle.

"For immediately after I had learned these things of you I inquired of the Lord concerning the matter. And the word of the Lord came to me by the power of the Holy Ghost, saying:

"Listen to the words of Christ, your

The Book of Mormon complements the Holy Bible and resolves the disputations among men.

Redeemer, your Lord and your God. Behold, I came into the world not to call the righteous but sinners to repentance; the whole need no physician, but they that are sick; wherefore,

---

[11] 3 Nephi 11:21-28.

little children are whole, for they are not capable of committing sin; wherefore the curse of Adam is taken from them in me, that it hath no power over them; and the law of circumcision is done away in me.

"And after this manner did the Holy Ghost manifest the word of God unto me; wherefore, my beloved son, I know that it is solemn mockery before God, that ye should baptize little children.

"Behold I say unto you that this thing shall ye teach—repentance and baptism unto those who are accountable and capable of committing sin; yea, teach parents that they must repent and be baptized, and humble themselves as their little children, and they shall all be saved with their little children.

"And their children need no repentance, neither baptism. Behold, baptism is unto repentance to the fulfilling the commandments unto the remission of sins.

"But little children are alive in Christ, even from the foundation of the world; if not so, God is a partial God, and also a changeable God, a respecter to persons; for how many little children have died without baptism!

"Wherefore, if little children could not be saved without baptism, these must have gone to an endless hell.

"Behold I say unto you, that he that supposeth that little children need baptism is in the gall of bitterness and in the bonds of iniquity, for he hath neither faith, hope, nor charity; wherefore, should he be cut off while in the thought, he must go down to hell.

"For awful is the wickedness to suppose that God saveth one child because of baptism, and the other must perish because he hath no baptism.

"Wo be unto them that shall pervert the ways of the Lord after this manner, for they shall perish except they repent. Behold, I speak with boldness, having authority from God; and I fear not what man can do; for perfect love casteth out all fear.

"And I am filled with charity, which is everlasting love; wherefore, all children are alike unto me; wherefore, I love little children with a perfect love; and they are all alike and partakers of salvation.

"For I know that God is not a partial God, neither a changeable being; but he is unchangeable from all eternity to all eternity.

"Little children cannot repent; wherefore, it is awful wickedness to deny the pure mercies of God unto them, for they are all alive in him because of his mercy.

"And he that saith that little children need baptism denieth the mercies of Christ, and setteth at naught the atonement of him and the power of his redemption."[12]

In the light of the above passage, controversy in these vital matters is swept away.

The Sacrament of the Lord's Supper

Likewise, there are deficiencies in the Bible concerning the administration of the sacrament of the Lord's Supper, which are supplied by the *Book of Mormon*. The *Book of Mormon* reveals the real purpose of the sacrament in these recorded words of Jesus:

"And it came to pass that Jesus commanded his disciples that they should bring forth some bread and wine unto him.

"And while they were gone for bread and wine, he commanded the multitude that they should sit themselves down upon the earth.

"And when the disciples had come with bread and wine, he took of the bread and brake and blessed it; and he gave unto the disciples and commanded that they should eat.

"And when they had eaten and were filled, he commanded that they should give unto the multitude.

"And when the multitude had eaten and were filled, he said unto the disciples: Behold there shall one be ordained among you, and to him will I give power that he shall break bread and bless it and give it unto the people of my church, unto all those who shall believe and be baptized in my name.

"And this shall ye always observe to do, even as I have done, even as I have broken bread and blessed it and given it unto you.

"And this shall ye do in remembrance of my body, which I have shown unto you. And it shall be a testimony unto the Father that ye do always remember me. And if ye do always remember me ye shall have my Spirit to be with you.

"And it came to pass that when he said these words, he commanded his disciples that they should take of the wine of the cup and drink of it, and that they should also give unto the multitude that they might drink of it.

"And it came to pass that they did so, and did drink of it and were filled; and they gave

---

[12]Moroni 8:5-20.

unto the multitude, and they did drink, and they were filled.

"And when the disciples had done this, Jesus said unto them: Blessed are ye for this thing which ye have done, for this is fulfilling my commandments, and this doth witness unto the Father that ye are willing to do that which I have commanded you.

"And this shall ye always do to those who repent and are baptized in my name; and ye shall do it in remembrance of my blood, which I have shed for you, that ye may witness unto the Father that ye do always remember me. And if ye do always remember me ye shall have my Spirit to be with you."[13]

Also, the *Book of Mormon* contains the words to be used in the sacramental prayers.

"The manner of their elders and priests administering the flesh and blood of Christ unto the church; and they administered it according to the commandments of Christ; wherefore we know the manner to be true; and the elder or priest did minister it—

"And they did kneel down with the church, and pray to the Father in the name of Christ, saying:

"O God, the Eternal Father, we ask thee in the name of thy Son, Jesus Christ, to bless and sanctify this bread to the souls of all those who partake of it; that they may eat in remembrance of the body of thy Son, and witness unto thee, O God, the Eternal Father, that they are willing to take upon them the name of thy Son, and always remember him, and keep his commandments which he hath given them, that they may always have his Spirit to be with them. Amen.

"The manner of administering the wine— Behold, they took the cup, and said:

"O God, the Eternal Father, we ask thee, in the name of thy Son, Jesus Christ, to bless and sanctify this wine to the souls of all those who drink of it, that they may do it in remembrance of the blood of thy Son, which was shed for them; that they may witness unto thee, O God, the Eternal Father, that they do always remember him, that they may have his Spirit to be with them. Amen."[14]

Had these instructions been found in the Holy Bible the confusion of the Christian world on this matter might

have been avoided. In the *Book of Mormon* the true form and purpose of this sacrament is fully restored, and that in language a child can understand.

Light Upon the Beatitudes

The Gospel of Jesus Christ as summarized in what is called the "Great Sermon" or the "Sermon on the Mount"[15] has been the subject of many a gospel discourse. Some of these discourses have been masterpieces of literature and have often carried a beautiful message. The interpretations vary so greatly, however, that all cannot agree with the meaning of Jesus. The *Book of Mormon* contains an account of a "Great Sermon," delivered by the resurrected Christ to the Nephites in America. While portions of the two great sermons are different, much of the discourses were upon identical subjects and include the same related thoughts. The record of this second "Great Sermon," insofar as it parallels the great sermon in Galilee, should cast light upon the great meanings of the Master. This it does. Consider the following comparisons:

In Matthew 5:1-3 we read,

"And seeing the multitudes, he went up into a mountain: and when he was set, his disciples came unto him:
"And he opened his mouth, and taught them, saying,
"Blessed are the poor in spirit: for theirs is the kingdom of heaven."

The last sentence has proven a stumbling block for centuries. The term "poor in spirit" has had a distinct meaning both in the English, and in the Greek and Aramaic expressions from which it was translated. In other literature than the Bible it unquestion-

---

[13]3 Nephi 18:1-11.
[14]Moroni 4; 5.

[15]Matthew 5; 6; 7.

ably means the "down-and-outer," the person who has lost courage and hope. But if that meaning were applied to the passage in Matthew it would be inconceivable how such a spiritually impoverished individual would have the Kingdom of God as a reward. Scholars faced with this incongruity have sought for some other interpretation for the "poor in spirit," and have sometimes ascribed them to be the "humble" and "penitent." This plain shunting of the true meaning has remained a thorn in the side of the conscientious reader of the Bible.

The *Book of Mormon* introduction to the same message, delivered in America to the Nephites, is enlightening.

"And it came to pass that when Jesus had spoken these words unto Nephi, and to those who had been called, (now the number of those who had been called, and received power and authority to baptize, was twelve) and behold, he stretched forth his hand unto the multitude, and cried unto them, saying: *Blessed are ye if ye shall give heed unto the words of these twelve* whom I have chosen from among you to minister unto you and to be your servants; *and unto them I have given power that they may baptize you with water;* and after ye are baptized with water, behold, I will baptize you with fire and with the Holy Ghost; *therefore blessed are ye if ye shall believe in me and be baptized,* after that ye have seen me and know that I am.

"And again, *more blessed are they who shall believe in your words* because ye shall testify that ye have seen me, and that ye know that I am. Yea, *blessed are they who shall believe in your words, and come down in the depths of humility and be baptized, for they shall be visited with fire and with the Holy Ghost, and shall receive a remission of their sins.*

"Yea, blessed are the poor in spirit *who come unto me,* for theirs is the kingdom of heaven." [Emphasis added.][16]

The light thrown by the above passages upon the so-called "Beatitudes" revolutionize the meaning. The "poor in spirit" are not blessed because of

[16]3 Nephi 12:1-3.

their present condition, but may be blessed if they will accept the principles Jesus taught and come unto His Church through the waters of baptism.

It cannot be a blessed condition to mourn. It crushes out hope and happiness. But blessed indeed are those mourners who come unto Christ and receive from Him the assurance of immortality.

Likewise with all other groups of people in whatsoever condition, if they will believe and come into the fold of Christ they will be blessed.

This contribution to the interpretation of the great message of the Savior gives the true meaning scholars have sought through the centuries.

Space will not permit a detailed analysis and comparison of the two great sermons. The student, however, would do well to follow them through for further contributions. One other illustration will suffice for our purpose here. In the sixth chapter of Matthew in the last part of verse twenty-four we read, "Ye cannot serve God and mammon." Jesus had been speaking to the multitude. Verse twenty-five continues, "Therefore I say unto you, Take no thought of your life, what ye shall eat, or what ye shall drink; nor yet for your body what ye shall put on, etc." This passage taken literally would present an impractical doctrine highly disastrous to any nation which might attempt to follow it. To avoid the conclusion that Jesus was an idealist whose teachings would not work, lovers of the Bible have manufactured meanings other than the literal. They have said that Jesus did not intend that we should not till our fields and tend our cattle, and turn the wheels of our mills, but that He is emphasizing the futility of making these things our masters. The explanation is not without merit and beauty in and of itself, but it remains in the last analysis the doctrine of its sponsors and not necessarily the meaning intended by Jesus.

The *Book of Mormon* passage found in the thirteenth chapter of 3 Nephi clarifies the problem. In the latter part of verse twenty-four we read as in Matthew,

"Ye cannot serve God and Mammon."

But in verse twenty-five there is a change.

"And now it came to pass that when Jesus had spoken these words *he looked upon the twelve whom he had chosen, and said unto them: Remember the words which I have spoken. For behold, ye are they whom I have chosen to minister unto this people. Therefore, I say unto you, take no thought for your life,* what ye shall eat, or what ye shall drink; nor yet for your body, what ye shall put on." [Emphasis added.]

There is no longer any necessity for hedging, for manufacturing meanings. The doctrine of Jesus becomes at once both sensible and practical. All people were not asked to give up the ordinary occupations of life, but the entire time and talent of the twelve men called to head His organization should be devoted to the Church.

The *Book of Mormon* is a challenge to faith. It is an invitation to Christian thinking. It introduces to the world a new conception of the Christ.

And the challenge of the book is like the challenge of the resurrected Lord to the doubting Apostles at Jerusalem.

"Handle me, and see; for a spirit hath not flesh and bones, as ye see me have."[17]

The last writer of the book breathes the same spirit when he says,

"When ye shall receive these things, I would exhort you that ye would ask God, the Eternal Father, in the name of Christ, if these things are not true; and if ye shall ask with a sincere heart, with real intent, having faith in Christ, he will manifest the truth of it unto you, by the power of the Holy Ghost."[18]

Supplementary Readings

Accounts of other ancient writings found in America are contained in the following:

1. Roberts, *New Witness for God,* Vol. 3, pp. 50-56.
2. *Ibid*—Vol. 3, pp. 57-66.
3. Sjodahl, *Introduction to the Study of the Book of Mormon.*
4. Widtsoe and Harris, *Seven Claims of the Book of Mormon,* Chapter 1.

---

[17]Luke 24:39.
[18]Moroni 10:4.

CHAPTER 7

WHAT WITNESSES HAVE
TO SAY CONCERNING THE
ORIGIN OF THE
BOOK OF MORMON

Three of the Witnesses Speak

Everyday truth is established in courts of law through the testimony of witnesses. Although many witnesses are desirable to establish truth, the testimony of a single witness, if it be consistent and straightforward, is often considered sufficient. The testimony of two or three witnesses, if in agreement on the essential items, can seldom be overthrown.

Joseph Smith proclaimed to the world that he had translated the *Book of Mormon* by the aid of the Lord, from the engravings on a set of metal plates which had the appearance of gold, and which had been delivered into his hands by an angel, for that purpose. This is a bold assertion, and we naturally ask, are there any witnesses to speak for the truth of such a statement? Did any others behold the angel?

We need but open the *Book of Mormon* to find not only the names of such witnesses, but a written statement of their testimony placed where all the world may see—a statement published repeatedly for over one hundred years and never changed or retracted by any one of those whose signatures appear there. And this in view of the fact that all of the witnesses lived for many years after that testimony was first published, and also in view of the fact that six of the eleven men whose names appear, left the Church which they had helped organize, or were excommunicated from it.

No document in religious history is vouched for by such an array of witnesses—or by such consistency in the testimony of the witnesses.

Above the signatures of Oliver Cowdery, Martin Harris, and David Whitmer, three of the witnesses, we find the following:

"Be it known unto all nations, kindreds, tongues, and people, unto whom this work shall come: That we, through the grace of God the Father, and our Lord Jesus Christ, have seen the plates which contain this record, which is a record of the people of Nephi, and also of the Lamanites, their brethren, and also the people of Jared, who came from the tower of which hath been spoken. And we also know that they have been translated by the gift and power of God, for his voice hath declared it unto us; wherefore we know of a surety that the work is true. And we also testify that we have seen the engravings which are upon the plates; and they have been shown unto us by the power of God, and not of man. And we declare with words of soberness, that an angel of God came down from heaven, and he brought and laid before our eyes, that we beheld and saw the plates, and the engravings thereon; and we know that it is by the grace of God the Father, and our Lord Jesus Christ, that we beheld and bear record that these things are true. And it is marvelous in our eyes. Nevertheless, the voice of the Lord commanded us that we should bear record of it; wherefore, to be obedient unto the commandments of God, we bear testimony of these things. And we know that if we are faithful in Christ, we shall rid our garments of the blood of all men, and be found spotless before the judgment-seat of Christ, and shall dwell with him eternally in the heavens. And the honor be to the Father, and to the Son, and to the Holy Ghost, which is one God. Amen."

Of the occasion referred to by the

Oliver Cowdery   David Whitmer   Martin Harris

The Three Witnesses to the existence of the Gold Plates of the Book of Mormon, to the correctness of Joseph Smith's translation, and to the declaration of the Lord that it is true.

witnesses, Joseph Smith writes in his journal that it occurred immediately after the completion of the translation. He says:

"Martin Harris, David Whitmer, Oliver Cowdery, and myself agreed to retire into the woods, and try to obtain, by fervent and humble prayer, the fulfilment of the promises given in the above revelation—that they should have a view of the plates.[1] We accordingly made choice of a piece of woods convenient to Mr. Whitmer's house, to which we retired, and having knelt down, we began to pray in much faith to almighty God to bestow upon us a realization of these promises.

"According to previous arrangement, I commenced by vocal prayer to our Heavenly Father, and was followed by each of the others in succession. We did not at the first trial, however, obtain any answer or manifestation of divine favor in our behalf. We again observed the same order of prayer, each calling on and praying fervently to God in rotation, but with the same result as before.

"Upon this, our second failure, Martin Harris proposed that he should withdraw himself from us, believing, as he expressed it himself, that his presence was the cause of our not obtaining what we wished for. He accordingly withdrew from us, and we knelt down again, and had not been many minutes

engaged in prayer, when we presently beheld a light above us in the air, of exceeding brightness; and behold an angel stood before us. In his hands he held the plates which we

Monument erected to the memory of The Three Witnesses at Richmond, Missouri. Picture was taken soon after its dedication in 1911.

[1]The revelation referred to is found in *Doctrine and Covenants*, Sec. 17, and was given to Oliver Cowdery, David Whitmer and Martin Harris at Fayette in June, 1829, a few days before the events here described.

had been praying for these to have a view of. He turned over the leaves one by one, so that we could see them, and discern the engravings thereon distinctly. He then addressed himself to David Whitmer, and said, 'David, blessed is the Lord, and he that keeps His commandments,' when, immediately afterwards, we heard a voice from out of the bright light above us, saying, 'These plates have been revealed by the power of God, and they have been translated by the power of God. The translation of them which you have seen is correct, and I command you to bear record of what you now see and hear.'

"I now left David and Oliver, and went in pursuit of Martin Harris, whom I found at a considerable distance, fervently engaged in prayer. He soon told me, however, that he had not yet prevailed with the Lord, and earnestly requested me to join him in prayer, that he also might realize the same blessings which we had just received. We accordingly joined in prayer, and ultimately obtained our desires, for before we had finished, the same vision was opened to our view, at least it was again opened to me, and I once more beheld and heard the same things; whilst at the same moment, Martin Harris cried out, apparently in an ecstasy of joy, ' 'Tis enough mine eyes have beheld; mine eyes have beheld;' and jumping up, he shouted 'Hosanna,' blessing God, and otherwise rejoicing exceedingly."[2]

The Witnesses Remain Faithful

In the years of trial and persecution which followed, all three of these men were found outside the Church, with feelings of bitterness toward it or its leaders. Not one of them denied at any time his aforementioned testimony, although they were afforded ample opportunity and inducement to do so. Three short incidents are typical of the faithfulness with which they clung to their original story.

Some time after leaving the Church, Oliver Cowdery, who had studied law, became prosecuting attorney in one of the counties of the state of Michigan. During the course of a murder trial the attorney for the defendant challenged Oliver Cowdery in the following words:

"May it please the court, and gentlemen of the jury, I challenge Mr. Cowdery, since he seems to know so much about the poor defendant, to tell us something about his connection with Joe Smith, and the digging out of the hill of the Mormon Bible, and how Mr. Cowdery helped Joe Smith to defraud the American people out of a whole lot of money selling the Mormon Bible and telling them that an angel appeared to them from heaven, dressed in white clothes."

When it came Oliver Cowdery's turn to reply he arose in calm dignity and in a clear voice said:

"If your honor please, and gentlemen of the jury, the attorney on the opposite side has challenged me to state my connection with Joseph Smith and the *Book of Mormon*: and as I cannot now avoid the responsibility, I must admit to you that I am the very Oliver Cowdery whose name is attached to the testimony, with others, as to the appearance of the Angel Moroni; and let me tell you that it is not because of my good deeds that I am here, away from the body of the Mormon Church, but because I have broken the covenants I once made, and I was cut off from the Church, but, gentlemen of the jury, I have never denied my testimony, which is attached to the *Book of Mormon*, and I declare to you here that these eyes saw the angel, and ears of mine heard the voice of the angel, and he told us his name was Moroni; that the book was true, and contained the fulness of the gospel, and we were also told that if we ever denied what we heard and seen that there would be no forgiveness for us, neither in this world nor in the world to come."[3]

Elder Edward Stevenson, who was instrumental in later years in inducing Martin Harris to re-enter the Church in 1870 relates an experience of Martin Harris:

"On one occasion several of his old acquaintances made an effort to get him tipsy by treating him to some wine. When they thought he was in a good mood for talk

---

[2] *History of the Church*—Period I, Vol. I, pp. 54-55.

[3] From the affidavit of Judge C. M. Nielson of Utah, under date of December 3, 1909. The affidavit is on file in the Church Historian's office, Salt Lake City, Utah.

they put the question very carefully to him, 'Well, now, Martin, we want you to be frank and candid with us in regard to this story of your seeing an angel and the golden plates of the *Book of Mormon* that are so much talked about. We have always taken you to be an honest good farmer and neighbor of ours but could not believe that you did see an angel. Now, Martin, do you really believe that you did see an angel, when you were awake?' 'No,' said Martin, 'I do not believe it.' The crowd were delighted, but soon a different feeling prevailed, as Martin, true to his trust, said, 'Gentlemen, what I have said is true, from the fact that my belief is swallowed up in knowledge; for I want to say to you that as the Lord lives I do know that I stood with the Prophet Joseph Smith in the presence of the angel, and it was in the brightness of day.'"[4]

On the 7th of September, 1878, thirty-nine years after David Whitmer had affixed his signature to the testimony to the *Book of Mormon*, he was visited by Orson Pratt and Joseph F. Smith at his home in Richmond, Missouri. Among other things confirming the *Book of Mormon* story he said:

"It was in June, 1829, (when we saw the plates) the latter part of the month, and the eight witnesses saw them, I think the next day or the day after. Joseph showed them the plates himself, but the angel showed us the plates. * * * I saw them just as plain as I see this bed and I heard the voice of the Lord, as distinctly as I ever heard anything in my life, declaring that the records of the plates of the *Book of Mormon* were translated by the gift and power of God."[5]

Oliver Cowdery returned to the Church in 1848, at a time when there was nothing of earthly value to gain in joining a homeless people on their way to the barren valleys of the Rocky Mountains. In the midst of his touching sermon to the Saints in Kanesville (now Council Bluffs), Iowa, at the time of his return, October 21, 1848, we read these words, "I beheld with my eyes and handled with my hands the gold plates from which it (the *Book of Mormon*) was transcribed. I also saw with my eyes and handled with my hands the 'Holy Interpreters.' That book is true." In January, 1849, while paying a last visit to his friend, David Whitmer, he died.

Martin Harris returned to the Church in later life, due to the efforts and influence of Elder Edward Stevenson. He died at Clarkston, Utah, July 10, 1875, at the age of ninety-three years. "On the afternoon of his death he was bolstered up in his bed, where with the *Book of Mormon* in his hand, he bore his last testimony to those who were present."[6]

David Whitmer lived out his life at Richmond, Missouri, without returning to membership in the Mormon Church. But he never denied his testimony. In his advanced age, to refute all claims that he had denied his original testimony, he wrote a remarkable pamphlet entitled "Addressed to all Believers in Christ," in which he says:

"It is recorded in the American Cyclopedia and the Encyclopedia Britannica, that I, David Whitmer, have denied my testimony as one of the Three Witnesses to the divinity of the *Book of Mormon;* and that the two other witnesses, Oliver Cowdery and Martin Harris, denied their testimony to that book. I will say once more to all mankind, that I have never at any time denied that testimony or any part thereof. I also testify to the world, that neither Oliver Cowdery nor Martin Harris ever at any time denied their testimony. They both died reaffirming the truth of the divine authenticity of the *Book of Mormon*."[7]

On the Temple grounds in Salt Lake City, we may see an unusual monument erected in memory of these three men. Engraved on plaques set into the granite shaft is a perpetuation

[4]Letter of Elder Edward Stevenson to the *Millennial Star*.
[5]*Millennial Star*, Vol. 40, pp. 49, 50.
[6]*Millennial Star*, Vol. 28, p. 390. See also *Deseret News*, issue of July 28, 1875.
[7]Pamphlet published in Richmond, Missouri, March 19, 1881.

of the testimony which fell from the lips of these men whom only death could still. Had these three men been hailed as witnesses before the bar of God, they could not have accounted themselves more nobly than in sustaining their testimony to the *Book of Mormon* among the children of men.

The Testimony of the Eight Witnesses

Remarkable and convincing as is the testimony of the Three Witnesses as to the divine origin and translation of the *Book of Mormon*, such evidence is still further supported by the testimony of eight additional men. The eight witnesses were shown the plates in a little grove of trees by the Smith residence near Palmyra, some two or three days after the experience of the Three Witnesses at Fayette. Above their signatures we find in the *Book of Mormon* the following:

"Be it known unto all nations, kindreds, tongues, and people, unto whom this work shall come: That Joseph Smith, Jun., the translator of this work, has shown unto us the plates of which hath been spoken, which have the appearance of gold; and many of the leaves as the said Smith has translated we did handle with our hands; and we also saw the engravings thereon, all of which has the appearance of ancient work, and of curious workmanship. And this we bear record with words of soberness, that the said Joseph Smith has shown unto us, for we have seen and hefted, and know of a surety that the said Smith has got the plates of which we have spoken. And we give our names unto the world, to witness unto the world that which we have seen. And we lie not, God bearing witness of it."

Of the eight men whose signatures appear after this declaration, five lived and died members of the Church Joseph established, namely Christian Whitmer, Peter Whitmer, Joseph Smith, Sr., Hyrum Smith, and Samuel H. Smith.

The remaining three, Jacob Whitmer, John Whitmer, and Hyrum Page, left the Church or were excommunicated from it during the trying days of 1838 in Missouri.

But like the Three Witnesses, all of these eight remained true to their testimony. Never at any time did any one of them deny it or alter it in the slightest degree. Even those who left the Church and had every opportunity to renounce their testimony did not do so, but on the contrary, repeatedly declared it to be the sober truth, and died with that testimony unchanged and unrefuted.

John Whitmer, who was excommunicated from the Church in 1838, had a bitter quarrel with Joseph Smith and sought in many ways to bring him into disrepute, but never would he retract one single word of his sworn testimony concerning the plates of the *Book of Mormon*.

The experience related by both sets of witnesses occurred in the bright light of day, under the open sky, where reality is uppermost in the minds of men. All were honest and God-fearing men and were so recognized by the communities in which they lived. They were practical men, used to the hard realities of the frontier. Those who became witnesses to the *Book of Mormon* were those who had at that early date acquainted themselves with Joseph's account concerning the plates and had believed. As Joseph, desiring peace and quiet for his translation, had told but relatively few of his experiences, the witnesses were necessarily drawn largely from the Smith and Whitmer families. Many others, while not permitted to examine the plates, nevertheless knew of their existence and testified in journals and letters concerning them. Lucy Smith, the Prophet's mother, testifies as to the existence of the plates and their various hiding places, as well as to her examination of the breastplate accompanying them.[8] Parley P. Pratt, in his autobiography, refers to the statements of several verifying the existence of the plates.[9] Mr. John Reid, Esq., testified to such knowledge in a speech before the state political convention held in Nauvoo, 1844.[10] Under date of December 19, 1843, Mrs. Martha L. Campbell wrote a letter to Joseph Smith at the request of Josiah Stoal which sets forth his knowledge of the existence of the plates and to having carried the wrapped plates into the Smith home at the time Joseph first obtained them.[11]

At this date, more than one hundred years after the testimonies of these men were first given, they stand entirely unrefuted and unchanged, despite all the attacks which have been launched against them.

Supplementary Readings

1. *History of Joseph Smith by His Mother Lucy Mack Smith*, Chapter 30. (An account of the eight witnesses viewing the plates.)

2. Evans, *Heart of Mormonism*, pp. 68-71. (Incidents in the life of Oliver Cowdery which verify his testimony.)

3. Cannon, *Life of Joseph Smith*, pp. 69-72. (The story of the plates being shown to the three witnesses.)

4. Roberts, *Comprehensive History of the Church*, Vol. I, pp. 150-156. (A discussion of criticisms made against the story of the witnesses.)

5. *Millennial Star*, Vol. 40, Nos. 49, 50. (Visit of Orson Pratt and Joseph F. Smith to David Whitmer.)

6. Roberts, *New Witnesses for God*, Vol. 2, Chapters 15-20. (An interesting summary of the life and testimony of each witness.)

7. Osbourne J. P. Widtsoe, *The Restoration of the Gospel*, pp. 43-45 (Hidden Gospel Records). (The *Book of Mormon*, a New Witness for God.)

8. *Ibid.*, pp. 137-140. (Testimonies of the truthfulness and Divine Authority of the *Book of Mormon*.)

[8]*History of Joseph Smith by His Mother Lucy Mack Smith.*
[9]*Autobiography of Parley P. Pratt*, 1964 edition, p. 110.
[10]*History of the Church*, Period I, Vol. I, pp. 94-96.
[11]The original of Mrs. Campbell's letter is on file at the Church Historian's office, package 4.

CHAPTER 8

THE BOOK OF MORMON
AND THE VERDICT OF TIME

The Book is Still a Matter of Controversy

Between 1960 and 1970, 3,700,000 copies of the *Book of Mormon* were sold to the world. The total number of volumes now in circulation runs well into many millions. At the end of a century it remains the greatest missionary in the Church, its reading being directly responsible for large numbers of converts each year. It has been translated into the languages of all the peoples where the Church maintains branches, and the circle of its readers is continually widening.

Well into its second century the Book remains a subject of controversy. It has neither lost its power to attract belief or to provoke criticism and antagonism.

Never, at any time in its history, have the Latter-day Saints felt the book more inspired. The testimonies of men who have read the book and claim divine assurance of its truth run into the thousands and tens of thousands. The wholesome religious philosophy which breathes from its pages permeates the whole structure and belief of the Church, and has made a lasting imprint upon the lives of its members.

Publications, almost without number, have appeared denouncing the *Book of Mormon* as a hoax and a fraud. Most of them have enjoyed briefly the popularity occasioned by curiosity, and then largely been forgotten. To date, few have reached a second edition. None have influenced the members of the Church against the book or interfered with its sales to the people of the world.

Rarely has the Church deigned to answer the critics of the *Book of Mormon*, deeming the content of the volume and the evidences of its origin sufficient refutation for all time to any who attack its divinity or challenge its claims. Subsequent critics of the volume have almost universally attacked the criticisms of earlier non-Mormon writers as a prelude to the importance of their own arguments and have done a fair job in eliminating one another.

Events and findings subsequent to the first publication of the *Book of Mormon* have largely eliminated the earlier objections to the book—so that it stands today more secure than ever in all its broad assertions.

In order to understand why the critics of the book have been largely discredited, and why the Mormon people have increased their faith in its divinity, it will be necessary to briefly review some of the claims of the book and what the findings of men over a one hundred year period have shown in regard to them.

The *Book of Mormon* declares that two races of people came to America in ancient times from the continent of Asia. One group reached America a short time after the destruction of Babel.[1] The other left the vicinity of Jerusalem about 600 B. C. and reached

---

[1] (Note) As Babel has never been definitely located, it is but a supposition that these people came from Asia. However, most historians indicate that the legend of the Tower of Babel concerns people of the Mesopotamia River valley. It is impossible to place a date for this migration. It was certainly earlier than 2000 B.C.

America some fourteen years later. According to the account, both races, but especially the latter, became highly civilized, developing a culture and language different from any then existing in the world.

As to the first part of this claim, the world is still in controversy—the *Book of Mormon* theory at the date of this writing, having been neither proved nor disproved by the researches of scientific men.

The second part of the claim, namely, that great successive civilizations existed on the American continent, prior to the coming of the Spaniards, has been definitely established by archaeological findings.

It must be remembered by those who believe the *Book of Mormon*, that the great mass of archaeological findings in America do not all relate to the story of the Jaredite or Nephite civilizations. It is easy for the person untrained in archaeology to misunderstand or misinterpret these discoveries. To draw hasty conclusions on such things may definitely injure the cause of the *Book of Mormon* and bring the scholarship of the Church into disrepute.

In the light of the contents of the book itself it is highly absurd to suppose that the volume contains the answers to all the puzzling discoveries which face the archaeologist in America. The *Book of Mormon* is not a history of the entire American continent, nor a complete history of any part of it.

The ancient historians whose records appear in the book made no attempt to write a profane[2] history. Details in culture are generally omitted and there is little reference to the geography of the land. The *Book of Mormon* leaves us without a map of its

cities nor does it indicate clearly in what part of the Americas they were located.[3] Perhaps that secret may yet be found by a close perusal of the text of the book itself, but at this date there is no such thing as a *Book of Mormon* map which can be generally accepted.[4] Consequently, none of the ancient cities which have been unearthed can be identified as yet as being cities mentioned in the *Book of Mormon*. To attempt to make such a claim at the present stage of research is to invite disaster and ridicule. Neither can the book be used as a geographical guide in an attempt to locate cities as yet not unearthed. The use of the *Book of Mormon* by the Smithsonian Institute and other archaeological societies is confined entirely at this time to a study of the *Book of Mormon* stories and names, in an attempt to decipher the inscriptions found on ancient American buildings.

Modern Evidences Supporting the Book

The great claims of the *Book of Mormon* to the existence of successive civilizations in America have been substantiated by archaeological discovery and, in the light of this, many of the earlier criticisms of the book have disappeared.

While the *Book of Mormon* writers made no attempt to describe fully their civilization, the following assertions are of interest:

Use of Metals. "And they did work in all manner of ore, and they did make gold, and silver, and iron, and brass, and all manner of metals; and they did dig it out of the earth; wherefore they did cast up mighty heaps of earth to get ore, of gold, and of

---

[2]Profane—Secular or civil.

[3]Report of the Washburn Committee on "Book of Mormon Geography"—filed with the Department of Education, 1934, offers some interesting suggestions and findings.
[4]The several theories of *Book of Mormon* geography fail to agree.

silver, and of iron, and of copper. And they did work all manner of fine work."[5]

Manufacture of cloth. "And they did have silks, and fine twined linen; and they did work all manner of cloth, that they might clothe themselves from their nakedness."[6]

Construction of highways. "And there were many highways cast up, and many roads made which led from city to city, and from land to land, and from place to place."[7]

Use of cement. "And there being but little timber upon the face of the land, nevertheless the people who went forth became exceedingly expert in the working of cement; therefore they did build houses of cement in the which they did dwell."[8]

Evidences of a civilization having those items enumerated above have been found in Central America. The knowledge of metals and their use by the early inhabitants is now universally recognized. One of the most prominent archaeologists, A. Hyatt Verrill, writes:

"Less than two years ago I was scoffed at for suggesting that an entirely new and unknown culture of great antiquity had existed in Panama, but we have now undeniable proof of the fact. Moreover, at the depth of five and a half feet below the surface, at the temple site, among broken pottery embedded in charcoal, I found a steel hardened iron implement. The greater portion is almost completely destroyed by corrosion, but the chisel-shaped end is in good condition. It will scratch glass, and with such an instrument it would be a simple matter to cut and carve the hardest stone."[9]

Of the existence of highways we read:

"In ancient times Chi-Chen Itza and all the great and lesser cities of the Yucatan Peninsula were linked by a network of smooth hard-surfaced highways. The Mayas of today call these old roads 'Zac-be-ob,' or 'white ways.' The name is of ancient origin, used, perhaps, by the very builders themselves and no doubt these roads were like ribbons stretching mile after mile through field and forest and deserving quite as much the appellation of 'white way' as any of our blazing night-lighted thoroughfares."[10]

Cement is also recognized as one of the chief building materials.

"Looming high above the lesser structures are the ruins of immense palaces with imposing facades, walls, and patios, while the dry bed of an irrigation canal that once supplied the city with water may be traced to its source at the Moche River, several miles distant. No stone was used in building this immense city whose ruins cover hundreds of acres: neither were the walls and buildings of ordinary adobe. Instead, the Chimus and their predecessors employed a cement-like clay mixed with gravel which hardened to form a material of great strength and durability, a material which has withstood earthquakes, floods, winds, and human hands for countless centuries."[11]

Knowledge of the Hebrew Scriptures in America

One of the interesting assertions of the *Book of Mormon* is that the ancestors of the American Indian were well acquainted with the Hebrew scriptures from the Books of Moses down to Jeremiah. We read:

"Lehi took the records which were engraven upon the plates of brass, and he did search them from the beginning. And he beheld that they did contain the five books of Moses, which gave an account of the creation of the world, and also of Adam and Eve, who were our first parents; and also a record of the Jews from the beginning even down to the commencement of the reign of Zedekiah, king of Judah."

This assertion met with ridicule and contempt in 1830 from practically all students of ancient American history. At the end of a century the extraordinary claim is no longer laughed at. While it is not an established fact acceptable to all students of the subject, some of the outstanding authorities find

[5]*Book of Mormon*, Ether 10:23.
[6]*Book of Mormon*, Ether 10:24.
[7]*Book of Mormon*, III Nephi 6:8.
[8]*Book of Mormon*, Helaman 3:7.
[9]A. Hyatt Verrill, working for the Museum of the American Indian, Heye Foundation, *American Magazine*, 1926.

[10]T. A. Willard — *The City of the Sacred Well*, pp. 88, 89.
[11]A. Hyatt Verrill, *Under Peruvian Skies*, p. 25.

it extremely probable. Nor can they account for what they have found in any other way—for it is quite evident from Indian traditions and legends that such stories as the creation, first parents, the flood, the twelve tribes, etc., were well-known among them before the advent of the European.

The most authentic source book for these legends is the Popol Vuh, a rare manuscript written in the Quiche language[12] and translated into the Spanish by Francisco Jimenez, a well-known Catholic priest who lived among the Indians of Guatemala during the early Spanish rule of America. This interesting volume is replete with stories so closely akin to those of the Hebrews that one noted scholar, Le Plongeon, declared that these stories originated in America and were later carried to the old world where the Hebrews adopted and improved upon them.[13] Le Plongeon claimed to have found upon the walls of old buildings at Chichen-Itza and Uxmal, in Central America, mural paintings of the creation, the temptation of Eve in the garden of Eden, the story of Cain and Abel, and many others of the Hebrew legends.

In the Chimalpapoca manuscript, one of the few native records not destroyed when the Spaniards conquered Central America, the Creator is represented as having fashioned the world in several successive periods, creating plants and animals and finally making man from dust, which was then animated.

"In Michoacan, the Indians tell us that a great flood covered the earth and that Tezpe, with his wife and children and a collection of animals and seeds, were saved in a spa-cious vessel which Tezpe constructed. When the waters began to subside, Tezpe sent out a vulture, that it might go to and fro on the earth and bring him word when dry land began to appear."[14]

The multitude of such legends would fill volumes. They seem to be indisputable evidence that the Hebrew tradition was common to the early inhabitants of America.

A Great Destruction in America

A great destruction of cities and people and a mighty cataclysm of the earth took place on the American continent at the time of the death of Jesus. Cities were buried beneath volcanic eruptions, some sunk beneath the sea, some burned, and some were carried upon the tops of mountains, while a large number of inhabitants were destroyed.[15] So claims the *Book of Mormon*, and for over one hundred years has challenged the world to search and see. Considerable searching and considerable seeing has been done, most of it confirming the story.

Indian traditions point definitely to some such happenings on the American continent. Bancroft, the historian, gives us such a Toltec tradition as follows:

"The sun and moon were eclipsed, the earth shook, and the rocks were rent asunder, and many other things and signs happened though there was no loss of life. This was in the year Ce Calli, which, the chronology being reduced to our system, proved to be the same date when Christ, our Lord, suffered—33 A. D."[16]

Nadaillac, another writer on the subject, gives a quotation of Brasseur de Bourbourg as follows:

"If I may judge from allusions in the documents that I have been fortunate enough to collect, there were in these regions, at that remote date, convulsions of nature, de-

[12]The Quiche Indians are natives of Guatemala, Central America.
[13]Ivins, *Mormonism and Free Masonry*, pp. 211-217.

[14]Ivins, *Mormonism and Free Masonry*, p. 220. Compare with Genesis 6, 7, and 8.
[15]*Book of Mormon*, 3 Nephi 8, 9.
[16]*Native Races*, Vol. V, p. 210.

luges, terrible inundations, followed by the upheaval of mountains, accompanied by volcanic eruptions. These traditions, traces of which are also met with in Mexico, Central America, Peru, and Bolivia, point to the conclusion that man existed in these various countries at the time of the upheaval of the cordilleras, and that the memory of that upheaval has been preserved."[17]

The historian Prescott also records a multitude of Indian traditions covering a great catastrophe, and places its happenings about the time of the death of Christ."[18]

The findings of archaeology point to such an occurrence as the *Book of Mormon* describes. Cities have been located beneath lava flows, or buried beneath lakes. Ruins have been found in the tops of mountains. In the valleys north of Mexico City, great cities and temples have been found buried beneath some twelve feet of volcanic ash. The beds of old cement highways show indications of terrific earth disturbances after their completion.

While these items do not prove the divine origin of the *Book of Mormon*, the strange assertions in the book no longer can be called absurd. One marvels indeed that a volume offering such a challenge has so well survived the test to which time has subjected it.

The World and the Religious Philosophy of the Book of Mormon

The *Book of Mormon* presents to the world a definite religion, declaring that God is and that he is the Creator in whose image man appeared.

The book teaches that God is really a Father to all mankind, and that all men are brothers. As a Father he is interested in the happiness and welfare of

his children, declaring that "Men are that they might have joy."

The Son, who is also a God, is that person who lived among men in the flesh, as Jesus of Nazareth. He is so intimately associated with the Father that, in his relationship with men, he is both the Father and the Son, reigning over the earth in God's stead. He is the savior of the world, chosen for that calling from the beginning. He was born of a Virgin who conceived "by the power of the Holy Ghost."

He was slain upon a cross, after which he arose from the tomb with a resurrected immortal body of flesh and bone, appearing to His apostles and some five hundred others in Palestine, and to thousands of Nephites on the American continent.

The Holy Ghost is variously called the "Holy Spirit" and the "Spirit of God." He bears record of the Father and the Son. He is represented as an exalted personage, who confers divine sanction upon the servants of God, sanctifies those ordained to the priesthood, imparts knowledge, enables men to speak in tongues, prophesy, see visions, have faith, and obtain many other precious gifts.

Revelations and other answers to prayers are realities and constitute the only source of man's knowledge of God and his relationship to man.

The gospel is the law of eternal progress, by which mankind may attain a fulness of joy. It was made known to the first man, Adam, and the knowledge of it has been preserved, or at times restored, by revelation to those who asked in faith concerning it. These have been called prophets. Those who became aware of the gospel, of the law of progress and had faith in it, were initiated through baptism by immersion

[17]Marquis De Nadaillac, *Pre-Historic America*, pp. 16-17.
[18]See William H. Prescott, *Conquest of Mexico*, 1873 edition, Vol. I, pp. 105-106.

into "The Kingdom of God." Members of this kingdom upon the earth, where numerous enough, have organized themselves into a church, or earthly organization, designated in any age, or among any people, as "The Church of Jesus Christ."

Authority to form and perpetuate such an organization and officiate in its ordinances is given directly from Jesus Christ and is termed priesthood. It is power delegated to man to act in God's stead.

This life is a step in progression from a previous existence, toward a future life. Heaven is a state of happiness obtained through obedience to divine law, and hell is a remorse of conscience which eventually must follow disobedience.

In this life man is given his free agency in a world of opposites, the bitter and the sweet, that which produces misery and that which results in happiness, that he may come to seek the one and shun the other.[19] The consequences of his choices result in a state of paradise or a state of misery when the spirit has gone into the Spirit World.[20]

The fall of Adam was a blessing for mankind. "Adam fell that men might be, and men are that they might have joy."[21]

"And it is requisite with the justice of God that men should be judged according to their works; and if their works were good in this life and the desires of their hearts were good, that they

should also at the last day be restored unto that which is good.

"And if their works are evil, they shall be restored unto them for evil."[22]

This is in brief the religious philosophy of the *Book of Mormon*. After more than one hundred years it remains the most beautiful philosophy of the world. It stands unparalleled in its simplicity. Its concepts have never been disproved or successfully controverted. All who read and accept them become members of "The Church of Jesus Christ," which has been again established in these "latter days."

It was to preserve this philosophy of life that the book was written, and therein lies its great value. But now, as a century and a half ago, the truth of this gospel message can only be obtained by prayer to that God who "giveth to all men liberally and upbraideth not."[23]

Supplementary Readings

The field for interesting reading on this subject is very broad. Students might find articles in current magazines to supplement the following:

1. *Widtsoe, Restoration of the Gospel*, pp. 50-52. (Value of the *Book of Mormon* from the viewpoint of the world.)
2. Talmage, *Vitality of Mormonism*, pp. 45-49. (The influence of the *Book of Mormon* on thinking people.)
3. *Ibid*, pp. 22-23. (The term "Mormon" a nickname given the Saints.)
4. *Ibid*, pp. 46-47. (A knowledge of good and evil is taught by the *Book of Mormon* as essential to progress.)
5. *Book of Mormon, Alma*, Chapters 40-41. (Book of Mormon Philosophy.)
6. Book of Mormon, II Nephi, Chapter 2. (Book of Mormon Philosophy.)

[19]See 2 Nephi 2.
[20]Alma 34, 40.
[21]2 Nephi 2:25.

[22]Alma 41:3-4.
[23]James 1:5.

CHAPTER 9

THE PRIESTHOOD AT WORK

Called of God

While translating the *Book of Mormon* from the Gold Plates, Joseph Smith and Oliver Cowdery came to many passages on baptism, among which was the following:

"And again the Lord called others, and said unto them likewise; and he gave them power to baptize. And he said unto them: On this wise shall ye baptize; and there shall be no disputations among you.

"Verily I say unto you, that whoso repenteth of his sins through your words and desireth to be baptized in my name, on this wise shall ye baptize them—Behold, ye shall go down and stand in the water, and in my name ye shall baptize them.

"And now behold, these are the words which ye shall say, calling them by name, saying:

"Having authority given me of Jesus Christ, I baptize you in the name of the Father, and of the Son, and of the Holy Ghost. Amen.

"And then shall ye immerse them in the water, and come forth again out of the water."[1]

These passages caused them to wonder exceedingly and to desire to be properly baptized into the Kingdom of God. But they knew not how to proceed.

Accordingly, on May 15, 1829, they retired to a small grove of trees on the bank of the Susquehanna River near Joseph Smith's residence in Harmony. Here they sought knowledge through prayer. Their compliance to that law by which knowledge may be obtained from God, was recognized. In the midst of their prayer a bright light overspread them and a messenger of the Lord confronted them. He announced himself as John the Baptist, who held the keys of baptism in the day of Jesus of Nazareth.

After giving them instructions concerning those topics uppermost in their minds, he laid his hand upon their heads and conferred upon them that priesthood and authority which he himself held. His words, as received by Joseph Smith, are significant:

"Upon you my fellow servants, in the name of Messiah I confer the priesthood of Aaron, which holds the keys of the ministering of angels, and of the gospel of repentance, and of baptism by immersion for the remission of sins; and this shall never be taken again from the earth, until the sons of Levi do offer again an offering unto the Lord in righteousness."[2]

Joseph records in his journal:

"He said this Aaronic Priesthood had not the power of laying on hands for the gift of the Holy Ghost, but that this should be conferred on us hereafter; and he commanded us to go and be baptized, and gave us directions that I should baptize Oliver Cowdery, and afterwards that he should baptize me. Accordingly we went and were baptized. I baptized him first, and afterwards he baptized me—after which I laid my hands upon his head and ordained him to the Aaronic Priesthood, and afterwards he laid his hands on me and ordained me to the same Priesthood—for so we were commanded.

"The messenger who visited us on this occasion, and conferred this Priesthood upon us, said that his name was John, the same that is called John the Baptist in the New Testament, and that he acted under the direction of Peter, James and John, who held the keys of the Priesthood of Melchizedek, which Priesthood, he said, would in due time be conferred on us, and that I should be called the first elder of the Church, and he (Oliver Cowdery) the second. . . .[2a]

---

[1] *Book of Mormon*, 3 Nephi 11:22-26. See also 2 Nephi 31:5.

[2] *Doctrine and Covenants*, Sec. 13. In an article in the *Messenger and Advocate*, 1834, Oliver Cowdery, ends the quotation thus, "Which shall remain upon the earth, that the sons of Levi might yet offer an offering unto the Lord in righteousness."

[2a] Joseph Smith 2:70-72, Pearl of Great Price.

"Immediately on our coming up out of the water after we had been baptized, we experienced great and glorious blessings from our Heavenly Father. No sooner had I baptized Oliver Cowdery, than the Holy Ghost fell upon him, and he stood up and prophesied many things which should shortly come to pass. And again, so soon as I had been baptized by him, I also had the spirit of prophecy, when, standing up, I prophesied concerning the rise of this Church, and many other things connected with the Church, and this generation of the children of men. We were filled with the Holy Ghost, and rejoiced in the God of our salvation."[3]

What joy must have been theirs! The power to act in God's name had been conferred upon them! A power that had been manifest in the days of Christ was again restored! Oliver Cowdery said of this event:

"I shall not attempt to paint to you the feelings of this heart, nor the majestic beauty and glory which surrounded us on this occasion; but you will believe me when I say, that earth, nor men, with the eloquence of time, cannot begin to clothe language in as interesting and sublime a manner as this holy personage. No; nor has this earth power to give the joy, to bestow the peace, or comprehend the wisdom which was contained in each sentence as it was delivered by the power of the Holy Spirit! . . . The assurance that we were in the presence of an angel, the certainty that we heard the voice of Jesus, and the truth unsullied as it flowed from a pure personage, dictated by the will of God, is to me past description, and I shall ever look upon this expression of the Savior's goodness with wonder and thanksgiving."[4]

Melchizedek Priesthood Restored

Some time later, perhaps in the early part of June,[5] Joseph and Oliver again sought knowledge from the Lord in regard to the higher authority which had been promised them. In answer to their petition, another remarkable occurrence took place. Peter, James, and John, the ancient apostles of Jesus, ap-

peared, gave them the gift of the Holy Ghost by the laying on of hands, and conferred upon them the Holy Melchizedek Priesthood.

Thus was restored to earth that priesthood so distinctive of the Church of Jesus Christ of Latter-day Saints today.

The effect of the Holy Ghost upon Joseph and Oliver is portrayed in the Prophet's journal:

"Our minds being now enlightened, we began to have the scriptures laid open to our understandings, and the true meaning and intention of their more mysterious passages revealed unto us in a manner which we never could attain to previously, nor ever before had thought of."[6]

The spirit of missionary work which they had not previously experienced came upon them. Despite the opposition which was gathering against them, and the necessity for secrecy in their work, the spirit would not be stilled. Joseph says:

"After a few days, however, feeling it to be our duty, we commenced to reason out of the scriptures with our acquaintances and friends as we happened to meet with them."[7]

The story of the restoration of the priesthood is one of the most significant stories of all time. Priesthood assumes the significance it had in the days of the Apostles. It becomes a power so real and vital as to be cherished above wealth, position, or fame.

The Test

The truth of this story is evident as we follow the history of the Priesthood in the Church, and the power manifested by its exercise.

After the Church was organized, Joseph conferred upon others, by the lay-

---

[3]Joseph Smith 2:73, Pearl of Great Price.
[4]Pearl of Great Price, p. 58.
[5]The exact date is not recorded.

---

[6]Joseph Smith 2:74, *Pearl of Great Price.*
[7]*History of the Church*—Period I, Vol. I, p. 44.

ing on of hands, the powers of the priesthood he held and sent them forth into the world to preach the gospel, with this mighty announcement previously received from Jesus, the Christ:

"Therefore, as I said unto mine apostles I say unto you again, that every soul who believeth on your words, and is baptized by water for the remission of sins, shall receive the Holy Ghost.

And these signs [of the Priesthood] shall follow them that believe—

"In my name they [that is, those holding the Priesthood] shall do many wonderful works;

"In my name they shall cast out devils;

"In my name they shall heal the sick;

"In my name they shall open the eyes of the blind, and unstop the ears of the deaf;

"And the tongue of the dumb shall speak;

"And if any man shall administer poison unto them it shall not hurt them;

"And the poison of a serpent shall not have power to harm them."[8]

The promise was made to those who should receive the Holy Ghost through the laying on of hands by men holding the proper priesthood, that some should prophesy, others obtain knowledge, acquire faith, work miracles, discern spirits, speak in tongues or have the gift of interpreting tongues.[9] Later he said to his people:

"If there are any sick among you, let him call for the Elders of the Church * * * and they shall lay their hands upon their heads * * * and their faith shall raise them up."

This was a bold announcement. If there is no power, there is no priesthood! Joseph stands like Elijah, on Mount Carmel, saying to the world, "Come and let us test the authority from God which we claim. Let us pray to God, in the name of that authority and be judged by the results." If the evidences of signs follow, who among men can sensibly deny that John, the Baptist, actually stood on the banks of the Susquehanna that spring morning in 1829, or that Peter, James, and John also appeared as Joseph and Oliver narrated?

In the face of this mighty test the petty arguments about the actuality of angels and the possibility of their appearance unto men sinks into utter insignificance.

A Church Is Organized by the Priesthood

When Joseph Smith and Oliver Cowdery, exercising the priesthood they had received, baptized each other in the waters of the Susquehanna River, and later had that ordinance confirmed by the laying on of hands by Peter, James and John, they became the first members of the Kingdom of God in these latter days. They had complied with the entrance requirements to that Kingdom. They had been received into it by those who had the proper authority to baptize others into the Kingdom of God and to organize the members of that Kingdom upon the earth into a church.

Samuel Smith, a younger brother of Joseph, arrived in Harmony a short time afterward. He heard of the ordinance of baptism and desired to enter into the Kingdom of God. Accordingly, Oliver Cowdery led him into the waters of the Susquehanna and baptized him. In June, 1829, Hyrum Smith and David Whitmer were baptized by Joseph Smith, and Peter Whitmer by Oliver Cowdery.

From the time of the first vision in the grove at Palmyra, Joseph had looked forward to the day when a definite organization of those who believed in the latter-day restoration of the gospel could be effected. Now he had the needed authority and a nucleus of individuals eligible for membership. He again sought the Lord in prayer and re-

---

[8]*Doctrine and Covenants*, Section 84, verses 64-72.
[9]*Ibid.*, Section 46, verses 17-25.

ceived an instructive answer, setting forth the method of procedure in beginning the church. This revelation was received as early as June, 1829, in a room of Father Whitmer's house in Fayette, New York.

Subsequently, in answer to further prayers, the Lord revealed other matters concerning the organization and declared the exact date when the church should come into being, namely, April 6, 1830. These various revelations were grouped together and later published as section twenty in the *Book of Doctrine and Covenants*.

During the interval between June, 1829, and April 6, 1830, other baptisms were performed and meetings in some of the homes of friends were held, in which the restoration of the gospel was discussed.

On the date designated, April 6, 1830, Joseph Smith, Oliver Cowdery, and members of the Smith and Whitmer families, met in the home of Peter Whitmer, Sr., in Fayette, Seneca County, New York. After appropriate songs and prayer the revelations concerning the organization of the church were read to the assembled people.[10] These revelations set forth the order of the priesthood and the duties of the officers in the church. Around this pattern the entire church organization of today has been built.

"According to previous commandment, the Prophet Joseph called upon the brethren present to know if they would accept himself and Oliver Cowdery as their teachers in the things of

[10]Probably the same revelation as contained in *Doctrine and Covenants*, Section 20.

Picture of a scene from "The Message of the Ages" pageant depicting the organization of the Church of Jesus Christ of Latter-day Saints on April 6, 1830 at the home of Peter Whitmer.

the Kingdom of God; and if they were willing that they should proceed to organize the church according to the commandments of the Lord. To this they consented by unanimous vote. Joseph then ordained Oliver an Elder in the Church of Jesus Christ;[11] after which Oliver ordained Joseph an Elder of the said church. The sacrament was administered and those who had been previously baptized were confirmed members of the church and received the Holy Ghost by the laying on of hands. Some enjoyed the gift of prophecy and all rejoiced exceedingly.[12]

Articles of incorporation of the Church of Jesus Christ had been previously drawn up in conformity to the laws of New York State concerning the organization of religious bodies. As the state law required six signatories to this document, the first six baptized in this dispensation affixed their signatures. These were in order of their baptism, Oliver Cowdery, Joseph Smith, Jr., Samuel H. Smith, Hyrum Smith, David Whitmer, and Peter Whitmer, Jr. While only six signed their names to the legal document, at least nine participated in the organization of the Church.[13]

Thus was the Church, now known as The Church of Jesus Christ of Latter-day Saints, ushered into being. The Priesthood had been previously restored. The Church was the creation of the Priesthood. It was a means for the efficient and orderly functioning of the priesthood and for carrying the gospel to the world.

During the meeting Joseph received another revelation directing that a record should be kept and that, in it, Joseph should be called

"a seer, a translator, a prophet, and apostle of Jesus Christ, an Elder of the Church through the will of God the Father and the grace of your Lord Jesus Christ."[14]

In this manner was set forth the will of God in relation to the organization of the Church. But nothing was to be effective except by the consent and vote of the people. For the Lord said,

"And all things shall de done by common consent in the church, and by much prayer and faith."[15]

Further,

"No person is to be ordained to any office in this church, where there is a regularly organized branch of the same, without the vote of that church; . . ."[16]

Thus the members were taught that God would give counsel, and use persuasion in guiding the Church, but never compulsion. Further, the Lord expected his officers in the Church to follow the same high moral principle. A short time later God revealed the high standard by which the priesthood should govern the affairs of the Church, and Joseph stated the revelation as follows:

"The rights of the priesthood are inseparably connected with the powers of heaven, and . . . the powers of heaven cannot be controlled nor handled only upon the principles of righteousness.

"That they may be conferred upon us, it is true; but when we undertake to cover our sins, or to gratify our pride, our vain ambition, or to exercise control or dominion or compulsion upon the souls of the children of men, in any degree of unrighteousness, behold, the heavens withdraw themselves; the spirit of the Lord is grieved; and when it is withdrawn, Amen to the priesthood or the authority of that man.

"No power or influence can or ought to be maintained by virtue of the priesthood, only

---

[11]The words, "of Latter-day Saints," were used at times, but not consistently until commanded in 1838. Doc. & Cov. Sec. 115. See Berrett & Burton *Readings in LDS Church History*, Vol. I pp, 75-76.
[12]*Comprehensive History of the Church*, Vol. I, p. 196.
[13]*Ibid.*, Vol. I, footnote, p. 195.

[14]*Doctrine and Covenants*, Section 21:1.
[15]*Ibid.*, Section 26:2.
[16]*Ibid.*, Section 20:65.

by persuasion, by long-suffering, by gentleness, and meekness, and by love unfeigned."[17]

Nearly all great religious movements have had humble beginnings, but none more so than that begun in the humble dwelling of Peter Whitmer, Sr., in the western borders of New York in 1830.

Founded by divine command, like "a stone cut out of the mountain without hands,"[18] it has rolled forth until it has branches in every state of the Union, in nearly every civilized nation of the earth and upon the isles of the sea. The roster of six members has grown to over three million and the movement is yet in its infancy.

The Story of Divine Authority in the World

The scriptures reveal that God's authority in this world actually began before the physical world came into being.

Abraham, who lived nearly two thousand years before Christ came in the flesh, recorded these significant words:

"Now the Lord had shown unto me, Abraham, the intelligences that were organized before the world was; and among all these there were many of the noble and great ones;

"And God saw these souls that they were good, and he stood in the midst of them, and he said: These I will make my rulers; for he stood among those that were spirits, and he saw that they were good; and he said unto me: Abraham, thou art one of them; thou wast chosen before thou wast born.

"And there stood one among them that was like unto God, and he said unto those who were with him: We will go down, for there is space there, and we will take of these materials, and we will make an earth whereon these may dwell;

"And we will prove them now herewith to see if they will do all things whatsoever the Lord their God shall command them;

"And they who keep their first estate shall be added upon; and they who keep not their first estate shall not have glory in the same kingdom with those who keep their first estate; and they who keep their second estate shall have glory added upon their heads for ever and ever.

"And the Lord said: Whom shall I send? And one answered like unto the Son of Man: Here am I, send me. And another answered and said: Here am I, send me. And the Lord said: I will send the first.

"And the second was angry, and kept not his first estate; and, at that day, many followed after him."[19]

From the above quotation we find that man existed before the creation of the world. After the plans for creation had been made, One, like unto God, was chosen and given authority to carry out the plans. The One chosen was Jesus Christ, our elder brother.

After the earth had been prepared by Christ, under the direction of God the Father, until it was suitable as a home for man, Adam and Eve were placed upon it and the gospel was made known unto them. Adam was later baptized and received the Holy Ghost.[20] Also, he was given priesthood, or authority to act in God's name in the performance of ordinances, and the right to delegate this authority to others.[21] This authority, handed down from Christ, from the beginning, has been bestowed from one individual to another in a particular way. The individual to receive the priesthood must be called by one already holding that authority. He must accept the call, and must be ordained. The ordination is accomplished by the person or persons holding that authority who lay hands upon the head of the individual and pronounce the words of the ordination. After this manner Adam received the priesthood, and after this manner be-

---

[17]*Doctrine and Covenants*, Section 121:36-37, 41.
[18]*Ibid.*, Section 65:2. Also see Daniel 2:34-35, 45.

[19]*Pearl of Great Price*, Abraham 3:22-28.
Note: For an explanation of why Satan was rejected and Christ chosen and given authority, see *Pearl of Great Price*, Moses 4:1-4; 5:4-12.
[20]*Ibid.*, Moses 6:53-68.
[21]*Ibid.*, Moses 6:7; Abraham 1:2-3; *Doctrine and Covenants* 8:6-17.

stowed it upon his sons and so on continually until the days of Moses.[22]

Concerning the Priesthood from the day of Moses to John the Baptist, so far as that part of Israel living in Palestine is concerned, we read in the Doctrine and Covenants:

"And this greater priesthood administereth the gospel and holdeth the key of the mysteries of the kingdom, even the key of the knowledge of God.

"Therefore, in the ordinances thereof, the power of godliness is manifest.

"And without the ordinances thereof, and the authority of the priesthood, the power of godliness is not manifest unto men in the flesh;

"For without this no man can see the face of God, even the Father, and live.

"Now this Moses plainly taught to the children of Israel in the wilderness, and sought diligently to sanctify his people that they might behold the face of God;

"But they hardened their hearts and could not endure his presence; therefore, the Lord in his wrath, for his anger was kindled against them, swore that they should not enter into his rest while in the wilderness, which rest is the fulness of his glory.

"Therefore, he took Moses out of their midst, and the Holy Priesthood also;

"And the l e s s e r priesthood continued, which priesthood holdeth the key of the ministering of angels and the preparatory gospel;

"Which gospel is the gospel of repentance and of baptism, and the remission of sins, and the law of carnal commandments, which the Lord in his wrath caused to continue with the house of Aaron among the children of Israel until John, whom God raised up, being filled with the Holy Ghost from his mother's womb.

"For he was baptized while he was yet in his childhood, and was ordained by the angel of God at the time he was eight days old unto this power, to overthrow the kingdom of the Jews, and to make straight the way of the Lord before the face of his people, to prepare them for the coming of the Lord, in whose hand is given all power."[23]

While the Lord took the Higher or Melchizedek Priesthood as an institu-tion out of Israel, afterward special dispensations of that Priesthood were given to individual prophets, such as Samuel, Nathan, Elijah, Isaiah, Jeremiah, Ezekiel, and Daniel, as these men exercised powers and enjoyed privileges which belong exclusively to the Melchizedek Priesthood.[24] So also Lehi who led a colony of Israelites to America in 600 B. C. possessed the Melchizedek Priesthood and conferred it upon his posterity. This higher priesthood in America continued in an unbroken chain for a thousand years, being lost only with the death of the Prophet Moroni about 421 A. D.[25]

The Melchizedek Priesthood thus existed in America at the time of the coming of Christ but had been lost so far as the inhabitants of Judah were concerned, although the lesser or Aaronic Priesthood continued among them. Christ conferred upon His Apostles this higher authority as shown by the subsequent functions and activities of these men.

The Priesthood in the apostolic church was organized with various offices and callings. Aside from the authority given them members of the church could not act for God. The chief authorities were the Apostles[26] with Peter, James and John acting as a Presidency over them. The Seventy were also selected and set apart.[27] Seven men were chosen to administer to the poor,[28] and were at first given only the lesser priesthood enabling them to teach and to baptize people but not to confirm them or bestow the Holy Ghost upon

---

[22]*Doctrine and Covenants*, Section 84:6-17.
[23]*Ibid.*, Section 84:19-28.

[24]Joseph Fielding Smith, *Teachings of the Prophet Joseph Smith*, pp. 180-181.
[25]See 2 Nephi 5:26; 6:2; Alma 4:20; 13:6-18; Roberts, *New Witnesses for God*, Vol. III, p. 469.
[26]Mark 6:7.
[27]Luke 10:1.
[28]Acts 6:2-6.

them. Thus we read in the Book of Acts of the Apostles:

"Now when the Apostles which were at Jerusalem heard that Samaria [the inhabitants of] had received the word of God, they sent unto them Peter and John:
"Who, when they were come down, prayed for them, that they might receive the Holy Ghost:
("For as yet he was fallen upon none of them: only that they were baptized in the name of the Lord Jesus.)
"Then laid they their hands on them, and they received the Holy Ghost."[29]

As the church grew bishops were appointed,[30] high priests ordained,[31] and evangelists (patriarchs) chosen.[32]

In a letter, to the Saints at Ephesus, Paul mentions many of the offices of the priesthood:

"And he gave some, apostles; and some, prophets; and some, evangelists; and some, pastors, and teachers;
"For the perfecting of the saints, for the work of the ministry, for the edifying of the body of Christ.[33]

Just how long this authority and these offices continued in the early Christian church is a matter of some dispute. Both the Roman Catholic and Greek Orthodox churches claim continuous priesthood authority from the days of Christ until now. The Latter-day Saints, while not ascribing the priesthood as being lost in any particular century, maintain that neither the priesthood nor its offices were to be found upon the earth in 1820 at which time the Prophet Joseph received his first great vision.

Supplementary Readings

1. Widtsoe, *The Restoration of the Gospel*, p. 68. (Signed statement of Oliver Cowdery regarding the Higher Priesthood.)
2. *Ibid.*, pp. 34-35; 70. (Joseph did not assume authority.)
3. *Ibid.*, p. 61. (Significance of the visits of John the Baptist.)
4. Evans, *Heart of Mormonism*, pp. 85-87. (Signs and symbols in the Church.)
5. Widtsoe, *Joseph Smith as Scientist*, pp. 83-85. (There is in science an equivalent to baptism.)
6. Talmage, *Vitality of Mormonism*, pp. 38-39. (A discussion of the claim of the Church to Priesthood.)
7. Joseph Fielding Smith, *Essentials in Church History*, pp. 91-94.
8. Cannon, *Life of Joseph Smith*, p. 65. (Samuel H. Smith receives a testimony and is baptized.)
9. B. H. Roberts, *Comprehensive History of the Church*, Vol. I, pp. 189-195. (A discussion of Section 20—Doctrine and Covenants.)
10. *Ibid.*, pp. 197-198. (Democracy in the Church.)

[29]Acts 8:14-17.
[30]Philippians 1:1.
[31]Hebrews 5:1.
[32]II Timothy 4:5.
[33]Ephesians 4:11-12.

CHAPTER 10

THE TRUTH SPREADS

The Zeal of the New Testament

"On Sunday, April 11, 1830, Oliver Cowdery preached the first public discourse that was delivered by any of our number."[1]

In those few simple words Joseph Smith relates the beginning of a missionary movement which has made of Mormonism a most dynamic religion. At the close of his discourse Oliver baptized six new members into the Church. A week later he baptized seven more. The beautiful Seneca Lake was his baptismal font.

In reality the first conversions came

[1]*History of the Church*, Period I, Vol. I, p. 81.

through the Prophet Joseph Smith, and he might be called the first missionary. But his missionary efforts had previously not been directed to the converting of the public nor to the bringing of members into an organization. Rather his conversations and informal talks, in the homes of his friends, had been for the purpose of satisfying their curiosity and arousing their faith in his experiences. And their faith had been aroused. His father and mother, his brothers and sisters, his wife, his neighbors, Martin Harris and Josiah Stoal, the schoolteacher Oliver Cowdery, the

Seneca Lake where first baptisms were performed after the organization of the Church.

family of Whitmers, and the Knights; all who came to know him felt the truth of his simple testimony and were ready to follow his leadership.

Through the missionary efforts of its members and the influence of the *Book of Mormon* the Church grew rapidly. At the first conference, held June 9, 1830, there were some ninety people in attendance, about thirty of them already members.[2] At the September conference, held on the 26th day of the month the number had more than doubled. When a conference was held on January 2, 1831, in Fayette, New York, the New York Saints numbered seventy, with several hundred new members in Ohio. By the time of the first annual conference in April the number of members in Ohio alone numbered over one thousand.[3] At the June conference held in Kirtland, Ohio, two thousand Saints were in attendance.

The growth was nothing short of marvelous. There were three important reasons for this rapid expansion: First, the missionary spirit which came upon the members of the Church; second, the effect of the *Book of Mormon;* third, the preparation which had been going on for some time in the minds of people along the frontier for just such a dynamic religion. The step into Mormonism was a short one indeed for great numbers of people who were already dissatisfied with their old creeds.

In the days of Jesus, the missionary zeal came to his apostles at the feast of Pentecost, following the resurrection of the Master, on which occasion the Holy Ghost came upon them. Under the influence of the Holy Ghost the twelve men became irresistible and Christian-ity spread like a conflagration over the Mediterranean world. So, too, in this "Latter-day Church of Christ" the missionary zeal follows the reception of the Holy Ghost by the laying on of hands.

The Missionary Spirit

A new spirit seems to have possessed Joseph Smith and Oliver Cowdery after receiving the Priesthood and the Holy Ghost on the banks of the Susquehanna. One cannot read carefully the story of their respective lives without being made aware of it. A new energy and power seems to have possessed them. It is as if they had suddenly increased in stature. A newborn desire to carry their message to the world and to effect an organization for that purpose gave direction to their energies. So, too, with all who were baptized into the Church and received the same rights to the influence of the Holy Ghost.

Shortly after the organization had been completed, Samuel Smith, getting a desire to preach the gospel, was called by revelation to go into northern New York State. His work resulted in the distribution of a number of copies of the *Book of Mormon,* one of which was directly responsible for the later conversion of Brigham Young, Heber C. Kimball and others. Others followed in the work. The Lord announced to those who might have the urge to labor:

"Behold, the field is white already to harvest, therefore whoso desireth to reap, let him thrust in his sickle with his might, and reap while the day lasts, that he may treasure up for his soul everlasting salvation in the Kingdom of God."[4]

David Whitmer, preaching in the vicinity of Fayette to his friends and neighbors, baptized eleven people into the Church about the middle of June.

---

[2]*History of the Church*, Period I, Vol. I, p. 84
[3]Roberts, *Comprehensive History of the Church,* Vol. I, p. 250.

[4]*Doctrine and Covenants,* Sec. 6:3.

Thirteen more were baptized by Oliver Cowdery at Coleville later in the same month, the result of the missionary work of Joseph Smith, Oliver Cowdery, John and David Whitmer in that vicinity. The missionary work continued, with little branches formed in Fayette, Palmyra, Manchester, and Coleville, in New York and at Harmony in Pennsylvania.

The Mission to the Western Border

The first extended mission and one which was destined to influence the Church for many years, followed the conference of September 26, 1830. At this conference Oliver Cowdery and Peter Whitmer were called to go and preach the good news to the Lamanites, or American Indians.

In October Parley P. Pratt and Ziba Peterson were called to accompany them. Their mission caused them to travel on foot more than fifteen hundred miles to the West and paved the way for a rapid Church expansion. Visiting the Indian tribe of Catteraugus, near Buffalo, New York, for a few days, with meager results, they pushed on to Kirtland, Ohio.

Parley P. Pratt had previously lived in that vicinity and had received a commission from the Campbellites there as a minister. He now sought out his former pastor, Sidney Rigdon, a preacher in the Church of the Disciples (Campbellites). He was well received. The privilege was gained of speaking to the congregation of the Disciples and the promise of Sidney Rigdon that he would read and study the *Book of Mormon*. The gospel preached appealed to the congregation. The *Book of Mormon* won over the scholarly and intelligent pastor. The roots of the Church were spreading with amazing rapidity. When the missionaries departed from Kirtland to continue on to their original goal, they took with them Dr. Frederick G. Williams, a new convert. They left a thriving branch of the Church with twenty members who were in the succeeding weeks to bring into the Church practically that entire group of the so-called Disciples.

Walking day after day westward the intrepid missionaries came to the Wyandot tribe of Indians near Sandusky, Ohio, where they spent several days. Parley P. Pratt writes:

"We were well received, and had an opportunity of laying before them the records of their forefathers, which we did. They rejoiced in the tidings, bid us Godspeed and desired us to write to them in relation to our success among the tribes further west, who had already moved to the Indian territory where these expected soon to go."[5]

On December 20th, they took passage on a steamer for St. Louis. Reaching the mouth of the Ohio, they found the Mississippi blocked with ice, and were compelled to walk the remaining two hundred miles to St. Louis. The weather was severe and the snow sometimes three feet deep. Occasional homes were found and in each the gospel message was preached.

In January, 1831, the little party left St. Louis for a journey of 306 miles on foot through a trackless waste to Independence, Missouri. It was a journey accompanied by much hardship. The snow was deep and wood for fires scarce. Parley P. Pratt writes:

"We carried on our backs our changes of clothing, several books, and corn bread and raw pork. We often ate of frozen bread and pork by the way, when the bread would be so frozen that we could not bite or penetrate any part of it but the outside crust."[6]

[5]*Autobiography of Parley P. Pratt*, 1964, p. 51.
[6]*Ibid.*, p. 52.

A Visit to the Delaware Indians

In February they reached Independence, 1500 miles from the beginning of their mission, with most of the distance being traversed on foot. But still they had not reached their destination. While two of them hired out as tailors in Independence for the purpose of securing funds to continue the missionary labors, the remaining three crossed over the frontier into the Indian country. They visited the powerful Shawnees, and then crossed the Kansas River into the region of the Delawares.

After considerable difficulties, Chief Anderson (as the whites called him), head of the ten nations of Delawares, granted them an opportunity to speak to the united council of the ten nations. Forty chieftains met in the council chambers of Chief Anderson. The council fires were lighted. The pipe of peace was passed around. Then Oliver Cowdery, with a *Book of Mormon* in his hand, addressed them through an interpreter:

"Aged Chief, and venerable council of the Delaware Nation, we are glad of this opportunity to address you as our red brethren and friends. We have traveled a long distance from towards the rising sun to bring you good news; we have traveled the wilderness, crossed the deep and wide rivers, and waded in the deep snows, and in the face of the storms of winter, to communicate to you great knowledge which has lately come to our ears and hearts and which will do the red man good as well as the pale face."[7]

Oliver Cowdery then told them of the *Book of Mormon* and of their ancestors who had written it, and how that Book had come again to the knowledge of men. After a pause and some palaver among the council, the venerable old Chief replied:

" 'We feel truly thankful to our white

friends who have come so far and been at such pains to tell us good news, and especially this good news concerning the book of our forefathers; it makes us glad in here'— placing his hand on his heart. 'It is now winter; we are new settlers in this place; the snow is deep; our cattle and horses are dying; our wigwams are poor; we have much to do in the spring—to build houses and fences and make farms; but we will build a council house and meet together, and you shall read to us and teach us more concerning the book of our fathers and the will of the Great Spirit.' "[8]

Elder Parley P. Pratt in his report of the matter adds:

"We continued for several days to instruct the old chief and many of his tribe. The interest became more and more intense on their part, from day to day, until at length nearly the whole tribe began to feel a spirit of inquiry and excitement on the subject. We found several among them who could read, and to them we gave copies of the book, explaining to them that it was the book of their forefathers. Some began to rejoice exceedingly and took great pains to tell the news to others in their own language. The excitement now reached the frontier settlements in Missouri, and stirred up the jealousy and envy of the Indian agents and sectarian missionaries to that degree that we were soon ordered out of the Indian country as disturbers of the peace, and even threatened with the military in case of non-compliance. We accordingly departed from the Indian country and came over the line, and commenced laboring in Jackson County, Missouri, among the whites. We were well received and listened to by many, and some were baptized and added to the Church."[9]

That work among the dark-skinned Lamanites, so auspiciously begun, was destined to wait many years for its accomplishment, during which time the scene of Mormonism was to shift twenty-five hundred miles west from the place of beginning, into the mighty Rockies.

But the spirit of the little group of missionaries was undaunted. Without

[7]*Ibid.*, p. 54.

[8]*Ibid.*, p. 56.
[9]*Ibid.*, p. 57.

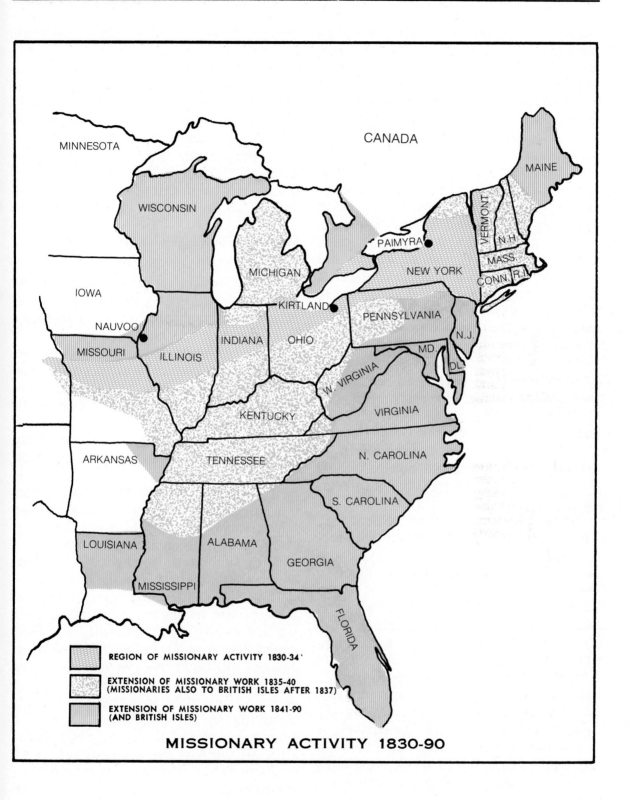

REGION OF MISSIONARY ACTIVITY 1830-34

EXTENSION OF MISSIONARY WORK 1835-40
(MISSIONARIES ALSO TO BRITISH ISLES AFTER 1837)

EXTENSION OF MISSIONARY WORK 1841-90
(AND BRITISH ISLES)

MISSIONARY ACTIVITY 1830-90

money or supplies, other than some extra clothing, depending upon the hospitality of the few red and white inhabitants, they had traversed sixteen hundred miles of wilderness and opened the way for thousands to hear of the restored Gospel. When Parley P. Pratt returned east in the Spring of 1831, to report his labors, he found the little branch which he and his companions had organized in Kirtland, Ohio, grown to a membership well over a thousand.

This one missionary journey, so rich in results, is but typical of many, and the spirit in which it was carried out is the spirit of all missionary activities in the Church from the beginning. There was no thought of pay; no expectations of earthly rewards; no hope of earthly fame.

A great urge to teach had come upon the members of the Church and the enthusiasm was contagious. Men who had but recently received the Gospel themselves found such comfort and joy in its message that they could not rest until they had taught the good news to relatives and friends.

While Oliver Cowdery, Parley P. Pratt, and their companions were journeying to the west, Ezra Thayre and Northrop Sweet were called to labor in the east.[10]

In November, 1830, Orson Pratt, who had been converted by his brother, Parley, was called to labor as a missionary.[11] In December, Sidney Rigdon and Edward Partridge received a similar call.[12] The numbers of missionaries doubled and redoubled again. At the June Conference, 1831, twenty-eight missionaries were called to labor in pairs, the majority to work westward to Independence, Missouri, where already the seeds of the Gospel had been planted.

The missionary spirit was later to cause men to go into Canada, across the ocean to England, to the Islands of the Sea, and finally into the whole world. That spirit has never died out. A century later finds over 13,000 missionaries constantly in the field, at a cost to themselves and friends of millions of dollars annually.

Whence Comes this Missionary Zeal?

What spirit prompted the new converts to The Church of Jesus Christ of Latter-day Saints to leave home, friends, and comforts, in order to carry the Gospel to others?

If we can understand what prompted the ancient apostle Paul to encompass land and sea, endure privations, beatings, shipwreck, prisons, and even walk cheerfully to his death in order that men might hear the message of Jesus—if we can answer why Jesus himself trod the certain road to the cross when he realized so clearly what lay ahead—then we can understand the spirit of the missionaries in early Mormonism. To them privation and sufferings were nothing compared to the priceless joy which they attest to having received.

In each case the individual testifies to a happiness in the work, a new-found joy in the service of humanity and God which becomes an irresistible driving power. Obstacles may be met; barriers and pitfalls thrown in their paths, but as well attempt to stop the flow of Mt. Vesuvius in its eruptions. And the movements had all the energy of a Vesuvius, all the fire and irresistibleness of the lava flow. Men and women everywhere caught the contagion of it. The discontented in religion felt its pull, and severed the few remaining ties with

---

[10]*Doctrine and Covenants*, Section 33.
[11]*Ibid.*, Section 34.
[12]*Ibid.*, Sections 35 and 36.

their old creeds. For the new religion breathed power and attained results. It had uttered a challenge to the world and was making good.

Prayer had again become a vital force, and many who had previously prayed with doubts and misgivings now received the needed bolstering which brought them the spirit of God. Men prayed for a testimony concerning Joseph Smith's message and their prayers were answered. Men read the *Book of Mormon* with a prayer in their hearts that they might know of its truth, and the Lord remembered his promise.

Men are always lifted by the faith of their associates. Confidence inspires confidence. When the Savior walked the earth, his presence, his voice, and his touch dispelled fear and doubt and the sick arose from their beds of affliction and the blind opened their eyes. His apostles finally acquired that same faith and confidence and rejoiced in the power they possessed. So in this new dispensation, Christ had revealed himself—a tangible book had appeared. The confidence and faith of Joseph Smith had opened the heavens and prayers were being answered. Others caught the same faith and, having been vested with the powers of priesthood, went forth to instill faith in others.

The fire and enthusiasm of the movement dwarfed all other motives in life. The desire for gain or power seemed to disappear. In the giving of service to others, self was forgotten and a new social brotherhood began—a true Kingdom of God. The principle, that he who "loseth his life" in the service of others "shall find it"—is still the fundamental principle of Mormon missionary activity, at home, or abroad. It cools when service cools, and bursts into new flame when service is resumed. In the early Mormon society it permeated everything and enriched all it touched. The spirit of service and brotherhood entered into home life and community life and brought dreams of a new Zion—a place of brotherly happiness and service to one another—where there should be no rich and no poor—where greed and selfishness should be banished forever.

Supplementary Readings

Only part of the events of this period could be included in the text. The reading of some of the following will help get a complete picture of the early days of the church.

1. Accounts of the first miracles performed in the Church are contained in the following:
   a. *History of the Church*, Period I, Vol. I, pp. 82-86.
   b. Roberts, *Comprehensive History of the Church*, Vol. I, pp. 201 ff.
   c. Cannon, *Life of Joseph Smith*, 1964, pp. 83-85, also footnote pp. 208-210.
   d. Evans, *Joseph Smith an American Prophet*, pp. 95-96.
   e. Smith, *Essentials in Church History*, pp. 95-96.

2. The first Conference. Arrest and trial of the Prophet:
   a. *History of the Church*, Period I, Vol. I, pp. 86-96.
   b. Roberts, *Comprehensive History of the Church*, Vol. I, pp. 203-208.
   c. Smith, *Essentials in Church History*, pp. 96-103.
   d. Cannon, *Life of Joseph Smith*, pp. 87-90.

3. The power of the Priesthood manifested.
   a. *History of the Church*, Period I, Vol. I, pp. 108-109. (Eyes of the mob blinded).
   b. Widtsoe, *The Restoration of the Gospel*, pp. 103-104. (Spiritual gifts manifest.)
   c. *Autobiography of Parley P. Pratt*, 1964, pp. 68-72. (Power of Priesthood to heal.)

4. Attempt to lead the Church astray.
   a. Cannon, *Life of Joseph Smith*, pp. 91-93.
   b. *History of the Church*, Period I, Vol. I, pp. 104-105.

5. Missionary activity and results.
   a. Evans, *Joseph Smith, an American*

Prophet, pp. 71-75. (The Missionary System Begins.)
b. *The History of Joseph Smith by His
Mother Lucy Mack Smith*, pp. 215-
217. (A prophecy of conversion fulfilled.)
c. *Ibid.*, pp. 191-192. (Edward Partridge converted.)
d. Evans, *Heart of Mormonism*, pp.

112-113. (Conversion of Rigdon and
Partridge.)
e. *History of the Church*, Period 1, Vol.
I, pp. 122-123. (Note) (Conversion
of Sidney Rigdon.)
f. *Ibid.*, pp. 120-125, 183-185. (Note)
(The Lamanite Mission.)

CHAPTER 11

THE MORMON COMMUNITIES
ALONG THE
AMERICAN FRONTIER

Kirtland and Vicinity

In its earlier years, The Church of Jesus Christ of Latter-day Saints found its greatest number of converts along that part of the American frontier which lay north of the city of St. Louis to the Canadian border. The settlers in that area were largely from New England and the Central Atlantic states. English stock predominated. The majority belonged to various Protestant sects and a large part of the remainder were free from any church affiliation. Further, there were some religious groups such as the Campbellites or "Disciples," whose doctrines were in many respects in harmony with those of the restored Church.

This area proved to be a fertile field for missionary activities. A few months after the organization of the Church, missionaries had carried the message to Ohio and Missouri. Its growth there was rapid. By the spring of 1831, the center of the Church population had shifted to Kirtland, Ohio, the number of members living in that vicinity being several times the number residing in New York and Pennsylvania branches.

It is not surprising that Joseph Smith should turn his attention to the West. He records that he sought the Lord in prayer upon the subject and received the following:

"Behold, verily, verily, I say unto thee, thou art not called to go into the eastern countries, but thou art called to go to the Ohio.

"And inasmuch as my people shall assemble themselves at the Ohio, I have kept in store a blessing such as is not known among the children of men, and it shall be poured forth upon their heads. And from thence men shall go forth into all nations."[1]

Advising the converts in New York and Pennsylvania to sell their properties and move to Ohio, Joseph prepared for his own departure. In the latter part of January, 1831, in company with Sidney Rigdon and Edward Partridge, he and his wife, Emma, arrived in Kirtland, Ohio. Here they were joyfully received. The Prophet and his wife were taken temporarily into the house of Newel K. Whitney, a member of the Church, and a successful young merchant.

This was the beginning of a general exodus of the Saints from New York. As fast as they could dispose of their property and equip themselves for the journey, they moved into the frontier settlements of Ohio. They were attracted to those settlements where branches of the Church were already established. Kirtland, and the two nearby towns of Thompson and Hiram, received the great majority. The group from Colesville, New York, moved en masse to Thompson, while the Palmyra Branch migrated to Kirtland and Hiram.

Before Mormonism had reached the vicinity of Kirtland, a group of Campbellites or Disciples had commenced the experiment of holding all property in common and living as one large family.

---

[1]*Doctrine and Covenants*, Section 39:14-15.

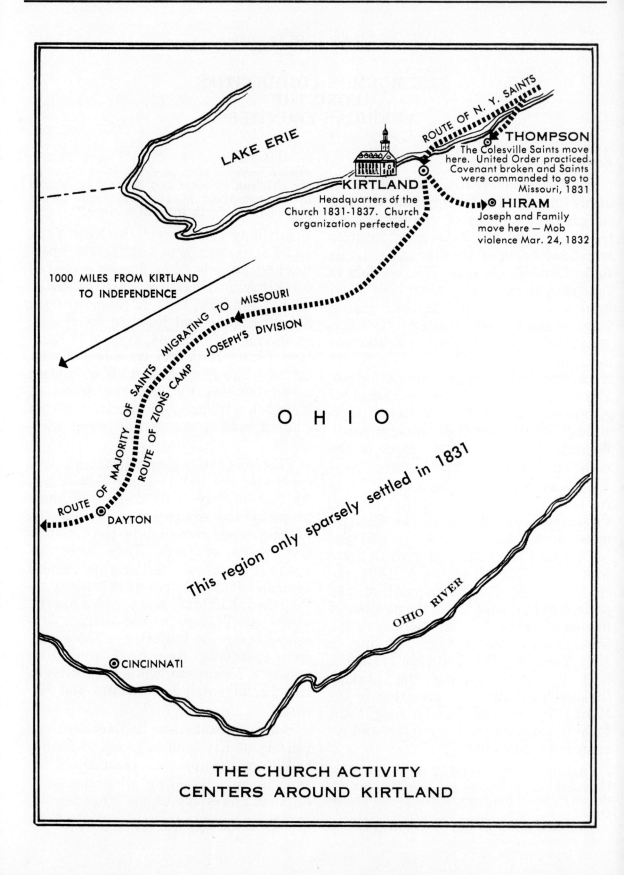

THE CHURCH ACTIVITY
CENTERS AROUND KIRTLAND

Practically the entire group had embraced the new faith after the visitation of Parley P. Pratt and his companions on their way to the Lamanite Mission. They continued, however, their social experiment until the arrival of Joseph Smith. If they expected him to approve of the order, they were disappointed. Commending them for their brotherly spirit he soon persuaded them to abandon the enterprise as not being patterned upon God's law for such societies.

The Saints, being anxious to know what the law of God was in that matter, and being desirous of living it, Joseph inquired of the Lord through prayer. On February 9th he gave to the people of Kirtland a revelation on the subject.[2] The new law given was called the Law of Consecration of property. Edward Partridge was called and ordained to the office of bishop, the first to hold that office in the latter-day Church. He was to leave his business and devote his entire time to the affairs of the Church in putting the Law of Consecration into operation among the Saints in Kirtland.

Property for the Use of all the People

Under the plan, all of the members of the Church within a given community were to deed their property in fee to the bishop over that community. The bishop in turn, as trustee of the property for the entire community, would then, by a special deed, convey back to each head of a family such lands, store, mill, shop, or other property of the individual, subject to certain conditions. A person might not hold more land than he could properly use. Further, the surplus in goods or money produced from the land or other property over and above that required for the immediate well-being of the family, and the improvement of the property, should be turned over annually into the general fund or storehouse of the community. This community surplus was then to be used for the benefit of the whole group. Out of it the poor were to be provided for; the sick, the orphans, and the widows relieved of their wants. Roads were to be built and an educational system maintained. Churches and community centers were to be erected and all enterprises which would be for the benefit of the whole group, carried out. The system was designed to prevent the rise of class, to abolish hoarding and selfishness and those elements which, in a modern community, tend to prevent a spirit of Christian brotherhood. Products and services were to be bought and sold as usual, and he that was idle should not eat the bread nor wear the garment of the laborer.[3]

The Law of Consecration was first followed in settling those Saints who were arriving from the Eastern States in the two settlements of Kirtland and Thompson. Not all of the members of the Church in either place participated in the plan and both experiments came to an early end.

The settlements of the Saints in Ohio was considered by Joseph Smith as temporary. The permanent settlement was to be farther to the west, in a place unknown at that time. In a revelation received at Kirtland in May, 1831, we read the following:

"I consecrate unto them this land for a little season, until I, the Lord, shall provide for them otherwise, and command them to go hence;

"And the hour and the day is not given unto them, wherefore let them act upon this land as for years, and this shall turn unto them for their good."[4]

---

[2] *Doctrine and Covenants*, Sec. 42.

[3] *Ibid.*, Section 42:42.
[4] *Ibid.*, Section 51:16-17.

The spirit of community fellowship and cooperation which reached its finest expression in the Law of Consecration, set the Latter-day Saints apart, socially and economically, from their neighbors. It struck deep at the roots of the American economic system, and served notice upon the profit motive as a basis of human activity. This spirit bound the Mormon people closer and closer together as units in the various communities. The fact that the Law of Consecration was short-lived must not be interpreted as meaning that the spirit of brotherhood disappeared. That spirit was to grow stronger with the years until Mormons came to be known as a "people different." It was the very youth of the Church, and the newness of the movement, which brought about the failure of a law which they desired but had not sufficient experience to live.

But the spirit of brotherhood continued and found expression in community enterprises and missionary activity.

The fact that the Mormons were animated by a different conception of community life aroused suspicion, and eventually persecution, on the part of other people who witnessed the number in the Church double and redouble with amazing rapidity. Ministers who witnessed their own flocks dwindle, as converts by the score moved away to the Mormon settlements, or set up a new Mormon community in the same locality, became alarmed. Often they became embittered and active in stirring up feeling against the new religion.

A New Zion

The Mormon communities in Ohio were scarcely in their infancy before Joseph Smith turned his attention farther west. In December, 1830, while in New York State, he had announced the revelation that a New Zion would be built somewhere in the West by the borders of the Lamanites. From that time he had been besieged with inquiries as to its exact location. In the spring of 1831, Parley P. Pratt arrived in Kirtland with a glowing report of the mission to the western border. The Indian mission had been brought to an abrupt close, but a small branch of the Church had been organized in Jackson County in the western part of Missouri. Elder Pratt's account of the country stirred the Prophet to make new inquiries of the Lord. During the conference of the Church at Kirtland in June, he received by revelation the following:

"I, the Lord, will make known unto you what I will that ye shall do from this time until the next conference, which shall be held in Missouri, upon the land which I will consecrate unto my people, which are a remnant of Jacob, and those who are heirs according to the covenant.

"Wherefore, verily I say unto you, let my servants Joseph Smith, Jr., and Sidney Rigdon take their journey as soon as preparations can be made to leave their homes, and journey to the land of Missouri."[5]

In the same revelation, twenty-six other elders were called to start on missions to the West. They were to travel by twos, preaching the gospel on the way. All were to meet at Independence, Missouri, where the Lord would reveal the location of the New Zion.

The idea that there would be a New Zion upon the earth in the latter days may be obtained from a reading of the Bible. It was not the study of ancient prophecies, however, which so fired the Saints with a zeal for Zion. To them God had spoken anew. Zion was to be realized.

To the Prophet Joseph Smith the

---

[5]*Ibid.*, Section 52:2-3.

word Zion had two meanings: "The pure in heart," and, "The place where the pure in heart dwell together in righteousness." It is quite evident that a successful "Zion community" is impossible without a "Zion people." Such an achievement could hardly be attained while the Saints were among people, in Ohio and elsewhere, who were not of their faith. Thus Joseph Smith contemplated a gathering place in the unsettled West, to which the pure in heart might gather from the four quarters of the earth. There, a new society, patterned after God's law, might reach fruition. From the Central Zion community the idea would grow, until eventually Zion would embrace the whole of the American continent.

Napoleon, in his wildest dreams, never advanced a more ambitious program. And Napoleon would reach his goal through force, while this new kingdom would win over men's hearts by loving persuasion.

It was approximately one thousand miles from Kirtland, Ohio, to Independence, Missouri. In the latter part of June and the early part of July, 1831, Joseph Smith, accompanied by Sidney Rigdon, Martin Harris, Edward Partridge, William W. Phelps, Joseph Coe, and Algernon S. Gilbert and wife, traversed this distance. The journey was by wagon, boat, and stage as far as St. Louis. From there Joseph and part of the company completed the journey on foot, the rest going by boat up the Missouri river. The region traversed was largely wilderness without suitable roads or accommodations. It was a tremendous journey in that day, yet leaders of the Church were to travel back and forth many times without complaint, and with no thought of material reward. And over that great dis-

tance thousands of covered wagons were to carry Mormon men, women and children during the succeeding years, to the New Zion. One such company, the group of Saints from Colesville, who had stopped for a few months at Thompson, Ohio, arrived in Jackson County two weeks in advance of the Prophet and his party. They were led by Newel Knight. This group, about sixty in number, settled in Kaw township, twelve miles west of Independence.

A New Zion Announced

Shortly after arriving in Missouri, the Prophet received a revelation announcing that Missouri was Zion, the gathering place for the Saints, and,

"The place which is now called Independence is the center place; and the spot for the temple is lying westward, upon a lot which is not far from the courthouse.

"Wherefore, it is wisdom that the land should be purchased by the saints, and also every tract lying westward, even unto the line running directly between Jew and Gentile;[6] And also every tract bordered by the prairies, inasmuch as my disciples are enabled to buy lands. Behold, this is wisdom that they might obtain it for everlasting inheritance."[7]

The land chosen for the New Zion was a land rich in those things needful to man. It was a beautiful country. Joseph Smith seeing it for the first time in mid-summer, wrote of it:

"As far as the eye can reach the beautiful rolling prairies spread out like a sea of meadows; and are decorated with a growth of flowers so gorgeous and grand as to exceed description; and nothing is more fruitful or a richer stockholder in the blooming prairie than the honey bee. Only on the water courses is timber to be found. There, in strips from one to three miles in width, and following faithfully the meanderings of the streams, it grows in luxuriant forests.

---

[6](Note) Has reference to the line separating the Whites and Indians, the Indians being referred to here as Jews.
[7]*Doctrine and Covenants*, Sec. 57:3-5.

The forests are a mixture of oak, hickory, black walnut, elm, ash, cherry, honey locust, mulberry, coffee bean, hackberry, boxelder and basswood; with the addition of cottonwood, butterwood, pecan, and soft and hard maple upon the bottoms. The shrubbery is beautiful and consists of plums, grapes, crab apple, and persimmons.

The soil is rich and fertile; from three to ten feet deep, and generally composed of a rich black mould, intermingled with clay and sand. It yields in abundance, . . . buffalo, elk, deer, bear, wolves, beaver and many smaller animals here roam at pleasure. Turkeys, geese, swans, ducks, yea a variety of the feathered tribe, are among the rich abundance that grace the delightful regions of this goodly land—the heritage of the children of God."[8]

Independence, in 1831, was a small frontier town, the outfitting place for trapper and hunter and a rendezvous for many rough characters of the west. It had a brick courthouse, two or three general stores, and some twenty log houses. The type of settlers presented a sharp contrast to the New England people who were now searching for a new Zion in that land. The old settlers were generally unschooled, ignorant of the ways of civilization, and unskilled in the arts of the newcomers.

On the second day of August, 1831, twelve men including the Prophet, representing the twelve tribes of Israel, laid the first log for a Mormon dwelling in Jackson County. This scene was enacted twelve miles west of Independence, in Kaw Township, now part of Kansas City, where the Coleville saints were preparing to settle.

Sidney Rigdon dedicated the land for the gathering of Israel and asked the assembled people:

"Do you receive this land of your inheritance with thankful hearts from the Lord?"

Answered from all: "We do."

"Do you pledge yourselves to keep the law

of God on this land which you never have kept in your own lands?"

"We do."

"Do you pledge yourselves to see that others of your brethren who shall come hither keep the laws of God?"

"We do."

After prayer he arose and said "I now pronounce this land consecrated and dedicated unto the Lord for a possession and inheritance for the saints, and for all the faithful servants of the Lord to the remotest ages of time, in the name of Jesus Christ, having authority from Him. Amen."[9]

On the third day of August, 1831, Joseph Smith in company with Sidney Rigdon, Edward Partridge, W. W. Phelps, Oliver Cowdery, Martin Harris and Joseph Coe, repaired to the place designated by revelation for the temple and the Prophet dedicated the temple site. The following day a conference was held at Kaw Township, after which all those not appointed to remain, started their return to their wives and families in Ohio.

Bishop Edward Partridge was appointed to remain in Independence and divide unto the Saints their inheritance. Sidney Gilbert, a young merchant, was appointed to remain as agent of the Church to purchase lands for the Saints. William W. Phelps was appointed printer of the Church, with Oliver Cowdery to assist him. Under the leadership of these men the Law of Consecration was put into effect in Independence and other parts of Jackson County. The growth of the Mormon settlement. was rapid. Thrift was rewarded with prosperity. Funds from the Saints in Ohio for the purchase of lands in Missouri began to pour into the hand of the purchasing agent, and Bishop Partridge had to work feverishly to settle the constant stream of incoming Saints satisfactorily.

---

[8]*History of the Church*, Period I, Vol. I, p. 197.

[9]John Whitmer, *History of the Church*, Ms. Chapter 9.

Independence, Jackson County, Missouri Temple Site (in triangle) and vicinity as it appears today looking toward the Northwest.

1. Original Temple Land: 63.46 acres
2. Mission Home and Office
3. Independence Ward Chapel
4. Reorganized LDS Auditorium
5. Gleaner Harvester Division of Allis Chalmers
6. Old Swope Man Property: Reorganized LDS Recreation Center
7. Waggoner Estate

8. Church of Christ Temple Lot, Hedrikites, Joseph Smith stood here to dedicate the temple site
9. Old Stone Church: Reorganized LDS
10. Reorganized LDS School of Restoration
11. Resthaven Old Folks Home: Reorganized LDS
12. Independence Hospital: Operated by the Reorganized LDS

Two Centers of Activity and Influence

It is necessary to keep in mind that the Mormon settlements in Ohio and Missouri were developing at the same time. Kirtland, Ohio, and Independence, Missouri, became the important centers of church activity for a number of years. These centers were a thousand miles apart, with the country between them largely unsettled. Communication and travel were exceedingly slow and difficult, making the Prophet's task of directing the Church a hard one.

By the summer of 1832, nearly all of the New York members of the Church had migrated to Jackson County, Missouri. Some of these had stopped for a short time in Ohio, while others had made the fifteen hundred mile journey directly to the New Zion.

The converts of the Church in Ohio were content to remain in the vicinity of Kirtland. The Prophet, in fact, urged them to remain and build a temple to the Lord, and reap the blessings God had promised them in that land.

Having announced the location for the New Zion and dedicated it as a gathering place for the Saints, the Prophet devoted most of his time to the building up of the Church at Kirtland. This he did for several reasons. The main body of the Church membership were settled in and around Kirtland. The city offered a more convenient center for directing the affairs of the Saints everywhere, and for directing missionary activity in Canada and the Eastern States. Further, God had given Joseph commandments which necessitated his remaining at Kirtland until they were carried out.

Of the two communities, Independence offered the better opportunity for putting into effect God's complete law of consecration and for establishing a city which would serve as a model for all future centers of Zion. The Law of Consecration, begun in Kirtland, was soon abandoned and that at Thompson came to an end when the Coleville Saints who had settled there moved in a body to Missouri. Joseph made no attempt to re-establish the Law of Consecration in Ohio. He did, however, insist that all who journeyed to the New Zion in Missouri must be willing to abide that law and they were required to enter into covenant with God that they would do so.

While the greater Law of Consecration was not continued in Kirtland, there did develop a very marked community spirit of cooperation among the Saints. This segregated them from non-members and brought upon them the envy and hatred of many outside the new society. The Church demanded high standards of its members, resulting in the apostasy or falling away of those who were lukewarm in the faith, or had joined the Church for ulterior motives. These apostates did much to ferment accusations and hatreds against the Latter-day Saints. Often the opposition from various classes of people against the Church expressed itself in open mob action.

One of the most brutal of such mobbings involved Joseph Smith and Sidney Rigdon as victims. At the time, both were living at Hiram, sixteen miles northwest of Kirtland, whence the Prophet had returned with his family to work on a revision of the English Bible.

About midnight of March 24th, 1832, Joseph Smith and Sidney Rigdon were dragged from their beds by a mob estimated at forty or more, led by a Church apostate, Simon Ryder. The Prophet was beaten into insensibility. Recover-

Plan for the "City of Zion," as evolved by Joseph Smith, to be founded at Independence, and which was to be a model for other cities to be established.

ing, he was carried a distance from the house, stripped of his clothing and covered with tar and feathers. Elder Rigdon was dragged by the heels over the frozen earth until he was unconscious.

This incident is but typical of the opposition which, in time, rose against the Saints wherever they settled and was to eventually culminate in driving them from the confines of the United States.

A Model for all Future Cities of Zion

In the Spring of 1833, a general plan for building "cities in Zion" was evolved. In June of that year the Prophet sent a copy of the plan of the city to the branch of the Church at Independence. The central city of Zion was to be laid out according to the model. Elder B. H. Roberts in his *Comprehensive History of the Church* has condensed the elaborate instructions to the Bishop in Zion as follows:

"The city plat is one mile square, divided into blocks containing ten acres each—forty rods square—except the middle range of blocks running north and south; they will be forty by sixty rods, containing fifteen acres, having their greatest extent east and west. The streets will be eight rods wide, intersecting each other at right angles. The center tier of blocks forty by sixty rods will be reserved for public buildings, temples, tabernacles, school houses, etc.

"All the other blocks will be divided into half-acre lots, a four rod front to every lot, and extending back twenty rods. In one block the lots will run from the north and south, and in the next one from east and west, and so on alternately throughout the city, except in the range of blocks reserved for public buildings. By this arrangement no street will be built on entirely through the street; but on one block the houses will stand on one street, and on the next one on another street. All of the houses are to be built of brick or stone; and but one house on a lot, which is to stand twenty-five feet back from the street, the space in front being for lawns, ornamental trees, shrubbery, or flowers, according to the taste of the owners; the rest of the lot will be for gardens, etc.

"It is supposed that such a plat when built up will contain fifteen or twenty thousand population, and that they will require twenty-four buildings to supply them with houses for public worship and schools. These buildings will be temples, none of which will be less than eighty-seven feet by sixty-one, and two stories high, each story· to be fourteen feet, making the building twenty-eight feet to the square. None of these temples will be smaller than the drawing of the one sent with the plat of the city to Independence; but of course there may be others much larger; the above, however, are the dimensions of the one the saints were commanded to build first.

"Lands on the north and south of the city will be laid off for barns and stables for the use of the city, so there will be no barns or stables in the city among the homes of the people.

"Lands for agriculturalists sufficient for the whole plat are also to be laid off on the north and south of the city plat, but if sufficient land cannot be laid off without going too great a distance, then farms are to be laid off on the east and west also; but the tiller of the soil as well as the merchant and mechanic will live in the city. The farmer and his family, therefore, will enjoy all the advantages of schools, public lectures and other meetings. His home will no longer be isolated, and his family denied the benefits of society, which has been, and always will be, the great educator of the human race; but they will enjoy the same privileges of society, and can surround their homes with the same intellectual life, the same social refinement as will be found in the home of the merchant or banker or professional man.

" 'When this square is thus laid off and supplied, lay off another in the same way,' said the Prophet to those to whom the city plat was sent, 'and so fill up the world in these last days, and let every man live in the city, for this is the city of Zion.' "[10]

Persecution prevented the carrying out of this plan. The general principles involved were later used in remodeling the city of Kirtland and became the basis for other Missouri settlements, for Nauvoo, and later for Salt Lake City and practically all the Mormon settlements in the Rocky Mountain region.[11]

[10]Roberts, *Comprehensive History of the Church*, Vol. 1, pp. 311-12.

[11](Note) A later chapter is devoted to the unique features of the Latter-day Saint settlements in the West.

Supplementary Readings

1. *History of the Church*, Period 1, Vol. I, pp. 145-146. (Story of the unusual meeting of the Prophet and Newel K. Whitney at Kirtland.)

2. *Ibid.*, pp. 182-183. (Oliver Cowdery's letter from Independence, Missouri, to the Prophet dated May 7, 1831.)

3. *Doctrine and Covenants*, Sec. 37. (The Church commanded to go to Ohio.)

4. *Ibid.*, Sec. 42. (The Moral Law given to the Church.)

5. *Ibid.*, Sec. 58. (The law of the Lord to the inhabitants of the New Zion.)

6. Roberts, *Comprehensive History of the Church*, Vol. I, pp. 244-246. (*Doctrine and Covenants*, Sec. 42—the moral law of the Church analyzed.)

7. *Ibid.*, pp. 246-247. (Law of Consecration.)

8. Cowley, *Wilford Woodruff*, p. 45. (Wilford Woodruff consecrates property to the Church.)

9. Cannon, *Life of Joseph Smith*, pp. 108-110. (Attitude of Joseph Smith toward the poor.)

10. Evans, *Joseph Smith an American Prophet*, pp. 66-71. (Movement of the Church to Ohio.)

11. *Ibid.*, pp. 75-81. (Dedication of the land of Zion.)

12. *Ibid.*, pp. 171-172. (Zion to be in America.)

13. *Ibid.*, pp. 102-104. (Joseph Smith tarred and feathered.)

14. *The History of Joseph Smith by His Mother Lucy Mack Smith*, pp. 218-221. (Joseph's own account of the tarring and feathering.)

15. *History of the Church*, Period I, Vol. I, pp. 259-266. (Mobs at Hiram—The Prophet and Sidney Rigdon are victims.)

CHAPTER 12

CHURCH GOVERNMENT
EXPANDS

The Foundation of Church Government is the Priesthood

The period from 1831-1837, during which the headquarters of the Church remained at Kirtland, witnessed a rapid development in organization. Strangely enough, the development was always a growth upon the foundation which had been already laid, and never the substitution of one form of organization for another. This is one of the most remarkable things in Church history. Had the Prophet been able to look down the vista of the future for many generations he could not have laid the foundations of the growing organization more surely or more wisely.

It is significant that he did not claim the credit for this wisdom. Each forward step follows the pronouncement of a Divine Commandment.

The foundation of Church Government is the Holy Priesthood. All Church organizations are creations of this priesthood. They are designed to meet the needs of the times. All offices in the Church are creations of the Priesthood designed to carry out the functions of the Priesthood. The entire Church organization is also a creation of the Priesthood.

After the Holy Priesthood was given to Joseph Smith and Oliver Cowdery they had all of the power necessary to bring into existence a Church and to create such offices and functions within the Church as was necessary for its efficiency. This power was subject, however, to the common consent of those

who had accepted the Restored Gospel and had been baptized into the Kingdom of God.

Free agency is a fundamental doctrine of Mormonism. God might command those holding the Priesthood to establish a church, or to ordain men to different offices or functions, but those offices do not come into existence until the membership votes for them, and men or women may not occupy any position in the Church, big or little, without the consent of the Church members involved.

It must be borne in mind, in any study of church government, that there are two grand divisions of Priesthood. The "Lesser," or "Aaronic," carries the power to officiate in temporal, or material things. The "Higher," or "Melchizedek," which also includes the "Lesser," carries the power over spiritual things. One who holds the Melchizedek Priesthood holds all the Priesthood there is. He may be called to function in many capacities as an Elder, Seventy, High Priest, Patriarch, Apostle, President, etc., but receives no additional Priesthood.

"Then again, if it were necessary . . . and there was no man left on earth holding the Melchizedek Priesthood, except an Elder— that Elder, by inspiration of the Spirit of God and by the direction of the Almighty, could proceed, and should proceed to organize the Church of Jesus Christ in all its perfection, because he holds the Melchizedek Priesthood."[1]

As God's house is one of order it is necessary that some be called to preside

---

[1]Joseph F. Smith, *Gospel Doctrine*, p. 148, also October Conference Report, 1903, p. 87.

over the Priesthood and the affairs of the Church. This directing power is called "Keys of the Priesthood." The person holding the "Keys," directs the activity of those holding the Priesthood under him.

When Joseph Smith was called and ordained First Elder in the Church he held the "Keys," or directing power over the Church, as effectively as though he had been termed President of the Church. He had the power, and the right with the consent of the Church, to bring into existence all the offices in the Priesthood and all organizations within the Church necessary for its proper functioning.

The Further Organization of the Aaronic Priesthood

By a revelation received at the time of the organization of the Church,[2] those ordained to the Aaronic Priesthood were to be called Deacons, Teachers, or Priests, according to their functions. Their duties and privileges were also set forth.

In the early months of the Church, but few, however, were ordained to the Aaronic Priesthood. Most of the converts to the Church were adults. The male members were usually ordained directly to the office of Elder in the Melchizedek Priesthood where they would be most useful to the Church as missionaries.

In February, 1831, the temporal affairs of the Church necessitated further organization. The Saints moving to Ohio needed land and homes. Often the removal could not be made without financial aid. To meet this situation Edward Partridge was called to the office of Bishop over the Church. This office carried with it the Presidency over the Aaronic Priesthood and the care of the temporal affairs of the people. Bishop Partridge was called to put into operation the "Law of Consecration," previously discussed. To this work he devoted his entire time.

In July, 1831, he was called to go with Joseph Smith and others to Missouri. At the close of that mission he was appointed to remain in Independence as Bishop over the Saints in Missouri.

After the Prophet returned to Kirtland, Newel K. Whitney was ordained Bishop over the Saints in Ohio and the Eastern States.

As the duties of these two Bishops increased, two counselors were ordained to assist each.

As the Church grew the office and functions of Bishops were retained. The number of Bishops steadily increased. This necessitated that one Bishop function as a presiding Bishop to look after the temporal affairs of all the members of the Church by counseling and advising the various Bishops. When the need arose, the Presiding Bishop also elected counselors to aid him in his duties.

On March 5, 1835, while at conference in Kirtland, Joseph Smith received a revelation which provided among other things for the organization of those holding the Aaronic Priesthood into Quorums.[3] Each Deacon's quorum was to have twelve members, the Teachers twenty-four, and the Priests forty-eight. Each quorum was to have a presidency, with the Bishop as president of the quorum of Priests.

Further Organization in the Melchizedek Priesthood

On January 25, 1832, a conference of

---

[2]*Doctrine and Covenants*, Sec. 20.

[3]*Ibid.*, Section 107:13-17, 85-88.

the Church was held in Amherst, Lorain County, Ohio, and here Joseph, the Prophet, was sustained as President of the High Priesthood of the Church and ordained to that Office.[4] This ordination carries with it the office of President over the whole Church. In a revelation received by Joseph Smith we read:

"And again, the duty of the President of the office of the High Priesthood is to preside over the whole church, and to be like unto Moses—

Behold, here is wisdom; yea, to be a seer, a revelator, a translator, and a prophet, having all the gifts of God which he bestows upon the head of the church."[5]

Joseph Smith was sustained in that office by the vote of the Church, both in Ohio and Missouri. He was as yet without counselors, and continued so for a little over a year. In response to a prayer on the matter of counselors, Joseph received on March 8, 1833, a revelation calling Sidney Rigdon and Frederick G. Williams to serve in that capacity, and to be equal with the Prophet "in holding the keys of this last Kingdom."

In the same revelation Joseph Smith was assured that,

"The keys of this kingdom shall never be taken from thee while thou art in the world, neither in the world to come."

"Nevertheless through you shall the oracles be given to another, yea, even unto the Church."[6]

Ten days later the two counselors were ordained to that office by Joseph Smith and were sustained by the vote of the members of the Church at their earliest conferences.

Thus was brought into existence the First Presidency of The Church of Jesus Christ of Latter-day Saints. The President and his counselors constitute a quorum called the quorum of the First Presidency. This quorum has been perpetuated in the Church to the present day, as the directing power.

On the 5th day of December, 1834, the quorum of the First Presidency met and ordained Oliver Cowdery as Assistant President of the Church. Later Hyrum Smith was ordained to this office.

This was the only time in the history of the Church when there has been an Assistant President. More than two counselors were sometimes chosen when more were needed to care for the affairs of the Church. The organization of the Church is highly flexible and may be changed at any time to meet new conditions.

The Organization of Church Units

Early in the Church, provisions were made to organize the Saints into stakes and wards. Each was a territorial subdivision. The size of the territory comprising a ward depended upon its membership. Several wards were organized into a stake. The first stakes organized were at Kirtland, Ohio, and Clay County, Missouri. Zion, established at Independence, Missouri, was not organized as a stake but was the "Center Place," the Holy City, to be supported and strengthened by the stakes, like unto the stakes to which tent lines are tied.

In February, 1834, a Stake Organization was effected at Kirtland with the First Presidency of the Church acting as the Stake Presidency. A High Council consisting of twelve high priests was ordained to act within the stake, for the purpose of settling important difficulties which might arise in the Church, which could not be settled by the Church or the Bishop's Council to the satisfaction of the parties.[7]

---

[4]*History of the Church*, Period I, Vol. I, p. 243 (footnote.)
[5]*Doctrine and Covenants*, Section 107:91-92.
[6]*Ibid.*, Section 90:3-4.
[7]*Ibid.*, Section 102:2.

Later in 1834, a stake was organized in Clay County, Missouri, with David Whitmer as president and W. W. Phelps and John Whitmer as counselors. A High Council for that stake was also chosen and ordained.

We must bear in mind that Joseph Smith and his counselors were acting in a double capacity. The office of "First Presidency of the High Priesthood," which is the "First Presidency of the Church," was separate and distinct from their office as a Stake Presidency. In the former capacity they were at the head of the whole Church. In the latter capacity their authority was limited to the stake at Kirtland. We will find that as the Church progressed in numbers, the quorum of the First Presidency found their time fully occupied with that office and, after abandoning Kirtland, a dual capacity was never held again by the Church Presidency.

The duties of the Stake High Councils increased as the Church grew and developed. It must be constantly kept in mind that from the beginning, the duties of the various members holding offices and callings in the Priesthood fluctuate or grow with the needs of the Church. Hence the duties evolve as the Church evolves.

Twelve Apostles Are Chosen

As early as June, 1829, it was known that twelve apostles would be chosen and ordained in the Church. Their nomination was to be made by Oliver Cowdery, David Whitmer and Martin Harris, the three special witnesses of the *Book of Mormon*.[8] They were to be special witnesses of Christ to all the world, a traveling High Council of the whole Church, officiating under the di-

rection of the Presidency of the Church. This quorum was not organized, however, until the Church had grown to need it.

Quorums of Seventy were also to be chosen to assist the Quorum of Twelve, in bearing witness of Christ to all the world, acting under the direction of the Twelve.

After the famous march of Zion's Camp, which we will treat in a separate chapter, a special conference of the Church was called at Kirtland. On the 18th day of February, 1835, the three special witnesses of the *Book of Mormon* selected those to be apostles as follows:

Lyman E. Johnson   Wm. E. M'Lellin
Brigham Young   John F. Boynton
Heber C. Kimball   Orson Pratt
Orson Hyde   William Smith
David W. Patten   Thomas B. Marsh
Luke S. Johnson   Parley P. Pratt

These were unanimously sustained by the conference and later by the Saints in Missouri.

The Seventies Are Organized

Two weeks later, on the 28th day of February, 1835, the first quorum of the Seventy was organized.[9] Its seventy members, like the Twelve, were chosen from among those who had been members of Zion's Camp. Seven of them were ordained as presidents of the quorum as follows:

Hazen Aldrich   Zebedee Coltrin
Leonard Rich   Levi W. Hancock
Joseph Young   Lyman Sherman
          Sylvester Smith

The Seventies were to constitute traveling quorums "to go into all the earth, whithersoever the Twelve Apostles shall call them."[10]

---

[8]*History of the Church*, Period I, Vol. II, Chapter 12 and notes.

[9]*Ibid.* p. 201.
[10]*Ibid.*, p. 202.

A second quorum of Seventy was ordained shortly afterward. The number of Quorums was later increased as the need arose. By January 1, 1845, there were fourteen quorums of Seventy. By 1970 the number had increased to 389 active quorums.

During this early period of the Church there were no auxiliary organizations. Sacrament meetings were held each Sunday and Priesthood meetings were also regular. Quarterly conferences of the Church were held, with many special conferences to consider vital problems.

The rapid change of the organization proved upsetting to many members who had failed to understand the purpose of the Church. This became a contributing cause of apostasy, and cries of "usurper" followed the Prophet in his organization movements.

Supplementary Readings

1. *History of the Church*, Period 1, Volume 2, pp. 194-200. (Interesting instructions to the Twelve by Oliver Cowdery and Joseph Smith.)

2. *Ibid.*, pp. 220-222. (Special instructions to the Twelve and Seventy by Joseph Smith.)

3. *Ibid.*, pp. 229-230 footnote. (Interesting letter of Joseph Smith instructing the Priesthood in their duties.)

4. Roberts, *Comprehensive History of the Church*, Volume I, p. 271 footnote 20. (Call of Newel K. Whitney to be Bishop.)

5. *Ibid.*, pp. 306-308. (The Presidency of the High Priesthood.)

6. *Ibid.*, pp. 371-378. (Finding approved witnesses—Apostles—Seventies.)

7. *Ibid.*, pp. 384-386. (The Three Great Councils of the Priesthood.)

8. *Ibid.*, pp. 386-388. (Patriarchs—Evangelists: organization of.)

9. *Doctrine and Covenants*, Section 20. (Organization and Duties of the Priesthood.)

10. *Ibid.*, Section 107, verses 1-40; 60-76. (Powers of Priesthood.)

11. *Autobiography of Parley P. Pratt*, pp. 118-126. (Interesting account of ordaining the Twelve and instructions by Oliver Cowdery.)

12. *Contributor*, January, 1885. (Call of Newel K. Whitney to be Bishop.)

13. Widtsoe, *The Restoration of the Gospel*, p. 60. (The Aaronic Priesthood.)

14. Evans, *Joseph Smith, an American Prophet*, pp. 83-86. (The beginning of Church Organization.)

CHAPTER 13

THE GLORY OF GOD IS
INTELLIGENCE

Joseph Smith Continues His Search for Knowledge

In the early period of the Church of Jesus Christ of Latter-day Saints there was a thirst for knowledge among its members which was unusual for the time and conditions under which the people lived. Generally the hard struggle for bread along the frontier dwarfed all efforts to advance in the arts and the higher fields of learning. Elementary schools were crude and adult education unknown. In contrast to this general condition in the West is the attitude of the Latter-day Saints toward education. The Prophet, himself, was indefatigable in his search for knowledge, and his severest critics today marvel at his accomplishments.

The knowledge which Joseph Smith acquired during his short lifetime did not come to any great extent from books. He recognized God as the source of all knowledge and had the requisite faith to apply to Him. Whatever he gleaned from books, or evolved from the workings of his own mind, or the association with men, was generally presented before the Lord for approval or disapproval. If he made fewer errors than most men it was due to this characteristic. He was a firm believer in the maxim that "the Lord helps those who help themselves."

He appealed to the Lord many times for knowledge and guidance, but never expected Him to do those things which he could, with proper diligence, do for himself.

Joseph Smith had been unable to translate the Book of Mormon without divine aid. That divine help was given.

But Joseph did not expect the Lord to forever aid him in understanding ancient languages. He could learn many of these for himself and he set about to do so. He began a study of Egyptian, Hebrew and Greek to enable him to better understand the Bible and ancient documents concerning God's people. This study continued at intervals until his death. His most notable achievement was the development at Kirtland of a grammar for the Egyptian hieroglyphic form of writing. This was used by him, as well as divine aid, in translating ancient writings of the Patriarch Abraham, now published as the Book of Abraham in the Pearl of Great Price. This grammar was never published, and was perhaps never used by any one other than the Prophet. It was, however, the first Egyptian grammar in America and was developed entirely independent of Champollion's Egyptian Grammar.[1] The latter, which is the basis for all modern scholarship on the subject, made its appearance in 1836, the result of thirty years of European study.

From the time Joseph Smith had first been visited by the Angel Moroni, who quoted to him from the Bible, it was apparent to the Prophet that the Sacred Hebrew Volume contained many errors. In the work of translating the Book of Mormon he and Oliver Cowdery became aware that the quotations from the plates of brass did not always agree

---

[1] (Note) Jean Francois Champollion (1790-1832) was a French Egyptologist. In his later life he was employed by the French government in an attempt to decipher Egyptian hieroglyphics. His premature death was the result of overwork. His Egyptian Grammar for which he became famous was not published until four years after his death.

with the same quotations in the King James' translation of the Bible.

When that work was completed, Joseph Smith turned his attention to the Bible with a view to correcting its inaccuracies. The Book of Genesis offered many puzzling problems and, after exhausting his own mind on the matter, he appealed to God in prayer. In answer he received a vision which he called the "Vision of Moses." At later intervals the vision was enlarged. A part was called the "Vision of Enoch." These visions were first made known to the Church in 1830 and references to them are found in writings of that date. They were published in Joseph Smith's Journal in 1838, and are found in the Pearl of Great Price, one of the standard scriptures of the Church.

Sometime between June and October 1830, Joseph Smith began what has come to be known as "An Inspired Revision of the Authorized Version." It was in large part not a translation at all. It was rather a revision of the King James Bible. The work resulted in revelation being given to the Prophet which increased his knowledge of gospel principles. During the Ohio and Missouri period he worked at short intervals. The heavy work of directing the affairs of a scattered church, the difficulties encountered in setting up the new economic and social ventures, and the untimely persecution heaped upon him, prevented this work from ever reaching completion.

He was engaged in this work at Hiram, with Sidney Rigdon, when the mobbing, previously alluded to, occurred.

The desire of Joseph Smith for knowledge concerning the problems confronting the Church during this period sent him, time and again, to his knees in prayer for divine help and makes this the greatest period for revelation in Church history.

The Importance of Knowledge in the Church

The Prophet's zeal for learning soon permeated the Church. In December 1832, he organized at Kirtland, the "School of the Prophets." The upper story of Newel K. Whitney's mercantile establishment was first used for this purpose. Although the objective of the school was to prepare the membership of the Church to carry the gospel to the world, the subjects taught and discussed were as broad as human interests.

In a revelation received by Joseph Smith, December 27, 1832, and addressed to the brethren assembled to attend the School of the Prophets, we read:

"And I give unto you a commandment that you shall teach one another the doctrine of the kingdom."

"Teach ye diligently and my grace shall attend you, that you may be instructed more perfectly in theory, in principle, in doctrine, in the law of the gospel, in all things that pertain unto the Kingdom of God, that are expedient for you to understand:"

"Of things both in heaven and in the earth, and under the earth; things which have been, things which are, things which must shortly come to pass; things which are at home, things which are abroad; the wars and the perplexities of the nations, and the judgements which are on the land; and a knowledge also of countries and of kingdoms."[2]

"Yea, seek ye out of the best books words of wisdom; seek learning even by study and also by faith."[3]

This revelation has become the charter for learning given by God to the church. It is a commandment to learn, which is further strengthened by the words of the revelation:

"Cease to be idle; cease to be unclean; cease to find fault one with another; cease to sleep longer than is needful; retire to thy bed early, that ye may not be weary; arise

[2]*Doctrine and Covenants*, Sec. 88:77-79.
[3]*Ibid.*, Sec. 88:118.

early, that your bodies and minds may be invigorated."[4]

"The School of the Prophets" was the first organized school for adult education in America. Its sessions were held chiefly in the evenings and were attended by all the male leaders of the Church in and around Kirtland. A school for Elders had been conducted in Missouri, but would hardly be recognized under the formal name "school."

Among the many fine expressions of Joseph Smith upon the subject of learning, first expressed to the School of the Prophets, are the following:

"You cannot be saved in ignorance."

"A man can be saved no faster than he gains knowledge."

"The Glory of God is intelligence."

In these crisp sentences the Prophet epitomizes* the law of the Latter-day Church on the importance of learning. The influence of this law has done much to shape the educational policies of the Church for over a century.

Those participating in the School of the Prophets were required to keep fully the commandments of God. The members of the school were received into fellowship only after participation in prayer, the sacrament, and the ordinance of the washing of feet. The school was to be a sanctuary or tabernacle where the Holy Spirit might edify them.[5]

The Word of Wisdom Given to the Church

On February 27, 1833, Joseph Smith entered the chamber where the School of the Prophets held forth. The room was filled with tobacco smoke, and the odor of it, to this man fresh from the pure outside, was offensive. Without

saying a word he retired from the room and sought the Lord in prayer on the matter.[6] In answer he received a revelation which has become known to the Church as the "Word of Wisdom."

1. A Word of Wisdom, for the benefit of the Council of High Priests, assembled in Kirtland, and the church; and also the Saints in Zion.

2. To be sent greeting: not by commandment or constraint, but by revelation and the word of wisdom, showing forth the order and will of God in the temporal salvation of all saints in the last days.

3. Given for a principle with promise, adapted to the capacity of the weak and the weakest of all saints, who are or can be called saints.

4. Behold, verily, thus saith the Lord unto you, in consequence of evils and designs which do and will exist in the hearts of conspiring men in the last days, I have warned you and forewarn you, by giving unto you this word of wisdom by revelation—

5. That inasmuch as any man drinketh wine or strong drink among you, behold it is not good, neither meet in the sight of your Father, only is assembling yourselves together to offer up your sacraments before him.

6. And, behold, this should be wine, yea, pure wine of the grape of the vine, of your own make.

7. And, again, strong drinks are not for the belly, but for the washing of your bodies.

8. And, again, tobacco is not for the body, neither for the belly, and is not good for man, but is an herb for bruises and all sick cattle, to be used with judgment and skill.

9. And again, hot drinks are not for the body or belly.

10. And again, verily I say unto you, all wholesome herbs God hath ordained for the constitution, nature, and use of man—

11. Every herb in the season thereof, and every fruit in the season thereof; all these to be used with prudence and thanksgiving.

12. Yea, flesh also of beast and of the fowls of the air, I, the Lord, have ordained for the use of man with thanksgiving; nevertheless, they are to be used sparingly;

13. And it is pleasing unto me that they should not be used only in times of winter, or of cold, or famine.

14. All grain is ordained for the use of man and of beasts, to be the staff of life, not only for man but for the beasts of the field,

---

[4]*Ibid.*, Sec. 88:124.

*epitomizes—summarizes concisely.

[5] (Note) See *Doctrine and Covenants*, Sec. 88:-137-141.

[6]Smith and Sjodahl, *Doctrine and Covenants Commentary*, p. 705.

and the fowls of heaven, and all wild animals that run or creep on the earth;

15. And these hath God made for the use of man only in times of famine and excess of hunger.

16. All grain is good for the food of man; as also the fruit of the vine; that which yieldeth fruit, whether in the ground or above the ground—

17. Nevertheless, wheat for man, and corn for the ox, and oats for the horse, and rye for the fowls and for swine, and for all beasts of the field, and barley for all useful animals, and for mild drinks, as also other grain.

18. And all saints who remember to keep and do these sayings, walking in obedience to the commandments, shall receive health in their navel, and marrow to their bones;

19. And shall find wisdom and great treasures of knowledge, even hidden treasures;

20. And shall run and not be weary, and shall walk and not faint.

21. And I, the Lord, give unto them a promise, that the destroying angel shall pass by them, as the children of Israel, and not slay them. Amen."[7]

More Revelation Received as Scripture

The numerous revelations received by Joseph Smith in answer to his earnest inquiries for knowledge, constitute a unique latter-day scripture. These revelations became standards for the Church only after each of them was received as such by the vote of the Church. This is the law of common consent and is the fundamental principle of Church government.

Many of the revelations received by Joseph Smith were accepted by the Church before any collection of such revelations appeared. Section 20 of the Book of Doctrine and Covenants was accepted at the time of the organization of the Church.

In the latter part of 1831, it was decided by a council of Church leaders to compile the revelations concerning the origin of the Church and its organization. The collection was to be called the "Book of Commandments." Such a collection was made and presented to a con-

ference of the Priesthood at Hiram, Ohio, November 1, 1831. On the first day of the conference Joseph Smith received a revelation which was made the preface for the new volume and is now Section 1 of the Book of Doctrine and Covenants. In this preface we read:

"Search these commandments, for they are true and faithful, and the prophecies and promises which are in them shall all be fulfilled."[8]

On the second day of the conference the brethren arose in turn and bore witness to the divine origin of the revelations in the collection. The Prophet challenged those who doubted that the revelations were of God to attempt to write such a revelation themselves. William E. M'Lellin made such an attempt, which ended in a confessed failure.

After accepting the collection as scripture it was voted to print 10,000 copies. Oliver Cowdery and John Whitmer were chosen to carry the manuscript to Independence, Missouri, for printing. The Saints had set up a printing press at the place for the publication of the first Latter-day Saint newspaper, *The Evening and Morning Star*.

The journey was delayed and at the April Conference of 1832, it was voted to reduce the issue to 3,000 copies. The publication was destined to wait a considerable time. The preparations for printing were well under way in August, 1833, when a mob in Jackson County destroyed the printing establishment and much of the material prepared for publication. The "Book of Commandments," as such, was never published by the Church.*

The continuous revelations received by the Prophet soon made the first collection inadequate. In September,

---

[7]*Doctrine and Covenants*, Sec. 89.

[8]*Ibid.*, Section 1, Verse 37.
*(Note) The Book of Commandments has, in recent years, been published by the Church of Christ (Hedrickites) at Independence, Missouri.

1834, a committee composed of Joseph Smith, Oliver Cowdery, and Frederick G. Williams was chosen to bring the collection up to date. This collection was presented by Oliver Cowdery to the general assembly of the Church at Kirtland, August 17, 1835, as "The Book of Doctrine and Covenants of the Church." A testimony of the twelve apostles concerning the truthfulness of the Revelation was read. The assembly then voted to receive the collection of revelations as scripture. Then publication followed in the same year.

Subsequent revelations, accepted by the vote of the Church, were added to later editions until the book reached its present proportions. No attempt was made to place in the book all of the revelations which the Prophet had received,

Modern publication of Doctrine and Covenants

but those which set forth in plain language the doctrines of the Church, and the commandments of God to his people. Not all of the sections are revelations. Remarks of the Prophet Joseph, on several occasions, so clearly set forth the principles of the gospel, that they were received by vote of the Church as doctrine and included in the volume. An account of the martyrdom of the Prophet and his brother Hyrum is now included, also a revelation to Brigham Young, concerning the organizing of the Camps of Israel.

The Origin of the Book of Abraham

In July, 1835, the Prophet Joseph Smith came into possession of ancient records, the value of which is not even yet fully appreciated.

Sometime in 1828, a French explorer by the name of Antonio Sebolo secured permission from Mehemit Ali, Viceroy of Egypt, to make a certain excavation in Egypt. In 1831, Sebolo, having secured the proper license, employed some 433 men for four months and two days, paying them about six cents per day each, in excavating a catacomb or tomb

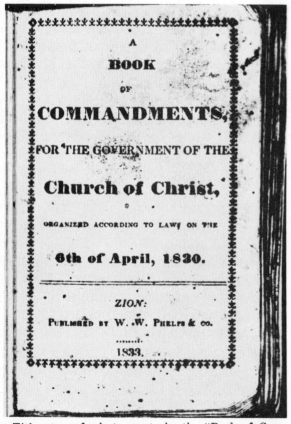

Title page of what was to be the "Book of Commandments." The press in Independence, Missouri was destroyed before the book, as such, could be printed.   Used by permission, Church Historian's Office

near the site of ancient Thebes."[9] The ancient tomb was of the multiple type, containing several hundred mummies of the three separate orders of burial. Only eleven mummies of the highest order were in suitable condition for removal.[10] With these mummies still encased, Sebolo started for Paris. On the way to Paris, however, M. Sebolo put in at Trieste, where he died after a ten-day illness.

The mummies were left by will to a nephew, Michael H. Chandler. Mr. Chandler was then a resident of Philadelphia, Pennsylvania, but it being supposed that he was a resident of Ireland, the mummies were first forwarded there. After a devious course of two years' duration, the mummies finally landed in New York, addressed to Michael H. Chandler, in the winter, or spring, of 1833.

In April, 1833, Mr. Chandler paid the customs duties and took possession. In opening the caskets Chandler was disappointed to find nothing in the way of jewels or precious ornaments, but attached to two of the bodies were rolls of linen preserved with the same care and, apparently by the same methods, as the bodies. Within the linen coverings were rolls of papyrus bearing a perfectly preserved record in black and red characters, carefully formed. "With other of the bodies were papyrus strips bearing epitaphs and astronomical calculations."[11] Mr. Chandler was, of course, curious to know the nature of the characters upon the papyrus, but, "he was immediately told, while yet in the customhouse, that there was no man in that city who could translate the roll, but was referred by the same gentleman (a stranger) to Mr. Joseph Smith, Jr."[12]

Mr. Chandler took the mummies and rolls to Philadelphia, but none of the learned men there could decipher the characters.

In the *Life of Joseph Smith* by George Q. Cannon[13] we read:

"The learned men of Philadelphia and other places flocked to see these representatives of an ancient time, and Mr. Chandler solicited their translation of some of the characters. Even the wisest among them were only able to interpret the meaning of a few of the signs."[14]

Mr. Chandler then formed a syndicate for the purpose of touring the country with the mummies, together with lectures concerning them. With only four of the mummies and the rolls of papyrus, he reached Kirtland, Ohio, July 3, 1835[15] where he sought and obtained an interview with the Mormon Prophet.

Oliver Cowdery says, "Mr. Chandler was told (by Joseph Smith) that his writings could be deciphered, and he very politely gave me the privilege of copying some four or five separate pieces, stating at the same time, that unless he found someone who could give him a translation soon, he would carry them to London."[16]

Mr. Chandler solicited an opinion concerning his antiquities or a translation of some of the characters. "Brother Smith gave him the interpretation of a few for his satisfaction." Upon the

[9]Oliver Cowdery's letter to Wm. Frye under date of December 25, 1835, published in *Messenger and Advocate*, December, 1835, Vol. 2, No. 3.

[10]Compare account in Cannon's *Life of Joseph Smith*, p. 180-1.

[11]Cannon, *Life of Joseph Smith*, 1964 edition, p. 197, compare also, *History of the Church*, Vol II, pp. 348-351, Widtsoe, *The Restoration of the Gospel*, p. 116.

[12]Oliver Cowdery's letter to Wm. Frye, December 25, printed in the *Messenger and Advocate*, December, 1835, Vol. 2, No. 3.

[13]Cannon, *Life of Joseph Smith*, p. 181.

[14]*History of the Church*, Period I, Vol. II, p. 235. Widtsoe, *The Restoration of the Gospel*, p. 116.

[15]Oliver Cowdery's letter to Wm. Frye, *Messenger and Advocate*, December, 1835. Vol. II. No. 3.

[16]*Ibid.*

request of Joseph Smith, but before any offer to purchase the rolls and mummies had been made, Mr. Chandler wrote a letter to the Prophet certifying to this effect:

Kirtland, July 6, 1835.

"This is to make known to who may be desirous concerning the knowledge of Joseph Smith Jr., in deciphering the ancient Egyptian hieroglyphic characters in my possession, which I have in many eminent cities showed to the most learned; and from the information that I could ever learn, or meet with, I find that of Mr. Joseph Smith Jr., to correspond in the most minute matters."

MICHAEL H. CHANDLER
Traveling with and proprietor
of Egyptian Mummies.[17]

Some conversation took place between Joseph Smith and Mr. Chandler and a comparison was made with a transcript of characters from the Book of Mormon plates, "resulting in the discovery of some points of resemblance."[18]

Later, friends of the Prophet living in Kirtland, purchased the four mummies, together with the rolls of papyrus from Mr. Chandler. The "Prophet with William W. Phelps and Oliver Cowdery as scribes began to translate."[19]

Translation of the Manuscript

The method by which the translation was undertaken is a subject of some dispute. Doubtless it was a matter of intensive study, aided by the inspiration which so frequently came in answer to the Prophet's prayers. Brigham H. Roberts in writing of the translation says:

"Then he (Joseph) took up the study of the letters and grammar of the Egyptian language. In this research he found himself virtually on pioneer ground, but like Champollion, he had an almost intuitive linguistic sense. The work, however, proceeded slowly. It was begun in 1835. Not until seven years

later, in 1842, could he begin the publication, and it was never completed."[20]

That considerable study preceded the translation is evidenced by the Prophet's own writings. Under date of October 1, 1835, he writes: "This afternoon I labored in the Egyptian alphabet, in company with brothers Oliver Cowdery and W. W. Phelps, and during the research, the principles of astronomy as understood by Father Abraham and the ancients, unfolded to our understanding."[20a] Under date of October 7, and November 24, of the same year, and in other places, he refers to his labors in translating the papyrus. On December 16, 1835, the Prophet records: "Elders William E. M'Lellin, Brigham Young, and J. Carter called and paid me a visit, with which I was much gratified. I exhibited and explained the Egyptian records to them, and explained many things concerning the dealing of God with the ancients, and the formation of the planetary system."[21]

From the above it would appear that considerable translating had been done before the end of 1835, but the difficulties which faced the Church and harassed the Prophet during the years immediately following, prevented the Prophet completing the work. As no grammar of the Egyptian language had appeared in America by 1835, some idea of the task which faced the Prophet may be realized, and the results of his labor become the more remarkable. Under date of December 25, 1835, Oliver Cowdery writes:

"The language in which this record is written is very comprehensive, and many of the hieroglyphics exceedingly striking. The evidence is apparent upon the face that they were written by persons acquainted with the

---

[17]*History of the Church*, Period I, Vol. II, p. 235.

[18]Roberts, *Comprehensive History of the Church*, Vol. 2, p. 126.

[19]Widtsoe, *The Restoration of the Gospel*, pp. 116-117.

[20]Roberts, *Comprehensive History of the Church*, Vol. 4, p. 519.

[20a]*History of the Church*, Period I, Vol. II, p. 286.

[21]*Ibid.*, p. 334. See Reynolds *Book of Abraham*, p. 3, see *Millennial Star, History of Joseph Smith*, a description of the records Vol. 15, p. 519, *Millennial Star*, Vol. 15, p. 550.

history of the creation, the fall of man, and more or less of the correct ideas or notions of the Deity.

The representation of the Godhead—three yet in one, is curiously drawn to give simply, though impressively, the writer's views of that exalted personage. The serpent represented as walking, or formed in a manner to be able to walk, standing in front of or near a female figure, is to me one of the greatest representations I have ever seen upon paper, or a writing substance; and must go far towards convincing the rational mind of the correctness and divine authenticity of the Holy Scriptures."[22]

Only part of the scrolls dealing with

---

[22]Letter of Oliver Cowdery to Wm. Frye, Esq., Gilead, Calhoun County, Ill., dated December 25, 1835.

the life of Abraham were completed by the Prophet. It appears that one of the rolls of papyrus containing the writings of Joseph, who was sold into Egypt, was never translated sufficiently for publication. That some of it was deciphered by the Prophet appears from the published *Life of Joseph Smith*, by Cannon. We read:

"In the record of Joseph who was sold into Egypt is given prophetic representation of the judgment, the Savior is shown seated upon his throne, crowned, and holding the sceptres of righteousness and power; before him are assembled the twelve tribes of Israel and all the kingdoms of the world; while Michael an Archangel holds the keys to the

A FACSIMILE FROM THE BOOK OF ABRAHAM
No. 1.

EXPLANATION OF THE ABOVE CUT.

Fig. 1. The Angel of the Lord. 2. Abraham fastened upon an altar. 3. The idolatrous priest of Elkenah attempting to offer up Abraham as a sacrifice. 4. The altar for sacrifice by the idolatrous priests, standing before the gods of Elkenah, Libnah, Mahmackrah, Korash, and Pharaoh. 5. The idolatrous god of Elkenah. 6. The idolatrous god of Libnah. 7. The idolatrous god of Mahmackrah. 8. The idolatrous god of Korash. 9. The idolatrous god of Pharaoh. 10. Abraham in Egypt. 11. Designed to represent the pillars of heaven, as understood by the Egyptians. 12. Raukeeyang, signifying expanse, or the firmament over our heads; but in this case, in relation to this subject, the Egyptians meant it to signify Shaumau, to be high, or the heavens, answering to the Hebrew word, Shaumahyeem.

Interesting page preceding "The Book of Abraham" in the Pearl of Great Price.

bottomless pit in which Satan has been chained."[23]

Publication

Publication of the Book of Abraham began in the *Times and Seasons*, March, 1842,[24] at Nauvoo with facsimiles of certain portions of the papyrus.[25] The wood engravings for the cuts were done by Reuben Hedlock, an engraver from Canada. John Taylor, a worker in wood, was also present and working on the *Times and Seasons* at that time.[26] For years after the publication of the facsimiles, the original documents remained in existence. They were considered as the property of the Smith family and, after the Prophet's martyrdom, were retained by his wife, Emma. They were later sold by her to a museum at St. Louis, from whence they found their way into the Museum of Chicago. During the Great Fire in 1871 in Chicago the museum was also destroyed. Hence it was believed that the precious ancient manuscripts were also destroyed. But recently, in 1966, the original of the so-called facsimile No. 1 from the Book of Abraham was rediscovered. An Egyptian scholar, Dr. Aziz Atiya, who taught in New York, found it together with ten other papyri in the New York Metropolitan Museum of Art. He recognized it as part of the manuscript that had once belonged to Joseph Smith and requested the directors of the museum to return it to The Church of Jesus Christ of Latter-day Saints. This took place November 27, 1967. The papyri from which the text of the Book of Abraham was translated was not among the recovered papyri.

The translation made by Joseph Smith, and facsimiles of some of the engravings, remain as one of the greatest contributions to the field of religion. The translated part of the scrolls contained Abraham's personal account of his early life, the creation of the world as revealed to him by God, and a graphic description of the astronomy of the heavens.

The system of rotating planets, described by Abraham, presents a knowledge of the astronomy which is startling to the modern world.

No prophet ever gave to the world a stronger challenge of his divine calling than did Joseph Smith in his publication of the Book of Abraham.

Supplementary Readings

1. *History of the Church*, Period I, Vol. 1, p. 226. (Testimony of the High Priesthood concerning the Book of Commandments.)

2. *Ibid.*, Volume II, p. 200. (Interesting report of Wm. E. M'Lellin on the progress of the Kirtland School.)

3. Roberts, *Comprehensive History of the Church*, Vol. I, pp. 214-216. (A brief analysis of the Book of Moses.)

4. *Ibid.*, pp. 247-248. (Note—Joseph Smith's inspired revision of the Bible.)

5. *Ibid.*, pp. 293-304. Joseph Smith's prophecies on war, especially a prophecy of the Civil War.

6. Parley P. Pratt, *Autobiography*, pp. 61-62. (Description of how Joseph Smith received revelation.)

7. *Ibid.*, (Adult education in the School of Elders, Jackson County, 1833.)

8. Evans, *Joseph Smith, an American Prophet*, pp. 92-96. (The School of the the Prophets.)

9. *Ibid.*, pp. 212-222. (The Sanctity of the Body.)

10. *Ibid.*, pp. 276-282. (The Glory of God is Intelligence—Wilful Ignorance is sin.)

11. Widtsoe, *Joseph Smith as Scientist*, pp. 142-144. (Joseph Smith taught the importance of schools.)

12. *Ibid.*, p. 92. (Science and the Word of Wisdom.)

13. *Doctrine and Covenants*, Section 55, Verse 4, (Revelation on Education.)

14. *Ibid.*, Section 67:4-14. (A challenge from the Lord to those who would write a revelation.)

15. Smith and Sjodahl, *Doctrine and Covenants Commentary*. (Preface.)

---

[23]Cannon's *Life of Joseph Smith*, p. 182.

[24](Note) The *Times and Seasons* was a Mormon newspaper published by the Church at Nauvoo, from 1840-46. The publication is especially valuable for the editorials, letters and articles written by Church leaders at that time.

[25]*Times and Seasons*, Vol. 3, Nos. 9, 10, 19.

[26]See *Improvement Era*, Vol. 16, p. 314.

CHAPTER 14

THE GREATNESS OF THE
EARLY LEADERS

The Church Developed Leadership

The Ohio and Missouri period in the history of the Church is significant for the development of the men and women who were attracted to the restored gospel. In general, the membership was drawn from the great middle class of society. Few of these, at the time of entering the Church, had received any wide distinction or notoriety. It is doubtful if they would have been long remembered but for their connection with the Church. True, most of them were highly respected members of their several communities and some were prominent in local affairs. None were nationally important.

It was the spirit within the Church which turned the commonplace into greatness. When Joseph Smith remarked, "I am a rough stone. The sound of the hammer and chisel were never heard on me until the Lord took me in hand,"[1] he spoke a truism which might be applied to hundreds and thousands within the Church.

The Church offered opportunities for expression. It encouraged learning. It called men to be leaders and expected them to grow big enough to fill the call. "Not what you are—but what you may become," was often the criterion of selection. The job might be bigger than the man—but not so big as the man might become. This fundamental faith in the possibilities of human beings, when actuated by a desire to serve, is one of the distinguishing characteristics

[1]*Scrapbook of Mormon Literature*, Vol. 2, p. 6.

of the Church. This faith in human possibilities has been justified. *The Church did not attract great men. It produced great men.* The Church attracted fine men, intelligent men. It gave them an opportunity for growth. It heaped upon them responsibilities which forced them to grow or to die. Every man became a leader,—a holder of priesthood. Every man was called to be a doer of the word, and not merely a hearer of it. Under such a system talent does not long remain hidden. Men rose to greatness who might have lived lives of relative obscurity outside the Church organiation.

Among those who rose to greatness within the Church we find Joseph Smith, Oliver Cowdery, Parley P. Pratt, Orson Pratt, Sidney Rigdon, Edward Partridge, Brigham Young, Heber C. Kimball, John Taylor, Wilford Woodruff, Lorenzo Snow, Orson Hyde, Willard Richards and a multitude of others.

The accounts of the conversion of each of these men to the gospel, and the story of their individual growth within the Church organization, are to be found in their journals and biographies and constitute some of the richest bits of romance in American history. Five of those men became presidents of the Church in succession, namely, Joseph Smith, Brigham Young, John Taylor, Wilford Woodruff, and Lorenzo Snow. The remainder held high positions. All were young men when the gospel found them. The average age was under thirty. With the exception of John Taylor, who was born in England, they were all descendants of early New England stock.

Four of them, Sidney Rigdon, Parley P. Pratt, Orson Hyde and John Taylor, had been preachers. Joseph Smith and Orson Pratt had been farmers, Oliver Cowdery a schoolteacher, Wilford Woodruff a miller, Brigham Young a carpenter, Willard Richards a physician, Heber C. Kimball a potter. All were respected citizens of their several communities, but all might have lived and died in relative obscurity but for the gospel touching their lives.

As indicated in Chapter Three, these men were among those who had become discontented with existing religious creeds, and had formulated many doctrines closely akin to that of the restored Church. The step into the Latter-day Church was not a great one.

A brief story of how some of these men developed into leaders will illustrate in a general way its effect upon them all.

The Coming of Brigham Young

In September, 1832, three men near thirty years of age, entered the town of Kirtland in a wagon and sought out the Prophet Joseph Smith. They introduced themselves as Brigham Young, Joseph Young, his brother, and Heber C. Kimball. They had recently been baptized into the Church at Mendon, New York.

Brigham Young wrote of the meeting:

"We found the Prophet, and two or three of his brothers, chopping and hauling wood. Here my joy was full at the privilege of shaking the hand of the Prophet of God, and receiving the sure testimony, by the spirit of prophecy, that he was all that any man could believe him to be as a true Prophet."

"In the evening a few of the brethren came in, and we conversed upon the things of the Kingdom. He called upon me to pray; in my prayer I spoke in tongues. As soon

Brigham Young, early convert to the Church who became its second president.

as we arose from our knees, the brethren flocked around him, and asked his opinion concerning the gift of tongues that was upon me. He told them it was the pure Adamic language. Some said to him they expected he would condemn the gift Brother Brigham had, but he said, 'No, it is of God, and the time will come when Brigham Young will preside over this church.' The latter part of this conversation was in my absence."[2]

Thus was introduced into the Church a man who was to become one of its greatest leaders.

This Brigham Young, in 1832, was not a great man. Joseph Smith had never before heard of him, although in

[2]Brigham Young, *Autobiography — Millennial Star*, Vol. 25, p. 439.

New York State they had lived, for ten years, only some forty miles distant from each other.

Brigham Young was born June 1, 1801, in a log house at Whittingham, Windham County, Vermont. He was the ninth child of John Young, a Revolutionary War veteran, and Abigail Howe Young.

He worked on his father's farm as a youth. His mother died when he was fourteen and he was hired out as an apprentice to learn the trade of carpenter and painter. At sixteen he was in business for himself. In the years which followed he became an expert carpenter and cabinet maker, painter, and glazier. He was not greatly interested in religion as a youth. He says:

"I was taught by my parents to live a strictly moral life. Still, it was not until my twenty-second year that I became serious and religiously inclined. Soon after this I attached myself to the Methodist church."[3]

His formal schooling consisted of eleven days under a traveling schoolmaster. His mother had taught him to read and his father had taught him considerable from the Bible. He was, however, a natural student, a keen observer of events, and judge of men.

His family early moved to New York State. Several towns there lay claim to being the place of his permanent residence. His occupation forced him to move from place to place and often he returned to the occupation of farming during the summers. At the age of twenty-three he married Miriam Angeline Works, October 8, 1824. Two daughters were born to them, Elizabeth and Vilate. Following the birth of the latter, his wife became invalided, and was nearly helpless in the latter years of her life. Brigham built a colonial house of fine workmanship for his wife at Mendon, New York.

Of the years which followed, his biographers say of him:

"He was in fairly comfortable circumstances, for he had the foresight to seize upon opportunity and use self-restraint to husband his resources. However, he did not display any unusual or ambitious traits. He was content with his good parents, brothers and sisters, his beautiful and loving wife and two little girls, his friends and neighbors. It is doubtful if he would have moved far or traveled much but for the thrilling appeal from God which was soon to enter his soul and drive out every thought but to "gather up to Zion" where Christ and his Prophet were re-establishing righteousness in the last days."[4]

A copy of the Book of Mormon, which came into his hands was Brigham's introduction to the restored Church. After months and months of study of the volume, he was baptized at Mendon, April 14, 1832. In turn he converted all his brothers and sisters, his aged father, and his wife. A few weeks later his wife died. Shortly thereafter he went to Kirtland, where his contact with the Prophet changed his entire life.

Almost immediately, this man, who had led hitherto a quiet and secluded life, was thrown into the maelstrom of rapidly moving events. During the winter of 1832-33 he was sent on a mission to Canada. He had scarcely returned from the duties involved there when he was given a major task. He was sent by the Prophet to·New York State to gather out the converts and lead a caravan of them to Kirtland. The carpenter and painter suddenly had to become a leader. Returning successfully from that assignment, he was sent on another mission during the winter of 1833-34.

Arriving back in Kirtland in Febru-

---

[3]Brigham Young, *Autobiography — Millennial Star*, Vol. 25.

[4]Gates and Widtsoe, *Life Story of Brigham Young*, pp. 5-6. Macmillan Company, 1930.

ary he met and married Mary Ann Angel, a convert from New England. Together they passed through many trials during the ensuing years. The winter of 1833-34 brought sad news from the Saints in Missouri. Early summer found him on the march with "Zion's Camp," one thousand miles on foot to relieve the Saints in Jackson County. It was a rare experience under the Prophet, now turned soldier. The lessons in organization were keenly learned and formed the ground work for his own great accomplishments at a later day.

Back in Kirtland again, he labored on the temple, supervising the carpenter work. On February 14, 1835, he was chosen as an apostle.

Always it was activity—a call to responsible positions—to leadership—to service in God's Kingdom. Under the load placed upon him his shoulders broadened—his talents found opportunity for expression, and a man emerged to whom not only his own people, but eventually the whole nation, could point with pride.

The Great Advocate of the Restored Church

In the same year that the Church was organized a young man, then nineteen years of age, was praying frequently to God for just such a restoration. Orson Pratt was a promising youth. Born and reared on a farm in Washington County, New York, he had early shown an interest in other things. Despite heavy duties on the farm, he managed to get some schooling. His special interest was mathematics, but he also gained some knowledge of grammar, bookkeeping, geography and surveying.

From early youth the teachings of his father had turned his mind toward religion. He was a firm believer in prayer, often retiring into the woods for that purpose. When his brother Parley appeared suddenly at the old homestead in September of that year and announced that he had found the restored church, Orson was immediately interested. Parley would not have left his home in Ohio and his job as minister unless he had found something genuine.

In a few days Orson was ready for baptism, and followed his brother to Fayette to see the Prophet.

From the time of that meeting the real development of his native talent began. His conversations with Joseph Smith so filled him with a desire to do God's will, that he asked the Prophet to inquire of the Lord concerning him. The answer was received by revelation:

"My son Orson, hearken and hear and behold what I, the Lord God, shall say unto you, even Jesus Christ your Redeemer;
"The light and the life of the world, a Light which shineth in darkness and the darkness comprehendeth it not;
"Who so loved the world that he gave his own life, that as many as would believe might become the sons of God. Wherefore, you are my son;
"And blessed are you because you have believed; and more blessed are you because you are called of me to preach my gospel—
"Wherefore, lift up your voice and spare not, for the Lord hath spoken; therefore, prophesy, and it shall be given by the power of the Holy Ghost.
And if you are faithful, behold I am with you until I come."[5]

Orson Pratt accepted that call of the Lord and with voice and pen became a mighty guardian and teacher of the restored gospel.

Although just twenty years of age when this call came he started northward on a mission alone. In 1833 he made a journey into Canada, where he

[5]*Doctrine and Covenants*, Section 34:1-5, 10-11.

Orson Pratt, one of the first missionaries of the Church to Canada.

had the honor of being one of the first missionaries to that land. His work during the next few years carried him on successful missions to the Eastern States. In 1834 he marched with Zion's Camp to Missouri, along with Brigham Young and others. In 1835 he was selected as one of the Twelve Apostles. He was but twenty-four years of age, one of the youngest men to ever hold that office in the Church. His many duties and responsibilities called for all the talent he possessed. Always he strove to be able to fill the job assigned

him, only on mastering it to find a still harder task appointed him.

With the years came the development of a great intellect. He attracted the attention of the world by his writings in the *Millennial Star*, the official Church publication in England. His published discourses fill many volumes. The quality of his writings stamp him as the greatest philosopher the Church has yet produced.

When the Saints later immigrated to the Rockies he won great recognition by his engineering and skill and mathematical accuracy. He and Erastus Snow were the first of the Saints to enter Salt Lake Valley. He was given the job of laying our Great Salt Lake City, determining the latitude, longitude, altitude, etc. The accuracy of his calculations is a lasting monument to the man.

Introducing John Taylor

The coming of John Taylor to the Church, near the close of the Ohio period, was an important addition to Church leadership. Although the real greatness of the man is shown in connection with later events, we will introduce him at this time as an example of fine scholarship which ripened under the opportunities within the Church.

John Taylor was born November 1, 1808, in Milnthorpe, County of Westmoreland, England. He was the second son of a family of ten. Until the age of fourteen, his summers were spent on the farm and his winters in school. At fourteen he was bound as an apprentice to a cooper.[6] In a year his employer went bankrupt, and John Taylor started to learn the trade of turner[7] in Penrith, Cumberland. Here he remained until

---

[6]Cooper—Maker and mender of casks, barrels, etc.

[7]Turner—One who fashions objects with a lathe.

his twentieth year, surrounded by most beautiful scenery, which affected deeply his natural poetical nature. The effect of these years is reflected in his later speaking and writing.

He had been brought up in the Church of England, but his natural vivacity caused him to have little regard for the stiff formalities of Church creed.

He had, however, a deep reverence for God, which caused him to investigate other religions. At the age of sixteen he left the Church of England and joined the Methodists. At seventeen we find him an exhorter or local preacher.

At the age of twenty he returned to his family estate at Hale and went into business for himself. In 1830, his father and family migrated to Canada leaving him to sell some property and settle the affairs of the estate. Two years later he followed them to the American Continent, and settled at Toronto, Canada. Here he affiliated with the Methodist Church of that city and became a preacher.

On January 18, 1833, he married Lenora Cannon, an English lady, who was visiting in Toronto, and had become a student in one of his Bible classes.

Endowed with so many natural talents John Taylor might have gone far in any society. He soon exerted an influence on the more independent of the Methodist sect of that city. His teachings were not confined to the established doctrines of his church. He says:

"My object was to teach what I then considered the leading doctrines of the Christian religion, rather than the peculiar doctrines of Methodism."[8]

Several others shared his views and these met in regular meetings several times a week and investigated the doctrines of the various churches. They

[8]Roberts, *Life of John Taylor*, p. 30.

developed a belief quite at variance with the Methodist church.

John Taylor. converted in Canada by Parley P. Pratt.

"They believed that men who accepted the gospel should have bestowed upon them the Holy Ghost; that it should lead them into all truth, and show them things to come. They believed also in the gift of tongues, the gift of healing, miracles, prophecy, faith, discerning of spirits and all the powers, graces and blessings as experienced in the Christian Church of former days. They believed that Israel would be gathered, the ten tribes restored; that judgments would overtake the wicked, and Christ return to the earth and reign with the righteous; they believed in the first and second resurrection, and in the final glory and triumph of the righteous. But while they believed all these things, they recognized the fact that they had no authority to act in the premises and organize a church with apostles and prophets, and all other officers, and teach the letter of their principles; but whence should they look for the Spirit to give it life and make their dream of a restored, perfect Christian church a reality? It was evident to them they could not perform this work unless called of God to do it, and they were painfully conscious of the fact that not one among them was so called. They could only wait, and pray that God would send to them a messenger if he had a church on the earth."[9]

The intensive study of religion by this small group led to an investigation by the prominent Methodists of the region. They advised them to retain their views privately but not to teach them. This they refused to do and were deprived of their offices in the Methodist church, but retained as members.

His Conversion

In the spring of 1836 Parley P. Pratt called at the home of John Taylor. He carried a letter of introduction from a merchant acquaintance, Mr. Moses Nickerson. John Taylor had heard so many rumors about the Mormons that he was not highly impressed by the visit of the missionary. He listened, however, to the strange story of the restoration.

The story of how Parley had come to Canada was equally strange. He told this story to John Taylor:

"I had retired to rest one evening at an early hour, and was pondering my future course, when there came a knock at the door. I arose and opened it, when Elder Heber C. Kimball and others entered my house, and being filled with the spirit of prophecy, they blessed me and my wife, and prophesied as follows:

"Brother Parley, thy wife shall be healed from this hour, and shall bear a son, and his name shall be Parley; and he shall be a chosen instrument in the hands of the Lord to inherit the priesthood and to walk in the steps of his father. He shall do a great work in the earth in ministering the Word and teaching the children of men. (Note) Arise,

therefore, and go forth in the ministry, nothing doubting. Take no thought for your debts, nor the necessaries of life, for the Lord will supply you with abundant means for all things.

"Thou shalt go to Upper Canada, even to the city of Toronto, the capital, and there thou shalt find a people prepared for the fulness of the gospel, and they shall receive thee, and thou shalt organize the church among them, and it shall spread thence into the regions round about, and many shall be brought to the knowledge of the truth and shall be filled with joy; and from the things growing out of this mission, shall the fulness of the gospel spread into England, and cause a great work to be done in that land."[10]

John Taylor continued for a time to turn a deaf ear to the message Parley P. Pratt proclaimed and gave him little aid. All places of meeting were closed against Parley and he was about to leave Toronto, disappointed, when the way was opened. A Mrs. Walton opened her house for him to preach in and offered him food and lodging. He began holding meetings and interest began to be manifest. He attended the investigation meetings held by John Taylor and his religious friends. They were delighted in his teachings until he mentioned Joseph Smith and the *Book of Mormon*. At this time the spirit of John Taylor which characterized his life came to the front. He addressed the assembly as follows:

"We are here, ostensibly in search of truth. Hitherto we have fully investigated other creeds and doctrines and proven them false. Why should we fear to investigate Mormonism? This gentleman, Mr. Pratt, has brought to us many doctrines that correspond to our own views. We have endured a great deal and made many sacrifices for our religious convictions. We have prayed to God to send us a messenger, if he has a true church on earth. Mr. Pratt has come to us under cir-

[9]Roberts, *Life of John Taylor*, p. 32.

(Note) This prophecy promising a son to Parley P. Pratt was unusual in that he and his wife had been married ten years and were without children. The illness alluded to was consumption, considered incurable. This prophecy was literally filled.

[10]*Autobiography of Parley P. Pratt*, 1964 edition, pp. 130-131.

cumstances that are peculiar; and there is one thing that commends him to our consideration; he has come among us without purse or scrip, as the ancient apostles traveled; and none of us are able to refute his doctrine by scripture or logic. I desire to investigate his doctrines and claims to authority, and shall be very glad if some of my friends will unite with me in this investigation. But if no one will unite with me, be assured that I shall make the investigation alone. If I find his religion true, I shall accept it, no matter what the consequences may be; and if false, then I shall oppose it."[11]

The investigation led John Taylor to be baptized into the Church, and true to his declaration he never swerved from his choice regardless of the trying circumstances which did follow.

The conversion of great numbers followed. John Taylor was ordained an Elder and assisted in preaching the newly accepted gospel. For the first time in his life he was contented at heart in his preaching. The work progressed so rapidly that Apostles Orson Hyde and Orson Pratt were sent to Canada to assist Parley P. Pratt in organizing the converts into branches of the Church. When the three apostles returned to Kirtland, John Taylor was appointed to preside over the Canadian branches.

Responsibility and opportunity came fast on the heels of his conversion.

In March, 1837, he visited the Prophet at Kirtland. From that time nothing could shake his faith in the Church. During the trying times which came to Kirtland that year, John Taylor earned the title of the "Lion" by his spirited defense of the Prophet in the temple

during the Prophet's absence. During the apostasy of that year, the strength and faith of John Taylor did much to hold those who were wavering in their faith loyal to the Prophet of God. In the fall of 1838 he was chosen an apostle. From his entrance into the Church until his death, at which time he was its third president, his life showed the development of great leadership and untiring devotion to the cause he had espoused.

Supplementary Readings

A. Special Readings.

1. Cowley, *Wilford Woodruff*, pp. 33-35. (Conversion of Wilford Woodruff and its effect upon him.)

2. Cowley, *Wilford Woodruff*, pp. 46-56. (Wilford Woodruff receives an answer to prayer, goes on a remarkable mission.)

3. *Ibid.*, last half of p. vi. (Unusual missionary accomplishments of Wilford Woodruff summarized.)

4. *Ibid.*, pp. 88-98. (Incidents in a leader's life.)

5. *Autobiography of Parley P. Pratt*, pp. 36-46. (Conversion to the Church—meeting with the Prophet—description of him.)

6. Eliza R. Snow, *Biography and Family Record of Lorenzo Snow*, pp. 6-17. (The coming of Lorenzo Snow into the Church.)

7. Evans, *Heart of Mormonism*, pp. 119-122. (Summary of early leaders.)

8. *Ibid.*, pp. 123-126. (Sketch of John Taylor.)

9. *Ibid.*, pp. 127-131. (Some missionary adventures of Parley P. Pratt.)

10. *Ibid.*, pp. 412-416. (Inspiring sketch of the life of Orson Pratt.)

11. Evans, *Joseph Smith, an American Prophet*, pp. 59-62. (Three men af ability —Oliver Cowdery, Parley P. and Orson Pratt.)

12. *Ibid.*, pp. 89-92. (A galaxy of stars.)

13. Cowley, *Wilford Woodruff*, pp. 70-81. (Converting the people on the Fox Islands.)

---

[11]Roberts, *Life of John Taylor*, pp. 37-38.

CHAPTER 15

CONFLICT OF MORMONS AND
NON-MORMONS IN MISSOURI

The Underlying Causes of the Conflict

It was inevitable that conflict would arise between Mormons and non-Mormons in Missouri. The stage was set for conflict and it would have been strange indeed had it not occurred. There were five great underlying causes:

First: The Mormons were a different people from those already living in Missouri.

The early settlers in Missouri were mainly from the mountain regions of the Southern States. They were largely poor people, with small acreage in the south, who had been induced by politicians to move into Missouri before 1820 and swell the slave-holding population. Due to this movement of Southern families into Missouri, the region had been admitted to the Union as a slave state, in 1820. These settlers were contented with a few acres of cleared land along the river bottoms. They had few home comforts, little education, and a totally undeveloped appreciation of the arts. They were hospitable and honest. They believed in the institution of slavery and were suspicious of all Northerners.

Another class of people, found along the western border of Missouri near the Mormon settlements, were the outcasts from society generally, who found safety from the arm of the law in these western outposts. To these people the Mormons presented a marked contrast. They were New England stock, thrifty,
ambitious, desirous of fine homes and broad acres. They had a strict respect for the law of the land and a reverence for the law of the Lord.

Second: The Mormons' zeal for Zion aroused the suspicions of the old settlers.

While the commandment to settle in Jackson County had included the injunction that the lands settled should be purchased, the assertion that all that land would become Zion, the property of the Latter-day Saints, was disturbing to the old settlers. The Saints were contemplating an exclusive Zion where only "The Righteous" could dwell and from which all others must necessarily move. This attitude may have seemed innocent enough to those inspired to work for a New Zion, but it did not encourage the love of the old settlers.

Third: The economic and social phases of the new society aroused the suspicions and enmity of the old inhabitants.

The Saints, even among outsiders, lived apart, as a unit. They isolated themselves socially. Young people were discouraged from association with non-Church members. Marriage outside the Church was severely frowned down. Buying and selling were done collectively. Homes, stores, and other buildings arose like magic under community cooperation. The Saints purchased the broad prairie lands which were ready for the plow without the clearing of timber, and organized large cooperative farms. It was inevitable that the old settlers should find the economic competition too keen for them, or, sensing its coming, seek to prevent it.

Fourth: The great numbers of incoming Yankees aroused the slave holders.

The movement of Saints to the New Zion was a surprisingly rapid one. In the first two years the number increased to over a thousand. Not a great number in a thickly populated community, but sufficient to alarm the few old settlers of Jackson County. Further, the stream of incoming Mormons was growing. New wagon caravans were constantly on the way, and rumors were that thousands of people in Ohio would soon join the Missouri group.

The Saints were not seeking to upset the slavery status of Missouri, but inevitably they would upset it if the migration continued. For Missouri had been admitted as a slave state by a narrow margin, and whether or not these Northerners preached the freedom of the slaves, it was a foregone conclusion that they would not vote for slavery at the polls.

As the slavery question was to pursue the Saints for the next thirty years, it is necessary that we understand the status of slavery at the time in question.

The Constitution of the United States provided that Congress should pass no law against slavery prior to 1808.[1] As that date approached, the number of free states and slave states was the same, giving equal numbers of Senators in Congress. This balance in the Senate prevented the passage of any anti-slavery law. After the Louisiana purchase in 1803, settlers began to push west into Missouri. Southern statesmen saw the possibility of a new free state and the destruction of slavery's safe-

guard. To the South, slavery was important. So important that they were willing, as later years proved, to spill their blood in its defense. It is not surprising, then, to find in the archives of the South that money was used freely to induce the poor whites of the mountain region to migrate to Missouri and later demand of Congress that Missouri be admitted as a slave state. This movement was successful. Missouri voted for slavery, Maine was admitted under the same agreement as a free state, and the balance of power in the Senate was maintained.

But after 1831, the status of Missouri was threatened by an influx of Northerners. True, they had not come to oust slavery, and were careful to say nothing about it. They came out of a religious zeal for a New Zion. But nevertheless slavery in Missouri was threatened. There were no slaves in the New Zion, and the Saints boasted that Zion would grow until it would encompass the whole of Missouri. It is necessary that the student of this period understand the tension within the nation if he would understand why the slave-holding Governor of Missouri did not interfere in the subsequent mobbings, and why the President of the United States himself felt that "Your cause is just, but I can do nothing for you."

George Q. Cannon, well acquainted with the conditions prevailing in that period writes:

"The Latter-day Saints were men from the eastern states—Yankee—and consequently open to the suspicion of being Abolitionists. In upper Missouri in those days no charge could be made that would arouse more intense hatred and violence than that of being an abolitionist. The mere whisper of such a suspicion was sufficient to inflame anger and arouse a mob. By such cries Pixley and others of his kind induced every dissolute idler

---

[1] *U. S. Constitution*, Article I, Sec. 9, Par. 1.

TEMPLE SITE IN FAR WEST, MISSOURI, designated by revelation to Joseph Smith on April 26, 1838.

ADAM-ONDI-AHMAN, located on the north side of Grand River in Daviess County, Missouri.

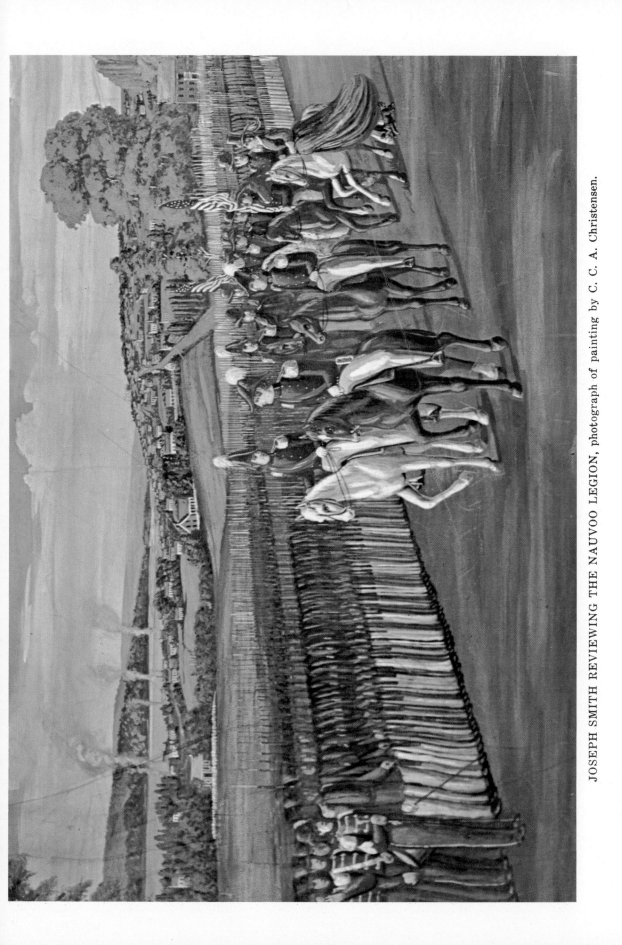

JOSEPH SMITH REVIEWING THE NAUVOO LEGION, photograph of painting by C. C. A. Christensen.

in that region to join in an onslaught for plunder."[2]

How serious this struggle on the part of the South was to defend slavery is well illustrated in the later settlement of the Kansas-Nebraska territory immediately west of the old Mormon homes in Missouri. There, in 1856, open warfare flamed. The slave holders seeking to drive the non-slave holders from the region, plundered, burned, and killed, and the Northerners, unlike the Mormons in Missouri, retaliated in kind until the total damage ran into millions of dollars and hundreds of lives.[3] It is significant that many who took part in driving the Mormons from Missouri were instrumental in fomenting the strife in the Kansas-Nebraska disturbance.

A fifth cause of conflict was the jealousy and enmity aroused among Protestant ministers in Jackson County.

These ministers had been sent into Missouri by their respective churches to build communities of members. But the zeal of the New Zion stole the whole show. It overshadowed and dwarfed their own movement and their individual importance. Their efforts in urging the rough border element to a religious life had not been encouraging. The funds for church building had not been forthcoming, while the incoming Latter-day Saints were making inroads upon their small congregations. It is little wonder that the majority became embittered and sought to recover their influence by driving the Mormons out.

The Saints are Driven out of Jackson County

The earliest rumblings of conflict occurred in the spring of 1832. Unknown individuals threw rocks through the windows of several Latter-day Saint homes. A few shots were fired into houses, with little damage. A number of stacks of hay were burned, and the people were often insulted by abusive language.

This was the prelude to the gathering storm. In the Spring of 1833 the Reverend Finis Ewing stirred the opposition to the Saints by a publication which declared among other things, "The Mormons are the common enemies of mankind and ought to be destroyed."[4] Mass meetings were held. Early in July a document known as the *Secret Constitution* was circulated among non-Mormons. This document charged them as being "idle, lazy, and vicious," as being the very dregs of society, as professing to have direct revelations from God, "to perform all the wonder-working miracles wrought by the inspired apostles and prophets of old." This was declared "derogatory of God and religion and to the utter subversion of human reason."[5]

This document was signed by many persons of note in Jackson County, and called for a mass meeting July 20, 1833.

The scheduled meeting was held. A committee was sent to demand of the Saints the immediate discontinuance of the printing press, the closing of the cooperative store, and the cessation of all mechanical labors. The Saints refused to comply. A mob was formed, which broke open the house of W. W. Phelps, containing the printing establishment. The printing press was taken and many valuable documents destroyed. Edward Partridge, the Bishop of the Church in Zion, was tarred and feathered. In his autobiography he says of the occasion:

[2]George Q. Cannon, *The Life of Joseph Smith*, p. 155.
[3]Muzzey, *History of the United States*, p. 11.

[4]*History of the Church*—Period I, Vol. I, p. 392.
[5]*Ibid.*, pp. 375-376.

"I was taken from my house by the mob, George Simpson being their leader, who escorted me about half a mile to the courthouse, on the public square of Independence; and then and there, a few rods from said courthouse, surrounded by hundreds of the mob, I was stripped of my hat, coat and vest and daubed with tar from head to foot, and then had a quantity of feathers put upon me; and all this because I would not agree to leave the country, and my home where I had lived two years.

"Before tarring and feathering me I was permitted to speak. I told them that the Saints had suffered persecution in all ages of the world; that I had done nothing which ought to offend anyone; that if they abused me they would abuse an innocent person; that I was willing to suffer for the sake of Christ, but to leave the country, I was not then willing to consent to it. . . . I bore my abuse with so much resignation and meekness, that it appeared to astound the multitude, who permitted me to retire in silence, many looking very solemn, their sympathies having been touched as I thought; and as to myself, I was so filled with the Spirit and love of God, that I had no hatred toward my persecutors or anyone else."[6]

Others shared the same treatment. Sidney Gilbert escaped a similar fate by agreeing to close his store.

The work of the mob was resumed July 23. A large group of non-Mormons gathered outside of Independence armed with rifles, old sabres, and other weapons, and bearing a red flag. To prevent bloodshed the Saints entered into a treaty to remove from the county by the first of the ensuing year. A committee of non-Mormons was appointed to aid the Saints in disposing of their property and to prevent mob uprisings.

The treaty offered a temporary breathing spell, and Oliver Cowdery was sent posthaste on the thousand mile journey to confer with the Prophet at Kirtland.

A petition was also prepared and sent "To His Excellency, Daniel Dunklin, Governor of the State of Missouri,"[6a] setting forth the grievances of the Saints and acquainting them with the true state of affairs. The petition asked that the state troops be raised for the protection of property, and martial law be declared in the county.

Meanwhile, depredations of a minor character continued in direct violation of the agreement of the mob.

It appears from a letter written by Joseph Smith on September 4, 1833 to Sister Vienna Jacques at Independence, Missouri, that the report of Oliver Cowdery of the troubles in Independence had not discouraged the Prophet in his expectations that Zion would be established.[7] He appears to have thought the trouble to have been temporary, the result of the disobedience of the Saints, and seemed at that time unaware of the gravity of the situation.

On October 19, 1833, Governor Dunklin replied to the petition of the Saints in a kindly manner. He regretted their difficulties and urged them to appeal to the courts of law to establish their rights, to preserve the peace, and secure redress for their grievances.[8] Lawyers from Clay County were hired and a number of lawsuits prepared and filed. This seemed the signal for a fresh attack. The officers of the courts were induced to join with the opposition, or were threatened with violence if the court actions were allowed.

On Thursday night, October 31st, a mob armed with guns, unroofed and demolished ten dwelling houses of the Saints west of the Big Blue River. The Mormon men were beaten and the women and children driven into the woods.

---

[6]Ibid., pp. 390-399.
[6a]A copy of this petition is found in Ibid., pp. 410-415.
[7](Note) The letter appears in full in Ibid., pp. 407-408.
[8](Note) For a copy of the letter see Ibid., pp. 423-424.

The depredations continued in every quarter. On November 1st one mob proceeded to attack a small prairie settlement, while another stoned houses and shops in Independence, and attacking the houses in groups, drove the men from their homes.

On November 2nd, all the families of Saints in Independence, despairing of help from the civil authorities, moved with some of their personal goods about one mile out of town and organized themselves for defense. Meanwhile, the mobs continued their work of turning the Saints out-of-doors and destroying their homes in the smaller settlements. The reign of terror lasted until the middle of November, by which time twelve hundred Saints had been driven out of Jackson County and two hundred and three of their homes destroyed.

Big Blue River in Jackson County, Missouri.
Used by permission, Church Historian's Office

The Saints had not been expelled without making some opposition. But the opposition was disunited. While some believed that God would justify them in defending their homes, the ma-

jority were opposed to the use of force as contrary to their religious beliefs.[9]

Some of the more militant Saints took up arms under the leadership of Lyman Wight and had several skirmishes with the mob, the main encounter being referred to as the battle of the Big Blue (after the river by that name.) Lyman Wight's defense movement was short-lived. On November 5th, the militia was called out, at the instigation of Lieutenant-Governor Lilburn W. Boggs, a sympathizer of the mob and a slave holder. Colonel Thomas Pitcher, a deputy constable of Jackson County and an energetic leader in the movement to oust the Saints, was placed in charge. Colonel Pitcher, with a promise that the mob would be forced to give up their arms, persuaded the Saints to turn over to the militia all their weapons of defense. They did so, with a feeling that they might then return to their homes in peace.

Their hopes were soon blasted by a fresh series of mobbings that did not halt until every Saint had been removed from Jackson County.

The number of slain on both sides of the conflict is not known.

The exiles moved northward to the Missouri River bottoms and crossed as rapidly as possible on ferry boats into Clay County, the only county which had extended to them a welcome. Elder Parley P. Pratt, who was with the exiles, leaves a vivid picture:

"The shore [of the Missouri River] began to be lined on both sides of the ferry with men, women and children: goods, wagons, boxes, provisions, etc., while the ferry was constantly employed; and when night closed upon us the cottonwood bottom had much the appearance of a camp meeting. Hundreds of

⁹(Note) The Lord's word on such matters had been received by Joseph Smith in a revelation of August 6, 1833, but this was not known generally in Zion. See *Doctrine and Covenants*, Sec. 88.

people were seen in every direction, some in tents and some in the open air around their fires, while the rain descended in torrents. Husbands were inquiring for their wives, wives for their husbands; parents for children, and children for parents. Some had the good fortune to escape with their families, household goods, and some provisions; while others knew not the fate of their friends, and had lost all their goods. The scene was indescribable and, I am sure, would have melted the hearts of any people on earth except our blind oppressors, and a blind and ignorant community."[10]

The March of Zion's Camp

While the twelve hundred Saints of Jackson County were undergoing their trying experiences, the main body of the Church, living in Ohio, was facing many difficulties of its own. A temple had been started at Kirtland, which event had drained the treasury of the Church and most of the ready cash of its members. The work of completing the $60,-000 structure was a tremendous one. Besides, persecution of the Saints had broken out in that vicinity. The Prophet, especially, was hounded and harassed by lawsuits, which, though groundless, hampered his movements. Problems in organization constantly confronted him. Every little branch of the Church had its troubles to lay at his feet.

It is not surprising, that in the midst of the almost super-human burden placed upon him, the Prophet failed to realize the deep underlying causes of the Missouri persecutions.

Twice in the two years following the dedication of Zion, Joseph Smith made hasty journeys to Missouri to straighten out the tangled matters which had arisen. A great deal of correspondence had been carried on between Independence and Kirtland. The Saints in Missouri felt that the Prophet had deserted them. They fully expected him to remove to the New Zion and could not reconcile themselves to his continued residence at Kirtland. News that a temple was being erected at the latter place, while the ground at the temple site in Independence was yet unbroken, aroused bitter feelings, which were ill-concealed.

Charges that the Prophet was usurping power in further organizing the Church were frequent in the record of correspondence. We find the Prophet and the High Priesthood in Ohio, upbraiding the Saints in Zion and calling upon them to repent, before the judgments of the Lord should come upon them. The Prophet uttered predictions of troubles if the attitude of the Saints in Zion did not change.[11]

When the Saints were driven out of Jackson County the Prophet looked no further than the apparent disobedience of the Saints as the chief cause. Hence, he looked forward to their restoration to their homes, when those who were blameworthy among them were sufficiently chastened. By letter he called them again to repentance and promised the re-establishment of Zion in the same place.

In looking back upon the events of the time, it is no reflection upon the greatness of Joseph Smith or upon his calling, as a Prophet of God, that he saw only a part of the problem and not the whole of it in that fateful winter of 1833-34. He was, after all, a human being with human limitations, but faced with unusual problems. If the subsequent failure in reestablishing Zion at Independence caused a new bitterness in the hearts of some toward the Prophet, it

---

[10] *Autobiography of Parley P. Pratt*, pp. 102-103.

[11] *History of the Church*—Period I, Vol. I. p. 402, See also *Doctrine and Covenants*, Section 97:26-27.

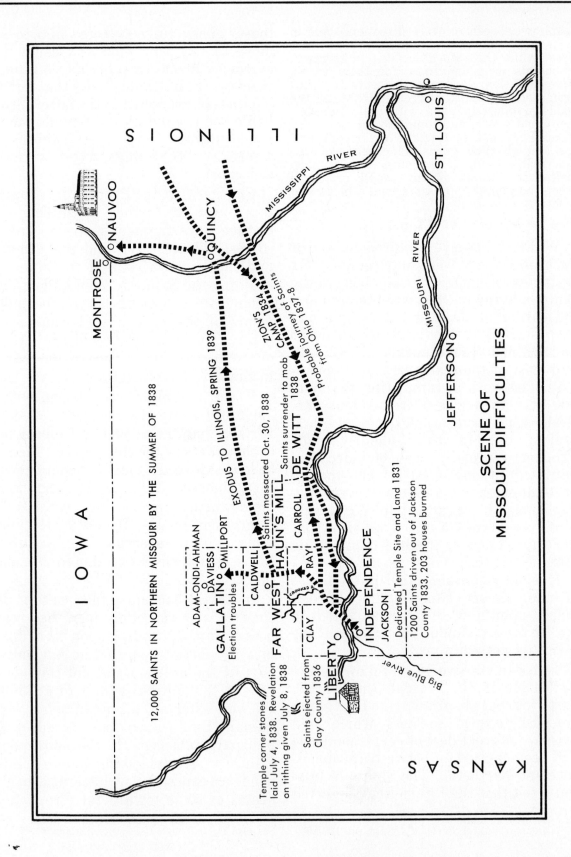

12,000 SAINTS IN NORTHERN MISSOURI BY THE SUMMER OF 1838

IOWA

MONTROSE

NAUVOO

QUINCY

ILLINOIS

MISSISSIPPI RIVER

ST. LOUIS

MISSOURI RIVER

JEFFERSON

SCENE OF
MISSOURI DIFFICULTIES

ZION'S CAMP 1834

Saints surrender to mob 1838

Probable journey of Saints from Ohio 1837-8

DE WITT

CARROLL

Saints massacred Oct. 30, 1838

EXODUS TO ILLINOIS, SPRING 1839

HAUN'S MILL

RAY

CROOKED R.

ADAM-ONDI-AHMAN

DAVIESS

GALLATIN   MILLPORT
Election troubles

CALDWELL

FAR WEST

CLAY

Saints ejected from
Clay County 1836

LIBERTY

Temple corner stones
laid July 4, 1838. Revelation
on tithing given July 8, 1838

INDEPENDENCE

JACKSON
Dedicated Temple Site and Land 1831
1200 Saints driven out of Jackson
County 1833, 203 houses burned

Big Blue River

KANSAS

was all the more a bitter disappointment to the Prophet himself.

In the correspondence with Governor Dunklin during the months of November, December and January of 1833-34, the Saints were encouraged to attempt to regain their rights by organizing as an armed militia.

However, the mob in Jackson County would also be armed and would outnumber them two to one. It was useless to attempt to settle again in their homes without additional military aid. The courts were powerless to protect them.

To relieve this situation, Joseph Smith, early in the spring of 1834, organized a group of some two hundred volunteers in Ohio to march to the aid of their brethren in Missouri. This organization came to be known as Zion's Camp. The men were heavily armed, and well provisioned. They were organized into companies of tens, fifties, and hundreds, with officers over each. The men marched the entire one thousand miles, while the supplies were hauled in wagons; several recruiting officers and scouts were on horseback.

It was a remarkable march of unseasoned infantry, and the order and dispatch with which the expedition was carried out attests the organizing and commanding genius of the Prophet. From the letters of Joseph Smith, sent to the brethren in Missouri, it is evident that the Prophet was ready to fight for the rights of the Saints if that seemed feasible upon his arrival.

Word of their coming reached the old settlers of Jackson County long before their arrival, and armed bands were directed to meet and turn them back.

As Zion's Camp neared Jackson County, Parley P. Pratt and Orson Hyde were dispatched to Governor Dunklin with a request that he carry out his promises to the Saints and call out the Militia to aid in restoring the exiles to their homes.

The Governor who had previously indicated great sympathy for the Saints and appeared ready to champion their cause, refused. In his letters of refusal to aid the exiles, he expressed a fear of a Civil War if a resort to arms was had. In his later letter of July 18, 1836, the charge that the Saints were opposed to slavery appears as the chief accusation against them.[12] The question of slavery, coming before the Governor in such force at this time was unquestionably the factor which caused him to about-face in his attitude toward the Saints. Feelings on the slave question were tense and a Civil War not at all improbable, as future events showed. And this, in spite of the fact that slavery did not particularly concern the Saints.

Several attempts had been made to settle the difficulties between the Saints and the old settlers peaceably. Offers and counter offers were made. These proved fruitless. The Saints were not able financially to buy out all the old settlers of Jackson County at the terms offered, and were unwilling to sell their own lands because of their belief that Zion would yet be established in that place. This latter attitude was heightened by a revelation which Joseph Smith had received December 16, 1833. Among other things we read:

"Therefore, it is my will that my people should claim, and hold claim upon that which I have appointed unto them, though they should not be permitted to dwell thereon!"[13]

Also by a letter from Joseph Smith dated December 10, 1833, in which we read:

---

[12]*History of the Church*, Vol. II, pp. 461-462.
[13]*Doctrine and Covenants*, Section 101:99.

"It is better in the eyes of God that you should die, than that you should give up the land of Zion, the inheritances which you have purchased with your moneys; for every man that giveth not up his inheritance, though he should die, yet when the Lord shall come, he shall stand upon it, and with Job in his flesh he shall see God."[14]

On June 19th, while Zion's Camp was settled for the night on a piece of elevated ground between Big and Little Fishing Rivers, the mobs, sent to intercept them, made an appearance. Sixty men from Ray County and a mob of seventy from Clay County were to be joined by some 200 men from Jackson County, directly across the Missouri River. A sudden and terrific storm scattered the mobs and made it impossible for them to join forces. The next day the majority of them returned to their homes.

In a revelation received by Joseph Smith at this place on the 22nd of June, the Saints were counseled to

". . . wait for a little season for the redemption of Zion—

"For behold, I do not require at their hands to fight the battle of Zion; for, as I said in a former commandment, even so will I fulfill—I will fight your battles."[15]

With the Governor turned against them and the strength of the opposition being realized, and considering their small numbers and lack of funds, the necessity of disbanding the camp, and awaiting a future redemption was wisdom.

Zion's Camp continued peaceably into Clay County, where, on July 3rd, it was disbanded, and the members given leave to return home.

Thus ended the attempts to restore the Saints to their lands in Jackson County. Henceforth they directed their energies to building up new communities in the counties north of the Missouri River.

---

[14]*History of the Church*—Period I, Vol. I, p. 455.
[15]*Doctrine and Covenants*, Section 105:9, 14.

Zion's Camp had failed in its initial mission. The Governor had refused the aid of the militia, and, without that aid, the camp was insufficient. But it had nevertheless been of great value, and in the minds of its members was a glorious experience. The form of organization was later the pattern used in guiding the great Exodus to the Rocky Mountains. Brigham Young and others received here a splendid training for the leadership they were later to assume. From the members of this Camp was chosen the first Quorum of Twelve Apostles. The willingness of two hundred men to give their all, even to their life's blood, to help establish Zion in her place, is a lasting monument to the faith and courage of the Saints.

Supplementary Readings

1. *History of the Church*, Period I, Volume I, pp. 453-456. (Letters from Joseph Smith to Saints in Missouri.)

2. *Ibid.*, Volume II, pp. 61-62. (Letters from W. W. Phelps to Joseph. Mob in Jackson preparing for war as Saints tried to return.)

3. *Ibid.*, pp. 64-68. (Organization of Zion's Camp—incidents of journey.)

4. *Ibid.*, pp. 78-80. (Finding a Nephite skeleton.)

5. Roberts, *Comprehensive History of the Church*, Volume I, pp. 315-317. (Letters from the Prophet to W. W. Phelps in Missouri, warning of coming troubles.)

6. *Ibid.*, pp. 334-336. (Notes—the charges of the old settlers against the Saints.)

7. Smith, *Essentials in Church History*, pp. 170-178. (The story of Zion's Camp.)

8. Evans, *Heart of Mormonism*, pp. 176-180. (The causes of conflict in Missouri.)

9. Evans, *Joseph Smith, An American Prophet*, pp. 104-110. (Conflict in Missouri.)

10. *Ibid.*, pp. 114-122. (The story of Zion's Camp.)

11. Whitney, *Life of Heber C. Kimball*, 1967 edition, pp. 57-66. (Cholera in Zion's Camp.)

12. *Autobiography of Parley P. Pratt*, pp. 114-117. (Events during march of Zion's Camp.)

13. Cowley, *Wilford Woodruff*, pp. 40-45. (Incidents in the march of Zion's Camp.)

CHAPTER 16

THE BEGINNING OF TEMPLE BUILDING

The Kirtland Temple is Constructed

On the 4th day of May, 1833, a conference of High Priests was held in Kirtland, Ohio, and plans were laid to erect a temple in that city. The building was to be fifty-five by sixty-five feet, inside measurement; two stories in height, with class rooms above in an attic. On the following day the ground was broken for the foundation, and a work started which was to take three years to complete, and was to cost the Saints, in material and labor, $60,000.[1]

It was a courageous undertaking for a church three years old! A treasury empty! The members few and relatively poor! But courageous as the undertaking was, the remarkable thing was its accomplishment and the manner in which that accomplishment was brought about.

No miracle was performed to produce funds. No millionaire endowed it. The beautiful colonial-styled structure arose, a monument to cooperation—to the power of a people imbued with a common objective and inspired with a common faith. Greater and more costly temples were later erected—none so taxed the energies of the people.

The temple was erected during trying times. Persecution hindered it. Apostasy from the Church threatened its completion, yet despite these difficulties it was completed. It is refreshing to read in a letter of the First Presidency to the Saints in Missouri, dated June 25, 1833. "We have commenced building the House of the Lord, in this place, and it goes on rapidly."[2]

The persecutions in Missouri diverted some of the Temple funds. It failed to divert the work. Zion's Camp took the majority of the Temple workmen, but old men and boys filled their places. The men, disbanded in Missouri, returned a thousand miles on foot to take up the mason's trowel and don the carpenter's apron anew.

And all this with no thought of pay! No hope of those rewards for which men ordinarily labor. And the women of the Church played a part seldom equalled in the world's history for its utter unselfishness. Heber C. Kimball, who labored much upon the temple, wrote in his journal of those trying times:

"Our women were engaged in knitting and spinning, in order to clothe those who were laboring at the building; and the Lord only knows the scenes of poverty, tribulation, and distress which we passed through to accomplish it."[3]

While Heber C. Kimball was marching with Zion's Camp a thousand miles on foot to aid the brethren in Missouri, his wife, and the wives of the others, were laboring for the temple. Heber C. Kimball says:

"My wife had toiled all summer in lending her aid toward its accomplishment. She took a hundred pounds of wool to spin on shares, which, with the assistance of a girl, she spun, in order to furnish clothing for those engaged in building the temple; and although she had the privilege of keeping half the quantity of wool for herself, as a recompense for her labor, she did not reserve so much as would make a pair of stockings but gave it to those who were laboring at the house of the Lord. She spun and wove, and got the cloth dressed and cut and made up into garments, and gave

[1] See Whitney, *Life of Heber C. Kimball*, pp. 80-81.
[2] *History of the Church*—Period I, Vol. I, p. 366.
[3] Orson F. Whitney, *Life of Heber C. Kimball*, 1967 edition, p. 67.

The Kirtland Temple, dedicated on March 27, 1836, still stands—the property of the Reorganized LDS.
Used by permission, Church Historian's Office

Interior of the Kirtland Temple, showing the four compartments at one end.
Used by permission, Church Historian's Office

them to the laborers in the temple. Almost all the sisters in Kirtland labored in knitting, sewing, spinning, etc., for the same purpose; while we went up to Missouri to endeavor to reinstate our brethren on the lands from which they had been driven."[4]

The spirit of cooperation which made the temple a realization is well shown by a further reading of Kimball's journal.

"Those who had not teams went to work in the stone quarry and prepared the stones for drawing to the house."

"The Prophet, being our foreman, would put on his tow[5] frock and tow pantaloons and go into the quarry. The Presidency, High Priests, and Elders all alike assisting. Those who had teams assisted in drawing the stone to the house. These all laboring one day in the week, brought as many stones to the house as supplied the masons through the whole week. We continued in this manner until the walls of the house were reared."[6]

Hyrum Smith, Reynolds Cahoon, and Jared Carter were in general charge of the building, and they used every exertion in their power to forward the work. The committee appointed to collect donations visited the several branches of the Church, but met with difficulties, for money was scarce. At the end of building operations the committee was still some $13,000 in debt.

By the latter part of 1835 meetings were held in the completed portions of the building. So urgent was the need for the temple that, at its dedication on the 27th day of March, 1836, the second story was still unfinished.

The first and second stories comprised single rooms, each 55 by 65 feet and 22 feet high. There were two pulpits in each room, one at each end. Each pulpit had four compartments, rising one above the other, and each compartment contained three seats. They were de-

signed for the Presidencies of the Melchizedek and Aaronic Priesthoods. White canvas curtains were so arranged that, when desired, each room could be divided into four. Heber C. Kimball says:

"The first story or lower room was dedicated for divine worship alone. The second was finished similar in form to the first, but was designed wholly for instructing the Priesthood, and was supplied with tables and seats instead of slips. In the attic, five rooms were finished for the convenience of schools and for the different quorums of the Church to meet in."[7]

The Saints could well be pardoned their pride in the building. The Historian Bancroft says of it:

"The building of this structure by a few hundred persons, who, during the period between 1832 and 1836, contributed voluntarily of their money, material, or labor, the women knitting and spinning and making garments for the men who worked on the temple, was regarded with wonder throughout all northern Ohio."[8]

The Dedication and Subsequent Events

The dedication of the temple was a joyous event in the lives of the Saints living in Ohio. Those from all the nearby branches of the church, and a few even from Missouri, journeyed to Kirtland afoot, on horses, or in wagons to witness the event.

Nearly nine hundred crowded into the building for the initial dedicatory service. Many could not get in. This service was repeated on Thursday, March 31, in order that all might have an opportunity to participate.

The dedicatory prayer repeated by Joseph Smith on that occasion has become a model in thought for all succeeding dedicatory prayers for temples of the Church.[9]

[4]*Ibid.*, pp. 67-68.
[5]Tow—The coarse or broken part of a flax or hemp.
[6]Orson F. Whitney, *Life of Heber C. Kimball*, p. 68.

[7]*Ibid.*, p. 90.
[8]Bancroft's *History of Utah*, p. 112.
[9]*Doctrine and Covenants*, Section 109.

These words contained in the prayer reflect its general spirit:

"And do thou grant, Holy Father, that all those who shall worship in this house may be taught words of wisdom out of the best books, and that they may seek learning even by study, and also by faith, as thou hast said;

"And that this house may be a house of prayer, a house of fasting, a house of faith, a house of glory and of God, even thy house; And that no unclean thing shall be permitted to come into thy house to pollute it;

"Remember the kings, the princes, the nobles, and the great ones of the earth, and all people, and the churches, all the poor, the needy, and afflicted ones of the earth;

"That their hearts may be softened when thy servants shall go out from thy house, O Jehovah, to bear testimony of thy name; that their prejudices may give way before the truth, and thy people may obtain favor in the sight of all;

"That all the ends of the earth may know that we, thy servants, have heard thy voice, and that thou hast sent us."[10]

We find, in the journals of many who were in attendance at the services, the assertion that angels appeared in the congregation and that heavenly choirs were heard.

On April 3rd, one week after the initial dedicatory service, a lengthy service was again held in the temple. Joseph Smith records that at the close:

". . . I retired to the pulpit, the veils being dropped, and bowed myself, with Oliver Cowdery, in solemn and silent prayer. After rising from prayer, the following vision was opened to both of us. . . .

"The veil was taken from our minds, and the eyes of our understanding were opened.

"We saw the Lord standing upon the breastwork of the pulpit, before us; and under his feet was a paved work of pure gold in color like amber.

"His eyes were as a flame of fire; the hair of his head was white like the pure snow; his countenance shone above the brightness of the sun; and his voice was as the sound of the rushing of great waters, even the voice of Jehovah, saying:

"I am the first and the last; I am he who liveth, I am he who was slain; I am your advocate with the Father.

"Behold, your sins are forgiven you; you are clean before me; therefore lift up your heads and rejoice.

"Let the hearts of your brethren rejoice, and let the hearts of my people rejoice, who have, with their might, built this house to my name.

"For behold, I have accepted this house, and my name shall be here; and I will manifest myself to my people in mercy in this house.

"After this vision closed, the heavens were again opened unto us; and Moses appeared before us, and committed unto us the keys of the gathering of Israel from the four parts of the earth, and the leading of the ten tribes from the land of the north.

"After this, Elias appeared, and committed the dispensation of the gospel of Abraham, saying that in us and our seed all generations after us should be blessed."

"After this vision had closed, another great and glorious vision burst upon us; for Elijah the prophet, who was taken to heaven without tasting death, stood before us, and said:

"Behold, the time has fully come, which was spoken of by the mouth of Malachi—testifying that he [Elijah] should be sent, before the great and dreadful day of the Lord come—

"To turn the hearts of the fathers to the children, and the children to the fathers, lest the whole earth be smitten with a curse—

"Therefore, the keys of this dispensation are committed into your hands; and by this ye may know that the great and dreadful day of the Lord is near, even at the doors."[11]

These statements, testified to by Joseph Smith and Oliver Cowdery, were accepted as a revelation by the solemn assembly of the Church and are considered as scripture. The authority for doing temple work in the Church, which has grown to tremendous proportions today, is based upon this restoration of the keys of Priesthood necessary to those functions, and especially upon the restoration of the keys held by Elijah.

The Kirtland temple was not constructed for the ordinances referred to by Elijah. It contained no baptismal

---

[10]*Doctrine and Covenants*, Section 109: 14, 16, 20, 55-57.

[11]*Ibid.*, Section 110: Preface, Verses 1-7, 11-16. See also *History of the Church*, Vol. II, p. 435.

font for work for the dead. Nor was it designed for other work now performed in Latter-day Saint temples. It was a holy meeting place, a place for instruction under the Spirit of God. A place of preparation for the great temple building era which followed.

Supplementary Readings

1. *History of the Church*, Period I. Vol. 2, pp. 427-428. (Angels are seen at the dedicatory services.)

2. Whitney, *Life of Heber C. Kimball*, pp. 88-94. (Description of the Kirtland Temple and an account of the heavenly manifestation at the time of its dedication.)

3. Smith, *Essentials in Church History*, pp. 188-192. (Spiritual manifestations in the Kirtland Temple.)

4. Widtsoe, *The Restoration of the Gospel*. pp. 99-100. (A partial fulfillment of the dedicatory prayer given at the Kirtland Temple.)

5. Evans, *Joseph Smith, an American Prophet*, pp. 73-74. (Elijah and temple work.)

6. *Doctrine and Covenants*, Sec. 109.

7. *Ibid.*, Sec. 110.

CHAPTER 17

TRYING TIMES IN THE CHURCH

Far West Becomes a New Gathering Place in Missouri

While the Saints in Ohio were rejoicing over the completion of the temple, those who had sought refuge in Clay County, Missouri, from earlier persecutions, were receiving disheartening news. Clay County no longer wanted them. They must leave.

The citizens of Clay County had shown great kindness in harboring the refugees from Jackson County when no other county had extended a welcome. It was understood, however, that the stay was but temporary, until the Saints could be restored to their homes. Two years had passed and such a restoration seemed more remote than ever. Besides, great caravans of eastern Saints kept pouring into Missouri, until the numbers became alarming to the old inhabitants.

On the 29th day of June, 1836, a mass meeting of citizens at Liberty formulated reasons for their expulsion:

"They are eastern men, whose manners, habits, customs, and even dialect, are essentially different from our own. They are non-slaveholders, and opposed to slavery, which in this peculiar period, when Abolitionism has reared its deformed and haggard visage in our land, is well calculated to excite deep and abiding prejudices in any community where slavery is tolerated and protected."[1]

In a document addressed to the Saints and asking them to peaceably leave we find the suggestion that the Saints settle in territory where slavery was prohibited. The document added:

"If they (the Saints) have one spark of

gratitude, they will not willingly plunge a people into Civil War, who held out to them the friendly hand of assistance in that hour of dark distress, when there were few to say, 'God save them.' We can only say to them, if they still persist in the blind course they have hitherto followed in flooding the country with their people, that we fear and firmly believe that an immediate Civil War is the inevitable consequence. We know that there is no one among us who thirsts for the blood of that people.

"We do not contend that we have the least right, under the Constitution and laws of the country, to expel them by force. But we would indeed be blind, if we did not foresee that the first blow that is struck, at this moment of deep excitement, must and will speedily involve every individual in a war, bearing ruin, woe, and desolation in its course. It matters but little how, where, or by whom, the war may begin, when the work of destruction commences, we must all be borne onward by the storm, or crushed beneath its fury. In a Civil War, when our home is the theatre on which it is fought, there can be no neutrals; let our opinions be what they may, we must fight in self-defense.

"We want nothing, we ask nothing, we would have nothing from this people, we only ask them, for their own safety, and for ours, to take the least of two evils."[2]

The Civil War, to which the citizens of Clay County referred, did begin twenty-four years later and cost the nation a million lives and billions in property. During that war, Missouri became a scene of plunder and bloodshed. In the years between 1830 and 1840 the nation tottered on the verge of war. Missouri was the hotbed of dissension during those years and the heavy immigration of Yankee Saints might well have aggravated the war long before it came.

On July 1, 1836, the leading brethren

---

[1]George Q. Cannon, *Life of Joseph Smith*, pp. 211-212.

[2]*Ibid.*, p. 196.

of the Church in Missouri met, with William W. Phelps as chairman, and considered the situation. It was resolved to thank the citizens of Clay County for their hospitality in the past, and to avoid further troubles by moving peaceably from the country.

When the citizens of Clay County witnessed the willingness of the long-suffering Saints to leave their new homes and give up their constitutional rights rather than to bring trouble to the old settlers, they offered their services to assist the Saints and to guarantee the peace.

Ill-fitted as the Saints were for the new migration, it was carried out peaceably and efficiently. Ray County lay to the east of Clay County.* The county was large and the upper part practically uninhabited. There was little timber and the land had proved unattractive to the ordinary settler. Into this place, known as the Shoal Creek region, the Saints moved in a body. Seven bee-hunters, the sole occupants of the region, were bought out, leaving the Saints in undisputed possession to enjoy a short period of peace.

The sound of the ax and hammer was heard for the first time on that virgin prairie as the Saints feverishly prepared homes for the coming winter. Sod that had fed trampling hordes of buffalo that very spring was plowed for gardens. The hand of industry began its transformation of a wilderness.

In December, 1836, a petition for the State Legislature to organize the Shoal Creek region and surrounding territory into a new county was granted. Caldwell County began its turbulent existence. Near the center of the region the city of Far West was laid out after the

*See map on p. 122.

pattern for cities of Zion. In the spring of 1837, a temple site was dedicated. Again the star of hope for a Zion in Missouri was in the ascendary.

The Church Opens a Mission in England

During the trying times in Missouri and Ohio the missionary spirit never lagged. Persecution, dissension, and apostasy failed to quench it. Wilford Woodruff went on an extended mission to the Southern States with great success. In 1837, he converted almost the entire population of the Fox Islands, off the coast of Maine.

Parley P. Pratt, Apostle and missionary to Canada.

Parley P. Pratt extended the Canadian Mission in 1836 and converted John Taylor at Toronto, in that year.

The Prophet himself went on two extended missions, one to the Eastern States in 1836 and another to Canada in 1837.

The most important development came in 1837 with the opening of the British Mission. Many of the Canadian Saints had relatives and friends in England to whom they were anxious to carry the gospel message. About June 1, 1837, Apostle Heber C. Kimball was called by revelation to preside over such a mission. Accompanied by Apostle Orson Hyde, and Elders Willard Richards and Joseph Fielding (the latter from Canada) he journeyed to New York City. Here they were joined by three other brethren from Canada, John Goodson, Isaac Russell and John Snyder.

On the 20th day of July, 1837, they alighted from the ship "Garrick" in the harbor at Liverpool, England. The majority were penniless. They were in a land strange to them, five thousand miles from home and loved ones. But the spirit in which these missionaries set about their task made all difficulties seem trivial.

Three days after landing they preached at Preston, in the Chapel of Reverend James Fielding, a brother of Elder Fielding. Seven days later nine converts were led into the waters of baptism. The foundations for a great missionary achievement had been laid.

The success of the Elders was far beyond their expectations. The Church membership in England in the succeeding years doubled and redoubled at an amazing rate. Soon a stream of emigrants was to cross the ocean in search of the New Zion. Branches of the Church were established in Eccleston, Wrightington, Heskin, Euxton Bath, Daubers Lane, Chorley, Whittle, Ley-land Mass, Ribchester, Thornley, Clithero, Waddington, Downham, and other places around Preston.

The "Cock Pit" (Temperance Hall), a large and convenient building in Preston, was rented by the Elders for meetings. On Christmas Day, 1837, the first conference was held in England. Over three hundred members of the Church were in attendance.

At this conference the Word of Wisdom was preached for the first time in that land.

On April 1, 1838, a second conference of the Church in England was held at Preston. Joseph Fielding was ordained as President of the whole British Mission, with Willard Richards and William Clayton as counselors. Following the conference Apostles Kimball and Hyde returned to America.

Apostasy and Persecution Cause the Saints to Leave Ohio

While the gospel was being carried into England, the Church in Ohio was facing dark, troublesome days. Scarcely had the temple been completed before apostasy began to break the ranks of the Church. This apostasy reached a climax in the latter months of 1837, when over half of the Kirtland membership either left the Church or were excommunicated from it, and the temple itself was abandoned to them.

The cause of the apostasy is not difficult to find. The failure to establish "Zion" in Jackson County had made it imperative that the location of the Saints in Kirtland be prolonged. Saints migrating from the east must be provided for there, rather than in Missouri. This made necessary an extended program of buying lands and establishing industrial and mercantile institutions. A financial institution was also needed.

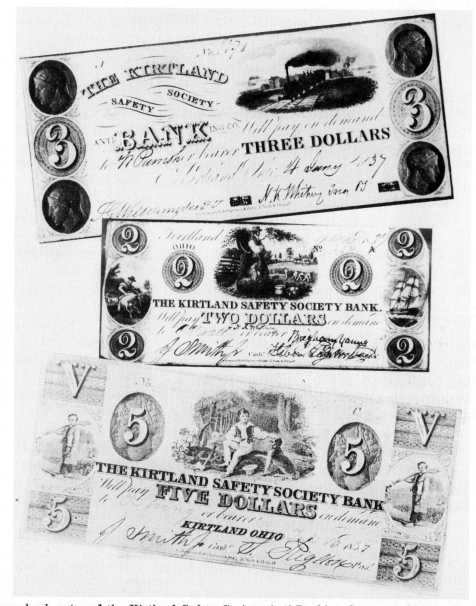

Promissory bank notes of the Kirtland Safety Society Anti-Banking Company showing the signature of Joseph Smith as cashier.

Photographed by permission of the
Church Bureau of Information

In November, 1836, the Church at Kirtland petitioned the State Legislature for a Bank Charter, and Oliver Cowdery was sent to Philadelphia to purchase the necessary plates for the printing of bank notes.

Due to the growing opposition to the Saints, the Ohio Legislature refused to grant the Charter. Desiring a central financial institution which would be an aid in the economic program of the Church, there was organized the "Kirtland Safety Society Anti-Banking Company."

The capitalization was to be four million dollars, to be raised by the selling of shares at fifty dollars per share. Fifty per cent was to be paid in cash and the balance subject to call. Without a Banking Charter, bank notes could not be issued, but promissory notes were issued in the stead and these circulated within the Church as a medium of exchange.

Scarcely had the Kirtland Safety Society got well under way before a spirit of wild speculation swept the nation. Land values rose so rapidly that profits in buying and selling were often great and enticing. Some of the Saints also caught this spirit of speculation. Money was borrowed from the Society and issued to the borrower in the form of promissory notes. These were then given as a security for the purchase of lands for speculative purposes. The issue of promissory notes soon exceeded the paid-in capital.

In the early spring of 1837, Joseph Smith warned the officers of the Kirtland Safety Society to cease lending more money and to collect the unpaid balance of the capital stock. The warning was unheeded and Joseph Smith withdrew from the Society.

The wild orgy of speculation in the United States was followed in the summer of 1837 by widespread financial panic. Hundreds of banks throughout the country failed. In that panic the small financial institution of the Saints at Kirtland was hopelessly crushed. Land values fell rapidly and borrowers could not sell their lands or otherwise repay the amount borrowed from the Society. The holders of the Society's promissory notes rushed to the Society for payments until the funds were exhausted. The unpaid balance of the subscribed capital was called for, but the subscribers were unable to pay. Merchants and manufacturers refused to accept the promissory notes of the Society for purchases of the Saints. Within one year from its opening the Kirt-

land Safety Society was forced to close its doors in bankruptcy.

Nearly every family in Kirtland, and many in other branches of the Church, lost money in the financial crash of 1837. The Prophet Joseph Smith received the brunt of the blame and the Church generally came under the condemnation of those whose hearts had been set on the acquiring of earthly wealth.

The historian vindicates the Prophet and frees him from blame—but those who had lost their money did not wait for the verdict of the historian. Joseph Smith had been instrumental in starting the Society, had written letters encouraging the members of the Church to buy stock—and the Society had failed— their money was gone. Cries of "Fallen Prophet," arose on every hand. Five of the quorum of Twelve Apostles broke with the Prophet. Among those who were embittered against him at this time was Elder Parley P. Pratt. Of this incident in his experiences he says:

"About this same time [summer of 1837], after I had returned from Canada, there were jarrings and discords in the Church at Kirtland, and many fell away and became enemies and apostates. There were envyings, lyings, strifes, and divisions, which caused much trouble and sorrow. By such spirits, I was also accused misrepresented and abused. And at one time, I also was overcome by the same spirit in a great measure, and it seemed as if the very powers of darkness which war against the Saints were let loose upon me. But the Lord knew my faith, . . . and he gave me the victory. I went to Brother Joseph Smith in tears, and, with a broken heart and contrite spirit, confessed wherein I had erred in spirit, murmured or done or said amiss. He frankly forgave me, prayed for me, and blessed me."[3]

So general did the feeling of bitterness within the Church become that the Prophet wrote of the occasion, "It

---

[3]*Autobiography of Parley P. Pratt*, p. 168.

seemed as though all the powers of earth and hell were combining their influence to overthrow the Church."[4]

The integrity of all the Church members was tested. While many broke away from the Church, the faithfulness and devotion of others stand out like lights in the midst of darkness. Brigham Young, John Taylor, Wilford Woodruff, Heber C. Kimball, Hyrum Smith and many other great leaders remained faithful in their allegiance to the Church and to the Prophet.

Joseph Forced to Flee

In the midst of the Ohio difficulties, conditions in Missouri made necessary a journey by Joseph Smith to that land. In company with Sidney Rigdon he left Kirtland in October, 1837, attended to affairs there and returned about the 10th of December.

He found the Church in greater dissension than ever. His enemies openly accosted him in the streets and blamed him for their financial losses and difficulties. During his absence Warren Parrish, a leading Seventy, and John F. Boynton, Luke S. Johnson, and Lyman E. Johnson, former members of the Quorum of Twelve, with others, had formed a new organization. They called themselves "The Church of Christ," claimed ownership of the Temple, and declared Joseph Smith and all who followed him heretics.

From the time of his return to Kirtland, Joseph Smith was kept constantly in the courts on one trumped-up charge after another, until he was unable to lend the weight of his personality in straightening out the troubled affairs.

The meetings of the Priesthood in the temple threatened several times to break into armed fights, and swords were worn to the temple meetings. John Taylor, by his vigorous defense of the Prophet in such meetings, earned the title of the "Lion," and for a time prevented open hostilities.

Brigham Young, in public and private, continued to assert he knew by the power of the Holy Ghost that Joseph Smith was a Prophet of God. On December 22, 1837, he was forced to flee from Kirtland in order to save his life from an infuriated mob of apostates.

On the 12th of January, 1838, the Prophet Joseph Smith and Sidney Rigdon followed. Their flight was by horseback in the night time in order to escape the mobs who followed.

About sixty miles from Kirtland they paused among Saints residing at that place until their families could join them. From thence, the party, including Brigham Young and family, proceeded with covered wagons over nine hundred miles into upper Missouri. Joseph Smith writes of the journey:

"The weather was extremely cold, we were obliged to secrete ourselves in our wagons, sometimes to elude the grasp of our pursuers, who continued their pursuit of us more than two hundred miles from Kirtland, armed with pistols and guns, seeking our lives. They frequently crossed our track, twice were in the houses where we stopped, once we tarried all night in the same house with them, with only a partition between us and them; and heard their oaths and imprecations and threats concerning us if they could catch us; and late in the evening they came into our room and examined us, but decided we were not the men. At other times we passed them in the streets, but they knew us not."[5]

The close of 1837 and the year 1838 witnessed a general exodus of those Saints in the region of Kirtland who remained loyal to the Prophet.

One company, comprising over five

[4]George Q. Cannon, *Life of Joseph Smith*, p. 124.

[5]*History of the Church*—Period I, Vol. 3, pp. 2-3.

hundred souls, designated as "The Kirtland Camp," made the journey from Kirtland under the direction of the first Council of Seventy, and arrived in Far West, Missouri, October 4, 1838.*

Far West was further increased by the arrival in the same year of another large body of Saints with two hundred wagons. These had journeyed from Canada and the eastern states, some a distance of fifteen hundred miles.

The Prophet and the Saints from Ohio and the east were greeted joyously by their brethren in Missouri. Hope for Zion rose again in the hearts of the people.

Supplementary Readings

1. *History of the Church*, Period I, Vol. 2, pp. 498-499, 503-507. (The mission to England.)

*See Map p. 122.

2. *Ibid.*, Vol. 3, pp. 43-44.
3. Roberts, *Comprehensive History of the Church*, Vol. I, pp. 408-411. (Joseph Smith's connection with the Kirtland Safety Society.)
4. *Ibid.*, Vol. I, pp. 431-437. (Charges against Oliver Cowdery and David Whitmer, resulting in excommunication from the Church.)
5. Snow, Eliza R., *Biography and Family Record of Lorenzo Snow*, pp. 20-24. (Near bloodshed in the Kirtland Temple in 1837.)
6. Evans, John H., *Joseph Smith, An American Prophet*, pp. 122-127. (False accusations against the Prophet.)
7. *Ibid.*, pp. 96-100. (The door of salvation opened in England.)
8. *History of Joseph Smith by His Mother Lucy Mack Smith*, pp. 255-256, (Joseph's personality wins over his enemies.)
9. *Autobiography of Parley P. Pratt*, p. 168. (P. P. Pratt nearly leaves the Church.)
10. Roberts, B. H., *Life of John Taylor*, pp. 39-41. (A visit to Kirtland during the apostasy.)
11. Whitney, O. F., *Life of Heber C. Kimball*, p. 104. (Call to go to England.)
12. *Doctrine and Covenants*, Section 119. (The Law of Tithing.)

CHAPTER 18

THE SAINTS ARE DRIVEN OUT
OF THE STATE OF MISSOURI

The Rapid Growth of the Latter-day Saint Population in Northern Missouri Promotes a Crisis

From every human appearance in the fall of 1837, the Church was rapidly approaching a dissolution. Apostasy had rocked the organization to the very center. Even such great leaders as Oliver Cowdery, Martin Harris and David Whitmer, the special witnesses of the *Book of Mormon*, had left the fold.

It is significant that, during that trying period, the optimism of the Prophet Joseph Smith and his assurance that the Church would stand forever, never faltered. In the darkest hours of apostasy he initiated two movements which strengthened the Church and illustrate his remarkable vision of the work ahead. He sent missionaries, with Heber C. Kimball at their head, to open a mission in England. Then he made a journey into northern Missouri and engineered the laying out of new towns to accommodate a great influx in population.

Both moves were timely. The British people were anxious for the gospel. Despite all the apostasy in the Church, the membership continued to grow by leaps and bounds. When the Saints in Ohio were forced to flee to a new land, that land was ready for them in Missouri.

Among the new towns laid out in northern Missouri was Adam-ondi-Ahman, Gallatin and Millport in Daviess County, Haun's Mill in Caldwell County and De Witt in Carroll County.

The Prophet's advice to the Saints in all of these settlements was to live within the cities with their farms on the outside. Small clusters of homes away from the central locations were discouraged. The centers were laid out as nearly as possible according to the plan for cities of Zion.

Some new social experiments are worthy of our notice. Large farming corporations were organized for cooperative farming. One of these cooperative farms, the "Western Agricultural Company," voted to inclose one field for grain containing twelve sections of land, or 7680 acres. A similar area was to be farmed by the "Southern Agricultural Company," and one by the "Eastern Agricultural Company." The Saints were driven from the state before the plan could be carried out.

The population of the Church in Daviess, Caldwell, Ray, and Carroll Counties was swelled rapidly by the steady stream of immigrants from the East. The long caravans of covered wagons cut deep ruts across the Missouri prairies. Twelve hundred had been driven out of Jackson County. By the summer of 1838, the numbers in northern Missouri totaled fifteen thousand.

Persecution is Renewed

It was inevitable that persecution would follow. All the old causes of disquiet were there intensified by numbers. One county would not hold the Mormons. They were overflowing into all northwestern Missouri. In a few years they might conceivably dominate the state. Even the finest citizens became alarmed, and in that alarm all the wild and lawless element of the frontier found an opportunity to plunder and ravage.

The renewed persecution began at Gallatin, Daviess County. It was election day, August 6, 1838. A group of Latter-day Saint men appeared at the polls to vote. A much larger group led by Colonel William P. Peniston, a candidate for the state legislature, sought to prevent the casting of ballots. A bitter fight ensued in which some heads were cracked. The Saints gained the upper hand and Peniston's men withdrew to take up arms.

It was the beginning of the end for the Saints in Missouri. Once trouble began, misunderstandings grew apace. Distorted reports circulated rapidly. Inflamed speeches against "Abolitionists" and "Yankees" were daily occurrences. Ministers renewed their charges against Mormon healings, signs, visions, etc. The whole population of northern Missouri became alarmed. Nor can the general populace be blamed. The Southerners' prejudice against the "Yankee" was deep-seated. The reports of huge co-operative farms were disturbing to the agricultural element, and the competition of cooperative mercantile establishments was threatening disaster to non-Mormon merchants. The majority knew little of the Mormons, nor had any way of knowing, except from the ministers and the press. The bitterness of Protestant ministers did much to arouse the prejudices of the majority. The slave holders had real cause for alarm as previously discussed.[1]

---

[1]See Chapter 15, "Underlying Causes of the Conflict," pp. 116-118.

Among those well acquainted with the Saints we find a friendship for them which lasted throughout the persecution and manifested itself in many acts of kindness. It was unfortunate for the Saints and a sorrowful memory for the state of Missouri, that a certain lawless element, devoid of the finer sensibilities of human beings, had found refuge from the law in the western part of the state. It was this element, which under cover of the general feeling against the Mormons, committed those acts of wanton cruelty and shame so often referred to in the journals of those who suffered from their hands. These saw in the events of the times a chance to profit by the misfortunes of others. To them the improved farms and homes of the Saints offered a rich prize. Those of this class who had thus profited during the Jackson County persecutions, now crossed into northern Missouri to join in the onslaught.

It was a further misfortune that the office of governor had to pass into the hands of a shrewd politician, Lilburn W. Boggs.

Boggs had been Lieutenant Governor during the expulsion of the Saints from Jackson County. His course of action during that affair had been prompted by political ambition. His actions on that occasion, in opposing the Mormons, won for him the Governor's seat. As Governor he was well aware of public sentiment and conscious that the voters were stirred against the Saints.

From a politician an abused minority can expect no relief. The Saints expected none from Governor Boggs and received none.

The Conflict Centers Around Far West

The people who were most stirred up against the Mormons congregated together in illegal groups or mobs, armed themselves with weapons of various kinds and vowed that they would drive the Mormons from the state. The earliest movements were against the outlying settlements, especially those unprotected by militia.

One mob, led by a Dr. Austin, besieged Diahman. But Lyman Wight was then in Diahman and that courageous frontiersman organized a resistance which was too much for them. Further, General Doniphan, in command of a group of State Militia, was camped near Diahman, and Doniphan was a friend of the Mormons.

Dr. Austin next moved against De Witt in Carroll County. His mob was increasing daily. The Saints were ordered to leave the state or face extermination.

Under the leadership of Colonel George M. Hinkle, who had been authorized to raise a militia against the mobs, the Saints resisted. A state of siege followed, lasting from the 21st of September, 1838, to October 11th of that year. During this siege Joseph Smith risked his life to slip past the guards at night into the city.

He found the Saints destitute of food and suffering extreme hunger. A number had died. Few of the defenders possessed firearms, while the mob was growing constantly and General Parks, with a body of State Militia, refused to interfere. A petition to the Governor had gone unheeded. Joseph counseled surrender. On the afternoon of the eleventh of October, the defenders filed out of De Witt on the long road to Far West. They left behind them all their earthly possessions, except the few items which could be loaded into the available wagons. It was a sad procession of half-starved men, women, and

General Alexander W. Doniphan, friend to the Mormons in Missouri.

children. It was still further saddened by the death of some enroute.

The fate of De Witt became the fate of all outlying settlements. From every direction, during the following month, refugees filed into the city of Far West. Their lands and homes were occupied by the mobbers or burned to the ground. Crops went unharvested and cattle and hogs were wantonly killed to feed their pursuers.

Much praise must be given to Generals Atchison and Doniphan who, with small forces of militia under their command, exerted for a time great energy in defense of the Saints. Public opinion was too powerful for them and their appeal to the Governor was met with rebuke. Superior officers, pledged to drive the Saints from Missouri, were placed over Atchison and Doniphan. Disgusted with the state of affairs Atchison resigned.

The last hope of protection from the military power of the state was gone.

In the County of Caldwell, centering around Far West, there was, for a time, a measure of protection. The county was largely Mormon. They had a county militia officered by their members and judges of their own faith.

After the fall of De Witt, all the Saints in outlying settlements were counseled to move into Far West. Many heeded the counsel. Some, however, failing to sense their danger and the tenseness of the situation, remained in their scattered communities. Upon them much of the brutality of the mobs fell.

Those of the Saints who had hoped for peace in Caldwell County were bitterly mistaken. The "Mormon problem" had grown into a state issue. Slaveholders from Jackson and other counties south of the Missouri River crossed into the troubled area to stir the mobs anew. The majority of those who fought against the Saints knew nothing of their real character and peaceful nature. False reports and propaganda had poisoned their minds. No official investigation was ever held. General Parks in a letter to Governor Boggs, dated September 25, 1838, wrote:

"Whatever may have been the disposition of the people called Mormons before our arrival here, since we have made our appearance they have shown no disposition to resist the law or of hostile intentions. * * * There has been so much prejudice and exaggeration concerning in this matter, that I found things entirely different from what I was prepared to expect. It is true that a great excitement did prevail between the parties, and I am happy to say that my exertions, as well as those of Major General Atchison, and the officers and men under my command, have been crowned with success. When we arrived here, we found a large body of men from the counties adjoining, armed and in the field, for the purpose, as I learned, of assisting the people of this country against the Mormons, without being called out by the proper authorities."[2]

As the disturbances grew worse the State Militia was increased until it finally reached a total of 6,000 armed men. This militia was originally called out for the purpose of protecting ˏproperty and to keep the peace. But in order to raise that number, thousands were enlisted who had previously taken part in the mobbings of the Saints and these proved uncontrollable by the officers. Further, the officers themselves favored the mobs, with the exceptions before mentioned, and did little to restrain them. Major General Parks repeatedly asserted that he could not control his troops or prevent them siding with the mob.[3] At any rate the presence of the State Militia in no wise stopped their activities.

The Saints did not continue to submit peaceably to these repeated outrages. They would not, however, retaliate in kind. Two of their number, Colonel Lyman Wight and Colonel George M. Hinkle, held commissions in the State Militia under the immediate command of General Parks. When their enemies began to burn and pillage, General Parks authorized them to raise companies of militia and disperse the mobs.

The companies were raised, but the number never exceeded 500 men. The

[2]General H. G. Parks to the Governor. Documents, etc. Published by order of the General Assembly of Missouri, p. 32.
[3]See *History of the Church* — Period I, Vol. 3, p. 158.

settlements needing defense were widely scattered and the mobbers outnumbered them by many thousands. This show of resistance, however, prevented a complete destruction of the Saints and their property.

The encounters of the Caldwell militia with the mobs only served to fan the flames of persecution. Colonel Wight dispersed large mobs at Diahman and Millport. In the retreat of the mob from the latter place they burned some of their own dwellings and then spread the report, "The Mormons have 'riz' and are burning the houses, destroying property and murdering the 'old settlers.' "[4]

Battle of Crooked River

The chief clash between the Caldwell Militia and their enemies is known as the "Battle of Crooked River." A number of Saints had been carried away by a mob as prisoners. A detachment of the militia under Captain David W. Patten was sent in pursuit. He encountered some militia men of the state, under Captain Bogart, who fired upon him, and a battle occurred during the early dawn. Bogart and his men had formerly composed the mob which harassed the Saints in Carroll County. Patten was unaware that they had been enlisted as militia. He ordered a charge and put them to flight. He was, however, mortally wounded in the affray, as was Gideon Carter and Patrick O'Banion. A number were wounded on both sides and one of Bogart's men was killed.

Reports were soon circulated that Captain Bogart and all of his company had been massacred by the Mormons. This false cry aroused the entire coun-

try. Large mobs began to move toward Caldwell County.

A distorted report reached Governor Boggs. Without investigation other than these reports, he issued an order to the Commanding Officer in the field, General Clark, and others, sometimes referred to as the "extermination order," for in it he said:

"Your orders are therefore to hasten your operations with all possible speed. *The Mormons must be treated as enemies, and must be exterminated or driven from the state if necessary for the public peace—their outrages are beyond all description.*"

All hope of the Saints for peace in the state of Missouri was at an end.

The militia sent to disperse the mobs had been ordered to aid them instead.

The day after this executive order had been received, a company of so-called militia, under the command of Colonel Wm. O. Jennings, fell upon the unsuspecting Saints of the Haun's Mill settlement. Seventeen were massacred outright. Twelve escaped into the woods severely wounded. The houses were looted and women raped.

Treachery in Far West

On the 30th of October, General Lucas, in the absence of his superior, General Clark, massed the state militia within firing distance of Far West.

Some six hundred men and boys, with the news of the Haun's Mill Massacre still burning in their hearts, drew up in line of battle to defend their homes and loved ones in the last remaining city of the Saints.

Colonel George M. Hinkle, as the highest militia officer in Caldwell County, was in command of the defending forces. On the 31st day of October he received an interview with General Lucas, in command of the general forces of

---

[4]Roberts, *Comprehensive History of the Church*, Vol. I, p. 463.

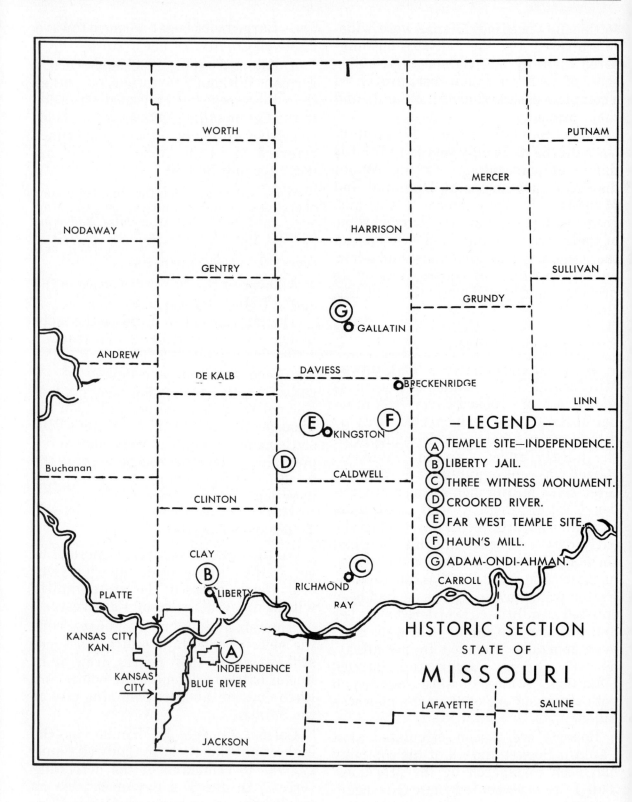

- LEGEND -
- A TEMPLE SITE—INDEPENDENCE.
- B LIBERTY JAIL.
- C THREE WITNESS MONUMENT.
- D CROOKED RIVER.
- E FAR WEST TEMPLE SITE.
- F HAUN'S MILL.
- G ADAM-ONDI-AHMAN.

HISTORIC SECTION
STATE OF
MISSOURI

state militia, seeking a compromise. General Lucas proposed the following terms to the Saints:

1. "To give up their leaders to be tried and punished.

2. "To make an appropriation of their property, all who had taken up arms, to the payment of their debts, and indemnity for damage done by them.

3. "That the balance should leave the state, and be protected out by the militia, but to be permitted to remain under protection until further orders were received from the commander-in-chief.

4. "To give up arms of every description to be receipted for."[5]

For some unknown reason Colonel Hinkle agreed to those absurd terms. Not only that, he returned to Far West and reported to Joseph Smith that General Lucas desired a conference with him, together with Sidney Rigdon, Lyman Wight, Parley P. Pratt, and George W. Robinson. The brethren consented to the interview but, on reaching the camp of Lucas, Colonel Hinkle said: "General, these are the prisoners I agreed to deliver up."[6]

They were then surrounded and marched away. That night they lay in chains, subjected to a cold drenching rain and the abuse of the guards.

On the following morning, the first of November, the militia were marched out of Far West by Colonel Hinkle and their arms delivered to General Lucas. The city was now at the mercy of the mobs, unless protected by the militia.

Either ignorantly or by design, General Lucas dismissed the greater portion of the militia, who immediately changed into looting mobs. These mobs, still bearing arms, ransacked the city, destroying property, beating defenseless men and ravishing their women. In a document addressed to the Missouri state legislature by M. Arthur, Esq., a non-Mormon, under date of November 29, 1838, we read:

"Respected friends:—Humanity to an injured people prompts me at present to address you thus. You were aware of the treatment (to some extent before you left home) received by that unfortunate race of beings called the Mormons, from Daviess, in the form of human beings inhabiting Daviess, Livingston, and a part of Ray County; not being satisfied with the relinquishments of all their rights as citizens and human beings in the treaty forced upon them by General Lucas, by giving up their arms, and throwing themselves upon the mercy of the state, and their fellow citizens generally, hoping thereby protection of their lives and property, are now receiving treatment from those demons that make humanity shudder, and the cold chills run over any man not entirely destitute of any feeling of humanity. Those demons are now constantly strolling up and down C a l d w e l l County, in small companies armed, insulting the women in any and every way, and plundering the poor devils of all their means of subsistence left them and driving off their horses, cattle, hogs, etc., and rifling their houses and farms of everything therein, taking beds, bedding, wardrobe and all such things as they see they want, leaving the Mormons in a starving and poor condition. These are facts I have from authority that cannot be questioned, and can be substantiated at any time."[7]

On the night of November 1st, in the camp of Lucas, a court-martial was held. The decision was arrived at, over some protest, that the prisoners were to be shot at sunrise, November 2nd, in the public square of Far West, as an example to all the Mormons.

The order was never carried out. General Doniphan to whom General Lucas sent the execution order made a curt refusal:

"It is cold-blooded murder. I will not obey

[5]Documents. Published by the Missouri Legislature, pp. 72-73.
[6]*Autobiography of Parley P. Pratt*, p. 187.

[7]Document, etc. Published by the Missouri Legislature, p. 94.

your order. My brigade shall march for Liberty tomorrow morning at 8:00 o'clock; and if you execute these men, I will hold you responsible before an earthly tribunal, so help me God."—A. Doniphan, Brigadier General.

Upon receiving that message, General Lucas was afraid to carry out the order and the matter was dropped. The prisoners were, however, marched into Far West that morning, momentarily expecting death. Some were permitted to say good-bye to their loved ones before being rushed away as prisoners to Independence.

A score of other leaders were arrested and lodged in the jail at Richmond. The Saints were left destitute even of the comforting assurance the Prophet and others might have given.

The Expulsion

When General Clark arrived at Far West he endorsed all that General Lucas had done. In an address to the Saints he stated, among other things:

Another article yet remains for you to comply with, and that is that you leave the State forthwith; and whatever may be your feelings concerning this, or whatever your innocence, it is nothing to me. * * * The orders of the governor to me were, that you should be exterminated, and not allowed to remain in the state, and had your leaders not been given up and the terms of the treaty complied with, before this you and your families would have been destroyed and your houses in ashes. * * * I do not say that you shall go now, but you must not think of staying here another season, or of putting in crops, for the moment you do this the citizens will be upon you. * * * As for your leaders, do not once think—do not imagine for a moment—do not let it enter your mind that they will be delivered, or that you will see their faces again, for their fate is fixed—their die is cast and their doom is sealed."[8]

The hope for relief was gone. Nor were the Saints permitted to wait until

spring. The drivings began immediately, so that the majority were forced to vacate their homes amid the snow and cold of winter.

The imprisonment of the majority of the Church leaders left the responsibility of directing the affairs of the people in the hands of Brigham Young and Heber C. Kimball. The remarkable executive ability of Brigham Young immediately came to the front. Under his leadership the greater portion of the members of the Church bound themselves in solemn covenant, "to stand by and assist each other, to the utmost of our abilities in removing from this state and that we will never desert the poor who are worthy till they shall be out of the reach of the exterminating order of General Clark, acting for and in the name of the state."[9] Two hundred and eighty men signed this covenant the first two days it was circulated. A finer expression of brotherly love and affection has never been expressed or so generally been carried into action.

The non-Mormons were appealed to for aid and many came forward generously. Agents were sent down the Missouri River to make caches of corn for the use of the Saints while making their way out of the state. The agents were to arrange for ferries and other necessary things.

The great activity of Brigham Young aroused the enemies of the Church and he was forced to flee for his life before the general exodus began. But so well had committees been organized that the work of removal continued to go forward in an orderly fashion. A long line of covered wagons was soon trailing eastward, back over the long miles they had traversed but a few short years be-

[8]*History of the Church*—Period I, Vol. III, p. 203.

[9]*Ibid.*, p. 250.

fore. It was a sorrowful and poverty-stricken procession in charge of Heber C. Kimball and John Taylor.

In the *History of Caldwell County,* by Crosby Johnson, a non-Mormon, we find this description of the exodus:

"The surrender took place in November. The days were cold and bleak, but the clamor for the instant removal of the Mormons was so great that the old and young, the sick and feeble, delicate women and suckling children, almost without food and without clothing were compelled to abandon their homes and firesides to seek new homes in a distant state. Valuable farms were sold for a yoke of oxen, an old wagon or anything that would furnish means of transportation. Many of the poorer classes were compelled to walk. Before half their journey was accomplished the chilly blasts of winter howled about them and added to their general discomfort."[10]

Brigham Young, with a few families, had found his way to Illinois and had received the encouragement and welcome of the inhabitants of Quincy to settle his people in that vicinity. By the twentieth of April, nearly all the Saints, between twelve and fifteen thousand, had left Missouri. They found temporary refuge either in the State of Illinois or Iowa.

Their condition was truly pitiable. Thousands lined the shores of the Mississippi on both the Iowa and Illinois sides, living in tents or dugouts, sleeping on the ground and subsisting chiefly on corn. Sickness and disease due to exposure took a heavy toll. Practically all that the people possessed had been left behind. Property, with an estimated value of two million dollars, fell into the hands of their enemies.

Petitions were forwarded to the Governor of Missouri, and to the legislature of the state, for redress. Neither made any move to relieve the afflicted people;

$200,000, however, was voted to pay the expenses of the state militia in the Mormon war.

Not all of the Saints moved from Missouri. The continued persecutions and the keen disappointment in failing to establish Zion destroyed the faith of many. Some of these became bitter against the Prophet and the Church, and joined forces with the persecutors. Others, while remaining friendly, broke their affiliations with the Church leaders and refused to undergo more for the sake of the gospel These were generally left unmolested by the old citizens. Among those who became disaffected at this time was David Whitmer who was excommunicated, as was Oliver Cowdery during the apostasy of 1837, which spread even into Missouri. Martin Harris was also excommunicated,* drifted away from the Church, and later supported the claims of James J. Strang.

The Church Leaders in Prison

While the mobs were plundering the Saints in Far West and driving them from the state, the Church leaders, who had been taken prisoners, passed through many bitter experiences. As before stated they were taken by General Wilson into Independence and paraded before the populace. From Independence they were marched under guard to Richmond, where they were placed in chains. Abuse by the guards over them and suffering from the severe cold weather was their lot. Parley P. Pratt gives a graphic description of a scene in the Richmond jail:

"In one of those tedious nights we had lain as if in sleep till the hour of midnight had passed, and our ears and hearts had been pained, while we had listened for hours to the obscene jests, the horrid oaths, and the dreadful blasphemies and filthy language of

---

[10]Crosby Johnson, *History of Caldwell County.*

*Church Historian's Office Journal History—from a letter by John Smith, Counselor to Joseph Smith.

our guards, Colonel Price at their head, as they recounted to each other their deeds of rapine, murder, robbery, etc., which they had committed among the Mormons while at Far West and vicinity. They even boasted of defiling by force wives, daughters, and virgins, and of shooting or dashing out the brains of men, women and children. I had listened until I became so disgusted, shocked, horrified, and so filled with the spirit of indignant justice that I could hardly refrain from rising upon my feet and rebuking the guards; but had said nothing to Joseph or anyone else, although I lay next to him and knew he was awake. On a sudden he arose to his feet, and spoke with a voice of thunder, or as a roaring lion, uttering as nearly as I can recollect, the following words:

" 'Silence, ye fiends of the infernal pit! In the name of Jesus Christ I rebuke you, and command you to be still; I will not live another minute and hear such language. Cease such talk or you or I die this instant!'

"He ceased to speak. He stood erect in terrible majesty. Chained, and without weapon; calm, unruffled, and dignified as an angel, he looked upon the quailing guards, whose weapons were lowered or dropped to the ground; whose knees smote together, and who, shrinking into a corner, or crouching at his feet, begged his pardon, and remained quiet until a change of guards."

"I have seen the ministers of justice, clothed in magisterial robes and criminals arraigned before them, while life was suspended on a breath, in the courts of England; I have witnessed a congress in solemn session to give laws to nations; I have tried to conceive of kings, of royal courts, of thrones and crowns; and of emperors assembled to decide the fate of kingdoms; but dignity and majesty have I seen but once, as it stood in chains, at midnight in a dungeon, in an obscure village in Missouri."[11]

During the long sojourn in prison Sidney Rigdon suffered considerably. He was ill when arrested and the privations of the prison steadily undermined him. His daughter, Mrs. Robinson, was permitted to accompany him in prison, where she remained until she had nursed him back to health.

The Preliminary Hearing

On Tuesday, November 10th, they

were arraigned before the Court of Richmond, Austin A. King as Judge. A great number of the Saints who had been arrested were tried at the same time. The trial lasted two weeks, at the end of which time all but the original prisoners were released or admitted to bail, as nothing could be found against them.

Joseph Smith, Lyman Wight, Caleb Baldwin, Hyrum Smith, Alexander McRae, and Sidney Rigdon were sent to the jail at Liberty, Clay County, to await trial for treason and murder. Parley P. Pratt, Morris Phelps, Lyman Gibbs, Darwin Chase, and Norman Shearer were placed in the Richmond jail to stand trial for the same crimes.

The testimony upon which Joseph and his companions were held for investigation before grand juries was the sworn testimony of apostates. Among these were Dr. Sampson Avard, John Corrill, W. W. Phelps, George M. Hinkle and John Whitmer, all of whom had been prominent in Church affairs in Missouri.

Dr. Avard charged the Saints with having organized a band of avengers called "The Daughter of Zion," and afterwards called the "Danite Band." Joseph Smith was charged with being the prime instigator. Such a band as the "Danites" did exist, as historians affirm; but that Joseph Smith had nothing to do with it and exposed the participants when he became aware of it, is equally well-confirmed. History further affirms that Dr. Avard himself was the author of the organization and that he was cut off from the Church when his guilt was discovered. The organization had been for the purpose of plundering and murdering the enemies of the Saints. It was foreign to the spirit of the Church. Joseph Smith wrote to his

---

[11]*Autobiography of Parley P. Pratt*, pp. 210-211. See also *History of the Church*, Vol. III, p. 208.

people: "Let no one hereafter, by mistake or design, confound this organization of the Church for good and righteous purposes, with the organization of the 'Danites' of the apostate Avard, which died almost before it had existed."[12]

Despite the lack of evidence against Joseph Smith and the other Church leaders, and despite the efforts of their attorneys, Doniphan and Reese, to secure their release, the imprisonment dragged on during the winter and into the summer.

Counsel from Prison

From his prison cell at Liberty the Prophet carried on a correspondence with the Church which gives a great insight into the man's nature. Some of the finest bits of Mormon literature came from his pen during that time.[13]

From Liberty prison the Prophet, by his words of counsel and encouragement, kept faith and hope alive in the Church. It is characteristic of Joseph Smith that his mind did not long dwell on the afflictions of the moment, but turned toward a glorious future. And this abounding optimism was caught by the great majority of the Church members, so that the historian says of them:

"Their trials and sufferings instead of dampening the ardor of the Saints, increased it tenfold. 'The blood of the martyrs became the seed of the Church.'"[14]

To a people with every cause for bitterness and hatred, he counseled love and tolerance:

"We ought always to be aware of those prejudices which sometimes so strangely present themselves, and are so congenial to human nature, against our friends, neighbors, and brethren of the world, who choose

to differ from us in opinion and in matters of faith. Our religion is between us and our God. Their religion is between them and their God. There is a love from God that should be exercised toward those of our faith, who walk uprightly, which is peculiar to itself, but it is without prejudice; it also gives scope to the mind, which enables us to conduct ourselves with greater liberality towards all that are not of our faith, than what they exercise toward one another."[15]

Joseph Escapes

In April the prisoners held at Liberty jail were removed for Grand Jury trial, first to Daviess County, and later to Boone County. While enroute to the latter place it was hinted to them that it would be pleasing to the authorities if they would escape. They were allowed by the guards to purchase two horses. On the night planned for the escape, the guards conveniently went to sleep, with the exception of one who helped them mount their horses and get away. Eventually they found their way out of the state and joined their friends in Illinois.

While the escape was welcomed at the time, it was a source of embarrassment later. Their trial had been near at hand and, being innocent, no charges could have been sustained against them and they must certainly have been set free. Because of the escape they were considered fugitives from justice and their later arrest could be demanded whenever some charge against them might be substantiated. Such demands for the arrest of the Prophet were made of the State of Illinois at a later period.

The leaders in Richmond jail were given no such opportunity. An escape was planned, however, and carried off successfully during the Fourth of July Celebration of 1839. Eventually, these also escaped from Missouri and rejoined their loved ones in a new land.

[12]*History of the Church*—Period I, Vol. III, pp. 178-182.
[13](Note) The finest of these writings are now published in the *Doctrine and Covenants*, Sections 121, 122, 123.
[14]Crosby Johnson, *History of Caldwell County*.

[15]Letter from Liberty Jail — Dated March 25, 1839. *History of the Church* — Period I, Vol. III, p. 304.

The Liberty Jail in Missouri where the Prophet Joseph Smith spent several months as a prisoner during the winter of 1838-39.

Supplementary Readings

1. *History of the Church*, Period I, Vol. III, pp. 183-186. (Joseph Young's narrative of the Massacre at Haun's Mill.)

2. *Ibid.*, Vol. 3, pp. 238-240. (The case of the Saints before the legislature.)

3. *Ibid.*, Vol. 3, pp. 256-259. (Letters of Alexander McRae to the *Deseret News*.)

4. *Autobiography of Parley P. Pratt*, pp. 186-187 (Leaders taken prisoners.) p. 188 (Prisoners part with friends.)

5. Evans, *Heart of Mormonism*, pp. 200-204. (Final expulsion of the Saints from Missouri and their vain pleas for justice.)

6. *Ibid.*, p. 208. (The Prophet subdues the guards.)

7. Cowley, *Wilford Woodruff*, p. 103. (A survivor of the Haun's Mill massacre. Shot several times but lives.)

8. Roberts, B. H., *Joseph Smith, the Prophet-Teacher*, pp. 68-73. (Joseph Smith taught that the Constitution of the United States was inspired of God.)

9. Evans, J. H., *Joseph Smith, An American Prophet*, pp. 139-142. (His majesty in chains.)

10. *Ibid.*, Ch. VI, pp. 127-139. (The expulsion of the people from Missouri.)

11. *History of Joseph Smith by His Mother Lucy Mack Smith*, pp. 300-302. (His mother sees Joseph and Hyrum in a dream as they escape jail. She announces their homecoming.)

12. Smith, Joseph Fielding, *Essentials in Church History*, pp. 238-241. (The Church leaders surrender themselves for peace, but were ordered to be shot. General Doniphan's refusal to carry out the order to save their lives.)

13. *Ibid.*, pp. 233-236. (The Haun's Mill Massacre as an example of the extremes to which men will go while dominated by mob spirit.)

14. *Doctrine and Covenants*, Sec. 121; 122.

CHAPTER 19

A FAITH STRONGER THAN STEEL

"Seek Ye First the Kingdom of God"

In the early summer of 1839, a man traversed a swampy terrain in western Illinois. The swamp was covered with underbrush and scattered trees. Around it on three sides, in a mighty horseshoe-like sweep, rolled the muddy waters of the Mississippi.

The land was practically deserted. Save for a half dozen stone and log houses squatting near the river bank and mockingly designated as "Commerce," one might have counted the dwellings for miles around upon the fingers of his two hands. Swarms of mosquitoes, the then-unknown carriers of malaria fever, were everywhere. The place was unhealthy, shunned by settler and wayfarer.

This man was a fugitive from persecution, an escaped prisoner from the state of Missouri. He was haggard and pale from his long confinement. He was penniless. His people—those who called him "Prophet"—and who had followed his leadership through nine eventful years, were as stripped and penniless as he. They lay, twelve thousand of them, in miserable encampments on both sides of the Mississippi and in the vicinity of Quincy, living in tents, in dugouts,—some shelterless under the open sky. Without homes, comforts, sufficient food, or fields to produce it. Disease taking its heavy toll, and sickness knocking at every door. A people driven, despised—unwanted.

This mosquito-infested swamp over which the Prophet walked had just been purchased for their home. This land which nobody wanted was to be the dwelling place of this unwanted people. More attractive lands were to be had on the Iowa side—for money—but the Saints had no money. The owners of this land had been glad to take even promissory notes, payable over a term of years.

Poverty forced the settlement of this place—poverty, and the vision of a Great Man.

Little more than two weeks had passed since Joseph Smith had crossed the Mississippi into Illinois to escape further imprisonment. But those two weeks had been full of activity. On April 24, the second day after his arrival, he had started with Newel Knight and Alanson Ripley, as a Church Committee, to find land for a new gathering place.

That purchase was made. A total sum of $14,000 in promissory notes was paid to Dr. Isaac Galland and Hugh White for the initial tracts of land.

A scattered people suddenly had an objective again—a place of gathering —and a Prophet as leader.

Characteristic of the Prophet, he renamed the place to meet his desires. Not what it was, but what, with the faith and work of man, the region might become—"Nauvoo, the City Beautiful."

On the 10th of May, Joseph moved his family into a small log house on the bank of the river, a mile south of Commerce. Following the Prophet's example the Saints, during the summer, began to arrive in numbers and were allotted lands according to their needs. A large group remained on the opposite side of the river at Montrose. Those who had previously gone to Quincy began to file into Nauvoo.

Remarkable Healings

There was much sickness, the dreaded malaria taking a heavy toll of the weakened people. President Smith's home was crowded with the sick. Many of the newly-arrived camped in his dooryard under tents. In his care of them Joseph himself was stricken.

Of the events occurring at this time Wilford Woodruff, who was present, wrote:

"After being confined to his house several days, and while meditating upon his situation, he had a great desire to attend to the duties of his office. On the morning of the 22nd of July, 1839, he arose from his bed and commenced to administer to the sick in his own house and dooryard, and he commanded them in the name of the Lord Jesus Christ to arise and be made whole; and the sick were healed upon every side of him.

"Many lay sick along the bank of the river; Joseph walked along up to the lower stone house, occupied by Sidney Rigdon, and he healed all the sick that lay in his path. Among the number was Henry G. Sherwood, who was nigh unto death. Joseph stood in the door of his tent and commanded him in the name of Jesus Christ to arise and come out of his tent, and he obeyed him and was healed. Brother Benjamin Brown and his family also lay sick, the former appearing to be in a dying condition. Joseph healed them in the name of the Lord. After healing all that lay sick upon the bank of the river as far as the stone house, he called upon Elder Kimball and some others to accompany him across the river to visit the sick at Montrose. Many of the Saints were living at the old military barracks. Among the number were several of the Twelve. On his arrival, the first house he visited was that occupied by Elder Brigham Young, the president of the quorum of the Twelve, who lay sick. Joseph healed him, then he arose and accompanied the Prophet on his visit to others who were in the same condition. They visited Elder Wilford Woodruff, also Elders Orson Pratt, and John Taylor, all of whom were living in Montrose. They also (arose and) accompanied him."[1]

The remarkable faith of the Prophet in the destiny of his people, caused him to forget their poverty, their miserable homes and past bitter experiences. *Faith is mightier than steel.* While it lived in the hearts of men, Zion could never be destroyed.

Those people on the banks of the Mississippi, who like Jesus of Nazareth had nowhere to lay their heads, were nearer to Zion than they had ever been before. Their heartrending troubles had swept them clean of all sordid desires. Those who were not pure in heart unconsciously remained behind. For the first time it began to dawn upon the Church that a "Zion People" was infinitely more important than a "Zion Place," for without a "Zion People" no spot in all the world could remain holy.

While the Church seemed at its lowest ebb to the casual observer, the strength within was greater than before. The faith of these people, their loyalty to the Prophet, and the missionary zeal which swept over them has never been paralleled in history. That deep and abiding strength was to change a swamp into a great city; miserable shelters into splendid houses; penniless people to the most prosperous citizens of Illinois. That missionary zeal was to carry the gospel into many lands and double the membership of the Church. And all of this in the short time of five years!

What a program. And what an accomplishment! A people stripped of all earthly possessions, money, homes, factories, lands, rebuilt in five short years a city-state which was the envy of long-settled communities.

[1] Wilford Woodruff, *Leaves from My Journal*. See also, *Autobiography of Parley P. Pratt*, pp. 293-294.

become their nursing fathers, and queens with motherly fondness wipe the tear of sorrow from their eye.

"Thou, O Lord, did once move upon the heart of Cyrus to show favor unto Jerusalem and her children. Do Thou now also be pleased to inspire the hearts of kings and the powers of the earth to look with friendly eye towards this place, and with a desire to see Thy righteous purposes executed in relation thereto. Let them know that it is Thy good pleasure to restore the kingdom unto Israel— raise up Jerusalem as its capital, and constitute her people a distinct nation and government, with David Thy servant, even a descendant from the loins of ancient David, to be their King.

"Let that nation or that people who shall take an active part in behalf of Abraham's children, and in the raising up of Jerusalem, find favor in Thy sight. Let not their enemies prevail against them, neither let pestilence or famine overcome them, but let the glory of Israel overshadow them, and the power of the Highest protect them; while that nation or kingdom that will not serve Thee in this glorious work must perish, according to Thy word—'Yea, those nations shall be utterly wasted.'"[7]

On the Mount of Olives and also upon Mt. Moriah in Jerusalem, Elder Hyde built stone altars after the fashion of the early Israelites, as a memorial of his prayer. From Alexandria, Egypt, he wrote to the Latter-day Saint *Millennial Star* at Liverpool, England, the following:

"It was by political power and influence that the Jewish nation was broken down, and her subjects dispersed abroad; and I will here hazard the opinion that by political power and influence they will be gathered and built up; and further, that England is destined in the wisdom and economy of heaven, to stretch forth the arm of political power and advance in the front ranks of this glorious enterprise."[8]

These facts in the history of the Church give peculiar significance and meaning to the events in Palestine since

World War I and the change in heart which has come over the Jewish race toward Jesus of Nazareth.

On December 11, 1917, General Allenby of the British Army marched his military forces into the Holy City of Jerusalem and wrested the control of that land from the Turks. Shortly afterward, Lord Balfour, then Secretary of the Foreign Affairs for Great Britain, made an important announcement to the world: England would foster the return of the Jews to Palestine. Other nations were invited to lend their encouragement to the same movement. To show their good faith, Great Britain appointed a Jew as Governor, and accepted a mandate from the League of Nations over that land.

A movement of Jews to Palestine has gone on continually since that time, the number of immigrants in a single year often exceeding 50,000. Renewed interest in an old dream has been awakened among the Jewish people of the world. An independent state Israeli has been established. The prayer of Orson Hyde now has added significance.

Supplementary Readings

1. *History of the Church*, Period I, Vol. 4, pp. 3-5. (Wilford Woodruff's account of the healings at Montrose.)

2. Roberts, *Comprehensive History of the Church*, Vol. 2, pp. 12-13. Note. (Reason for welcoming the Saints into Illinois.)

3. *Ibid.*, pp. 21-22. (A day of healing.)

4. *Ibid.*, pp. 41-43. (Death of Joseph Smith Sr., and Don Carlos Smith.)

5. Cannon, *Life of Joseph Smith*, pp. 302-304.

6. Cowley, *Wilford Woodruff*, pp. 104-106. (The sick are healed in Commerce and Montrose.)

7. *Ibid.*, pp. 107-108. (Instructions of Joseph Smith to the Apostles departing for England.)

---

[7]Contained in a letter from Orson Hyde to Parley P. Pratt in England, dated November 22, 1841. See *History of the Church*—Period I, Vol. 4, pp. 454-459.

[8]*Millennial Star*, March issue, 1842.

8. *Ibid.*, pp. 108-110. (Incident connected with the departure of the Twelve.)

9. *Ibid.*, pp. 117-118. (Remarkable conversions in England.)

10. *Ibid.*, pp. 140-141. Wilford Woodruff bids farewell to friends in England.)

11. Snow, Eliza R., *Biography and Family Record of Lorenzo Snow*, pp. 46-47. (The English Mission presenting *Book of Mormon* to Queen Victoria—healings.)

12. Evans, *Heart of Mormonism*, pp. 222-224. (A day of healing in Nauvoo and vicinity.)

13. *Ibid.*, pp. 227-230. (Converting the United Brethren in England.)

14. Evans, *Joseph Smith, An American Prophet*, pp. 165-167. (Good news from England.)

15. *Ibid.*, pp. 149-155. (Nauvoo, the Beautiful.)

16. Smith, Joseph Fielding, *Essentials in Church History*, pp. 312-314. (The dedication of Palestine by Orson Hyde.)

17. Wilford Woodruff, *Leaves From My Journal*, Ch. 19. (Healing at Montrose, Mission to England.)

CHAPTER 20

A CITY STATE IS DEVELOPED
IN AMERICA

A Prophet Plans a City

The story of the development of Nauvoo constitutes one of the most progressive chapters in social history. A people inspired by a great faith do not long remain in poverty. Swamps were soon drained, and with their disappearance went the mosquito and the dread malaria. Underbrush gave way to gardens. Tents and hastily devised shacks were replaced by beautiful dwellings.

Nauvoo did not develop in the usual haphazard way of cities. It was fashioned in the mind of its founder before a stone was laid or a ditch dug.

As early as 1833 the Prophet had received revelations concerning the construction of cities of Zion. In that year he had sent a plan for such a city to Independence, Missouri. Persecutions in that state had prevented more than a partial conformity to the plan.

Nauvoo offered the first real opportunity to show what the Prophet might accomplish in solving the problems of city life. The planning of the city came under three heads:

Physical Construction

The city was laid out with streets, eight rods in width, running directly

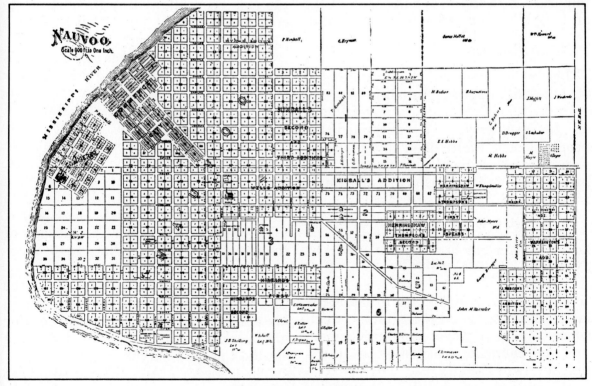

Plat of Nauvoo, Illinois.

north and south, and east and west, and crossing each other at regular intervals. Sections of the city were designated for the erection of public buildings and recreational centers. Building restrictions controlled the location of manufacturing plants, mercantile establishments, etc. In the residential sections, houses were erected a uniform distance from the street and were fronted with lawns and shrubs. Unsightly structures were prohibited. The plan embraced most of those features now common in the "zoning" of cities.

Nauvoo became the pattern for future cities built by the Saints in the Rocky Mountains. Salt Lake City presents an example, and an amazing revelation in city planning to those who visit it. The material welfare and happiness of his people was ever of great importance to the Prophet. The "City of Joseph" was a reflection of the man.

Political Government

The bitter lessons of the Missouri period had an important bearing upon the organization of the political government of the new city. To safeguard his people, Joseph Smith drew up the provisions for an unusual city charter and presented it to the legislature of Illinois for approval. He says of it:

"I concocted it for the salvation of the church, and on principles so broad that every honest man might dwell secure under its protecting influence, without distinction of sect or party."[1]

The charter provided for broad legislative powers resting in a city council consisting of a mayor, four aldermen, and nine councilors elected by the qualified voters of the city.

It provided for a municipal court, independent of any but the Supreme

[1] History of the Church, Period I, Vol. 4, p. 249.

Court of the State and the Federal Courts.

It provided for a city militia to be known as the Nauvoo Legion, to be equipped by the State and officered by citizens of Nauvoo.

The many enumerated powers which were granted created practically a city-state. Within the limits of the city— and these might be extended indefinitely by the vote of residents in the area to be added—the city was independent of all other agencies in the state. Only the repeal of the charter by the state legislature could curtail these powers. No other municipality in America before or since has enjoyed such complete control of its own affairs. The charter was a protection to the Church from mobs, illegal court proceedings, and the whims of higher governmental agencies. Had the city been allowed by its enemies to continue, it might have well become a model for city governments in America.

Political circumstances aided the people of Nauvoo in getting the charter passed. The Saints were a numerous people in that sparsely settled state and both political parties sought their friendship. The Mormon vote could easily sway an election in the state. Even political opponents like Stephen A. Douglas and Abraham Lincoln, then members of the Illinois legislature, joined hands to vote for the passage of the charter. In December, 1840, Nauvoo began its official existence.

John C. Bennett, who joined the Church at Nauvoo, had been tireless in his efforts in securing its passage. For his work he was rewarded by being elected the first mayor.

The isolation of the Saints from those of another faith, which had been attempted in Missouri, was abandoned. Indeed, people of all religious denominations were invited to dwell with the Saints in Nauvoo. In a proclamation by the First Presidency we read:

"We wish it likewise to be distinctly understood that we claim no privileges but what we feel cheerfully disposed to share with our fellow citizens of every denomination, and every sentiment of religion; and therefore say, that so far from being restricted to our own faith, let all those who desire to locate in this place (Nauvoo) or the vicinity, come and we will hail them as citizens and friends, and shall feel it not only a duty, but a privilege to reciprocate the kindness we have received from the benevolent and kind-hearted citizens of the State of Illinois."

In keeping with this spirit, one of the first acts of the city council was to pass an ordinance protecting people in the undisturbed enjoyment of their several religions.

Another early ordinance prohibited the sale of hard liquor and practically made Nauvoo a prohibition city.

Educational and Religious Facilities

In drawing up the proposed charter for Nauvoo the Prophet had been careful to include a grant of power to the city to organize and control its own educational system. This included a charter for a municipal university, the first of its kind in America.

In accordance with this power an educational system, including all grades from elementary to university classes, was organized by the city council. University buildings and campus were planned, but the plans were never carried out before the people were driven from Nauvoo. Instructors were hired and university classes held, however, in such buildings as the city afforded. The organization for the control of the university was later adopted in Utah for the University of Deseret, now the University of Utah.

It was the aim of the Prophet to edu-cate his entire people, young and old. Nearly all who attended classes at the University of Nauvoo were adults.

One of the first thoughts of the Prophet in planning Nauvoo, was a site for a temple. A well constructed city, enjoying wise governmental powers, would not alone make for a happy people. Even the addition of education would not assure success. The true Zion must have people who are pure in heart. To the Prophet the most important item was correct thinking. When asked on one occasion how he governed his people, Joseph replied, "I teach them correct principles and they govern themselves."[2] So the "City of Joseph" should be built around a Temple of God, and be provided with other suitable places of worship, where the Gospel of Jesus might be taught to his people.

A city organized under such principles was not long in attracting the attention of thinking men. As early as the summer of 1841, the St. Louis "Atlas" referred to Nauvoo as follows:

"The population of Nauvoo is between 8,000 and 9,000, and of course the largest town in the State of Illinois. How long the Latter-day Saints will hold together and exhibit their present aspect, it is not for us to say. At this moment they present the appearance of an enterprising, industrious, sober and thrifty population, such a population indeed, as in the respects just mentioned, have no rivals east and we rather guess, not even west of the Mississippi."[3]

The Growth and Influence of Nauvoo

The growth of Nauvoo was naturally rapid as it became the gathering place for the majority of the exiles from Missouri and was the destination of converts migrating from eastern states and foreign lands.

---

[2]Cannon, *Life of Joseph Smith, the Prophet*, p. 496.
[3]See *Liverpool Route*, p. 62.

In June of 1844, Franklin D. Richards, the Church Historian, placed the population at 14,000. Governor Ford in his *History of Illinois*, estimates the population of the city at the close of 1845 as 15,000.[4] No actual census was taken and the number is variously estimated from twelve to twenty thousand.

As this growth had occurred in the short space of time following 1839, the city attracted many visitors who came largely out of curiosity to see the Mormon metropolis. Eastern newspapers sent representatives to interview the founder of the city and make observations on the unusual features of the Mormon center.

The wharf at Nauvoo became a busy place. All the important river steamers stopped to unload or pick up passengers and freight. The growth of the city overshadowed that of the neighboring towns of Warsaw, Carthage, and Quincy, and caused considerable loss of prestige to the older places. This provoked jealousy and envy, especially among the speculators in lands.

Nauvoo became a social center. It was easily accessible to settlements up and down the river, and great celebrations held on U.S. Indepddendence Day and other holidays attracted people for many miles. Excursion boats from Warsaw and even St. Louis were common, the vessels docking at Nauvoo amidst much laughter and gayety. Dances were held on such occasions, usually lasting until the early hours of the following morning. The beauty of the city and the hospitality of its people became known far and wide.

The parade of the Nauvoo Legion was a colorful event which seldom failed to attract an audience. At its height the Legion contained 5,000 men, armed and in uniform. On many occasions mock battles were held, both for the better training of the soldiers and for the entertainment of the people.

Wrestling, racing, jumping at a mark, pitching horseshoes, etc., were features of the usual holiday, the Prophet being an active and able participant in them all.

Buildings in Nauvoo

The most hospitable place in the city was the Mansion House, home of Joseph Smith. The Mansion was also used to accommodate travelers stopping at Nauvoo and to care temporarily for arriving converts. It early gained a reputation for fine meals and accommodations. Men of renown visiting Nauvoo slept beneath its roof; the humblest were equally welcome. While the Prophet was at home, he was accessible to all and life in the city gravitated about the Mansion.

To better accommodate travelers and converts who were constantly arriving in the city, a larger building, "The Nauvoo House," was begun. The cornerstone was laid October 2, 1841, in obedience to a revelation that such a house should be erected.[5] It was built with funds raised by the selling of stock to worthy Church members. Within the cornerstone Joseph Smith deposited the original manuscript of the *Book of Mormon* translation. The building was never completed as originally designed, the martyrdom of the Prophet and the contemplated exodus West causing a change in plans. The part completed is still standing in Nauvoo not far from the Mansion House; but has been changed to make a dwelling.

Brick homes of large proportions

[4]Ford, *History of Illinois*, p. 403.

[5]*Doctrine and Covenants*, Sec. 124.

(2)

(3)

(5)

(4)

(6)

Some of the homes and buildings the Saints built in Nauvoo, as they appear today: (1) The Times and Seasons Building; (2) The Nauvoo House; (3) Joseph Smith's first home in Nauvoo; (4) Heber C. Kimball's home; (5) John Taylor's home and (6) Joseph Smith's home known as the "Mansion House."

Used by permission, J. M. Heslop (Nos. 1, 2, 4, 5, 6) and W. Claudell Johnson, No. 3).

were common in Nauvoo and attest the industry, skill, and civic pride of the inhabitants.

The Temple, begun in 1841, was a never-failing source of interest to the visitor. Although not completed until 1846, its position on the highest point of the city made even the unfinished walls visible from the surrounding country. Except on Sundays and holidays it was always a scene of some activity. At times building operations slackened for lack of funds.

Extending to the east of the city, and to the north and south, were broad cultivated acres. It was easily one of the most advanced agricultural areas in that section of the nation. It was the most unusual in America in that none of the people lived upon their farms, but resided in the city, passing to and from their fields in the morning and evening. This gave to all the advantages of education and social contacts which the city afforded, and promoted the unity of the people.

While the phenomenal growth of the Church, the rapid rise of the city, and the prosperity of the Saints were gratifying to the founders of the Church and city, these factors attracted a class of men quite undesirable.

"Adventurers seeking for place and power and wealth; demagogues who, by fulsome flattery of the people, hoped to attain through their political influence a realization of their ambitious dreams; knaves who by falsely professing conversion, thought to cover up corrupt, licentious lives, and thrive by villainy; thieves and counterfeiters who saw their opportunity to live by roguery, and steal, on the credit of the Mormons, of whom the people of Illinois were too ready to believe anything that savored of evil, because prejudiced against their religon—all these characters were attracted to Nauvoo by the prosperity that reigned there; and their ungodly conduct hastened the evil day of the city's destruction."[6]

[6]Roberts, *Life of John Taylor*, pp. 107-108.

Among these reckless adventurers, none was more skillful in winning his way into the confidences of the people than John C. Bennett, previously alluded to as the first Mayor of the city. He is often referred to by historians as a "moral leper." When his promiscuous sexual practices were discovered he was excommunicated from the Church and deprived of all his civic positions. Other men of the same stamp as Bennett helped to bring discredit upon the community, especially among those who were searching for charges against the Saints.

Nauvoo Publications

In each of the locations the Saints had gathered, a printing press and a Church publication had been started. So in Nauvoo one of the first achievements was the establishment of a printing press. On the night that the mob forces of General Lucas had surrounded Far West, the Church printing press, used at that place for the publication of the *Elders Journal*, was hidden from the enemy and buried in the dooryard of a Brother Dawson. Later it was secretly dug up and shipped to Commerce, Illinois. There it was set up again in a cellar during the fall of 1839. On this press was published the fourth periodical of the Church, the *Times and Seasons*. In the beginning it was a sixteen page monthly. Later it became a semimonthly publication. Don Carlos Smith, youngest brother of the Prophet, was the first editor, assisted by Ebenezer Robinson. After the death of Don Carlos Smith, August 7, 1841, Ebenezer Robinson assumed the duties for a time. At the end of a year the editorial chair was assigned to John Taylor, who conducted the publication until its final issue, February 15, 1846.

The Prophet wrote numerous editorials and articles which appeared in the publication. Much historical material also appeared in its issues, so that it is considered a great repository of historical material.

The *Nauvoo Neighbor* also espoused the cause of the Saints and was owned by the Church. It was perhaps read more widely outside of Mormon circles than was the *Times and Seasons* and was frequently quoted by other papers published in the west.

During the time the Saints occupied Nauvoo no other city of the Mississippi Valley could boast such rapid growth. Few could match its civic pride or economic prosperity. Yet the unseen faith of its inhabitants was mightier than its masonry. This faith had been responsible for the building of a city where a swamp had been, and when the people who possessed that faith were gone, Nauvoo quickly sank to the common level of its neighbors.

Supplementary Readings

1. *History of the Church*, Period I, Volume 6, p. 3. (Quotation from *New York Sun*.)

2. *Ibid*, Volume 5, pp. 457-458. (Extract from Nauvoo City Charter concerning strangers.)

3. Roberts, *Comprehensive History of the Church*, Volume 2, p. 54, footnote. (A brief, interesting story associating Abraham Lincoln with the Nauvoo Charter.)

4. *Ibid*, Volume 2, pp. 53-60. (An excellent account of the Nauvoo Charter. Note especially the carefully selected extracts from the Charter. The last two paragraphs of this section on p. 60 challenge us to attain a real understanding of the charter, its implications, and its influence on "Mormon-Gentile" relations, and Mormon history of the period.)

5. *Ibid*, Volume 2, p. 54b. (Mormon avowal of their readiness to share all the powers and privileges of the Nauvoo Charter with all peoples. Note especially the statement of the First Presidency of the Church, and section I of the charter.)

6. Evans, *Joseph Smith, An American Prophet*, p. 151a. (Joseph Smith's basic purpose in city planning.)

7. *Ibid*, pp. 149-155a. (Joseph Smith, power in government, and the Nauvoo Charter. This entire section will reward a thoughtful reading. Give attention to remarks quoted from the Prophet. 152d-153, and quotation from the charter, p. 155.)

8. *Ibid*, p. 150. (President Taft, Salt Lake City, Mormon city-planning. Joseph Smith vs. Brigham on Mormon city-planning.)

9. *Ibid*, p. 196a. ("An astounding thing" —City of Nauvoo asked to be made a "Territory.")

10. *Ibid*, pp. 143-147. (Commerce vs. Nauvoo the Beautiful. Joseph Smith, man of vision. An attractive story.)

11. Smith, Lucy Mack, *Joseph Smith the Prophet*, p. 265. (Joseph Smith, Sr., blesses each member of his family just before his death.)

12. Evans, *Heart of Mormonism*, pp. 210-221. (An easy, pleasant story of Joseph's insight and impelling leadership. Note pp. 215-216. The real story here is pp. 217-221.)

13. Little, James A., *From Kirtland to Salt Lake City*, pp. 35-37. (A vivid picture of Commerce when the Mormons first settled there. An unusual prayer by Joseph Smith, Sr., Joseph's father, on the first ear of corn grown in Commerce.)

CHAPTER 21

THE TRIALS OF A
MODERN PROPHET

Missouri Enemies Pursue the Prophet

If we follow Joseph Smith during the years in which Nauvoo rose to its splendid height, we come to know and appreciate a great American. The development and growth of the man would become to us more amazing than the development and growth of the city. We would see him in the role of prophet, statesman, soldier, student, and martyr. We would witness the vile hatred of his enemies and the warm sympathy and devotion of his friends. We would see him in his intensely human reactions and yet witness him, at times, rise among the stars. Out of this experience we would emerge with a greater faith and a finer appreciation.

It is doubtful if Joseph Smith, after the expulsion from Missouri, seriously expected to be reinstated in that land at that time or even to receive compensation for the losses incurred. That hope had not died out, however, among the Saints. Sidney Rigdon even proposed a scheme to oust Missouri from the Union of States and worked up considerable feeling over it. To allay this feeling and satisfy his people, Joseph Smith started for Washington, D.C., October 29, 1839, accompanied by Sidney Rigdon and Judge Elias Higbee, to lay the cause of the people before the Federal Government. Rigdon, becoming ill, was left in Columbus, Ohio. The others reached their destination.

A short time in the National Capital convinced the Prophet of the folly of expecting help from that source. President Van Buren informed them in a meeting, "Gentlemen, your cause is just, but I can do nothing for you. If I take up for you I shall lose the vote of Missouri."[1]

President Van Buren must not be criticised too harshly. At that time there existed in the states a jealousy of the Federal power which threatened the existence of the Union. When the Civil War later broke out, the immediate cause was the attempt on the part of the Federal Government to regulate affairs which the Southern States considered exclusively their own business. At the time of the Missouri persecutions, the power of the Executive of the United States had seldom been exercised in State affairs, and there was a considerable weight of opinion which would have denied the Federal Government any right of interference unless the existence of the Union was threatened.

While the Prophet returned to Nauvoo, convinced that the Saints must forget their cause against Missouri, the Missourians were in no wise willing to forget the Saints. The hospitality displayed by the citizens of Illinois and the blame poured upon Missouri by the eastern press seems to have stirred those responsible for the Missouri mobbings to a fresh determination. Their previous treatment of the Mormons must be justified by condemning the Mormon leader to punishment for some crime.

A few incidents will serve to illus-

---

[1] *History of the Church*, Vol. I, p. 80.

trate the attempts on the part of enemies outside the Church and within it to bring about the fall and, if possible, the death of the Prophet. The legal justification of the Missourians in attempting to retake the Prophet and others was the fact that they had escaped from the hands of civil authorities in Missouri while being taken to trial. Joseph Smith was now in another state. But he could be extradited; that is, the Governor of a State may give up one who has sought refuge in his State, upon the request of another Governor for his arrest, where he is convinced that there is a sufficient charge laid against the refugee.

Missouri appealed to Governor Carlin of Illinois for such a writ, authorizing the arrest of Joseph Smith. Governor Carlin granted the request and issued the writ.

The Prophet was innocent of any crime, but was convinced that if he fell into the hands of his Missouri enemies again, he would never return to Nauvoo alive. Thinking men generally agreed with him. A leading publication, the *Whig*, of Quincy, printed the following:

"We repeat, Smith and Rigdon should not be given up. The law requiring the Governor of our State to deliver up fugitives from justice is a salutary and a wise one, and should not in ordinary circumstances be disregarded; but there are occasions when it is not only the privilege but the duty of the Governor to refuse to surrender the citizens of his state upon the requisition of the executive of another, and this we consider the case of Smith and Rigdon.

"The law is made to secure the punishment of the guilty, and not to sacrifice the innocent."[2]

The Prophet and the other leaders named in the writ went into hiding and the writ was returned unserved.

This was the beginning of a trouble

which was to last the remaining years of the Prophet's life and greatly hamper his work. Sheriffs from Missouri constantly were in search of him and he was freed from one writ only to be pursued by another. Only the devotion of his people enabled him to escape arrest or being kidnaped and rushed across the border into Missouri. Part of the time he secluded himself on the little island lying mid-stream between Nauvoo and Montrose, and from that tiny island came important teachings and some of his finest writings. Part of the time he spent in his own home, although it was watched closely by his enemies, who kept careful check on the goings and comings of the Prophet's wife.

The writs issued by Governor Carlin called for the arrest of all those who had escaped from Missouri prisons. The real objective, however, was to get hold of Joseph Smith. Some outrages were perpetrated, however, against some of the other brethren. On the 7th of July, 1840, Alanson Brown, Benjamin Boyer, Noah Rogers and James Allred were kidnaped by an armed mob of Missourians and taken into Missouri. They were severely handled before being released.[3]

New Attempts to Get the Prophet

In May, 1842, an attempt was made in Missouri to kill ex-Governor Boggs. He recovered from the assassin's bullet, but the assassin was never found.

On July 20, 1842, Boggs swore out an affidavit that Orrin Porter Rockwell, a resident of Illinois, had done the shooting and charged Joseph Smith as "accessory before the fact." He asked Governor Reynolds of Missouri to de-

---

[2] *Quincy "Whig"* 1841.

[3] (Note) For full account see *History of the Church*, Period I, Vol. 4, pp. 154-157. *Essentials in Church History*, Smith, p. 299.

mand that Governor Carlin of Illinois deliver Joseph Smith to be dealt with according to law. Governor Reynolds complied, and Governor Carlin issued a writ for the Prophet's arrest. On August 8, 1842, both he and Orrin Porter Rockwell were taken into custody. The Prophet demanded the right of "habeas corpus,"[1] and the court of Nauvoo issued a writ requiring the prisoners to be brought before it. The sheriff was afraid either to obey or to disobey the order, and rushed away to Governor Carlin for instructions. When he returned, the prisoners were not to be found, nor could any threat against the people of Nauvoo disclose their hiding place.

The whole proceeding on the part of Missouri was a legal farce, but nothing probably would have saved the Prophet and Rockwell from their Missouri enemies had they been taken. Every type of scheming was used to get Joseph to come out of hiding or to get his people to betray him. Rumors were that he had gone to Europe, or at least to Washington, while all the time he was never farther from Nauvoo than the island in the river.

The faith of the people in their Prophet was unshakable. Emma, his wife, made an appeal to Governor Carlin to rescind his order, without success. On the 8th of December, 1842, the term of office of Governor Carlin expired and Thomas Ford took the Governor's seat.

Affidavits were secured immediately to prove that Joseph Smith was not in Missouri at the time of the crime against Boggs and, on the basis of these,

the Supreme Court of Illinois declared the writ to be illegal but decided that a trial should be held before the Governor should interfere. The Prophet submitted to arrest and in the subsequent trial was discharged, January 5, 1843.

For a brief period he was to enjoy peace. The people of Nauvoo rejoiced that their Prophet could once more walk openly among them.

Reynolds and Wilson

The respite was, however, short-lived. On June 13 of that year, a new conspiracy against him came to fruition. John C. Bennett, one time friend of the Prophet and first Mayor of Nauvoo, joined the Missouri forces. Bennett, who proved to be an unscrupulous and immoral individual, had been previously excommunicated from the Church. His bitterness toward the Prophet for exposing him knew no bounds. Both Governor Reynolds of Missouri and Ford of Illinois, joined with him in his new scheme against the Mormon leader.

On June 13, 1843, a secret requisiton was made to Governor Ford on the old charges. A writ was issued, and two Missouri officers, disguised as Mormon Elders, were appointed to serve it. An incidental remark of Governor Ford to Judge James Adams caused that esteemed friend of the Prophet to send him warning. Joseph was not in Nauvoo when the warning came. William Clayton and Stephen Markham mounted fast horses and rode 212 miles in 64 hours to the house of Mrs. Wasson, sister of Emma Smith, near Dixon in Lee County, Illinois. The Prophet was surprised at their appearance, but felt secure and refused to flee. Somehow the disguised officers had learned where he was and proceeded there. Still representing themselves as missionaries

[1]Habeas Corpus — name of a writ issued by a court in the locality where a person is arrested, demanding that the person held under arrest be brought before it, rather than be carried away to some court in another jurisdiction.

they came into the Prophet's presence, when they immediately sprang upon him and made him prisoner. Without permitting him to say "good-bye" to his wife, Emma, who was within the house, they rushed him away.

The object was to get him into the hands of waiting Missourians before his friends could rise to protect him. In this they underrated the loyalty of his friends and the magnetism of Joseph Smith's personality. Stephen Markham, who was present at the time of the arrest, rode posthaste to Dixon to secure a writ of *habeas corpus*. When Joseph arrived at Dixon he was imprisoned in a tavern and denied the privilege of consulting a lawyer. Seeing a man pass the window, Joseph shouted for an attorney. Two of them came but were refused admittance by the sheriffs. This aroused the neighborhood. Led by the proprietor, Mr. Dixon, they threatened violence to the sheriffs if they did not give their prisoner his civil rights. Word was sent to a Mr. Chamberlain, master in chancery[5] to come to Dixon, and Cyrus Walker, a great criminal attorney, was engaged to defend the Prophet.

During this time, Stephen Markham had not been idle. He had secured a warrant for the arrest of Reynolds and Wilson for having made a threat upon his life and another warrant for threatening the life of Joseph Smith and for false imprisonment. Ten thousand dollars damage was claimed on the ground that the writ under which Joseph was arrested was void in law. As these men were far from their friends they could not obtain bondsmen. They were therefore arrested and placed in custody by Sheriff Campbell of Lee County. It

was a strange picture—Joseph Smith in the custody of Reynolds and Wilson, while they in turn were in custody of Campbell.

Meanwhile William Clayton had raced over two hundred miles to Nauvoo to acquaint Hyrum Smith with the circumstances and request his aid.

It was well known that large groups of Missourians had crossed over the river into Illinois and now were waiting to get possession of the Prophet and whisk him into Missouri. Hyrum Smith hastily called the Nauvoo Legion. Of this group 175 marched out of Nauvoo determined to prevent any force from taking Joseph Smith out of Illinois. Convinced as these men were that such extradition would result in their beloved leader's death, they were ready to shed their blood in his defense. After leaving Nauvoo the force divided to watch to better advantage those avenues through which the Missouri officers might attempt to carry off the Prophet. One detachment boarded the river vessel, *Maid of Iowa*. Passing for a distance down the Mississippi, the vessel was turned up the Illinois river to shut off any party attempting to carry off the Prophet by the water route. The remainder separated to traverse the various roads.

The officers, Reynolds and Wilson, had by this time, however, become so enmeshed in legal writs that they could not carry out their designs. Sheriff Campbell was convinced by the Prophet that Nauvoo was the closest place where a court of competent jurisdiction might be found to handle the case. The party was proceeding to that place when the first detachment of troops from Nauvoo encountered it. Joseph Smith remarked, "Well, I guess I won't go to Missouri this time. There are my boys." As far

[5]Chancery—Judge of one of the higher courts—a court of equity, as distinguished from a common-law court.

as the Prophet was concerned it was a triumphal procession from there to Nauvoo. At Nauvoo Joseph Smith entertained his captors at his home and treated them with all courtesy.

The Municipal Court, upon convening discharged the Prophet on the grounds that the writ against him was illegal. A general rejoicing swept over Nauvoo.

Reynolds and Wilson repaired to Carthage and circulated petitions urging the Governor to raise militia to march on Nauvoo and retake the Prophet. They claimed that the municipal court had usurped authority and that they had been coerced to take their prisoner into Nauvoo by Stephen Markham and a group of Nauvoo men under arms.

Tension ran high. Petitions were sent from Nauvoo to Governor Ford to dispel the falsehoods and calm the troubled waters. Governor Ford recognized the jurisdiction of the municipal court of Nauvoo and upheld its decision in discharging Joseph Smith. The Prophet was a free man—only to find the net of his enemies tightening further about him. Even this was not so disturbing nor so dangerous as when some members of the Church began to turn against him and lay plots for taking his life.

Apostates Within the Church Seek the Prophet's Life

It is a sad thing that among those who came into prominence during the Nauvoo period were some who lost their faith in the Prophet and sought his destruction. A study of the lives of those disaffected shows immorality, selfishness, or ambition as the cause for loss of the spirit.

One of the early ones to fall from his station was John C. Bennett, previously referred to for his great energy in securing the Nauvoo Charter. On the

eve of his intended marriage to a young woman of Nauvoo it was learned that he had deserted a wife and children in the East. Other disclosures of immoral conduct followed and he was excommunicated in May or June of 1842. He had previously resigned from the office of Mayor. In June he left Nauvoo and set about to undermine the Prophet. He later wrote a book, *The History of the Saints*. It was full of misrepresentations and base charges and proved to be of little interest to thinking people.

With Bennett, a number who had been influenced by his teachings on sex, were cut off from the Church. The majority of these remained in Nauvoo. It was not until 1844 that their smoldering hatred of the Prophet was fanned into an open flame. In January of that year the Prophet addressed some newly appointed officers of the peace. In the course of his remarks he said:

"I am exposed to far greater danger from traitors among ourselves than from enemies without, although my life has been sought for many years by the civil and military authorities, priests, and people of Missouri; * * * I have had pretended friends betray me. All the enemies upon the face of the earth may roar and exert all their power to bring about my death, but they can accomplish nothing, unless some who are among us and enjoy our society, have been with us in our councils, participated in our confidence, taken us by the hand, called us brother, saluted us with a kiss—, join with our enemies, turn our virtues into faults, and by falsehood and deceit, stir up their wrath and indignation against us, and bring their united vengeance upon our heads. * * * We have a Judas in our midst."[6]

William and Wilson Law, William Marks, Leonard Soby, Dr. Robert D. Foster, and some others took offense at the Prophet's remarks. It soon was shown that these men were in a secret league to assassinate the Prophet and destroy the Church.

A Story of Intrigue

The story of the two young men, Denison L. Harris and Robert Scott, shows something of the nature of the conspiracy within the Church against the Prophet:

These two young men, then but seventeen years of age, had been invited to attend a secret meeting of the conspirators. In a spirit of comradeship they confided in each other, wondering what course to pursue. They took the matter to Denison's father, Emer Harris, brother of Martin Harris. He advised them to lay the whole matter before Joseph Smith. The Prophet requested the two boys to attend the meeting and report to him its proceedings.

The meeting was held on the Sabbath day at the house of William Law, counselor to the Prophet. A multitude of charges were laid against Joseph and Hyrum Smith.

"It seems that the immediate cause of these wicked proceedings was the fact that Joseph Smith had recently presented the Revelation on Celestial Marriage to the High Council for their approval, and certain members were most bitterly opposed to it, and denounced Joseph as a fallen Prophet and were determined to overthrow him."[7]

The two boys were silent observers, and after the meeting was over met the Prophet secretly and reported to him. Following the Prophet's advice they attended similar meetings the two following Sundays, and received an invitation to attend a fourth meeting. In each meeting the spirit of bitterness against the Prophet increased. Before they attended the last meeting Joseph Smith said to them:

"This will be your last meeting; this will be the last time that they will admit you into their councils! They will come to some determination. But be sure that you make no covenants, nor enter into any obligations, whatever, with them." After a pause he added, "Boys, this will be their last meeting, and they may shed your blood, but I hardly think they will, as you are so young. If they do I will be a lion in their path! Don't flinch. If you have to die; die like men. You will be martyrs to the cause and your crowns can be no greater. But I hardly think they will shed your blood."[8]

When Denison and Robert approached the house of William Law on that Sabbath afternoon they were stopped at the door by armed guards. After a severe questioning and cross-examination they were admitted.

The house was filled with men, pouring out charges against the Prophet. Bitterness was everywhere. It was evident that a decision would be arrived at during the meeting. As the two boys took no part in the discussions, but remained by themselves, William Law and Austin Cowles spent some time explaining to them how the Prophet had fallen and why they should join in ridding the Church of him. As the meeting progressed, each member present was requested to take oath as follows:

"You solemnly swear, before God, and all the Holy Angels, and these your brethren by whom you are surrounded, that you will give your life, your liberty, your influence, your all, for the destruction of Joseph Smith and his party, so help you God."

The person being sworn would then say "I do," after which he signed his name in the presence of the justice of the peace.[9]

About two hundred took oath. Among them were three women heavily veiled, who testified to attempts by Joseph and Hyrum to seduce them. When all but

---

[7]Horace Cummings, "Historical Account," *Contributor*, Vol. 5:252.

[8]*Millennial Star*, Vol. 5:253 (1884).
[9]Horace Cummings Account, *Contributor*, Vol. 5:255.

the two boys had complied, the attention of the group was turned to them. The boys refused to take the oath and started to leave the room. One of the number stepped in their way, exclaiming:

"No, not by a d—n sight. You know all our plans and arrangements, and we don't propose that you should leave in that style. You've got to take the oath or you'll never leave here alive."[10]

The boys were in a dangerous position. Threatening could be heard on every hand. One voice shouted, "Dead men tell no tales."[11] Violent hands were laid on them. Swords and bowie knives drawn. One of the leading men said, "If you do not take that oath, we will cut your throats."[12]

Only the wisdom of the leader prevented their murder then and there. The house of William Law stood close to the street and there was danger that the disturbance would be heard by passers-by. Better to execute them in the cellar.

Accordingly, a guard with drawn swords and bowie knives was placed on either side of the boys, while two others armed with cocked muskets and bayonets at their backs, brought up the rear, as they were marched off in the direction of the cellar. William and Wilson Law, Austin Cowles, and others accompanied them to that place. Before committing the murderous deed, however, they gave the boys one last chance for their lives. One of them said, 'Boys, if you will take that oath your lives will be spared; but you know too much for us to allow you to go free and, if you are determined to refuse, we will have to shed your blood."[13]

With their death as the immediate alternative the two boys grimly refused to turn against their Prophet. Trembling and white with fear they awaited the sword. As the sword was raised by an angry participant, a sharp voice from the crowd halted it in midair.

"Hold on! Hold on there! Let's talk this matter over before their blood is shed."[14] A hurried consultation followed, during which the young men were relieved to hear a strong voice say, "The boy's parents very likely know where they are, and if they do not return home, strong suspicion will be aroused, and they may institute a search that would be very dangerous to us."[15] That counsel prevailed. The boys were threatened with death if they revealed a word of what had transpired, and sent away. A guard accompanied them for a distance to prevent some of the more bloodthirsty individuals following to kill them. The parting words of the guards were, "Boys, if you ever open your mouths concerning anything you have seen or heard in any of our meetings, we will kill you by night or by day, wherever we find you, and consider it our duty."[16]

The boys continued to the river bank, where they met the Prophet, who had become anxious and had gone in search of them. Retiring to a secluded spot below the Prophet's home they told the entire story. The bravery and loyalty of the two young men melted the Prophet to tears. For fear that harm might come to them he urged them to promise never to reveal their story for twenty years. This secrecy was faithfully kept.

The heroism of two boys saved the life of the Prophet for a time from the

---

[10]*Contributor*, Vol. 5:255.
[11]*Ibid.*, Vol. 5:255.
[12]*Ibid.*, Vol. 5:256.
[13]*Ibid.*, Vol. 5:256.

---

[14]*Contributor*, Vol. 5:256.
[15]*Ibid.*, Vol. 5:256.
[16]*Ibid.*, Vol. 5:256.

net closing about him. Subsequently, the conspirators were excommunicated from the Church, after which they openly allied themselves with all those forces seeking its overthrow.

Apostates Bring Charges

On May 25, 1844, William Law, Robert D. Foster, and Joseph H. Jackson had the Prophet indicted at Carthage for adultery and perjury. The Prophet promptly appeared in court and demanded trial. His enemies, becoming frightened, were unwilling to press the charges against him, and asked for a postponement of the case. A plot to take the Prophet's life while he was at Carthage was disclosed by two of the conspirators, Charles A. and Robert D. Foster. These men repented of their part in the proceedings and confessed to the Prophet in tears.

The apostates next purchased a printing press and prepared to publish a paper, *The Nauvoo Expositor*, for the avowed purpose of advocating "the unconditional repeal of the Nauvoo City Charter and to expose immoral practices in the Church." The only number appeared June 7, 1844. It was filled with slander against Joseph Smith and the Church leaders in Nauvoo. The charter was also bitterly attacked.

The people in Nauvoo were incensed. The City Council met and declared the "Expositor" press a public nuisance. Under orders the City Marshal, John P. Green, forcibly entered the printing establishment, pied the type, and destroyed the printed papers. The conspirators, seeing what was done, set fire to their own building, and fleeing the city, circulated reports that their property had been destroyed and that their lives were in danger. The event was like a lighted match dropped in a powder house. The resulting conflagration swept the Prophet and his brother to their deaths and rocked the foundations of the Church organization.

Supplementary Readings

1. *History of the Church*, Period I, Volume 5, p. XXVIII. ("Development of the Prophet's character." A revealing page on the growth of the Prophet's character during a period of terrible experience. Here is revealed the growth of insight, strength and courage, gentleness and sympathy, etc., which the Prophet possessed.)

2. *Ibid*, pp. 458b-475. (Joseph's own account of his release from the officers of Missouri in their attempt to take him back to Missouri for trial.) pp. 465d-473a. (The Prophet's speech to his people in Nauvoo.) See especially touches on pp. 467-469. Note last paragraph of speech, p. 473a.

3. Roberts, *Comprehensive History of the Church*, Volume 2, pp. 148-150.

4. *Ibid*, Volume 2, p. 152. (The spirit in which the Prophet met his trials.)

5. *Ibid*, Volume 2, p. 153. (The Prophet speaks on mob violence.)

6. *Ibid*, Volume 2, pp. 160-162. (Quotations from Prophet in small type expressing his appreciation of his wife Emma, his brother Hyrum, and loyal friends.)

7. *Ibid*, Volume 2, pp. 47-50. (Regarding John C. Bennett.) p. 47 footnote. (A good brief discussion. Bancroft, the historian, on Bennett.)

8. *Ibid*, Volume 2, pp. 65; 221-225. (William Law and the Prophet.) See footnote 3.

9. *Ibid*, Volume 2, pp. 226-227. (Law's charges against Joseph the Prophet. These volumes are full of interesting material.)

10. *Ibid*, pp. 27-30. Appeal to General Government for redress of Missouri grievances. Perhaps our best account of this venture. The Prophet in Washington, pp. 29-31. Especially see note, pp. 38-39.

11. Evans, *Joseph Smith, An American Prophet*, pp. 167-176. ("Echoes from Missouri." An appealing and stimulating story of the attempts of Missourians to get Joseph back in Missouri.)

12. *Ibid*, pp. 158-163. (The Prophet in the Nation's capital.)

13. *Ibid*, pp. 176-184. ("The Pinnacle of Power." A pleasing picture of Joseph Smith attempting to reveal the character and soul of the man.)

14. *Autobiography of Parley P. Pratt*, pp. 289-291. (The Mormons a Nation of Heroes.)

15. *Ibid.*, pp. 170-176. (The Missouri fires begin.)

16. *Ibid.*, pp. 158-163. (The Prophet visits the President of the United States.)

17. *Doctrine and Covenants*, Section 124: 16. (John C. Bennett called by revelation to help Joseph.)

18. *Ibid.*, Section 124:82, 91, 97, 126. (William Law called by revelation to be a counselor to Joseph Smith.)

CHAPTER 22

A MILLION-DOLLAR SACRIFICE

On April 6, 1841, an unusual gathering took place on the brow of the highest eminence of land overlooking Nauvoo. A large rectangular excavation had been made. Near the edge of it Joseph Smith, Sidney Rigdon, and a score of Church leaders, were gathered. Enclosing both the excavation and the leaders, stood sixteen companies of the Nauvoo Legion in full uniform, forming a hollow square. Beyond them thousands of men, women, and children had assembled.

This people, so lately impoverished, were laying the cornerstone for a million dollar structure—a Temple to the Living God. A people of great faith were obeying the commandment of the Lord.

". . . let this house be built unto my name, that I may reveal mine ordinances therein unto my people;

For I design to reveal unto my church things which have been kept hid from before the foundation of the world, things that pertain to the dispensation of the fulness of times.

And I will show unto my servant Joseph all things pertaining to this house, and the priesthood thereof. . . .

And ye shall build it on the place where you have contemplated building it, for that is the spot which I have chosen for you to build it"[1]

The cornerstones were laid and the spot dedicated. A great undertaking had been commenced. The faith so auspiciously displayed on that occasion was never relinquished. People gave in labor and money—in provisions and encouragement. Stone quarries were opened a short distance down the river and the grey sandstone blocks were transported to the Temple site. When

the year ended, the foundations had become visible from the surrounding country.

They were five years in erecting the building. When the capstone was laid the Prophet and his brother were dead, the city lay practically deserted and its inhabitants spread out over the Iowa plain—exiles seeking another home.

The story of those grey walls, once the glory of Western Illinois, parallels that of the "City Beautiful." The rise and glory and fall of the Temple was but typical of the city upon which it looked. When the Saints were gone the great structure seemed to invite the lightning of heaven to crack it asunder and let out its lifeblood.

Beneath the walls of that rising symbol of faith, the varied pattern of the city's life passed in interesting review.

Near the walls of the temple the Saints erected a bowery, in what was termed "The Grove." There, in the open air, the people met in solemn worship. There they listened to the words of the Prophet or his associates. It was an historic spot—that old bowery or "grove"—so near the temple. The sermons delivered there would fill volumes, and the faith displayed there in worship was sufficient to move mountains. Men of national renown sat, at times, beneath its shade Ministers of a dozen creeds, upon invitation, had there expressed their views.

Not far from the temple was the greensward where athletic events were staged. There the Prophet might have been wrestling or jumping at a mark,—engaging in that intensely human side

[1]*Doctrine and Covenants*, Sec. 124:40-43.

of a prophet's life which the artist has missed and the historian neglected.

Within the Temple Walls

Within the walls of the temple built through the sacrifice of a unique people, were performed the finest acts of sacrifice and love for which the human race is capable.

Deep within its bowels there rested upon the backs of twelve bronze oxen a great bowl filled with water—a baptismal font—like unto that font in the Ancient Temple of Solomon. Within this font the living were baptized for their dead ancestors, a practice which prevailed in the early Church at the time of the Apostle Paul.[2] The doctrine of baptism and ordinance work for the dead had been developing in the Church from the time of the visitation of the Angel Moroni when he quoted from the Book of Malachi as follows:

"Behold, I will reveal unto you the Priesthood by the hand of Elijah the prophet, before the coming of the great and dreadful day of the Lord. And he shall plant in the hearts of the children the promises made to the fathers and the hearts of the children shall turn to their fathers; if it were not so, the whole world would be utterly wasted at his coming."[2a]

Knowledge concerning this doctrine was received by the Prophet from time to time. On April 3, 1836, as related in a previous chapter, Elijah appeared to Joseph Smith and Oliver Cowdery in the Kirtland Temple and conferred upon them the keys of sealing. These keys included the authority necessary for temple ordinances for both the living and the dead.

In Nauvoo the Saints had been commanded to build a temple to the Lord, for only in such temples are these ordinances acceptable to God, unless circumstances make the use of a temple impossible.

"For this ordinance belongeth to my house," says the Lord, "and cannot be acceptable to me [i.e., outside of the temple] only in the days of your poverty, wherein ye are not able to build a house unto me."[3]

While the temple was in course of construction some sealing ordinances were performed in the upper story of Joseph Smith's store in Nauvoo. Baptisms for the dead were performed during this time in the Mississippi River.

As soon as a portion of the temple was completed the Lord, by revelation, commanded the Saints to cease performing those ordinances outside the proper house.

The work performed in the temple was for the salvation of men, and consisted of performing for both the living and the dead those ordinances in the gospel which pertain to the mortal stage of existence.

For those who were already members of the Church, temple ordinances consisted in receiving "endowments," a promise of blessings based on obedience to God's laws, and the "sealing of family ties." Within the temple walls was taught the beautiful doctrine of eternal marriage given by revelation from the Lord:

"Behold, mine house is a house of order, . . . and not a house of confusion. . . . Therefore, if a man marry him a wife in the world, and he marry her not by me nor by my word, and he covenant with her so long as he is in the world, and she with him, their covenant and marriage are not of force when they are dead, and when they are out of the world; therefore, they are not bound by any law when they are out of the world;

"Therefore, when they are out of the world, they neither marry nor are given in marriage; but are appointed angels in heaven, which angels are ministering servants, to

---

[2]Read *I Corinthians* 15:29.
[2a]*History of the Church*, Vol. I, p. 12.

[3]*Doctrine and Covenants*, Sec. 124:30.

minister for those who are worthy of a far more, and an exceeding, and an eternal weight of glory.

"For these angels did not abide my law; therefore, they cannot be enlarged, but remain separately and singly, without exaltation, in their saved condition, to all eternity; and from henceforth are not gods, but are angels of God forever and ever.

"And again, verily I say unto you, if a man marry a wife, and make a covenant with her for time and for all eternity, if that covenant is not by me or by my word, which is my law, and is not sealed by the Holy Spirit of promise, through him whom I have anointed and appointed unto this power, then it is not valid neither of force when they are out of the world, because they are not joined by me, saith the Lord, neither by my word; when they are out of the world it cannot be received there, because the angels and the gods are appointed there, by whom they cannot pass; they cannot, therefore, inherit my glory, for my house is a house of order, saith the Lord God.

"And again, verily I say unto you, if a man marry a wife by my word, which is my law, and by the new and everlasting covenant, and it is sealed unto them by the Holy Spirit of promise, by him who is anointed, unto whom I have appointed this power and the keys of this priesthood; and it shall be said unto them—Ye shall come forth in the first resurrection; and if it be after the first resurrection, in the next resurrection; and shall inherit thrones, kingdoms, principalities, and powers, dominions, all heights and depths— then shall it be written in the Lamb's Book of Life that he shall commit no murder whereby to shed innocent blood, and if ye abide in my covenant, and commit no murder whereby to shed innocent blood, it shall be done unto them in all things whatsoever my servant hath put upon them, in time, and through all eternity; and shall be of full force when they are out of the world; and they shall pass by the angels, and the gods, which are set there, to their exaltation and glory in all things, as hath been sealed upon their heads, which glory shall be a fulness and a continuation of the seeds forever and ever.

"Then shall they be gods, because they have no end; therefore shall they be from everlasting to everlasting, because they continue; then shall they be above all, because all things are subject unto them. Then shall they be gods, because they have all power, and the angels are subject unto them."[4]

---
[4]*Doctrine and Covenants*, 132:8, 15-20.

Before the people were driven from Nauvoo, most of the adults had received their endowments, and the husbands had had their wives and children sealed to them by the power of God.

Justice for All Men

The second phase of the work was equally important. Millions upon millions of people had died in the world without hearing or understanding the gospel of Jesus Christ. Joseph Smith said of them:

"The Mussulman condemns the heathen, the Jew, and the Christian, and the whole world of mankind that reject his Koran, as infidels, and consigns the whole of them to perdition. The Jew believes that the whole world that rejects his faith and are not circumcised, are Gentile dogs, and will be damned. The heathen is equally as tenacious about his principles, and the Christian consigns all to perdition who cannot bow to his creed, and submit to his *ipse dixit*.[5]

"But while one portion of the human race is judging and condemning the other without mercy, the Great Parent of the universe looks upon the whole of the human family with a fatherly care and paternal regard; He views them as His offspring, and without any of those contracted feelings that influence the children of men, causes 'His sun to rise on the evil and on the good, and sendeth rain on the just and on the unjust.' He holds the reins of judgment in His hands; He is a wise Lawgiver, and will judge all men, not according to the narrow, contracted notions of men, but 'According to the deeds done in the body, whether they be good or evil,' or whether these deeds were done in England, America, Spain, Turkey, or India. He will judge them, 'Not according to what they have not, but according to what they have,' those who have lived without law, will be judged without law; and those who have a law, will be judged by that law. We need not doubt the wisdom and intelligence of the Great Jehovah; He will award judgment or mercy to all nations according to their several deserts, their means of obtaining intelligence, the laws by which they are governed, the facilities afforded them of obtaining correct information, and His inscrutable designs in

---
[5]*Ipse dixit*—dogma, dictum; an assertion to be accepted without proof.

NAUVOO TEMPLE, photograph of painting by C. C. A. Christensen.

NAUVOO TEMPLE IN FLAMES, photograph of painting by C. C. A. Christensen.

SUNSTONE, salvaged from the ruins of the Nauvoo Temple.

relation to the human family; and when the designs of God shall be made manifest, and the curtain of futurity be withdrawn, we shall all of us eventually have to confess that the Judge of all the earth has done right."[6]

Joseph taught that all men would have equal opportunity to hear and embrace the laws of God whether in this life or in the life to come.

"All who have died without a knowledge of this Gospel, who would have received it if they had been permitted to tarry, shall be heirs of the celestial kingdom of God; also, all that shall die henceforth without a knowledge of it, who would have received it with all their hearts, shall be heirs of that kingdom, for I, the Lord, will judge all men according to their works, according to the desire of their hearts."[7]

Those who in the spirit world accepted the Gospel and wished to conform to its principles and ordinances would find a way provided. People upon the earth could perform by proxy those necessary things which they themselves had failed through lack of opportunity or understanding to do. This is temple work for the dead, and consists in the performance of all those ordinances which God ordained to be performed during man's mortal existence. These ordinances are impossible of performance in a later life. God has so designed this law, and in the performance of it we perceive a glorious purpose. For nothing that man can do will so promote a bond of love between himself and his departed ancestor as the sacrifice involved in building temples and devoting his time and service therein for that practically unknown member of his family.

All the love of the human race from birth to the grave is the by-product of sacrifice—doing something for others

which those others cannot do for themselves. It is not strange then to find that God has so chosen to bind together in love all the members of his Kingdom, and he who will not accept the sacrifice of another in his behalf or he who is not willing to sacrifice on behalf of another has not attained those qualities worthy of the Kingdom.

The temple represented the beauty of Nauvoo—the purity of thought which actuated its people—the love of all mankind embraced in the Church doctrines. Those who entered it left behind all sordid desires, and the acts of sacrifice performed in it purified the soul.

Supplementary Readings

1. *History of the Church*, Period I, Volume 4, pp. 326-331. (Laying foundation stones of Nauvoo Temple on eleventh anniversary of organization of the Church. Note prominence of Nauvoo Legion. Very interesting source of material.) Marginal note.

2. *Ibid.*, Volume 4, p. 517. (Interesting note by Joseph Smith on temple labor and laborers.)

3. *Ibid.*, Volume 4, pp. 608-610. (Editorial from *Times and Seasons* on the temple.)

4. Roberts, *Comprehensive History of the Church*, Volume 2, pp. 133-136. (First endowment ceremonies introduced and discussed. See especially footnote 11, p. 135.)

5. *Ibid.*, Volume 2, pp. 66-68. (Note the spirit of joyousness on this occasion.)

6. *Ibid.*, Volume 2, pp. 471-473. (Laying the capstone of the Nauvoo Temple.)

7. *Ibid.*, Volume 3, pp. 22-23. (Nauvoo Temple destroyed by fire and wind.)

8. *Ibid.*, Volume 2, pp. 183-189; footnote 8. (Joseph Smith and Stephen A. Douglas.)

9. *Ibid.*, Volume 2, pp. 189-190. (A Methodist minister describes Nauvoo.)

10. *Ibid.*, Volume 2, p. 179. (Destruction of Nauvoo mansion.)

11. Evans, *Joseph Smith, An American Prophet*, pp. 297-301.

12. *Ibid.*, pp. 308-311. (Sacrifice in the history of religion.)

13. *Ibid.*, pp. 259-266. (Mormon doctrine

---

[6]*History of the Church*, Period I, Vol. IV, pp. 595-596.

[7]*Ibid.*, Vol. II, p. 380.

on the sanctity of woman, marriage, and the home.)

14. Smith, *Essentials of Church History*, pp. 250-251. (Revelation on Nauvoo Temple.)

15. *Ibid.*, pp. 255-257. (Building and dedication of font of Nauvoo Temple.)

16. *Ibid.*, p. 263. (Ordinance work in Nauvoo. Dedication of Nauvoo Temple.)

17. Talmage, *House of the Lord*, pp. 17-62. (Temples of earlier times.)

18. *Ibid.*, pp. 126-135. (The Nauvoo Temple. A rather complete story and study.)

CHAPTER 23

A CLASH OF SOCIAL ORDERS

Throughout history, those who have attempted to change radically the society in which they lived faced persecution, and often, violent death. The only exceptions are those who have, through force and violence, seized the control of government and, by a reign of terror, crushed all opposition. Joseph Smith was essentially a peaceful man, winning his way through love and not through fear. But his doctrines were revolutionary. The social order he wished to create was a radical departure from that to be found anywhere in America. And it was the clash of the doctrines he taught with those of established society which caused his death.

During the period of time that the Saints lived in Nauvoo, three features of the "Mormon Society," aroused opposition and finally caused expulsion.

First: The Solidarity and Exclusiveness of the Saints.

We have witnessed in the Ohio and Missouri settlements how the Saints acted as a unit economically, politically, and socially to the exclusion of others. We have noted also the opposition and jealousy it aroused. But this characteristic became the more pronounced at Nauvoo. Practically all of the Saints congregated there, and while non-Mormons were invited and some came, nevertheless the city remained almost exclusively Mormon. The broad powers of the Nauvoo Charter heightened this exclusiveness. It set the city apart, almost as a state within a state. It bestowed upon it powers which other cities

did not possess. It provoked jealousy and suspicion.

This solidarity of the Saints was especially felt at the polls. From the time when the Saints had been invited to settle at Quincy, politicians had sought favor with them. For a time they held the balance of power between the political parties of Illinois, and registered a solid vote for the candidates, promising them a greater interest in their welfare. During the period while the Mormons held the balance in power, the government lent them every favor. As opposition against the Saints grew, this solidarity became a thorn in the flesh of some candidates who hoped to gain the Mormon's vote, while retaining the vote of the non-Mormons. This midway position of the politician became more and more impossible as the opposition to the Saints increased. By 1843 the politicians of the state and nation had sided with the majority against the Saints in order to save their own political careers.

It soon became impossible for the Saints to support the candidates of either political party, a condition which meant the end of political protection for them in Illinois, and eventually the repeal of those rights and privileges which they had obtained. In fact, a repeal of the Nauvoo Charter was attempted in 1843, and the bill for repeal succeeded in passing the House of Representatives which had most readily responded to feelings within the state against the Mormons.

During the latter part of the year

1843, Joseph Smith communicated with the prospective political aspirants for the United States Presidency. Clay, Calhoun, Cass, and Van Buren were asked for their views toward the Mormon people. The answers were evasive. It was evident that the Saints could expect little help, whichever candidate was elected. Anxious to exercise their right of the ballot and especially anxious to place their cause and views before the nation, the Mormon leaders made a surprising move. In a council meeting it was decided to place their own candidates in the field. A State convention of a "Reform Party" was called and met at Nauvoo, May 17, 1844. From that convention Joseph Smith emerged a candidate for the office of President of the United States. None expected him to be elected, least of all himself. But it offered a real opportunity to lay before the nation the Mormon cause. The press would eagerly publish the views of a candidate to the office of President of the United States while spurning those same views as the expressions of a Prophet. The Twelve Apostles and other special missionaries were called to go into the Eastern States to further the cause. To these Joseph jokingly remarked, "There is enough oratory in the Church to put me in the Presidential chair the first slide."

The political views set forth by Joseph Smith and printed throughout the nation are worthy of comment. They display the vast scope of interests of the Prophet and something of his aggressive, fearless nature. We find him advocating the following:[1]

1. A central banking system owned by the government, with the mother bank at Wash-

ington, and branch banks in the several states.

2. The annexation of Texas upon her application, and the extending of an invitation to Mexico and Canada to become parts of the United States of America.

3. The immediate occupation and settlement of the Oregon region.

4. The reduction of the National Congress, the House two-thirds and the Senate one-half.

5. The freedom of the slaves through purchase by the Federal Government; the funds to be obtained by the sale of public lands.

6. A reform of the prison system, which would make the prisons workhouses and seminaries of learning.

7. The building by the government of a dam across the Mississippi River at Keokuk (just below Nauvoo) and the construction of locks to aid shipping around the rapids at that place.

8. A reform of the strict military punishment for desertion in time of war.

9. A high tariff to protect young industries.

These views created wide interest and newspapers commented upon the new candidate. The *Iowa Democrat* published the following:

A New Candidate in the Field

"We see from the *Nauvoo Neighbor* that General Joseph Smith, the great Mormon Prophet, has become a candidate for the next Presidency. We do not know whether he intends to submit his claims to the National Convention, or not, but, judging from the language of his own organ, we conclude that he considers himself a full team for all of them.

"All that we have to say on this point is, that if superior talent, genius, and intelligence, combined with virtue, integrity, and enlarged views, are any guarantee to General Smith's being elected, we think that he will be a 'full team of himself.' "[2]

A National Convention of a "Reform Party" was to be called in July, but before that time the Mormon leader was slain by his enemies.

The second phase of the solidarity and exclusiveness of the Mormon commu-

[1]Views of the Power and Policy of the Government of the United States. A pamphlet reprint in *History of the Church*, Vol. 6, p. 197.

[2]*History of the Church*, Vol. 6. p. 268.

nity is evident in their economic policy. Although the law of consecration was never attempted at Nauvoo, the spirit of that social order was very manifest. Cooperation, rather than ruthless competition, was the core of the Mormon economic life. Cries of "Communism," the first in the modern world, were frequent. The real conflict with the economic order of other communities was prospective, however, rather than real. The very success of the Mormon society drew the attention of its neighbors and aroused imaginary fears.

The land speculators were perhaps the only class directly affected. These found it impossible to operate in the region of Nauvoo. The Church purchased land in tracts and sold it to the Saints at non-profit prices. While private land deals were made, the Church land policy dominated the situation and discouraged profit-taking. To see Nauvoo develop into the largest city of the State without deriving a cent of profit for themselves enraged the class of land speculators common to that period.

Further, the rapid growth of Nauvoo had a retarding effect upon the growth of surrounding cities. Business naturally gravitated to the larger centers. This was a blow to those speculators who had invested money in the surrounding towns with a view to profiting by their expected growth.

The exclusiveness of the Saints was further manifest in their social and religious life. This was true in their recreation, marriages, and general neighborliness.

Second: The Proselyting Activities of Missionaries.

The work of converting their neighbors to the faith the Saints embraced continued during the Nauvoo period.

The missionary activity also increased abroad. The effect of the successful proselyting of the Mormons has been seen in the Missouri period of the Church. This effect followed the Saints everywhere. The active opposition of Christian ministers who were losing their congregations to the new religion was a powerful factor in every persecution.

Third: Differences in Religious Beliefs.

The religious beliefs of the Saints, as we have witnessed in the Missouri troubles, clashed with those of other people. Some new elements, however, are presented in the Illinois situation. At Nauvoo the power of the Prophet over his people became more and more evident, and belief in revelations affected every phase of community life. The Prophet leader became a power feared in the state, because of the aggressive nature of his religious teachings. Mormonism was not a passive religion. The Saints did not sit quietly by their hearthsides satisfied with their own peculiar beliefs. They had a mission to perform in carrying the message of the restored Church to their neighbors and to the whole world. So strong was the desire and the feeling of duty in this matter that, as we have witnessed, men were willing to sacrifice all their earthly possessions if necessary to further that cause. The assertion on the part of the Saints that they possessed the gospel in its fulness while all other denominations were wrong, continued as it had done from the time of the first vision, to arouse opposition.

Further, in Nauvoo the Prophet proclaimed a number of additional doctrines. These had to do with marriage and temple work and set the Saints apart still further from the rest of the world.

One of these doctrines was especially responsible for bringing persecution upon the Church. That was the doctrine of plural marriage by divine sanction. As early as 1831, Joseph Smith claimed a revelation upon the subject and spoke of it to a few close associates. It was not, however, placed in writing, practiced or generally made known at that time. In 1840, the doctrine was taught to a few leading brethren who, with the Prophet, secretly married additional wives in the following year. This secrecy could not be long kept, yet the doctrine was not openly discussed. This state of affairs gave rise to serious slander outside the Church.

Revelation on Marriage

On July 12, 1843, the Prophet caused the revelation on the "Eternity of the Marriage Covenant and Plural Marriage" to be set down in writing and read to the High Council at Nauvoo. Perhaps no doctrine of the early Church so caused dissension within and without the organization. It is well that we pause for a moment and contemplate the way in which the doctrine was received.

For years after learning of the doctrine, through revelation from God, Joseph could not bring himself to practice it or to teach others to do so. The whole Anglo-Saxon training of the Church was opposed to Plural Marriage, although it had never been forbidden by either the State or Federal Constitution. Even after settling in Nauvoo, when the Prophet says he was commanded of the Lord to put the Law of Plural Marriage into operation, he hesitated to do so. Night after night he paced the banks of the Mississippi, at times accompanied by his brother, Hyrum, wrestling with the problem. He was convinced that the practice of the doctrine would bring bitter persecution upon the Church and eventually cause him to lose his life.

No greater mistake could be made than to suppose that Joseph Smith, Brigham Young, or any of the Church leaders hailed the Doctrine of Plural Marriage with delight or introduced it through lustful desires. Brigham Young later said:

"If any man had asked me what was my choice when Joseph Smith revealed that doctrine (Plurality of Wives) provided that it would not diminish my glory, I would have said, 'Let me have but one wife. * * * I was not desirous of shrinking from any duty, nor of failing in the least to do as I was commanded, but it was the first time in my life that I had desired the grave and I could hardly get over it for a long time."[3]

John Taylor, who became the third president of the Church adds:

"I had always entertained strict ideas of virtue, and I felt as a married man that this was to me, outside of this principle, an appalling thing to do. The idea of going and asking a young lady to be married to me when I already had a wife! It was a thing calculated to stir up feelings from the innermost depths of the human soul. I had always entertained the strictest of chastity. * * * With the feeling I had entertained nothing but a knowledge of God, and the revelations of God, and the truth of them, could have induced me to embrace such a principle as this."[4]

To Heber C. Kimball and his wife, Vilate, the commandment of the Prophet that Heber take another wife was an unusually severe trial. This commandment was kept from Heber's wife for a time. Vilate noticed that Heber was greatly perplexed. She claimed that in answer to her prayer, concerning what

---

[3]Discourse at Provo, July 14, 1855. See Roberts, *Comprehensive History of the Church*, Vol. 2, p. 102.
[4]Roberts, *The Life of John Taylor*, p. 100

it was that was causing her husband such concern, she received a vision of the eternal world. Just what she witnessed is not known, but at any event, thereafter she became a staunch advocate of the doctrine of plural marriage.

If the doctrine caused such a struggle on the part of the staunchest men of the Church, is it little wonder that large numbers would not receive it. Only the secrecy surrounding its practice prevented a wholesale apostasy from the Church in 1844. When the doctrine was publicly announced in the mission fields, opposition to the Church greatly increased and mob violence was often resorted to.

The secrecy which surrounded the introduction of the practice led to gross misrepresentations and charges of adultery. This was a most important factor in embittering both Mormon and non-Mormon against the Prophet. None of the teachings of the Church clashed so directly with the social order of the day or aroused such bitter resentment.

The Philosophy of Mormonism and the Circumstances of the Time Led to the Introduction of Plural Marriage

It must be constantly borne in mind that the doctrine of marriage for time and eternity, contained in Section 132 of the *Doctrine and Covenants*, with all the blessings promised therein, does not necessarily involve plural marriage. The doctrine that marriage may be eternal when that ordinance is performed by the Priesthood of God is one of the unique contributions to religious thought, and gives definite meaning to Mormon philosophy.

The fundamental principles of the philosophy Joseph Smith introduced must be kept before us. First, the primary purpose of existence is to develop

human personality to its greatest capacity for happiness. Secondly, this development of God-like attributes can be best accomplished when individuals pass through the experience of fatherhood or motherhood and share the responsibilities of a home. This marriage relationship is obtained for life and eternity when sanctioned by God, through his Priesthood. Joseph Smith taught that those who were married for time and eternity might, after gaining their exaltation, continue to propagate spirit children, and eventually become as gods to those children.

Naturally under such a plan the greatest development for the race would be accomplished where every man and every woman, fit mentally and physically for marriage, would enter into the marriage relationship and become parents. As the sexes are approximately equal in number under normal conditions, a system of monogamous marriage, one man and one woman, would normally prevail. Such a law was given by the Lord to the Nephites,

"For there shall not any man among you have save it be one wife; and concubines he shall have none."[5]

If, when the sexes are equal, a system of plural marriage should prevail, many men physically and mentally fit would be deprived of an opportunity for marriage and the subsequent development of personality.

In the early period of The Church of Jesus Christ of Latter-day Saints an unusual condition prevailed. More women than men joined the Church. This was true of the period at Nauvoo and for a number of years after the arrival of the Saints in Utah.[6] It re-

---

[5]*Book of Mormon*, Jacob 2:27.
[6]Roberts, *Comprehensive History of the Church*, Vol. 3, p. 291. Also *Ibid.*, p. 488.

mained true so long as converts made up the mass of Church membership. The Saints were as isolated a people as if they had been on an island of the sea. Marriage outside the Church was discouraged. There were not enough men to go around. Many women must live and die singly, deprived of the opportunity for development which marriage and a home brings. The alternative was plural marriage. It was not to stop prostitution that plural marriage was introduced. It was not to satisfy the lusts of himself or his followers that Joseph Smith taught and practiced the doctrine. The men and women who entered into plural marriage were among the most moral people this world has ever known. It is true that among the early Mormons prostitution was unknown, but that would have been true with such a people if plural marriage had never been practiced.

Plural marriage was never at any time a general law for the entire Church, and was never at any time practiced by over two per cent of the male population. The President held the keys to its practice, and only those supposedly able to live the law in righteousness were permitted to enter into such relationships. That the surplus women of the Church were absorbed into family life is an undeniable fact. That some of the best people of the Church and of the world came from such plural households is equally undeniable. It is a sad fact that some few abused the law and the trust which was placed in them and gave grounds for slander and ridicule against the Church.

Despite the social reasons which may be advanced in justification of plural marriage, it must be admitted that it was directly contrary to the traditions of the people both in and out of the

Church. The very secrecy involved prevented any explanations to these people. The vaguest of rumors were multiplied and enlarged by the tongue of gossip.

The Prophet Anticipates the Crisis

The Prophet was aware that the social order he contemplated would arouse bitter opposition in Illinois. The experiences of the Church in Ohio and Missouri had made this apparent. The presence of the Mormons in a large body in any part of settled America at that time would have produced a similar story. *And this not because the Mormons were hard to get along with, or because non-Mormons were wicked, but because the teachings of the Church and the existing social orders were so directly in conflict.* It was to prepare for such an expected opposition and perhaps in a measure to avoid it, that Joseph Smith had written the unusual Nauvoo Charter and secured its passage. It was to prepare against illegal arrests that he insisted upon an independent municipal court at Nauvoo. It was to protect his people from expected mob violence that he organized and trained the famous Nauvoo Legion.

Nor did he believe that even these precautions would long protect his people. He saw ahead an inevitable crushing opposition. As early as 1842, he began to look for an unsettled section of America where his people might accomplish their "Zion" without conflict. His attention necessarily turned west and in that year he uttered a famous prophecy to a group of Saints at Montrose, Iowa. In his journal for August 6, we read:

"I prophesied that the Saints would continue to suffer much affliction and would be driven to the Rocky Mountains, many would apostatize, others would be put to death by our persecutors or lose their lives in consequence of exposure or disease, and some of you will live to go and assist in making settlements and build cities and see the Saints become a mighty people in the midst of the Rocky Mountains."[7]

From that time he anxiously gleaned such knowledge of the West as was available and began to lay plans for a westward exodus. These plans were hastened when the circle of his enemies began to tighten about him early in the year 1844. On the 20th of February of that year, he instructed the Twelve Apostles to send out a delegation to explore the region called Oregon and California (which regions so named at that time included the entire Rocky Mountain area) with a view of finding a suitable place to locate the Saints after the temple at Nauvoo should be completed. From his recorded sermons it is evident that he expected the temple to be completed by the spring of 1845.

In regard to the raising of the expedition, Joseph Smith said to the Twelve, "Let that man go that can raise $500, a good horse and mule, a double barrel gun, one barrel rifle, and the other smooth bore, a saddle and bridle, a pair of revolving pistols, bowie knife and a good sabre."[8]

Those who volunteered for this expedition were organized as the "Western Exploration Company." Preparations were begun for the proposed journey. On February 25, 1844, Joseph Smith wrote in his journal:

"I gave some important instructions and prophesied that within five years we should be out of the power of our old enemies, whether they were apostates or of the world; and told the brethren to record it, that when it comes to pass they need not say they had forgotten the saying."[9]

On March 26, Joseph Smith sent a memorial to the National Congress requesting that an ordinance be passed *"for the protection of the citizens of the United States emigrating to the adjoining territories, and for the extension of the principles of universal liberty."*[10]

The ordinance proposed by President Smith would have empowered him to raise a force of one hundred thousand volunteers, and with them safeguard and insure the settlement of the West under the principles suggested.

Congress rejected the proposed ordinances, partly because of existing treaties with England for the joint occupation of the Oregon country, and partly because of the personal nature of the ordinance and the great power it would have placed in the hands of one man.

Events in Nauvoo became so turbulent thereafter that those called for the Western Expedition were assigned other duties, and the proposed journey was postponed until after the election.

The very provisions of the Nauvoo Charter which the Prophet had desired to protect his people, namely, the independent judiciary and the militia, provoked greater opposition to the Saints.

Supplementary Readings

1. *History of the Church*, Period I, Volume 5, pp. 85-86. (Joseph Smith's brief statement and Anson Call's detailed account of the prophecy about the Saints moving to the Rocky Mountains. Text, and footnote.)

2. *Ibid.*, Volume 5, pp. 393-394; 395c-398 Note. (Joseph Smith and Stephen A. Douglas from William Clayton's account, and note by editor Roberts. Here is the story of the much discussed prophecy by Joseph regarding Douglas. This seems to be the chief source for this story.)

3. *Ibid.*, Volume 6, pp. 187-189a. (Launching movement to make Joseph Smith a candidate for President of the United States.)

[7]*History of the Church*, Period I, Vol. V, p. 234.
[8]*Ibid.*, Vol. VI, p. 224.
[9]*Ibid.*, p. 225.

[10]*Ibid.*, p. 275.

4. *Ibid.*, Volume 6, pp. 197b-209. ("Views of the Powers and Policy of the Government of the United States" by Joseph Smith.)

5. *Ibid.*, Volume 5, p. 526. ("The Prophet's Attitude on Politics." An earlier, brief, rather informal statement by Joseph.)

6. *Ibid.*, Volume 6, pp. 32-33. (Joseph Smith comments on Socialism.)

7. *Ibid.*, Volume 6, p. 46a. (Brief comment on plural marriage.)

8. Roberts, *Comprehensive History of the Church*, Volume 2, pp. 121-125. (Church attitude on politics.)

9. *Ibid.*, Volume 2, pp. 202-209. (Joseph Smith a candidate for President of the United States.)

10. *Ibid.*, Volume 2, pp. 181-183a Note 4. (Prediction of Saints moving West.)

11. *Ibid.*, Volume 2, pp. 182b-189 (Note 8), pp. 190b-192. Also pp. 210-216a. (Joseph Smith and Stephen A. Douglas. Joseph's prophecy regarding Douglas. Joseph's plan and preparations for the western movement.)

12. Evans, *Joseph Smith, An American Prophet*, pp. 191-200. (We have a Judas in our midst.)

13. *Ibid.*, pp. 167-170. ("Porter Rockwell, Joseph Smith's guardian.")

14. *Ibid.*, pp. 185-191. (Politics and the Mormon question, Joseph Smith a candidate for President, etc. An interesting account.)

15. *Ibid.*, pp. 266-275. ("Mormon Polygamy." Social theories of polygamy from Mormon leaders: "surplus theory" of Orson Pratt; "limitation" theory of Parley P. Pratt; "equalizing" theory of George Q. Cannon. Here Evans makes a skillful use of story, quotation, philosophy.)

16. *Ibid.*, pp. 241-244. (Joseph Smith and the United Order.)

17. *Ibid.*, pp. 200a-202. (Story of the Prophet giving up his purpose and plan to go West, and returning to Nauvoo and Carthage.)

18. *Doctrine and Covenants*, Section 132.

19. Whitney, Orson F., *Life of Heber C. Kimball*, pp. 331-339. (Interesting experiences involving Joseph Smith, Heber C. Kimball, and Vilate Kimball, his wife, and their daughter, Helen Kimball, gathering around the Prophet's revelation and teaching on plural marriage.)

20. Smith, Joseph Fielding, *Essentials in Church History*, pp. 481-486. Plural marriage.)

21. *Ibid.*, pp. 493-496. (The Woodruff manifesto regarding plural marriage.)

22. *Ibid.*, pp. 296-302. (Attempts of false brethren to overthrow the Prophet Joseph.)

23. *Ibid.*, pp. 283-295. (Joseph Smith and the Presidency of the United States.)

24. Snow, Eliza R., *Biography and Family Record of Lorenzo Snow*, pp. 69, 76, 77. (Joseph Smith teaches plural marriage to Lorenzo Snow, Joseph plans to move West. Candidate for President of the United States.)

NAUVOO EXPOSITOR.

THE TRUTH, THE WHOLE TRUTH, AND NOTHING BUT THE TRUTH.

NAUVOO, ILLINOIS, FRIDAY, JUNE 7, 1844.

Page one of the *Nauvoo Expositor*.

CHAPTER 24

THE PRICE OF GREATNESS

The Net is Closed About the Prophet

The destruction of the *Nauvoo Expositor* June 10, 1844, proved to be the spark which ignited all the smoldering fires of opposition into one great flame. It offered the occasion for which the apostates from the Church were waiting, a legal excuse to get the Prophet and other leaders into their hands. The cry that the "freedom of the press" was being violated, united the factions seeking the overthrow of the Saints as perhaps nothing else would have done.

Protest meetings were held throughout Hancock and neighboring counties. Bitter enemies of the Prophet stirred these meetings into threats of open violence. Newspapers displayed the matter in bold type. At the headquarters of the anti-Mormons the Warsaw *Signal*, after publishing the apostate Foster's account of the destruction of the *Expositor* press, added:

> "We have only to state that this is sufficient! War and extermination is inevitable! *Citizens arise, One and All!!!* Can you stand by, and suffer such *Infernal Devils* to rob men of their property and rights, without avenging them? We have no time to comment; every man will make his own. Let it be made with powder and ball!!!!"[1]

On the same day this article appeared, Constable David Bettisworth came from Carthage to Nauvoo and arrested for "riot" Joseph Smith, Samuel Bennett, John Taylor, William W. Phelps, Hyrum Smith, John P. Greene, Stephen Perry, Dimick B. Huntington, Jonathan Holmes, Jesse P. Harmon, John Lytle, and Levi Richards. The

brethren submitted to arrest but demanded trial before the justice of the peace in Nauvoo. The Constable objected. Upon writs of habeas corpus they went before the Municipal Court of Nauvoo and were discharged. Harsh as the action in destroying the press was, it appeared, nevertheless, perfectly legal. On the advice of a circuit judge a second trial was held before Judge Daniel H. Wells, a non-Mormon. A second discharge followed. These trials failed to appease the opposing faction who demanded that Joseph and the brethren be tried at Carthage. Joseph did not feel that their lives would be safe there and refused. Mobs were increasing in the neighboring towns. The Mayor sent to Governor Ford a statement of the situation and awaited his advice. None came. On the 16th, Joseph Smith issued a proclamation to clarify the situation, and a warning against mobs approaching the city.

The situation only grew worse. Carthage and Warsaw began to resemble military camps. Five pieces of cannon were forwarded to the latter point. Resolutions were passed in both cities to "Massacre the whole Mormon Community."

Martial Law in Nauvoo

To protect his people the Prophet called out the entire force of the Nauvoo Legion and proclaimed martial law in Nauvoo, June 18. In a last address to his soldiers and people he said:

> "I call God and angels to witness that I have unsheathed my sword with a firm and unalterable determination, that this people

[1] *Warsaw Signal*, Issue of June 12, 1844.

shall have their legal rights and be protected from mob violence, or my blood shall be spilt upon the ground like water, and my body be consigned to the silent tomb. While I live I will never tamely submit to the dominion of cursed mobocracy."[2]

The militia of the Saints at Ramus and at Montrose came into Nauvoo and joined forces with the defender of the city. On June 20, letters were forwarded to the ten of the apostles who were on missions, bidding them return speedily to Nauvoo. Theodore Turley was instructed to commence the manufacture of artillery.

On June 21, Governor Ford arrived at Carthage and requested by letter, of the Nauvoo City Council, that representative men be sent to present their case before him. Dr. Willard Richards, Dr. John M. Bernhisel and John Taylor were elected by the City council for that mission.

Richards was later detained by Joseph Smith for other duties and on the following day Lucien Woodworth was sent in his place. Woodworth carried a letter to Governor Ford inviting him to come to Nauvoo and make a complete investigation.

It appears that Governor Ford was strongly influenced by the feeling which prevailed at Carthage. In his reply letter, late in the day, he charged the Nauvoo City Council with an abuse of power, ordered the Legion disbanded and martial law discontinued. He requested that Joseph Smith submit to arrest to be tried at Carthage. His letter ended with a promise and a threat:

"If it should become necessary to have witnesses on the trials, I will see that such persons are duly summoned, and I will also guarantee the safety of all such persons as may be thus brought to this place from Nauvoo, either for trial or as witnesses for the accused.

"If the individuals accused cannot be found when required by the Constable it will be considered by me as an equivalent to a refusal to be arrested, and the militia will be ordered accordingly."[3]

In answer, Joseph dispatched a second letter, a brilliant defense of the action of the City Council, to the Governor. He added:

"We would not hesitate to stand another trial according to your Excellency's wish, were it not that we are confident our lives would be in danger. We dare not come. Writs, we are assured, are issued against us in various parts of the country. For what? To drag us from place to place, from court to court, across the creeks and prairies, till some bloodthirsty villain could find his opportunity to shoot us. We dare not come, though your Excellency promises protection. * * * You have expressed fears that you could not control the mob, in which case we are left at the mercy of the merciless."[4]

A meeting of the leading brethren who were in Nauvoo was held in the evening of June 22nd at the Mansion House. After reading the letter from Governor Ford to the Council the Prophet remarked, "There is no mercy—no mercy here." Hyrum added, "No; just as sure as we fall into their hands we are dead men." A little later the Prophet's countenance lighted up and he said, "The way is open. It is clear to my mind what to do. All they want is Hyrum and myself; then tell everybody to go about their business, and not to collect in groups, but to scatter about. There is no doubt they will come here and search for us — let them search; they will not harm you in person or property and not even a hair of your head. We will cross the river tonight and go away to the west."[5]

The personal journal of the Prophet

---

[2]History of the Church, Period I, Vol. 6, p. 499.

[3]Letter: Governor Ford to Mayor and City Council of Nauvoo. June 22, 1844. See History of the Church, Period I, Vol. 6, pp. 533-537.

[4]History of the Church, Period I, Vol. VI, pp. 538-541.

[5]Ibid., pp. 545-546.

closes with these words uttered on that occasion:

"I told Stephen Markham that if I and Hyrum were ever taken again we would be massacred, or I was not a prophet of God. I want Hyrum to live to avenge my blood, but he is determined not to leave me."[6]

That night Joseph and Hyrum, with Willard Richards, secretly crossed the Mississippi River into Iowa. The sheriff who had been waiting in Nauvoo to arrest the Prophet and members of the City Council, on the morning of June 23rd, without attempting any arrests, returned to Carthage and reported that the accused had fled.

Joseph and Hyrum Make a Decision

About 1 P.M. on June 23, 1844, three men were busily engaged in the house of William Jordan in Montrose, Iowa. They were packing supplies for a journey on horseback to the Great Basin, in the Rocky Mountains. That journey meant freedom for them and eventually for their people. They were awaiting the arrival of Orrin Porter Rockwell with horses for the journey.

Rockwell came, but without horses. Instead, he was accompanied by Reynolds Cahoon with a letter from the Prophet's wife, Emma. His people in Nauvoo were calling him a coward. Those who should have been his friends were denouncing his running away. Even Emma, in her letter, pleaded for him to return and submit to trial. Cahoon likened him to the shepherd who left his flock to the wolves.

Stung by the taunt of cowardice, Joseph exclaimed: If my life is of no value to my friends, it is of none to myself." That night he crossed over the river into Nauvoo, and sent word to the Governor that he would submit to ar-

rest. Joseph was confident that arrest would mean his death.

Safety had lain within his grasp. The open West had beckoned to him. The Spirit had whispered to him the wisdom of flight. But safety without the faith and devotion of his beloved people was an empty shell.

For some time Joseph had felt that a continuation of his teachings would result in his death. Death was no longer an improbability to him. As early as April 9, 1842, he had declared:

"Some have supposed that Brother Joseph could not die; but this is a mistake; it is true that there have been times when I have had the promise of my life to accomplish such and such things; but, having now accomplished those things, I have not at present any lease on my life; I am as liable to die as other men."[7]

The Prophet requested of Governor Ford by letter that a posse conduct him into Carthage. Due to influence of apostates with the Governor the request was denied. Instead, Joseph was ordered to appear in Carthage by 10 o'clock the next morning without a posse. If General Smith did not come, "Nauvoo would be destroyed and all the men, women and children that were in it."[8]

Early on the morning of the 24th, President Smith and the members of the City Council, with a few friends, started from Nauvoo. They were bound for Carthage to give themselves up for trial. It was a sorrowful procession. The Prophet's gaze rested long upon the uncompleted temple and upon his beloved people. Out of a heart full to bursting he exclaimed: "This is the loveliest place, and the best people under the heavens. Little do they know the trials that await them."[9]

[6]Ibid., p. 546.

[7]Funeral Sermon, April 9, 1842
[8]Ibid., p. 552.
[9]Ibid., p. 554.

The Arrest

About four miles west of Carthage, they were met by a company of sixty mounted militia under Captain Dunn. It was during the approach of these troops that the Prophet exclaimed:

"I am going like a lamb to the slaughter; but I am calm as a summer's morning; I have a conscience void of offense toward God and toward all men. If they take my life I shall die an innocent man, and my blood shall cry out from the ground for vengeance, and it shall be said of me 'He was murdered in cold blood.' "[10]

Captain Dunn presented an order from the Governor for the State arms in the possession of the Nauvoo Legion, and asked President Smith, in his capacity as Lieutenant General of the Legion, to countersign it. This was done. Captain Dunn appeared fearful of entering Nauvoo with his men and induced the Prophet to return with him and see that the Governor's order was complied with.

Reluctantly the people of Nauvoo surrendered their arms—their weapons of defense against mob violence.

As evening approached, the company of militia, with Joseph and his party, again started for Carthage. It was midnight when they arrived, but the public square swarmed with militia men known as the "Carthage Greys," who, with cursing and yelling, seemed ready to finish the Prophet then and there. The intervention of Governor Ford from his hotel window quieted them, and the company was permitted to retire to the Hamilton House for the night.

On the morning of the 25th, Joseph and his brethren voluntarily surrendered themselves to Constable Bettisworth. At 8:00 A.M. Joseph and Hyrum were again arrested on the charge of "treason" against the State of Illinois. The alleged treason consisted in declaring martial law in Nauvoo.

Later in the day Joseph and Hyrum were paraded before the troops by Governor Ford, who seemed anxious to appease the militia men. When introduced as "Generals" to the "Carthage Greys" a near riot ensued.

Shortly afterward, in the Hamilton House, militia officers complained that, although General Smith's appearance indicated a peaceful character, "We cannot see what is in his heart, neither can we tell what are your intentions." To which the Prophet replied:

"Very true, gentlemen, you cannot see what is in my heart, and you are, therefore, unable to judge me or my intentions; but I can see what is in your hearts, and I will tell you what I see. I can see that you thirst for blood, and nothing but my blood will satisfy you. It is not for crime of any description that I and my brethren are thus continually persecuted, and harassed by our enemies, but there are other motives, and some of them I have expressed, so far as relates to myself; and inasmuch as you and the people thirst for blood, I prophesy in the name of the Lord that you shall witness scenes of blood and sorrow to your entire satisfaction. Your souls shall be perfectly satiated with blood, and many of you who are now present shall have an opportunity to face the cannon's mouth from sources you think not of, and those people that desire this great evil upon me and my brethren shall be filled with sorrow because of the scenes of desolation and distress that await them. They shall seek for peace and shall not be able to find it. Gentlemen, you will find what I have told you to be true."[11]

Illegal Imprisonment

During the day the members of the Nauvoo City Council were brought before Robert F. Smith, a justice of the

[10]Ibid., p. 555. See also Doctrine and Covenants, Section 135:4.

[11]History of the Church, Vol. VI, p. 566.

peace, and Captain of the Carthage Greys. Here they were bound over on bail to appear at the next term of the Circuit Court for Hancock County, on the charge of "riot destroying the printing press of the *Nauvoo Exposi- tor*."[11a] The total bail was $7500, an excessive amount. To the surprise of their accusers it was soon raised and the brethren departed for Nauvoo that night, but Joseph and Hyrum, while seeking an interview with Governor Ford, were arrested again by Constable Bettisworth. Despite their protests they were thrust into prison on a false mit- timus,[12] which declared that they had appeared on a charge of "treason" be- fore Justice Robert F. Smith and had been committed to prison to await trial. As no such appearance on that charge had been made the imprisonment was illegal. When the Governor was in- formed of the affair by John Taylor, he refused to interfere.

That night Joseph and Hyrum, to- gether with Willard Richards, John Taylor, John P. Greene, Stephen Mark- ham, Dan Jones, John S. Fullmer, Dr. Southwick, and Lorenzo D. Wasson, who accompanied them, slept on the prison floor of the debtor's cell.

The following morning Joseph Smith requested again an interview with the Governor, who came to the jail for that purpose. A long conversation ensued. The Governor promised them protec- tion and that, if he marched his troops into Nauvoo the following day, Joseph and Hyrum should probably be taken along to insure their safety. Nothing was promised in regard to their false imprisonment.

The day wore on, with the prisoners writing letters to their friends, discus- sing plans with Attorney Reid, and hearing reports of public utterances against their lives.

In the afternoon Justice of the Peace Robert F. Smith sent for the prisoners, but the jailer refused to give them up as contrary to his sworn duty. This caused considerable excitement. A mob gathered and a company of Carthage Greys was sent to bring the prisoners before the justice.

Seeing the multitude and its threat- ening aspect, Joseph walked boldly out of the prison into the hollow square of Carthage Greys, politely locked arms with the worst mobocrat he could see and started for the Court House. The brethren followed, surrounded by a guard, and expecting to be massacred at any moment.

As witnesses could not be immediate- ly procured, the court postponed the case until the following noon and later to the 29th.

The prisoners had been given the privilege of occupying the upper story of the jail which offered greater com- fort and contained one bed and extra mattresses. The evening was passed with pleasant conversation. Long after the rest had gone to sleep, Joseph con- versed with John Fullmer and Dan Jones, who were sleeping on either side of him. "I would like to see my family again," he said, "I would to God that I could preach to the Saints in Nauvoo once more."

Later he was heard to say to Dan Jones, "Are you afraid to die?" To which Jones replied, "Has that time come, think you? Engaged in such a cause, I do not think that death would have many terrors." And then the

[11a]*Ibid.*, p. 567.
[12] A person arrested for a crime must be taken before a Justice of the Peace, or other Court Of- ficer. If the Justice believes there is reasonable cause for trial the prisoner is committed to jail or released on bail until a trial may be had.

Prophet said, "You will yet see Wales, and fulfill the mission appointed you before you die."[13] So passed the last earthly night of the Mormon Prophet.

The Fateful Day

The part played by Governor Ford on that fateful day of June 27th was an ignoble one. A man of high position, he was nevertheless weak and vacillating, anxious to please all parties and factions. Whether by design or ignorance, his actions on that day laid the stage for the perpetration of the tragedy. Early on the morning of the 27th he marched the militia toward Nauvoo his promise to Joseph disregarded. Fifty men of the "Carthage Greys" were left to guard the prisoners at the jail. As these were the avowed enemies of the Prophet, it caused his friends alarm, and Cyrus H. Wheelock overtook and appealed to the Governor. Ford replied, "I was never in such a dilemma in my life; but your friends shall be protected and have a fair trial by law; in this pledge I am not alone; I have obtained the pledge of the whole of the army to sustain me."[14]

Governor Ford had planned a display of military force in Nauvoo to awe the inhabitants and had ordered the militia from Warsaw to join his forces at Golden Point, to disband and return to their homes. Some of them did so. About one hundred fifty, however, disappointed in their expectation to sack Nauvoo, were aroused by radical officers to a reckless spirit of vengeance. These started for Carthage, vowing death to Joseph and Hyrum. Some seventy-five, disguised by blackened faces, arrived in time to join in the terrible deed of that day.

Meanwhile the prisoners at Carthage jail had used the morning in writing messages and preparing for the ensuing trial. John S. Fullmer was sent to Nauvoo to procure witnesses. Dan Jones departed with a letter to O. H. Browning, an attorney, engaging him as counsel. Jones had a narrow escape from mobs which threatened his life. Dr. Richards was somewhat ill that morning and Stephen Markham left the jail to procure some medicine. He was not allowed to return, but the Carthage Greys put him on his horse and forced him out of town at the point of the bayonet. This left but the four men in the jail, Joseph and Hyrum, Dr. Willard Richards and John Taylor.

One of the touching incidents of this mid-afternoon was the singing of the following song by John Taylor:

A Poor Wayfaring Man of Grief

A poor wayfaring man of grief
Had often crossed me on my way,
Who sued so humbly for relief
That I could never answer, Nay.

I had not power to ask his name,
Whither he went or whence he came;
Yet there was something in his eye
That won my love, I knew not why.

Once, when my scanty meal was spread,
He entered—not a word he spake!
Just perishing for want of bread;
I gave him all; he blessed; he brake,

And ate, but gave me part again;
Mine was an angel's portion then,
For while I fed with eager haste,
The crust was manna to my taste.

I spied him where a fountain burst,
Clear from the rock—his strength was
    gone,
The heedless water mock'd his thirst,
He heard it, saw it hurrying on.

I ran and raised the suff'rer up;
Thrice from the stream he drain'd my cup,
Dipp'd, and returned it running o'er;
I drank and never thirsted more.

[13]*History of the Church*, Vol. VI, p. 601.
[14]*Ibid.*, p. 607.

'Twas night, the floods were out, it blew
A winter hurricane aloof;
I heard his voice, abroad, and flew
To bid him welcome to my roof.

I warmed, I clothed, I cheered my guest,
I laid him on my couch to rest;
Then made the earth my bed, and seem'd
In Eden's garden while I dreamed.

Stripp'd, wounded, beaten nigh to death,
I found him by the highway side;
I rous'd his pulse brought back his breath,
Revived his spirit, and supplied

Wine, oil, refreshment—he was heal'd;
I had myself a wound conceal'd;
But from that hour forgot the smart
And peace bound up my broken heart.

In pris'n I saw him next—condemned
To meet a traitor's doom at morn;
The tide of lying tongues I stemmed,
And honored him 'mid shame and scorn.

My friendship's utmost zeal to try,
He asked, if I for him would die;
The flesh was weak, my blood ran chill,
But the free spirit cried, "I will!"

Then in a moment to my view,
The stranger started from disguise;
The tokens in his hands I knew,
The Savior stood before mine eyes.

He spake—and my poor name he named—
"Of me thou hast not been asham'd;
These deeds shall thy memorial be;
Fear not thou didst them unto me."[15]

[15]*History of the Church*, Vol. 6, pp. 614-615.

Carthage Jail, where the Prophet Joseph Smith was martyred with his brother Hyrum.
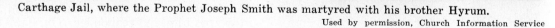
Used by permission, Church Information Service

At 4 p.m. the guard at the jail was changed. Only eight men were left to protect the prisoners from violence. The jailer, Stigall, noticing this, suggested to the prisoners that they would be safer in the cell on the lower floor. They promised to go there after supper. Joseph said to Dr. Richards, "If we go into the cell will you go with us?" The doctor answered, "Brother Joseph, you did not ask me to cross the river with you—you did not ask me to come to Carthage—you did not ask me to come to jail with you—and do you think I would forsake you now? But I will tell you what I will do; if you are condemned to be hung for treason, I will be hung in your stead, and you shall go free."[16]

About that time the guard asked for money to buy wine and Joseph supplied it. The events thereafter happened with startling rapidity. A cry of "Surrender" and a discharge of muskets was heard. About one hundred men rushed the jail. The guards made a half-hearted show of resistance. Some

Hyrum Smith, faithful brother to the Prophet Joseph Smith.

[16]Dr. Richards' description of the tragedy. See Whitney, *The Mormon Prophet's Tragedy*, pp. 79-83.

of the mob rushed into the jail and commenced firing up the stairway, while others fired through the open window. A graphic description by Willard Richards of what followed, was later printed in the *Times and Seasons*, entitled:

TWO MINUTES IN JAIL[17]

"A shower of musket balls were thrown up the stairway against the door of the prison in the second story, followed by many rapid footsteps.

"While Generals Joseph and Hyrum Smith, Mr. Taylor and myself, who were in the front chamber, closed the door of our room against the entry at the head of the stairs, we placed ourselves against it, there being no lock on the door, and no catch that was usable.

"The door is a common panel, and as soon as we heard the feet at the stairs' head, a ball was sent through the door, which passed between us, and showed that our enemies were desperadoes, and we must change our position.

"General Joseph Smith, Mr. Taylor and myself, sprang back to the front part of the room, and General Hyrum Smith retreated two-thirds across the chamber, in front of and facing the door.

"A ball was sent through the door, which hit Hyrum on the side of the nose, when he fell backwards, extended at length without moving his feet.

"From the holes in his vest (the day was warm, and none had their coats on but myself), pantaloons, drawers and shirt, it appears evident that a ball must have been thrown from without, through the window, which entered his back on the right side, and passing through lodged against his watch, which was in his right vest pocket, completely pulverizing the crystal and face, tearing off the hands, and mashing the whole body of the watch. At the same time the ball from the door entered his nose.

"As he struck the floor he exclaimed emphatically, 'I'm a dead man.' Joseph looked towards him and responded, 'Oh, dear Brother Hyrum!' and opened the door two or three inches with his left hand, discharged one barrel of a six shooter (pistol) at random in the entry, from whence a ball grazed Hyrum's breast and entering his throat passed

[17]Whitney, *The Mormon Prophet's Tragedy*, pp. 79-83.

into his head, while the other muskets were aimed at him, and some balls hit him.

"Joseph continued snapping his revolver round the casing of the door into the space as before, three barrels of which missed fire; while Mr. Taylor, with a walking stick stood by his side and knocked down the bayonets and muskets which were constantly discharging through the doorway, while I stood by him ready to lend any assistance, with another stick, but could not come within striking distance without g o i n g directly before the muzzles of the guns.

"When the revolver failed, we had no more firearms, and expected an immediate rush of the mob, and the doorway full of muskets half way in the room, and not hope but instant death from within.

John Taylor's watch, struck by an assassin's bullet.

"Mr. Taylor rushed into the window, which is some fifteen or twenty feet from the ground. When his body was nearly on a balance, a ball from the door within entered his leg, and a ball from without struck his watch, a patent lever, in his vest pocket, near the left breast, and smashed it into 'pie,' leaving the hands standing at 5 o'clock, 21 minutes and 26 seconds; the force of which ball threw him back on the floor, and he rolled under the bed which stood by his side, where he lay motionless, the mob continuing to fire upon him, cutting away a piece of flesh from his left hip as large as a man's hand, and were hindered only by my knocking down muzzles with a stick, while they continued to reach their guns into the room, probably left-handed, and aimed their discharges so far around as almost to reach us in the corner of the room, to where we retreated and dodged, and then I recommenced the attack with my stick.

"Joseph attempted as the last resort, to leap the same window from whence Mr. Taylor fell, when two balls pierced him from the door, and one entered the right breast from without, and he fell outward, exclaiming, 'O Lord, my God!' As his feet went out of the window, my head went in, the balls whistling all around. He fell on his left side, a dead man.

"At this instant the cry was raised, 'He's leaped the window!' and the mob on the stairs and in the entry ran out.

"I withdrew from the window, thinking it of no use to leap out on a hundred bayonets, then around General Smith's body.

"Not satisfied with this I again reached my head out of the window, and watched some seconds to see if there were any signs of life, regardless of my own, determined to see the end of him I loved. Being fully satisfied that he was dead, with a hundred men near the body and more coming around the corner of the jail, and expecting a return to our room, I rushed towards the prison door, at the end of the stairs, and through the entry from whence the firing had proceeded, to learn if the doors into the prison were open.

"When near the entry, Mr. Taylor cried out, 'Take me.' I pressed my way until I found all the doors unbarred; returning instantly, I caught Mr. Taylor under my arm, and rushed by the stairs into the dungeon, or inner prison, stretched him on the floor and covered him with a bed in such a manner as not likely to be perceived, expecting an immediate return of the mob.

"I said to Mr. Taylor, 'This is a hard case to lay you on the floor, but if your wounds are not fatal, I want you to live to tell the story.' I expected to be shot the next moment, and stood before the door awaiting the onset."

A loud cry from without, "The Mormons are coming!" saved the lives of Dr. Richards and John Taylor. Who uttered the cry is unknown. It was entirely without foundation. Had it been the truth, however, it could have had no more effective results. The mobbers fled in all directions. The militia from Warsaw returned home with haste.

"The town was instantly put in such attitude of defense as its limited means permitted. The women and children were ferried across the river to a village on the Missouri shore. The men kept guard night and day in the hazel thickets around the town. Everybody expected sudden and exemplary vengeance from the Mormons."[18]

No vengeance came. The whole city of Nauvoo, on hearing of the tragedy, were like sheep without a shepherd. They were stunned by the blow that had fallen. Their beloved Prophet and Patriarch were dead.

Supplementary Readings

1. *History of the Church*, Period I, Volume 6, pp. 432-631. The fourteen chapters in these pages are truly a rich storehouse of information, story, letter, oratory, invective, etc., revealing the spirit and heart of the men and times involved. Note especially the personal and official correspondence between Joseph and his friends, and their enemies.

2. Roberts, *Comprehensive History of the Church*, pp. 210-216. ("Western movement of the Church projected by Joseph Smith.")

[18]John Hay, Article in *Atlantic Monthly*, December, 1869.

3. *Ibid.*, pp. 217-220a. ("Peace efforts of Saints in Illinois.")

4. *Ibid.*, p. 220, ("A Wolf Hunt" proposed. See also note 16.)

5. *Ibid.*, pp. 221-233. (False brethren turn against the Prophet Joseph. The newspaper of these "false brethren," the Nauvoo Expositor, destroyed. This is the incident that started the fires of hatred that consumed the Prophet Joseph and his brother, Hyrum.

6. *Ibid.*, pp. 234-273. (An interesting comprehensive study of the "Storm of Mobocracy" led to the martyrdom of Joseph and Hyrum.)

7. *Ibid.*, pp. 274-287. (An excellent condensed account of the martyrdom of Joseph and Hyrum. See note at end of chapter.)

8. *Ibid.*, pp. 288-308. ("Aftermath of the Carthage Tragedy." Note Governor Ford's letter, and footnotes.)

9. *Ibid.*, pp. 309-343. (Trial and acquittal of the murderers of Joseph and Hyrum Smith.)

10. *Ibid.*, pp. 332-334. (Legends and errors about the martyrdom of Joseph and Hyrum corrected.)

11. *Doctrine and Covenants*, Section 135. (L.D.S. Church's official account of the martyrdom of Joseph Smith and his brother Hyrum.)

12. Evans, *Joseph Smith, An American Prophet*, pp. 191-200; 200b-207. ("And after that the dark.")

13. Cannon, George Q., *Life of Joseph Smith, the Prophet*, p. 53, 1st paragraph. (Joseph Smith's statement of perils through which he must pass.)

14. Smith, Joseph Fielding, *Essentials in Church History*, pp. 296-302. (Enemies without, and false friends within.)

15. Evans, John Henry, *Heart of Mormonism*, pp. 238-246. (Forces that caused the martyrdom of Joseph and Hyrum.)

CHAPTER 25

THE GREATNESS
OF THE MAN JOSEPH

The Judgment of Time

At the height of his power at Nauvoo Joseph Smith was visited by Josiah Quincy, later mayor of Boston. This learned gentleman was so impressed by his contact with the Mormon Prophet that he wrote an account of that visit and later published it in his book, *Figures of the Past.* In a chapter entitled "Joseph Smith," we read:

"It is by no means improbable that some future textbook, for the use of generations yet unborn, will contain a question something like this: What historical American of the nineteenth century has exerted the most powerful influence upon the destinies of his countrymen? And it is by no means impossible that the answer to that interrogatory may be thus written: *Joseph Smith the Mormon Prophet.* And the reply, absurd as it doubtless seems to most men now living, may be an obvious commonplace to their descendants. History deals in surprises and paradoxes quite as startling as this. The man who established a religion in this age of free debate, who was and is today accepted by hundreds of thousands as a direct emissary from the Most High—such a rare human being is not to be disposed of by pelting his memory with unsavory epithets."[1]

The influence of Joseph Smith is indeed being felt in wider and wider circles as the years progress. Today, more than one hundred years after his death, over three million people revere his memory and testify that he was a Prophet of the living God. These followers represent nearly all the civilized nations of the earth. Perhaps no man, aside from Jesus of Nazareth, can claim disciples from so many lands.

The missionary spirit, so manifest in the day when Joseph lived, has shown no signs of abating. At the end of a century the missionary movement is more wide-spread and better organized than ever before. Wherever the gospel is preached, the name of Joseph Smith is known. It divides men into two camps, those who revere his memory and those who ridicule and scorn his claims.

The critic may not thrust lightly aside one who wielded such an influence during his life as did the Prophet Joseph Smith. The historian cannot forever brush lightly past the account of a man whose influence grows stronger with the years. The religionist cannot long cast the shadow of ridicule upon a system of religion which has produced such remarkable results.

Today, as in the day Joseph Smith lived, thousands and tens of thousands would die rather than relinquish the religion he established. They would leave home and friends for the faith they have acquired. Indeed, many are leaving home and friends in all those parts of the world which continue to deny to the followers of this man the right to worship the living God as his teachings proclaimed.

When we search for the secret to this startling development, this unusual devotion, this vital Latter-day Saint religion, the search leads us into interesting roads and acquaints us with revealing truths.

First of all, there was the man himself. The story of his life is one of the greatest American stories of accom-

[1]George Q. Cannon, *Life of Joseph Smith,* p. 338.

plishment yet written. Born in the backwoods of Vermont, of humble parentage, and lacking the opportunities for scholastic training, this man carved his name across the centuries.

Those who visited the Prophet at Nauvoo, and these comprised learned men from every walk of life, came away with the impression of having met a charming and intelligent individual. They were amazed at the power he possessed over his people and the unbounded confidence which these same people placed in him.

A Non-Mormon Speaks

The Masonic Grand Master, in the State of Illinois, wrote of Joseph to the *Advocate*:

"Having recently had occasion to visit the city of Nauvoo, I cannot permit the opportunity to pass without expressing the agreeable disappointment that awaited me there. I had supposed from what I had previously heard, that I would witness an impoverished, ignorant and bigoted population, completely priestridden and tyrannized over by Joseph Smith, the great Prophet of these people.

"On the contrary, to my surprise, I saw a people apparently happy, prosperous and intelligent. Every man appeared to be employed in some business or occupation. I saw no idleness, no intemperance, no noise, no riot; all appeared to be contented, with no desire to trouble themselves with anything except their own affairs. With the religion of this people I have nothing to do; if they can be satisfied with the doctrines of their new revelation, they have a right to do so. The Constitution of the country guarantees to them the right of worshiping God according to the dictates of their own conscience, and if they can be so easily satisfied, why should we, who differ with them, complain?

"During my stay of three days I became well acquainted with their principal men, and more particularly with their Prophet. I found them hospitable, polite, well-informed and liberal. With Joseph Smith, the hospitality of whose house I kindly received, I was well pleased. Of course, on the subject we widely differed, but he appeared to be quite as willing to permit me to enjoy my right of opinion as I think we all ought to let the Mormons enjoy theirs. But instead of the ignorant and tyrannical upstart, judge my surprise at finding him a sensible, intelligent companion and gentlemanly man. In frequent conversations with him he gave me every information that I desired and appeared to be only pleased at being able to do so. He appears to be much respected by all the people about him, and has their entire confidence. He is a fine-looking man, about thirty-six years of age, and has an interesting family."[2]

A writer for the *New York Herald* had visited the Prophet, and in 1842 that paper said:

"Joseph Smith is undoubtedly one of the greatest characters of the age. He indicates as much talent, originality and moral courage as Mahomet, Odin or any of the great spirits that have hitherto produced the revolutions of past ages. In the present infidel, irreligious, ideal, geological, animal-magnetic age of the world, some such singular prophet as Joseph Smith is required to preserve the principle of faith, and to plant some new germs of civilization that may come to maturity in a thousand years. While modern philosophy, which believes in nothing but what you can touch, is overspreading the Atlantic States, Joseph Smith is creating a spiritual system, combined also with morals and industry, that may change the destiny of the race. * * * We certainly want some such prophet to start up, take a big hold of the public mind—and stop the torrent of materialism that is hurrying the world into infidelity, licentiousness and crime."[3]

The Estimate of His Friends

It is from those who knew him best—those who ate, and walked and slept with him—that we get the truest appraisal of the man. These were not always enthusiasts in religion. They comprised a broad cross-section of individuals. John Taylor, the refined and educated English minister who became the third president of the Church, wrote in his journal:

---

[2]George Q. Cannon, *Life of Joseph Smith*, pp. 345-346.

[3]George Q. Cannon, *Life of Joseph Smith*, p. 337.

"In the midst of difficulties he was always the first in motion; in critical positions his counsel was always sought. As our Prophet he approached our God and obtained for us His will."[4]

Parley P. Pratt, the great missionary and writer, says:

"He possessed a noble boldness and independence of character; his manner was easy and familiar; his rebuke terrible as the lion; his benevolence unbound as the ocean; his intelligence universal, and his language abounding in original eloquence studied—not smoothed and softened by education and refined by art; but flowing forth in its own native simplicity, and profusely abounding in variety of subject and manner. He interested and edified, while, at the same time, he amused and entertained his audience; and none listened to him that were ever weary of his discourse. I have even known him to retain a congregation of willing and anxious listeners for many hours together, in the midst of cold or sunshine, rain or wind, while they were laughing at one moment and weeping the next. Even his most bitter enemies were generally overcome, if he could once get their ears."[5]

Brigham Young, the successor to the Prophet, and one who knew him intimately, said late in life after his own great accomplishments had been widely heralded:

"Who can say aught against Joseph Smith? I was as well acquainted with him as any man. I do not believe that his father and mother knew him any better than I did. I do not think that a man lives upon the earth that knew him any better than I did; and I am bold to say that, Jesus Christ excepted, no better man ever lived or does live upon this earth. I am his witness. He was persecuted for the same reason that any other righteous person has been or is persecuted at the present day."[6]

Among those who admired the Prophet and would have given their lives for him were two of the roughest men, in externals, that have found membership within the Church. Both had hearts of gold and the Prophet's tolerance of their outward roughness is characteristic of his ability to look beyond mere externals to the human heart.

Lyman Wight was attracted to the Church by the magnetism of the Prophet's character. He was a rough frontiersman, a deadly shot, whose reckless courage was well known along the border. While the Prophet lived, Wight was as plastic clay in his hands, as gentle as a lamb. After the death of his "beloved Joseph," no one could govern him. He was tolerated in the Church only because of his former devotion to the Prophet. His independent missionary ventures and his garbled teachings finally led, however, to excommunication from the Church.

Orrin Porter Rockwell, whose devotion has been mentioned, was a similar character. In 1841, he was accused, along with Joseph Smith, of attempting to assassinate ex-Governor Boggs of Missouri. For a time he escaped arrest by going east. Thinking that the falsity of the charges had been found and that the matter had been dropped, he started to return to Nauvoo. He was mistaken. At St. Louis, Missouri, he was arrested, taken to Independence, and thrown into jail. He was kept there for nearly a year and foully treated. He was placed in irons. Once he escaped, was caught, and was nearly lynched.

The reason for keeping Rockwell so long without a trial was the thought that he might be used as a decoy to get the Prophet across the Missouri line.

"Port," said Sheriff Reynolds, "Joe Smith has unlimited confidence in you. He'll come to the line, if you ask him to. Do that for us, and we'll let you go; and you can name your pile."

Rockwell answered, "I'll see you all damned first—and then I won't."

[4]Roberts, *Life of John Taylor*, p. 141.
[5]*Autobiography of Parley P. Pratt*, pp. 45-46.
[6]*Journal of Discourses*, Vol. 9, p. 332.

The Growth Which Produced a Prophet

At this period, so long removed from the Prophet's life, it is easy to forget the process by which he became a Prophet of God—the thorny path he trod to the heights. Nothing so clearly points the way by which the boy Joseph became a Prophet as his own teaching.

"There is a law, irrevocably decreed in heaven before the foundations of this world, upon which all blessings are predicated—

And when we obtain any blessing from God, it is by obedience to that law upon which it is predicated."[7]

Orrin Porter Rockwell, known for his devotion to the Prophet Joseph Smith.
Used by permission, Utah State Historical Society

The first vision came through obedience to a divine law and so did all the

[7]*Doctrine and Covenants*, Sec. 130:20-21.

knowledge of God which Joseph Smith acquired. The founder of Nauvoo was an immeasurably greater man than the Joseph Smith who organized the Church ten years earlier. The finest quality of the man was his determination to grow. He had that rare genius which recognized faults in himself and the moral courage to repent of them. Such expressions as: "I often felt condemned for my weakness and imperfections,"[8] appear frequently in his personal journal and give a rare insight into the inner soul of the man.

In the personal revelations received of the Lord, he did not hesitate to write down those parts condemning his own actions. We find such expressions as:

"And, behold, how oft you have transgressed the commandments and laws of God, and have gone on in the persuasions of men."[9]

And again:

"Thou art not excusable in thy transgressions; nevertheless, go thy way and sin no more."[10]

His energy seemed drawn from an inexhaustible fountain. When one considers the trials and persecutions which pursued the Prophet at every turn and the multitudinous tasks which faced him in molding the Church, his accomplishments become the more amazing. During the fourteen years which elapsed from the founding of the Church until his martyrdom, he scarcely had a moment of peace. During that time he was driven from three states, imprisoned by one and martyred in another. He was the victim of mob violence on more than one occasion. Thirty-eight times he was arrested on false charges by his enemies and hailed into courts to stand trial.[11] The charges varied from

[8]*History of the Church*, Period I, Vol. II, p. 10.
[9]*Doctrine and Covenants*, Section 3:6.
[10]*Ibid.*, Section 24:2.
[11]*Journal of Discourses*, Vol. I, pp. 40-41.

theft to treason. The courts, as well as the accusers, were ordinarily unfriendly toward him, but in each case carried to trial, he was acquitted.

Besides the persecution of those unaffiliated with his religious organization he was confronted with apostasy and dissatisfaction within the ranks. His courage in attacking all forms of unrighteousness and striking off the membership rolls—regardless of where the ax might fall—those who failed to conform to a high standard, preserved the Church from corruption, but multiplied tenfold his own personal problems and responsibilities.

In those fourteen years, he fashioned an organization which has stood the test of time and stands today unequalled for effectiveness. He formulated religious philosophy which has met the needs of a changing world. So complete was his work, and so far ahead of his people was he, that at the end of a century but little has been added either to the organization or the doctrines of the Church.

During those same years he advanced the cause of education, delved into the eccentricities of law and government, laid out cities, organized a military body, served as Mayor of a thriving city and interested himself in manufacturing and industry.

Perhaps nowhere is the progress of Joseph Smith so noticeable as in the literary quality of his writings. The earliest preserved fragments of his own handwriting show mistakes in spelling and grammar. Those written in his later life show rare literary form and beauty of expression. Joseph Smith was not a perfect man—far from it, but he was never contented with his imperfections. He recognized those imperfections and sought to overcome them.

His collected literary works fill many volumes and his uncollected sermons and editorials would fill dozens more. His finest contribution was in translation of the *Book of Mormon*, a major task in itself. But, in addition, there is the *Book of Moses*, the *Book of Abraham*, and the *Doctrine and Covenants*. His personal journal is now printed with annotations in six large volumes and is the finest historical document in the Church. Without the advantages of a formal education he gained a fair knowledge of five languages, became a master of the contents of the Bible, became conversant with general history and developed into an interesting conversationalist upon any common subject.

Supplementary Readings

1. Roberts, *Comprehensive History of the Church*, Vol. II, pp. 344-348a. (Varied estimates classified. The voice of enemies. It is interesting, and well, perhaps, to know what those who hated our Prophet said of him.)

2. *Ibid.*, pp. 348-351. ("The Voice of the Mystified." Here we hear the voice of some who honestly wanted to be fair, but who did not know Joseph Smith well enough to really understand him.)

3. *Ibid.*, pp. 351b-355a. ("The Testimonies of friends and interested parties." John Taylor, Brigham Young, and Parley P. Pratt are quoted.)

4. *Ibid.*, pp. 355-358. ("The Prophet's Self-Revealment to the Intelligent Disciple." "A view that would in itself be truer and even more just to the Prophet than unreasoning adulation.")

5. *Ibid.*, pp. 358-359. ("The Limitations of a Prophet." Only God is without limitations. To know truly Joseph Smith we must keep him human; so we call attention to this and the next reference.)

6. *Ibid.*, pp. 358-360a. ("The Limitations of a Prophet," and "The Tendency to Autocracy in the character and life of Joseph Smith.")

7. *Ibid.*, pp. 362-380. ("The Prophet's Work." Here, we may have Brigham H. Roberts' estimate and witness of the work and achievement of the Prophet Joseph Smith. Section headings, throughout the

chapter, enables the student to select reading in line with his immediate interests.)

8. *Ibid*, pp. 360-361. ("The Summary." A Testimony, and a challenge.)

9. *Ibid*, pp. 381-412. ("The New Dispensation, a System of Philosophy." Here Roberts gives us a condensed statement of the Religious Philosophy revealed to, and through the Prophet Joseph Smith, as he (Roberts) knows and understands it.)

10. Evans, *Joseph Smith, an American Prophet*, pp. 3-5. (Impressions Joseph made on strangers: Josiah Quincy, Stephen A. Douglas, a writer for the *New York Times*.)

11. *Ibid*, pp. 5-7. (Impressions of his friends: Amasa Lyman, John Taylor, Brigham Young.)

12. *Ibid*, pp. 7-10. ("The Prophet's Magnetic Power.")

13. *Ibid*, pp. 10-12. (Joseph compared with Jonathan Edwards, and Mrs. Eddy.)

14. *Ibid*, pp. 12-15. ("Joseph Smith Still an Enigma," "There have been many attempts to explain the puzzling individuality of the Mormon leader.")

15. *Ibid*, pp. 15-19. ("The Key to the Riddle.")

16. *Ibid*, pp. 319-371. Especially 353. (A Panorama of the Prophet's Life. Some of the headings of this chapter called "The Spiritual Expert," "Egoism of the Prophet," "Joseph Smith in Need of an Explanation," "A Glance at the Visions.")

17. *Ibid*, pp. 211-215. (Dynamic Power of the Prophet's Religious Philosophy.)

18. *Ibid*, pp. 372-399; 176-184. (Joseph Smith's Personality and Power.)

19. *Ibid*, pp. 321-326. (Joseph the Seer.)

20. *Ibid*, pp. 280-288. (A new definition of immortality.)

21. *Ibid*, pp. 415-416; 421-433. (Joseph Smith takes his place among the great characters of history.)

22. Cowley, M. F., *Wilford Woodruff*, pp. 38-39. (Woodruff's first meeting with the Prophet Joseph. "Joseph was not an old, sanctified Prophet, but a human being.")

23. Cannon, George Q., *Life of Joseph Smith*, pp. XXV-XXVII. (Characteristics of Joseph Smith as man, and as seer.)

24. Evans, *Heart of Mormonism*, pp. 276-312. (An exciting career. What Joseph Smith looked like, p. 282. The magnet and steel filing, p. 286. Characteristics of the Prophet, p. 219. Prophet and Seer, p. 296. The Martyrs, p. 302. The Greatness of Joseph Smith, p. 307.)

25. Evans, *Joseph Smith, An American Prophet*, pp. 225-231. ("Dignity and worth of human personality.")

PREVIEW OF UNIT II

We are about to follow the Saints during the second great period of Church History. This period begins with the consternation in Nauvoo over the death of the Prophet and closes with the end of conflict between Mormons and non-Mormons in Utah. In these chapters we will witness the restored gospel at work in the hearts of men and women. We will thrill at the faith which accompanies the exodus of a whole people west to the Rocky Mountains. We will make a march of 2,000 miles with the Mormon Battalion to the Pacific Ocean. In these pages we will delve into camp life on the plains—see its joys and its tragedies—and we will thrill at the faith which prompted mighty sacrifices. Above all, we will come to realize that part played by faith in conquering the Great American Desert, and the powerful spirit of gathering which is filling these desert lands with converts from all the earth.

CHAPTER 26

THE CHURCH OF JOSEPH SMITH
OR THE CHURCH OF GOD?

A People Mourn

On the morning of June 28, 1844, Nauvoo lay as in a pall. The sound of industry had wholly ceased. The unfinished temple stood silent as the great sphinx. A hush, like death, enveloped the entire city. People spoke in whispers on the street corners and saluted one another in grave tones.

All anger toward their persecutors and feelings of malice toward those who had laid their Prophet and his brother Hyrum low, were forgotten in the one, overpowering emotion, an overwhelming grief at the loss of their leaders. It was as if a permanent cloud had obscured the face of the sun.

In the Nauvoo Mansion, home of the Prophet, there was sorrow indeed. Emma Smith had followed her husband with a rare faithfulness. She had maintained her courage while he lived, in the face of bitter slander, persecution and forced migrations. But now that sustaining strength had ebbed out with his lifeblood. Lucy Mack Smith, the mother, that worthy character, was at last crushed by the sudden loss of her two sons. Her husband and three sons lost to her in three short years! To these women there seemed nothing left for which to strive, nothing further for which to sacrifice. It is not then to be wondered at, that when the Church was driven again, they remained behind near the graves of their dead and the places of their last association together.

The feeling of depression was not confined to Nauvoo. The apostles in the mission field sensed it even before the news of the tragedy reached them. Parley P. Pratt writes:

"A day or two previous to this circumstance I had been constrained by the Spirit to start prematurely for home, without knowing why nor wherefore; and on the same afternoon I was passing on a canal boat near Utica, New York, on my way to Nauvoo. My brother, William Pratt, being then on a mission in the same state (New York) happened, providentially, to take passage on the same boat. As we conversed together on the deck, a strange and solemn awe came over me, as if the powers of hell were let loose. I was so overwhelmed with sorrow I could hardly speak; and after pacing the deck for some time in silence, I turned to my brother, William, and exclaimed, 'Brother William, this is a dark hour; the powers of darkness seem to triumph, and the spirit of murder is abroad in the land; and it controls the hearts of the American people, and a vast majority of them sanction the killing of the innocent. My brother, let us keep silence and not open our mouths. If you have any pamphlets or books on the fulness of the gospel lock them up; show them not, neither open your mouth to the people; let us observe an entire and solemn silence, for this is a dark day, and the hour of triumph for the powers of darkness. * * * This was June 27, 1844, in the afternoon, and as near as I can judge, it was the same hour that the Carthage mob were shedding the blood of Joseph and Hyrum Smith, and John Taylor, nearly one thousand miles distant."[1]

The Burial

About noon on June 28th, the bodies of Joseph and Hyrum were brought into the city of Nauvoo. Sorrowfully the people gathered behind the procession and filled the streets around the Nauvoo mansion. Several of their brethren

---

[1]*Autobiography of Parley P. Pratt*, p. 330.

Stone marker over the graves of Joseph Smith, his wife Emma, and his brother Hyrum in Nauvoo, Illinois.   Used by permission, J. M. Heslop

addressed them and urged them to keep the peace and leave vengeance unto God.

On the 29th thousands filed past the bodies as they lay in state in the mansion. At 5 o'clock in the evening the doors were closed. The coffins were removed from the outer boxes. These outer boxes were then filled with bags of sand, taken to the cemetery, and buried with the usual ceremony. At midnight, the bodies were taken by trusted friends and buried in the basement of the Nauvoo House, then in course of construction. This precaution was taken through fear that the enemies of the Prophet and Hyrum would return to mutilate their remains.

In the fall of 1844, at the request of Emma Smith, the bodies were removed secretly to a spot near the Nauvoo Mansion overlooking the Mississippi River.

The visitor to Nauvoo may view at that place a beautiful and fitting monument recently erected by the descendants of these men.

A few days later John Taylor, seriously and painfully wounded, was brought into Nauvoo on a sleigh. The sight of his suffering and the graphic nature of his story aroused a new surge of anger at their persecutors. A cry of revenge against Carthage was heard for a brief time. However, anger soon gave way to wisdom and tolerance. The forbearance of the Saints during those trying times is a remarkable tribute to them as a people.

The Priesthood Holds the Keys to the Succession

Despite the tenseness of the times the members of the Church had not anticipated their Prophet's death. Time after time, a kind Providence had permitted him to escape his enemies. They had felt that somehow he would be spared again. The blow which had fallen left them like sheep without a shepherd. What would happen next? Would the solidarity of the Mormon people be forever broken? Non-Mormon observers sincerely thought so. The enemies of the Church expected it. The newspapers in Illinois proclaimed such a result. Had the Church been built solely around a great personality that result would certainly have followed. But the succeeding events point to a deeper foundation. The Church was not the Church of Joseph. It was the Church of Jesus Christ. The heart of the Church was not a great personality— it was the restored priesthood of the Lord and Master.

All the powers and rights of this Priesthood had been conferred by Joseph upon the Twelve, and this included the power to ordain a new President of the Church. But it took some time for the people to realize this. Sidney Rigdon, previous to the death of the Prophet, became dissatisfied with the Church and went to Pittsburgh, Pennsylvania, to live. Joseph Smith had recommended at the last conference he attended that the people reject Rigdon as first counselor in the Presidency. But the people had sustained him. Upon hearing of the death of the Prophet, Sidney Rigdon returned to Nauvoo, arriving August 1st. He had a plan for the government of the Church. No one, in his opinion, could be a Prophet and take Joseph's place by mere appointment. The people must wait for God to call a Prophet. A guardian was needed to act as the head until such a time. Being first councilor in the Presidency he should

naturally be that guardian. So he taught the people before the arrival of the Twelve. Many of the people, including the Prophet's wife and mother, believed, and became staunch supporters of Rigdon's plan.

The apostles who were in Nauvoo, Willard Richards, John Taylor, and Parley P. Pratt, counseled the people to wait until the return of the remainder of the Twelve.

Sidney Rigdon, on his own initiative, called a meeting for August 8th to decide the matter of a guardian. By the time for the meeting a number of the Twelve, sufficient for a quorum, had arrived. The meeting was carried out, the gathering taking place in the Grove or Bowery. Sidney Rigdon talked at great length, during the morning, on the matter of a guardian, but did not put it to a vote. When he sat down, Brigham Young arose and announced a meeting called by the Council of the Twelve for two o'clock in the afternoon.

When that time arrived a large congregation had gathered, the Priesthood being seated by quorums. Brigham Young, President of the Quorum of the Twelve, was the first speaker. He spoke with great power—reminded the people that the Church was the Church of Jesus Christ and would continue until that Personage should return to earth to reign in righteousness. All the powers of the Priesthood were vested in the Twelve. Upon the death of the Church's president, the quorum of the First Presidency was dissolved and the governing power of the Church rested upon the Twelve until a new Presidency should be nominated by them through the spirit of revelation and sustained by the vote of the people.

Some of those present testify that while he spoke it appeared to them that the Prophet Joseph was standing before them and that the Prophet's voice was speaking to them. The great majority were convinced and voted to sustain the Twelve as the leaders of the Church.

On this occasion Brigham Young said to the congregation:

"All that want to draw away a party from the Church after them, let them do it if they can, but they will not prosper."

The Dissatisfied Break from the Main Body of the Church

The unity of opinion among the Twelve Apostles concerning the organization of Church government, convinced the great mass of the Saints that the organization had been so well laid that it was self-perpetuating. The Church was bigger than any man or set of men.

A few, however, remained unconvinced. These grouped themselves around some leader and drew away from the Church. After the meeting of August 8th, Sidney Rigdon outwardly seemed to agree with the Twelve; he was, however, holding meetings with disgruntled members of the Church, telling them that he was called by revelation of God to lead them. Of the powers he claimed we read:

"Telling them * * * he was the proper person to lead the Church—to be its 'guardian' for to that position he had been called of God, and held the keys of authority higher than any conferred upon the Prophet Joseph —'the keys of David,' which, according to his representations, gave him power to open and no man could shut; to shut and no man could open; and the power to organize armies for the destruction of the Gentiles. In fact his fervid imagination pictured himself as a great military chieftain, and by his prowess all the enemies of God were to be subdued. He secretly ordained men to be prophets, priests, and kings to the Gentiles.

He also chose and appointed military officers to take command of the armies that were to be raised ere long to fight the battles of the great God."[2]

Sidney Rigdon, when called to account by the Quorum of the Twelve, confessed to holding the meetings and ordaining the officers. He refused, however, to correct his views or to be subordinated to the Twelve. At a subsequent hearing, which he refused to attend, he was excommunicated from the Church. Much disappointed, he returned to Pittsburgh. There he organized a church on the pattern laid down by the Prophet and gathered a few followers. The movement did not prosper and soon dissolved. Sidney Rigdon died in obscurity in Allegheny County, New York, in 1876.

The Strangites

James J. Strang, a convert living at Voree, Walworth County, Wisconsin, also became dissatisfied with the new leadership of the Church and drew away. He laid claim to a letter from Joseph Smith under date of June 18, 1844, appointing him as the Prophet's successor. Several hundred of the discontented believed his claim, among them William Smith, the only surviving brother of the Prophet, John C. Bennett, and John E. Page, one of the Council of the Twelve.

Strang established himself with his followers on Beaver Island, one of the Manitou group in upper Lake Michigan. He organized a county which he represented in the Michigan State Legislature and finally had himself crowned as king of Beaver Island. In 1856, he was killed during an uprising on the Mani-

---

[2]Roberts, *Comprehensive History of the Church*, Vol. 2, p. 426.

tou Island. His followers, generally nicknamed Strangites, disbanded.[3]

William Smith

Another to lead a group away from the Church was William Smith, brother of the martyrs. At the time of the Prophet's death he was an apostle. He was in the East, however, at that time and did not return to Nauvoo until the spring of 1845. He was then ordained as Presiding Patriarch. Soon he was claiming authority over all of the Priesthood in the Church. At the conference of October, 1845, the congregation refused to sustain him either as an apostle or as the Presiding Patriarch. Later in that month he was excommunicated.

He associated himself for a time with the movement started by Strang. The spring of 1850 found him starting another movement. In that year he called a conference to assemble at Covington, Kentucky, where he effected an organization, with himself as "President pro tem." of the Church, with Lyman Wight and Aaron Hook as counselors. His claim was that the office of President was a right of lineage in Joseph Smith's family. Hence Joseph Smith's eldest son should become President. As this son, Joseph, was then too young to take that office it naturally followed, he said, that he, the only surviving brother of the Prophet and the natural guardian of the "seed of Joseph," should act as President for the time being. The organization scarcely endured for a year. Later William Smith became nominally connected with what is known as the

"Reorganized Church of Jesus Christ of Latter Day Saints," but took little active part. He died at Osterdock, Iowa, 1893.

Lyman Wight

Lyman Wight was not among those who claimed the Presidency of the Church, but after the death of the Prophet none could rule him. In the latter part of August, 1844, he led a group of about 150 Saints into the sparsely settled territory of Wisconsin and settled them on government lands, about 450 miles above Nauvoo. For some years he had advocated the movement of the Church to Texas. In 1845, he led his small colony there. Upon his death in 1858 the *Galveston News* said of him:

"Mr. Wight first came to Texas in November, 1845, and has been with his colony on our extreme frontier ever since, moving still farther west as settlements formed around him, thus always being the pioneer of advancing civilization, affording protection against the Indians. He has been the first to settle five new counties, and prepare the way for others."[4]

During his life his small company of Saints lived a form of the United Order. On his death the order broke up and the Saints scattered. Lyman Wight was excommunicated from the Church at Salt Lake City in 1848.

James C. Brewster, while sixteen or seventeen years of age, claimed certain visions in connection with the books of Esdras.[4a] He was then a member of the Church at Kirtland. In 1840 he was severely rebuked by the Prophet at Nauvoo for advancing the claim that he had learned from the books of Esdras that the gathering place, or "place of refuge," was to be in the valleys of the Colorado and Gila rivers and on the

---

[3] (Note) *Bickertonites and Baneemyites.* From the factions mentioned came a number of subfactions. From the Rigdonite group came the Bickertonites. From the Strangites came the Baneemyites. Both movements died out in a few years. See Roberts, *Comprehensive History of the Church,* Vol. 2, pp. 436-438.

[4] See *Succession in the Presidency of the Church,* Second Edition, p. 122, et. seq.

[4a] (Note) The Books of Esdras are found in the Apocrypha. See McConkie, *Mormon Doctrine,* pp. 41-42; also *Doctrine and Covenants,* Section 91.

shores of the Gulf of California. Four years after the Prophet's death, in 1848, Hazen Aldrich revived Brewster's views and organized a church at Kirtland, Ohio, with himself as president and James E. Brewster and Jackson Goodale as counselors. A quorum of apostles with seventies, priests, teachers and deacons, constituted the remainder of the organization. A small colony moved West and established "Colonia" on the Rio Grande. By 1852, the entire movement was broken up by internal disputes on doctrine. Brewster subsequently became a preacher on Spiritualism in California.

Hedrickites

Granville Hedrick joined the Church in Illinois, prior to the death of the Prophet. After the Prophet's death he followed several factions, but became dissatisfied with all of them. In 1863-64, he made independent claims of being the true successor to Joseph Smith and effected an organization called the "Church of Christ."

He laid claim to revelations in which Joseph Smith was termed a fallen Prophet. "The Truth Teller" was the official publication. Jackson County, Missouri, was to be the place of gathering. All the followers of Hedrick were to gather to Jackson County prior to "judgments," which were to begin in 1871, and destroy the nation in 1878.

John E. Page, once an apostle under Joseph Smith, joined this movement. The "Hedrickites" have remained in Jackson County until the present time (1972). They purchased plots of ground in Independence, and still own part of the plot designated by Joseph Smith as the temple site. In recent years revelations have been claimed by the "Hedrickites," commanding them to construct a temple. The foundations were started, but the movement has been temporarily abandoned for lack of funds. The members have never constituted more than a few hundred souls.

The Whitmerites

In 1847, three years after the death of the Prophet, William E. M'Lellin, formerly one of the Twelve Apostles, and Martin Harris, one of the three witnesses of the *Book of Mormon*, started a reorganizing movement at Kirtland, Ohio. M'Lellin visited David Whitmer at Richmond, Missouri, and induced him to join the movement together with the Whitmers in that vicinity.

David Whitmer was sustained as president of the church, which was designated as "The Church of Christ." Whitmer's claim was based on an alleged commandment of the Lord to Joseph Smith in 1834 to ordain David Whitmer as his successor. In 1838, at a meeting of the High Council at Far West, Joseph Smith referred to this commandment and said that it was conditioned upon his own falling from the Church. At this time Joseph approved of the action of the High Council in excommunicating David Whitmer from the Church.[5]

On the refusal of David Whitmer to remove to Kirtland a quarrel ensued between the two branches and the organization broke up.

A second attempt to organize the Whitmerites occurred two years before the death of David Whitmer, which occurred January 25, 1888. Nothing came

[5]See *Far West Council Record*, March 15, 1838. Also *History of the Church*, Period I, Vol. 3, pp. 31-32, footnote.

of the movement. In a few years' time the organization was completely dropped.

It must be remembered that the members of one faction which broke from the Church often became members of succeeding factions, and that the total number of members breaking away from the Church was but a mere handful considering the total membership. The failure of these factions and subfactions emphasize the prophecy of Brigham Young.

"All that want to draw away a party from the Church after them let them do it if they can, but they will not prosper."

"The Reorganized Church"

Sixteen years after the death of Joseph Smith one more faction arose. On April 6, 1860, at Amboy, Illinois, Joseph Smith III, son of the first Prophet of the Church, was accepted as the head of the "Reorganized Church of Jesus Christ of Latter-day Saints." The congregation on that occasion was less than one hundred fifty and the total membership of the organization about three hundred.

This organization was the culmination of a movement which began during the years from 1850-1853. In those years several meetings were held in Wisconsin, Illinois and Michigan by a group of men who believed that the principle of "lineal descent" applied to the presidency of the Church. William Smith, brother of the Prophet, was a leader in that movement. In April, 1853, an organization was effected under a revelation alleged to have been received by H. H. Deam.

In 1856 the "Reorganized Church" urged Joseph Smith III, the predicted head, to come and take his place. The messengers sent to Mr. Smith's home near Nauvoo, were not cordially received, and their insistent demands that he comply with the wishes of the church were rejected.

In the winter of 1859, Joseph Smith, having failed in various occupations, resolved to communicate with the "Reorganized Church." The result was an invitation to attend the April conference at Amboy, Illinois. The conference voted to accept him as president as stated above.

The church was then presented to Mr. Smith, who accepted it. Four men proceeded to ordain him to the office of "President of the high priesthood and president of the church." These four were William Marks, former president of the Nauvoo Stake, until his excommunication in 1844; Zenos H. Gurley, Samuel Powers, and W. W. Blair, the latter three "apostles" in the "Reorganized Church."

This organization drew to it the discontented remnants of the early movements away from the Church. Headquarters of the church was made at Plano, Illinois, and later moved to Independence, Missouri, where the majority of the members reside today. The church has shown little growth or continuous vitality. Missionaries were sent to Utah in 1863, and again in 1869, and succeeded in attracting a number of discontented Church members. Upon The Church of Jesus Christ of Latter-day Saints generally, the effect was unimportant.

Supplementary Readings

1. Roberts, *Comprehensive History of the Church*, pp. 413-428. (Succession in the Presidency of the Church. A brief statement of temporary confusion of the people immediately after the Prophet's death, and of the struggle for the leadership of the Church between Sidney Rigdon and President Brigham Young and the Quorum of the Twelve.)

2. *Ibid.*, pp. 415-417. (Brigham Young's reply to Rigdon.)

3. Talmage, *The Vitality of Mormonism*, pp. 15-18. (The vital character of the Church of Jesus Christ of Latter-day Saints.)

4. Smith, *Essentials in Church History*, pp. 318-322. (The problem of choosing a new leader for the Church.)

5. Evans, *Heart of Mormonism*, pp. 242-246. (The crash of hopes.)

6. *Ibid.*, pp. 314-319. (Choose a new leader.)

———

"For a full discussion of the "Reorganite" movement see:

Roberts, *Succession in the Presidency of the Church*, second edition, 1900, subdivision 6, pp. 50-87; and subdivision 7, pp. 88-96.

Joseph Fielding Smith, *Origin of the Reorganized Church, and the Question of Succession*.

CHAPTER 27

NEW LEADERS AND
OLD PROBLEMS

A New Leader

June 18, 1844, President Joseph Smith said in an address to the Nauvoo Legion:

"It is thought by some that our enemies would be satisfied with my destruction; but I tell you that as soon as they have shed my blood, they will thirst for the blood of every man in whose heart dwells a single spark of the spirit of the fulness of the gospel. The opposition of these men is moved by the spirit of the adversary of all righteousness. It is not only to destroy me, but every man and woman who dares believe the doctrines that God hath inspired me to teach in this generation."[1]

This prophecy had a speedy fulfillment. The death of Joseph and Hyrum created a brief breathing spell for the Saints in Illinois. As soon as it became apparent that under new leadership the Saints were as united as ever and that nothing had really been changed, opposition began anew.

Three lines of activity carried forward by the Saints under the leadership of the Twelve made declaration to the world that Mormonism was but in its infancy. First—the temple was pushed to completion. Due to the activity of Brigham Young and the Twelve this work moved forward with great rapidity. When the Prophet and his brother were killed, only one story of the temple had been completed. Eleven months later, May 24, 1845, the capstone was laid. These were months of feverish activity and great sacrifice. Wilford Woodruff under date of February 8, 1857, writes of those times:

---
[1]*History of the Church*, Period I, Vol. VI, p. 498.

"President Young preached in the tabernacle, followed by H. C. Kimball. In the afternoon at a prayer circle the President spoke of a blank in the *History of the Church*, and related the following: 'A few months after the martyrdom of Joseph the Prophet, in the autumn and winter of 1844, we did much hard labor on the Nauvoo Temple, during which time it was difficult to get bread and other provisions for the workmen to eat. I counseled the committee who had charge of the temple funds to deal out all the flour they had, and God would give them more; and they did so; and it was but a short time before Brother T o r o n t o came and brought me twenty-five hundred dollars in gold. The bishop and the committee met, and I met with them; and they said that the law was to lay the gold at the Apostle's feet. Yes, I said, and I will lay it at the bishop's feet; so I opened the mouth of the bag and took hold at the bottom end, and gave it a jerk toward the bishop, and strewed gold across the room and said, now go and buy flour for the workmen on the temple and do not distrust the Lord any more; for we will have what we need!'"

The capstone was laid at six o'clock in the morning because the Twelve were in semi-seclusion to avoid arrest on fraudulent charges brought against them by their enemies to harass them. Of the occasion John Taylor writes:

"On the morning of Saturday, May 24, 1845, we repaired to the temple with great secrecy, for the purpose of laying the (cap) stone. There were but few that knew about it, (but) the band playing upon the walls, and the people hearing it hurried up. About six o'clock a.m. the brethren being assembled, we proceeded to lay the stone; at a quarter past six the stone was laid; after which Brother Brigham prayed, his voice being heard distinctly by the congregation below; and the congregation shouted, 'Hosanna, Hosanna to God and the Lamb, Amen and Amen!' Brother Kay sang a song, composed for the occasion by W. W. Phelps, called 'The Capstone.' Although there were several officers watching for us to take us, yet we escaped without their knowledge; when the singing commenced we left unnoticed, and they had not an opportunity of seeing us."[2]

A second movement was the increased missionary activity under the direction of the Twelve. The states of the Union and eastern Canada were divided into ecclesiastical divisions and a mission president placed over each. The number of missionaries was greatly increased. Wilford Woodruff was sent to Great Britain to lend his leadership to the Church there. A number of missionaries were sent into Wales. In the next three years several thousand converts were baptized in Wales alone. Despite the heavy migration of Church members from England to Nauvoo, the Saints in that land in January, 1846, numbered 12,247. Every month witnessed one or more shiploads of English Saints leaving the river steamers at Nauvoo. The Eastern States Mission, under the leadership of Parley P. Pratt, took on renewed vigor.

Third: The Saints displayed increased vigor in industrial growth. Capitalists were invited to Nauvoo and encouraged to establish factories. Elder John Taylor took a prominent part in industrial affairs. On his recommendation and under his supervision a "trades union" was formed. This organization had for its object the establishment of industries which would produce as far as possible everything which the Saints at Nauvoo might need, and a surplus for exportation.

As it was unlikely that a charter could be obtained for that purpose from an unfriendly state legislature, John Taylor devised a novel plan:

First, twelve men to be appointed forming a *Living Constitution,* with a president, sec-

retary, etc., to take the lead in all affairs of the association.

Second, separate trustees to organize themselves and have their own laws, but to be subject to the living Constitution.[3]

These movements were successful and gave such an impetus to industry that a new era of prosperity dawned upon Nauvoo. Factories sprang into existence and absorbed the population which was rapidly increasing through immigration. The material welfare of the Saints seemed assured.

Zion Must Flee

The great energy displayed by the Church and especially its activity along cooperative commercial lines fed the fires of growing opposition. Mob violence was threatened as early as the forepart of July, 1844, and a movement was begun to have the charter granted to Nauvoo repealed. Unless the charter could be repealed the Saints with the powerful Nauvoo Legion might prove too powerful for the factions aiming to overthrow them.

On July 22, 1844, Governor Ford addressed a letter to W. W. Phelps, acting editor of the *Times and Seasons,* which set forth the state of the public mind, and that of the Governor, concerning the Saints. Among other things he said:

"The naked truth, then, is, that most well informed persons condemn in the most unqualified manner the mode in which the Smiths were put to death, but nine out of every ten of such accompany the expression of their disapprobation by a manifestation of their pleasure that they are dead. * * *

"The unfortunate victims of this assassination were generally and thoroughly hated throughout the country, and it is not reasonable to suppose that their death has produced any reaction in the public mind resulting in active sympathy; if you think so, you are mistaken.

---

[2]Taylor's *Journal,* Ms. Entry of May 25, 1845.

[3]Roberts, *Life of John Taylor,* p. 159.

"Most that is said on the subject is merely from the teeth out; and your people may depend on the fact, that public feeling is now, at this time, as thoroughly against them as it has ever been.

"I mention this, not for the purpose of insulting your feelings, but to show you clearly how careful your people ought to be in future to avoid all causes of quarrel and excitement, and what little reliance could be placed on any militia force which I could send in your favor.

"I ought, perhaps, to qualify what I have said, by remarking that but few persons from the surrounding counties could now be procured to join a mob force against you, without further cause of excitement to be ministered by some misguided imprudence of your people. But what I mean to say, and to say truely, is, that in the present temper of the public mind I am positively certain that I cannot raise a militia force in the state who would be willing to fight on your side, or to hazard their lives to protect you from an attack of your enemies."

The attempt on the part of State officials to bring the murderers of Joseph Smith and Hyrum to justice was a farce. Nine known members of the mob were arrested. A trial was held and the nine acquitted. Nothing further was ever done.

A Wolf Hunt

In the month of September an armed movement to drive out the Saints was inaugurated. The object of the military movement was kept in the background. The historian, Gregg, refers to it as the "Grand Military Encampment."[4] Governor Ford in his *History of Illinois*, says of it:

"In the fall of 1844, the anti-Mormon leaders sent printed invitation to all the militia captains in Hancock and to the captains of militia in all the neighboring counties in Illinois, Iowa, and Missouri, to be present with their companies at a great wolf hunt in Hancock; and it was privately announced that the wolves to be hunted were the Mormons

and Jack-Mormons.[5] Preparations were made for assembling several thousand men, with provisions for six days; and the anti-Mormon newspapers, in aid of the movement, commenced anew the most awful accounts of thefts and robberies, and meditated outrages by the Mormons."[6]

To prevent this "Wolf Hunt" Governor Ford issued a proclamation calling for 2,500 volunteers. Only 500 responded. With these he marched into Hancock County and the "Malcontents" abandoned their enterprise.

Nauvoo Charter Repealed

The anti-Mormons then concentrated on an effort to repeal the Nauvoo Charter. In January, 1845, the repeal measure passed the Legislature, and Nauvoo was left without civil authority. Only the Church organization and the respect of the members for the law prevented an outbreak of confusion and crime. Of this act on the part of the State Legislature, Josiah Lamborn, the state's attorney, wrote to Brigham Young as follows:

"I have always considered that your enemies have been prompted by political and religious prejudices and by a desire for plunder and blood, more than the common good. By the repeal of your charter, and by refusing all amendments and modifications, our legislature has given a kind of sanction to the barbarous manner in which you have been treated. Your two representatives exerted themselves to the extent of their ability in your behalf, but the tide of popular passion and frenzy was too strong to be resisted. It is truly a melancholy spectacle to witness the law makers of a sovereign state condescending to pander to the vices, ignorance and malevolence of a class of people who are at all times ready for riot, murder, and rebellion."[7]

---

[5]Jack-Mormons—A name applied to non-members of the Church who showed special friendship for the Saints.

[6]Ford, *History of Illinois*, p. 364.

[7]See *Times and Seasons*, January 15, 1845, for the full letter.

---

[4]Gregg, *History of Hancock County*, pp. 326-327.

Mobbings Begin

The continued growth and prosperity of Nauvoo, despite the repeal of her charter, aroused the anti-Mormons to more drastic actions. Early in September, 1845, they commenced mobbing the Saints in the outlying settlements and burning their homes. The Saints offered no armed resistance, believing that any movement on their part would be misjudged and bring upon them all the opposing forces. They appealed to the sheriff of Hancock County for protection. That worthy gentleman, Mr. J. B. Backenstos, proved himself a courageous champion of law and order. He announced to the people of Hancock County that:

"The Mormon community had acted with more than ordinary forbearance, remaining perfectly quiet, and offering no resistance when their dwellings, their buildings, stacks of grain, etc., were set on fire in their presence. They had forborne until forbearance was no longer a virtue."[8]

Between the 10th and 25th of September the Sheriff issued five proclamations, setting forth the outrages against the Saints and calling upon honest citizens to help put down mob violence. His appeal to the non-Mormons for a posse to aid him in that purpose having met with failure, he accepted a posse from among the Saints, led by Orrin P. Rockwell, and had soon driven the mobbers from the county or broken up their gatherings.

Anti-Mormons reported to the Governor that Backenstos was carrying affairs with a high hand. Governor Ford thereupon sent a detachment of 400 militia into Hancock County under the command of General John J. Hardin and declared the county under martial law. Sheriff Backenstos was sheared of power and left the county, and his life was in grave danger from the mob.

Immediately following the first burnings of homes of the Saints a council of the Twelve was called in Nauvoo, September 11. Of this meeting John Taylor says:

"We (the Twelve) held a council and thought it advisable, as we were going West in the spring, to keep all things as quiet as possible and not resent anything. Thinking by these pacific measures that they would be likely not to molest us; and to show the surrounding county that we were orderly disposed people and desirous of keeping the peace. It was also counseled that the brethren from the surrounding settlements should come into Nauvoo with their grain. After the trouble we had had to finish the temple to get our endowments, we thought it of more importance than to squabble with the mob about property, seeing that houses were not of much importance and no lives were lost."[9]

Demand for Removal

On September 22, 1845, the citizens of Quincy held a mass meeting. It was generally known that Joseph Smith had contemplated moving his people into the West. A resolution was passed demanding that that removal begin at once. A committee from Quincy waited upon the Quorum of Twelve. On September 24, 1845, a reply was published as follows:

"We would say to the committee above mentioned and to the Governor, and all the authorities and people of Illinois, and the surrounding states and territories, that we propose to leave this country next spring, for some point so remote that there will need to be no difficulty with the people and ourselves, provided certain propositions necessary for the accomplishment of our removal shall be observed, as follows to wit:

"That the citizens of this and surrounding counties, and all men, will use their influence and exertion to help us to sell or rent our properties, so as to get means enough that

---

[8]Roberts, *Comprehensive History of the Church*, Vol. 2, p. 477.

[9]Taylor's *Journal*, Ms. Entry of September 11, 1845.

we can help the widow, the fatherless and the destitute to remove with us.

"That all men will let us alone with their vexatious lawsuits so that we may have time, for we have broken no law; and help us to cash, dry goods, groceries, good oxen, beef-cattle, sheep, wagons, mules, horses, harness, etc., in exchange for our property, at a fair price, and deeds given at payment, that we may have means to accomplish a removal without the suffering of the destitute to an extent beyond the endurance of human nature.

"That all exchanges of property shall be conducted by a committee, or by committees of both parties; so that all the business may be transacted honorably and speedily.

"That we will use all lawful means, in connection with others, to preserve the public peace while we tarry; and shall expect, decidedly, that we be no more molested with house-burning, or any other depredations, to waste our property and time, and hinder our business.

"That it is a mistaken idea, that we have proposed to remove in six months, for that would be so early in the spring that grass might not grow nor water run; both of which would be necessary for our removal. But we propose to use our influence to have no more seed time and harvest among our people in this community after gathering our present crops; and that all communications to us be made in writing. 'By order of the Council.'"

"W. RICHARDS,"   "BRIGHAM YOUNG,"
    "Clerk."   "President."[10]

On the 2nd of October a great anti-Mormon convention met in Carthage. An organization was effected and the following resolutions passed:

"Resolved, that it is the settled and deliberate conviction of this convention that it is now too late to attempt the settlement of the difficulties in Hancock County upon any other basis than that of the removal of the Mormons from the State; and we therefore accept the proposition made by the Mormons to remove from the State next spring, and to wait with patience the time for removal."

The enemies of the Saints did not wait until spring. Plundering began anew. Vexatious lawsuits were stirred

up and officers with writs were constantly in Nauvoo seeking to arrest the Church leaders. Even Governor Ford attempted to hasten their departure by circulating a false story that the Secretary of War would send a force to prevent the Mormons from going West to the Rocky Mountains for fear that "they would there join the British and be more trouble than ever."[11]

Throughout the winter of 1845-46 the work of preparation went forward for removal to the Rocky Mountains. Every available building in Nauvoo became a workshop and the sound of the hammer and anvil could be heard early and late. Timber was purchased and brought into Nauvoo where it was dried in a kiln. Wagons were sent into the surrounding counties to gather up scrap iron. This was converted into tires, axles and other necessary metal parts of wagons. Piles of hides were purchased and the harness maker began to use many assistants to work long hours overtime. Horses were purchased in the surrounding territory until a rise in price made such purchases prohibitive. Oxen were then purchased and yokes manufactured.

Meanwhile work in the interior of the temple continued and temple work for the living and dead went forward feverishly, as if there was no thought of removal. This continued until most of the Saints had started the long trek west. On May 1, 1846, after the majority had left, the completed temple was publicly dedicated in the presence of about three hundred people.

Supplementary Readings

1. Roberts, *Comprehensive History of the Church*, pp. 446-541. (A comprehensive

---

[10] J. F. Smith, *Essentials in Church History*, p. 396.

[11] (Note) Governor Ford admitted his deceit in his *History of Illinois*, p. 413.

account of the tragic period between the martyrdom of Joseph and Hyrum and the beginning of the movement west.)

2. *Ibid.*, p. 448, note 5. (A brief statement of the political situation of the Saints and the two major parties, from the Mormon view.)

3. *Ibid.*, p. 473. (An interesting one-page story of the laying of the capstone of the Nauvoo Temple. Vivid and informing.)

4. *Ibid.*, p. 475. (Quotation from editor of Quincy *Whig*. Small type.) (An appealing, vivid picture of the wrongs suffered by the Mormons during this period written by a fair-minded non-Mormon.)

5. *Ibid.*, p. 485, under 3. (Mr. Babbitt, a non-Mormon member of the Illinois legislature, defends the Mormons against the attack on the Nauvoo Charter.)

6. *Ibid.*, pp. 486-488, No. 4 ("Backenstos" —charges against the anti-Mormons.)

7. Evans, *One Hundred Years of Mormonism*, pp. 384-388. (Clear, brief account of the period immediately following the martyrdom, and of Brigham Young's qualities of leadership.)

8. *Ibid.*, pp. 389-394.

9. Evans, *Heart of Mormonism*, pp. 320-329. (Interesting and easily read account of the time between the martyrdom of Joseph and the movement west.)

10. Smith, *Essentials of Church History*, pp. 391, growth of the work—400. (A clear, condensed report of this period.)

11. James A. Little, *From Kirtland to Salt Lake City*. pp. 42-56. (Here is a graphic picture of persons and incidents during those last tragic days at Nauvoo, revealing the suffering and heroism of the Saints.)

12. Cowley, *Wilford Woodruff*, pp. 227-232. (In these pages Brother Woodruff tells of his visiting Emma and Lucy Smith, the wife and mother of the Prophet Joseph, soon after the death of Joseph, to comfort them.)

CHAPTER 28

AN EXILED PEOPLE

Leaving the Beloved City

Beginning February 4, 1846, an observer on the bank of the Mississippi River, opposite Nauvoo, would have witnessed an unusual succession of events. On that date a number of wagons drawn by horses and oxen, surmounted by great white canvas covers, and loaded with household goods, provisions, and farming implements, drove off the wharf at Nauvoo onto flat boats and were ferried across the mighty Father of Waters. Reaching the Iowa side the wagons struck west onto the prairie and disappeared in the distance, leaving a deep trail through the freshly fallen snow.

On February 6, six other wagons similarly equipped, followed. They, too, were soon lost to view in the west. About six and one-half miles from the river these wagons came to a halt on the banks of Sugar Creek. The snow was cleared away and tents pitched. These wagons belonged to people who were exiles from comfortable homes—the advance group of 15,000 men, women and children who were being driven from their beloved city of Nauvoo.

During the days which followed hundreds of wagons crossed the river, and lumbered across the white expanse in long caravans. The migrating people became an almost unbroken line.

"Several flatboats, some old lighters, and numbers of skiffs, forming altogether quite a fleet, were at work day and night, crossing the Saints."[1]

On February 15, Brigham Young

and members of the Twelve crossed the river with their families and moved on to Sugar Creek. The weather was extremely cold, the thermometer hovering below zero. On the 25th Charles C. Rich walked across the river near Montrose, on the ice. The next few days witnessed the strangest sight of all, long caravans streaking out across the mighty river over a solid floor of ice which stretched from bank to bank a distance of one mile. A few days later this unique roadway cracked up and the line of caravans was halted while great blocks of ice choked the river. The delay was but temporary. The ferry boats began to ply the river again and fresh caravans spotted the prairie. The great exodus of the Mormon people had begun.[2]

Sugar Creek Camp

The camp on Sugar Creek assumed the appearance of a white city. Over four hundred wagons had congregated there. Some had been in the encampment for two weeks awaiting the arrival of the leaders. Brigham Young had found many of the people in want, their provisions gone, their shelter insufficient and their clothing scanty. Many things had contributed to this. The cry of the citizens of Hancock and neighboring counties had become so insistent for their removal that the exodus began two months before the Saints had anticipated. It had become absolutely vital that the exodus begin if bloodshed

---

[1]*History of the Church*, Period 2, Vol. 7. p. 582.

[2](Note) The facts for the above are taken from the Manuscript Journal of Brigham Young, which corrects the view that the Mississippi River in 1846 was frozen over before February 25th.

was to be averted. Brigham Young had counseled the brethren to leave Nauvoo prepared with sufficient provisions for several months and with an adequate supply of tents and clothing. This advice had not always been followed, because time had not permitted the raising of funds by the sale of property in Nauvoo. Then there were a number of families who seemed fearful of being left behind the Twelve and crowded into the vanguard, despite their lack of preparation. Eight hundred men reported themselves at the camp at Sugar Creek the last two weeks of February without more than a fortnight's provisions for themselves and teams. Brigham Young entered the camp with a year's supply of provisions in his wagons for his family. Within two weeks he had nothing left, so freely did he give to those in need. It was Brigham Young who, in the Missouri troubles of 1838, secured the pledge of 200 brethren with himself that they would use all their means to aid the deserving poor in removing from Missouri. That had been done. Before leaving Nauvoo, Brigham Young and the leading brethren entered into a similar covenant. How quickly they were called upon to fulfill it! They did so with little or no complaint. The great leader, Brigham Young, took upon himself the care of the poor and the destitute. Upbraid his people he did—many times—but never for their being poor.

He was highly pleased with the patience and courage of his people. Many, many times, however, he corrected them. On February 17, he said to the camp:

"I wish the brethren to stop running to Nauvoo, hunting, fishing, roasting their shins, idling away their time, and fix nose buckets for their horses, and save their corn, and fix comfortable places for their wives and children to ride, and never borrow without asking leave, and be sure and return what was borrowed lest your brother be vexed with you. * * * All dogs in the camp should be killed if the owners will not tie them up. * * * We will have no law we cannot keep but we will have order in the camp. If any want to live in peace after we have left this they must toe the mark."[3]

The Suffering of the Saints

Despite all the efforts of the leaders, the intense cold and the lack of preparation and organization produced much suffering while at Sugar Creek. An account of the incidents which occurred there would fill volumes. A few extracts will, however, reveal the feelings and the hardships of this people.

"By the first of March over five thousand exiles were shivering behind the meager shelter of wagon covers and tents, and the winter-stripped groves that lined the creek. Their sufferings have never been adequately told; and to realize how cruel and ill-timed was this forced exodus, one has only to be reminded that in one night nine children were born under these distressing conditions. * * *

"By ascending a nearby hill we could look back upon the beautiful city and see the splendid temple we had reared in our poverty at a cost of one and a half million dollars.[4] Moreover, on a clear, calm morning we could hear:

"The silvery notes of the temple bell
That we loved so deep and well:
And a pang of grief would swell the heart
And the scalding tears in anguish start
As we silently gazed on our dear old homes."[5]

Violent storms and excessive cold sapped the energy and vitality of the people. Especially did the women and new-born infants suffer. Eliza R. Snow, who was present in the camp at Sugar Creek, writes:

"We had been preceded from Nauvoo by thousands and I was informed that on the

[3]*History of Brigham Young*, Ms.; see *History of the Church*, Period I, Vol. 7, pp. 585-586.
[4]Most authorities place it at about one million dollars.
[5]*Memoirs of John R. Young*, Utah Pioneer, 1847. Ch. 2, pp. 14-15.

first night of the encampment, nine children were born into the world, and from that time as we journeyed onward mothers gave birth to offspring under almost every variety of circumstances imaginable, except those to which they had been accustomed; some in tents, others in wagons—in rainstorms and in snow-storms. I heard of one birth which occured under the rude shelter of a hut, the sides of which were formed of blankets fastened to poles stuck in the ground, with a bark roof through which the rain was dripping; kind sisters stood holding dishes to catch the water as it fell, thus protecting the new-comer and its mother from a shower bath as the little innocent first entered on the stage of human life."

The following is another picture from the same pen illustrating the situation:

"Many of our sisters walked all day, rain or shine, and at night prepared suppers for their families, with no sheltering tents; and then made their beds in and under wagons that contained their earthly all. How frequently, with intense sympathy and admiration, I watched the mother, when, forgetful of her own fatigue and destitution, she took unwearied pains to fix up, in the most palatable form, the allotted portion of food, and as she dealt it out was cheering the hearts of her homeless children, while, as I truly believed, her own was lifted to God in fervent prayer that their lives might be preserved."[6]

Of these scenes an unknown poet of the camp wrote:

God pity the exiles, when storms come down—
When snow-laden clouds hang low on the ground,
When the chill blast of winter, with frost on its breath
Sweeps through the tents, like the angels of death
When the sharp cry of child-birth is heard on the air,
And the voice of the father breaks down in his prayer,
As he pleads with Jehovah, his loved ones to spare![7]

Reflecting upon the sufferings endured at Sugar Creek, Brigham Young recorded in his journal:

"The fact is worthy of remembrance that several thousand persons left their homes in midwinter and exposed themselves without shelter, except that afforded by a scanty supply of tents and wagon covers, to a cold which effectually made an ice bridge over the Mississippi River, which at Nauvoo is more than a mile broad.

"We could have remained sheltered in our homes had it not been for threats and hostile demonstrations of our enemies, who, notwithstanding their solemn agreements, had thrown every obstacle in our way, not respecting either life, or liberty, or property so much so that our only means of avoiding a rupture was by starting in midwinter."[8]

The Order to Move West

To remove the ever present invitation to grief and sorrow which came from being camped within the sight of the "Beloved Nauvoo," the leaders wisely counseled to move on. In the *Memoirs of John R. Young* we read:

"I remember hearing the ringing voice of President Young as standing early in the morning in the front end of his wagon, he said:

" 'Attention, the camps of Israel. I propose to move forward on our journey. Let all who wish follow me; but I want none to come unless they will obey the commandments and statutes of the Lord. Cease, therefore, your contentions and back-biting, nor must there be swearing or profanity in our camps. Whoever finds anything must seek diligently to return it to the owner. The Sabbath day must be hallowed. In all our camp, prayers should be offered up both morning and evening. If you do these things, faith will abide in your hearts; and the angels of God will go with you, even as they went with the children of Israel when Moses led them from the land of Egypt.' "[9]

On March 1, five hundred wagons moved out of camp. They struggled five miles through snow and mud. Then, the wagons were stopped, the snow cleared away and tents raised for the night. The journey continued daily un-

---

[6]James A. Little, *From Kirtland to Salt Lake City*, pp. 42-47-48.
[7]*Memoirs of John R. Young*, Utah Pioneer, 1847, Ch. 2, p. 14.

[8]*History of Brigham Young*, Ms., p. 69.
[9]*Memoirs of John R. Young*, Utah Pioneer, 1847, Ch. 2, pp. 15-16.

til the Chariton River was reached, when a halt was called for a few days.

The main camp—that is, the camp of Brigham Young and most of the Twelve —was called the "Camp of Israel." Ahead of this camp a group of "Pioneers" were sent to seek out the best roads, build bridges and construct ferry boats. In the meantime, the provisions of the camp were nearly exhausted. To supply the Saints with food, companies were organized to go north and south of the line of march to the Iowa and Missouri settlements, to trade watches, feather beds, shawls and all the items which the Saints were finding that they could dispense with, for grain and flour. Crops, the season before, had been bountiful in Iowa and Missouri, and the forests were full of hogs. The farmers were glad for such an exchange. The Saints asked for no gratuities. They were willing to pay for all they obtained. A great number of the unmarried men found employment on the farms and in the towns of Iowa and Missouri.

A Story of Sacrifice

Many were the sacrifices made by these people for their religion. One such story is told by John R. Young in his *Memoirs*:

"Orson Spencer was a graduate from an eastern college, who having studied for the ministry, became a popular preacher in the Baptist Church. Meeting with a Mormon elder, he became acquainted with the teachings of Joseph Smith and accepted them. Before doing so, however, he and his highly educated young wife counted the cost, laid their hearts on the altar and made the sacrifice! How few realize what it involved to become a Mormon in those early days! Home, friends, occupation, popularity, all that makes life pleasant, were gone. Almost overnight they were strangers to their own kindred.

"After leaving Nauvoo, his wife, ever delicate and frail, sank rapidly under the ever-accumulating hardships. The sorrowing husband wrote imploringly to the wife's parents, asking them to receive her into their home until the Saints should find an abiding place. The answer came, 'Let her renounce her degrading faith and she can come back, but never until she does.'

"When the letter was read to her, she asked her husband to get his Bible and to turn to the book of Ruth and read the first chapter, sixteenth and seventeenth verses: 'Entreat me not to leave thee or to return from following after thee; for whither thou goest I will go, and where thou lodgest I will lodge. Thy people shall be my people and thy God my God.'

"Not a murmur escaped her lips. The storm was severe and the wagon covers leaked. Friends held milk pans over her bed to keep her dry. In those conditions, in peace and without apparent suffering, the spirit took its flight and her body was consigned to a grave by the wayside."[10]

The exodus, however, was not without its bright side. John Taylor, after recounting the trials and hardships, in a communication to the Saints in England said:

"We outlived the trying scenes—we felt contented and happy—the songs of Zion resounded from wagon to wagon—from tent to tent; the sound reverberated through the woods, and its echo was returned from the distant hills; peace, harmony, and contentment reigned in the habitations of the Saints. * * * The God of Israel is with us. * * * And as we journey, as did Abraham of old, to a distant land, we feel that like him, we are doing the will of our Heavenly Father and relying upon His word and promises; and having His blessing, we feel that we are children of the same promise and hope, and that the great Jehovah is our God."[11]

Organization Enroute

Captain Pitt and his brass band accompanied the Camp of Israel and after the toils of the day were over, music, dancing and singing caused the people to forget their woes and look with hopes upon the future. To the inhabitants of

[10]*Memoirs of John R. Young*, Utah Pioneer, 1847, Ch. 2, pp. 17-18.
[11]*Millennial Star*, Vol. 8, Nos. 7 and 8.

SAINTS CROSSING THE MISSISSIPPI RIVER IN THE DEAD-COLD OF WINTER, photograph of section of the Lynn Fausett mural in the tourist center adjacent to the "This Is The Place" Monument.

PIONEERS, section of the Lynn Fausett mural in the tourist center adjacent to the "This Is The Place" Monument.

HANDCART PIONEERS, photograph of oil painting by C. C. A. Christensen in the library of the Church Historian's Office.

Iowa it was incomprehensible that a people so driven, in the midst of such hardships, could accompany the exodus with such gay scenes of festivity. Pitt's band was invited to play in towns on both sides of the line of march, and did so, often receiving pay, which helped the camps financially.

Before leaving Nauvoo, an organization of four companies of migrating Saints, with captains of hundreds and fifties, had been effected. This organization was nearly useless, as the people designated to belong to a particular company could not all leave Nauvoo at the advanced date. Further, great numbers who had not been assigned to the advance companies, crowded into the first encampments. Disunion and waste was the result. Some independent spirits, like Bishop George Miller, pushed ahead without waiting for the main camp. Parley P. Pratt and Orson Pratt were also ahead with their teams. This condition led Brigham Young to call a halt and reorganize the Camps of Israel. He sent word ahead severely rebuking Miller, Pratt, and others for their independent action and threatened to disfellowship them if they did not meet with the main camp on the Chariton River for organization. They complied. Brigham Young was unanimously chosen to preside over all the camps. The Saints were organized into companies of "hundreds" and "fifties," with captains over each. Each fifty had also appointed a contracting commissary for the purpose of contracting for grain and work, and a distributing commissary to distribute food in the camp. A clerk was also appointed for each fifty, while William Clayton was chosen as clerk for the entire camp. Instructions were given:

"No man to set fire to the prairies. No man to shoot off a gun in camp without orders. No man to go hunting unless he is sent, and all to keep guns, swords and pistols out of sight."[12]

From the camp on the Chariton the migration moved forward in orderly and commendable fashion. The "Pioneers" were divided among the fifties. The captain of fifty further organized his camp by appointing captains of "tens," buglers, blacksmiths, etc., until every man had his assigned duties.

The Vision of a Great Leader

Under the leadership of Brigham Young the Saints early assumed the aspect of an industrial column on the march. From the first it was evident that sufficient provisions to last out the journey to the mountains could not be taken from Nauvoo, even had a sufficient supply been available. The migrating Saints must be self-sustaining during the march. To accomplish this, herds of cattle and sheep, hogs, chickens, etc., were taken with them across the plains. Further, Brigham Young planned for the planting of huge areas into grain by the advance companies, which might be harvested by the succeeding companies. The movement to the West might well continue for years after the Saints of Nauvoo had reached the Rocky Mountains. Converts from the Eastern States, Canada, and England would be following in the wake of the Pioneers. With rare vision Brigham Young prepared for this continuing migration. Scouting parties were sent ahead to select permanent camping sites which might be utilized for many years. As most of Iowa was still public land and unsurveyed, such selections and settlements could be made without great expense or difficulty.

---

[12]*William Clayton's Journal*, p. 10.

Garden Grove

The first of such encampments was located on a branch of the Grand River, 150 miles from Nauvoo. It was named "Garden Grove." Upon reaching this vicinity, selected by the advance Pioneers, the Camp of Israel halted for a time. It was now the latter part of April. A council was called. One hundred men were appointed to make rails, forty-eight to build houses; twelve to dig wells; ten to build a bridge, and the rest to plow the ground and plant grain.[13]

Almost as if by magic an orderly town arose on the prairie. Seven hundred fifteen acres of sod were broken and planted to grain and other crops. These were enclosed by a neat rail fence. Log houses were built along hastily laid out streets, in orderly fashion. "The camp was like a swarm of bees, every one was busy. And withal the people felt well and happy."[14]

Elder Samuel Bent was appointed to remain at Garden Grove and preside over the settlement, with Aaron Johnson and David Fullmer as counselors. The harvested crops were to be put in a storehouse and distributed to the needy emigrants. Large flocks of sheep and herds of cattle were also to be maintained at the encampment.

Mount Pisgah

The second permanent camp was made another hundred miles to the west. Parley P. Pratt, who had been sent ahead and who selected the location, said of it:

"I came suddenly to some round and sloping hills, grassy and crowded with beautiful groves of timber; while alternate open groves and forests seemed blended in all the beauty and harmony of an English park. While beneath and beyond, on the west, rolled a main branch of Grand River, with its rich bottoms of alternate forest and prairie. As I approached this lovely scenery, several deer and wolves, being startled at the sight of me, abandoned the place and bounded away till lost from my sight amid the groves. Being pleased and excited at the varied beauty before me, I cried out, 'This is Mount Pisgah.'"

Upon reaching this place the Camp of Israel halted again. The organized laborers went to work and soon produced another magic city. A farm of several thousand acres was enclosed, the ground broken and planted. Scores of log cabins were erected. William Huntington was made president of the encampment, and with Ezra T. Benson and Charles C. Rich as counselors, remained behind to supervise the tending of flocks and herds, the harvesting of grain, and the care of incoming and outgoing Saints.

The main camp of Israel now moved forward again and by June 14, reached Council Bluffs, on the banks of the Missouri River, where a third permanent camp was made. The season was late for planting, but preparations for fencing, plowing and planting were begun. Bishop Miller was detailed, with a group of men, to build a ferry with which to cross the river.

It was at this stage of the journey that a call was made by the United States Government for volunteers in the war against Mexico, which will be treated in the following chapter. This call altered the previous plan of the Saints, to send one hundred men without families over the Rocky Mountains that year, to select a site for settlement.

As soon as it was apparent that winter must be spent on the plains, preparations were begun, so that it might

---

[13]See *William Clayton's Journal*, p. 25.
[14]Cannon, "History of the Church," *Juvenile Instructor*, Vol. 17, p. 325.

be endured with the least possible hardship.

Winter Quarters

A site, across the river and a short distance above Council Bluffs, was selected as a fourth permanent camp and designated "Winter Quarters." This encampment was located on the present site of Florence, Nebraska, about six miles from the present city of Omaha. Five hundred thirty-eight log houses, and eighty-three sod houses were built before winter began. These were sufficient to shelter about three thousand souls. By spring, the houses and people were twice that number. The buildings were generally of a single room, twelve by eighteen feet, with sod floor and roof and a good chimney. Thousands of tons of prairie hay were cut with scythes and stacked for the winter, while the meat of wild game was salted down or dried. Along the river bottoms hundreds of bushels of wild berries were gathered. These were preserved in various forms for winter use. Scouting parties went out in various directions to locate the best route to be followed in the spring. Details were sent to St. Louis to procure much needed supplies for the winter, which were not available on the plains. Emptied of their loads, the wagons were sent back over the prairies to aid other companies. Boys were placed to herd sheep and cattle.

The swimming of the cattle across the Missouri to Winter Quarters was an interesting feat. John R. Young says of the occasion:

"Boy that I was, the swimming of the cattle was an achievement of great interest. Early in the morning, so that the sun might not shine in the cattle's faces, a boatload was taken across and held on the opposite shore. Then a thousand head were driven some distance up the stream and forced into the river.

Good swimmers would climb upon the backs of some of the strongest oxen, and slapping them on the sides of the faces would guide them into the current. Soon we had a string of animals reaching from one shore to the other. Of course it was lively and exciting, and called for courage and physical endurance."[15]

The city of Winter Quarters was divided into thirteen wards. A bishopric was appointed over each, with instructions to look after both the temporal and physical welfare of the people, to supervise industrial activities and provide for sanitation in the community. The number of wards was later increased to twenty-two. High councils were selected for Winter Quarters and also for the other permanent camps.

During the winter, schools were held and the majority of young people had an opportunity of gaining some formal instruction. An improvised mail service had been instituted. Many men had gone with the advance companies as drivers, leaving their families. Letters were sent with them from the camps back to individuals started on the return journey to Nauvoo to get their families. Letters were sent with them from the camps back to their friends. Mail was also forwarded from Nauvoo to the headquarters of the Camp of Israel. Willard Richards was known as the general postmaster both for outgoing and incoming mail. This mail system kept the people informed of their friends in Nauvoo, of their daily prayers on behalf of the Camp of Israel and, finally, of the great tragedy at that place in the fall of the year.

The Final Chapter at Nauvoo

During the spring and summer of 1846, Nauvoo rapidly assumed the ap-

---

[15]*Memoirs of John R. Young*, Utah Pioneer, 1847, Ch. 3, pp. 26-27.

pearance of a deserted city. There were many Saints, however, too poor to provide themselves with the necessities of travel. These must wait until the advance wagons could be sent back for them. To have attempted to move all the people to the West at once, ill-prepared as they then were, and in the cold of early spring, would have been to invite a major tragedy. Further, there were many too sick to travel and these must wait until health returned before undertaking the hard journey. Besides, the Saints had for the most part been unable to dispose of their property. A number of people remained behind for this purpose.

As the mobs witnessed the departure of thousands of the Saints during the early spring, they ceased for a time their depredations. When some of the remaining people commenced the planting of grain and indicated that they might remain until another spring, new hostilities began. These hostilities were directed alike toward the Mormons and the non-Mormons who had purchased property of the Saints in Nauvoo and had come there to dwell.

The mobs scoured the country outside the city limits, occasionally beating some Saint who fell into their hands. It became dangerous to go into the fields without an armed guard.

Meanwhile the finishing touches were done on the interior of the Temple. In the latter part of April, Wilford Woodruff and Orson Hyde reached Nauvoo from the British Mission. Under date of April 30, 1846, Elder Woodruff's journal contains the following:

"In the evening of this day, I repaired to

An artist's drawing of the ruins of the Nauvoo Temple.

the Temple with Elder Orson Hyde and about twenty other elders of Israel. There we all dressed in our priestly robes and dedicated the Temple of the Lord, erected in His most holy name by the Church of Jesus Christ of Latter-day Saints. Notwithstanding the predictions of false prophets and the threat of the mobs that the building should never be completed or dedicated, their words. had fallen to the ground. The Temple was now finished and dedicated to Him. After the dedication, we raised our voices in a united shout of 'Hosanna to God and the Lamb.' "[16]

On May 1, a public dedication was held, attended by about three hundred people.

As the summer progressed mass meetings were held in Hancock and neighboring counties demanding the immediate evacuation of Nauvoo by every Mormon. In May, Governor Ford sent Major Warren to Nauvoo with a small military force to keep peace. He was empowered to enlist the aid of Nauvoo citizens to put down mob riots. For a time he did much to enlist public sympathy for the departing exiles by informing the people in the surrounding counties of the fact that the Saints were leaving with all possible speed. On May 14, he reported that 450 teams and 1,350 souls had left Nauvoo during the week. On the 22nd he reported:

"The Mormons will continue to leave the city in large numbers. The ferry at this place averages about 32 teams per day, and at Fort Madison, 45. Thus it will be seen that 539 teams have left during the week, which average about three persons to each, making in all 1,617 souls."[17]

The State Retreats While Mobs Rule

The publishing of these facts did not stop the outrages of the mob, and on May 20, Major Warren issued a proclamation setting forth the nature of these attacks and warning the people of Hancock County against their repetition. No attention was paid to the proclamation. On June 6, a movement started at Warsaw to drive out the remaining Mormons at the point of the sword. The mob militia assembled at Golden Point for this purpose, but at this time it was rumored that Stephen Markham had returned to Nauvoo with several hundred armed men. As Markham's name was a terror among his enemies, the mob hastily disbanded. Markham had returned to Nauvoo to remove some Church property but had brought no more than a few teamsters and wagons for that purpose.

The mob soon reassembled and issued an ultimatum against any Saints leaving the city limits, except to go westward. In the latter part of July a party of Mormons and non-Mormons, who went outside the city limits to harvest grain, were captured and severely beaten. Attempts to bring the perpetrators to punishment failed.

Conditions went from bad to worse. Major Warren resigned. On August 24, 1846, Major James R. Parker was sent with ten men and power to raise a posse and defend the city of Nauvoo. His entreaties to the gathering mobs to disperse were met with contempt. He received a counter proclamation from the mob leader, Singleton:

"When I say to you the Mormons must go, I speak the mind of the camp and county. They can leave without force or injury to themselves or property, but I say to you, sir, with all candor, they shall go—they may fix the time within sixty days, or I will fix it for them."[18]

Parker, on behalf of the citizens of Nauvoo, agreed to the terms allowing sixty days for removal. The mobs rejected the treaty made by their officers

---

[16]Cowley, *Wilford Woodruff*, p. 247.
[17]Gregg, *History of Hancock County*, pp. 346-347.

[18]Conyer, *Hancock County Mob*, pp. 53-54.

and these withdrew from command. Thomas S. Brockman was placed over the mob forces. Parker also resigned and Major Clifford succeeded him in command at Nauvoo.

In total disregard for the legal government of Illinois, Brockman marched a force of 700 men against Nauvoo. His propositions to the Saints were so outrageous that a force of 150 to 300 men was raised to resist him.[19] These threw up breastworks on the north side of Mulholland street facing the mob camp. Some steamboat shafts were converted into crude cannon.

On September 10, 11, and 12, firing on both sides ensued. On the 13th, a real battle took place. The resistance was so determined that the attacking force was driven back to their encampment. Esquire Daniel H. Wells, an old friend of the Mormons, and a recent convert, distinguished himself in this defense of the city. The number of the mob killed in the battle of Nauvoo is not definitely known. Three of the defenders were killed and several wounded.

Nauvoo Surrenders to the Mob

As the state made no move to aid the stricken city, it was decided in council to surrender rather than to shed more blood in defending a city they were so soon to abandon anyway. The treaty of surrender guaranteed the Saints protection until they could move across the river and provided for a committee of five Saints to remain in the city for the purpose of disposing of property.

Under the terms of the treaty the mob forces entered the city in perfect order, on September 17, and marched to camp on the southern side of the city. This constraint on the troops was not

kept. In Governor Ford's *History of Illinois* we read:

"When the posse arrived in the city, the leaders of it elected themselves into a tribunal to decide who should be forced away and who remain. Parties were dispatched to hunt for Mormon arms and for Mormons, and to bring them to the judgment, where they received their doom from the mouth of Brockman, who there sat, a grim and unawed tyrant, for the time. As a general rule, the Mormons were ordered to leave within an hour or two hours; and by rare grace some of them were allowed until next day, and a few cases longer. The treaty specified that the Mormons only should be driven into exile. Nothing was said in it concerning the new citizens, who had, with the Mormons, defended the city. But the posse no sooner obtained possession, than they commenced expelling new citizens. Some of them were ducked in the river, being in one or two instances actually baptized in the name of the leaders of the mob, others were forcibly driven into the ferry boats, to be taken over the river, before the bayonets of armed ruffians; and it is believed that the houses of most of them were broken open and their property stolen during their absence. Many of these new settlers were strangers in the county from various parts of the United States, who were attracted there by the low price of property, and they knew but little of previous difficulties, or the merits of the quarrel. They saw with their own eyes that the Mormons were industriously preparing to go away, and they knew of their own knowledge of that effort. To expel them with force was gratuitous and unnecessary cruelty."[20]

A Graphic Description

Colonel Thomas L. Kane, in a speech before the Historical Society of Philadelphia, gives a graphic picture of the fate of Nauvoo:

"A few years ago, ascending the upper Mississippi in the autumn, when its waters were low, I was compelled to travel by land past the region of the rapids. My road lay through the Half Breed tract, a fine section of Iowa, which the unsettled state of its land titles had appropriated as a sanctuary for coiners, horse thieves and other outlaws. I had left my steamer at Keokuk at the foot of

---

[19] (Note) Authorities disagree on the number. Governor Ford places the number at 150.

[20] Ford, *History of Illinois;* see also Roberts, *Comprehensive History of the Church,* Vol. 3, p. 18.

Col. Thomas L. Kane who, on many occasions, was a friend to the Mormons.

the lower falls, to hire a carriage and to contend for some fragments of a dirty meal with the swarming flies, the only scavengers of the locality.

"From this place to where the deep water of the river returns my eye wearied to see everywhere sordid vagabond and idle settlers, and a country marred without being improved by their careless hands. I was descending the last hillside upon my journey, when a landscape in delightful contrast broke upon my view. Half encircled by a bend of the river, a beautiful city lay glittering in the fresh morning sun. Its bright new dwellings, set in cool green gardens ranging up around a stately dome-shaped hill, which was crowned by a noble marble edifice, whose high tapering spire was radiant with white and gold. The city appeared to cover several miles, and beyond it, in the background, there rolled off a fair country chequered by the careful lines of fruitful husbandry. The unmistakable marks of industry, enterprise and

educated wealth everywhere, made the scene one of singular and most striking beauty. It was a natural impulse to visit this inviting region. I procured a skiff, and rowing across the river, landed at the chief wharf of the city. No one met me there. I looked and the quiet everywhere was such that I heard the flies buzz and the water ripples break against the shallow beach. I walked through the solitary streets. The town lay as in a dream, under some deadening spell of loneliness, from which I almost feared to wake it, for plainly it had not slept long. There was no grass growing up in the paved ways, rains had not entirely washed away the prints of dusty footsteps, yet I went about unchecked. I went into empty workshops, rope walks and smithies. The spinner's wheel was idle, the carpenter had gone from his work bench and shavings, his unfinished sash and casings, fresh bark was in the tanner's vat, and fresh chopped light wood stood piled against the baker's oven. The blacksmith's shop was cold; but his coal heap and ladling pool and crooked water horn were all there, as if he had just gone for a holiday. * * *

"Only two portions of the city seemed to suggest the import of this mysterious solitude. On the eastern suburb the houses looking out upon the country showed, by their splintered woodworks and walls battered to the foundations, that they had lately been a mark of destructive cannonade, and in and around the splendid temple, which had been the chief object of my admiration, armed men were barracked, surrounded by their stacks of musketry and pieces of heavy ordnance. These challenged me to render an account of myself and why I had the temerity to cross the water without a written permit from the leader of their band. Though these men were more or less under the influence of ardent spirits, after I had explained myself as a passing stranger, they seemed anxious to gain my good opinion. They told the story of the dead city—that it had been a notable manufacturing and commercial mart, sheltering over twenty thousand persons. That they had waged war with its inhabitants for several years, and had finally been successful only a few days before my visit, in an action fought in front of the ruined suburb, after which they had driven them at the point of the sword. * * *

"They also conducted me inside the wall of the curious temple, in which they said the banished inhabitants were accustomed to celebrate the mystic rites of an unhallowed worship. They particularly pointed out to me certain features of the building, which having been the peculiar objects of a former superstitious regard, they had as a matter of duty sedulously defiled and defaced. * * *

"They permitted me also to ascend into the steeple to see where it had been lightning struck on the Sabbath before, and to look out East and South on wasted farms, like those I had seen near the city, extending till they were lost in the distance. Here in the face of pure day, close to the scar of divine wrath left by the thunderbolt, were fragments of food, cruses of liquor, and broken drinking vessels, with a bass drum and a steamboat signal bell, of which I afterwards learned the use with pain.

"It was after nightfall when I was ready to cross the river on my return. The wind had freshened after sunset, and the water beating roughly into my little boat, I headed higher up the stream than the point I had left in the morning, and landed where a faint glimmering light invited me to steer. Here among the dock and rushes, sheltered only by the darkness, without roof between them and the sky, I came upon a crowd of several hundred creatures, whom my movements roused from uneasy slumber upon the ground. Passing these on my way to the light I found it came from a tallow candle in a paper funnel shape, such as as used by street vendors of apples and peanuts, and which flaring and fluttering away in the bleak air off the water, shone flickeringly on the emaciated features of a man in the last stage of a bilious remittent fever. They had done their best for him. Over his head was something like a tent made of a sheet or two, and he rested on a but partially ripped open old straw mattress, with a hair sofa cushion under his head for a pillow. His gaping jaw and glazing eye told how short a time he would enjoy these luxuries.

"Dreadful indeed were the sufferings of these forsaken beings, bowed and cramped by cold and sunburn, alternating as each weary day and night dragged on. They were, almost all of them, the crippled victims of disease. They were there because they had no homes, nor hospitals, nor poor house, nor friends to offer them any. They could not satisfy the feeble cravings of their sick. They had not bread to quiet the fractious hunger cries of their children. Mothers and babes, daughters and grandparents, all of them alike, were bivouacked in tatters, wanting even covering to comfort those whom the sick shiver of fever was searching to the marrow.

"These were the Mormons, famishing in Lee County, Iowa, in the fourth week of the month of September, in the year of our Lord, 1846. The city—it was Nauvoo, Illinois. The Mormons were the owners of that city, and the smiling country around, and those who stopped their plows, who had silenced their hammers, their axes, their shuttles and their workshop wheels, those who had put out their fires, who had eaten their food, spoiled their orchards and trampled under foot their thousands of acres of unharvested grain, these were the keepers of their dwellings, the carousers in their temple, whose drunken riot insulted the ears of their dying. They were, all told, not more than six hundred forty persons who were thus lying on the river flats, but the Mormons in Nauvoo had numbered the year before over twenty thousand. Where were they? They had last been seen, carrying in mournful trains their sick and wounded, halt and blind, to disappear behind the western horizon, pursuing the phantom of another home. Hardly anything else was known of them and people

Samuel Brannan who was appointed to take charge of the Saints aboard the ship Brooklyn enroute to California.

asked with curiosity—what had been their fate, what their fortune!"[21]

A Voyage of Ten Thousand Miles

When the ultimatum came to leave Nauvoo, not all the Saints were living in that vicinity. Thousands of converts were as yet in the Eastern States, Canada, and England. In January, 1846, Brigham Young advised the Saints in

[21]Thomas L. Kane, Address before the Historical Society of Philadelphia. *Memoirs of John R. Young*, Utah Pioneer, 1847, pp. 31 to 38.

(Note) The Temple was always a source of envy to the enemies of the Saints, and a painful reminder of their own misdeeds. On November 10, 1848, an incendiary set it on fire. The tower was destroyed and the building so weakened that a tornado which struck it May 27, 1850, blew down the north wall. Finally all the walls were torn down and the stone hauled away. The Saints received nothing for the building stone. Two hundred thousand dollars was offered for the Temple in April, 1846, while the greater part of the Saints were on the plains, but the offer had been withdrawn. (See William Clayton's *Journal*, pp. 25-26.)

the Eastern States to join the Church in its western exodus the following spring, or to charter ships and sail around South America to California.

Samuel Brannan, an energetic Elder of the Church in the New York branch, was appointed to take charge of the Saints who should go to California by water. The ship "Brooklyn" was finally chartered at a cost of $1,200 a month for the journey. Over three hundred Saints asked for places. Two hundred and thirty-eight were finally taken at a total cost for passage of $50 each.

Samuel Brannan was led to believe that the United States Government might interfere to prevent the Mormons going west. He was induced to agree to a scheme of A. G. Benson and Company who, with Amos Kendall, had

The ship Brooklyn left New York with two hundred and thirty-eight Saints on February 4, 1846 and arrived in Yerba Buena, California (San Francisco) on July 29, 1846. (Photograph of painting by Arnold Friberg.)

Used by permission, The Improvement Era

great influence at Washington. By the contract Benson and Company drew up, the Mormons were guaranteed that no interference would be made with their departure west and the company would use its influence to have the government protect them in their future home. In payment for this consideration the Mormons were to deed to the company every alternate section of land acquired in the region to which they might go. The contract was sent by Samuel Brannan to Brigham Young and the Twelve, who turned it down with contempt.

The ship, "Brooklyn," by a coincidence, sailed on February 4, 1846, the same day the first wagons of the Saints left Nauvoo for the West. After a voyage of more than five months the ship sailed through the Golden Gate in San Francisco harbor, July 29, 1846, and docked at Yerba Buena, now the city of San Francisco. To the surprise of the Saints, the Stars and Stripes were already floating over the city, having been raised some two weeks previous.

A contract had been drawn up on board the "Brooklyn," whereby the Saints of that group should give the proceeds of their labors of the next three years into a common fund from which all were to draw their living. The plan did not work and was soon abandoned. The people found work wherever they could. Some twenty, however, were detailed to select a place for a settlement, put in crops, build houses, etc., preparatory for removing the Brooklyn colony to the site in the spring. The place selected was called New Hope. It was situated on the north bank of the Stanislaus, about a mile and a half from the San Joaquin river.

The uncertainty of where the main body of Saints were going to settle, and quarrels as to the purpose of the enclosed plot, prevented the project being carried out. Brannan finally acquired title to the entire tract at New Hope.

In January, 1847, Brannan began the publication of the *Yerba Buena California Star*, using the press on which *The Prophet* had been printed by the Saints in New York. This was the first newspaper printed in San Francisco and the second English paper in California.

Of the "Brooklyn" Company, near 140 found their way to Salt Lake Valley between 1848-1850, and joined the main body of the Church. Some of those who remained in California, together with Samuel Brannan, their leader, left the Church. Some later joined Mormon colonies in San Bernardino and in Arizona.

Samuel Brannan was a capable, energetic man, but disappointed in the failure of his plans to get the main body of the Church to settle in California. He became California's first millionaire. Through unwise investments he lost his entire fortune and spent the final years of his life in poverty.[22]

Supplementary Readings

1. Roberts, *A Comprehensive History of the Church*. pp. XIX-XXII. ("Exodus." A compact summary or epitome of a 544 page story of the Mormon Exodus.)

2. *Ibid*, pp. 2-20. (Impatience of mob forces. Warren proclamation, Golden Point incident. Harvest party and picket incidents. Daniel Wells, defender of Nauvoo. Nauvoo Treaty surrender.)

3. *Ibid*, pp. 42-59. (The march of an industrial column. Sufferings on Sugar Creek. Sufferings made light of — God vindicated planting that others may reap.)

4. *Eventful Narratives: The Faith Promoting Series*; pp. 68-76. (A thrilling personal story of a young man's devotion, and daring heroism in the last battle at Nauvoo between the mob and the Mormons.)

---

[22] (Note) An account of Samuel Brannon's journey, to meet Brigham Young and the pioneers, will be told in a subsequent chapter.

5. Cowley, *Wilford Woodruff*, pp. 247-261. (President Woodruff's account of the last days in Nauvoo, and early stages of the movement West.)

6. *Autobiography of Parley P. Pratt*, pp. 337-347. (Incidents of the early stages of the Mormon exodus.)

7. Smith, *Essentials of Church History*, pp. 401-421. (A clear, concise account of this period.)

8. Evans, *One Hundred Years of Mormonism*, pp. 389-403. (The last days of Nauvoo.)

9. *Ibid.*, pp. 404-419. (Westward Ho!)

10. *Ibid.*, pp. 421-429. (Wayside stations.)

11. Evans, *Heart of Mormonism*, pp. 332-346. (The Mormons across the Mississippi. A long, long trail. Some plant, others reap.)

CHAPTER 29

THE MORMON BATTALION

A Story in Stone and Bronze

A visitor to the Utah State Capitol at Salt Lake City, may see at the right hand corner of the grounds as he approaches from the south, a beautiful monument. (See illustration.)

If he takes the time to examine this remarkable work of art he will see, carved in enduring stone and bronze, one of the most thrilling stories of western history.

The bronze figure of a soldier confronts the beholder. Flanking him on the left is a scene of pioneers enlisting as soldiers under the flag of the United States; on the right, these soldiers are on the march, some assisting in pulling wagons up and over a precipitous ascent, while still others are ahead, widening a cut to permit the passage of the wagons between the outjutting rocks. In the background are rugged mountains. And on the third side of this triangular monument may be seen the end of a great story and the dim and receding figure of a vanishing race, the American Indian.

Over the bronze man and the thrilling scene on either side of him, symbolizing the brooding spirit of the mighty West, is chiseled a beautiful head and upper body of a woman. She personifies the impulsive power and enduring courage that sustained these men and led them, as a vanguard of civilization, across trackless plains and over rocky defiles.

"The bronze figure of the battalion man is dignified, strong and reverential. He typifies that band of pioneer soldiers which broke a way through the rugged mountains and over trackless wastes.

"Hovering over and above him the beautiful female figure, with an air of solicitous care, guards him in his reverie. Her face stands out in full relief. The hair and diaphanous drapery waft back, mingling with the clouds, while the figure fades into dim outline in the massive peaks and mountains, seeming to pervade the air and the soil and her very soul.

"It is the Spirit back of the breaking of the soil by the farmer, back of the institution of our schools, back of our mines, back of our government and our very hearthsides. It permeates the air, the soil and the hearts of men. It tempers the character of all who come within the influence of the boundless plains and majestic peaks. It has led men to make a garden of a desert and a treasure house of the mountain. It has justified and approved every sacrifice to make this part of the world a better place in which to live. It is constant, never-ending—infinite."[1]

The Setting of the Story

The beginning of this story takes us back more than a century—to an exiled people camped on the Iowa plains—an unwanted people—leaving the confines of the United States. It takes us still farther, into the Blue Room of the White House in Washington, D.C., into the presence of James K. Polk, President of the United States. Elder Jesse C. Little, representative of the Church of Jesus Christ of Latter-day Saints, and Amos Kendall, ex-Postmaster-General of the United States, had just completed a three hour conference with the President on the subject of the Mormon migration to the West, then under way.

Elder Little had just received the assurance of the President that he would

[1]From the description of the Monument contained in a written report of Mr. Samuel C. Park, former Mayor of Salt Lake City, to the Monument Commission after viewing the model done by the sculptor, Mr. G. P. Griswold.

aid the Mormons to go to the West and protect them in their place of settlement. That was on June 3, 1846.

Before his death, Joseph Smith had made some preparations for moving his people into the Rocky Mountains. Desiring governmental sanction and protection for the enterprise, he had carried on negotiations with the Federal Government, with that end in view. Maps and other information of the West had been collected. After the martyrdom, Brigham Young carried the Prophet's plans forward. Before any government help could be obtained, however, the Saints were driven out of Nauvoo. Unable to dispose of much of their property they were destitute of cash. A contract with the Federal Government to build a line of blockhouses to protect the Oregon migration was sought. Such a contract would ease the financial problem and lend governmental sanction to the western movement of the Mormons.

On January 26, 1846, President Young wrote to Elder Jesse C. Little, then in New Hampshire, to go on a mission to Washington, D.C., with the objective of embracing "any facilities for emigration to the western coast which our government shall offer."

By the time Little reached Washington, war had been declared against Mexico. Little carried letters of introduction from a number of notable men, among them Judge John K. Kane, and his son, Captain Thomas L. Kane.

One of his first important contacts was with Amos Kendall, who had considerable influence in Washington. Of this meeting Little reports:

"We talked upon the subject of emigration and he thought arrangements could be made to assist our emigration by enlisting one thousand of our men, arming, equipping and

establishing them in California to defend the country."[2]

The Action of President Polk

This is the first indication of what was to be the Mormon Battalion. Elder Little, following Kendall's suggestion, wrote to the President asking for such a privilege. In a series of conferences with President Polk from June 1 to June 8, 1846, he secured the assurance of the President that when the Mormons reached the Rocky Mountains, a few companies would be received as volunteers by the United States Army to defend that area.

Elder Little was pleased with his success and forwarded his assurances to Brigham Young. President Polk seems to have been prompted by other motives than mere sympathy for the Saints. In his diary for June 2, he notes:

"Col. Kearny was also authorized to receive into service as volunteers a few hundred of the Mormons on their way to California, with a view to conciliate them, attach them to our country, and prevent them from taking part against us."[3]

The Mormons were becoming powerful enough to oblige the President to fear their allegiance to another nation. The President was also fearful of having a predominant force of Mormons in the United States army which should occupy California, and the final instructions to General Kearny from the War Department on this matter states:

"June 3, 1846—War Department, Washington.

"It is known that a large body of Mormon emigrants are en route to California for the purpose of settling in that country. You are desired to use all proper means to have a good understanding with them to the end that the United States may have their cooperation in taking possession of and holding that

[2]Little's report to Brigham Young.
[3]President Polk's *Diary*. Entry for June 2, 1846.

country. It has been suggested here that many of these Mormons would willingly enter the service of the United States, and aid us in our expedition against California. You are hereby authorized to muster into service such as can be induced to volunteer, not, however, to a number exceeding one-third of your entire force. Should they enter the service they will be paid as other volunteers and you can allow them to designate, as far as it can be properly done, the persons to act as officers thereof."[4]

Colonel Kearny, to whom this order was sent, was recruiting volunteers in Missouri and Illinois for a conquest of California. Kearny sent Captain Allen to intercept the Mormons on their journey west and receive the enlistments.

Exiles Become Soldiers

Captain Allen reached the camps of the Saints before Elder Little, who left Washington on June 9. Thus, although Brigham Young and the leaders were well aware of Elder Little's activities, and expected some sort of enlistment in the government service, the exact nature of that service was not known until Captain Allen appeared. To the leaders, the call to raise a Battalion at that time, which was to leave the main body of the Saints and march by a totally different route to the West, came as a surprise and was rather disconcerting. Eighteen hundred wagons, with the attendant teamsters and families, were encamped in various places between Nauvoo and Council Bluffs. A great number of the young unmarried men had gone into adjoining states to look for work, the wages of which would aid their destitute families. Five hundred teamsters, the majority with families, could hardly be spared. Brigham Young, upon hearing the enlistment order, said:

"I would rather have undertaken to raise two thousand men a year ago in twenty-four hours than one hundred in a week now."[5]

Why the Leaders Approved the Call

The leaders were, however, quick to see the advantages which the enlistment offered. In the first place the realization was now clear that it was too late in the season to expect to move Saints with their families into the Rocky Mountains that year. The plan had suddenly been changed to move the people into a place suitable for spending the winter and of sending a group of young men into the valleys of the mountains to prepare the way. Thus the raising of a Battalion of men to serve for one year's time, although it would interfere with the advance scout plan, would not greatly hamper the western movement, which could not get really under way until the following spring.

In the second place, the camps of Israel were in desperate need of funds. The committee, left in Nauvoo to dispose of their properties, were not finding cash buyers. All the surplus beds and bedding had been traded to the Missourians for corn and flour. Unless funds were forthcoming from some source the Saints could not survive the coming winter. The Battalion call presented an opportunity to get five hundred of the men to the West, feed them through the coming winter and pay them a wage which would be a godsend to their families.

In the third place, the Saints, certain now that they must remain on the plains of Iowa and Nebraska during the winter of 1846-47, were facing perplexing problems which enlistment in the United States Army would solve. The only suitable places for spending the

[4] *Executive Document* No. 60, order of Secretary of War W. L. Marcy to General Kearney to muster the Mormons into service.

[5] *Journal History*, 1846, entry of July 13.

winter were located on Indian lands. While the Indians were especially friendly to the Mormons, both peoples being exiles, the Indian Agents were not. It became increasingly evident, during the early summer of 1846, that an attempt to winter in the Iowa or Nebraska territory would be fraught with trouble. If a Battalion of soldiers was raised to march in the cause of the United States, the Government must of necessity protect the families of these men who wished to winter on the Indian lands.

Further, the State of Missouri was deeply agitated by the presence of the Mormons along her northern borders. This agitation was prompted by a fear that the large gathering of Mormons might attempt some sort of revenge against those who had driven them out, or try to re-establish themselves in the northern part of the state. The fact that these fears were groundless did not alter their efforts. Letters complaining against the presence of the Mormons so near Missouri, poured into Washington, D.C. The following letter from L. Marshall, prominent citizen of Putnam County, nearest the encampment of the Saints, shows how serious the situation had become. This letter was written July 4, 1846, and was addressed to the President of the United States.

"There is a set of men denominating themselves Mormons hovering on our frontier, well armed, justly considered as depredating on our property, and in our opinion, British emissaries, intending by insidious means to accomplish diabolical purposes, if circumstances favor, we consider it the duty of our common American father, to assume the responsibility, in defense of the 'brave and hardy men of the frontier' to take the necessary measures to disarm them and expel them from our border."[6]

---

[6]Old record A. G. O. Munitions Building; see also Golder, *The March of the Mormon Battalion*, p. 96.

A note of alarm, and the hint of the necessity of keeping troops in Missouri "to keep the Indians and Mormons in check," is found in a letter from Governor Edwards of Missouri to W. L. Marcy, Secretary of War, under date of August 11, 1846.

An enlistment in the United States Army would dispel these fears and assist the government in the Saints' behalf. A refusal might well lead to a belief in all the false charges being brought against them.

Brigham Young was also desirous that the Saints should not only have a part in settling the West but in conquering it as well. This would assure them security and establish a right to the country.

All of these various factors were known to Brigham Young and prompted his reply that Captain Allen should have his Battalion. Despite the hardships which the absence of 500 able-bodied men from Israel's Camp would entail, it would, however, prove a blessing. When Elder Little later arrived he was highly complimented for the success of his negotiations in Washington.

Reactions to the Call

If the leaders of the Saints foresaw the advantages of raising a Mormon Battalion for the United States Army, the followers generally did not. The appearance of Captain Allen filled them with dismay. The call to enlist seemed another blow added to the already crushing load. It took all the persuasion of Brigham Young, Heber C. Kimball, Parley P. Pratt, Orson Pratt, and others to change their suspicions of the government into gratitude. These brethren journeyed from camp to camp with Captain Allen, explaining the call and its advantages. Near Mount Pisgah Brigham Young and Heber C. Kimball met Elder Little, who made his report and confirmed all that Captain Allen had said. In a letter written from Mount Pisgah to the Saints at Garden Grove we get the gist of Brigham Young's plea for volunteers:

"The United States wants our friendship, the President wants to do us good and secure our confidence. The outfit of this five hundred men costs us nothing, and their pay will be sufficient to take their families over the mountains. There is war between Mexico and the United States, to whom California must fall a prey, and if we are the first settlers the old citizens cannot have a Hancock (county) or Missouri pretext to mob the Saints. The thing is from above for our good."[7]

In a letter to the Saints still in Nauvoo he adds:

"This is the first time the government has stretched forth its arm to our assistance, and we receive their profits with joy and thankfulness. We feel confident they (the Battalion) will have little or no fighting. The pay of the five hundred men will take their families to them. The Mormons will then be the old settlers and have a chance to choose the best locations."[8]

The final enrollment took place at Council Bluffs on July 13. An American flag was brought out from the supply wagons, "hoisted to a tree mast, and under it the enrollment took place."[9]

The afternoon before the departure of the troops a dance was held. Colonel Thomas L. Kane, who was paying a visit to Brigham Young at Council Bluffs, later wrote this description:

"There was no sentimental affection at their leave-taking. The afternoon before was appropriated to a farewell ball; and a more merry dancing rout I have never seen, though the company went without refreshments, and their ball-room was of the most primitive. It was the custom, whenever the larger camps rested for a few days together, to make great

arbors or boweries, as they called them, of poles and brush, and wattling, as places of shelter for their meetings of devotion or conference. In one of these, where the ground had been trodden firm and hard by the worshipers of the popular Father Taylor's precinct, was gathered now the mirth and beauty of the Mormon Israel.

"If anything told the Mormons had been bred to other lives, it was the appearance of the women, as they assembled here. Before their flight, they had sold their watches and trinkets as the most available resource for raising ready money; and, hence, like their partners, who wore waistcoats cut with useless watch pockets, they, although their ears were pierced and bore the loopmarks of rejected pendants, were without earrings, finger-rings, chains, or brooches. Except such ornaments, however, they lacked nothing most becoming the attire of decorous maidens. The neatly darned white stocking, and clean, bright petticoat, the artistically clear starched collar and chemisette, the something faded, only because too well washed, lawn or gingham gown, that fitted modishly to the waist of the pretty wearer these, if any of them, spoke of poverty, spoke of a poverty that had known its better days."[10]

Benefits and Effects of the Enlistment

Some of the results of the enlistment were immediately felt. On July 1, Captain Allen had been assured by Brigham Young that the Battalion would be raised. On the following day ten Indian chiefs, then near Council Bluffs, were brought before Captain Allen and induced to put their marks as signatures to a treaty guaranteeing to the Mormons the right to stop upon the Indian lands, to cultivate the soil, and to pass to and fro through it without molestation.[11]

On July 16 Captain Allen gave a written approval for the Mormons to reside in the Pottawattamie country. A similar document was executed, permitting the Saints enroute to the West to

[7]*History of Brigham Young*, Ms., Bk. 2, pp. 3-34.
[8]*Ibid.*
[9]Kane's Lecture before the American Historical Society. "The Mormons," p. 80.
[10]Thomas L. Kane, "Address delivered before the Historical Society of Pennsylvania on March 26, 1850." See also Tyler, *The Mormon Battalion*, pp. 80-82.
[11]*Journal History*, pp. 91-100.

make such stopping places as were necessary.

"To facilitate the emigration of the whole people to California and for such time as may be reasonably required for this purpose.

"At such stopping points they may entrench themselves with such stockade works or other fortifications as may be necessary for their protection and defense against the Indians. This during the pleasure of the President of the United States."[12]

These documents were subsequently approved by President Polk, largely through the influence of Thomas L. Kane, who had found the Mormons a delightful people and had become their staunch friend.

A further benefit was soon realized. The Battalion men were allowed to wear their regular clothing rather than uniforms, and were paid in advance for this clothing when the companies reached Fort Leavenworth. A year's pay in advance for their clothing, at the rate of $3.50 per month, would mean $42.00 each, or $21,000 for the entire Battalion. The greater part of this was sent back to their families, together with their first month's pay. Secret agents were also sent by the Saints to Santa Fe through which the Battalion would pass to bring back to the Camps of Israel the pay checks which would then have accrued. In a letter to the Battalion, Brigham Young said:

"We consider the money you have received, as compensation for your clothing, a peculiar manifestation of the kind providence of our Heavenly Father at this particular time, which is just the time for the purchasing of provisions and goods for the winter supply of the camp."[13]

The pay of the Battalion men ranged from $7.00 a month for privates to $50 a month for captains. At the end of

one year's service their equipment was to become the personal property of the men, on their discharge in California.

The Families Left Behind

The raising of the Battalion had been done from the advance companies, which left five hundred wagons without men as teamsters. To fill in the gaps President Young wrote to the Saints camped at Garden Grove under date of July 7:

"The places of these five hundred teamster-soldiers must be immediately supplied, and we want you to gather up all the old men and boys and all the others who are capable of going into the army, driving oxen, herding cattle and sheep, milking cows, chopping wood, drawing water, cutting grass, pitching and stacking hay, etc., from the farm, and those who may be in Missouri at work and all others within your call, and dispatch them to Council Bluffs forthwith, or five hundred teams must be left without drivers." * * *

"The demand we are making on you for every man and boy (only enough left to watch the farm crops and herds), we shall take immediately in all the regions of Nauvoo and there must be no deafness on this subject."[14]

Brigham Young promised the Battalion members who left their families that he would see that all were provided for and either taken forward with the main camp or cared for in one of the stopping places.[15]

This promise was faithfully kept. Brigham Young later asserting with justifiable pride, that the families of the Battalion men had fared even better than the others.

The plan, at the time the Battalion was called, was to winter the Saints on Grand Island in the Platte River. This island was fifty-two miles long, with an average width of a mile and three-quarters, and was well timbered. Near at

[12]*Journal History*, pp. 98-100.
[13]*History of Mormon Church*, American, March, 1912, p. 310.

[14]*Journal History*, 1846, pp. 30-34.
[15]*History of Brigham Young*, Ms., Bk. 2, pp. 4, 5.

hand were wide prairies covered with grass that might be cut for hay.

This plan was later changed and the Saints moved into Winter Quarters, across the river from Council Bluffs, not far from what is now Omaha, Nebraska.

Carving Out a Road For a Nation

The march of the Mormon Battalion is often called the greatest march of infantry in the history of the world. At the end of the journey Lieutenant Colonel P. St. George Cooke, in an order to the Battalion, wrote:

"The Lieutenant Colonel commanding congratulates the Battalion on their safe arrival on the shores of the Pacific ocean, and the conclusion of their march of over two thousand miles. History will be searched in vain for an equal march of infantry."[16]

The route followed by the Battalion led its members from Ft. Leavenworth, across the arid regions of the Southwest, to historic Santa Fe. Captain Allen, who had become a friend of the Battalion men, died at Fort Leavenworth after having ordered the Battalion to proceed on their journey without him. His death was deeply lamented by the Battalion. Lieutenant A. J. Smith was sent from the regular army to replace him. As the Battalion was part of the army of General Kearny whom it was trying to overtake, the Battalion felt that their own Captain Jefferson Hunt, of Company A, should command them until Kearny himself should appoint a command. Smith was accepted as commander, however, when the officers were brought to realize that their own commissions were not yet sanctioned by the War Department and they would be unable to draw on government supplies.

[16]Roberts, *The Mormon Battalion*, p. 2.

The march to Santa Fe was conducted at a rapid pace, which told severely on the men who had been already weakened by their journey across Iowa from Nauvoo. A number of Battalion men had been allowed to take their wives and families where private wagons were provided. The march was extremely hard for the women, but they bore the burdens of army life without complaint.

From the journals of Battalion men we get an insight into their trials. Henry Standage, under date of August 17, wrote in his journal:

"We traveled 25 miles this day across one of the most dreary deserts that ever man saw, suffering much from the intense heat of the sun and for want of water. The grass, not more than two inches high, and as curly as the wool on a Negro's head, and literally dried up by the heat of the sun. The teams also suffered much from the sand. I drank some water today the buffaloes had wallowed in. * * * Saw many buffaloes today and many wounded by the Battalion. Some killed. Camp'd without water in this desert and not a blade of grass for our mules."

Day after day the march continued into the Southwest. Feet blistered by the hot sands and shoulders galled by the heavy packs, there was no time to rest. Often men, so weary they could not endure the grind, fell behind and trudged into camp hours after the rest. It soon became apparent that this was no march for women and children, even where private wagons had been brought for them. On September 16, at the last crossing of the Arkansas River, the commanding officer insisted that the families accompanying the Battalion, twelve or fifteen in number, should be detached and sent under a guard of ten men up the Arkansas to Pueblo at the east base of the Rockies. There were many protests, but future events proved the wisdom of this procedure.

MARCH OF THE MORMON BATTALION, photograph of oil painting by G. M. Ottinger in the Bureau of Information on Temple Square.

MORMON PIONEER MEMORIAL BRIDGE, Omaha, Nebraska, near the site first ferry placed in operation across the Missouri River by Brigham Young at Winter Quarters in the fall of 1846.

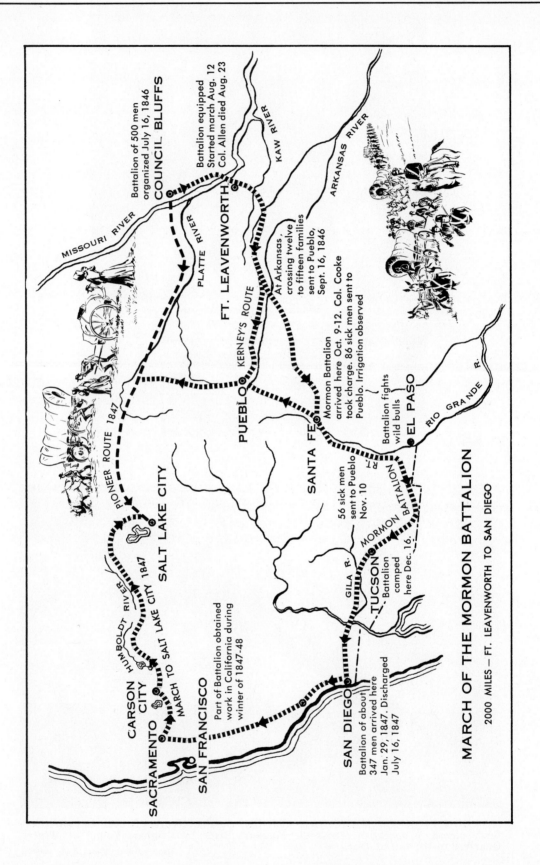

MARCH OF THE MORMON BATTALION

2000 MILES — FT. LEAVENWORTH TO SAN DIEGO

Hardships For the Battalion

During the days which followed there was much to discourage the soldiers. The Journal of James A. Scott, under date of September 26, reads:

"March! march! march! is the daily task. Daybreak brings the reveille, sick or well must go either to roll call or to the doctor; next get your breakfast and strike your tents with all possible speed; then left! left! all day over the sand, through dust, over hills and across valleys, sometimes twelve, fifteen and eighteen miles. Halt, stack arms, pitch tents, run all over creation gathering buffalo chips or a little brush and getting water, draw rations, cook supper, eat, then roll call, and by the time the evening chores are finished it is dark. Attend to evening duties, go to bed and sleep on the rough, cold ground, with only one blanket and a thin tent to shelter from the cold. Say, sympathetic reader, is not the condition of the Mormon soldier hard? But dwell not my mind on these things; gloom, perhaps repentance at having started the journey, might overcome thee. Cheer up, drooping Saint, and look forward to green fields, pleasant gardens and neat farm houses that will soon adorn the valleys of California and think thy hand had a part in the accomplishment of this."[17]

On October 9, the first detachment of the Battalion reached Santa Fe. This is the oldest city of the Southwest, a place of 6,000 inhabitants and an important trade center between Mexico and the United States.

General Kearny had entered Santa Fe without opposition and taken the city in the name of the United States. Leaving Colonel Doniphan in charge, Kearny had gone on to the West. Doniphan had shown friendship for the Mormons in the Missouri troubles. When the battalion entered the city, he had a salute of a hundred guns fired in its honor.

At Santa Fe Lieutenant-Colonel P. St. George Cooke, appointed by Kearny before his departure, took over the command of the Battalion. Speaking of the condition of the Battalion at the time of taking over command, Cooke says:

"Everything conspired to discourage the extraordinary undertaking of marching that Battalion eleven hundred miles, for the much greater part through an unknown wilderness, without road or trail, and with a wagon train.

"It was enlisted, too, much by families; some were too old and feeble, and some too young; it was embarrassed by many women; it was undisciplined; it was much worn by traveling on foot, and marching from Nauvoo, Illinois; their clothing was very scant; there was no money to pay them, or clothing to issue; their mules were utterly broken down; the quartermaster department was without funds, and its credit bad; and animals were scarce. Those procured were very inferior, and were deteriorating every hour for lack of forage or grazing."[18]

The Battalion was now inspected and eighty-six men, found sick or unable to endure the march ahead, were detached with nearly all the women to Pueblo, to join those already sent there for the winter. It was understood that the Pueblo detachment would have the privilege of going north in the spring to join the main body of the Saints in their westward trek and move with them to the West "at government expense." Five wives of Battalion officers were reluctantly allowed to accompany the expedition, but furnished their own transportation.

It was at Santa Fe that the Battalion saw irrigation for the first time. Tyler thus describes it:

"Canals for irrigation purposes were found all along the banks of the river. Some of them several miles in length. They conveyed water to the farms, or as they were called in that country, ranches. There being little or no rain during the growing season, the water was made to flow over the ground until it was sufficiently saturated, and then shut off until needed again for the same purpose."[19]

---

[17]*Journal History*, p. 273. Journal of James A. Scott.

[18]Cooke, *Conquest of New Mexico and California*, pp. 91-92.

[19]Tyler, *History of the Mormon Battalion*, pp. 180-183.

West From Santa Fe

On October 10, the Battalion left Santa Fe behind. The difficulties had just begun. The long journey to California across the roadless waste was enough to test the endurance of the strongest of men. Often wells had to be dug before water of any sort could be obtained.

The march took them 220 miles down the Santa Fe River; thence, the Battalion turned west to the San Pedro, which was reached December 9. At this place the only fighting the Battalion engaged in took place—a fight with wild bulls.

That country abounded in herds of cattle which had become wild. These, through curiosity, gathered along the line of march and a large number of infuriated bulls charged upon the wagon train. Several mules were gored to death and one of the wagons upset. Sergeant Albert Smith was run over by a bull and severely bruised. Amos Cox, of Company D, was tossed into the air on the horns of one of the animals and received a deep wound. It is variously estimated that from twenty to sixty of the wild bulls were killed before the infuriated animals would desist from their periodic attacks.

Leaving the San Pedro, the command marched northeasterly to Tucson, a Mexican town of four or five hundred inhabitants. When within sixteen miles, word was sent to Captain Comanduran, commanding a Mexican force there of 200 men, demanding the giving up of arms and a token that the inhabitants would not fight against the United States. Captain Comanduran declined and the Battalion prepared for battle. Upon arriving at Tucson the next day, however, the Battalion found that the garrison had fled. The march through the town was accomplished without a shot being fired.

In three days' march from Tucson the command reached the Gila River, down which the march continued. Attempting to lighten the load by floating the provisions on a raft down the river, the Battalion lost most of its supplies, which had to be unloaded to get the craft over frequent sandbars.

Southern California

From the mouth of the Gila the journey lay for a hundred miles across what is termed, in Southern California, the Colorado desert. Here there was intense suffering. Although the men were weakened by insufficient food, the burden was nevertheless doubled. Great stretches of sand forced the men to aid the teams by pulling on ropes. No water was to be had except by digging deep wells in the desert sands, and often these turned out to be dry holes. The animals were without forage. Tyler writes of these days:

"We found here the heaviest sands and hottest days, and coldest nights, with no water and but little food. At this time the men were nearly barefooted; some used, instead of shoes, rawhide wrapped around their feet, while others improvised a novel style of boots by stripping the skin from the leg of an ox. To do this a ring was cut around the hind leg above and below the gambrel joint, and then the skin was taken off without cutting it lengthwise. After this the lower end was sewed up with sinews, when it was ready for the wearer, the natural crook of the hide adapting it somewhat to the shape of the foot. Others wrapped cast-off clothing around their feet to shield them from the burning sand during the day and the cold at night.

"Before we arrived at the garrison many of the men were so nearly used up from thirst, hunger and fatigue, that they were unable to speak until they reached the water or had it brought to them. Those who were strongest reported, when they arrived, that they had passed many lying exhausted by the wayside."[20]

From Garrison Creek to San Phillipe proved the most difficult part of the journey for the wagons. In many places a way had to be cut through the solid rock and at times wagons were taken apart, lowered over a precipice, and put together again, so that they might reach camp while the road was being made. From here the march was somewhat more pleasant except for the meals, which had become entirely beef.

The march was scheduled to the city of San Diego to join General Kearny, but as it was supposed that the enemy was concentrated at Los Angeles, the direction was changed to come upon the city from the east. The first sight of the Pacific Ocean filled the tired travelers with an exaltation they had not known for months. Finding that all of California was already in the hands of the Americans, the company turned south to San Diego. The end of the journey was reached January 29, 1847. The Battalion had conquered the desert and made a wagon road of sorts over one of the most difficult sections of North America.

The Battalion was highly congratulated by Lt. Colonel Cooke for its splendid achievement in the face of such difficulties and for the fine calibre of its men.

Duty Versus Wealth

As no fighting remained to be done in California the Battalion was divided and placed to garrison the San Luis Rey Mission, San Diego and Los Angeles. Time was spent in building a fort at Los Angeles, in guarding the passes to the northeast, in building roads, and digging ditches. So faithfully did the Bat-

talion members discharge their duties, and so free were they from the vices of the usual soldiers, that great inducements were offered to get them to re-enlist when the term of service had expired. A few did re-enlist for a period of six months. The majority, however, had families which they were anxious to rejoin. Some of these families were, by that time, nearing Salt Lake Valley, while others were yet in the encampments on the plains. The destination of the main body of Saints had been determined by that time, and the Battalion members desired to join them in the Great Basin. It was a long trek to their future home and was accompanied by great hardship.

The Battalion members journeyed north to the Sacramento valley, thence east over the high Sierra Nevada mountains, and across the Nevada desert to Salt Lake Valley, where they arrived about the first of October, 1847. The greatest achievement of that journey was the cutting of a wagon road over the lofty Sierras, in the midst of dangerous Indian bands. Three of the men who volunteered to go in advance and blaze the trail were killed by Indians.

Meanwhile the Pueblo detachment of the Battalion had followed the Pioneers into Salt Lake Valley. There, their term of enlistment having expired, they were mustered out of service with full pay.

A few of the returning Battalion members remained for the winter in California. These found employment at Sutter's Mill in the Sacramento Valley, and were present at the time of the discovery of gold. It is from the journal of a Battalion man, Henry Bigler, that the authentic date for the discovery of gold in California is learned. On Monday, January 24, 1848, Bigler wrote:

---

[20]Tyler, *The Mormon Battalion*, pp. 244-245.

"This day some kind of metal was found in the tail race that looks like gold." A short time later Battalion members discovered gold on an island in the American river, which became famous as the rich "Mormon Diggin's."

The Battalion men, however, had hired out to Sutter by contract. Their contract was kept despite the fact that many times the amount of their wages could be obtained digging for gold.

The cry of "gold" was the signal for a mad scramble which turned the eyes of the civilized world to California. In the next seven years, $500,000,000 was added to the world's store of gold.

The call of duty and religion was greater than the appeal of riches. Spring found the Battalion members heading for the Great Basin with their savings—leaving the gold fields to which all the world seemed rushing. The Historian Bancroft could not pass unnoticed this remarkable test of character. He writes:

"As the wagons rolled up along the divide between the American river and the Cosumnes on the National 4th, their cannon thundered independence above the high Sierras. * * * Thus amidst the scenes now everyday becoming more and more absorbing, bringing to the front the strongest passions in man's nature, * * * at the call of what they deemed duty, these devotees of their religion unhesitatingly laid down their wealth-earning implements, turned their backs on what all the world was just then making ready with hot haste and mustered strength to grasp at, and struggle for, and marched through new toils and dangers to meet their exiled brethren in the desert."[21]

---

[21]Bancroft, *History of California*, Vol. 5.

Supplementary Readings

1. Roberts, *Comprehensive History of the Church*, pp. 60-121. Volume 3. (A full, comprehensive account of the Mormon Battalion.) pp. 65-66 (Kearny's instruction to Captain Allen), pp. 66-67 (Appeal of L.D.S. Church to the Federal Government for employment), pp. 67-75 (Jesse C. Little representing the Church in Washington on Battalion matters) pp. 77-79. (Captain Allen and Church leaders.)

2. *Ibid.*, pp. 84, note 61. (Colonel Kane describes a dance held for the Battalion before leaving for their Westward adventures.)

3. *Ibid.*, p. 84, notes. (Brigham Young and Father DeSmet.)

4. *Ibid.*, pp. 92-94. (Mental attitude of the Saints toward the United States.)

5. *Ibid.*, pp. 113-114. ("Blow the Right"—"God bless the colonel!" This is a charming, dramatic little story of vigorous, daring men, prayer, and a hard-headed, hard-hitting colonel.)

6. *Ibid.*, pp. 114-115, including note 24. ("The Fight with the Bulls." A real fight between desperate, enraged wild bulls, and men with courage and nerve. A true story of the wild West.)

7. *Ibid.*, pp. 115-117. (The Tucson incident, shows the decisive firmness of Colonel Cooke, and the manliness and kindly hearts of the Battalion boys.)

8. Roberts, *The Mormon Battalion, Its History and Achievements*, pp. 1-4. (The march of the Battalion compared with other historical marches.)

9. *Ibid.*, (See and study the map inside the front cover.)

10. *Ibid.*, pp. 85-96. (Anecdotes.)

11. Leah D. Widtsoe and Susa Young Gates, *Life Story of Brigham Young*, pp. 63-70. (An interesting account interspersed with appealing bits of verse and story.)

12. Evans, *The Heart of Mormonism*, pp. 357-361. (A Lift and a Blow. A brief readable story of the Mormon Battalion.)

13. Evans, *One Hundred Years of Mormonism*, pp. 430-438. ("A Ram in the Thicket." Evans gives a somewhat different view here than in his later book, cited above No. 12.)

14. Smith, *Essentials in Church History*, pp. 422-432. (The Mormon Battalion.)

CHAPTER 30

PIONEERS

Faces to the West

During the trying winter of 1846-47 one thought dominated the encampment of the Saints—"West in the Spring." The expression became a symbol of hope, which lightened people's loads, eased their sorrows, and assuaged their griefs. Colonel Kane, who spent much time among them, said:

"The Mormons took the young and hopeful side. They could make sport and frolic of their trials, and often turn the sharp suffering into right sound laughter against themselves. I certainly heard more jests while in this camp than I am likely to hear again in all the remainder of my days."[1]

Yet underneath the great hope for the future were hearts mellowed by griefs and sorrows which few people have known. Before the cold of winter prevented the spread of disease, 300 fresh graves appeared in the cemetery outside "Winter Quarters."[2] Weakened by the long trek from Nauvoo and the lack of sufficient vegetables in their diet, people became easy victims of malaria, scurvy, and other then little-known maladies. Scurvy, called by the Saints "Blackleg," caused the greatest sufferings and the majority of deaths. When the disease became rampant, wagons were sent into Missouri to get potatoes, which proved effective in checking and curing the disease. Horseradish found in an abandoned fort some distance from the camp, proved an ex-

cellent antidote. The disease was totally checked during the winter, but not until it had made inroads upon nearly every family.

The Indians, especially the tribe of Omahas wintering in the river bottoms, though professing the greatest of friendship, lived either by gift or theft, upon the cattle belonging to the Saints. Indian thieves were often caught and severely punished, but this did not greatly lessen the loss of cattle. It was during this winter that Brigham Young became well acquainted with Indian nature and formulated the policy for which he became famous—"It is cheaper to feed the Indians than to fight them." In the war which occurred during the winter between the Omahas and the Sioux and Iowas the Saints kept aloof.

Long months before the movement west could begin again, preparations were under way. Wagons were repaired and some new ones made. Canvas was sewed into covers and tents. Shoes were fashioned and socks knitted. A gristmill was constructed, and all the grain, except that needed for the animals, was ground into flour. Those who had no other tasks set about gathering willows and weaving them into baskets and half-bushel measures. Some of the men manufactured washboards. These were for sale to the people of Iowa and Missouri. Brigham Young, in a letter to the Apostles who had gone to England, said in reference to these articles, "Hundreds of dollars' worth have already been completed and there is a

[1]Kane, *The Mormons*, p. 48.
[2]Kane, *The Mormons*, in Tyler, *History of the Mormon Battalion*, p. 94. (Note) See also Roberts, *Comprehensive History of the Church*, Vol. III, p. 151.

prospect of quite an income from this source in the spring."[3]

Revelation of Brigham Young

On January 14, 1847, Brigham Young gave to the Saints the only formal revelation he ever set down in writing, "The Word and Will of the Lord" upon the march of the camps of Israel to the West.[4]

The following are excerpts:

"Let all the people of the Church of Jesus Christ of Latter-day Saints, and those who

"Winter Quarters" Monument at Florence, Nebraska, erected to the memory of the nearly six hundred who lie buried in the Pioneer cemetery.

---

[3] Brigham Young's letter to Elders Hyde, Pratt, and Taylor, dated January 6, 1847, *Millennial Star*, Vol. 9, p. 100.

[4] It must not be supposed that this was the only revelation he received. From the journals of his associates it is evident that the Spirit of the Lord was constantly relied on by him in his decisions.

journey with them, be organized into companies, with a covenant and promise to keep all the commandments and statutes of the Lord our God.

"Let the companies be organized with captains of hundreds, captains of fifties, and captains of tens, with a president and his two counselors at their head, under the directions of the Twelve Apostles.

"And this shall be our covenant, that we will walk in all the ordinances of the Lord.

"Let each company provide themselves with all the teams, wagons, provisions, clothing and other necessaries for the journey that they can.

"When the companies are organized, let them go to with their might, to prepare for those who are to tarry.

"Let each company with their captains and presidents, decide how many can go next spring; then choose out a sufficient number of able-bodied and expert men, to take teams, seeds, and farming utensils, to go as pioneers to prepare for putting in spring crops.

"Let each company bear an equal proportion, according to the dividends of their property, in taking the poor, the widows, the fatherless, and the families of those who have gone into the army, that the cries of the widow and the fatherless come not up into the ears of the Lord against this people.

"Let each company prepare houses, and fields, for raising grain, for those who are to remain behind this season, and this is the will of the Lord concerning his people.

"Let every man use all his influence and property to remove this people to the place where the Lord shall locate a stake of Zion.

"And if ye do this with a pure heart, in all faithfulness, ye shall be blessed; you shall be blessed in your flocks, and in your herds, and in your fields, and in your houses, and in your families. * * *

"And let my servants that have been appointed go and teach this my will to the Saints, that they may be ready to go to a land of peace.

"Go thy way and do as I have told you, and fear not thine enemies; for they shall not have power to stop my work.

"Zion shall be redeemed in mine own due time.

"And if any man shall seek to build up himself, and seeketh not my counsel, he shall have no power, and his folly shall be made manifest.

"Seek ye and keep all your pledges, one with another, and covet not that which is thy brother's.

"Keep yourselves from evil to take the

name of the Lord in vain, for I am the Lord your God, even the God of your fathers, the God of Abraham, and of Isaac, and of Jacob."[5]

The Pioneer Company

As spring slowly approached, Brigham Young sent word to all the camps selecting those who were to go west with the advance company of "Pioneers" to make roads and prepare the way.

This company was to be composed of 144 men who were to go forward, without their families, so as to be less handicapped in the hard work which lay ahead. They were to be the vanguard of the movement. The remainder of the people were to march by families under appointed leaders when the grass should be high enough for their cattle and sheep.

The unity and cooperation of the people in preparing for the long trail west is one of the remarkable elements of the Exodus. This unity was marred, however, by a few defections. Bishop Miller, who had showed an independent spirit during the entire journey from Nauvoo, and had, with sixteen teams, traveling ahead of the Camp of Israel, now broken with the Twelve. Contrary to the advice of Brigham Young he had wintered with sixty-two wagons, among which were those of Anson Call, on the Running Water, eleven days drive due north of the line of travel of the Saints. Following orders from the Twelve, Miller's encampment moved into Winter Quarters in the spring. Here Bishop Miller came out in open opposition to Brigham Young and the Council and declared that it was his conviction that the Saints should settle in Texas. When his views were not accepted he withdrew from the camp. With a few followers, mostly his own relatives, he went to Texas and joined Lyman Wight.

On April 5, the journey of the Pioneers had its initial march. Heber C. Kimball, with six of his company's wagons, moved out to Cutler's Park, about four miles west of Winter Quarters. Other wagons joined as they were ready, and the company moved westward to the Elkhorn River and commenced building a ferry.

Meanwhile President Young presided at the seventeenth Annual Conference of the Church held at Winter Quarters, April 6. On the seventh, Brigham Young left Winter Quarters with twenty-five wagons and encamped ten miles west. He returned to Winter Quarters the next day, with members of the Apostles' Quorum, to meet Parley P. Pratt, who was returning from the British Mission. Together with John Taylor and Orson Hyde, Pratt had journeyed to England during the winter to straighten out difficulties in the mission and encourage the English Saints.

As John Taylor was reported enroute with some scientific instruments, the leaders awaited his arrival. On April thirteenth he brought into Winter Quarters, "two sextants, one circle of reflection, two artificial h o r i z o n s, two barometers, several thermometers, telescopes, etc."[6]

These had been brought from England at the suggestion of Orson Pratt that such instruments would be needed in the new land.

John Taylor also brought a number of maps of the West which he had obtained in Washington, D. C., from General Atchison, then Senator from Missouri. The brethren were especially pleased

---

[5]*Doctrine and Covenants*, Section 136:1-11, 16-21.

[6]Orson Pratt's Journal, *Millennial Star*, Vol. 12, p. 18.

with Fremont's maps of routes west. One of these was the route followed by Fremont to California, via Great Salt Lake, in 1843. Fremont's maps also included one of his return from California, "in 1844, via Southern California, Mojave River, Las Vegas, Rio Virgin, the Sevier, Utah Lake, Spanish Fork Canyon, Uintah River and so to Pueblo and the East."[7] Thomas Bullock made sketches of these maps for the use of the Pioneers.[8]

The real start of the Pioneers was made from the Platte River April 16. From this point there was but one objective, the valleys of the Rocky Mountains.

The company numbered one hundred forty-three men, three women, and two children. As previously mentioned, no women or children were to accompany the Pioneers. During the final preparations Harriet Page Wheeler Young, wife of Lorenzo Young, being stricken with malaria, persuaded the Council to let her go with the camp and get away from the river bottoms. Her two children accompanied her. Her going led to the addition of Clara Decker Young, wife of Brigham Young, and Ellen Sanders Kimball, wife of Heber C. Kimball.

The outfit consisted of 73 wagons, 93 horses, 52 mules, 66 oxen, 19 cows, 17 dogs and some chickens.

The camp had a dual organization, one following the revelation received at Winter Quarters, and the other a military organization. Under the first, the camp was divided into hundreds, fifties, and tens with a captain over each. Stephen Markham and A. P. Rockwood were appointed captains of hundreds,

with five captains of fifties, and fourteen captains of tens.[9] In the military organization Brigham Young was elected Lieutenant General; Stephen Markham, Colonel; John Park and Shadrach Roundy, Majors. The organization of the tens remained the same for both purposes.

The camp carried with them a cannon mounted on wheels. The captains of tens appointed forty-eight men as a constant night guard, "who were divided into four watches to be on duty half the night at a time."[10]

The order of travel as given by Brigham Young is recorded by William Clayton in his journal:

"After we start from this spot, every man must carry his loaded gun, or else have it in his wagon where he can seize it at a moment's notice. If the gun is cap-lock, he should take off the cap and put on a piece of leather to exclude moisture and dirt; if a flint-lock, he must take out the priming and fill the pan with tow or cotton. The wagons must now keep together while traveling, and not separate as heretofore they have separated. Every man is to keep beside his own wagon and is not to leave it, except by permission.

"At five o'clock in the morning the bugle is to be sounded as a signal for every man to arise and attend prayers before he leaves his wagon. Then the people will engage in cooking, eating, feeding teams, etc., until seven o'clock, at which time the train is to move at the sound of the bugle. Each teamster is to keep beside his team with loaded gun in hand or within easy reach, while the extra men, observing the same rule regarding their weapons, are to walk by the side of the particular wagons to which they belong; and no man may leave his post without the permission of his officers. In case of an attack or any hostile demonstration by Indians, the wagons will travel in double file—the order of the encampment to be in a circle, with the mouth of each wagon to the outside and the horses and cattle tied inside the circle. At half-past eight each evening the bugles are

[7]Roberts, Comprehensive History of the Church, Vol. 3, p. 162 (also footnote).
[8]See History of Brigham Young, Ms., 1847, p. 80. For copies of Fremont's maps see Roberts, Comprehensive History of the Church, Vol. 3, pp. 199, 234.

[9]For details and names see Roberts, Comprehensive History of the Church, Vol. III, p. 164.
[10]History of Brigham Young, Ms., 1847, p. 83.

to be sounded again, upon which signal all will have prayers in their wagons, and be retired to rest by nine o'clock."[11]

William Clayton who kept a journal of the advance company of "Pioneers."

Used by permission, Utah State Historical Society

The Mormon Exodus Part of a Great Western Movement

The Mormon exodus to the West was unique in that it was a movement of an entire people under unfavorable circumstances to a land which had been uninviting to other emigrants. It was not, however, the only movement of people to the West nor by any means the first.

[11]*William Clayton's Journal*, Entry for April 17. See also, *Juvenile Instructor*, Vol. 21, p. 230.

The Lewis and Clark expedition, which traversed the western regions to the Oregon country and back in 1804-6, turned the attention of America to the West. Adventurous spirits saw the unsettled region a golden opportunity for a life of freedom and profit.

The first of these adventurers to push into the little-known region were the fur hunters. The early ventures were individual enterprises in trapping, and in trading with the Indians for furs. Those who penetrated the valleys of the Rockies came to be known as "Mountain Men." The individual trapper was superseded by the organized fur companies. Both American and British companies penetrated the Rocky Mountain area. Every stream and lake were visited by these intrepid forerunners of civilization, who left a lasting imprint on the names of streams, mountains and places of rendezvous. Further, these "Mountain Men" carried back to civilization a store of knowledge concerning the mountain country. The forts established by them for protection from hostile Indians became objectives and guide posts for every caravan of emigrants who later came west.

By the time of the "Mormon Exodus," the fur-bearing animals were rapidly disappearing and the fur trade was swiftly declining. Most of the trading posts in the Great Basin had been abandoned. Fort Bridger, about 100 miles east of Salt Lake, was one of the last outposts of the fur trade and this was abandoned in 1853.

The fur hunter was followed by the missionary to the Indian. Aside from the work of the early Catholic Priests, who pushed northward from Mexico into California, Arizona, and Southern Utah, little work had been done among the Indians. The missionary activity in the Northwest was a Protestant movement beginning in 1834, in which year Jason and Daniel Lee were sent to that region by the Missionary board of the Methodist Episcopal Church. They journeyed to Oregon via the Oregon Trail. In 1835, the Presbyterian Church sent Rev. Samuel Parker and Dr. Marcus Whitman to the Oregon country. Their party was under the protection of sixty trappers of the American Fur Company and traveled in wagons as far as Fort Laramie. In 1836, Dr. Whitman took his wife west and induced Rev. H. H. Spaulding and his wife to join them. The wives of these missionaries were the first white women to make the overland journey to the northwest.

After 1836, companies of settlers headed west each year over the Oregon Trail. None of the companies were of any size until 1841. In that year John Barlism's company, consisting of 48 men and 15 women, joined by 17 missionaries and adventurers, made the journey to California via the Oregon Trail to Fort Hall, then down the Bear River, through Cache Valley, around the north end of Salt Lake to the sinks of the Humboldt and thence to California.[12]

In 1842 Elijah White led a company of 112 men, women and children from Jackson and Platte Counties, Missouri, to Oregon. Wagons were taken as far as Green River and there cut up to make pack saddles.

In 1843, a larger company was led from Independence, Missouri, made up of emigrants from various states. This company comprised about 1,000 people, 120 wagons, 5,000 cattle. It went west from Fort Laramie as far as Fort

Bridger before turning north to Fort Hall and thence to Oregon. In the following year, 1,400 people migrated to Oregon, and in 1845 over 3,000 persons passed over the Oregon Trail to the Columbia River Valley. By the end of that year 7,000 Americans had reached Oregon. In 1846, about 2,500 persons migrated to the West. Nearly half of these journeyed to California, some passing through Salt Lake Valley via the Echo and Weber Canyons in Utah and around the south end of Great Salt Lake.

One company, the Donner party, in 1846 made the first wagon trail down Emigration Canyon to the road around the south end of Great Salt Lake. The next year the Mormon migration followed the wheel tracks of the Donner party into Salt Lake Valley.

In the same year, 1847, nearly 5,000 emigrants passed over the Oregon Trail to the northwest.

Thus, by the spring of 1847, the Oregon Trail had become a great national highway which had been used for forty years by the forerunners of an empire. The Exodus of the Saints was part of a great surge to the west of an adventurous people moving the confines of a nation to the shores of the Western Sea. Of all the emigrant trains which passed to the west, the Mormons alone were forced to go. They alone were seeking a home, where they might preserve their faith. The search for wealth, for gold, for fame, did not prompt their journey. Therefore it was easier for them to prepare homes in barren valleys and to find a contentment in seclusion which none others desired.

---

[12]See Bancroft, *History of California*, Vol. 4, pp. 268-271.

The Mormon Trail

Strangely enough the Pioneers did not start westward on the Oregon Trail. They made a new road to the west which came to be known as the "Mormon Trail." This road ran to the north of the Platte River, while the Oregon Trail was on the south of it. The two routes nearly paralleled each other, with often no more than the width of the river between. The reasons for this are not at first clear. The Oregon Trail was easy to follow. There was no road to make or bridges to build; south of the river the grass was green, while the Pioneers passed for days through blackened stubble, where prairie fires had left scarcely a vestige of feed for cattle or horses.

It was the vision of the leaders which prompted the making of the Mormon Trail. Had the Pioneers been the only company of Saints traveling west, they would certainly have crossed the Platte and followed the Oregon Trail, saving weeks in travel and hard labor. But the Pioneers were not looking for easy travel for themselves. They had in mind the moving of 15,000 people in their wake, and probably countless other thousands as the years progressed. The route they chose was somewhat shorter than the Oregon Trail, with a better grade.[13] The grass, though scanty for the Pioneer company, would be plentiful by the time the larger companies should follow.[14]

Further, the greater part of the emigrants going west on the Oregon Trail

---

[13](Note) This route is now followed by the Union Pacific Railway between Omaha and Laramie.

[14](Note) The Indians fired the old grass of the prairies each spring, so that the new growth of tender grass would entice the buffalo herds to come into their hunting grounds during the summer. Along the Oregon Trail the trappers fired the prairies in the fall so that the spring burning by the Indians would not hinder an early growth of grass to feed the animals of their pack trains.

were from Missouri. Many were old enemies of the Mormons. A trail to the north of the Platte would avoid contacts which might have proved unpleasant, to say the least. Many times, from Winter Quarters to Fort Laramie, when the going was difficult, a council was called to consider the advisability of crossing the river to the Oregon Trail. Each time the consideration of the camps to follow outweighed inconveniences to the Pioneers. The years which followed show the wisdom of their judgment.

Buffalo on the Plains

As the Pioneers moved forward a few miles each day, the monotony was broken by unusual events. For accounts of these we are indebted to William Clayton, Thomas Bullock and others, who kept daily journals. The sight of buffalo herds created considerable interest. Orson Pratt writes:

"During the time of our halts we had to watch our teams to keep them from mingling with the buffalo. I think I may safely say that I have seen ten thousand buffalo during the day. Some few antelope, which came near our wagons, we killed for food, their meat being very excellent, but we did not allow ourselves to kill any game only as we wanted it for food. * * * Young buffalo calves frequently came in our way and we had to carry them away from the camp to prevent their following us.

"About this time, between the buffalo and the prairie fires, the animals of the camp were nearly famished. The buffalo became very numerous. It was impracticable to give an approximate estimate of their numbers, say one hundred thousand or more. They were poor in flesh, and no more were killed than the necessities of the camp required. At one time a herd of several miles in extent was seen. The prairie was literally a dense, black mass of moving animals."[15]

Thomas Bullock adds:

"Our camps had to stop two or three miles while the droves went around us. As soon as

---

[15]James A. Little, *From Kirtland to Salt Lake City*, pp. 82-83.

they passed many would stop and look at us, as if amazed at such a sight. We caught several calves alive. Remember, catching a buffalo calf and a domesticated one, are two different things. A swift horse is sometimes pushed to catch up with him. They are as swift as horses, and although the old animals are the ugliest racers of any brutes, they get over the ground very fast, and an inexperienced rider is soon left to admire their beauty in the distance."[16]

Indians often visited the camp and these were generally given gifts of tobacco, beads, and fishhooks. While the Pioneers were passing through the country of the Pawnees, some animals were stolen. Often a double guard was kept at night for fear of an Indian attack. Fortunately the Mormon Exodus occurred at a time when the Indians of the plains were at peace with the whites. The friendly attitude of the Mormon emigrants toward their "red brothers"

[16]James A. Little, *From Kirtland to Salt Lake City*, p. 83.

caused the latter to gradually distinguish between Mormons and other white men. This produced an immunity from attack for later Mormon emigrant trains which has been often remarked by the historian.

Recording the Journey

The pioneer camp had somewhat the nature of a scientific expedition. Orson Pratt, who had a keen scientific mind, made almost daily observations of the latitude, longitude, and altitude of the camping places. He also noted the atmospheric conditions and the changes in flora and fauna along the way. The accuracy of his calculations is attested by modern day calculations.

A record was made of distances traveled each day, and the total distances between landmarks. This was chiefly the work of William Clayton.

The "Odometer," invented by William Clayton and Appleton M. Harmon to indicate the miles traveled by the "Pioneers."

Used by permission, Utah State Historical Society

For a time the estimate of distances traveled was a matter of guess. Then Clayton devised the method of tying a red rag on the spoke of a wheel and of computing the miles traveled by the number of revolutions of the wheel. This was a tiring job, but its very tiresomeness led to the invention of an instrument to do the counting. This instrument was made on the principle of the endless screw and, by a system of wooden wheels and cogs, registered the miles and tenths of miles traveled. It was called the "Odometer," and was the work of William Clayton and Appleton M. Harmon, a skillful mechanic.[17] After its installation on the 10th or 12th of May, accurate mileage was kept until the company reached Salt Lake Valley. Data concerning the route was left from time to time for the companies which were following. This information was carved into the face of trees or on the face of a post set in the ground. For example, on the 8th of May a cedar post was planted on a north bluff of the Platte Valley, approaching near the river, on which was written:

From Winter Quarters, 295 miles
May 8th, '47. Camp all well.
W. Clayton

Sometimes letters were sealed in a groove sawed into a board or post, with a sign to indicate their whereabouts. On the open plain, whitened buffalo skulls were commonly used as bulletins.[18] Westward of Fort Laramie the Pioneers planted posts every ten miles. Letters were often sent back to the

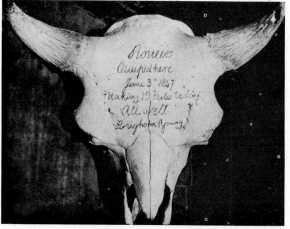

"Bulletin of the plains."
Used by permission, Church Historian's Office

Saints by parties of trappers and guides who were on their way East.

The Sabbath day was strictly observed, except for the necessities of keeping the camp in order and the stock tended, or when the necessity of reaching water or feed made camping impracticable.

Most of the members of the camp were young men, full of exuberance, which often led them to waste their time in numerous frivolities. Dancing, checkers, dominoes, cardplaying for amusement, scuffling, wrestling, telling humorous jokes, loud laughter, the playing of practical jokes, etc., were indulged in. When the love of these amusements threatened the welfare of the camp, Brigham Young gave his severest rebuke of the journey. On May 29, as the camp was preparing to move, he called the Pioneers together and, according to Wilford Woodruff, said to them:

"I think I will take for my text to preach my sermon—these words:
'I am about to revolt from traveling with this camp any further with the spirit they now possess.'
"I had rather risk myself among the sav-

---

[17](Note) For an illustration of the Odometer, and a minute description, see Roberts, *Comprehensive History of the Church*, Vol. III, p. 174, and note 3, pp. 190-191. This machine is now in the Deseret Museum at Salt Lake City.

[18](Note) For an illustration of a buffalo skull used as a bulletin by Brigham Young see Roberts, *Comprehensive History of the Church*, Vol. III, p. 178.

ages with ten men that are men of faith, men of mighty prayer, men of God, than to be with this whole camp when they forget God and turn their hearts to folly and wickedness. Yes, I had rather be alone; and I am now resolved not to go any further with the camp unless you will covenant to humble yourselves before the Lord and serve Him and quit your folly and wickedness. For a week past nearly the whole camp has been cardplaying, and checkers and dominoes have occupied the attention of the brethren, and dancing and 'hoeing down'—all this has been the act continually. Now, it is quite time to quit it. And there has been trials of law suits upon every nonsensical thing; and if those things are suffered to go on, it will be but a short time before you will be fighting, knocking each other down and taking life. It is high time it was stopped."[19]

He continued to admonish the camp for some time, after which the brethren voted to abstain from the offensive practices. The following day, Sunday, was set apart for fasting and prayer. The repentance of the camp was genuine, and not a single complaint of their conduct is thereafter mentioned.

Pioneers Reach Fort Laramie

On June 1, the Pioneers arrived opposite Fort Laramie, having covered

one-half the distance to Salt Lake Valley. They were now 543 miles from Winter Quarters. Four hundred miles of new road had been broken and the Mormon Trail begun.

Fort Laramie was situated on the river of that name a mile and a half above its confluence with the Platte. It was built of clay or unburnt brick, the walls being about fifteen feet high. It was

"Of a rectangular construction, measuring on the exterior 116 by 118 feet. Ranges of houses were built on the interior adjoining the walls, leaving a central yard about 100 feet square. The post belonged to the American Fur Company, and was occupied by about eighteen men with their families under the charge of Mr. Boubeau."[20]

Finding that the north bank of the Platte could no longer be followed, the Pioneers obtained the use of a flatboat from the fur company for $15 and spent three days in ferrying the seventy-three wagons over to the south side of the Platte.

At Fort Laramie the Pioneers received their first news of the outside world. Part of the Mississippi Com-

[19]Roberts, *Comprehensive History of the Church*, Vol. III, p. 184.

[20]Orson Pratt, *Journal*, entry for June 1.

An artist's sketch of old Fort Laramie, about half way on the Pioneer route to Great Salt Lake City.

pany of Saints had been waiting for two weeks at Fort Laramie for Brigham Young to arrive. The Mississippi Company of Saints were converts from Monroe County, Mississippi. Under instructions from Brigham Young they had started westward in April, 1846, to join the main body of the Church, in their journey to the mountains. At Independence, Missouri, they were joined by some Saints from Illinois and the company journeyed west to within a few miles of Fort Laramie. As the main body of the Church had not come west, the Mississippi Saints went south to Pueblo for the winter. There they were joined by part of the Mormon Battalion, sent there for the winter because of sickness. In the spring of 1847, the entire company of Mississippi Saints and Battalion members with their families started for Fort Laramie to intercept the advance companies of the Pioneers. Most of this group were still some distance from Fort Laramie.

A party of four men was detailed to go to meet the detachment of the Mormon Battalion and the remainder of the Mississippi Saints. At Fort Laramie the pioneer company also learned of the heavy migration enroute to Oregon and California that year. A total of nearly 2,000 wagons, in detached companies, had been passed by trappers between the Missouri River and Fort Laramie.

On leaving Fort Laramie the Saints followed the Oregon Trail to Fort Bridger. On that great highway they frequently met parties traveling to the East, loaded with peltries. Several wagon caravans enroute for Oregon were also encountered.

The Choice of Salt Lake Valley

It is difficult to determine the time at which Salt Lake Valley was selected as the destination of the Saints. Joseph Smith, in 1842, had prophesied that the Saints would go "West to the Rocky Mountains" without designating a particular place. In the spring of 1844, he had started a move to send 25 men to explore the "Great Basin," but there is nothing to indicate that he had Salt Lake Valley in mind.

After the death of the Prophet, there was still more uncertainty as to the future location of the Saints. Brigham Young and the Twelve even wrote a letter to the governor of Arkansas asking his sanction for the settlement of the Saints in that State.[21] The plea was curtly refused. Arkansas was not anxious to have a repetition of the Missouri and Illinois affairs.[22] A similar response met their petitions to other states. From the correspondence of the Church for the year 1845-6, it is evident that the chief desire of the Saints was to go to a region where they would be by themselves, and as the Great Basin was the only place which offered such isolation, it was naturally given first choice. Oregon and California were filling up too rapidly with emigrants from Missouri, Illinois, and Iowa, for Brigham Young to desire to go there if the Great Basin proved habitable. In the minds of the leaders there were greater considerations than opportunities for wealth in the land which should be chosen.

As the Saints gained knowledge of the Great Basin, the descriptions of Salt Lake Valley seemed to appeal to them. Just why, they did not know. Certainly the reports concerning the valley were not encouraging for the set-

[21] See Golder, *The Mormon Battalion*, p. 41. Letter from the Council of Twelve to Governor Drew of Arkansas.
[22] *Ibid.*, p. 46. Reply of Governor Drew to Brigham Young.

tlement of a numerous people. Nevertheless a mental picture of the valley remained in their minds, which became sharper during the journey westward from Fort Laramie.

On June 8, the Pioneers met a small number of wagons loaded with peltries, traveling East from Fort Bridger, led by James H. Grieve.

Brigham Young records:

"From him we learned that Mr. Bridger was located 300 miles west, that the Mountaineers could ride from Bridger to Salt Lake in two days, and that the Utah country was beautiful."[23]

Mr. Grieve told them of a boat made of skins hidden on the Sweetwater and gave them permission to use it for crossing.

On June 9, the Pioneers were overtaken by a pack train of 15 to 20 horses enroute to San Francisco Bay, via the Great Salt Lake.[24]

The main company of the Pioneers, on June 12 reached the Black Hills where the Oregon Trail crossed the Platte River. The advance company of Pioneers who had been sent ahead to the crossing were busy ferrying Oregon emigrants. For this purpose the Pioneers were using a leather boat called the "Revenue Cutter," which they had carried across the plains in a wagon. It was capable of carrying from 1,500 to 1,800 pounds. For the work of crossing the emigrant party the Pioneers received:

"1,295 pounds of flour, at the rate of two and a half cents a pound; also meal, beans, soap, and honey. At corresponding prices, likewise two cows, total bill for ferrying $78."[25]

Of the occasion Wilford Woodruff wrote:

"It looked so much of a miracle to me to see our flour and meal bags replenished in the midst of the Black Hills, as it did to have the children of Israel fed on manna in the wilderness."[26]

Seeing the possibility of conducting a profitable ferry at that place, the Pioneers constructed a large one and left a company of ten men under the leadership of Thomas Grover in charge.[27]

Parties Encountered at South Pass

The Pioneer company now followed up the Sweetwater to South Pass, a broad expanse of country some 7,080 feet above sea level.

"It was with great difficulty that we could determine the dividing point of land which separates the waters of the Atlantic from those of the Pacific. * * * The South Pass, some system of twenty miles in length and breadth, is a gently undulating plain or prairie, thickly covered with sage from one to two feet high."[28]

Near the South Pass the company met Major Moses Harris and a party from Oregon. Harris had an extensive knowledge of the mountains. Especially he acquainted the Pioneers with the Salt Lake Valley. Orson Pratt relates:

"We obtained much information from him, in relation to the great interior basin of the Salt Lake, the country of our destination. His report, like that of Captain Fremont's, is rather unfavorable to the formation of a colony in this basin, principally on account of the scarcity of timber. He said that he had traveled the whole circumference of the lake and there was no outlet to it."[29]

Harris had with him some copies of Oregon newspapers, and a copy of the

[26]*Woodruff's Journal*, entry for June 13.

[27](Note) The ferry was especially for the use of the large caravans of Saints to come later in the season. Between that day, June 18 and July 1, 500 wagons with 1,553 of the Saints left the Elkhorn River to follow the trail the Pioneers had blazed. These companies had 2,213 oxen, 124 horses, 887 cows, 358 sheep, 716 chickens and number of pigs.

[28]*Orson Pratt's Journal*, entry for June 26, 1847.

[29]*Orson Pratt's Journal*, entry for June 26.

[23]*History of Brigham Young*, Ms., 1847, p. 92.
[24]*Orson Pratt's Journal*, entry for June 9.
[25]*History of Brigham Young*, Ms., 1847, p. 94.

"THIS IS THE PLACE" MONUMENT, dedicated on the centennial anniversary of the entrance of the "pioneers" into the valley through Emigration Canyon on July 24, 1847.

"California Star," published by Samuel Brannan.

Near the South Pass the company also met Thomas L. Smith, who had a trading post on the Bear River. He described Bear Lake, Cache, and Marsh Valleys, in all of which he had trapped. Erastus Snow later wrote:

"He earnestly advised us to direct our course northwestward from Bridger, and make our way into Cache Valley; and he so far made an impression upon the camp, that we were induced to enter into an engagement with him to meet us at a certain time and place, some two weeks afterwards, to pilot our company into that country. But for some reason, which to this day has never to my knowledge been explained, he failed to meet us; and I have recognized his failure as a providence of the Allwise God. The impressions of the Spirit signified that we should bear rather to the southwest from Bridger than to the north of west."[30]

Two days later the Pioneers met that picturesque character of the West, James Bridger. Bridger was, at this time, the best known character of the mountains and had a first-hand knowledge of the entire area. The Pioneers had desired to interview him but had expected to find him at his home—Fort Bridger. Having previously heard that the Mormons wished to see him, he suggested that they call a halt and camp for the night together. Various versions of this interview have been given. Orson Pratt records:

"Being a man of extensive acquaintances with the interior country, we made inquiries of him in relation to the Great Basin and the country south. His information was rather more favorable than that of Major Harris."[31]

Brigham Young in his journal adds:

"Bridger considered it imprudent to bring a large population into the Great Basin, until it was ascertained that grain could be raised;

James Bridger, who was interviewed by the Pioneers concerning the Great Basin.
Used by permission, Utah State Historical Society

he said he would give $1,000 for a bushel of corn raised in that basin."[32]

President Young replied: "Wait a little and we will show you."[33]

The statement of Bridger, concerning corn being raised in the Basin, was not to discourage the Saints settling there, but to express a hope that it might be done successfully.

This view is expressed by Wilford Woodruff in his Journal:

"He (Bridger) spoke more highly of the Great Basin for a settlement than Major Harris did: *that it was his paradise*, and if this people (i.e. the Saints) settled in it, he wanted to settle with them. There was but one thing that could operate against it be-

[30]Erastus Snow, *Utah Pioneers*, pp. 44-45.
[31]*Orson Pratt's Journal*, entry for June 28.

[32]*History of Brigham Young*, Ms., Bk. 3, p. 95.
[33]Erastus Snow, *Utah Pioneers*, p. 43.

coming a great country, and that would be the frost. He did not know but the frost would kill the corn."[34]

From the time of the meeting with Bridger there seems to have been but one place for settlement in the minds of the Pioneers—Salt Lake Valley.

From the South Pass to the Green River was the most pleasant part of the journey, the grass was high and game plentiful. The downhill grade eased the teams and rested the men.

Meeting with Samuel Brannan

At the Green River it was necessary to build another ferry. While the Pioneers were camped there, Samuel Brannan rode into camp, having crossed the mountains from California, with two companions. Brannan had made a dangerous journey of 800 miles to meet the Church leaders and persuade them to go to California. He brought news of the ill-fated Donner party, the greater number of which had perished in the mountains, while many of the survivors had turned cannibal.[35]

[34]*Woodruff's Journal*, entry for June 28.
[35]See *Millennial Star*, Vol. 12, p. 161.

The efforts of Brannan to convince Brigham Young of the wisdom of going on to the Sacramento Valley were unavailing. The great leader had made up his mind. He knew where he was going. Brannan remained with the Pioneers until they reached Salt Lake Valley and it became evident that nothing would alter their choice of location. Disappointed, he returned to California and soon left the Church. The reception given Brannan by the Saints had not been cordial, as they had remembered the contract he had made with A. G. Benson and Company, which would have placed an intolerable burden upon them.

From Green River, five volunteers were sent back to guide the main body of Saints, who were now somewhere on the plains.

A small detachment of the Mormon Battalion from Pueblo also overtook the company at Green River, with news that the Pueblo Company was but seven days journey behind. The Battalion members were still in the pay of the United States Army and had been ordered to proceed west to California. Thomas S. Williams, a Battalion officer, and Sam-

An artist's sketch of Fort Bridger where the Pioneers arrived July 9, 1847.

uel Brannan were detailed to meet the Battalion and conduct its members to their destination. As their term of enlistment had expired by the time of reaching Salt Lake, they were later mustered out of service at that place.

The company reached Fort Bridger July 9. From here the Pioneers left the Oregon Trail and followed the dim trail left by the wagons of the Donner party the year before. This route was called "Mr. Hasting's new route to the Bay of San Francisco," and was the most direct route into Salt Lake Valley. July 10 the company met Miles Goodyear, who was acting as guide for a party traveling East from San Francisco. Goodyear had what he termed a farm at the mouth of Ogden Canyon, on the site of the present city of Ogden. Respecting Salt Lake Valley as a promising place of settlement,

"He, too," says Erastus Snow, "was unable to give us any hope; on the contrary, he told us of hard frosts, cold climate; that it was difficult to produce grain and vegetables in any of this mountain region. The same answer was given to him as to Mr. Bridger, "Give us time and we will show you!"[36]

To Salt Lake Valley

From the Green River the camp had considerable sickness from "mountain fever." President Young was severely stricken and remained behind at Bear River, with eight wagons, while the main company moved forward. Orson Pratt was sent ahead with 23 wagons and 42 men to lay out the route. The route chosen followed closely that taken by the Donner party into Salt Lake Valley, as Goodyear had reported the Weber Canyon impassable with wagons. Orson Pratt followed down Echo Canyon and, after some difficulty, passed through East Canyon and over "Big

Mountain" into the head of what is now called Parley's Canyon. From here the road led over "Little Mountain" in Emigration Canyon, called by them "Last Creek." From the top of Big Mountain, on July 19, the first sight of Salt Lake Valley had been obtained. The main body of Pioneers was now close behind Orson Pratt's camp. President Young sent word to Orson Pratt to proceed on into Salt Lake Valley, bear northward, and commence the planting of potatoes, as the season was late and he was desirous of raising seed for another year. Accordingly, Orson Pratt moved for-

Orson Pratt and Erastus Snow give a shout upon viewing the Salt Lake Valley. (One of the pieces of sculpture from the "This is the Place" Monument.)

Used by permission, Utah State Historical Society

---

[36]*Erastus Snow's Journal*, entry for July 10.

ward. Leaving his camp on July 21, he rode forward accompanied by Erastus Snow. From a hill at the mouth of Emigration Canyon they obtained an unobstructed view of the Valley. Orson Pratt records:

"Mr. Snow and myself ascended this hill, from the top of which a broad open valley, about twenty miles wide and thirty long, lay stretched out before us, at the north end of which the broad water of Great Salt Lake glistened in the sunbeams, containing high mountainous islands from twenty-five to thirty miles in extent. After issuing from the mountains, among which we had been shut up for many days, and beholding in a moment such an extensive scenery open before us, we could not refrain from a shout of joy which almost involuntarily escaped from our lips the moment this grand and lovely scenery was within our view."[37]

Seeing what appeared to be a field of waving grain some distance to the South, they rode over to see. They discovered only canes growing on the banks of what is known today as Mill Creek. They retraced their steps. As they had but one horse between them, Orson Pratt rode to the present site of Salt Lake City, while Erastus Snow walked back up the canyon to find a coat he had lost. The next day the advance company entered the valley and, on July 23, formed an encampment at the spot now occupied by the City and County Building. Orson Pratt called the camp together, dedicated the land, and asked God's blessing upon the seed they were about to plant. It was a prayer of thanksgiving which touched the hearts of all the camps.

Following the dedication, the men were divided into groups, some to clear the sagebrush from the land preparatory to plowing; others to unpack the wagons and do the plowing; others to make an encampment and care for the stock. A company was set to work to put a dam in the creek (City Creek) and flood the land. This was the beginning of Utah irrigation and the transformation of a desert into a garden. Several acres were plowed the first day and some potatoes planted.

The following day, July 24, 1847, Brigham Young and the main Pioneer company entered the valley. There was no special demonstration in the camp on their arrival. Brigham Young's own narrative simply says:

"July 24th: I started early this morning and after crossing Emigration Canyon Creek eighteen times, emerged from the Canyon. Encamped with the main body at 2 p. m. About noon, the five-acre potato patch was plowed, when the brethren commenced planting their seed potatoes. At five, a light shower accompanied by thunder and stiff breeze."[38]

Wilford Woodruff relates that:

"When we came out of the canyon in full view of the valley I turned the side of my carriage around open to the West, and President Young arose from his bed and took a survey of the country. While gazing on the scene before us, he was enrapt in vision for several minutes. He had seen the valley before in vision, and upon this occasion he saw the future glory of Zion and of Israel, as they would be, planted in the valleys of these mountains. When the vision had passed, he said: 'It is enough. This is the right place. Drive on!' "[39]

Supplementary Readings

1. Roberts, *Comprehensive History of the Church*, pp. 122-231. (A rich, indispensable source of information and an interesting story, stimulating and challenging.)

2. *Ibid.*, pp. 124-128. (A project to make money out of the interest of the converts in England in the movement of the Mormons to the west.)

3. *Ibid.*, pp. 140-142. (The problem of car-

---

[37]*Orson Pratt's Journal*, entry for July 21.

(Note) Goodyear claimed an immense tract of land by Mexican grant. These rights were later purchased by members of the Mormon Battalion and the settlement of Ogden was begun.

---

[38]*History of Brigham Young*, Ms., 3, Journal entry for July 24, 1847.

[39]*Utah Pioneers*, p. 23.

ing for their stock during the movement West.)

4. *Ibid.*, pp. 163-164. (Who went with this first Pioneer company and what they took with them.)

5. *Ibid.*, pp. 164-167. (The order of the journey of the Pioneers. Interesting personal details that made this movement human and real, and hence interesting.)

6. *Ibid.*, p. 168. (Quotation from Brother Wilford Woodruff's Journal, May 4, 1847. This quotation reveals the finest spirit of these Pioneers that permeates so much of their decisions and policies and actions.)

7. *Ibid.*, pp. 174-175. Footnotes 40, 43. (The Buffalo herds.)

8. *Ibid.*, pp. 181-182. Read footnote 56. "More Redmen Visitors." (Note the Indian's use of the flag.)

9. *Ibid.*, pp. 182-184. Footnotes 57, 61, 62. Note especially quotations from address by President Young on page 184. ("The Lord's Day" — "Brigham Young's Reproof." It is interesting to note the ages of those who made up this company of Pioneers. Note the nature of their amusements. President Young's sharp reproof.)

10. Gates and Widtsoe, *Life Story of Brigham Young*, pp. 81-82. ("There is no fiddling, there is no music in hell. Music belongs to heaven, to cheer God, angels and men.")

11. *Ibid.*, pp. 84-85. (The women of this first company of Pioneers. Suffering for worthy causes.)

12. *Ibid.*, p. 90. Last paragraph. (An amusing illustration of President Young's sense of humor and his practical wisdom.)

13. Cowley, *Wilford Woodruff*, pp. 271-275. (Indian scares, thefts, fights. Buffalo hunt. Porter Rockwell in the midst of all this. Brother Woodruff delighted in "Hunting.")

14. Evans, *One Hundred Years of Mormonism*, pp. 439-442.

15. Smith, *Essentials of Church History*, pp. 356-370. (Pioneers)

16. Walt Whitman, *Leaves of Grass*. Pioneers! O Pioneers! (This great poem of Whitman's is one of the really great and worthy tributes written to *Pioneers*. It is in many anthologies and collections of poems. In *Heart of Mormonism*, p. 332, Evans quotes two verses.)

17. Evans, *Heart of Mormonism*, pp. 332; 362-366. (Brigham Young A Pioneer of Pioneers.)

18. Roberts, *Life of John Taylor*, pp. 188-197. (In these pages may be found story, humor, song or poetry, bits of biography, facts with vital meanings and values; all revealing the very life and character of these Pioneers. Especially do these pages reveal that unique, manly Pioneer, John Taylor. Roberts says, "It was a bold undertaking, this moving over fifteen hundred souls— more than half of whom were women and children—into an unknown country, through hostile tribes of savages."

19. James A. Little, *From Kirtland to Salt Lake City*, pp. 53-54. (Zina D. Young's description of the sufferings at Mt. Pisgah on the plains.)

20. *Ibid.*, pp. 74-75. (People fed on quails.)

21. *Ibid.*, pp. 82-83. (Orson Pratt's description of the great herds of buffalo, and other animals encountered on the plains.)

22. *Ibid.*, pp. 42-48. (Suffering of Saints at Sugar Creek.)

CHAPTER 31

THE NEW GATHERING PLACE

The Challenge of the Great Basin

It is easy to forget that the rich valleys of Utah with their fine irrigated fields were, in 1847, part of the Great American Desert; that Salt Lake Valley was then considered worthless for the raising of crops and entirely unfitted for the habitation of large populations.

When the Pioneers drove their wagons onto the site of the present Salt Lake City, the valley floor was a dry and treeless plain. Grey sage, the natural home of the jack rabbit and the rattlesnake, stretched in every direction until it became a grey haze beneath the distant hills. The hot July sun had scorched the grass and baked the earth. Had the Saints arrived while the freshness of spring was in the air, the prospect might have been more pleasant. But a dry blistering heat welcomed them and smote on the thin canvas coverings which sheltered the women and children and offered a pitiless challenge to its dominion.

For centuries the hot rays of the sun in summer and the cold blasts of wind in winter had ruled in this vast inland basin, which owed no allegiance to either sea. A few Indian tribes, their skins bronzed beyond further hurt of sun and wind, here eked out an existence. A few intrepid trappers had, for some thirty years, drained it of its only apparent wealth—its furs. But the Great Basin was unconquered. It presented a challenge to civilization—to the ingenuity of man—to his ability to survive. When the Mormons accepted this challenge many predicted that the desert would come off victor in the struggle. Tyler reports that Samuel Brannan, in meeting the returning members of the Mormon Battalion in the Sierra Nevada in September, 1847, said that:

"The Saints could not possibly subsist in the Great Salt Lake Valley, as according to the testimony of the mountaineers, it froze there every month of the year, and the ground was too dry to sprout seeds without irrigation, and irrigated by the cold mountain streams the seeds planted would be chilled and prevented from growing; but if they did grow they would be sickly and fail to mature. He considered it no place for an agricultural people and expressed his confidence that the Saints would emigrate to California the next spring. On being asked if he had given his views to President Brigham Young, he answered that he had. On further inquiry as to how his views were received, he said in substance that the President laughed and made some rather insignificant remarks, 'but,' said Brannan, 'when he has fairly tried it, he will find that I was right and he was wrong, and will come to California.' "[1]

To men of vision the Salt Lake Valley presented great possibilities, the realization of which would involve years of toil and hardship. To the women it was a picture of utter desolation. Many a tear came to the eyes of the brave women who found only a barren waste at the end of their long journey. Clara Decker Young, wife of the leader, is reported to have said:

"I have come 1200 miles to reach this valley and walked much of the way, but I am willing to walk a thousand miles farther rather than remain here."

It was not only Salt Lake Valley

---

[1] Tyler, *History of the Mormon Battalion*, p. 315.

which was chosen to be the new home of the Saints. It was the whole Great Basin of which the valley was a small part. Dr. Talmage described this Basin as follows:

"The region to which this name is applied is of outline roughly triangular. * * * It extends about 880 miles in greatest length, running east of south and west of north, and 572 miles in extreme width from east to west. The area thus included is about 210,000 square miles, comprising the western half of Utah, the greater part of Nevada, and portions of eastern California, southeastern Oregon, southeastern Idaho and southwestern Wyoming."[2]

This vast area has no external drainage—all the water of the region loses itself in the sands, evaporates, or finds its way into streams emptying into inland lakes or seas. These have become salty through years of evaporation.

Early Travelers to the Great Basin

Into this Great Basin came the Spanish priest, Escalante, in the same year that the American Colonies declared their independence from England, 1776. In a four month's journey the great Catholic Father left Santa Fe, crossed through western Colorado, up the Uintah, Duchesne and Strawberry Valleys and down Spanish Fork Canyon, up Utah Valley, which he called "The Valley and Lake of our Lady of Mercy of the Timpanogotsis." After preaching to the Indians and making some observations, Escalante's party headed South to find Monterey, California. Snow overtook them and, changing his plans, Escalante returned to Santa Fe, where he arrived January 2, 1777.

The Great Basin again became lost to mankind, bearing new names on lakes and rivers, but as forbidding and unconquered as before.

---

[2]Talmage, *The Great Salt Lake, Present and Past*, p. 88.

Nearly half a century rolled by before white men again reached the heart of this vast inland area. Beginning about 1820, trappers entered the Great Basin. Powerful fur companies struggled for control of the rich harvest of furs, while diplomats of three nations politely asserted claims of their respective countries to the disputed region. But when the fur-bearing animals had largely disappeared two decades later, the Basin had hardly seemed worth dispute and it remained barren and unoccupied.

The trapping period left its stamp on the Basin. Peter Skeen Ogden, working for the British Hudson Bay Fur Company, trapped throughout what is now northern Utah and made several large caches of furs in what is now called Cache valley. Another cache was made at the foot of the Wasatch Range, where the city of Ogden now stands, and where Ogden for a time remained a trading post.

Etienne Provost left his name to a river and later a city which stands on the spot where seventeen of his men lost their lives through Indian treachery.

General Ashley, founder of the Rocky Mountain Fur Company, left his name to a valley and a river. Of James Bridger, who was one of the first and the last of the Mountain Men, we have already heard.

None of these men came into the Basin to make their homes or to conquer the soil. Nor did Colonel Fremont or Captain Bonneville, who came into the valley prior to the Saints, do more than add to the world's store of information of the barren area.

The Saints came into the Great Basin to establish homes—to subsist from the soil—to preserve a faith, even though

SEAGULL MONUMENT, located on Temple Square it commemorates the part played by the birds in delivering the Saints from the plague of crickets.

SEGO LILIES, designated by legislative act as the Utah state flower because their bulbous roots provided food for early pioneers.

EAGLE GATE, originally the entrance to Pres. Brigham Young's estate. It was a landmark until 1960 when it was accidentally damaged and removed from its location on north State Street. This later was replaced by a new arch surmounted by an eagle.

THE LION HOUSE, home of the families of Pres. Brigham Young, was built in 1856.

that preservation would require the conquering of a desert.

Except for the desire of the Saints to exercise their faith unmolested, the Great Basin would likely not have been settled in 1847, or perhaps for many years afterward. The history of attempts at establishing agricultural communities in similar areas of the United States, where settlement was not prompted by such religious faith, has been a story of failure. This phase of the settlement of the Great Basin will be given in greater detail in a later chapter.

Founding the First City

When the Saints erected their tents on the present site of Salt Lake City, the land into which they had come technically belonged to Mexico. The treaty of peace with that country, whereby the Great Basin became part of the United States, was not signed until February 2, 1848. In actuality the region belonged to no nation. No governmental officers had ever lived in the territory, nor had the administration of any law been attempted there. The Mexicans called the region upper California, and the Mexican Governor at Monterey was technically its administrative officer, but that is as far as the attempt of government had gone. Miles Goodyear had obtained from the Mexican Government a grant of land of considerable extent where Ogden is now situated, but Goodyear lived alone with his gardens, undisturbed by government or law.

The Saints must of necessity establish their own law and their own government. On the first Sabbath day spent in the Valley, religious services were held in the forenoon and afternoon, and the sacrament of the Lord's Supper was administered. Several of the Apostles spoke. The law of the Lord was declared to be the law of the land. "The brethren were exhorted," says Wilford Woodruff, "to hearken to counsel, do away with selfishness, live humbly and keep the commandments of God, that they might prosper in the land."[3]

On that day Brigham Young laid down the principles which should govern the appropriation of property in the valley. Out of fairness to the thousands of Saints who were yet upon the plains, the President was determined that none should seize upon and monopolize the resources of the valley.

"No man should buy or sell land. Every man should have his land measured off to him for city and farming purposes, what he could till. He might till it as he pleased, but he should be industrious and take care of it."[4]

This land law is identical to that inaugurated at Garden Grove and Mount Pisgah, where Brigham Young had added, "that if a man would not till his land it should be taken from him."[5]

The law was also laid down that the timber in the mountains belonged to the community and could not be appropriated by individuals. This timber must be conserved and only the dead wood cut for fuel.

The water also belonged to the community. A man might appropriate that which he could profitably use on his land for irrigation, but no more. This theory of the use of water gradually developed into what is called the "appropriation theory of water rights," and is the basis of irrigation law in nearly all the intermountain country today.

No attempt was made in 1847 to set up a civil government.

Before definitely selecting the site of

---

[3]*Wilford Woodruff's Journal*, entry for July 25, 1847.
[4]*Ibid.*
[5]*History of Brigham Young*, Ms., p. 110.

the city, exploration parties were sent out in each direction for short distances. Some went into the canyons and located splendid timber. Others investigated the river flowing into the Great Salt Lake. Some bathed in the salt water of the lake and were amazed at its buoyancy.

President Young, in company with several of the Twelve and others, ascended a peak in the north. It was suggested that this peak was a fitting ensign to the nations, so Brigham Young named it "Ensign Peak." It was the ensign of Christ's Kingdom.

To the Saints gathered upon the peak it seemed that the ancient prophecy of Isaiah was about to be fulfilled.

"And it shall come to pass in the last days, that the mountain of the Lord's house shall be established in the top of the mountains, . . . and all nations shall flow unto it.

"And many people shall go and say, Come ye, and let us go to the mountain of the Lord, to the house of the God of Jacob; and he will teach us of his ways, and we will walk in his paths; for out of Zion shall go forth the law, and the word of the Lord from Jerusalem."[6]

"And it shall come to pass in that day, that the Lord shall set his hand again the second time to recover the remnant of his people, . . .

"And he shall set up an ensign for the nations, and shall assemble the outcasts of Israel, and gather together the dispersed of Judah from the four corners of the earth."[7]

"All ye inhabitants of the world, and dwellers on the earth, see ye, when he lifteth up an ensign on the mountains; and when he bloweth a trumpet, hear ye."[8]

No flag was raised on Ensign Peak, but in the minds of the people a new standard had been unfurled to all the world. Inspired by this idea, Parley P. Pratt later wrote:

See on yonder distant mountain
    Zion's standard wide unfurled,
Far above Missouri's fountain,
    Lo! it waves for all the world.

Freedom, peace and full salvation
    Are the blessings guaranteed,
Liberty to every nation,
    Every tongue, and every creed.
Come, ye Christian sects and pagan,
    Pope, and Protestant, and Priest,
Worshipers of God or Dagon,
    Come ye to fair freedom's feast.
Come, ye sons of doubt and wonder,
    Indian, Moslem, Greek, or Jew,
All your shackles burst asunder,
    Freedom's banner waves for you.
Cease to butcher one another,
    Join the Covenant of peace,
Be to all a friend, a brother,
    This will bring the world release.
Lo! Our King! the great Messiah,
    Prince of Peace, shall come to reign;
Sound again, ye heavenly choir,
    Peace on earth, good will to men.[9]

City of the Great Salt Lake

The results of the brief exploration satisfied the Saints with the selection of the site of the city and filled them with optimism for the future. July 28, the members of the Twelve met and designated the site for a temple block between the two forks of City Creek. By motion of Orson Pratt it was unanimously voted that the Temple should be built upon the site so designated. The Apostles at the same time voted to lay out the city in blocks of ten acres each with streets eight rods wide running at right angles. The blocks were to be divided into lots containing one and one-quarter acres in each. One house was to be built on a lot and must be twenty feet back from the street line, "that there might be uniformity throughout the city." Upon every alternate block, four houses were to be built on the West and four on the East. The intervening blocks were to have four houses on the North and four on the South. Thus, no houses confronted each other across the street and those on the same side were eight rods apart. This plan followed

---

[6]*Isaiah*, 2:2, 3.
[7]*Isaiah*, 11:11-12.
[8]*Isaiah*, 18:3.

[9]*Sacred and Spiritual Songs by The Church of Jesus Christ of Latter-day Saints*, 1851, London, p. 102.

that laid down by Joseph Smith for cities of Zion.

Four squares of ten acres each were designated for public grounds. The plans for the city were presented to the whole camp and unanimously accepted.

August 2, 1847, Orson Pratt began the survey of the city. The base line of Orson Pratt's survey was on the southeast corner of the Temple Block. Government officials later adopted this as the base meridian line for the survey of the entire mountain area. The survey made by Orson Pratt and Henry A. Sherwood, and their calculations of latitude, longitude, and altitude excite the admiration of modern surveyors.

Details of the city plan were gradually changed as time progressed, but still retain some of its unique features. The city was named "City of the Great Salt Lake." Subsequently it was changed to Salt Lake City.

season was too late, however, to secure much of a crop, the potatoes getting just large enough to be used for seed the following spring. During the same time, twenty-seven log houses were built. A portion of a fort was also erected on a ten-acre plot where one hundred sixty families could winter until they built on their own inheritances. The Old Fort was built on what is now Pioneer Park.

"The walls were twenty-seven inches thick and nine feet high on the outside. It was built as a continuation of huts joined together in rectangular form around the outside of the ten acres on which it stood. The east wall was built of logs, and the other three sides of adobe. They slanted but slightly inward, and were made of brush covered with earth. Each side had a loophole facing the outside and a door and windows facing the interior. The main entrances which were on the East and West sides of the stockade were carefully guarded by heavy gates which were locked at night."[10]

Later in the year, two additional

An artist's sketch of a view of early Great Salt Lake City.

During the first month after reaching the valley, the Pioneers plowed eighty-four acres of land, and planted it in corn, beans, potatoes, buckwheat, turnips and a variety of vegetables. The

blocks, one on the north and one on the south were joined to the original Old Fort. A bowery twenty-eight by forty feet, was erected as a place for public

[10]Smith, *Essentials in Church History*, p. 376.

worship and was the first community center.

Indian visits to the settlement were discouraged when they began to increase in number. Brigham Young ordered that no bartering be done with the Indians except at the latter's encampments. The Indians were mostly Utes, who proved friendly and not disposed to steal.

At the suggestion of Brigham Young, the majority of the Saints were rebaptized beginning August 6, as a renewal of their covenants with the Lord to keep His commandments. It was in no sense necessary, as their former baptisms were perfectly valid, but was a remarkable symbol of their desire to live in righteousness.

In the founding of the city the heroism of the pioneer women played a large part. Nine women had entered Salt Lake Valley with Brigham Young's company on July 24. Three were previously referred to as starting with the Pioneer company. The other six were Mississippi Saints who were among those who had overtaken the Pioneers at Green River. These were Elizabeth Crow, Harriet Crow, Elizabeth J. Crow, Vinda Exene Crow, Ira Minda Almarene Crow, and Martilla Jane Therlkill.

The main body of the Mississippi Saints and the Pueblo detachment of the Mormon Battalion entered the valley on July 29. This greatly increased the number of pioneer women and swelled the total population of the settlement to 400. By the close of the year the majority of the 2,095 who had entered the valley were women.

The first birth in the valley was that of Young Elizabeth Steele, daughter of John and Catherine Campbell Steele, a Battalion family, August 9. A second child, Hattie A. Therlkill, was born August 15, in the family of George W. Therlkill, a Mississippi Saint. The first death was also in this family, August 11, when a three-year-old child fell into City Creek and was drowned.

Of the pioneer women, Dr. Charles William Elliott, then President of Harvard University, said in a speech in the Salt Lake Tabernacle, March 17, 1892:

"Did it ever occur to you what is the most heroic part of planting a colony of people which moves into a wilderness to establish a civilized community? You think perhaps, it is the soldier, the armed man or the laboring man. Not so, it is the women who are the most heroic part of any new colony. Their labors are less because their strength is less. Their anxieties are greater, their dangers greater, the risks they run are heavier. We read that story in the history of the Pilgrims and Puritan Colonies of Massachusetts. *The women died faster than the men; they suffered more.* Perhaps their reward was greater, too. They bore children to the colony. Let us bear in our hearts veneration for the women of any Christian folk going out in the wilderness to plant a new community."[11]

The Main Body of the Church

While the Pioneers were building a road across plains and mountains and founding a new city, the main body of the Church was still upon the Indian lands of Iowa and Nebraska. Besides the three companies which had already entered Salt Lake Valley, however, ten companies of Saints were on the Plains enroute to their new home. These ten companies contained over sixteen hundred souls, the women and children greatly predominating. They were bringing with them large herds of sheep and cattle, hogs and chickens, and necessarily moved slowly along the route laid out by the Pioneers. Nearly 13,000 remained behind in the temporary settlements.

[11]*Deseret Evening News,* March 17, 1893.

Of the movement West, Brigham H. Roberts, the historian, says:

"To appreciate the heroism of this Latter-day Saint movement to the West, one must contemplate the chances taken by these companies which followed the Pioneers. It was late in the season when they started from the Elkhorn—the latter part of June—too late for them to put in crops that season even if they stopped far short of the Eastern base of the Rocky Mountains. They barely had provisions enough to last them eighteen months, and then if their first crop failed them in the new mountain home selected, starvation must follow, for they would be from eight to ten hundred miles from the nearest point where food could be obtained, and no swifter means of transportation than horse or ox teams. It was a bold undertaking, this moving over two thousand souls into an unknown country, and into the midst of tribes of savages of uncertain disposition, and of doubtful friendship. Had it not been for the assurance of the support and protection of God, it would have been not only a bold but a reckless movement—the action of madmen. But as it was, the undertaking was a sublime evidence of their faith in God and their leaders."[12]

Aside from the occasional letters which trappers carried to them, and the sign posts erected to mark the way, the companies on the plains under Pratt and Taylor knew nothing of the final destination of the Pioneers.

Ezra T. Benson and three companions started from Salt Lake Valley on August 2, to meet the Saints on the plains and give them the glad tidings that a gathering place had been found.

As many of the Pioneers and Battalion members had families still at Winter Quarters, preparations were made to return to that place and prepare for their removal in the Spring. Accordingly on August 16, a company of men was organized for the return journey. There were 24 of the pioneers and 46 of the Mormon Battalion, 34 wagons, 72 yoke of oxen, 18 horses, and 14 mules. It was generally referred to as the "ox train of returning pioneers." This company started ten days ahead of a second company, which intended to use horses and mules entirely. It was thought that the second company would overtake the first, but the oxen proved best adapted for the journey, being able to subsist nicely on the forage along the way, while the horses weakened unless grain-fed.

The second company returning to Winter Quarters left Salt Lake Valley, August 26. There were 107 persons, 71 horses and 49 mules. Brigham Young and the members of the Council of Twelve who were then in the valley headed this company. The returning pioneers were able to take few provisions as these were needed by the Saints in the valley. Accordingly, much fishing and hunting were necessary on the return journey in order to get food.

Father John Smith, uncle of the Prophet Joseph, was left in charge of the colony at Salt Lake City.

On September 4, the first of the westbound companies was met on the Big Sandy River. This company was in charge of Parley P. Pratt and Peregrine Sessions. Two days later Elder John Taylor's and Joseph Horne's companies were encountered on the Sweetwater. Several inches of snow had fallen which disheartened some of the Saints. Elder Taylor cheered them up and proposed to insure the lives of the whole company, "at $5 per head."[13]

A banquet was secretly prepared by the women in honor of the Twelve and a hearty time of feasting and dancing was had. On September 9, the last westbound company, led by Jedediah M. Grant, was met.

[12]Roberts, *Comprehensive History of the Church,* Vol. III, p. 301-302.

[13]Roberts, *Life of John Taylor,* p. 190.

SEAGULLS DEVOUR THE CRICKETS, photograph of oil painting by Vigos, Daughters of the Utah Pioneers Museum.
Used by permission, Kate B. Carter

The First Presidency and the Quorum of the Twelve Apostles under Brigham Young. Reading left to right they are: Top Row: Heber C. Kimball, President Brigham Young, and Willard Richards. Second Row: Orson Hyde, Parley P. Pratt, Orson Pratt, and Wilford Woodruff. Third Row: John Taylor, George A. Smith, Amasa Lyman, and Ezra T. Benson. Bottom Row: Charles C. Rich, Lorenzo Snow, Erastus Snow, and Franklin D. Richards.

All of these companies arrived safely in Salt Lake Valley, the last on October 10.

Brigham Young and the returning Pioneers reached Winter Quarters, October 31. When one mile out of the settlement the company was drawn up in order, and Brigham Young said to them:

"Brethren, I will say to the Pioneers: I wish you to receive my thanks for your kindness and willingness to obey orders. I am satisfied with you; you have done well. We have accomplished more than we expected. Out of one hundred forty-three men who started, some of them sick, all of them are well; not a man has died; we have not lost a horse, mule or ox, but through carelessness; the blessings of the Lord have been with us. If the brethren are satisfied with me and the Twelve, please signify it, (which was unanimously done.) I feel to bless you all in the name of the Lord God of Israel. You are dismissed to go to your own homes."[14]

The reunion of pioneers with their families at Winter Quarters was a happy one. Brigham Young and the Twelve were relieved to find that the Saints in Winter Quarters, Council Bluffs, Mount Pisgah, and Garden Grove had enjoyed an abundant harvest and would have ample food for the winter.

Organizing the First Presidency

On December 4, 1847, in a council meeting at Elder Orson Hyde's, Brigham Young was chosen and sustained by the Council to be the President, Prophet, Seer, and Revelator to the Church of Jesus Christ of Latter-day Saints, with Heber C. Kimball and Willard Richards as his first and second counselors.

For three and one-half years the Church had been without a First Presidency. The Quorum of Twelve with Brigham Young as its President, had successfully directed the Church throughout that period, but now it was thought proper to perfect the Church organization.

The action of the Council was ratified by the unanimous vote of the General Conference of the Church held in the Log Tabernacle, at Winter Quarters, December 27, 1847, and in the eighteenth annual conference of the Church at Kanesville,[15] April 6, 1848. Subsequently, the selected First Presidency was sustained at a conference of the Saints in Salt Lake Valley on October 8, 1848; and in England by a general conference of the English branches August 14, 1848.

Spring found Brigham Young and Heber C. Kimball leading two large companies of Saints toward the distant valley in the Mountains. Brigham Young had made his last trip to the East. He says in his journal:

"On the 26th (May) I started from Winter Quarters on my journey to the mountains, leaving my houses, mills, and the temporary furniture I had acquired during our sojourn there. This was the fifth time I had left my home and property since I embraced the Gospel of Jesus Christ."[16]

President Young arrived in Salt Lake Valley with his company of 1,229 souls, on September 20, 1848. President Kimball arrived with his company a few days later. By the end of the year there were 5,000 Saints in the valley.

Supplementary Readings

1. Roberts, *Comprehensive History of the Church*, Vol. 3, pp. 313-314. ("Peace with God, and good will to all men." The conclusion of a statement from the *Twelve* to the world.)

---

[14]*History of the Church*, Period 2, Vol. 7, pp. 616-617.

[15]Kanesville was the original Mormon settlement at Council Bluffs. The name was changed in honor of Colonel Kane.

[16]*History of Brigham Young*, Ms., entry for April 26, 1848.

2. *Ibid.*, p. 210 and footnote 53. ("The Fate of the Donner-Reed Party." A sad tragedy of the great migration to the West. One Mormon woman died in this tragedy.)

3. *Ibid.*, pp. 216-218. (The First Two of the Pioneers to enter Salt Lake Valley—Orson Pratt and Erastus Snow.)

4. *Ibid.*, pp. 218-219. (Second Party of the Pioneers to enter the Salt Lake Valley.)

5. *Ibid.*, pp. 219-221. (Third Party of Pioneers to enter the Salt Lake Valley.)

6. *Ibid.*, pp. 221-223. (Rear Section of the Pioneer Train.)

7. *Ibid.*, pp. 223-224. (Brigham Young enters Salt Lake Valley.)

8. *Ibid.*, pp. 232-243. ("Salt Lake Region: Fertile or Not Fertile.") Brigham Young vs. Samuel Brannan. The Schuyler Colfax and John Taylor bout. Anti-Mormon literature. Gunnison, and Fremont on the fertility issue.

9. *Ibid.*, pp. 244-267. (An intensely interesting chapter on the white man in the Salt Lake Region before the coming of the Mormon Pioneer: The Catholic Fathers. The Hunter and Trapper. Discovery and description of Great Salt Lake.)

10. *Ibid.*, Opposite page 264. A graphic picturesque map of Lake Bonneville. Note the extent of this lake of an age long ago.) See also pp. 259-260 (Discovery of Great Salt Lake.)

11. *Ibid.*, pp. 268-283. Note three-line quotation from President Young on p. 269. (The Founding of Salt Lake City. An interesting and informative chapter.)

12. *Ibid.*, pp. 284-304. Note especially paragraph quoted from President Charles W. Elliot of Harvard University on greater *heroism* of Pioneer *women*.

13. James A. Little, *From Kirtland to Salt Lake City*, pp. 130-132. (A vivid description of what the Saints accomplished during their first month in the Salt Lake Valley.)

14. *Ibid.*, pp. 120-121. (The Indians in Salt Lake Valley prepare crickets for food.)

15. Cowley, *Wilford Woodruff*, p. 459. (Wilford Woodruff's description of Cove Fort.)

16. *Ibid.*, p. 373. (A person is reviewed or questioned for re-baptism. An amusing report.)

17. *Ibid.*, pp. 342-343. (A Stampede on the Plains.)

18. Gates and Widtsoe, *Life Story of Brigham Young*, pp. 99-100. ("Down into the 'Valley of Promise' rode these hardy scouts." "This is the Place." An interesting phase of this famous saying.)

19. *Ibid.*, p. 101. (The Voice of the Three Pioneer Women in response to their first view and impressions of Salt Lake Valley.")

20. *Ibid.*, pp. 102-113. "The First Winter." An inspiring chapter. A personal letter from Clara I. Young to her husband, Brigham Young.)

21. Roberts, *Life of John Taylor*, p. 202. (Parts of a letter, from General Wilson about the Mormons in Salt Lake City, September 6, 1849, read in the United States Senate.)

22. *Ibid.*, pp. 202-203. (John Taylor called on a mission to France. Contrast between Salt Lake City, in 1849, and Paris, France.)

23. John G. Neihardt, *The Splendid Wayfaring*. (A classical story of exploration and fur trapping in Rocky Mountains between 1822-1831. The book centers about Jedediah Smith, one of the hardiest and bravest of the Western Explorers, who was as sensitive, as clean, as fine as the most gracious woman,—a noble man and a true, reverent Christian. A record of fact, biographical in nature.)

24. Emerson Hough. *Covered Wagons*. (Another classic story of exploration and life in the West.)

CHAPTER 32

THE SPIRIT OF GATHERING

To Every Tongue and People

In 1849, when the feverish haste for gold drew men in a steady stream across the nation to California, the strangest sight in all that dreary march was the Mormon missionary threading his way against that tide. It was so strange an event that few historians of the West have passed it by without comment. It was not that the Mormon missionary looked different from the gold seeker, for the casual observer might have perceived similarity in the appearance of the two; nor yet in the manner by which each traveled, for horses, or mules, or the covered wagons were common to both. The startling difference lay in the fact that, while the illusive lustre of the yellow metal was drawing all other men toward it, the missionary, who often had been at the very scene of the discovery and felt the thrill of the golden dust in his hands, was turning his back against it all, and was traveling out into the world to give, without thought of self and without a wage, two or three years of his time for the salvation of his fellow men.

It is significant that a religion might be found upon the earth promoting in its followers a faith so strong, and with a feeling of duty toward mankind so insistent, that worldly considerations sink into insignificance beside it. Yet that is the story of the great missionary movement of the Church during the very years when Saints were most in need of money, when an impoverished people were making a new start in a barren desert, and wealth in abundance was beckoning from the hills and streams of a neighboring land.

This great missionary movement, the third of its kind in the history of the Church, had its beginning, like those which preceded it, in the darkest days of trouble and persecution. It began during the spring of 1846, while the Saints were impoverished exiles on the plains of Iowa. A young man by the name of Orson Spencer had just lost his wife. The privations and hardships had been too much for her frail body. She had sacrificed her life for the Gospel, nor would she abandon it in order to secure the comforts her family might have provided her. To that same Gospel Orson Spencer resolved to devote his life. The summer of 1846 found him in England appointed to preside over that mission of the Church, throwing into his work all that great zeal and talent which he possessed. His remarkable work was the beginning of a missionary movement which, in the next few years, doubled the membership of the Church, and did much toward carrying the Gospel to every tongue and people. During the next two years the converts in the English mission increased by 8,467 souls, and when Orson Pratt replaced him in 1848, the number of Saints in the British Isles numbered 17,902. The missionary spirit which the elders, laboring under Orson Spencer, carried throughout the British Mission was soon to receive further impetus. From Winter Quarters, in the winter of 1847-48, Brigham Young directed an energetic missionary program. On November 23, 1847, seventeen elders were called upon missions from that place, and this number was greatly enlarged in the spring.

Jesse C. Little was sent to preside over the Eastern States Mission. Ezra T. Benson and Amasa M. Lyman were sent into the eastern and southern states to visit the Saints. Orson Pratt was sent to replace Orson Spencer in England, and Wilford Woodruff was sent to preside over the Canadian mission. The effect upon the missions was remarkable. With the exception of England, where already a new impetus had been given by Orson Spencer, the missions seemed to spring into new life. New members joined the restored Church by the tens, hundreds, and finally the thousands.

The missionary zeal reached its greatest height in 1849-50. On February 12, 1849, four men who took a prominent part in that Missionary expansion, were called to fill the vacancies in the Quorum of the Twelve. These vacancies were caused by the organization of the First Presidency, and the excommunication of Lyman Wight, who had refused to return to the fold. The new Apostles were Charles C. Rich, Lorenzo Snow, Erastus Snow, and Franklin D. Richards.

Charles C. Rich was called to assist Amasa M. Lyman in the California Mission. These elders succeeded in organizing the scattered Saints in that region and in doing much missionary work. In 1851, they purchased the San Bernardino Rancho of 80,000 acres for the settlement of the Saints. Five hundred migrated from Utah in 1851 and commenced a Mormon colony at that place.

Elders Addison Pratt, James Brown, and Hiram H. Blackwell were sent to the Society Islands in the Southern Pacific, in 1849, to extend the mission established there by Addison Pratt a few years earlier. The Church enrollment in those islands soon numbered many thousands.

Missions to Europe and Asia

In the same year (1849) Lorenzo Snow and Joseph Toronto were sent on a mission to Italy. In London they were joined by Elders T. B. H. Stenhouse and Jabez Woodward.

A Branch of the Church was formally organized in Italy, September 19, 1850. Apostle Snow, like Paul of old, catching the spirit of his calling, earnestly desired to carry the Gospel into the whole Mediterranean world. The year 1850 found him, accompanied by Elder Stenhouse, organizing a flourishing branch of the Church in Switzerland. Leaving Elder Stenhouse to preside over the mission there, Elder Snow sailed to the island of Malta in the Mediterranean Sea. Here another Branch was established and Elder Obrey, who had recently joined him from England, was left in charge.

Already Lorenzo Snow was looking for new lands in which to preach, and set his heart on going to distant India, circumnavigate the globe from there, and return to Utah via the Mormon settlements in California. Returning from Malta to London he sent Elder William Willis by ship to Calcutta, India, to open the way. Hugh Findlay was sent to Bombay in that same land. Before Lorenzo Snow could follow and begin his circumnavigation of the globe, he was recalled to Utah for other duties.

The mission to India met with temporary success. William Willis baptized 309 natives and 40 English residents, and established a branch at Calcutta. Before leaving England, Snow sent Elder Joseph Richards to assist Willis.

Four new missions had been opened, due to the great zeal of Lorenzo Snow and his companions. Besides, Elder Snow published a pamphlet, "The Voice of Joseph," in the French language which had a wide circulation.

Meanwhile, John Taylor had been sent to open a mission in France and had been successful in establishing a Branch of the Church in that land. Taylor's interest in the sugar beet industry and subsequent work in organizing a sugar beet company for Deseret, prevented his carrying the Gospel into Germany as he had planned.

In these same years Erastus Snow was sent to open missions in the Scandinavian countries. Accompanied by Peter O. Hansen and John Forsgren, he journeyed to Denmark. On September 15, 1850, a Branch was organized in the city of Copenhagen, with fifty members. In that year the party was joined by Elder George P. Dykes, then on a mission to England. Elder John Forsgren was sent to open the ministry in Sweden. At Geffle, in the northern part of that nation, Forsgren baptized twenty members and was about to organize a branch, when he was arrested and placed on a ship to be deported to America. The ship, however, while en route, docked for a few days at Elsinore, Denmark. At that place Elder Forsgren escaped, and rejoining Elder Snow, continued his mission in that land.

Erastus Snow sent Elder Dykes to Jutland in October, 1851, where within six months he baptized ninety-one persons and organized a branch.

In September, 1851, Elder Hans F. Peterson was sent by Elder Snow from Aalborg, Jutland, to open the Gospel door to Norway.

Erastus Snow also sent Elder Gudmund Gudmundson, a native Icelander, converted in Denmark, to Iceland, where the foundation was laid for a successful work.

When Elder Snow left Denmark for his return to Salt Lake City, at the end of twenty-two months, the Danish Church numbered 600 members. The Book of Mormon and the Doctrine and Covenants had been translated and published in the Danish language, and also a number of missionary pamphlets in both Danish and Swedish.

Missions to South America and the Pacific Islands

The Hawaiian Mission was opened in 1850-51 under the direction of Elder Charles C. Rich, then presiding in California. The first Branch was organized at Kula, upon the island of Maui, by George Q. Cannon. Elder Cannon translated the Book of Mormon into the Hawaiian language, which was published at San Francisco, in 1855. The mission proved a great success. A letter from Elder F. A. Hammond, laboring on the islands, under date of March 1, 1852, says:

"The missionaries (that is, other denominations) succeeded in putting a stop to our labors, but the government gave their full consent to our laboring here, and the United States Consul took an active part in getting granted to us the same rights as the other denominations, since which time the work has been increasing rapidly and we now number about six hundred members upon all the islands, four hundred and fifty of them upon this island (i.e. Maui). We baptized about two hundred and fifty since Christmas and the work is still going ahead."[1]

Parley P. Pratt was set apart in February, 1851, "to a mission to open the door and proclaim the Gospel in the Pacific Islands, in Lower California, and in South America."

Under the Presidency of Parley P.

[1] *Deseret News*, July 24, 1852.

Pratt the mission to the Hawaiian Islands was expanded. The mission to the Society Islands, u n d e r Addison Pratt, was extended to the Friendly Islands. Parley P. Pratt also sent Elders John Murdock and Charles W. Wandell to Australia in 1851, and 1852 nine other missionaries to Australia, New Zealand and Tasmania. Branches were established in each of these lands. At Sydney, Australia, a Church periodical called "Zion's Watchman" was published. All of these missions have been continuous since that time.

Accompanied by his wife and Rufus Allen, Elder Pratt journeyed to South America and commenced laboring at Valparaiso, Chile. Civil war in that land prevented the carrying out of their plans and the little mission returned to California in May, 1852.

An attempt to establish a mission at Berlin in Prussia, during January, 1853, failed. Elders Orson Spencer and Jacob Houtz were not allowed to preach and were ordered to leave the country.

Attempts in the same year, by Elders Edward Stevenson and Nathan T. Porter, to preach the Gospel at Gibraltar and in Spain also failed, due to the intolerant attitude of the authorities. An attempt to extend the mission in India also met with failure, and in 1855 the entire mission in India was closed by an order from Brigham Young, calling upon all the missionaries in that land to return home and bring with them all the converts who could conveniently come.

An attempt to establish the Church in China, in 1853, was cut short by the spread of revolution in that land. In Siam and Burma, the Elders were rejected. Elder Luddingham was stoned out of Bangkok.

Jesse Haven, William Walker, and Leonard I. Smith, succeeded, after many difficulties, in establishing small branches of the Church in South Africa, in 1853.

Attempts to preach the Gospel in the West Indies and British Guiana, in the same year met with failure, not a single meeting having been allowed.

Thus was made an heroic attempt to carry the Gospel to every "kindred, nation, tongue and people." In many parts of the world the time was not ripe for the success of the movement, but in the main, the foundation for a great work was laid.

The great missionary expansion of these years brought into the Church converts from many lands. As the numbers grew into thousands the Church was to become a great melting pot of nationalities and the predominance of the English membership was gradually to diminish.

A World Wide Gathering

With the selection of the valleys of the mountains as the future home of the Saints an "ensign" was truly raised, under which converts of the Church were called to gather from every land and clime. In a general epistle sent by Brigham Young and the Twelve from Winter Quarters, December 23, 1847, the Saints scattered from Nauvoo and those in Canada or the British Isles were advised to gather to the eastern bank of the Missouri River, preparatory to the further migration to the Rocky Mountains. They were called to settle temporarily on the land then vacated by the Pottawattamie Indians, and owned by the United States Government. Kanesville was to be the resting place and recruiting point for the western migration.

The English Saints were advised to ship, via New Orleans, on the all-water route to Kanesville. The gathering Saints were urged to bring:

"All kinds of choice seeds, of grain, vegetables, fruits, shrubbery, trees, and vines—everything that grows upon the face of the whole earth that will please the eye, gladden the heart, or cheer the soul of man; also the best stock of beasts, bird and fowl of every kind; also the best tools of every description, and machinery for spinning, or weaving, and dressing cotton, wool, flax, silk, etc., or models and descriptions of the same by kinds, or kinds of farming utensils and husbandry, such as corn shellers, grain threshers, and cleaners, smut machines, mills and every implement and article within their knowledge that shall tend to promote the comfort, health, happiness, and prosperity of any people. So far as it can be consistently done, bring models and drafts, and let the machinery be built where it is used, which will save great expense in transportation, particularly in heavy machinery, and tools and implements generally."[2]

The Saints in California were instructed to remain where they were, if they so chose; likewise the Saints on the islands of the Pacific, "until further notice." The Saints in Australia and the East Indies[3] were urged to ship to the "most convenient part in the United States" and from thence to the Great Basin.

The traveling ministry of the Church in the world were instructed in regard to the new converts:

"Teach them the principles of righteousness and uprightness between man and man; administer to them bread and wine, in remembrance of the death of Jesus Christ, and if they want further information, tell them to flee to Zion—there the servants of God will be ready to wait upon them and teach them all things that pertain to salvation. * * * Should any ask 'where is Zion?' tell them in

America, and if any ask 'what is Zion?' tell them the pure in heart."[4]

The Epistle closed with a stirring appeal to all of the Saints in the world:

"We are at peace with all nations, with all kingdoms, with all governments, with all authorities under the whole heavens, except the kingdom and power of darkness, which are from beneath and (we) are ready to stretch forth our arms to the four quarters of the globe, extending salvation to every honest soul; for our mission in the Gospel of Jesus Christ is from sea to sea, and from the rivers to the ends of the earth. * * *

"The kingdom which we are establishing is not of this world, but is the kingdom of the Great God. It is the fruit of righteousness, of peace, of salvation to every soul that will receive it, from Adam down to his latest posterity. Our good will is towards all men, and we desire their salvation in time and eternity; and we will do them good so far as God will give us power, and men will permit us the privilege; and we will harm no man. * * * The kingdom of God consists in correct principles. * * *

"Come, then, ye Saints of Latter-days, and all ye great and small, wise and foolish, rich and poor, noble and ignoble, exalted and persecuted, rulers and ruled of the earth, who love virtue and hate vice, and help us to do this work, which the Lord hath required at our hands; and inasmuch as the glory of the latter house shall excel that of the former, your reward shall be an hundred fold, and your rest shall be glorious.

"Our universal motto is, 'Peace with God, and good will to all men.' "[5]

At the date of the above instructions, fewer than two thousand souls were gathered in Salt Lake Valley. Twelve to fifteen thousand were in the temporary settlements in Iowa and Nebraska, and a greater number were in the Eastern States, Canada, England, and the islands of the sea. It was a colossal program to gather them to Zion.

This gathering would have been impossible but for the "Spirit of Gather-

[2]General Epistle from Winter Quarters under date of December 23, 1847. Millennial Star, Vol. 10, pp. 81-88.
[3]Note: The Australian Mission was opened in 1840 by Elder William Barrett, and the East Indies Mission by Elder William Donaldson, in 1840.

[4]General Epistle from Winter Quarters, December 23, 1847, Millennial Star, Vol. 10, pp. 81-88.
[5]General Epistle from Winter Quarters under date of December 23, 1847. Millennial Star, Vol. 10, pp. 81-88.

ing" which came upon the converts to the Gospel, and the spirit of sacrifice and brotherly kindness which prompted those already at their destination to reach out a helping hand.

The appeal of the Church Presidency for the Saints to gather struck a responsive chord in the hearts of converts, whether those converts were on the plains of Iowa or in foreign lands. There is an inner urge which has prompted the members of The Church of Jesus Christ of Latter-day Saints to gather.

The miracle of the Latter-day gathering is greater than the healing of the sick or the raising of the dead. It has been a continuous miracle of more than a century. The Mormon convert in every clime has undergone a change of spirit which has transformed a life's habits, severed the strongest of economic bonds and the closest of family ties in order to satisfy that longing which has come into his heart "to gather."

The Lord said to the Church, through Joseph Smith, in the year when the Church was founded:

"And ye are called to bring to pass the gathering of mine elect; for mine elect hear my voice and harden not their hearts;

"Wherefore the decree hath gone forth from the Father that they shall be gathered in unto one place upon the face of this land, to prepare their hearts and be prepared in all things against the day when tribulation and desolation are sent forth upon the wicked."[6]

The Perpetual Emigrating Fund

The extensive missionary activity of the Church in the years following the initial settlement of Salt Lake Valley, doubled and redoubled the Church membership. These new members were located in all parts of the world, but prompted by the "Spirit of Gathering,"

and the encouragement of the Church leaders, a continuous migration began to pour into the valley of the mountains.

The "Spirit of Gathering" took hold of the hearts of men without regard to financial standing. People without means sufficient to journey to a new land found the desire to come so overwhelming that the Elders of the Church were constantly meeting their appeals for aid.

Perhaps the Saints who were most in need were those who had been driven from Nauvoo and had spent two winters as exiles on the Indian lands of Iowa. Before leaving Nauvoo, Brigham Young and others had pledged themselves to use all their influence and, if necessary, their property, to remove all the Saints of that city to the Rocky Mountains. Accordingly, in September, 1849, Brigham Young and his counselors proposed the creation of a revolving fund for the purpose of helping the poor membership to reach Salt Lake City. The proposed plan was adopted, and Willard Snow, John S. Fullmer, Lorenzo Snow, John D. Lee, and Franklin D. Richards were appointed to raise the nucleus of an emigrating fund. At the General Conference in October, the congregation voted unanimously to support the emigration fund by contributions. Destitute as many of the Saints were, having barely reached the valley themselves, they gave liberally of their means to aid the needy emigrants. Lorenzo Snow relates:

"One man insisted that I should take his only cow, saying that the Lord had delivered him, and blessed him in leaving the old country and coming to a land of peace; and by giving his only cow, he felt that he would only do what duty demanded, and what he would expect from others, were the situation reversed."[7]

[6]*Doctrine and Coveants*, Sec. 29:7-8.

[7]Eliza R. Snow, *Biography and Family Record of Lorenzo Snow*, p. 108.

About $5,000 was raised that fall, and forwarded by Bishop Edward Hunter to Kanesville, to relieve the Saints residing on the Pottawattamie lands. Hunter had been appointed General Agent of the "Perpetual Emigrating Fund Company," under which name the enterprise had been incorporated.

Bishop Hunter carried with him a letter of instructions to Orson Hyde, who was in charge of the membership in Iowa. The letter sets forth in clearness the whole plan of aiding the emigrants:

"We write you more particularly at this time concerning the gathering and the mission of our general agent for the Perpetual Emigrating Fund for the coming year, Bishop Edward Hunter, who will soon be with you, bearing the funds already raised in this place, and we will here state our instructions to Bishop Hunter so that you may the more fully comprehend our designs.

"In the first place, this fund has been raised by voluntary donations, and is to be continued by the same process and by so managing as to preserve the same and then to multiply.

"Bishop Hunter is instructed to go direct for Kanesville and confer with the general authorities at that place and, by all means within his reach, procure every information so as to make the most judicious application of the funds in the purchase of young oxen and cows that can be worked effectually to the valley, and that will be capable of improving and selling after their arrival so as to continue the fund the following year. * * *

"As early in the spring as it will possibly do, on account of feed for cattle, Brother Hunter will gather all his company, organize them in the usual order, and preside over the camp, traveling with the same to this place; having previously procured the best teamsters possible, such as are accustomed to driving, and be gentle, kind, and attentive to their teams. When the Saints thus helped arrive here, they will give their obligations to the Church to refund to the amount of what they received, as soon as circumstances will permit, and labor will be furnished to such as wish on the public works, and good pay; and as fast as they can procure the necessaries of life, and a surplus, that surplus will be applied to liquidating their debt and thereby increasing the Perpetual Fund.

"By this it will readily be discovered that the funds are to be appropriated in the form of a loan rather than a gift; and this will make the honest in heart rejoice, for they love to labor and be independent by their labor, and not live on the charity of friends, which the lazy idlers, if such there be, will find fault and want every luxury furnished them on their journey and in the end pay nothing.

"The Perpetual Fund will help no such idlers; we have no use for them in the valley. * * *

"The few thousands we send out by our agent at this time is like a grain of mustard seed in the earth; we send it forth into the world and among the Saints, a good soil, and we expect it will grow and flourish, and spread abroad in a few years so that it will cover England, cast its shadow in Europe and in the process of time encompass the whole earth. That is to say these funds are designed to increase until Israel is gathered from all nations, and the poor can sit under their own vines, and inhabit their own homes, and worship God in Zion."[8]

Help to the Saints on the Plains

The immediate purpose of the revolving fund was to bring forward the exiles in Iowa. The ultimate object was to help the needy converts throughout the world gather to Zion. In a letter to Orson Pratt, President of the British Mission, dated October 14, 1849, an appeal was made for contributions to the Perpetual Emigrating Fund from the Saints in foreign lands, to be "expended for the gathering of the poor Saints."[9]

In 1850, there were 7,828 Saints on the Indian lands of Iowa. The movement of these Saints to the West was too slow to suit the presiding authorities of the Church. On September 21, 1851, the First Presidency issued a sharp order to all those remaining in Iowa to bestir themselves and remove to the mountains the following spring. Ezra

[8]James A. Little, *From Kirtland to Salt Lake City*, p. 216. Letter dated October 16, 1849.
[9]Linforth, *Route from Liverpool to Great Salt Lake Valley*, p. 8.

T. Benson and Jedediah M. Grant were sent to organize them and lead the caravans west. The result was that in 1852, the Pottawattamie lands were practically deserted, and the Nauvoo Saints were at last removed to the Rocky Mountains. In 1850, the population of Utah Territory had been given by the government at 11,380. By the close of 1852, the number was between 25,000 and 30,000.[10]

Help to the European Saints

In the Mormon migration from Europe there were two important functions: first, the work of the shipping office in England, charged with the responsibility of chartering ships and organizing the prospective emigrants; and second, the work of the outfitting agent at the landing place on the Mississippi River, whose duty it was to provide the proper equipment for the journey across the plains.

The shipping agent in England made his announcements through the medium of the Millennial Star in such items as the following:

"Notice of first ship of season will sail in January, 1853. Applications to be accompanied by name, age, occupation, and nativity of applicant, and deposit of one pound. Parties will provide own bedding, cooking utensils, etc."[11]

Charles Dickens, the famous novelist, visited a ship loaded with Mormon converts, to observe the general procedure, and later wrote of the occasion:

"Two or three Mormon agents stood ready to hand them (the emigrants) on to the inspector, and to hand them forward when they had passed. By what successful means a special aptitude for organization had been infused into these people, I am, of course, unable to report. But I know that, even now, there was no disorder, hurry or difficulty . . . I afterwards learned that a dispatch was sent home by the captain before he struck out into the wide Atlantic, highly extolling the behavior of these emigrants, and the perfect order and propriety of all their social arrangements . . . I went on board their ship to bear testimony against them, if they deserved it, as I fully believed they would; to my great astonishment they did not deserve it, and my predispositions and tendencies must not affect me as an honest witness. I went over the Amazon's side, feeling it impossible to deny that, so far, some remarkable influence had produced a remarkable result which better known influences have often missed."[12]

The efficiency of the Church shipping agent is manifest from an article in the Edinburgh Review for January, 1862:

"The select committee of the House of Commons on emigrant ships from 1854 summoned the Mormon Agent and passenger broker before it and came to the conclusion that no ships under the provisions of the "Passenger's Act" could be depended upon for comfort and security in the same degree as those under his administration. The Mormon ship is a family, under strong and accepted discipline, with every provision for comfort, decorum, and internal peace."[13]

"Conducting the emigrants from Europe was as patriarchal as the Church itself. As the emigration season came round, converts were brought from every branch and conferences to Liverpool by the Elders," who saw them on shipboard in vessels chartered for their use. Not a moment were they left to the mercy of "runners" and "shipping agents." When on board, the companies, which in some cases amounted to more than one thousand per ship, were divided into wards, each ward under its president, or bishop, and his two counselors, and besides these there were the doctor, steward, and cook, with assistants. Regular religious preaching service was observed daily, and council meeting as occasions required. Morning and evening prayers were observed; and occasional entertainments, concerts, and dances were enjoyed by the passengers and the officers of the ship as well."[14]

[10]Bancroft, History of Utah, p. 397.
[11]Millennial Star, Vol. 15, p. 618.
[12]Charles Dickens, Uncommercial Traveller, pp. 209-213.
[13]Rev. John Todd, D.D., Sunset Land, 182, states, "A committee of the British Parliament has sat at the feet of the Mormons to learn their system of aiding emigration."
[14]Gustive Larson, History of the Perpetual Emigration Fund Company, p. 23. Also see Tullidge, History of Salt Lake City, p. 100.

An idea of the procedure of the outfitting agent on the Missouri may be obtained from a letter written by Erastus Snow, then frontier agent, published in *The Luminary*,[15] February 16, 1855.

"My assent will not be given to any Saint to leave the Missouri River unless organized in a company of at least fifty effectual well-armed men, and that too, under the command of a man appointed by me.

"I will furnish at this point of outfit, for such as desire it, wagons, oxen, cows, guns, flour, bacon, etc.

"Choice wagons made to order and delivered to the point of outfit with bows, projectors, etc., will be about $78, without projectors[a] $75. Oxen with yokes and chains from $70 to $85 per yoke; cows from $16 to $25 cash.

"My experience, derived from six journeys over the plains, enables me to know what kind of teams and outfits are wanted for the plains.

"One wagon, two yoke oxen, and two cows will be sufficient (if that is the extent of their means) for a family of eight or ten persons, with the addition of a tent for every two or three families. Of course with that amount of teams, only the necessary baggage, provisions, and utensils can be taken, and then the persons ride but little."[16]

The period from 1852 to 1855 forms the first period of European emigration under the Perpetual Emigrating Fund. In those years over 125,000 pounds ($650,000) was expended by the company in emigrating poor converts.

"A total of 6,753 emigrants sailed during that period, 2,885 of whom were aided entirely by the Perpetual Fund Company. One thousand forty-three came under special rate arrangements and the remaining 2,825 were aided through the services of the purchasing agencies and general organization of the company."[17]

So successful were the efforts to aid the emigrating Saints during this period that Brigham Young wrote to the Church in England:

"Let all who can procure a loaf of bread and one garment on their backs, be assured there is water, plenty and pure, by the way, and doubt no longer, but come next year to the place of gathering even in flocks, as doves fly to their windows before the storm."[18]

Handcart Emigrants

The costs of transporting emigrants from England to Salt Lake Valley rose so rapidly during the early fifties that, in 1856, a new experiment was tried to cut down the cost. Wagons and carts made entirely of wood, the wheel looped with hickory or rawhide, were used by some of the Saints in crossing the plains earlier than 1851. It was now proposed that light carts be made entirely of wood and pulled or pushed by hand across the plains.

The first emigrants to use the "Handcarts" came from England in 1856. By this means of travel the emigrant could journey from Liverpool, England, to Salt Lake City for about forty-five dollars.

One company, led by Edmund Ellsworth, numbering 266 people, left Iowa City, June 9, 1856. Another followed two days later, under the leadership of Daniel D. McArthur. A third company under Edward Bunker, left on the 23rd of June. All of these people walked across the plains, pushing or pulling their handcarts. One of the emigrants thus describes the carts:

"In length the side pieces and shafts were about six or seven feet, with three or four binding crossbars from the back part to the fore part to the body of the cart. Then two or three feet space from the latter bar to the front bar or singletrees[b] from the lead horse or lead man, woman, or boy of the teams . . . Across the bars of the bed of the cart we usually sewed a strip of bed ticking or a counterpane.[c] On this wooden cart, of a thimbleless axle,[d] with about two and one-

---

[15]*The Luminary* was an L. D. S. publication printed in St. Louis.

[a]Projector—part of covered wagon top extending over driver's seat.

[16]*Millennial Star*, XVII:218.

[17]Gustive Larson, *History of the Perpetual Emigrating Fund Company*, p. 29.

---

[18]*Millennial Star*, Vol. 14, p. 325.

[b]Singletree—pivoted bar by which wagon is drawn.

[c]Counterpane—heavy cloth cover.

[d]Thimbleless axle—plain axle with no provisions for prevention of wear.

half inches shoulder and one inch point, were often loaded 400 to 500 pounds of flour, bedding, extra clothing, cooking utensils, and a tent."[19]

The first two companies arrived in Salt Lake Valley, September 26. They were met at the foot of Little Mountain, Emigration Canyon, by the First Presidency, a large number of people and a brass band, and were escorted into the city. Captain Edward Bunker received an enthusiastic welcome, October 2.

The Willie and Martin Companies

Two other Handcart Companies were fitted out in 1856. These were composed of British and Scandinavian Saints, who arrived in Iowa City in June, only to find that the tents and carts for the journey had not been provided. The delay was untimely. The first company under James G. Willie, left Iowa City, July 15, and reached Florence, Nebraska (Winter Quarters), August 19. The second, under Edward Martin, was nearly two weeks later. At Florence the companies, contrary to the advice of missionaries encountered, voted to continue the journey that year, despite the lateness of the season.

It was an unfortunate decision. Hasty construction of the handcarts led to constant trouble and delay. The wood in the carts had not been properly seasoned. Under the burning August sun they dried and fell apart, and precious days had to be taken, time and again, for repairs. The companies had been a month late in starting across the plains. An extraordinary early winter shortened the season still further. By the middle of September, heavy frosts made the nights uncomfortable. These increased with severity. Winter was fast approaching. The delays had produced

a shortage of rations. From Fort Laramie restrictions were placed on them which increased with severity as they progressed. Part of the handcarts had become so useless they had to be left by the wayside. The remainder were so heavily loaded that the steep sandy slopes west of Fort Laramie caused the Saints to cache articles of clothing and much bedding by the wayside, in order to proceed with greater speed before winter should come upon them.

Improperly clad for the winter weather encountered, and weakened by the meager rations, the delicate fell sick and were buried by the wayside. The fear that the entire company would perish prevented even proper ceremonies for the departed, but they wrapped their loved ones in sheets, lowered them into hastily dug graves, and covered them with rocks to keep away the wolves which hovered constantly along their trail.

Martin's company, coming later than Captain Willie's, suffered even greater hardships and loss of life. Heavy snows were encountered on the Sweetwater. During one of the severe storms fifteen died in one day.

Missionaries, returning to Salt Lake Valley from the East, passed the companies on the Sweetwater, and on reaching Salt Lake Valley, informed President Young of their condition.

Relief parties were immediately formed and started with provisions and bedding to meet the belated emigrants.

Joseph A. Young and Stephen Taylor were sent in a light wagon, as advance messengers, to inform the companies that help was on the way. John Chislett, a member of Captain Willie's Company, says of their arrival:

"More welcome messengers never came from the courts of glory than these two

[19]*Latter-day Saints Journal History*, November 9, 1856.

young men were to us. They lost no time, after encouraging us all they could to press forward, but sped on further to convey their glad news to Edward Martin and the fifth handcart company, who had left Florence about two weeks after us, and who it was feared were even worse off than we were. As they went from our view, many a hearty 'God bless you,' followed them."[20]

The two young men found the Martin Company encamped in a ravine between the Platte and the Sweetwater, now called "Martin's Ravine." Their food was gone, and the newly dug graves gave the place the aspect of a cemetery. The company had about given up hope and were waiting for the inevitable end when the word of relief arrived. New courage caused them to push forward again to meet the relief parties.

Even with the relief provisions and clothing their troubles were not over. The mountains had to be crossed, and the early snows lay deep upon them. Streams had to be forded, and floating ice lacerated their legs, while the waters chilled them to the marrow.

It was November 9 before Willie's company entered Salt Lake City, and the close of the month before Martin's survivors arrived. Of the first company of something over four hundred souls, seventy-five had died. Of Martin's Company of five hundred seventy-six, about one hundred fifty had found wayside graves.

The handcart, as a method of crossing the plains, had not failed, but the tragedy of 1856 had the effect of lessening the number of emigrants who relied on that method of transportation. Never again were handcart companies allowed to leave the outfitting point so late in the season or under such conditions. The handcarts continued to be used by a portion of the emigrants until 1860. Be-

ginning in 1861, the policy was adopted by the Church, acting through its emigration agency, of sending teams East, annually, to meet the Utah-bound emigrants. These teams and teamsters were supplied gratis by volunteers, who responded readily to calls from the First Presidency. Their sacrifice in time and means to aid brethren in the Gospel whom they had never yet seen is illustrative of the love which dominated the whole movement to upbuild the kingdom of God.

Supplementary Readings

1. Roberts, *A Comprehensive History of the Church*, Vol. 3, pp. 382-413. (The Founding of Missions.) Vol. 5, pp. 77-116. ("Survey of Missions.")

2. *Ibid.*, pp. 93-95, Note 6. ("The Prophetic and Historical Connection of Napoleon III with Mormonism.")

3. *Ibid.*, Vol. 5, pp. 106-115 ("A Change in Immigration Methods." "Benevolent Work of the Church Immigration of the Poor." "Romance.")

4. Gates and Widtsoe, *Life Story of Brigham Young*, pp. 24-25. Last paragraph p. 24, first on p. 25. (Beginnings of Mormon Emigration from Great Britain. Emigration Fund.)

5. *Ibid.*, p. 210. (Number, and cosmopolitan and representative character of emigrants.)

6. *Ibid.*, pp. 23-24. (Brigham Young as a Missionary.)

7. Roberts, *Life of John Taylor*, pp. 209-234. (John Taylor, Missionary in France and Germany. Missionary Experiences.)

8. Cowley, *Wilford Woodruff*, p. 192 ("The Spirit of Lord Jesus Christ is a gathering spirit."—Brigham so declared. A striking paragraph on "the gathering.")

9. *Ibid.*, pp. 412-413. (President Brigham Young instructs missionaries.)

10. Evans, *Heart of Mormonism*, pp. 127-131; 167-171; 479-483. Mormon Missionary. Wilford Woodruff an outstanding example of the ideal Missionary. Mormon Missionary System. A Marvelous Work and a Wonder.

11. Smith, *Essentials of Church History*, pp. 535-540. (Missions.)

12. Evans, *One Hundred Years of Mormonism*, p. 335. (Missionary System.)

---

[20]Joseph Fielding Smith, *Essentials in Church History*, pp. 397-398.

CHAPTER 33

CONQUERING THE DESERT

The Struggle for Existence

The outcome of great military battles has often decided the destiny of nations, but few battles have so affected the destiny of a people and the fate of a vast inland empire as the battle fought between man and the desert in the quiet valleys of the Rockies, between the fall of 1847 and the spring of 1849. Upon the outcome of that battle depended the future of the Great Basin.

If one large colony could survive in that barren land, others could be established. For two years the result was uncertain. Only a mighty faith in a Divine Providence and a wise leadership tipped the scales in favor of civilization and the establishment of a commonwealth.

Those who fought in that great battle against poverty, hunger, and disease, have never forgotten those terrible first winters when sugar was not to be had, even at one dollar a pound, and flour at fifty dollars a hundred.

Two thousand people had gathered into Salt Lake Valley by the fall of 1847. For these people there had been no harvest, as the summer had been spent traversing the plains. The food which had been brought from Winter Quarters was nearly exhausted, and it could not be replenished. As the heavy snows closed the mountain passes and shut off all contact with the outside world, the dread of starvation entered many a heart as the realization of the many months before a harvest came to them. And who knew there would be a harvest? To the knowledge of man, no large amount of food had ever been produced there. Then, too, the coming summer would see thousands more of the Saints pouring into the valley, depending upon that uncertain harvest for the preservation of their lives.

Before the winter was half over many families were destitute. Their flour was gone—their meat was gone. There were no vegetables or fruits. The oxen were needed for the plowing and the few cows for the milk they produced.

A public meeting was called and in that meeting was expressed the spirit of brotherly love and cooperation by which a people became unconquerable. So long as one pound of flour remained in that community no person would be allowed to starve. If there was to be hunger unsatisfied, then all would hunger together. A committee was called to gather the food supply and ration it out to the people. Bishop Edward Hunter and Tarlton Lewis were appointed to receive food from those who had it and to distribute it to the destitute.

By spring the hunger of many was intense. John R. Young, who lived through those scenes, says:

"By the time the grass began to grow the famine had waxed sore. For several months we had no bread. Beef, milk, pigweeds, segoes, and thistles formed our diet. I was the herd boy, and while out watching the stock, I used to eat thistle stalks until my stomach would be as full as a cow's At last the hunger was so sharp that father took down the old bird-pecked ox-hide from the limb; and it was converted into most delicious soup, and enjoyed by the family as a rich treat."[1]

---

[1]John R. Young, *Memoirs*, p. 65.

In the spring of the year the roots of the beautiful sego lily, which adorned the hills, were used for food,[2] as well as weeds and watercress. A few deaths occurred through the eating of poisonous roots of the wild parsnip.

Crickets and More Crickets

Fortunately for the Saints the winter had been a mild one and the plowing of fields continued throughout the winter months. The Saints rejoiced to see the first green grain which had been planted in the fall covering nearly two thousand acres of land. Between 3,000 and 4,000 acres more were planted into spring grain. A bounteous harvest was looked forward to. But wait!—Had the Pioneers forgotten those hordes of black crickets which they had observed in the foothills when they had entered the valley? The Pioneers had then been amused, watching the Indians gathering the black insects for winter food. Now they were painfully reminded of their existence. A drop of water is an insignificant thing, but added drop to drop it becomes a flood, and rushing from the mountains, sweeps to destruction all in its path. So the insignificant cricket, an inch and a half of clumsy, loathsome, black body, multiplied into millions, swept down upon the ripening fields of grain. All the ingenuity of man seemed powerless against this grinding, crawling sea of black, which allied itself with cold and famine and heat to drive civilization beyond the confines of the Great Basin.

It seemed for a time that the fight for human existence was lost—that the final chapter of a noble experiment at settlement was doomed; it must speedily vacate the mountain fastness or perish in the snows of the coming winter. And if these hardy pioneers, bolstered as they were by a mighty faith, were to admit defeat—if these could not survive in the great American desert, when would that barren land be settled—so momentous was the outcome of that battle. Men, women, and children labored with their might in the cause of life, but also in the cause of civilization. They beat and flayed the invading army, they drowned them in ditches, they drove them into fires, they buried them in trenches. As well attempt to stem the tide of the ocean, which, inch by inch, creeps higher on the beach. Men, thinking of the famine ahead—the long search for another home—the privations of loved ones, sweated and toiled until sheer exhaustion brought its accompanying despair. The women and the men prayed. Then came the gulls—those great grey birds, with their eerie cry, which nest upon the islands of the Inland Sea—they came in twos, in threes, in hundreds, in thousands—in great flocks which darkened the fields with their flying shadows—and the plague was stayed. They feasted upon the feasters. They devoured the devourers. They saved the fate of a civilization. They ate and gorged until they could hold no more—disgorged—only to eat and disgorge again. When night settled over the scene the two great forces retired, the gulls to their island home, the crickets to their rest from destruction. In early morn the conflict was resumed—day after day until the cricket army wavered and disappeared, and the green stocks of grain raised their heads again.

John R. Young says of that epic battle:

"As the summer crept on, and the scant harvest drew nigh, the fight with the crick-

---

[2]Note: By legislative enactment in 1917 the Sego Lily was made the Utah State Flower.

ASSEMBLY HALL, located on the southwest corner of Temple Square is used for numerous Church meetings and to accommodate the overflow crowds from the Tabernacle.

ets commenced. Oh, how we fought and prayed, and prayed and fought the myriads of black, loathsome insects that flowed down like a flood of filthy water from the mountainside. And we should surely have been inundated, and swept into oblivion, save for the merciful Father's sending of the blessed seagulls to our deliverance.

"The first I knew of the gulls, I heard their sharp cry. Upon looking up, I beheld what appeared like a vast flock of pigeons coming from the Northwest. It was about three o'clock in the afternoon. My brother Franklin and I were trying to save an acre of wheat of father's, growing not far from where the Salt Lake Theatre now stands. The wheat was just beginning to turn yellow. The crickets would climb the stalk, cut off the head, then come down and eat it. To prevent this, my brother and I each took an end of a long rope, stretched it full length, then walked through the grain, holding the rope so as to hit the heads, and thus knock the crickets off. From sunrise to sunset we kept at this labor; for as darkness came the crickets sought shelter, but with the rising of the sun they commenced their ravages again.

"I have been asked, 'How numerous were the gulls?'

"There must have been thousands of them. Their coming was like a great cloud; and when they passed between us and the sun, a shadow covered the field. I could see the gulls settling for more than a mile around us. They were very tame, coming within four or five rods of us.

"At first we thought that they, also, were after the wheat and this thought added to our terror; but we soon discovered that they devoured only the crickets. Needless to say, we quit drawing the rope, and gave our gentle visitors the possession of the field. As I remember it, the gulls came every morning for about three weeks when their mission was apparently ended, and they ceased coming. The precious crops were saved."[3]

It was a scanty harvest the gulls had saved the Saints, insufficient for all the thousands who were gathered in the valley. Another winter with insufficient food. Another winter on rations—with all distinctions of rich and poor forgotten. Again in 1849, despite a good har-

---

[3]*Memoirs of John R. Young*, Utah Pioneer, 1847, Chap. 8, pp. 65-66.

vest, the food supply ran low because of the great influx of Saints who had gathered to the mountains. Besides this, several thousand "gold seekers" bound for California passed through Salt Lake City, many of whom remained for the winter.

But the Saints survived. The settlement was a success. A mighty struggle, which tested the spiritual strength and physical fortitude of a great people, had been won.

A Unique Colonization

When President Brigham Young issued his call for the Saints throughout the world to gather to the valleys of the mountains, he did not contemplate that they should all dwell in Salt Lake City, or even in the valleys adjacent. The confines of "Deseret," as the Saints chose to call the territory to which they had come, was to embrace an area three times the present size of Utah. It was the dream of the Mormon leader to fill the habitable portions of this entire area with his people. The initial settlement at Salt Lake had succeeded. This could be repeated in other valleys until the Mormon State of Deseret would become the envy of the world—and "Zion" a reality. This was his dream, and the vigor with which he sought to bring it about and the success which he attained, mark him as a great colonizer in American history.

The success of the Church missionary activities gave him confidence in his plans, especially when converts by the thousands began gathering to Zion. The First Presidency wrote in 1850:

"The estimated population of 15,000 inhabitants in Deseret this past year, having raised grain sufficient to sustain the 30,000 for the coming year, inspires us confidently to believe that the 30,000 the coming year

Photograph of Main Street in Salt Lake City in the 1870's.

Used by permission, Utah State Historical Society

can raise sufficient for 60,000 the succeeding year, and to this object and end, our energies will be exerted, to double our population annually by the assistance of the Perpetual Emigrating Poor Fund, and otherwise provide for the sustenance of that population.

"Viewing the gathering of Israel which produces our increased population in the valleys of the mountains, an important part of the Gospel of Jesus Christ, and one of the most important at the present time, we shall send few, or no elders abroad to preach the Gospel this fall; but instruct them to raise grain and build houses and prepare for the Saints that they may come in flocks, like doves to their windows; and we say: Arise! Ye Saints of the Most High! rich and poor, and gather to the state of Deseret, bringing your plows and drills, your reapers and gleaners, your threshers and cleaners, of the most approved patterns so that one man can do the labor of twenty in the wheat field and we will soon send the Elders abroad by hundreds and thousands to a harvest of souls among the nations, and the inhabitants of the earth shall speedily hear of the salvation prepared by Israel's God for His people."[4]

As the converts to the Church poured into Salt Lake, that city became but a temporary outfitting place for a continued journey into new settlements.

The colonization of the Great Basin was not left to chance. The locations were determined by scouting parties, who traversed wide areas. The leaders chosen were called to that work by the authority of the Priesthood. They were carefully selected men. The founding of settlements became a religious duty to which families were called, in the same way that their sons were called to carry the gospel into the world. Some made converts—others prepared places for settlement into which those who

[4]James A. Little, *From Kirtland to Salt Lake City*, pp. 229-230.

were converted might gather. It was a comprehensive scheme of colonization, unique in the history of the world.

Without the religious motive it would have failed. Often the feeling of duty alone kept men and women battling for existence against mighty odds. Sometimes even that was not sufficient, and a colony would be abandoned.

An expedition leaving Salt Lake City to found a new colony had an interesting organization. It had its bishopric, or presidency, which would preside in the new settlement; its blacksmith, tailor, harness maker, tinsmith, miller, carpenter, mason, farmers, etc. If possible it contained a doctor, a merchant, and a skilled mechanic. It was a community prepared to labor at more-or-less designated tasks, and while men were not tied to follow the trade they professed, the great majority did so, and helped promote a harmonious and self-sustaining community. The few colonizing failures were not the results of an inadequate personnel, but because of an over-estimation of the life-sustaining possibilities of the site selected.

Within twenty years of the founding of Salt Lake City nearly every present settlement of importance in the Great Basin was begun. Into these settlements flowed the great migration of converts in the succeeding years.

The earliest settlements were started without the organization referred to above.

During the winter of 1847-8 the sites for later settlements were occupied by individuals charged with the care of wintering large herds of cattle. Thomas Grover settled on Deuel Creek, at what is now Centerville. Peregrine Sessions, accompanied by Samuel Brown, settled on East Mill Creek at what is now Bountiful. Heber C. Haight, with one of his sons, wintered on the present site of Farmington.

In the Spring of 1848, Captain James Brown, formerly of the Mormon Battalion, purchased the Goodyear tract of land at the mouth of Weber Canyon for $1,950 cash, which had been collected as Battalion wages and authorized by the members for that purpose. On September 3, 1849, Brigham Young selected the site for the present city of Ogden. A wall was built to enclose the settlement. The number of settlers increased so rapidly that in 1851 it was divided into two wards. Also in 1851, the colonization movement to the north reached Box Elder Creek, where Brigham City was settled by Welsh and Scandinavian emigrants under Simeon A. Carter. Logan, in Cache Valley, was occupied in 1859.

Meanwhile, settlements were extending to the South. On March 17, 1849, a company of one hundred fifty souls, organized with John S. Higbee as president and Isaac Higbee and Dimick B. Huntington as counselors, moved into Utah Valley to a site two miles northwest of the present Provo City. Here they hastily built Fort Utah, as the Indians were gathering in large numbers, and warnings were being received from Fort Bridger that an uprising was impending. In September, the settlement was visited by the First Presidency, who selected the present site of Provo for a city.

After a treaty of peace had been negotiated with the Indians, the settlement of Battlecreek (Pleasant Grove), American Fork, Evansville (Lehi), Springville, and Payson, were established.

Isaac Morley arrived in Sanpete County with two hundred twenty-four souls, in 1849. Manti was selected a site

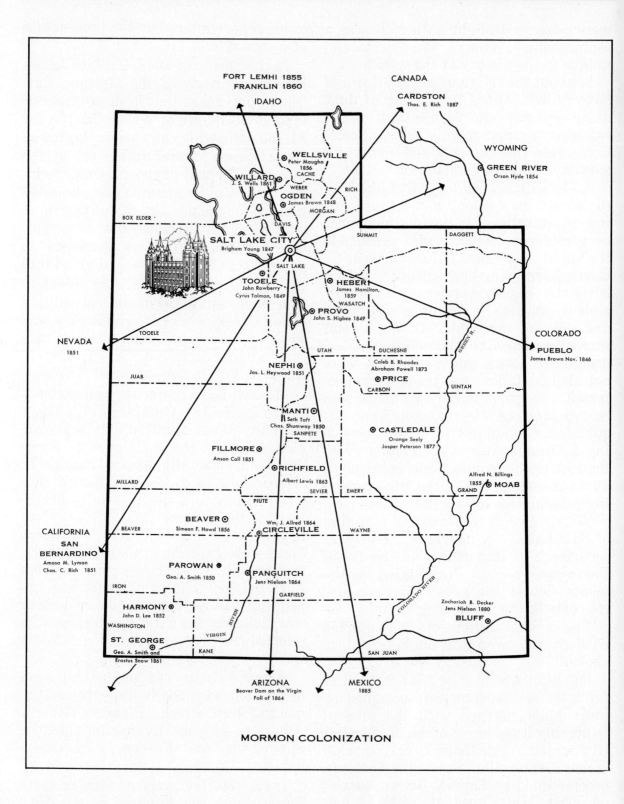

FORT LEMHI 1855
FRANKLIN 1860
IDAHO

CANADA

CARDSTON
Thos. E. Rich   1887

WYOMING

GREEN RIVER
Orson Hyde 1854

WELLSVILLE
Peter Maughn
1856
CACHE

WILLARD
J. S. Wells 1861

WEBER

RICH

OGDEN
James Brown 1848

MORGAN

BOX ELDER

DAVIS

SUMMIT

DAGGETT

SALT LAKE CITY
Brigham Young 1847

SALT LAKE

TOOELE
John Rowberry
Cyrus Talman, 1849

HEBER
James Hamilton,
1859
WASATCH

PROVO
John S. Higbee 1849

NEVADA
1851

TOOELE

UTAH

DUCHESNE

COLORADO

PUEBLO
James Brown Nov. 1846

Caleb B. Rhoades
Abraham Powell 1873

PRICE

CARBON

UINTAH

NEPHI
Jos. L. Heywood 1851

JUAB

MANTI
Seth Taft
Chas. Shumway 1850
SANPETE

CASTLEDALE
Orange Seely
Jasper Peterson 1877

FILLMORE
Anson Call 1851

RICHFIELD
Albert Lewis 1863

SEVIER

EMERY

Alfred N. Billings
1855
GRAND

MOAB

MILLARD

PIUTE

BEAVER
Simeon F. Howd 1856

Wm. J. Allred 1864
CIRCLEVILLE

WAYNE

BEAVER

CALIFORNIA
SAN
BERNARDINO
Amasa M. Lyman
Chas. C. Rich   1851

PAROWAN
Geo. A. Smith 1850

PANGUITCH
Jens Nielson 1864

GARFIELD

COLORADO RIVER

Zachariah B. Decker
Jens Nielson 1880

IRON

HARMONY
John D. Lee 1852

WASHINGTON

VIRGIN   RIVER

BLUFF

ST. GEORGE
Geo. A. Smith and
Erastus Snow 1861

KANE

SAN JUAN

ARIZONA
Beaver Dam on the Virgin
Fall of 1864

MEXICO
1885

MORMON COLONIZATION

for a city by Brigham Young, in August, 1850.

In this same year, George A. Smith led thirty families 200 miles to the South, and on January 13, 1850, settled "Parowan" in the Little Salt Lake Valley.

Tooele was established in 1849, by John Rowberry and Cyrus Tolman, who led a number of families west from Salt Lake City.

In November, 1849, Parley P. Pratt led an exploring party of fifty men southward. Part of the party explored the region of the Little Salt Lake Valley, while Elder Pratt and nineteen men continued South to the confluence of the Rio Virgin and Rio Santa Clara, before returning northward.

Fillmore, in Millard County, was settled by Anson Call, in October, 1851, and settled as the capital of the Utah territory. Also in the same year, Joseph L. Heywood established the town of Nephi.

At the general conference in October, 1853, a number of men were called to gather families and strengthen the various settlements. George A. Smith and Erastus Snow were to take fifty families to strengthen the settlements in Iron County; Wilford Woodruff and Ezra T. Benson, fifty families for the settlements in Tooele County; Lyman Stevens and Reuben W. Allred, fifty families for each of the settlements in San Pete County; Lorenzo Snow, fifty families to Box Elder County; and Orson Hyde to raise a company and make a permanent settlement in Green River, near Fort Bridger.

The population of the Mormon settlements numbered 76,335 by February, 1856. Of these 37,277 were males and 39,058 females.[5]

[5]Roberts, *Comprehensive History of the Church*, Vol. 3, p. 488.

Settlements in Distant Areas

A company of Elders, called on a mission to the Indians in April, 1854, opened the way to the establishment of settlements in the Southern part of the state. These missionaries built a small settlement on the Santa Clara. In 1855, forty men, under the presidency of Alfred N. Billings, founded Moab.

George A. Smith and Erastus Snow founded St. George in 1861, and set the colonists to work raising cotton.

Sevier Valley was settled in 1863, with Richfield and Monroe as centers.

In 1866-67 many of the settlements in Sevier Valley, as well as some in Kane, Piute, and Iron Counties, were temporarily abandoned, due to Indian troubles. In the fall of 1867, 163 missionaries with their families were called to strengthen the settlements in Southern Utah, and others were likewise called in 1868.

This was a tremendous program of settlement for a twenty-year period. Even this does not tell the whole story. The boundaries of present Utah did not limit the ambitions of the Saints. In 1851, a settlement was made at San Bernardino, in Southern California. McClintock summarizes the colonizing activities of the Mormons in Arizona and other neighboring states as follows:

"But in Arizona, in the valleys of the Little Colorado, the Salt, the Gila and the San Pedro and of their tributaries and at points where the white man theretofore had failed, if he had reached them at all, the Mormons set their stakes and, with united effort, soon cleared the land, dug ditches and placed dams in unruly streams, all to the end that farms should smile where the desert had reigned . . . Mormons also were Pioneers in Southern California, where in 1851, several hundred families of the faith settled at San Bernardino. * * *

"The first Anglo-Saxon settlement within the boundaries of the present state of Colorado was at Pueblo, November 15, 1846, by

Captain James Brown and about 150 Mormon men and women. * * *

"The first American settlement in Nevada was one of Mormons in the Carson Valley, at Genoa, in 1851. * * *

"In Wyoming, as early as 1854, was a Mormon settlement at Green River, near Fort Bridger, known as Fort Supply. * * *

"In Idaho, too, pre-eminence is claimed by virtue of a Mormon settlement at Fort Limhi, on the Salmon River in 1855, and at Franklin, in Cache Valley, in 1860." * * *[6]

In 1857, due to the uncertainties of the "Utah War," the colonists at Limhi, Idaho, Carson, Nevada, and San Bernardino, California, were advised to abandon their settlements and move nearer the main body.

The unsettled condition, due to the polygamy question, led to the establishment of colonies in Canada. In September, 1886, President John Taylor appointed Charles O. Card, President of the Cache Valley Stake, to investigate the possibilities of colonies in Canada. Card reported favorably on the Southern Alberta Province. In 1887, in company with Thomas E. Ricks of Rexburg, Idaho, and others, he located a colony in that Province, which was named Cardston. This was the beginning of a very important and prosperous settlement of the Church.

Colonies in Mexico

A group of Saints, seeking relief from the persecutions under the anti-bigamy laws, left the confines of the United States and migrated to Mexico in 1885. Ten years later, Charles W. Kendrick, U.S. Consul at Ciudad, Juarez, wrote a description of the colony, which not only depicts the success of colonization in that land, but might be equally applied to Mormon colonies everywhere:

[6]McClintock, *Mormon Settlement in Arizona*, pp. 2, 3, 5.

"The Mormon settlers came to Mexico in 1889. They were poor people. Many of them had not even the means of transportation, and when they arrived in the valley of the Cascas Grandes river, two hundred miles south of the New Mexican line and as many miles from a railroad, they had practically nothing but their physical strength and religious enthusiasm. Around them were high mountains, capped with snow; dark canyons, where wild beasts made their lair, and a narrow arid valley, without irrigation, and barren of vegetation except grama grass and cottonwood trees. Apache Indians lurked in the hills, drove away their herds, and sometimes attacked the settlements. But the Mormons prospered. No difficulty, no hardship was great enough to appall them or drive them back. They made ditches, turned the water of the river upon their lands, planted fruit trees, laid out gardens, tended their flocks, and plenty came to support and sustain them. Other colonies were established which were also prosperous. In a single "stake", comprising the colonies, or "wards," of Colonia Juarez, Colonia Diaz, Dublan, Oaxaca, Pacheco, Garcia, and Chuichupi, the Mormons number 2,523 persons and 477 families. * * * *

"The capital colony is a beautiful village comparable to any in New England. There is every evidence of thrift, cleanliness, industry, comfort, and good management. There is an absence of the vices common to modern communities. There are no saloons tobacco shops, jails, nor houses of ill-fame in the colony. The property is owned by Mormons, and the internal affairs of the several settlements are under the direction of the Church. There is a gristmill, a furniture factory, and other industries in Colonia Juarez. There is an academy with five teachers and 400 pupils. It is the policy of the Mormons to erect schoolhouses before churches and temples."

Laws and Government

As previously mentioned, the Great Basin in 1847 was not formally a part of the United States and no form of government had ever been provided for the territory.

The Mormons, however, had five hundred of their men enlisted in the United States Army and it was generally understood that sooner or later the

Utah region would become a part of the United States.

Brigham Young carried a United States flag across the plains in his wagon, and raised it over the camp at the time of the enlistment of the Battalion. In October, 1847, an American flag was raised over the fort at Salt Lake City.[7]

No attempt was made to organize a civil government until the return of Brigham Young from Winter Quarters, in the fall of 1848. On February 1, 1849, a call was signed by many citizens and issued to the people of the Basin to assemble their delegates to Salt Lake City, "for the purpose of taking into consideration the propriety of organizing a territorial or State government."[8]

The United States Government had taken no step to organize the new territory. Accordingly, the inhabitants at the convention organized a "State of Deseret," "until the Congress of the United States should otherwise provide by law."[9] The established government was therefore a "provisional government," to manage the affairs of the Basin until Congress should alter or affirm the procedure.

A constitution was drafted which followed the line of the constitutions of the older States, with a governor, legislative body, etc.

The convention which met to formulate the constitution sent a memorial to Congress asking for admission to the Union as the "State of Deseret." A petition signed by 2,270 individuals asking for a territorial form of Government, was forwarded to Congress by Dr. Bernhisel, on March 30. The

reason for the petition was the belief that Congress would act more promptly in establishing some form of government if two alternatives were proposed.

Dr. John M. Bernhisel was sent to Washington on behalf of the Saints. He and Wilford Woodruff, then presiding in the Eastern States Mission, conferred with Colonel Thomas L. Kane, who, in his great friendship for the Mormons, was exerting himself in Washington on their behalf. Colonel Kane advised them:

"You are better off without any government from the hands of Congress than with a territorial government. The political intrigues of government officers will be against you. You can govern yourselves better than they can govern you. I would prefer to see you withdraw the bill rather than to have a territorial government, for if you are defeated in the state government, you can fall back upon it again at another session, if you have not a territorial government; but if you have, you cannot apply for a state of government for a number of years. I insist upon it. You do not want corrupt political men from Washington strutting around you, with military epaulettes and dress, who will speculate out of you all they can. They will also control the Indian agency, and Land agency, and will conflict with your calculations in a great measure. You do not want two governments. You have a government now (alluding to the provisional state government of Deseret then in existence), which is firm and powerful, and you are under no obligation to the United States." * * * * If you have a state government, men may come along and say, 'I am judge,' 'I am colonel,' 'I am governor,' you can whistle and ask no odds of them. But while you have a territorial government they cannot do it. And then there are always so many intrigues to make political parties among you. The first thing you know, a strong political party is rising up in your midst, selfish, and against your interests."[10]

Acting upon the advice of Colonel Kane, Dr. Bernhisel took no steps to present the petition for a territorial

[7]Roberts, *Comprehensive History of the Church,* Vol. 3, p. 274.
[8]*History of Brigham Young,* Ms., 1849, entry of February, p. 3.
[9]*History of Brigham Young,* Ms., 1849, p. 26.

[10]*History of Brigham Young,* Ms., 1849, pp. 161-164.

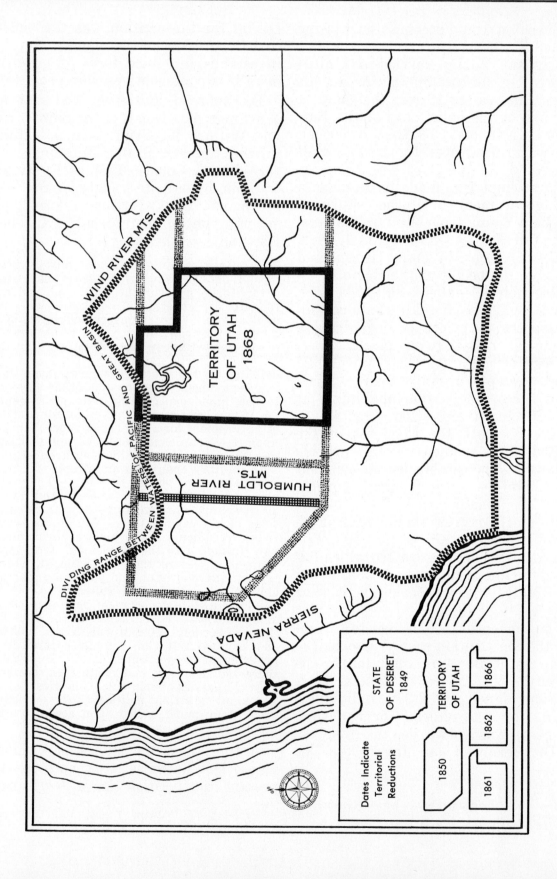

WIND RIVER MTS.

GREAT BASIN

DIVIDING RANGE BETWEEN WATERS OF PACIFIC AND

TERRITORY
OF UTAH
1868

HUMBOLDT RIVER
MTS.

SIERRA NEVADA

STATE
OF DESERET
1849

TERRITORY
OF UTAH

1866

1862

1850

1861

Dates Indicate
Territorial
Reductions

Picture taken at the dedication of the Brigham Young Monument which now stands at the head of Salt Lake City's Main Street.

form of government to Congress, but earnestly labored for a "State of Deseret."

Territory of Utah Organized

Congress, however, was in no mood to admit Deseret into the Union of States. The Southern congressmen were opposed to the admission of every "Free State," and many of the Northern congressmen, especially from Missouri, Illinois, and Iowa, opposed the admission of Deseret.

For a time it was proposed that Deseret and California be united under one state government for a period of two years, to offset the admission to the Union of the great slave state of Texas. This proposition was advanced by General John Wilson in a private mission to California which already had held a constitutional convention and was appealing for statehood. The Southern States opposed the admission of California because of the slavery question, but despite the opposition, California was accepted as a state under Henry Clay's compromise bill of 1850.

The entrance of California as a "Free State" doomed the chances of the State of Deseret until the Civil War period, as the South lined up solidly against the admission of another "Free State." By the time of the Civil War, the conflict over polygamy had arisen, which kept the region from Statehood until 1896.

In September, 1850, an act was passed by Congress creating not the "State of Deseret" but the "Territory of Utah." The change in name from

"Deseret" to "Utah" was a flat rejection of the desires of the Mormon people. "Utah," named after the Ute Indians living in the Territory, meant "the land of the Utes" and was used in early times by the "Mountain Men."

So rapidly had the population of Deseret and California increased, and so slowly did the wheels of government turn in providing a civil administration for them, that both territories had formed provisional state governments and had proceeded to manage their own affairs.

The creation of the provisional State of Deseret served a most useful purpose in the history of Utah. Brief as its existence was, 1849-1851, it nevertheless left its stamp upon the policies of the territory. This was especially true in the matter of the establishment of new settlements and new industries. The legislature and governor of the State of Deseret assumed a paternal policy toward these communities and industries. Money was frequently voted to protect the settlements from Indian depredations. The Nauvoo Legion was revived for this purpose, and, with the friendly policy adopted toward the Indian, effectively prevented Indian uprisings. This encouragement on the part of the government of Deseret induced many men of means to begin manufacturing enterprises and tended toward the industrial independence of the region.

Further, the policy adopted toward education was a far-sighted one. Had Deseret been granted statehood, greater stress would have been laid upon that important phase of civilization than became the case under territorial government. This paternal attitude is shown in the founding of the University of Deseret and the voting of State funds for its maintenance.

Brigham Young was elected as governor of the provisional State of Deseret. So efficient was his administration of affairs that, with the organization of Utah Territory in September, 1850, he was appointed by President Fillmore as its first governor. The oath of office was administered February 3, 1851, and the provisional State of Deseret came to an end.

New Territorial Officers

The majority of appointed officers for Utah Territory were non-Mormons from the Eastern States, who were wholly unacquainted with the peculiarities of the Mormon people and failed to understand and sympathize with them. The appointment to the far off Utah Territory was not considered an attractive assignment, and the abler men like Joseph Buffington of Pennsylvania, who was appointed as Chief Justice, declined proffered positions.

Then, too, the Saints had a deep and abiding mistrust for the Federal Government, which had grown out of a feeling that the government, if not responsible for the outrages against them in Missouri and Illinois, had at least, by failing to act, consented to their being persecuted. This was a most unfortunate viewpoint as it developed an antagonism against the "foreign" appointees to Territorial offices which was ill-concealed. Captain Stansbury, a keen observer and a friend of the Saints, wrote:

"That a deep and abiding resentment of injuries received and wrongs endured in Missouri and Illinois pervades the whole Mormon community, is perfectly true; and that many of the less informed, and, I regret to add, some even whose intelligence and education ought to have enabled them to form more correct opinions this exasperation has extended itself to the general government, because of its refusal to interpose for their protection at the time of these difficulties, is also true; but from all that I saw and heard, I deem it but simple justice to say but notwithstanding these causes of irritation, a more loyal and patriotic people cannot be found, within the limits of the Union."[11]

In the years which followed there was a constant clash between Federal appointees and the people of the territory. Many contributing factors, other than those before mentioned, must be kept in mind. Some of these appointed officers came into the territory with their minds poisoned by slander against the Mormons. The moral standards of others were offensive to a people who had accepted the mission of bringing "righteousness" to all the world. Further, the Saints were attached to their religious leaders, and followed their counsel, whether or not it coincided with the wishes and advices of the civil government. No man could possibly wield the same power and influence as Brigham Young in the territory, regardless of his civil position. To the Saints, Brigham Young was not only the founder of the State of Deseret, but their prophet and Church President. Obedient as they wished to be to the law of the land, there was yet in their hearts the higher law of the Gospel to which they owed the utmost allegiance and upon which they placed their reliance.

Captain Stansbury reports:

"Intimately connected with them from their exodus from Illinois, this man (Brigham Young) has been indeed their Moses, leading them through the wilderness to a remote and unknown land, where they have since set up their tabernacle, and where they are now building their temple. Resolute in danger, firm and sagacious in council, prompt and energetic in emergency, and enthusiastically devoted to the honor and interests of his people, he had won their unlimited

confidence, esteem and veneration, and held an unrivaled place in their hearts. With the establishment of the provisional government, he had been unanimously chosen as their highest civil magistrate, and even before his appointment by the President, he combined in his own person, the triple character of confidential advisor, temporal ruler, and Prophet of God."[12]

The Federal appointees from the East truly felt that they were outsiders, distrusted and unwanted. The ensuing bitterness and misunderstandings are an unfortunate chapter in the history of Utah.

Supplementary Readings

1. Roberts, *Comprehensive History of the Church*, Vol. 3, p. 330. ("The Community Placed on Rations." People eat thistles, sego lilies, and other native plants.)

2. *Ibid.*, Vol. 3, pp. 330-331. (The Sego Lily: Utah State Flower.) Also p. 353. Note 1. ("Our Sego Lily." A poem by John W. Pike. A beautiful bit of verse.)

3. *Ibid.*, Vol. 3, pp. 331-333. ("The Cricket War. The Miraculous Deliverance.")

4. *Ibid.*, Vol. 3, pp. 333-335, Notes 10, 11. ("The Harvest Home"—1848. A Pioneer celebration of joyous thanksgiving, gladness, and gayety, August, 1848.)

5. *Ibid.*, Vol. 3, pp. 499-501; 504; 506-509. ("The Right of Local Self-Government." "Premature Action of Governor Young in Administrative Action." "The Mental Attitude of the Saints Toward the United States Government.")

6. *Ibid.*, Vol. 3, pp. 509-512-516. ("A Territorial Government of our own." "Attachment of the Saints to their Religious Leaders.")

7. *Ibid.*, Vol. 3, pp, 537-543. ("Attack on Brigham Young." "Defense of Brigham Young by Colonel Kane." "President Young's Attitude on the Utah Situation." "Triumph of Governor Brigham Young and the People of Utah vs. the 'Ran-A-Way' Officials.")

8. *Ibid.*, Vol. 4, pp. 10-12. ("First State Capital. One and Only Session of the Legislature of the New Capital." Note picture of Old State House, at the First Capital, Fillmore.)

9. Cowley, *Wilford Woodruff*, p. 349. In general conference all the people vote to discontinue the use of tea, coffee, and tobacco.)

[11]*Stansbury's Report*, p. 144.

[12]*Stansbury's Reports*, pp. 146-147.

10. *Ibid.*, p. 36. (Philosophical society organized to improve their minds.)

11. Roberts, *Life of John Taylor*, pp. 274-279. (A daring speech by John Taylor on the rights and loyalty of the Mormon people in the Territory of Utah.)

12. Evans, *Heart of Mormonism*, pp. 385-389. (Political Government and the Mormons.)

13. Smith, *Essentials in Church History.* pp. 476-480. (Early political government in Utah.)

14. Gates and Widtsoe, *The Life Story of Brigham Young*, pp. 146-154. (Other Churches and Non-Mormons in Utah.)

15. *Ibid.*, pp. 155-171. (Territorial Government. Loyalty of Mormons. Gold Seekers. Judge Brocchus insults the people in a speech in conference, etc.)

16. Roberts, *A Comprehensive History of the Church*, Vol. 3, pp. 520-537; 543-544. Note. ("Clash of Federal Officials and Church Authorities. Brigham Young or Judge Brocchus, etc.)

CHAPTER 34

A SELF-SUSTAINING PEOPLE

Industrial Independence

When Brigham Young moved the Saints into the Rocky Mountain area it was evident that such a large number of people must supply their own wants, or perish. They were, in a very literal sense, isolated from the world. They must not only supply themselves with sufficient food, but they must produce their own building materials, manufacture their own clothing, provide for their own amusements, establish their own educational system, construct their own roads, and devise their own system of communication.

The isolation forced them to exercise an initiative which, for its accomplishments, has been rarely equaled in the world. Grim necessity developed a leadership and force of character which permeated the humblest household and made the founders of Mormon communities in the West a unique generation of men and women.

Fortunately for the Saints, the membership of the Church had been drawn from the great middle class of society, trained and inured to labor. It contained artisans from every walk of life. Especially was this true of the English converts. The system of apprenticeships in England had produced men efficient in the building trades, from architect to mason; shoemakers, harnessmakers, weavers, skinners, clothiers, cabinet makers, millers, skilled workers from every branch of industry. Even makers of musical instruments, builders of organs, composers, journalists, printers, and jewelers were found

among them. Never have the people of Utah and the surrounding territory been so blessed with an array of trained laborers as in the first generation of pioneers who settled in the valleys of the mountains. This was a vital factor in the success of the Mormons as colonizers.

The necessities of isolation forced the Saints to use their skill and talents to a degree uncalled for in the lands from which they came, leading to accomplishments which remain to this day unusual enough to attract the attention of the world. The most enduring of these accomplishments was the erection of buildings.

Many millions have visited the Temple Block at Salt Lake City, entered the unique Tabernacle and listened to a concert from the great Tabernacle organ. These attractions, together with the great Temple which stands upon the same block, were the work of a people who brought into the West little more than bare hands, energetic brains and a mighty faith.

While less spectacular than the building program of the Church, the industrial accomplishments were the foundation of the commonwealth. When the water of City Creek was flooded over the adjacent land in the afternoon of July 23, 1847, the Saints began their economic independence. Irrigation grew rapidly from a mere flooding of the soil to a scientific method of farming, which soon made the Mormon people independent of the entire world for their food

CHURCH OFFICE BUILDING, operations center in Salt Lake City, Utah of the world-wide activities of the Church of Jesus Christ of Latter-day Saints.

JERUSALEM TODAY, as seen from the Mount of Olives where Apostle Orson Hyde offered his dedicatory prayer.

Used by permission, Lynn M. Hilton

HEBREW UNIVERSITY, located in Jerusalem, the modern structure is indicative of advancement in higher learning since World War II.

Used by permission, Lynn M. Hilton

Long Sounds.

Letter.	Name.		Sound.
Ə	e	as in	eat.
Ɛ	"	"	ate.
Ə	ah	"	art.
Θ	aw	"	aught.
O	o	"	oat.
Ꝺ	oo	"	ooze.

Short Sounds of the above.

ɟ	as in		it.
	"		et.
	"		at.
	"		ot.
	"		ut.
	"		book.

Double Sounds.

i	as in		ice.
ow	"		owl.
ye			
woo			
h			

Letter.	Name.	Sound.
7	p	
8	b	
6	t	
0	d	
C	che	as in cheese.
9	g	
0	k	
0	ga	as in gate.
f	f	
	v	
L	eth	as in thigh.
Y	the	" thy
8	s	
6	z	
D	esh	as in flesh.
S	zhe	" vision.
+	ur	" burn.
U	l	
)	m	
4	n	
N	eng	as in length.

LESSON III.

A STORM.

The Deseret alphabet with a page from the second primer and the title page of the Book of Mormon taken from a subsequent publication containing parts of the Book of Mormon.

supply. Irrigation became the key which unlocked the fertility of the soil and made possible the establishment of a numerous people on a previously barren land.

The improvement of their herds of cattle and sheep, the raising of hogs and domestic fowls, further strengthened the independence of the region. The high cost of bringing freight across the plains, $250 per ton, and the great length of time involved in obtaining goods from the East, forced the Saints into the manufacturing field and broadened the agricultural base.

As early as 1849, Brigham Young wrote to the Elders presiding in the various mission fields, asking them to investigate any industry which might be suited to the Saints in their mountain home and urging converts with capital to migrate to Salt Lake Valley and enter the manufacturing field.

Domestic Manufactories

A sixth general epistle from the Church Presidency in 1851 contains the following and illustrates some of the accomplishments over a three-year period:

"The 'Deseret Pottery' is in successful operation; some good light yellow ware was drawn from the kiln, June 27, and white ware is soon expected. It is anticipated that the valley materials for making crockery and chinaware will be equal to any other place; and that the pottery will soon be able to supply this market. Good potters are wanted. A carding machine is in operation and doing extensive business in this valley; also one in Utah (Valley) and others in progress.

"There are four grain- and five sawmills in operation, or nearly completed in Great Salt Lake county; also two grain- and two sawmills in Weber County; one grain- and two sawmills in Davis county; two grain- and three sawmills in Utah county; one grain- and two sawmills in San Pete county; one grain- and one sawmill in Iron county; and one sawmill in Tooele county; and an in-

creasing desire and exertion to promote domestic manufacture prevails throughout the territory."[1]

In his message to the territorial legislature, in 1852, Governor Young gives the following information on the economic situation:

"Domestic manufacturers, I am happy to state, are in a flourishing condition; considerable quantities of leather and crockery have found their way into market, and a large amount of clothing has been made, principally by the hands of the good housewife; who thereby adds dignity to her station and reflects credit and honor upon her household. Specimens of iron have also been forwarded from the works in Iron County, which for the first run, was exceedingly flattering. It separates well, but owing to the sulphur in the coal not being sufficiently extracted, was thereby injured; but a little experience in combining materials, and continued effort, it is believed. will soon produce that article in great abundance, and of good quality. A liberal hand should be extended unto the enterprising men who have nobly devoted their time, under circumstances of penury and want, in producing an article of so much moment as iron, to the urgent necessities, and future wealth of the territory. It will soon pay its own way, and become a source of profit to the producers; but until returns can be received, the enterprise exhausts the means of operators, and they should be relieved by the public funds. * * * I am also happy to announce the arrival in our territory, of the machinery for the manufacture of sugar from the beet. The machinery, and operators who have been accustomed to the manufacture of that article from the beet, have come together from the 'Old World,' and being under the direction of energetic, enterprising, and able men, will doubtless soon furnish an abundant supply of that article, for the wants of the people."[2]

In the same message, the Governor notes that a Mr. Gaunt was succeeding in his enterprise of establishing a woolen mill. "He is now weaving and by another year, will be enabled to do an extensive business."[3]

[1]Roberts, Comprehensive History of the Church, Vol. 4, p. 24.
[2]Deseret News, December 25, 1852.
[3]Deseret News, December 25, 1852.

In speaking of the labors of the people in their homes to supply their wants, Brigham Young records in his Journal:

"Sister Hulda Duncan, of Davis County, between August 5, 1854, and January 27th (1855), wove 194 yards of jeans, 508 of linsey and 64 of flannel, besides doing other work. Much cloth of the kinds named, and large quantities of rag carpeting have also been manufactured the past year in Utah. This was done by looms, and spinning wheels of a very primitive character."[4]

Two years previously President Young had announced:

"We are going in for home manufactures pretty extensively. My own family alone this season manufactured over five hundred yards of cloth, and the homemade frequently makes its appearance in our streets and in our gatherings."[5]

Industry at Brigham City

Similar activities were conducted throughout the territory. Manufacturing by individual companies developed slowly, however, and paid small interest on the investments, due to the limited demand for manufactured articles in a new country, lacking in population and money. This factor gave rise to cooperative manufacturing enterprises which flourished until after the advent of the railroad. A brief study of the cooperative development at Brigham City will illustrate the nature and effect of such movements. Lorenzo Snow, who instituted and managed the enterprise, summarizes its accomplishments in a letter to Bishop Lunt of Cedar City under date of October, 1876:

"In accordance with your request, I send you the following brief account of the rise, progress and present condition of "Brigham City Mercantile and Manufacturing Association."

"We commenced over twelve years ago by

organizing a mercantile department which consisted of four stockholders, myself included, with a capital of about three thousand dollars. The dividends were paid in store goods, amounting, usually, to about twenty-five per cent, per annum.

"As this enterprise prospered, we continued to receive capital stock, also adding new names to the list of stockholders, until we had a surplus of capital, or means, and succeeded in uniting the interests of the people and securing their patronage. We resolved, then, to commence home industries and receive our dividends, if any, in the articles produced. * * *

"We erected a tannery building two stories, 45 x 80, with modern improvements and conveniences, at a cost of $10,000 (ten thousand). Most of the materials, mason and carpenter work were furnished as capital stock by such persons as were able and desired an interest in our institution.

"The larger portion of the work was done in the winter season, when no other employment could be had, one-fourth being paid in merchandise to such as needed. We gained, by this measure, additional capital, as well as twenty or thirty new stockholders, without encroaching much on any one's property or business. This tannery has been operated during the past nine years with success and reasonable profits, producing an excellent quality of leather, from $8,000 to $10,000 (eight thousand to ten thousand) annually. We connected with this branch of industry a boot and shoe shop; also, a saddle and harness shop, drawing our dividends in the articles manufactured in those departments.

"Our next enterprise was the establishing of a woolen factory; following the same course as in putting up the tannery—procuring the building materials, doing the mason and carpenter work in the season when laborers would otherwise have been unemployed. This, also, added to our capital—increasing the number of our stockholders without interrupting any man's business. The profits of the mercantile department, with some additional capital, purchased the machinery. During the past seven years this factory has done a satisfactory business, and we have not been necessitated to close for lack of wool, winter or summer, and have manufactured about $40,000 (forty thousand) worth of goods annually. This establishment, with its appurtenances, cost about $35,000 (thirty-five thousand).

"With the view of probable difficulty in obtaining wool, we now started a sheep herd,

---

[4]*History of Brigham Young*, Ms., Entry of February, 1855, p. 19.
[5]*History of Brigham Young*, Ms., Entry of February, 1852, pp. 15-16.

commencing with fifteen hundred head, supplied by various individuals who could spare them, as capital stock. They now number five thousand, and prove a great help to our factory in times like these, when money is scarce, and cash demanded for wool.

"Our next business was the establishment of a dairy; and, having selected a suitable ranch, we commenced with sixty cows; erected some temporary buildings, making a small investment in vats, hoops, presses, etc., all of which have gradually improved till, perhaps, now it is the finest, best and most commodious of any dairy in this Territory. The past two years we have had five hundred milch cows, producing, each season, in the neighborhood of $8,000 (eight thousand) in butter, cheese, and milk.

"Next we started a horn stock herd, numbering, at present, one thousand, which supplies, in connection with the sheep herd, a meat market, owned by our association.

"We have a horticultural and agricultural department, the latter divided into several branches, each provided with an experienced overseer.

"Also, we have a hat factory, in which are produced all our fur and wool hats. We make our tinware—have a pottery, broom, brush, and molasses factory, a shingle mill and two sawmills, operated by water power, and one steam sawmill; and also blacksmith, tailor and furniture departments, and one for putting up and repairing wagons and carriages.

"We have a large two-story adobe building, occupied by machinery for wood turning, planing, and working mouldings, operated by water power.

"We have established a cotton farm of one hundred and twenty-five acres, in the southern part of the Territory, for the purpose of supplying warps to our woolen factory, where we maintain a colony of about twenty young men. This enterprise was started about two years ago, and has succeeded beyond our expectations. The first year, besides making improvements in buildings, making dams, constructing water sects, setting our trees, planting vineyards, plowing, scraping, leveling and preparing the ground, they raised a large crop of cotton, which produced in the neighborhood of seventy thousand yards of warp. More than double the amount has been raised this season.

"We have a department for manufacturing straw hats, in which we employ from fifteen to twenty girls. Last year we employed twenty-five girls in our dairy, and have them in constant employ in our millinery and tailoring departments, also in making artificial flowers—as hat and shoe binders—as weavers in our woolen mills, and clerks in our mercantile departments. * * *

"The past two or three years we have paid our employees five-sixths in home products, one-sixth in imported merchandise, amounting in aggregate, at trade rates, to about $160,000 (one hundred and sixty thousand). In the year 1875 the value of products, in trade rates, from all our industries, reached about $260,000 (two hundred and sixty thousand)."[6]

Other Industries

Utah's Dixieland, so named because of the early cotton industry in that southern area, could have produced enough cotton to supply the entire territory. Mills for the spinning and weaving of the cotton were established in St. George and Orderville, but the bulk of it was transported to Provo, Salt Lake, and Brigham City.

Southern Utah also became noted for its silk industry. Silk worms were imported from Japan and fed upon mulberry trees which flourished in that part of the state. The natural thread produced by the worm in spinning his cocoon was wound upon spools and later woven into silk cloth.

The cotton and silk industries were profitable while the high prices for hauling freight across the plains or from the Pacific Coast continued. With the coming of the railroad in 1869, both industries were doomed. Only the loyalty of the Saints to their own establishments caused them to survive at all in the following years, and the enterprises were gradually abandoned.

The manufacture of paper was likewise a thriving business for a period. At the mouth of Big Cottonwood Can-

[6]Snow, Eliza R., *Biography and Family Record of Lorenzo Snow*, pp. 291-295.

Paper script which circulated throughout the early Mormon settlements.

yon in the Salt Lake Valley may still be seen the remains of one of the paper mills. Being built of granite rock the walls survived the fire which gutted the buildings April 1, 1893. In recent years the historic old building has been converted into a club house[7] for dancing purposes, and is now one of the best preserved landmarks of the state.

The history of the beet sugar industy is an industrial romance in itself. While on a mission to France in 1849-50, Elder John Taylor was urged by a special letter from President Young "to get ideas and machinery if necessary to send to 'Deseret' to further and build up her industries."[8]

In pursuance of this unique missionary duty, Elder Taylor, accompanied by a young French convert, Philip De La Mare, visited the region of Arras, in the department of Pas-De-Calais, which had become the center of the beet sugar industry in Northern France. This little town was putting on the market some two or three million pounds of sugar annually. A careful study was made of the sugar beet plant, the soil necessary to its growth, its care, and the process of manufacturing the sugar. Elder Taylor was convinced that he had found a suitable industry for the distant "State of Deseret."

The Attempt to Manufacture Sugar

The Deseret Manufacturing Company was formed, young De La Mare subscribing for $5,000 worth of stock. Elder Taylor went to England, and from four wealthy Saints (Mr. Colliston, John R. Winder, John W. Coward and Captain Russell.) raised the capital of the enterprise to $60,000. Under the

supervision of Elder Taylor, the English firm of Faucett, Preston and Company, manufactured the necessary machinery for a sugar factory at a cost of $12,500.

The difficulties of the company were just beginning. The heavy machinery was shipped to New Orleans. Here the customs officials unexpectedly assessed them $5,000 in tariff. From here the machinery was taken by river steamer to Fort Leavenworth, where fifty-two wagons had been gathered to transport it across the plains. The wagons proved too light and broke down under the heavy machinery. Those not broken down were given to Saints intending to migrate West with the "sugar train." The funds of the company were becoming depleted. Young De La Mare, who was supervising the shipping, met one Charles H. Perry, a non-mormon, at Fort Leavenworth, who furnished him with forty great Santa Fe wagons on credit.

On the 4th of July, 1852, the long caravan, with 200 yoke of oxen, started the twelve hundred mile trek to Salt Lake City. This was a unique journey in the history of American industry. For five months this heavily laden caravan labored through the heat and, finally, through two feet of snow to reach Salt Lake Valley. Provisions ran low and ox teams were eaten. Before reaching Salt Lake City the heavier machinery was left by the wayside. Elder John Taylor preceded the caravan to the valley and sent two relief expeditions with teams and supplies. These met the caravan on the way and conducted the migrating Saints, who were with the caravan, into Salt Lake City. The main company arrived in the latter part of November.

The sugar machinery was shipped

---

[7]The Old Mill Club.
[8]Philip De La Mare, *Manuscript History of the Deseret Manufacturing Company.*

first to Provo, then returned to Salt Lake City. Part of it was set upon the northeast corner of the temple block, where it was used for a short time making molasses. The entire plant was finally set up four miles southeast of the city. Its location became known as Sugar House.

The first attempt at sugar making was a further discouragement. The sugar beet seed, brought from France with the machinery, was planted in the wet bottom lands. When the crop was harvested and the beets ground, the sugar beet juice was found to be filled with minerals and was too dark.

Mr. Mollenhauer, an expert sugar maker, who had been induced to migrate to Utah, saw the condition of the juice and sought for the "retorts" to be used to clarify the syrup. There were none. The French Company which had drawn up the specifications for the plants had omitted the "retorts." It looked for a time as if the whole enterprise was doomed. Mr. Mollenhauer and Mr. De La Mare improvised some retorts for the burning of bones, and with the animal charcoal clarified the syrup "until it was clear as crystal; and 'satisfied ourselves,' writes De La Mare, 'that the sugar could be made and all that was needed was an abundance of animal clarifying matter.' "[9]

By this time the company was so heavily involved, with no means to pay their debts, that the entire plant was turned over to the Church with the understanding that the Church assume the debts. The plant was later used for manufacturing syrup but not for sugar.

The enterprise was not a total failure. It demonstrated that beet sugar could be produced in Utah and became the impetus for the establishment, later, of a great industry. The story illustrates the daring courage of the early Saints in industrial enterprises.[10]

Education

A people transplanted into a new country have always suffered, for a time, educationally. The hard struggle to establish homes and the total lack of schools and school facilities have retarded the education of their youth. The case of the Saints was no exception. The heroic efforts of this isolated people, however, to safeguard against a decline in learning and to promote the training of their young people, did much to bridge the gap and pave the way to the present splendid educational system.

When preparations for the great Exodus West was begun in Nauvoo in the Winter of 1845-46, the future education of the youth of the Church was considered. The eastern Saints who sailed for California on the ship *Brooklyn* carried with them a large quantity of school books on every scholastic subject. These had been gathered under instructions from Brigham Young.

At Nauvoo, the council of Twelve appointed W. W. Phelps, an enthusiast on education, to prepare and collect text books to be taken to the new gathering place for the education of the youth. Some of these books collected by Phelps were used in the schools conducted at Winter Quarters the latter part of the winter of 1846-47.

From Winter Quarters in December, 1847, a "General Epistle" was sent

---

[9]Philip De La Mare, *Manuscript History of the Deseret Manufacturing Company.*

[10]Note The sugar beet industry was successfully established in 1893, with the opening of a factory at Lehi, Utah. Wilford Woodruff, then president of the Church, was inspired of God to begin the industry as a Church enterprise. The organization for this purpose became known as the Utah-Idaho Sugar Company.

BRIGHAM YOUNG UNIVERSITY, Church institution of higher learning at Provo, Utah has an enrollment of 25,000 students.

to the Saints throughout the world. In it we read:

"It is very desirable that all the Saints should improve every opportunity of securing at least a copy of every valuable treatise on education—every book, map, chart, or diagram that may contain interesting, useful and attractive matter, to gain the attention of children and cause them to love to learn to read; and also every historical, mathematical, philosophical, geographical, geological, astronomical, scientific, practical, and all other variety of useful and interesting writing, maps, etc., to present to the general Church Recorder, when they shall arrive at their destination, from which important and interesting matter may be gleaned to compile the most valuable works on every science and subject, for the benefit of the rising generation."[11]

These suggestions were followed by the migrating Saints. As a result, a free public library was opened in Salt Lake City in 1850.

The problem of educating their youth under their impoverished condition, surrounded by circumstances which required that every hand, old and young, labor to establish homes, herd the cattle and till the fields, was an almost insurmountable one.

Nevertheless, courageous souls made the attempt. As soon as a portion of the Old Fort was completed in the latter part of October, 1847, Mary Dilworth opened the first school. One of the newly constructed buildings, comprising the wall of the fort and containing loopholes in case of Indian attack, was the first schoolroom. During the winter of 1848-49, a number of classes were conducted, many of them for missionaries. In the spring of 1849, the First Presidency of the Church announced:

"There has been a large number of schools the past winter, in which the Hebrew, Greek, Latin, French, German, Tahitian and English language have been taught successfully."[11a]

The University of Deseret

Before Utah had been organized as a territory of the United States (September, 1850) the Legislature of the provisional State of Deseret passed an act for the creation of the "University of Deseret," the forerunner of the present "University of Utah." The first institution of higher learning was given a chancellor and a board of twelve regents. Five thousand dollars a year for twenty years was voted as part of a maintenance fund. Orson Spencer, a graduate of the Theological Seminary at Hamilton, New York, was appointed to head the institution.

The founding of a university at such a time required greater means than the Saints possessed. The University was opened, however, in the Council House the second Monday in November, 1850. Dr. Cyrus Collins was the sole instructor. He was succeeded, during the year, by Orson Spencer, and he by W. W. Phelps. In a report issued by the board of regents in 1884-5 we read:

"Owing, however, to the immature conditions of its finances, as well as to its limited patronage, not withstanding it had been made a free school institution, the department of instruction was soon discontinued, the university continuing for many years in abeyance and having but a nominal existence until 1877."

From 1867-69, the University was conducted under Mr. D. O. Calder, and partook of the nature of a commercial college.

The University really dates from the appointment of Dr. John R. Park as chancellor, in 1869. From that date it has grown into an institution ranking with the best of the nation.

[11]*Millennial Star*, Vol. 10, pp. 81-88. See also Roberts, *Comprehensive History of the Church*, Vol. 2, p. 312.

[11a]James R. Clark, *Messages of the First Presidency*, Vol. I, p. 355.

Elementary schools, however, were conducted from the time of Mary Dilworth's school in 1847, although the school system throughout the territory was in a disorganized condition for many years, and the majority of the rising generation spent very little time under formal schoolroom instruction. Several conditions retarded the development of the schools. First, there was the lack of school facilities and funds with which to hire teachers. Second, in their isolated condition many communities could not find competent teachers. Those among the Saints who could have conducted schools were busily engaged in the task of subduing the soil, building a community, or in carrying on the extensive missionary system of the Church. In the third place, territorial government, especially where the governmental officers were non-Mormon, was not conducive to the establishment of a strong educational policy. The territorial government continued for forty years after Utah was prepared for statehood. During that time (until 1896) no public lands were set aside in Utah for the support of the schools, as was done in other States.

Development of Church Schools

The interest of the Church in the education of its youth prompted it to launch into the education field and to develop in the state an educational system independent of the state schools. This system of Church schools was inaugurated for the higher education of boys and girls who had graduated from the grades, especially where no secondary state schools were provided. To supervise its educational policy, the Church appointed a Church Board of Education and local boards of Education at each Church school or academy. The Church

schools were distributed throughout the territory in the larger centers of population and taught both secular and religious subjects.

In 1876, Brigham Young sent Dr. Karl G. Maeser to establish a university at Provo, which came to be known as the Brigham Young University. A college called Brigham Young College was also established at Logan in 1877. By 1913 there were three colleges, nineteen academies and eight seminaries.

Karl G. Maeser, sent by Brigham Young to Provo in 1876 to establish a university.

As the State high school system developed, the heavy tax burden of maintaining the State schools made it unwise for the Church to have its members also support a Church system of schools paralleling the courses taught in the State schools.

Beginning in 1913, with the abandonment of the Summit Academy in Utah, the Church has gradually withdrawn from the field of secular education. The majority of the Church school buildings have been purchased at a nominal price by school districts or by the State school system and maintained as high schools or State junior colleges. By 1961 the Church maintained the Brigham Young University at Provo, which has grown into one of the outstanding schools of the Rocky Mountain region, the Ricks Junior College at Rexburg, Idaho, and the Juarez Stake Academy at Colonia Juarez, Mexico. While leaving some areas of secular education, the Church has increased activity in the field of religious education. It has turned the major attention to the daily instruction of the young people of the church on religious subjects. In this field of week-day religious instruction it has been a pioneer in a fast growing movement toward week-day religious education in America.

In 1912, an experiment was conducted in week-day religious education for students attending high schools. The experiment, called the Seminary, involved the establishment of a classroom near the Granite High School under permission from the School District and the Utah State Board of Education. Students with free classroom periods crossed from the high school campus to the Seminary building where they received formal religious instruction during that released-time period and then returned to the high school. The participation in the program on the part of the students was entirely voluntary. The Seminary was an institution entirely independent of the high school. The program proved successful and was extended to other schools and eventually throughout the world. In the school year 1971-72, there were 230 seminaries operating on released-time; 15 special seminaries for handicapped students; 2,918 nonreleased-time seminary classes meeting in an hour prior to the regular school day and 1,774 home study classes, with a total enrollment of 138,069. In addition to the Seminary Program indicated above, religious instruction in the seminaries of the Church was extended by 1972 to some 17,000 Indian students in government schools for the Indians on and off Indian Reservations.

Institutes of Religion were established to serve students at colleges and universities located throughout the United States and Canada. By 1972, the total college student enrollment in Institutes of Religion had reached 53,395.

The total Seminary and Institute enrollment in 1972 had reached 208,477 with plans in progress for much further expansion.

Deseret Clubs operated by the Department of Education and which were forerunners to the Institutes of Religion had been established at more than 300 colleges by 1970. In that year, these clubs as such were discontinued and replaced by part-time Institute classes and by the Latter-day Saints Student Association which had been established on a world-wide basis to contact and aid all Latter-day Saint students of college age throughout the world wherever the Church was established.

Man is that He Might Have Joy

The philosophy of life as taught by the Prophet Joseph Smith had nothing in it of "asceticism."[12] The body, in his opinion, was not a prison for the spirit of man, but "the spirit and body inseparably united receive a fulness of joy."[12a] The *Book of Mormon* proclaimed "Men are that they might have joy."[13] The Prophet, quite to the dismay of other religious denominations, introduced dancing, sports, and the theatre among his people. At the same time he denounced those sensual pleasures which are but temporary and lead to misery and decay.

As the Pioneers took their weary journey to the valleys of the mountains, their load was lightened by song and dance.

It was well that these things became part of the life of the Saints in the valleys of the West, for they softened the hardness of the mountains and caused men and women to forget the past in the hope of the tomorrow.

Isolated as the people were, all of the entertainment which they enjoyed they had to provide. In this field they became independent of the world. Every community, for example, developed its theatrical company. Farmers and housewives, young and old, dropped their toils and adopted new roles upon the stage. Nor did entertainment wait until the homes were made. In 1848, plays were produced under the old bowery in Salt Lake City. In 1859, the Social Hall was erected for theatricals and dances. In 1861, Brigham Young ordered the construction of the Salt Lake Theatre. Within that historic building every great actor of America for more than one-half century performed. The structure was designed by the Church architect, Mr. William H. Folsom, and was a duplicate, outside and in, of the famous Drury Lane Theatre in London, England. Mr. Samuel Bowles, Massachusetts Editor, said of it:

"The building is itself a rare triumph of art and enterprise. No eastern city of one hundred thousand inhabitants — remember Salt Lake City has less than twenty thousand —possesses so fine a theatrical structure. It ranks, alike in capacity, and elegance of structure and finish, along with the opera houses and academies of music of Boston, New York, Philadelphia, Chicago and Cincinnati."[14]

The theatre was opened for dramatic performances March 8, 1862. For the first year the plays presented were prepared by the "Deseret Dramatic Association," with Hiram B. Clawson as general manager and John T. Caine as stage manager. After the first year, theatrical troupes crossing the continent furnished much of the entertainment in the theatre. It continued in steady use until 1929, when it was torn down to make way for commercial enterprises.

The example set by Brigham Young in building and maintaining the Salt Lake Theatre was followed to a lesser degree in every Mormon community. Amateur theatrical companies continued until the coming of commercialized motion pictures drove them from the field.[15]

In every Mormon community a recreation hall was erected and considered nearly as important as a chapel for happiness of the people. In some of the smaller communities the building which served for worship on the Sabbath day was utilized for recreation during the week.

---

[12]Asceticism—The philosophy that the spirit is imprisoned in the body and that man attains his greatest reward in after-life by conquering and suppressing his bodily desires.
[12a]See *Doctrine and Covenants*, Section 93:33-34.
[13]*Book of Mormon*, 2 Nephi, 2:25.

[14]Bowles, *Across the Continent*, p. 103.
[15](Note) This early interest in the play is being now revived by the M.I.A. and will be discussed in a later chapter.

The Salt Lake Theater, ordered constructed by Brigham Young in 1861. It stood where the Mountain States Telephone Building now stands on the intersection of State and First South Streets in Salt Lake City.
Used by permission, Utah State Historical Society

Communication

When the Pioneers entered Salt Lake Valley they found themselves cut off from the outside world. They knew nothing of what was transpiring beyond the valley. Even the fate of the emigrating Saints upon the plains was unknown.

Likewise, those emigrating companies knew nothing of the arrival of the Pioneers in the valley. There was but one way to communicate and that was by sending a messenger on mule or horseback over the intervening miles, or by entrusting letters to slow moving caravans or trappers enroute to the East or West. There was no mail service or post office. Such mail as reached Salt Lake City was distributed at the close of Sacrament services each Sunday.

In the winter of 1849, the Federal government established a post office in Salt Lake City and appointed Joseph L. Heywood postmaster. A bi-monthly mail was authorized between Kanesville and Great Salt Lake City. Almon W. Babbitt undertook to carry the mail under this authorization, at his own expense, in connection with his "carrying and transportation company."

In 1850, the United States Postal Service was extended to Salt Lake City and gradually included the principal settlements in the territory.

Petitions were constantly sent to the government for postal services or improvements by citizens of the various counties in the new territory, but the response was slow.

The first contract with the United States Postal Department for carrying mail from the Missouri River to Salt Lake City was let to Samuel H. Woodson of Independence, Missouri, in 1850. The first mail arrived in Salt Lake November 9, 1850. Feramorz Little, a Mormon, subcontracted to carry the mail between Fort Laramie and Salt Lake City. In Brigham Young's Journal we find this interesting entry:

"Brother Charles Decker arrived from Laramie with the eastern mail. He had to swim every river between this and Laramie. The mail coach and mules were lost at Ham's Fork, where the mail lay under water from one to seven p.m.; the lead horses were saved by being cut loose. Brother Decker was in the ice water with the mail all of the time, and then, exhausted, had no resources but to wrap himself in robes and blankets, wet as water could make them, till morning, when he found himself in a free perspiration, fully relieved from a fever he had been laboring with under most of the time since he left the city.

"Brother Ephraim K. Hanks (about the same time), had proceeded as far as Bear River with the eastern mail. At Weber river the raft on which he and party crossed was sucked under, forcing them to swim for their lives: the mail was carried down the stream and lay in the water upward of two hours. After a great deal of trouble and at the risk of their lives they secured it, but in bad condition. On reaching Bear River, which was a foaming torrent, extending from mountain to mountain, they found it impossible to proceed."[16]

The Pony Express

The carrying of the mail was an adventurous and dangerous occupation.

In 1859-60, great improvement was introduced in the postal system. This was the introduction of the "Pony Express." The system was organized by W. H. Russell of St. Louis, and others.

Under this plan, solitary horsemen carried the mail across the continent at the high rate of $5 per ounce. Stations were located on an average of twenty four miles apart, and fresh horses were kept at each station. Each rider would cover three laps in a day, using three horses. These men were to cover eight miles an hour. The mail time from New York to San Francisco was cut to thirteen days, a remarkable achievement. The heroic riders covered their routes regardless of storm, or heat, or attack of Indians. Lives were often sacrificed for the service. The Pony Express was popular in Salt Lake Valley. Many of the young men of the valley were among the successful riders George A. Smith wrote in April, 1861:

"The Pony Express proved to be quite an institution. The news of the surrender of Fort Sumpter reached here (Salt Lake City) in seven days."[17]

The Pony Express was discontinued in 1861 for lack of patronage. The high rate charged reduced the number of letters carried to less than 200 per carrier

With the completion of the overland telegraph in 1861 the patronage practically ceased. The completion of the telegraph line to Salt Lake City was largely the result of petitions to the Federal Government from the Utah territory, beginning as early as March 1852.

Brigham Young was permitted to send the first message over the wire. On October 18, he sent the following to Mr Wade, President of the telegraph company:

"Sir: Permit me to congratulate you upon the completion of the overland telegraph line west to this city, to commend the energy displayed by yourself and associates in the rapid and successful prosecution of a work so bene

[16]Roberts, *Comprehensive History of the Church*, Vol. 4, pp. 29-30.

[17]Letter to John L. Smith, *History of Brigham Young*, Ms., 1861, p. 165.

ficial; and to express the wish that its use may ever tend to promote the true interests to the dwellers upon both the Atlantic and Pacific slopes of our continent. *Utah has not seceded, but is firm for the Constitution and laws of our happy country, and is warmly interested in such useful enterprises as the one so far completed.*"[18]

The telegraph line from San Francisco was completed a few days later, and Brigham Young was given the privilege of sending the first wire to the Pacific coast. These courtesies to Brigham Young were in recognition of his great service in fostering the enterprise, and in recognition of the Mormon laborers who constructed much of the line.

A telegraph line connecting Salt Lake City with settlements south was extended as far as Pipe Springs, Arizona, in 1865-67. This was entirely a Church enterprise to promote greater unity and responsiveness within the Church. It was called the Deseret Telegraph and was operated by the Church until 1900 when it merged into the Western Union System.[19]

Supplementary Readings

1. Roberts, *A Comprehensive History of the Church*, Vol. 3, pp. 411-413; 395-402. ("Philip De La Mare, Early Utah Industrial Hero." The story of the Pioneer attempt to establish the sugar-beet industry in Utah, under John Taylor's leadership and interest. A dramatic story involving many persons and adventures, and touching three countries —France, England, United States of America.) (See also Reading No. 6, below, for a narrative account of this "Epic of the Sugar-Beet.")

2. *Ibid.*, Vol. 4, pp. 12-19. (Historic Buildings of the Pioneer Period which Became Famous.)

3. *Ibid.*, Vol. 6, pp. 506-521. (Review of Education, State and Church.)

4. *Ibid.*, Vol. 6, p. 513. ("Our schools began when Utah began, and they have grown as Utah has grown," quoted from official statement by Professor William Roylance, Assistant State Superintendent of Public Instruction, a non-Mormon. An excellent, compact statement of an important historical fact.)

5. *Ibid.*, Vol. 4, pp. 31-33, 46-52, 548-550. (Telegraph and National Railroad. Mormon interest in improved communication and transportation between the East and West.)

6. Evans, *Heart of Mormonism*, pp. 390-394. ("An Epic of the Sugar Beet. See above Reading No. 1, A clear, interesting account.)

7. Gates and Widtsoe, *Life Story of Brigham Young*, pp. 215-216. (The early adventure into the sugar-beet industry in Utah.)

8. *Ibid.*, pp. 210-223. ("Industrial Independence." An interesting, informing chapter.)

9. *Ibid.*, p. 24. (Brigham Young and his sympathy with and interest in the poor.)

10. Roberts, *Life of John Taylor*, pp. 323-324. (John Taylor elected to the office of Territorial Superintendent of district schools. Commended by Charles Warren, Commissioner of Education at Washington.)

11. *Education Review*, June, 1913. (Article on scholarship of early Pioneers.)

[18]*Deseret News*, October 23, 1861.
[19](Note) The coming of the railroad in 1869 marked the close of Utah isolation and will be treated in a later chapter.

CHAPTER 35

SOCIAL EXPERIMENTS

The Mormon Rural Community

In colonizing the West, Brigham Young made no early attempt to establish the "Law of Consecration." In the leader's plan of colonization, however, were several unique features which have made the Mormon rural community different from communities in other rural sections of the United States. These unique features have risen through an attempt to follow in part the Prophet Joseph Smith's plan for "cities of Zion." The need of protection from Indians and the necessity for culinary water has also played a part.

The traveler who has previously passed through the agricultural areas of Kansas and Nebraska, with their widely scattered farm houses and numerous one-room schools, is amazed to find the farmers in Mormon settlements all living in towns and cities. As he passes through Utah he notices towns as regular intervals some ten or twelve miles apart. Between these towns there are few or no houses, although the fields are cultivated and signs of careful husbandry are everywhere. The owners of these fields live in the towns.

It was the plan of Joseph that all of his people should enjoy the advantages which being in groups offered. Hence, in his contemplated "Cities of Zion," all of the farms were to be on the outside of the city, while the people were to live close together. In the Prophet's view, the purpose of life was to develop personality, and that development came best through social contact. Isolation of individual families was therefore to be avoided, regardless of the monetary return such isolation might bring.

In the rural settlements developed in the Great Basin by the Saints, much time was wasted in journeying to and from the farms which were often four or five miles out of town. However, to offset this economic loss there were many economic and cultural gains. The compact community made possible the erection of fine schools and churches. The one-room schoolhouse, so typical of rural sections of the United States, was practically unknown. The usual school and church were of the type found in metropolitan areas.

The consolidation of the rural population simplified the problem of transportation to school and church, and induced a larger attendance at both than could otherwise have been obtained. The result was a practically universal education in the elementary grades long before such a thing as compulsory education was tried.

Each rural community likewise had its recreation center and its dramatic clubs. Its women had their gatherings and sewing circles. Children found playmates of their own age. A people in close proximity freely exchanged ideas. Cooperation in community projects for the common good became an easy matter—civic pride was developed, and keen interest in governmental affairs. A community paper was usually published, which in a measure kept the community informed on current happenings. At a later period the town life brought to the people the benefits of electricity and all the comforts which have followed its introduction. The compact community also made possible the introduction of the telephone system. In the sections of widely scattered farm homes the introduction of these improvements has been slow and costly.

The Mormon settlements were more than rural communities. In the early days of colonization they of necessity were nearly self-supporting. The communities often produced their own clothing, milled their own grain, operated their own sawmills, manufactured their own brick and adobes, and in general supplied all their needs. Some of these settlements were isolated a good part of the year.

In these communities religion was the strongest factor in the unity of the people. The fact that many of the community were sent by the Church authorities into a given locality to settle, prompted them to a supreme effort to make the colony a success. Many a community in the Great Basin would have been abandoned but for the feeling of a religious duty to make it succeed.

The compact settlement offered protection from the Indians. The security afforded by numbers was usually enhanced by the building of a wall or stockade surrounding the settlement, or a part of it, so that the community partook of the nature of a fort.

The Mormon type of community was especially adaptable to arid regions where water suitable for domestic use was in widely separated places. This was especially true in southern Utah, where the communities became primarily interested in the raising of cattle and sheep rather than in agriculture. A given community often ranged their flocks and herds over an area one hundred miles square, and yet people enjoyed a compact community life.

"The United Order"

In the winter of 1873-1874 a reform movement within the Church was inaugurated by Brigham Young. The members of the Church were becoming careless of their duties toward fellow members. Classes were arising (within the Church) and the poor were not always provided for. To remedy this growing tendency to worldliness, Brigham Young advocated a return to the principle of consecration and stewardship of property as advocated by Joseph Smith. His purpose clearly was to secure a higher spiritual union among his people.

The movement was inaugurated at St. George while Brigham Young was wintering there in 1873-1874. The following rules of conduct were drawn up for those who entered the movement to be known as the "United Order of Zion":

"We will not take the name of the Deity in vain, nor speak lightly of His character or of sacred things.

"We will pray with our families morning and evening and also attend to secret prayer.

"We will observe and keep the Word of Wisdom, according to the spirit and the meaning thereof.

"We will treat our families with due kindness and affection, and set before them an example worthy of imitation. In our families and intercourse with all persons, we will refrain from being contentious or quarrelsome, and we will cease to speak evil of each other, and will cultivate a spirit of charity towards all. We consider it our duty to keep from acting selfishly or from covetous motives, and will seek the interest of each other and the salvation of all mankind.

"We will observe the Sabbath day to keep it holy, in accordance with the revelations.

"That which is committed to our care, we will not appropriate to our own use.

"That which we borrow we will return according to promise, and that which we find we will not appropriate to our own use, but seek to return it to its proper owner.

"We will, as soon, as possible, cancel all

individual indebtedness contracted prior to our uniting with the order, and, when once fully identified with said order, will contract no debts contrary to the wishes of the board of directors.

"We will patronize our brethren who are in the 'Order.'

"In our apparel and deportment we will not pattern after nor encourage foolish and extravagant fashions, and cease to import or buy from abroad any article which can be reasonably dispensed with, or which can be produced by combination of home labor. We will foster and encourage the producing and manufacturing of all articles needful for our consumption as fast as our circumstances will permit.

"We will be simple in our dress and manner of living, using proper economy and prudence in the management of all intrusted to our care.

"We will combine our labor for mutual benefit, sustain with our faith, prayers, and words those whom we have elected to take the management of the different departments of the 'Order,' and be subject to them in their official capacity, refraining from a spirit of fault-finding.

"We will honestly and diligently labor and devote ourselves and all we have to the 'Order' and to the building up of the Kingdom of God."[1]

On his return journey to Salt Lake in the spring of 1874, Brigham Young preached the "United Order" at the various settlements. In the 44th annual conference which had opened April 6, 1874, and then adjourned to May 7, to await his coming, the President spent much time discussing the United Order and urging the people to enter into it.

A general organization was formed with the Presiding Authorities of the Church and a council of leading businessmen at the head. The development of the "Order" was not uniform and was never adequately established. The aging of President Young, and his poor health, prevented him from lending the movement his usual weight and vigor.

---

[1]Roberts, *Comprehensive History of the Church,* Vol. 5, pp. 485-486.

"United Order" in Sevier Stake

The original "Law of Consecration," as introduced in Missouri in 1831-34, was not strictly followed in any instance. The nearest to it was the "United Order" set up in the Sevier Stake of Zion, presided over by Joseph A. Young, oldest son of President Brigham Young. Joseph A. Young explained the operation of the organization as follows:

"A year ago last April eight settlements of the county were organized into that system ('United Order') and about two-thirds of the people have since been steadily working in it. The qualification for membership is not the amount of property possessed by the individual, but his standing in the Church and general good conduct, and no one is admitted except those who put all they have into the association, which is organized under the laws of the Territory. In the admission of persons to membership, the question of capacity to render valuable service to the association is not considered; the Gospel theory and practice of 'the strong aiding the weak' is recognized and carried out, that the whole community may arise together.

"In Richfield, the leading settlement, 135 families work in the 'Order.' The capital of the organization is under the control of the board of directors, who are elected by the members, each person having credit according to the amount of property or means that he has placed therein.

"Most kinds of work is done by contract, based on cash prices, and the surplus credits accruing from a man's labor, over what he draws for the sustenance of himself and family . . . when a member wants a house built, and has not quite enough credit or stock to pay for it, the 'Order' builds it for him, and in course of a short time his credits increase and he pays for it, thus making the system one of the best mutual associations in existence.

"Besides the general stock concern, the people have stewardships' which are separate, and which include their homes, city lots, domestic animals, etc., which by industry and tact, they put to good use in procuring extras with their products, the substantials being furnished from the main source of supply.

"The 'Order' in Richfield now owns a gristmill which cost between $10,000 and $11,000, and also a steam saw, lathe, and shingle mill, at which about thirty men are employed. The horse herd of the association includes about 200 head of animals, the cattle herd 800, and the sheep herd 1,700, and a tannery belonging to the county.

"About half a dozen shoemakers are at work in the 'Order,' and carpenters, masons, and tenders to the number of about twenty, besides forty-five that are farming something over 1,100 acres of land, and a few men are at work making furniture, besides other branches of business that are in operation.

"A few of the older men stay around home and attend to the heavier labors in that department, such as wood hauling, attending to water ditches, plowing, etc., so that everybody has something to do.

"Some difficulty was met with the first year, but the organization and its operations, being based upon benign Gospel principles and a well-defined business system, obstacles are fast disappearing, and a feeling of brotherly kindness is increasing."[2]

In most places the initiations of the "Order" were accompanied by a renewal of the covenant of baptism, Brigham Young and his counselors setting the example at Ephraim, Utah, July 17, 1875.

In Orderville and Glenwood, Utah, the "Order" was launched on a community basis. Not only was property held in common, but the people ate at community tables, did their washing in community laundries, ran their cattle and sheep in community herds, and operated community farms and factories.

The Movement Abandoned

The movement generally did not get a fair start. Several factors contributed to an early abandonment: first, entrance into the "Order" was voluntary and, as great numbers in each stake were not willing or were not considered worthy to enter the "Order," two classes were created within the Church, a very

undesirable thing; second, there was lack of uniformity in the movement and lack of vigorous leadership which resulted from the failing health of Brigham Young; third, the great influx of non-Mormons into the territory and the increasing complexity of community life which produced friction.

By the time of Brigham Young's death in 1877 the majority of the stakes had abandoned the "United Order," and in 1878 the Richfield unit was dissolved.

Strong influence was brought to bear by the Church leaders for a time to make the "Order" at Glenwood and Orderville permanent, but the people finally rebelled against the monotonous existence which resulted from the communistic nature of those experiments. The United Order as given by Joseph Smith rests upon a basis of private property.[3]

Under date of May 1, 1882, the Presidency of the Church in a carefully prepared letter to stake presidents, high councils, bishops, and other authorities of the Church, said of efforts which had been made at establishing the United Order:

"Cooperation had been talked about considerably from time to time as being a stepping stone to something that would yet be more fully developed among the people of God, namely, the "United Order." We had no example of the United Order in accordance with the word of God on the subject. Our cooperation was simply an operation to unite us together in our secular affairs, tending to make us one in temporal things. * * * Our relations with the world and our own imperfections prevent the establishment of this system (the Law of Consecration) at the present time. As was stated by Joseph in the early day, it cannot yet be carried out. But cooperation and the "United Order" are a step in the right direction and are leading our brethren to reflect upon the necessity of union as one of the fundamental

---

[2]*Deseret News, Weekly,* of August 4, 1875, p. 417.

[3]See Geddes, *The United Order Among the Mormons,* Chap. 13. Also see the Preface in that volume.

principles of success in temporal things as well as in spiritual things."[4]

Plural Marriage

At a special conference held in Salt Lake City, August 28 and 29, 1852, the doctrine of "plural marriage" was first publicly declared. The revelation to Joseph Smith upon the subject was read, and Orson Pratt gave a discourse from the standpoint of the Bible. The bounds and restrictions of the law as laid down by modern revelation were clarified. As previously discussed, a number of the leading brethren were already practicing the doctrine. Following this conference, others received the sanction of President Young, who held the keys of this order of marriage, to enter its practice. In certain instances the President urged Church leaders to marry and provide a home for worthy women of the community, who had been denied the opportunity for the development of personality which comes from married life.

The philosophical reasons for the doctrine of plural marriage have been previously discussed. At the end of the first year's migration to Utah the number of women exceeded the number of men.[5] That excess of women continued for half a century. Under the Mormon practice of "plural marriage" these women were absorbed into family life in the several communities. The practice was necessarily limited, only about two percent of the men eligible for marriage having more than one wife. Nor was the law applicable to the general population of the territory or even to the general membership of the Church. Only those men who obtained the sanc-

tion of the President, who kept in mind the character and fitness of the individual, could marry a second wife, and then only with the consent of the first wife.

In the operation of such a social law there developed irregularities and abuses. The practice of the doctrine required a degree of self-sacrifice and an unselfish devotion to principle beyond the power of most people.

Opposition Aroused

The practice of plural marriage, or as it was erroneously called, "polygamy," created a considerable stir in the press and became the center of attack against the Church by its enemies. As Utah was a territory of the United States and as the laws for territories are passed by Congress, the discussion of "polygamy" was carried to that body and became the chief argument against the admission of Utah as a State.

So bitter did the attacks against the Church become that Congress, under the influence of lobbyists and of the press, passed an "anti-bigamy law" in 1862, aimed at the suppression of "polygamy" among the Mormons.

The bill was signed by President Lincoln, July 8, 1862, and made the contracting of a plural marriage punishable by a fine of $500 or imprisonment for a term of five years, or both.

In the main the President and members of Congress were not hostile to the Mormon people, but they were opposed to the practice of polygamy. They appear to have been conscientious and genuine in their feeling that polygamy was a bad social practice and should not be tolerated upon those grounds. The political platform upon which Lincoln was elected, contained a plank condemning the practice of polygamy.

---

[4]*Epistle of John Taylor*—Pamphlet, pp. 1-11.
[5]See Roberts, *Comprehensive History of the Church*, Vol. 3, p. 291.

Out of friendship for the Mormons, with whom he had become acquainted in Illinois, President Lincoln neglected to appoint officers to enforce the anti-bigamy law.

The enemies of the Church, who were seeking its destruction, were not content with letting the issue drop. The law contained a provision forbidding a religious body in a territory to hold real estate in value to exceed $50,000. This was aimed directly at the Church of Jesus Christ of Latter-day Saints. An effort made by Governor Harding of Utah in 1863 to have Brigham Young punished under this law failed, the constitutionality of the whole law being questioned.

The agitation against polygamy grew more bitter as the years progressed, but it was not until 1874 that the constitutionality of the "anti-bigamy law" was tried and an attempt made to enforce it. The Mormon people were confident that the law was unconstitutional and that if a trial case was carried to the higher courts it would be so declared and the uncertain state of affairs cleared up. Accordingly, George Reynolds, the private secretary of Brigham Young, volunteered to test the law. The Federal officers of the territory seemed equally desirous of clarifying the matter by a friendly suit. Accordingly, Reynolds was indicted. He voluntarily appeared in court and furnished the evidence of the facts whereby he had violated the law. He was convicted, sentenced to one year's imprisonment, and ordered to pay a fine of $500. The case was appealed to the Supreme Court of the territory, where it was dismissed on the grounds that the grand jury which found the indictment against Reynolds was an illegal jury.

Anti-Bigamy Laws Held Constitutional

The constitutionality of the law still being undecided, a second trial was held in 1875, before Alexander White, Chief Justice of Utah. The friendly nature of the previous trial was entirely lacking, the prosecution becoming bitter toward the accused, and the accused in his turn refusing to furnish the evidence to prove a violation of the law. A conviction was obtained, however, and Reynolds received the severe sentence of $500 fine and two years in the penitentiary at hard labor. The Supreme Court of Utah confirmed the decree, and the case was appealed to the United States Supreme Court, which upheld the constitutionality of the law, to the surprise of the Church and many constitutional lawyers. It was a stunning blow to the Church and the forerunner of a period of intense persecution. The decision was not given, however, until January 6, 1879. In the meantime Brigham Young had died, and the quorum of the Twelve Apostles became the presiding authority of the Church. An attempt to have the trial of George Reynolds reopened, and a petition to have him pardoned, met with failure. He was committed to prison, June 16, 1879.

In October, 1880, the first presidency was again organized with John Taylor as President of the Church. Upon his administration fell the brunt of the "anti-bigamy" campaign. Following the death of Brigham Young and especially after the decision of the Supreme Court on the Reynolds' case, an effort was made by bitter enemies to bring about the end of polygamy and to crush the Church. Their agitation and false representations through the press resulted in the passage of new legislation aimed at the suppression of polygamous practices. In March, 1882, Congress passed the "Edmunds' Bill," amending the "anti-bigamy law" of 1862. This measure added to the punishable offense of plural marriages, "polygamous living," which was defined as "unlawful cohabitation." The law deprived all who lived the polygamous relationship of the right to vote or to hold public office. Further it abrogated[6] the right of the traditional jury trial in that a mere belief in the doctrine of plural marriage was sufficient to bar an individual from jury service.

This law further declared all registration and election offices vacant in the territory and provided for Federal appointees in their place. The Edmunds law virtually deprived Utah of those rights of self-government which had become a definite factor in the government of territories. The law was made retroactive in regard to the franchise. No individual who had ever lived the law of plural marriage was allowed to vote, regardless of whether he was then living that law or not.

A campaign of bitter persecution began against those men who had entered into plural marriage before or after the passage of the law. This campaign lasted throughout the entire administration of President Taylor. Hundreds of homes were broken up, the fathers and husbands being sent to the penitentiary. Women were sent to prison for "contempt of court," because they refused to testify against their husbands. Following the severe sentence given Rudger Clawson in October, 1884, there developed what was termed the "segregation ruling." This was a ruling of the courts that separate indictments might be found against a man for every day he was found guilty of living with a plural wife.

This ruling of the courts was responsible for driving the leaders of the Church into exile, for it amounted to an announcement that a man who practiced polygamy, or even attempted to provide for his several wives, might by an accumulation of separate charges, be sent to prison for life.

This "segregation policy" was condemned by the Supreme Court of the United States in the case of Lorenzo Snow, which came before it in February, 1887.

Edmunds-Tucker Law

In March of 1887, Congress passed a still more rigid measure to suppress polygamy, known as the "Edmunds-Tucker Law." This law provided for the disincorporation of The Church of Jesus Christ of Latter-day Saints, which taught the doctrine, and of the Perpetual Emigrating Fund Company. The property of these corporations was to escheat[7] to the Federal Government to be used for the benefit of schools in the territory. Buildings and grounds used exclusively for religious services, and burial grounds, were alone exempted from the law. This infamous law was denounced in Congress by many notable non-Mormons, but the popular clamor against polygamy secured its passage.

The United States Marshal Dyer took charge of the real and personal property of the Church. In order to retain the use of the tithing offices, the historian's office, the Church was forced to pay the government an annual rental of $2,400. Four hundred fifty dollars a month was paid to retain the use of the Gardo House, and the use of the temple block was retained by paying a high rental.

---

[6]*Abrogate*—to annul or abolish.

[7]*Escheat*—to be forfeited.

During this period the Church was under heavy financial stress. It could not borrow a dollar. Only the faithful payment of tithes enabled it to weather the storm. From hiding places, generally called the "underground," the exiled First Presidency conducted the affairs of the Church. John Taylor died in exile July 27, 1887, at Kaysville, Utah.

After the death of John Taylor, the crusade against polygamy continued, but with considerable tolerance on the part of the officers. President Grover Cleveland pardoned a number of men who had been given extraordinarily severe sentences, among them Charles Livingston, Rudger Clawson and Joseph H. Evans.

In Idaho and Arizona the feeling against polygamy became intense. In 1885, the Idaho Legislature passed a law which disfranchised all members of the Church which taught such a doctrine and this deprived all Mormons of the right to vote or hold office, regardless of whether or not they practiced polygamy themselves. The constitutionality of the law was questioned. It was upheld by the United States Supreme Court in a decision of February 3, 1890. Such a bill was introduced in Congress for the Territory of Utah, called the "Struble Bill," but even prominent non-Mormons of Utah opposed it, and it was defeated.

The Manifesto

In the midst of these trying difficulties, Wilford Woodruff, who had been sustained President of the Church, April 7, 1889, appealed to the Lord in prayer. In answer he received a revelation suspending "plural marriage."

The anti-polygamy laws had placed the members of the Church on the horns of a dilemma. They must disobey the laws of God or the laws of the land. The revelation brought them relief. On September 25, 1890, President Woodruff issued his famous "Manifesto" which declared an end to the contracting of plural marriages in the Church and called upon the members to obey the law of the land. In the October conference the "Manifesto" was sustained and thus became binding upon the Church. In that conference President Woodruff said:

"I want to say to all Israel that the step which I have taken in issuing this manifesto has not been done without earnest prayer before the Lord. * * * I am not ignorant of the feelings that have been engendered through the course I have pursued. * * * The Lord will never permit me or any other man who stands as the President of this Church to lead you astray. It is not in the program. It is not in the mind of God. If I were to attempt that the Lord would move me out of my place."

The result of the manifesto was a noticeable change in attitude toward the Church. President Harrison issued a proclamation of amnesty on January 4, 1893, to those who had entered into "polygamous marriages" prior to November 1, 1890. The restrictions against voters were removed, and in 1893 the personal property of the Church was returned to its rightful owners. Three years later, when Utah achieved statehood, the real estate which had been confiscated was likewise returned to the Church.

Supplementary Readings

1. *Doctrine and Covenants*: Section 49:19-21; 51:3; 70-14; 82:17-18. ("It is not given that one man should possess that which is above another." Again. "You are to be equal, * * * you are to have equal claims on the properties, * * * every man according to his wants and his needs, * * * Read all the refer-

ences in the Doctrine and Covenants cited above. They are a striking commentary on economic principles, and on Joseph Smith as a Prophet.)

2. Talmage, *The Vitality of Mormonism*, pp. 209-212. ("The United Order." "No Longer Mine and Thine, But the Lord's and Ours." A brief chapter on God's will and way in economic affairs.)

3. *Book of Mormon*, 3 Nephi 26:19; 4 Nephi 1:3.

4. *New Testament*, 1st Timothy 6:10a, and Acts of The Apostles 2:44-47; 4:32-37.

5. Nelson, Lowry: *The Mormon Village*.

6. Roberts, *Comprehensive History of the Church*, pp. 268-270. (Land, Water and Timber Law Proclaimed.)

7. Gates and Widtsoe, *Life Story of Brigham Young*, pp. 199-209. (Practical Sociology. United Order, Cooperation, etc.)

8. Roberts, *Comprehensive History of the Church*, Vol. 2, pp. 92-110; Vol. 5, pp. 287-294; 295-301; 471-472; 472-474, (Notes 29, 30); 541-545 (Notes 7, 8); Vol. 6, pp. 226, 228, 229; 227-228. (A comprehensive study of plural marriage or polygamy.)

9. *Ibid.*, Vol. 5, pp. 484-490. ("Each one for the whole, and God for all. * * * It was for the strong to sustain the weak," says Erastus Snow. * * * Several attempts in the United Order are cited.)

10. *Ibid.*, Vol. 5, p. 498. (President John Taylor on the United Order.)

11. *Memoirs of John R. Young*, pp. 250-252. (An intimate glimpse at the United Order, and President John Taylor's response to a question about the Order.)

12. *Ibid.*, pp. 242-263. (Comments and incidents about polygamy, and his relations with his four wives, their children, etc. Pictures of three of his wives are given; glimpses of the persecutions against polygamy and polygamists.)

13. *Ibid.*, pp. 305-317. (Crusade Against Plural Marriage. Incidents and stories of Federal Marshals and Deputies attempting to run down and prosecute Mormon polygamists. Sometimes these prosecutions, or attempted prosecutions were *persecution*.)

14. Joseph A. Geddes. *The United Order Among The Mormons*. (An economic Study of the United Order Among the Mormons by an Economist, the Son of a Mormon Pioneer.)

CHAPTER 36

THE UTAH WAR

Mistakes and Misunderstandings

It was unfortunate that the early applications of the people of Utah for statehood were rejected by the Congress of the United States. It was inevitable that, under a territorial form of government, there would develop an antagonism between a people so "different" as the Saints and government appointees sent into the territory. A situation comparable to that of the Utah Territory has never existed within the confines of the United States.

The Mormons, as previously stated, were devoted primarily to the church of which they were members, and were suspicious of a government which had either been unable or unwilling to protect them. Further, the large majority of the Saints were of foreign birth. They had preferred The Church of Jesus Christ of Latter-day Saints to all else in life. They had preferred it to citizenship in their native lands. It is small wonder that, having endured so much for the gospel they professed, the Church and its leaders claimed it their first allegiance. The law of God was more important than the law of the land, although the latter would be observed so long as it did not interfere with the former.

Under favorable circumstances the Mormons have been a people little understood. The peculiar circumstances which surrounded them in the early days of Utah, inevitably led to mistakes and misunderstandings between the members of the Church and those who came in contact with them.

These difficulties arose when the first appointments were made by President Fillmore to federal offices in the territory. Scarcely had these appointees taken their oath of office when three of them: Chief Justice Brandebury, Associate Justice Brocchus and the Territorial Secretary, Broughton D. Harris, refused to stay longer in the Territory and returned to the eastern states. There they spread the report that first, they had been compelled to leave Utah because of the lawless and seditious acts of Governor Young; second, that Governor Young was wasting federal funds allotted to the Territory; third, that the Saints were immoral, and were practicing polygamy.

Governor Young anticipated the type of report these men would likely circulate. On September 29, 1851, he wrote to President Fillmore, setting forth the facts which clearly contradicted the accusations. Other letters were sent by Jedediah M. Grant, Mayor of Salt Lake City, and Colonel Thomas L. Kane, supporting Young's position. Daniel Webster, then Secretary of State, upon receipt of these letters, ordered the runaway officers to return to their positions or to resign. Accordingly, they resigned.

New appointees were sent. Lazarus H. Reid, of New York, became chief justice; Leonidas Shaver, associate justice, and Benjamin G. Ferris, Territorial secretary. These men were well received and became highly respected by the Mormon people.

Misunderstandings between the Saints and Federal appointees and the subsequent ill feelings and abusive actions on both sides, fill many pages of Utah history. Some of these, however, led to greater consequences than others and with these we are primarily concerned.

With the resignation of Chief Justice Reed in 1854, John F. Kinney was appointed in his stead. He proved an honest and impartial judge, honored and esteemed by Mormon and non-Mormon alike. But in 1855 there came to Utah as associate justices two men who were to arouse the resentment of the Saints and eventually cost the United States government forty millions of dollars.

Judge William W. Drummond replaced Judge Zerubbabel Snow, whose term of office had expired, and George P. Stiles, a Mormon apostate, replaced Judge Shaver who had died.

Drummond was an immoral and unprincipled man. Leaving a wife and children without support in his own state of Illinois, he appeared in Utah accompanied by a harlot, whom he introduced as his wife, and who often sat upon the bench with him. His drunken and dissolute habits caused the Saints to despise him and their feelings were ill-concealed. When his immorality and neglect of his own family was revealed he left the territory in disgrace.

In his resignation of office, tendered to Jeremiah S. Black, the attorney general of the United States, and in other reports, he spread a multitude of false accusations against the Saints. As reasons for resigning he stated the following:

"(1) That Brigham Young is the head of the Mormon Church; and, as such head, the Mormons look to him, and to him alone, for the law by which they are to be governed; therefore no law of congress is by them considered binding in any matter;

"(2) That he (Drummond) knew that a secret, oath-bound organization existed among all the male members of the Church to resist the laws of the country, and to acknowledge no law save the law of the priesthood, which came to the people through Brigham Young.

"(3) That there were a number of men 'set apart by special order of the Church,' to take both the lives and property of any person who may question the authority of the Church."

The judge also alleged—

"That the records, papers, etc., of the supreme court have been destroyed by order of the Church, with the direct knowledge and approbation of Governor B. Young, and the federal officers grossly insulted for presuming to raise a single question about the treasonable act.

"(4) That the federal officers of the territory are constantly insulted, harassed, and annoyed by the Mormons, and for these insults there is no redress.

"(5) That the federal officers are daily compelled to hear the form of the American government traduced, the chief executives of the Nation, both living and dead, slandered and abused from the masses as well as from all the leading members of the Church.

"(6) The judge also charged discrimination in the adminstration of the laws as against Mormon and Gentile; that Captain John W. Gunnison and his party were murdered by Indians, but under the orders, advice and direction of the Mormons'; that the Mormons poisoned Judge Leonidas Shaver, Drummond's predecessor; that Almon W. Babbitt, secretary of the territory, had been killed on the plains by a band of Mormon marauders, who were 'sent from Salt Lake City for that purpose, and that only,' under direct orders of the presidency of the Church of the Latter-day Saints, and that Babbitt was not killed by Indians, as reported from Utah."[1]

Judge Stiles forwarded an affidavit affirming much of Drummond's charges. These charges were further substantiated by a letter to President Buchanan, written by Mr. W. F. Magraw, who had been underbid by a Mormon firm for the mail contract between

---

[1]Roberts, *Comprehensive History of the Church*, Vol. 4, pp. 203-204.

Independence and Salt Lake City. This letter said in part:

"In relation to the present social and political condition of the territory of Utah." * * * "There is no disguising the fact that there is left no vestige of law and order, no protection for life or property; the civil laws of the territory are overshadowed and neutralized by a so-styled ecclesiastical organization, as despotic, dangerous, and damnable, as has ever been known to exist in any country, and which is ruining, not only those who do not subscribe to their religious code, but is driving the Mormon community to desperation."[2]

Buchanan Orders the Army to Utah

The Indian agent of the upper Platte, Thomas S. Twiss, also registered a complaint that the Mormons were invading the Indian lands along the Green River. These rank misrepresentations were relied on by the Federal Government as evidence of Mormon disregard for the law and as an excuse for the steps which followed. All the denials of the accusations seemingly were disregarded, and without waiting for a Federal investigation of the charges President Buchanan acted. On May 28, 1857, a portion of the Federal Army was ordered to mobilize at Fort Leavenworth and proceed thence to Utah.

While the reports of Judge Drummond and others stirred the President to issue his drastic order, the real causes of the "war" which followed were largely political.

In their platform of 1856 the Republican party had adopted a decided stand against the Mormons. This stand is embodied in the party plank adopted at Philadelphia June 17, 1856, which read:

"Resolved, that the Constitution confers upon Congress sovereign power over the territories of the United States for their government, and that in the exercise of this power it is both the right and the imperative duty of Congress to prohibit in the territories those twin relics of barbarism—polygamy and slavery."[3]

The Republican plan was to throw upon the Democratic party, which in their platform defended the right of the territories to determine for themselves the domestic problems of slavery, the position of defending also the right of a territory to determine for itself the domestic problems of marriage. So stirred up had the country become over the Mormons and their "plural marriage" doctrine, that the Democratic party had no desire to carry their platform to its logical conclusion. The "Expedition" against the Mormons by a Democratic administration would show to the voters of the Nation that the Democrats, no less than the Republicans, were opposed to the Mormon people and their practices.

John Taylor, who was editing an L.D.S. paper, the *Mormon*, in New York City, during the formative period of the Utah expedition, said later in the year during an address to the Saints in Utah:

"The Republicans were determined to make the Mormon question tell in their favor. At the time they were trying to elect Fremont they put two questions into their platform, viz., opposition to the domestic institutions of the South and to polygamy. The Democrats have professed to be our friends, and they go to work to sustain the domestic institutions of the South and the rights of the people; but when they do that the Republicans throw polygamy at them and are determined to make them swallow that with the other (i.e. slavery). This makes the Democrats gag and they have felt a strong desire to get rid of the Mormon question. Some of them, I know, for some time past, have been concocting plans to divide up Utah among the several territories around, and I

---

[2]Magraw's Letter to the President, House Executive Documents, 35th Congress, 1st session, X No. 71, pp. 2-3.

[3]Cooper, *American Politics*, book 2, platforms, p. 39.

believe a bill having this object in view was prepared once or twice and came pretty nearly being presented to Congress, but that was not done. * * * They wish now to steal the Republicans' thunder, to take the wind out of their sail, and to out-Herod Herod. Say they: 'We, who profess to be the friends of the Mormons and support free institutions, squatter sovereignty and equal rights, will do more to the Mormons than you dare do; and we will procure offices by that means and save our party.' "[4]

The sending of the "Expedition" was encouraged by the pro-slavery group on the grounds that it would definitely curtail the move for statehood which had begun with renewed vigor and insistence in 1855.

If it could be made to appear that the Mormons were in rebellion against the United States, whether the facts supported that view or not, the danger of Utah as a new "free state" would be inevitably postponed.

Thus it was that the charges of Drummond were eagerly seized upon. An investigation was neither desired, nor made, for fear that the true state of affairs might not warrant the political expediency offered.

The cries of conspirators in Utah for the removal of Governor Young led President Buchanan to appoint new territorial officers. Alfred Cumming was appointed as Governor and accompanied the "Expedition" West from Fort Leavenworth.

The Saints Prepare to Defend Their Homes

On July 24, 1857, a large concourse of people were gathered at Silver Lake, at the head of Big Cottonwood Canyon, thirty miles from Salt Lake City. The occasion was the celebration of the tenth anniversary of the arrival of the Saints in Salt Lake Valley. Led by Brigham

Young and the general Church officers, 2,587 people, including six large brass bands and several detachments of the Nauvoo Legion, were having a joyous celebration. Two United States flags were flying from nearby peaks and two from the tops of adjacent pine trees.[5] Three spacious board floors, with boweries built over them, were utilized for dancing.

At noon of the 24th four men rode into the encampment and sought out President Young. They were Abraham O. Smoot, Orrin Porter Rockwell, Judson Stoddard and Judge Elias Smith. To Brigham Young and his immediate counselors and associates they made the announcement that a United States army and supply trains were on the plains enroute to Utah. The exact purpose of the army was unknown, but the rumors were that they were coming "to suppress the Mormons."

The difficulty of communication in those days and the isolation of the Saints in the Utah valleys made it possible for the "Army" to be well under way to the West before the Utah people became aware of it.

Feramorz Little, assisting with western mail matters at Independence, Missouri, was the first Mormon to get an inkling of the movement. On June 1, Little left Independence with mail for Salt Lake City. At Fort Laramie he met Abraham O. Smoot, then Mayor of Salt Lake City, going east with the mail. Upon hearing of the rumors, which Little was inclined to disbelieve, Smoot determined on finding the facts. Some troops and supply trains were encountered on the plains, but Smoot could not find out their destination. At Independence, however, a Mr. Russell, who had contracted to carry supplies for the

---

[4]*Deseret News*, September 2, 1857.

[5]*Deseret News*, July 29, 1857.

army, disclosed that the army was bound for Utah.

Smoot returned as rapidly as possible toward the West. About one hundred miles east of Fort Laramie he met Orrin P. Rockwell, heading east with the mail.

It was decided that both would return speedily to Salt Lake City. Securing a small spring wagon at Fort Laramie to which they hitched two span of horses, and joined by Judson Stoddard, they covered the entire distance to Salt Lake City in five days. They arrived July 23, only to find the Mormon leader gone to Silver Lake.

Not even the news of an approaching army was allowed by Brigham Young to spoil the festivities of that glorious Twenty-fourth. But at the close of the day an assembly was called. Daniel H. Wells announced the "war news" and gave instructions for breaking camp and returning to Salt Lake City the following morning. Everything was done in order and without apparent haste.

So inured to opposition were the Saints and so confident were they in the ability of their leaders, that the "war news" created but little excitement throughout Salt Lake City and the settlements.

Saints Prepare For War

Preparations for "war" however, went quietly forward. Under date of August 1, 1857, General Wells reported to the officers and men of the Nauvoo Legion the approach of an army to invade Utah. He instructed the district commanders to hold their respective divisions of the militia in readiness to march at the shortest possible notice to any part of the territory. They were

General Daniel H. Wells who headed the Nauvoo Legion as organized in Salt Lake City.

Used by permission, Utah State Historical Society

cautioned to "Avoid all excitement, but be ready."[6]

Word was also sent throughout the settlements to conserve the grain supply, to use none for the feeding of cattle, and to sell none to emigrant trains for that purpose.

The members of the Apostles' quorum presiding over the missions were recalled home and nearly all the elders on missions were recalled. Samuel W. Richards was dispatched with instructions to Orson Pratt and Ezra T. Benson in the British Mission. Enroute he delivered a letter to Colonel Thomas L. Kane, addressed to President Buchanan

[6]*Contributor*, Vol. 3, p. 177. Article, "The Echo Canyon War."

and protesting against the actions of the government.

The message delivered to President Buchanan by Colonel Kane was a harsh arraignment of the Government and a brief history of the treatment of the Mormons at the hands of the government from the beginning of the Missouri troubles.

The people in the outlying settlements of San Bernardino, California, Carson, Nevada, and on the Salmon River in Idaho, were ordered to dispose of their property and return to Salt Lake Valley. The dispatch and spirit with which the Saints in those settlements carried out the orders of Brigham Young, sacrificed their homes and journeyed to Salt Lake Valley ready to die with the Saints rather than submit to further persecution, is one of the finest examples of the unity and faith of the Mormon people.

By way of further preparation, expeditions were sent out to locate the best places in the mountains for making a determined resistance to armed forces. Colonel Robert T. Burton of the Nauvoo Legion was sent on August 15, with a small detachment to the east, presumably to protect the incoming Mormon emigrants, but in reality to learn the location, strength, and equipment of the United States army, and to report their progress from day to day by "riders."

A volunteer company was called to proceed northward and establish a settlement near Fort Hall. This was in reality a detachment of militia to watch the northern route into Utah in the event the "Army" attempted to enter from that direction.

General Wells, with the main body of the militia, proceeded to Echo Canyon and fortified that natural barrier sufficiently to withstand a considerable force of troops.

The attitude of Brigham Young during this crisis was a firm and determined one. When the news reached him at Silver Lake he had said:

"Liars have reported that this people have committed treason, and upon their representations the President has ordered out troops to assist in officering the territory. We have transgressed no law, neither do we intend to do so; but as for any nation coming to destroy this people, God Almighty being my helper, it shall not be."[7]

This attitude, that with the help of the Lord, the Saints could successfully resist the United States Army, was maintained throughout by the Mormon leader.

It was unfortunate that the purpose of the administration in sending the Expedition to Utah was not understood by the Church leaders. Could they have known the nature of the splendid officers and personnel of the Expedition and been aware of the instructions to them from the war department, many of the complications which followed would not have occurred. But the Saints had no way of knowing those facts and the government had taken great pains to keep them in the dark rather than to inform them. Thus it was easy for a people who had endured so much in the way of persecution to believe the ribaldry of the rank and file of the camp.

Some of Burton's command of Scouts, disguised as California emigrants, mingled constantly with the camps of the Utah Expedition. Their reports were to the effect that the soldiers were boasting they would drive and plunder the Mormons and "scalp old Brigham."

Elder John Taylor said to Vice President Schuyler Colfax in 1869:

"We had men in all their camps, and knew what was intended. There was a continual boast among the men and officers even be-

[7]Joseph Fielding Smith, *Essentials in Church History*, 1st ed., p. 500.

fore they left the Missouri river, of what they intended to do with the Mormons. The houses were picked out that certain persons were to inhabit; farms, property, and women were to be distributed. 'Beauty and Booty' was their watchword. We were to have another grand Mormon conquest, and our houses, gardens, orchards, vineyards, fields, wives and daughters to be the spoils."[8]

It was natural in the face of such reports and without an acquaintance with the sealed orders to the Expedition commander, that the Saints expected the worst. Repeatedly they had been driven until there was no further place to which to flee. They decided to resist further persecution to the last drop of their blood.

Arrival of Captain Van Vliet

Such was the situation when Captain Van Vliet, advance courier of the "Army," arrived in Salt Lake City in September. On the 9th of that month the Captain met with the leading Church authorities in the old Social Hall. Van Vliet was seeking arrangements for food and forage, etc., for the army when it arrived in the city. The assurances of Van Vliet that the army was not coming to make war was not convincing to the Church leaders. The captain was courteously informed that no hostile army would be allowed to enter the territory. Federal officers would be welcomed without troops, if they came in peace. The attitude of the Saints is shown in the report of Van Vliet to his superiors:

"In the course of my conversation with the Governor and the influential men of the Territory, I told them plainly and frankly what I conceived would be the result of their present course. I told them that they might prevent the small military force now approaching Utah from getting through the narrow defiles and rugged passes of the

mountains this year, but that next season the United States Government would send troops sufficient to overcome all opposition. The answer to this was invariably the same: 'We are aware that such will be the case; but when those troops arrive they will find Utah a desert. Every house will be burned to the ground, every tree cut down, and every field laid waste. We have three years' provisions on hand, which we will cache, and then take to the mountains and bid defiance to all the powers of the Government.'

"I attended their services on Sunday, and, in course of a sermon delivered by Elder Taylor, he referred to the approach of the troops and declared they should not enter the Territory. He then referred to the probability of an over-powering force being sent against them, and desired all present who would apply the torch to their buildings, cut down their trees, and lay waste their fields, to hold up their hands. Every hand, in an audience numbering over four thousand persons, was raised at the same moment. During my stay in the city I visited several families, and all with whom I was thrown, looked upon the present movement of the troops toward their Territory as the commencement of another religious persecution, and expressed a fixed determination to sustain Governor Young in any measure he might adopt."[9]

Captain Van Vliet was impressed with the sincerity and orderliness of the Mormon people and felt convinced that the whole "Expedition" was a mistake. His report to the Secretary of War, delivered personally at Washington, D.C., opened the way for the sending of a peace commission.

After the departure of Van Vliet from Salt Lake City, Governor Young issued a proclamation declaring the territory under martial law. General Wells made his headquarters in Echo Canyon and commenced raising additional forces, amounting to 1,250 men at that place.

A Bloodless Conflict

The advance section of the Expedition, under Colonel E. B. Alexander,

[8]Smith, *Essentials in Church History*, p. 412, (note).

[9]Smith, *Essentials in Church History*, pp. 410-411.

crossed the border of the Territory September 29, determined to press on to Salt Lake City that fall. Acting upon the previous advice of Captain Van Vliet, Colonel Alexander waited in Ham's Fork, in a place called Camp Wenfield, for the arrival of the main body of the army.

The command of the Utah Expedition was originally given to General W. S. Harney, but late in the summer Harney was replaced by Colonel Albert Sidney Johnston.

While the "Army" was encamped in Ham's Fork, Governor Young sent a proclamation to the Commander of the "Utah Expedition" demanding the removal of troops from the Utah Territory. Colonel Alexander gave the only reply possible. He was there by orders of the President of the United States, and further movements would depend upon "orders issued by competent authority."

The Utah militia now took the initiative. A council of war was held at Fort Bridger, October 3. It was decided to begin operations against the Expedition. The methods of defensive war now used had been taught the Saints by their struggle for existence in their desert home and by their experiences in crossing the plains; these methods were more effective than rifle fire or cannons. A copy of the instructions to Utah militia officers was found upon the person of Major Joseph Taylor, of Weber County, when he was captured by United States troops early in October. From this document we get a picture of the Mormon campaign:

INSTRUCTIONS TO UTAH MILITIA OFFICERS

"Headquarters Eastern Expedition,
Camp Near Cache Cave,
October 4, 1857.

You will proceed, with all possible dispatch, without injuring your animals, to the Oregon road, near the bend of Bear river, north by east of this place. Take close and correct observation of the country on your route. When you approach the road, send scouts ahead, to ascertain if the invading troops have passed that way. Should they have passed, take a concealed route, and get ahead of them. Express to Colonel Burton, who is now on that road and in the vicinity of the troops, to proceed at once to annoy them in every possible way. Use every exertion to stampede their animals and set fire to their trains. Burn the whole country before them, and on their flanks. Keep them from sleeping by night surprises; blockade the road by falling trees or destroying the river fords where you can. Watch for opportunities to set fire to the grass before them that can be burned. Keep your men concealed as much as possible, and guard against surprise. Keep scouts out at all times, and communications open with Colonel Burton, Major McAllister and O. P. Rockwell, who are operating in the same way. Keep me advised daily of your movements, and every step the troops take, and in which direction.

God bless you, and give you success.

Your brother in Christ,
DANIEL H. WELLS.

P.S.—If the troops have not passed, or have turned in this direction, follow in their rear, and continue to annoy them, burning any trains they may have. Take no life, but destroy their trains, and stampede or drive away their animals, at every opportunity.

Major Joseph Taylor.

(Signed) "D. H. WELLS."[10]

Fort Bridger and Fort Supply, then owned by the Church, were burned to the ground to prevent their being utilized by the United States Army.

Before leaving Fort Bridger, October 3, General Wells sent Major Lot Smith, with a small company of men, to intercept the supply trains then advancing from South Pass and to either turn them back or burn them. Major Lot Smith's own account shows the spirit which prevailed among the defenders of the territory:

[10] *House Executive Documents*, 35th Congress, 1st Session, X No. 71, pp. 56-57.

"I was invited to take dinner with the commanding General and his aids. During the meal General Wells, looking at me as straight as possible, asked if I could take a few men and turn back the trains that were on the road or *burn them*. I replied that I thought I could do just what he told me to. The answer appeared to please him, and he accepted it, telling me that he could furnish only a few men, but that they would be sufficient, for they would appear many more to our enemies. As for provisions, none would be supplied, as we were expected to board at the expense of Uncle Sam. As this seemed to be an open order I did not complain."[11]

Major Lot Smith was remarkably successful in his mission and destroyed an immense quantity of supplies intended for the "Army." The manner in which he operated will be understood from his own account of one incident in his campaign, the burning of a supply train at the Big Sandy or "Simpson's Hollow." When Major Smith rode up to this train and asked for the train-master, he found that the "captain" was out after cattle. After disarming the teamsters the Major rode out to meet the Captain. Lot Smith writes:

"I told him," says Smith's narrative, "that I came on business. He inquired the nature of it, when I demanded his pistols. He replied: 'By G—d, sir, no man ever took them yet, and if you think you can, without killing me, try it.' We were all the time riding towards the train, with our noses about as close together as two Scotch terriers would have held theirs—his eyes flashing fire; I couldn't see mine—I told him that I admired a brave man, but that I did not like blood—you insist on my killing you, which will only take a minute, but I don't want to do it. We had by this time reached the train. He, seeing that his men were under guard, surrendered, saying: 'I see you have me at a disadvantage, my men being disarmed.' I replied that I didn't need the advantage and asked him what he would do if we should give them their arms. 'I'll fight you!' 'Then,' said I, 'We know something about that, too—take up your arms!' His men exclaimed, 'Not by a

d—n sight. We came out here to whack bulls, not to fight.' 'What do you say to that, Simpson?' I asked. 'Damnation,' he replied, grinding his teeth in the most violent manner, "If I had been here before and they had refused to fight, I would have killed every man of them.' "

"Captain Simpson was the bravest man I met during the campaign. He was a son-in-law of Mr. Majors, a large contractor for government freighting. He was terribly exercised over the capture of his train, and wanted to know what kind of a report he could make to the commander, and what he could do with his crowd of cowardly teamsters left on the plains to starve. I told him that I would give him a wagon loaded with provisions. 'You will give me two, I know it by your looks!' I told them to hurry up and get their things out, and take their two wagons, for we wanted to go on. Simpson begged me not to burn the train while he was in sight, and said that it would ruin his reputation as a wagon master. I told him not to be squeamish, that the trains burned very nicely, I had seen them before, and that we hadn't time to be ceremonious. We then supplied ourselves with provisions, set the wagons afire, and rode on about two miles from the stream to rest."[12]

From the burning of supply trains Lot Smith turned to the business of running off cattle from the army encampments. From his successive raids, 1,000 head of cattle were sent into Salt Lake Valley. The government cavalry, which at times attempted to pursue Lot Smith's forces, were easily outrun because of the lighter equipment and better condition of the latter's mounts.

The only shots of the war were fired by a party of United States cavalry, under Major Marcy, who came near to capturing Major Smith. The shots did no more damage than the killing of two horses, however. During the encounter between Marcy and Smith, some conversation took place, of which Major Smith says that Marcy was a "perfect gentleman" and expressed sympathy for the Mormon people.

[11]Major Lot Smith's Narrative, *Contributor*, Vol. 3, pp. 271-272.

[12]Lot Smith's Narrative, *Contributor*, Vol. 4, pp. 27-28.

Early in November, 1857, General Johnston arrived at the main "Army" camp on Ham's Fork. He was a capable officer and his enthusiasm revived the drooping spirits of the troops who were becoming dispirited.

For a time the question of turning north to enter Salt Lake Valley via Fort Hall was considered. For some reason that plan was abandoned and the command moved toward Fort Bridger. The distance was less than forty miles, but the army found it a barren desert. The grass for their stock was burned. The road was obstructed at every conceivable point. Fuel other than sagebrush could not be found. In addition, the troops faced one of the severest blizzards of the winter. The oxen weakened from lack of forage and many died. The journey took them fifteen days. When they reached Fort Bridger they found it in ashes, as well as Fort Supply twelve miles away.

It was apparent that Salt Lake Valley could not be reached that year. General Johnston reluctantly was forced to return and make winter quarters on Black's Fork.

The sufferings of the Army during the winter were intense. The weather was extremely cold and supplies scarce. The coming of winter to the aid of the Saints enabled the greater part of the militia to return to their homes, leaving squads of men to watch and report the Army's movements.

Clearing Away Misunderstandings

The failure of the Army to reach Salt Lake Valley in 1857 proved the undoing of the whole political scheme behind the Expedition. The excessive cost of the Expedition and the ill-conceived haste with which it had been begun, aroused criticism over the entire nation. It gave time for serious reflection. Senator Sam Houston, on the floor of the United States Senate, voiced the opinion of many:

"The more men you send to the 'Mormon War' the more you increase the difficulty. They have to be fed. For some sixteen hundred miles you have to transport provisions. The regiments sent there have found Fort Bridger and other places, as they approached them, heaps of ashes. They will find Salt Lake, if they ever reach it, a heap of ashes. They will find that they will have to fight against Russia and Russians. Whoever goes there will meet the fate of Napoleon's army when he went to Moscow. Just as sure as we are now standing in the senate, these people, if they fight at all, will fight desperately. They are defending their homes. They are fighting to prevent the execution of threats that have been made, which touch their hearths and their families; and depend upon it they will fight until every man perishes before he surrenders. That is not all. If they do not choose to go into conflict immediately, they will secure their women and children in the fastnesses of the mountains; they have provisions for two years; and they will carry on a guerrilla warfare, which will be most terrible to the troops you send there. They will get no supplies there. You will have to transport them all from Independence, in Missouri. When the fire will consume it, there will not be a spear of grass left that will not be burnt. * * * I know not what course will be taken on this subject. I hope it will be one of conciliation. As for troops to conquer the Mormons, fifty thousand would be as inefficient as two or three thousand; and in proportion as you send troops in that vast region, without supplies, and without the hope of them, with no means of subsistence after a certain period, unless it is transported to them, the greater will be your danger. Consider the facilities these people have to cut off your supplies. I say your men will never return, but their bones will whiten the valley of Salt Lake. If war begins, the very moment one single drop of blood is drawn, it will be the signal of extermination. Mr. President, in my opinion, whether we are to have a war with the Mormons or not, will depend on the fact whether our troops advance or not. If they do not advance; if negotiations be opened; if we understand what the Mormons are really willing to do; that they are ready to acquiesce in the mandates of the government, and render obedience to the Constitution; if you will take time to ascertain that, and not repudiate all idea of peace, we may have peace. But so sure as the troops advance, so sure they will be annihilated. You may treble them, and you will only add to the catastrophe, not diminish human suffering. These people expect nothing but extermination or abuse more intolerable than even extermination would be, from your troops, and they will oppose them."[13]

It became apparent in Washington before the winter was over that the administration was ready to withdraw peaceably from the whole affair, if a reasonable way offered.

During the winter two rival governments of Utah Territory were in existence. As Governor Young had received no official notice of his removal from office, and Governor Cumming had not been officially installed in office, the Mormon leader continued to function as governor of the Territory. Governor Cumming attempted to establish his authority from the army headquarters at Camp Scott, on Black's Fork. He issued a proclamation to the inhabitants of the Territory, in which he said:

"I come among you with no prejudice or enmities, and by the exercise of a just and firm administration I hope to command your confidence. Freedom of conscience and the use of your own peculiar mode of serving God are sacred rights, the exercise of which is guaranteed by the Constitution, and with which it is not the province of the Government or the disposition of its representatives in the Territory to interfere."[14]

All armed bodies in the territory were ordered to disband. Disobedience would "subject the offenders to the punishment due to traitors."[15]

Governor Cumming's Proclamation had little or no effect upon the territory,

aside from creating a favorable attitude toward him as an individual. A court was set up at Camp Scott to deal with the numerous civil offenses among the teamsters attached to the "Army." A grand jury, called for the purpose of the court, returned indictments for treason against Brigham Young and sixty of his associates.

Coming of Colonel Kane

On February 25, 1858, Colonel Thomas L. Kane arrived in Salt Lake City. He had traveled from New York via the Isthmus of Panama to Los Angeles and thence by the southern overland route.

From the beginning of the troubles in the Territory Colonel Kane was kept informed by the Mormons of the condition of affairs. During the winter of 1857-58, although in a delicate state of health and against the advice of his friends, he had made that long and dangerous journey, at his own expense, in order to aid his Mormon friends in their unfortunate situation. A finer Christian attitude has never been expressed. His mission, as events showed, was entirely private, and his actions prompted by a conviction of duty. He had traveled to Salt Lake under the name of Dr. Osborne and so he was known for a time among those residents of Salt Lake who were not previously acquainted with him. Even in his private capacity, as an ambassador of good will, his coming turned the tide in favor of peace and opened the way for a reconciliation.

Colonel Kane brought with him convincing evidence that the purpose of the "Expedition" was not to make war on the Mormons and an assurance that Governor Cumming was a man of fine integrity and sterling character. He also assured them that the Mormons

[13]*Congressional Globe*, 35th Congress, 1st Session, 25th February, 1858, p. 874.
[14]*House Executive Documents*, 35th Congress, 1st Session, 10, No. 71, p. 76.
[15]*Ibid.*

had friends in Congress. The coming of Colonel Kane cleared away the clouds of misunderstanding and eventually resulted in a change of viewpoint on the part of the Saints. His attempt to persuade Brigham Young to aid the Expedition to enter Salt Lake Valley that winter failed to move the Mormon leader. Afterward, in conversing with some of the brethren, Brigham Young said:

"When Colonel Kane came to visit us, he tried to point out a policy for me to pursue. But I told him I should not turn to the right or to the left, or pursue any course, only as God dictated. I should do nothing but what was right. When he found that I would not be informed, only as the Spirit of the Lord led me, he felt discouraged and said he would not go to the army. But finally he said, *if I would dictate, he would execute*. I told him that as he had been inspired to come here, he should go to the army and do as the Spirit of the Lord led him, and all would be right. He did so and all was right. He thought it very strange that we were not afraid of the army. I told him we were not afraid of all the world; if they made war upon us, the Lord would deliver us out of their hands if we did right. God controls all these matters."[16]

Colonel Kane left Salt Lake City on March 8, 1858, with a letter from Brigham Young, "accrediting him as a negotiator in the existing difficulties."[17] On March 12, he arrived at Camp Scott, where he was entertained by Governor Cumming. General Johnston opposed his interference in affairs and attempted to arrest him as a spy. The incident nearly resulted in a duel between General Johnston and Colonel Kane.

The result of Colonel Kane's visit of some three weeks with Governor Cumming was the convincing of the Governor that he should accompany Kane to Salt Lake City. The Governor was assured of a cordial reception. Accordingly the Governor journeyed to Salt Lake City, where he was amazed at the hospitality shown him. In a letter to General Johnston he said:

"I have been everywhere recognized as Governor of Utah; and so far from having encountered insults or indignities, I am satisfied in being able to state to you, that in passing through the settlements I have been universally greeted with such respectful attentions as are due to the representative authority of the United States in the territory."[18]

A change of mind had come to the Mormons after the visit of Colonel Kane. Where before the Saints had been ready to fight to the last for their homes, now it was determined not to resist with arms but to burn their homes and flee to the South. Brigham Young had obtained from the reports of trappers a mistaken idea that a large fertile land, capable of supporting a half million population, existed in the southwestern desert area. Two scouting parties sent out failed to locate such a place. Meanwhile the Saints were moving steadily southward. Daily the streets of Salt Lake were thronged with wagons and stock, starting the southward journey.

When Governor Cumming arrived he found that a large portion of the inhabitants had deserted their homes, leaving only sufficient to fire the dwellings when the time arrived. Large groups, whose destination he could not learn, were going south, driving their flocks before them. He could not persuade them to remain long, as they were menaced by an army.

Governor Cumming reported to Washington the true state of affairs and

[16]*History of Brigham Young*, Ms. Entry for August 15, 1858, p. 927.
[17]Utah Expedition, *Atlantic Monthy*, April, 1859, p. 479.
[18]*House Executive Documents*, 35th Congress, 2nd Session, Vol. 2, pt. 2, pp. 72-73.

the deliberate falseness of Drummond's charges.

Even before news of Colonel Kane's accomplishments and Governor Cumming's report reached the East, a storm of protest was raging against President Buchanan and his course in sending out the Utah expedition. Senators Henry Wilson, of Massachusetts, and Sam Houston, of Texas, and Representatives Warren, from Arkansas, and Zollicoffer, of Tennessee, openly demanded an investigation. The important newspapers of the East, especially the *New York Times*, *New York Tribune*, and the *Herald*, took up the fight.

In April, President Buchanan appointed a peace commission, composed of L. W. Powell, former governor of Kentucky, and Major Ben McCullock, of Texas. The commission carried with them a proclamation of pardon, under date of April 6, 1858. The proclamation declared the Church leader to be in a state of "rebellion" and "treason," yet in order to prevent the shedding of blood, granted a pardon to all who would submit to the authority of the federal government.

The peace commission reached Salt Lake City June 7, and were astonished to find so large a city with its inhabitants fled. Even the Church leaders had joined in the move south.

Brigham Young declared that the Church leaders were not guilty of treason or rebellion, but would accept the pardon.

It was agreed that the Army would be allowed to pass through the city unmolested, providing they were not permitted to stop and would camp at least forty miles away. The Commission forwarded a letter to that effect to General Johnston, and on June 26, 1858, the Army entered Salt Lake City. They passed through the city and camped on the Jordan River. Three days later they marched southward and established a permanent camp in Cedar Valley. The camp was called "Camp Floyd," after the Secretary of War.

Thus was brought to a close an unfortunate chapter in the history of the Church, and of the State. The army was maintained at Camp Floyd until the outbreak of the Civil War, when the camp was abandoned. While the camp remained it was a social problem to Salt Lake City and the adjacent settlements. Immoralities, gambling, drunkeness, thefts, etc., accompanied the army and its hangers-on into the territory. The police force in Salt Lake City was increased four-fold and crimes, unknown before, became commonplace.

The course taken by the Saints in the "Utah War" was vindicated in the eyes of the nation. It will ever remain one of the outstanding examples of the faith of a people in the power of the Almighty God to protect them. The unwavering position of Brigham Young, that with the help of the Lord the Saints could withstand the entire Army of the United States, won the respect and admiration of the world. It will forever cause him to rank with the great spiritual leaders of mankind.

Supplementary Readings

1. Roberts, *A Comprehensive History of the Church*, Vol. IV, pp. 181-471. ("The Utah War." The account includes official papers and documents, speeches and orations, sermons, personal letters, editorials, narratives, from the President of the United States, Generals and other officers in the U.S. Army, Senators and Representatives of the U.S. Congress, Governors of States and Territories, Governor of Utah and President of the Mormon Church, and Apostles of said Church, and others.)

2. *Ibid.*, Vol. 4, 266-272. (Brigham Young's threat to burn homes and everything that

fire can destroy, that the people could not carry away, if the Army entered Utah.) People vote to fire their own homes. John Taylor calls for the vote. *Ibid.*, Vol. 4, pp. 273-274. (Proclamation by Governor Brigham Young forbidding the United States Army entering Utah.)

3. *Ibid.*, Vol. 4, pp. 294-295. (Senator Sam Houston, hero frontiersman, from the floor of the United States Senate, warns the government against making war on the Mormons.)

4. Roberts, *Life of John Taylor*, pp. 263-299. (John Taylor's unbounded courage and loyalty to his people and their leaders during the trying days of the Utah War.)

5. Cowley, *Wilford Woodruff*, pp. 382-410. (A view or picture of the trying times, and the response of the Mormon people and their leaders during the Utah War Period, through the eyes and mind of Wilford Woodruff, is a valuable source of information and understanding of the times, and our people.)

6. Gates and Widtsoe, *The Life Story of Brigham Young*, pp. 155-171. (Government and Loyalty. Brigham Young appointed Governor. Justice Brocchus insults the people. Attempts to remove Brigham Young.)

7. *Ibid.*, pp. 172-186. (New Governor for Utah appointed. U.S. sends army to suppress "Rebellion among the Mormons." Army forbidden to enter Utah. Troops held up in the mountains. Troops enter the Valley. "Move South.")

8. *Ibid.*, p. 187. (The Army in Utah, marches through deserted streets and city. End of Utah War.)

9. Smith, Joseph Fielding, *Essentials in Church History*, pp. 407-417. ("Buchanan's Blunder," 24th of July Celebration. Captain Van Vliet. Governor Young's Ultimatum. Peace efforts of Colonel Kane. Arrival of the troops. "The President's Pardon.")

10. Evans, *Heart of Mormonism*, pp. 454-459. ("Insiders and Outsiders.")

11. Evans, *One Hundred Years of Mormonism*, pp. 462-472. (Pioneer Day. A strange exodus.)

12. *Memoirs of John R. Young*, p. 97. (A comment of President Brigham Young on The Utah War in a letter to his nephew, John R. Young, a missionary in the Sandwich Islands.)

CHAPTER 37

A GREAT TRAGEDY

Emigrant Trains in Utah

While the Army of the United States was approaching the territory of Utah, a courier rode posthaste into Salt Lake City. He had covered the three hundred miles from Cedar City in three days. As James Haslam stood before President Young he recounted a story and delivered a message which caused that beloved leader grave concern and galvanized him into action.

During this period of Utah's history there was a constant string of emigrant trains passing through the territory on their way to California. The feeling between such emigrants and the Saints was not always a wholesome one. The emigrants often entered the territory with a deep-seated prejudice against the Mormons. Often these companies contained Missourians who had taken part in driving the Saints from that State. Toward these, some of the Mormons could not help feeling resentful and suspicious.

These emigrant trains did much to antagonize the Indians throughout the territory. Easterners generally did not share the feeling of brotherliness toward the Red Man which the Mormons had manifested. They looked upon them as little higher than animals and often fired upon them without provocation. Indians entering their camps for peaceful trading were often treated badly, and some Indians were wantonly killed. This aroused the anger of the Indian tribes. This was especially true throughout the southern settlements. The ire of the white settlers was also aroused. The Indians had been difficult to control before, but now it became impossible to control them.

A crisis in feeling was reached during the time that a large company of Arkansas emigrants were on their way to California via southern Utah, in 1857. This company contained a group of Missourians who styled themselves the "Missouri Wildcats." Their spirit seemed to dominate the caravan. They boasted openly of having helped to oust the Mormons from Missouri and Illinois; that they were going to return and help the Army which was approaching Utah to exterminate the Saints.

The evidence concerning their actions in passing through the southern settlements is so conflicting that it is difficult to determine the entire truth. Among the charges against them was the assertion that they had poisoned a dead ox, which caused the death of a number of Piute Indians who ate it. It was also alleged that they had poisoned the springs, causing the death of a number of cattle, and illness to the settlers who attempted to save the fat of the animals.

The Indians were thoroughly aroused. All the accumulated insults of the many caravans caused them to seek vengeance. To the Indian mind all whites except the Mormons belonged to one tribe, the "Mericats." Their law demanded blood vengeance against any of the offending tribe.

Ordinarily the influence of the settlers was exerted to keep the peace, and at any cost prevent an attack upon emigrant trains. At this time it appears that this restraint was not used. Many of the whites were goaded by the taunts of the "Missouri Wildcats," and by their depredations to a point of extreme bitterness.

On the sixth of September, while the emigrant train was making an extended camp on "Mountain Meadows," forty miles southwest of Cedar City, a council of leading Saints was held in Cedar City. It was decided that a messenger should be sent to Brigham Young, acquainting him with the situation. James Haslam, of Cedar City, was that messenger.

After reading the message Haslam brought, Governor Young asked him if he could stand the return journey. He was answered in the affirmative. After several hours' sleep he mounted his horse for the return ride. As the President handed him an unsealed answer, he said:

"Go with all speed; spare no horse flesh. The emigrants must not be meddled with, if it takes all Iron County to prevent it. They must go free and unmolested."[1]

In the instructions Haslam carried back to Isaac C. Haight of Cedar City we read:

"In regard to emigration trains passing through our settlements we must not interfere with them until they are notified to keep away. You must not meddle with them. The Indians we expect will do as they please, but you should try and preserve good feeling with them."[2]

Haslam arrived at Cedar City on September 13, having made the remarkable ride of over six hundred miles in six days. As Isaac C. Haight read the message he burst into tears and said:

"Too late, too late!"

"The Massacre," added Haslam, "was all over before I got home."[3]

[1]Report of Lee trial. *Deseret News*, September 10, 1876. Also Penrose, *Mountain Meadows Massacre*, pp. 94-95.

[2]*Church Business Letter Book*, No. 3. See Roberts, *Comprehensive History of the Church*, Vol. 4, pp. 150-151.

[3]Haslam's testimony, Penrose, *Mountain Meadows Massacre*, Supplement p. 95.

The Mountain Meadows' Massacre

Mountain Meadows is a narrow valley five miles in length, situated three hundred and twenty miles south and a little west of Salt Lake City. It is on a plateau which forms the southern rim of the Great Basin. The Arkansas and Missouri emigrants, in the first week of September, 1857, went into encampment in the south end of the valley near a spring.

Several hundred Indians gathered in the vicinity, and at break of day on September 8 or 9 commenced an attack upon the emigrants. The attack was repulsed and the emigrants "dug in" for a siege.

The Indians, meanwhile, sent runners to the neighboring tribes to gather warriors. A number of white men also arrived upon the scene of conflict.

It was a deliberately planned massacre, treacherously carried into execution. On the morning of September 11, a flag of truce was sent to the emigrant camp and terms of surrender proposed. The emigrants were to give up their arms. The wounded were to be loaded into wagons, followed by the women and children, and the men to bring up the rear, single file. Thus they were to be conducted by the whites to Cedar City. This was agreed to, and the march began.

A short distance from the encampment, the white men at a given signal, fell upon the unarmed emigrant men. At the same time hundreds of Indians, who had lain in ambush, rushed upon the hapless party. In five minutes the terrible tragedy was enacted. Only three men escaped the first deadly assault. These were pursued by the Indians and killed. Only the smallest children were spared. These were taken into the homes of settlers and cared for. Later the United States Government provided a fund to father the children and transport them to relatives in Arkansas and Missouri and to an orphanage in St. Louis.

Responsibility of the Tragedy

News of the Mountain Meadows Massacre was a shock to the leaders of the Church, and brought a deep and sincere sorrow to the entire territory. Unfortunately, no thorough investigation to bring the perpetrators to justice was held until twenty years later. George A. Smith was sent by Brigham Young to investigate the affair and made formal report to Brigham Young in 1858. By that time Brigham Young had relinquished all civil authority to his successor, Governor Cumming. John D. Lee, the Indian Agent, in his report of Indian affairs to the government, gave his own story of the tragedy, but the government did not order an investigation.

Brigham Young urged Governor Cumming to investigate the charge of white men participating in the massacre. In 1876, Brigham Young said on the witness stand:

"Soon after Governor Cumming arrived, I asked him to take Judge Cradlebaugh, who belonged to the southern district, with him and I would accompany them with sufficient aid to investigate the matter and bring the offenders to justice."[4]

Governor Cumming, in the face of settling the difficulties of the "Utah War" and the pardoning of offenders against the United States Government, made no move to prosecute any participant in the crime.

An attempt was made by non-Mormons to hold Brigham Young responsible for the tragedy. Judge Cradlebaugh took the lead in that attack and made an attempt, in 1859, to probe into the affair. Of this effort, Forney, the Indian agent, reported:

"I fear, and I regret to say it, that there is with certain parties a greater anxiety to connect Brigham Young and other Church dignitaries with every criminal offence than diligent endeavor to punish the actual perpetrators of crime."[5]

For the deed at Mountain Meadows there is no excuse. The perpetrators were never held guiltless by the Church and the Church must not be condemned because of the vile deeds of a few of its members. The law of the Church was announced from the beginning by the Son of God:

"And now, behold, I speak unto the church. Thou shalt not kill; and he that kills shall not have forgiveness in this world, nor in the world to come. And again I say, thou shalt not kill, but he that killeth shall die. And it shall come to pass, that if any persons among you shall kill, they shall be delivered up and dealt with according to the laws of the land; for remember that he hath no forgiveness, and it shall be proven according to the laws of the land."[6]

Supplementary Readings

1. Gates and Widtsoe, *Life Story of Brigham Young*, pp. 142-145.
2. Cowley, *Wilford Woodruff*, pp. 387-389, (September 29, 1857, John D. Lee, in Wilford Woodruff's presence, makes a report to Brigham Young about the Mountain Meadows Massacre. Brother Woodruff wrote his memories and impressions of the report in his journal that evening. This is his journal record.)
3. Smith, *Essentials of Church History*, pp. 418-422. (A brief account of the affair.)
4. Penrose, *Mountain Meadows Massacre*. (A booklet.)
5. Roberts, *A Comprehensive History of the Church*, Volume 4, pp. 139-159.

---

[4]*Court Report*, second Lee trial, 1876. See Roberts, *Comprehensive History of the Church*, Vol. 4, p. 168.

[5]*Senate Documents*, 36th Congress, 1st Session, No. 2, p. 86. See also, Bancroft, *History of Utah*, p. 561.

[6]*Doctrine and Covenants*, Section 42:18-19, 79.

CHAPTER 38

ISOLATION COMES TO AN END

The Nation Pushes West

The isolation which Brigham Young obtained for his people in the valleys of the mountains gave the Church of Jesus Christ of Latter-day Saints the opportunity of becoming a permanent institution. The roots of the Church became firmly planted. Its organization and beliefs became fixed and crystallized. The isolation preserved the Church from destruction. It was not preserved, however, without terrific cost. Despite the interest of the Church in schools, the circumstances were such that a whole generation developed with little formal education. But for the continual influx of emigrants and the contact of missionaries with the outside world, the Mormons would have witnessed a period of stagnation in learning. As it was, the development of men of letters, scientists, artists, etc., suffered greatly. Further, isolated as the people were, deep-seated convictions crystallized into doctrines in the minds of many and religious forms into unchangeable laws.

This isolation, however, did not long continue. Nor was it the desire of Brigham Young or of the Church that it should continue. Once the Saints were established in the West, the Church exerted its full influence to open new channels of communication with the world—to invite industry to Utah —and to welcome contacts in every way with the rest of the Nation.

The forbidding nature of the country prolonged the isolation. Especially was this true of the outlying settlements. An easier living could be obtained in Oregon or California. So for many years the "Gentiles," or non-Mormons, avoided the Great Basin.

The first event to break into this isolation was the gold rush to California, which made of Utah a national highway to the gold fields. This brought numerous non-Mormons into Utah and resulted in a number of non-Mormon merchants establishing themselves in Salt Lake City.

The organization of a territorial form of government and the coming of federal appointees encouraged the other non-Mormons to enter the territory for political or economic purposes. In 1858 Johnston's army added to the Gentile population. The next development was the opening of the mining industry in Utah during, and immediately following, the Civil War. Camp Floyd had been abandoned at the beginning of that struggle (1861), but in 1862 Colonel P. Edward Connor was ordered to Salt Lake City with a company of California Volunteers, and established Fort Douglas on the bench east of Salt Lake City. This detachment of the Army had been sent to the territory to prevent the Mormons aligning themselves with the Southern States. Finding the Utah people loyal to the Union, General Connor found little active service for his soldiers, so granted them long furloughs. Many of these soldiers had been miners and gold seekers in California. These explored the mountains of Utah for ore and discovered every important mining area of the State. The development of the Utah mining industry followed. Foreign capital and laborers were attracted to the State and the non-Mormon population rapidly increased in the cities and mining centers.

In 1861, the overland telegraph, connecting Salt Lake City with the eastern and western centers and the development of the Deseret Telegraph in 1865-7, from Arizona to Idaho, was a large step in bring the settlements closer to each other and to the world.

In 1869, an event occurred which more than any other removed the barriers created by time and distance and revolutionized the economic conditions of the Territory. In that year the first transcontinental railroad was completed. For three years two large crews of men had been working feverishly to accomplish this objective — the Union Pacific pushing west from Omaha along the Old Mormon trail, and the Central Pacific pushing east from San Francisco.

When the two lines met at Promontory, Utah, forty-five miles west of Ogden, Utah, and the engines from east and west rubbed noses, the period of Utah isolation was at an end.

Although the Saints welcomed the railroad and had urged and aided its building, the realization brought some painful readjustments to the economic structure of the Territory. In the first place the economic independence of the Territory ended. Many industries had been possible only because the high costs of transportation made it possible to compete with eastern products. The coming of the railroad ended that condition. The silk industry, cotton raising, iron manufacturing, and a multitude of lesser activities were doomed

Celebration of the completion of the first transcontinental railroad. The two lines, the Union Pacific and the Central Pacific, met in 1869 at Promontory, Utah. Used by permission, Utah State Historical Society

and an adjustment had to be made. The railroad opened a market for agriculture and mining products, however, and eventually resulted in prosperity for the people of the Territory.

The disappearance of the frontier found the Church firmly established. It is fortunate that it was, for the conflict which ensued might otherwise have destroyed it. Part of this conflict we have previously discussed in relation to the social problem of polygamy.

Mormon and Gentile Again

When we realize that from the time of the organization of the Church the contact between Mormons and non-Mormons was attended by deep misunderstandings and mutual intolerance, it is to be expected that the contact between the Mormon and Gentile population in Utah would not be free from conflict.

During all the previous conflicts the Saints had been in the minority. The majority who were non-Mormons had ended the conflict by driving the Mormons out. In Utah the Saints were in the overwhelming majority. They would not be driven nor did they have any desire to drive out those who disagreed with them.

Of the many causes of conflict, four are especially manifest in Utah history. First, the Doctrine of Plural Marriage, which we have discussed at length. Second, the political solidarity of the people which followed the leadership of the Church. Third, the economic solidarity of the Saints. Fourth, the intolerance of the Saints toward vice and immorality.

The first cause of friction was eliminated in 1890 by the "Manifesto." The second disappeared, as the political forces operating against the Saints decreased. With the admission of Utah

to statehood in 1896 the Saints gradually aligned themselves with the major political parties. Only in the case of political problems, where moral issues are involved, does the political influence of the Church now assume any importance.

In the economic field, likewise the solidarity of the Mormon people has disappeared. As stated above, the coming of the railroad meant the end of many industries in Utah which had been built up by the Saints through cooperative methods.

The Church leaders anticipated the effects the coming of the railroad would produce on industry, and early in 1868 initiated a movement to organize the Mormon merchants and purchasers into cooperative merchandising enterprises. This movement was designed to aid the Saints in purchasing articles manufactured in the East, at a reasonable price, without being subject to prices set by "Gentile" merchants who were entering the territory. The capital for such enterprises was furnished in small amounts by a multitude of stockholders. The central objective of the movement was to enable the people to become their own merchants, to share in the profits of the business, and to prevent concentration of wealth in a few hands.

Cooperative Merchandising

The first of these cooperative merchandising organizations was begun in Provo in 1868. In 1869 the Zion's Cooperative Mercantile Institution, which became shortened in name to the Z. C. M. I. became a Churchwide institution. Local merchants in the various settlements were invited to join the movement and to sell stock in the local concerns to their customers.

The Eagle Emporium Building, place of operations of Z. C. M. I. in Salt Lake City in the 1870's.
Used by permission, Utah State Historical Society

In connection with the establishment of the Z. C. M. I. a boycott was urged against non-Mormon merchants. In the October conference of 1868 Brigham Young announced:

"I want to tell my brethren, my friends, and my enemies, that we are going to draw the reins so tight as not to let a Latter-day Saint trade with an outsider."[1]

Both of these movements were defensive. It was openly claimed by enemies of the Church that, with the coming of the railroad, Mormonism would be overthrown. An influx of Gentile merchants was expected. A crusade against Mormonism was to begin with the advent of the railroad. Hostile schemes were afoot, to deprive the Saints of their privileges as citizens and to attack their marriage program.

"It was a time of war—a struggle for community existence, and as a measure of self-preservation, until the danger was past, and normal conditions restored, 'the no trade intercourse' policy with Gentiles was naturally to be expected, and was justifiable, and was brave and wise."[2]

The Z. C. M. I. and its branches throughout the Territory proved, in the main, a great success as a commercial enterprise and served to level prices. It was, however, a contributing cause of feeling between Mormon and Gentile merchants, which lasted until the end of the century. The Z. C. M. I. was gradually abandoned as a cooperative enterprise, as the need for it disap-

[1]Sermon of October 8, 1868, *Journal of Discourses*, Vol. 12, p. 286.

[2]Roberts, *Comprehensive History of the Church*, Vol. 5, p. 228.

MANTI TEMPLE, dedicated by Lorenzo Snow, May 21, 1888.

HAWAIIAN TEMPLE, dedicated by President Heber J. Grant, Nov. 27, 1919.

CANADIAN TEMPLE, dedicated by President Heber J. Grant, August 26, 1923

ARIZONA TEMPLE, dedicated by President Heber J. Grant, October 23, 1927.

peared. At the present time the institution of that name contains none of its original cooperative features.

The fourth cause of friction between Mormons and non-Mormons has likewise disappeared to a large extent. Occasionally, Mormons and non-Mormons line up on opposite sides of such questions as anti-cigarette laws, and the prohibition of liquors.

During its formative years in the valleys of the mountains the Church was blessed with remarkable leadership. The faith of John Taylor, who became president in 1880, three years after the death of Brigham Young, held the Saints together during the polygamy persecutions.

Wilford Woodruff, his successor, was likewise a bulwark of strength and like John Taylor an early associate of the Prophet Joseph.

President Woodruff, who had done much to bring the Church out of its financial difficulties and to restore harmony with the civil government, died September 2, 1898. He was succeeded eleven days later by Lorenzo Snow, then eighty-five years of age. President Snow's three years of administration were vigorous ones and resulted in a great revival of spirituality and unity in the Church. At the close of his administration the Church was out of debt, missionary activity had been increased and a new mission opened in Japan.

Political Opposition

During President Snow's administration opposition to the Saints had flared afresh. Brigham H. Roberts, one of the general authorities of the Church, was elected by the State of Utah as representative to Congress. Some of the non-Mormons of Utah urged Congress to deny him a seat on the grounds that he was a polygamist. The dispute became nationwide and Roberts was finally excluded from Congress.

Bitter political feeling between Mormons and their enemies continued into the administration of President Joseph F. Smith, who was sustained to succeed President Snow at a special conference, November 10, 1901. When Reed Smoot, one of the Twelve Apostles, was chosen for the United States Senate in 1903, it was a signal for a fresh attack against the Church. The Ministerial Alliance of Salt Lake City and individual citizens petitioned the Senate to refuse him a seat on the grounds that he believed in the principles of polygamy. Smoot was not himself a polygamist. The case was before the Senate for two years during which time a Senate investigating committee made a journey to Utah to examine all phases of the matter. A spirit of prejudice ran high over the United States and thousands of petitions opposing the seating of the "Mormon Apostle" reached Congress.

The case was called up before the Senate December 13, 1906, and on February 20, 1907, Senator Smoot was admitted to membership.

For a short time opposition to the Church continued with the organization in Utah of the American Party designed to fight Mormonism. The organization was discontinued in 1911.

As the Church enters its second century, persecution of it has ceased throughout the United States and a more tolerant attitude is being adopted toward the Mormons by the peoples of the world.

The Church Loses its Hold Upon the Economic and Social Life of the People

The Church from its beginning has

been interested in both the spiritual and physical conditions of its members. Its primary function has been to promote the spiritual welfare of its people and of the whole world. This function has been kept actively alive throughout the history of the Church. Spiritual welfare and the happiness of a people is also dependent upon their material welfare. To Joseph Smith there was a close relationship between an economic system and a spiritual life. Thus the Church became instrumental in establishing a social order which would best promote Christian virtues. The "law of consecration" recognized the close relationship between the physical and spiritual sides of life.

The social order Joseph Smith desired was never obtained, and remained at his death, the "great unfinished enterprise." In the West it was never attempted except by isolated groups. The Church did, however, exercise a definite control over the economic and social life of its people. The reason for this was largely self-preservation, which demanded cooperation to conquer the desert. It became also a defensive movement against a world which sought to destroy the Saints.

It was but natural then, that as the conquering of the desert became a reality, and the attacks against the Church from outside ceased, that the Church would relinquish its efforts to direct the economic and social life of its people.

It has not, however, relinquished its interest in these fields. The Bishop is still in charge of the material welfare of his people, and under his direction the Relief Society administers to the needs of the poor. By the collection and disbursements of tithes the Church remains a great cooperative enterprise for the building of chapels, temples, etc., in educating its youth, and in the maintenance of missions throughout the world.

With the disappearance of frontiers, commercial entertainment has weakened the Church's hold on the social life of its people. This is regrettable. A movement to regain what the Church has lost in this field is now under way, and rapid strides have been made during the administrations of Heber J. Grant and successive presidents. This movement consists of a Church-wide recreational program conducted through the M.I.A., the building of recreational halls, and the training of recreational leaders.

Supplementary Readings

1. Roberts, *A Comprehensive History of the Church*, Vol. 5, pp. 216-238. ("The Cooperative Mercantile System—Proposed exclusiveness of Mormon trade—Attempted Anti-Mormon National Legislation — Action of Mormon Women in relation thereto.")

2. *Ibid.*, Vol. 5, pp. 239-252. (Advent of the railroads into Utah — Attitude of the Church toward the coming of the railroad—Salt Lake City as a railroad center.")

3. *Ibid.*, Vol. 5, pp. 253-271. (A chapter of one to two page character sketches of outstanding men and women; and some apostates, and opponents of Brigham Young or the Church. Sketches of Vilate Kimball, Leonard Taylor, Heber C. Kimball, Daniel Spencer, Ezra Benson. Apostates and apostate groups: W. S. Godbe, E. L. T. Harrison, Eli B. Kelsey, Henry W. Lawrence, and movements they aided.)

4. Smith, *Essentials of Church History*, p. 443. (The Cooperative Movement Among the Mormons.)

5. Gates and Widtsoe, *Life Story of Brigham Young*, pp. 202-207. (Cooperation among the Mormons in self-defense, after the coming of the railroad and rush of non-Mormon businessmen into Utah.)

PREVIEW OF UNIT III

THE CHURCH TODAY

Mormonism is now in its second century. It has established itself in the world as a vital, progressive religion. In this unit we shall delve deep into the working of the Church to find its underlying strength. We will come to marvel at its unique organization and amazing vitality. We will be thrilled by the program of love enacted in its temples; we will be touched by the burning testimony which causes the missionary movement to live; we will learn to appreciate God's concern in the happiness of His children; and finally we will come to realize that the laws of God's Kingdom are the laws of all life—the eternal truths.

UNIT III – THE CHURCH TODAY

CHAPTER 39

THE SECOND CENTURY
OF MORMONISM

The Centennial Celebration

On April 6, 1930, a great celebration marked the close of the first century of Mormonism and the ushering in of the second. On that occasion a centennial pageant, "The Message of the Ages," was presented in the Tabernacle at Salt Lake City, portraying the growth of the Church and the fruits of its teachings. For thirty days the pageant was repeated to the vast throngs which filled that historic structure.

During that occasion the Temple in Salt Lake City was illuminated at night by giant floodlights totaling 52,000 candlepower. The figure of the Angel Moroni, freshly covered with gold leaf, atop the Temple, symbolized anew to the world the prediction of the Apostle John on the Isle of Patmos:

"And I saw another angel fly in the midst of heaven, having the everlasting gospel to preach unto them that dwell on the earth, and to every nation, and kindred, and tongue, and people,

Saying with a loud voice, Fear God, and give glory to him; for the hour of his judgment is come: and worship him that made heaven, and earth, and the sea, and the fountains of waters."[1]

In contrast to the humble beginnings of the Church in Fayette, New York, April 6, 1830, this celebration was attended by hundreds of thousands. On April 7, 1930, the Mormon Tabernacle organ was heard over radio hookups by "seven to ten millions" throughout the world.

The Church reported a membership of 700,000 souls. Seven million baptisms had been performed for the dead. President Heber J. Grant reported:

"We have at the present time: 104 stakes of Zion, 930 Wards, 75 independent branches, 27 dependent branches, total Wards and Branches in the Stakes of Zion, from Canada to Mexico, 1032; Missions, 29; Mission branches, 800."[2]

The first century was distinctive for its remarkable leadership. The following table shows the succession of men

---

[1]*Revelation* 14:6-7.
[2]Adapted from *Conference Report*, Apr. 1930, p. 176.

(Chart of Presidents of the Church)

	Born	Died	Ordained an Apostle	President Council of Twelve	Sustained President of Church
Joseph Smith	Dec. 23, 1805	June 27, 1844	1829	——————	April, 1830*
Brigham Young	June 1, 1801	Aug. 29, 1877	Feb. 14, 1835	Jan. 19, 1841	Dec. 27, 1847
John Taylor	Nov. 1, 1808	July 25, 1887	Dec. 19, 1838	April 10, 1875	Oct. 10, 1880
Wilford Woodruff	March 1, 1807	Sept. 2, 1898	Apr. 26, 1839	Oct. 10, 1880	April 7, 1889
Lorenzo Snow	April 3, 1814	Oct. 10, 1901	Feb. 12, 1849	April 7, 1889	Sept. 13, 1898
Joseph F. Smith	Nov. 13, 1838	Nov. 19, 1918	July 1, 1866	——————	Oct. 17, 1901
Heber J. Grant	Nov. 22, 1856	May. 14, 1945	Oct. 16, 1882	Nov. 23, 1916	Nov. 23, 1918
George A. Smith	Apr. 4, 1870	April 4, 1951	Oct. 8, 1903	July 8, 1943	May 21, 1945
David O. McKay	Sept. 8, 1873	Jan. 18, 1970	Apr. 9, 1906	Sept. 30, 1950	April 9, 1951
Joseph Fielding Smith	July 19, 1876	July 2, 1972	Apr. 7, 1912	April 9, 1951	Jan. 23, 1970
Harold B. Lee	Mar. 28, 1899		Apr. 6, 1941	Jan. 23, 1970	July 7, 1972

*In 1830, Joseph Smith presided over the Church as its First Elder. He was sustained as President of the High Priesthood at a conference in Amherst, Ohio, January 25, 1832.

IDAHO FALLS TEMPLE, dedicated by President George Albert Smith, Sept. 23, 1945.

SWISS TEMPLE, dedicated by President David O. McKay, Sept. 11, 1955.

LOS ANGELES TEMPLE, dedicated by President David O. McKay, March 11, 1956.

who have presided over The Church of Jesus Christ of Latter-day Saints.

Of the eleven presidents, the four succeeding the Prophet Joseph were his close associates. They were nearly the same age. Their loyalty to the Prophet was an outstanding feature of their eventful lives.

As Mormonism entered its second century the eminent Dr. Thomas Nixon Carver, professor of political economy at Harvard University, said of it:

"I have never found more sound and wholesome personal habits than among the Mormons. I never mingled with people who showed fewer signs of dissipation. I have never studied groups of people who seemed better nourished and more healthful. I have never known people who took more pains to educate their children. This gives a clue to the success of the Mormons as colonizers and nation-builders. The power to save skill, talent and genius from going to waste, is as near to divine wisdom as anything we are ever likely to know in this world. Whether this power comes from superior organization, or from superior personal insight, it is equally valuable. The Mormon Church seems to have possessed it in high degree."[3]

Speaking of the cooperation among the Saints, Dr. Carver continues:

"It may have been the sheer necessity of the situation which forced the early Mormons to cooperate or starve. It may have been the bond of a common religion, it may have been superior intelligence and insight. Whatever the source, the result was good."[4]

The Mormon people stood ready to be judged by the great test set forth by the Master:

"Ye shall know them by their fruits. Do men gather grapes of thorns, or figs of thistles?

"Even so, every good tree bringeth forth good fruit.

"Wherefore by their fruits ye shall know them."[5]

---

[3]Thomas Nixon Carver, "A Positive Religion," *Westerner*, Apr. 1930, p. 7.
[4]*Ibid.*
[5]*Matthew* 7:16, 17, 20.

In order to understand the effects of the gospel upon the lives of Church members it is necessary to study the organization through which the members function and the gospel is taught. This organization has attracted the attention of thinking men throughout the world. It is recognized as the most complete church organization which has ever existed upon the earth.

The foundation of this organization is the Holy Priesthood. The Priesthood is the authority from God to officiate in his Church, to teach the gospel and perform its ordinances. The Priesthood can be held by the male members of the Church over twelve years of age. It is the possession of this authority and power from God which sets the Latter-day Saints apart from all other peoples in the world. The restoration of the Priesthood to the earth and its organization have been previously discussed.

The Priesthood for administrative purposes functions on three levels, general, stake, and ward. The relationship of these to each other may be ascertained by a close study of the accompanying chart.

During 1961 the First Presidency organized the Church Priesthood Correlation Committee under whose direction a far-reaching program was inaugurated to bring all of the activities of the Church under Priesthood leadership and control.

Four areas of Church activity, the Church welfare program, the missionary program, home teaching, and genealogical work, were brought directly under the General Authorities, stake and ward priesthood authorities, and the Melchizedek Priesthood quorums. This program centered Church activities and education in Priesthood quorums and established a line of Priesthood responsibility and communication through the quorums from the General Authorities to each individual family of the Church.

In the October conference of 1964, Elder Harold B. Lee, chairman of the Church Correlation Committee, announced:

"This next year will see some definite steps taken to strengthen the hands of the parents in carrying out these great God-given admonitions in placing stress upon the teaching of the gospel in the home. . . .

". . . The time has now come when the General Authorities have decided to correlate and co-ordinate all of these efforts under the direction of the priesthood, and we announce then, a new program designed to assist the parents in the teaching of the gospel in the home. The program 'Teaching and Living the Gospel in the Home' is to be inaugurated throughout the Church in January 1965."[6]

In January, 1965, this new program for teaching in the home was launched Churchwide. A family home evening manual was placed in every Latter-day Saint home, and home teachers were appointed to assist families in carrying out the program successfully.

Although the Priesthood remains the same, its functions have expanded and become better defined and it now provides more direct leadership to a number of auxiliary organizations which assist it in carrying out its functions. These auxiliaries, functioning under the authority of the Priesthood, have assumed a large and important role in the Church. A brief survey will show their origin and growth.

The Relief Society

The oldest auxiliary in the Church is the Relief Society. It was organized by the Prophet Joseph in Nauvoo, March 17, 1842, at which time it was called The Female Relief Society. In 1892, it was named the National Woman's Relief Society and in 1942 became The

Relief Society of The Church of Jesus Christ of Latter-day Saints. Its purpose during its entire existence has been a faithful carrying out of the Prophet's admonition that the society was to look after the needs of the poor, to search after objects of charity and to administer to their wants, and to assist in correcting the morals and strengthening the virtues of the community.

From an initial membership of eighteen, the society increased to a total membership of 377,840 at the close of 1971. The work of this organization in recent years has been outstanding and has received much praise. Its official organ, the *Relief Society Magazine*, was established in 1914 and attained a wide circulation before 1971 when it was absorbed into the new Church publications.

The Sunday School

The Sunday School was the second auxiliary established. In the winter of 1849, Richard Ballantyne held a Sunday School at his home in the Old Fort at Salt Lake City. From that humble beginning on December 9, 1849, the Sunday School grew into a churchwide movement. In the beginning there was no central organization or uniformity, but in 1866 a general meeting was called and the Deseret Sunday School Union came into existence, with Elder George Q. Cannon as president. In the same year the *Juvenile Instructor* was published as the official organ of the Sunday School. Under the new name of *The Instructor* its publication was continued until December 1970.

The Sunday School is devoted to the religious instruction of the entire membership of the Church. It is the great preparatory school for Church service, at home and in the mission field.

---

[6]Harold B. Lee in *Conference Report*, Oct. 1964, pp. 84-85.)

Relief Society Building, headquarters of the Relief Society of the Church of Jesus Christ of Latter-
day Saints in Salt Lake City.

From an initial membership of fifty, the enrollment now includes all Church members and had increased to 2,387,509 at the close of 1971.

The MIA

On June 10, 1875, an important meeting was held in the Thirteenth Ward, Salt Lake City. Junius F. Wells, acting under instruction from Brigham Young, organized during that meeting the Young Men's Mutual Improvement Association.

Brigham Young announced the purpose of the organization to be "the establishment in the youth of individual testimony of the truth and magnitude of the great latter-day work: the development of the gifts within them that have been bestowed upon them by the laying on of hands by the servants of God; cultivating a knowledge and an application of the eternal principles of the great science of life."[7]

The Young Women's Mutual Improvement Association had its origin in the Retrenchment Association, or-

ganized by Brigham Young at the Lion House on November 28, 1869. In 1880, general boards were set up for both associations. The combined organization is called the Mutual Improvement Association. Its work has been greater than the expectations of its founders. In recent years the movement has been extended to include adult members of the Church. Upon this organization has devolved the duty of providing, not only worthwhile instruction, but wholesome recreation and activities for its members. Through the MIA the Church is having an influence on the social life of its people. The production of plays, musicals, vaudevilles, the supervision of dancing and indoor and outdoor sports have been outstanding. The M Men Basketball League, a feature of the MIA program, is the largest basketball league in the world.

Since the young men's and young women's organizations were combined as the Mutual Improvement Association, the official publication was the *Improvement Era*. In 1970 this publication was discontinued. From that time the three Church publications, the

[7]Joseph Fielding Smith, *Essentials in Church History*, 24th ed., 1971, p. 678.

Priesthood Line of Authority

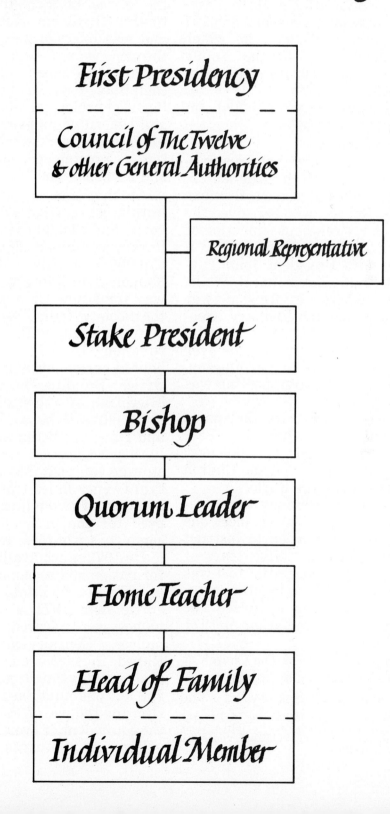

First Presidency

Council of The Twelve & other General Authorities

Regional Representative

Stake President

Bishop

Quorum Leader

Home Teacher

Head of Family

Individual Member

New Era, the *Ensign,* and the *Friend,* have given general help and inspiration to all Church members. The membership of the Young Men's Mutual Improvement Association reached 355,107 by the beginning of 1972, at which time the membership of the Young Women's Mutual Improvement Association reached 386,735. In 1973 the MIA was brought directly under the direction of the priesthood.

The Primary Association

The Primary originated at Farmington, Davis County, Utah, August 25, 1878. It was the result of the reflections of Aurelia S. Rogers, who perceived the need for weekday religious education of boys and girls. Her interest led to a consultation with President John Taylor, Eliza R. Snow, Emmeline B. Wells, and others, where a decision was reached to organize the Primary Association. On August 11, 1878, Aurelia S. Rogers was set apart to preside over a Primary Association in Farmington, and on August 25 the first meeting was held.

The movement spread to other parts of the Church and on June 19, 1880, Louie B. Felt was called to preside over the Primary Association of the Church of Jesus Christ in all the world.

Ward and branch Primary organizations throughout the Church meet one afternoon during the week to instruct children from four to twelve years of age. The official organ until 1970 was the *Children's Friend,*[7a] a monthly magazine devoted to young children. The membership of the association in 1971 totaled 487,951.

The Genealogical Society of The Church of Jesus Christ of Latter-day Saints

The Genealogical Society of The Church of Jesus Christ of Latter-day Saints, originally called the Genealogical Society of Utah, was organized at the office of Franklin D. Richards, Church Historian, November 13, 1894, and was incorporated November 20 of the same year. Its original purpose was declared "to be benevolent in collecting, compiling, establishing and maintaining a genealogical library for the use and benefit of its members and others; educational in disseminating information regarding genealogical matters; and also religious."

At the time of incorporation the library consisted of a donation of eleven books and 300,000 films. By 1968 the library contained 80,000 volumes and 670,000 microfilms. When the Smith Memorial Building was razed to make way for a new Church office building, the Society found itself in temporary quarters, but with greatly enlarged function. In 1972 it was moved to be housed permanently in the new Church Office Building in Salt Lake City. Microfilming of genealogical records in many parts of the world has accelerated, and films are being added daily to the library's collection. In addition, a huge storage vault cut into the granite mountain twenty miles from Salt Lake City at a cost of two million dollars is being used for the permanent home of one complete set of these important records.

By 1972 much available pertinent information had been placed in computers in order to facilitate its use. In one single year, 1971, a total of 1,750,416 names were cleared for temple ordinances. Genealogical records microfilmed in seventeen countries during that same year brought the total to 712,945 one-hundred-foot rolls of microfilm for the use of the Church. This is the equivalent of over 3,401,301 printed volumes of 300 pages each. Each year

---

[7a]This magazine was discontinued as of January 1, 1971. In its place *The Friend* (for children, their parents and teachers) is being published under the direction of the priesthood.

sees the work advance more rapidly than the year before.

In 1969 the Church held the World Conference on Records at Salt Lake City, Utah to which representatives came from forty-five nations, an indication of the worldwide interest in genealogical records. Out of that world conference came a new respect for the work of the Church in this field. Invitations which extended free access to their archives came from many nations, and workers have been continuously microfilming such records.

The early establishment of a general board for the Society, together with the stake boards and ward genealogical committees, was superseded in 1964 by the placing of all genealogical work under the Priesthood of the Church, with overall supervision by the Church Priesthood Correlation Committee. The Priesthood genealogical program thus became one of four programs directed by General Authorities with responsibility delegated to stake presidents and from stake presidents to bishops.

The auxiliaries are subject to the authority of the Priesthood and have no power apart from that authority. Through the Priesthood and its auxiliaries the Church reaches every member with an opportunity for service, learning, and growth.

Education

From the beginning the Latter-day Saints have fostered education. At Kirtland Joseph Smith organized an elementary school and a School of the Prophets for adults. At Nauvoo, schools ranging from elementary to the university levels were authorized and begun under a liberal charter granted by the state of Illinois.

In the Great Basin schools found a place in the earliest settlements with Mary Dilworth opening the first school in October, 1847. Before Utah became an official territory of the United States, the University of Deseret was organized.

During the latter part of the nineteenth century the Church established schools throughout the Rocky Mountain area. These consisted of elementary schools, academies, and colleges. The elementary schools were early taken over by the territorial government. At the beginning of the twentieth century there were three colleges and nineteen academies operated by the Church.

Beginning in 1912 the Church began to establish seminaries adjacent to high

Kaysville Seminary Building, typical of many buildings erected on Church property adjacent to high schools in Utah, Idaho, and Arizona where Seminary classes are taught on a released time basis.

NEW ZEALAND TEMPLE, dedicated by President David O. McKay,
April 20, 1958

LONDON TEMPLE, dedicated by President David O. McKay,
September 7, 1958.

OAKLAND TEMPLE, dedicated by President David O. McKay, November 17, 1964

schools for the purpose of giving daily religious instruction. By 1972 the number of seminary students was over 140,-000.

Beginning in 1926, institutes of religion were established adjacent to colleges and universities where Latter-day Saint students were found. From the beginning at Moscow, Idaho, the institute program spread throughout the United States and Canada and in

There was a total of 4,251 full-time and part-time paid teachers and an additional 1,774 teachers engaged in home study seminary on a voluntary basis.

Changes in Latter-day Distribution

During the latter half of the nineteenth century and the early years of the twentieth century the history of Mormonism is marked by the gathering of the Church adherents into the Great Basin region of the Rocky Mountains.

Pocatello Institute of Religion, typical of many buildings being erected on Church property adjacent to various university campuses throughout the western states.

the 1970s extended into England, Europe, Mexico, Central and South America, New Zealand, Australia, Japan, and Korea. In the 1971-72 school year there were 53,395 college students, other than those in Church colleges, taking courses in religion at the Church institutes located near some 350 colleges and universities.

Seminaries had been established on several Indian reservations adjacent to government schools, and in the year 1971-72 some 17,013 Indian students were enrolled. The total of seminary and institute students rose to 208,477.

Beginning in the third decade of the century this gathering movement slowed down, and a reverse process set in. With the rapid growth of the Church it was no longer practical for its members to be concentrated in a relatively small area, but rather the decision was made to organize branches, wards, and stakes wherever sufficient Church members could be found. The great financial depression of the 1930s hit the Great Basin area severely, and thousands moved away chiefly to the West Coast to find employment. In 1923 there was only one Latter-day

Saint stake on the entire Pacific Coast. By 1950 the number of stakes there had risen to 14, and by the close of 1971 to 118. Nearly every Sunday new stakes are organized in areas distant from the Church center. By the close of 1971 the total number of stakes was 562.

Foreseeing the time when the Church would be established throughout the world rather than gathering in one place, the First Presidency as early as October 18, 1921, made the following statement:

> Many of the saints who immigrate here (the United States), could make themselves much more useful if they would build up and strengthen the church in their own lands, rather than making the sacrifice to emigrate to Zion where their hopes will not be realized.
> . . . The teaching of the gathering has definitely had great meaning in our history but we must realize that times and conditions change and that therefore the application of the principles and teachings must change. For years now it has been evident that the emigration of the Saints to Utah and the surrounding area is not advantageous. . . . The Church cannot now be responsible for disillusionment suffered here which there would have to be if the missionaries were encouraging the emigration.[8]

Mission presidents for some decades have urged new converts to remain in the mission areas and build up the Church there with the promise that the full Church program, including the establishment of temples, would come to them.

An example of this counsel is shown in the following appeal by the presidents of three German-language missions to their people in 1958:

> "We still call all people to come out of the spiritual Babylon, which means to come out of spiritual darkness. We are still gathering scattered Israel. But we no longer urge them to emigrate to America. On the contrary, we tell the Saints exactly what the Lord required, namely to build up the stakes of Zion and to enlarge the boundaries of His kingdom.
> In the second period of church history the main task to be done is in the missions. Here there is a great growth yet to be achieved, enabling wards and stakes to be founded which will then continue to spread the Gospel throughout the world.[9]

To reinforce their counsel, the European mission leaders included as part of their appeal the above quoted statement of the First Presidency.

Changes in Distribution

In 1900, out of a total Church membership of 236,316, some 172,623 or 73 percent were living in Utah, with 90 percent in Utah, Idaho, and Arizona.

Between 1900 and 1938 the Church membership increased 332 percent. While the number of Latter-day Saints in Utah rose to 386,139, the percentage in relation to total Church membership had dropped to 49.2 percent and that of Utah, Idaho, and Arizona combined to 67.1 percent.

The change in the distribution of Church membership was very marked by 1972 with only 34.7 percent of the Church membership in the three Rocky Mountain states. Predictions were being made that before the end of the century half of the Church membership would be in non-English-speaking nations.

By August, 1972, there were seventy-five stakes outside the continental United States. The non-English-speaking stakes of the Church included thirteen Spanish, five German, five Tongan, four Samoan, four Portuguese, one Dutch, one Japanese, and one French. In addition over half a dozen other stakes use extensively both English and a non-English language.

By 1972 stakes had been organized in all parts of the United States, Can-

---

[8]Burtis F. Robbins, Jesse R. Curtis, and Theodore M. Burton, "Auswandering," *Der Stern* (Nov. 1958), pp. 343-346. Translated by Douglas Dexter Alder, "The German-Speaking Immigration to Utah," (Masters Thesis, University of Utah, 1958) pp. 114-118.

[9]*Ibid.*

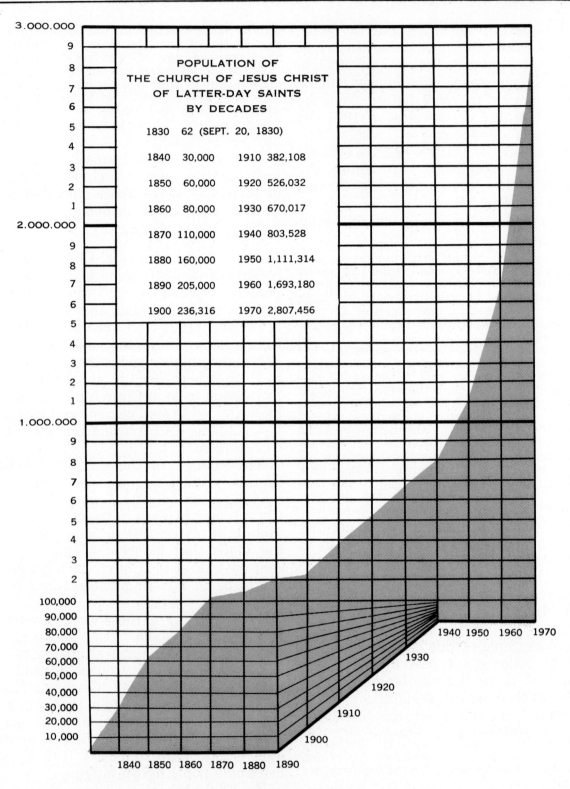

POPULATION OF
THE CHURCH OF JESUS CHRIST
OF LATTER-DAY SAINTS
BY DECADES

1830   62 (SEPT. 20, 1830)

1840   30,000   1910 382,108

1850   60,000   1920 526,032

1860   80,000   1930 670,017

1870   110,000   1940 803,528

1880   160,000   1950 1,111,314

1890   205,000   1960 1,693,180

1900   236,316   1970 2,807,456

ada, Great Britain, New Zealand, Uruguay, Peru, Chile, Guatemala, South Africa, Samoa, Tonga, Japan, Korea, and the Philippines. The Church program was truly being carried to the world.

Changes in Occupations

The rapid growth of the Church has been marked by a rapid change in the occupations of its members. From an agricultural base in the early days of the Church when 90 percent of the people lived in farming areas, the situation had changed by 1972 until only about 10 percent of the Church membership in the United States were engaged in agricultural pursuits. Members who had moved from the farms during the depression of the thirties rarely returned to them but found new jobs in industry or the professions. Most of the new converts were from nonagricultural areas. The occupational changes in the Church members gave rise to increased interest in education and in the arts.

Missionary Work

Missionary work, which had been increasing all during the twentieth century was accelerated in the sixties. The number of full-time missionaries in 1964 rose to twelve thousand, with another approximate six thousand in local missions. The number of converts per year rose 400 percent from 1955 to 1960. In 1963 there were 105,210 converts. Indications are for a continual increase in missionary activity.

A new energy seemed to pervade the Church. Attendance at Church meetings rose to surprising levels, and tithes increased proportionately.

This increased loyalty of Church members made possible an extensive building program, which extended into the mission fields, even into foreign lands. A new phase of this program was the erection of Church chapels and schools by labor missionaries who were called to donate their time and labor without recompense in the service of the Church. Under such a program, colleges and other schools were erected in Hawaii, New Zealand, Samoa, and Tonga. Following the same pattern, an extensive chapel-building program was initiated in England, the European missions, the South American missions, and in the islands of the sea.

Meeting the Problems of Today

Rapid growth also gave rise to changes in the Church to meet the growing problems. Additional Assistants to the Twelve Apostles were called to help in setting in order the affairs of the stakes and missions; financial aides were established to handle the details of business matters; and the Building Department of growing dimensions was established to handle the details of the vast building program. To house the needed administrative offices and Church services a huge building, launched in 1961 and completed in 1972, will make Church headquarters one of the great church administrative centers of the world.

As the second half of the twentieth century got under way new frontiers of power and influence were being penetrated by members of the Church. The Mormons were rapidly attaining national and international prominence for their achievements in politics, athletics, business and industry and several other fields. A general renaissance in art, literature, music, and drama arose in the Church, parts and aspects of which sometimes received wide recognition and held promise of greater cultural attainments in the future.

For the first time in the history of the Church, goodly numbers of men of

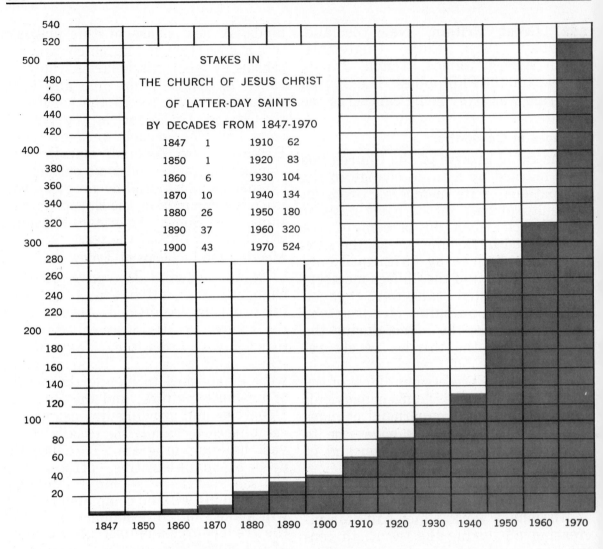

STAKES IN
THE CHURCH OF JESUS CHRIST
OF LATTER-DAY SAINTS
BY DECADES FROM 1847-1970

Year	Stakes	Year	Stakes
1847	1	1910	62
1850	1	1920	83
1860	6	1930	104
1870	10	1940	134
1880	26	1950	180
1890	37	1960	320
1900	43	1970	524

wealth appeared, accompanied by a remarkable spirit of Christ that led to generous giving to their fellowmen and the cause of the kingdom.

The Saints also were living longer and seemed to be freer from disease than their average contemporaries. The death rate by 1971 had sunk to a low of 4.92 per thousand, and the birth rate had risen to 28.50 per thousand.

The Latter-day Saints had become so intermingled with the world by the middle of the twentieth century that many factors affecting the nations as a whole began to have a marked effect upon them. Thus, the Saints followed in large measure the style of the world in clothing, entertainment, literature, mechanical equipment, etc. Other worldly trends were also reflected by such things as increased divorce rate, especially among those married outside the temples of God. To hold the youth of the Church to the faith and practices of their fathers, the educational program of the Church was accelerated. Seminaries and institutes of religion were established wherever concentrations of Saints were found. Church colleges were expanded and the program of the Mutual Improvement Association improved.

The Living Prophets

Of foremost importance to the study of Church history is the effect each living prophet of God has had upon his generation. Each appears to have been chosen of God because of his preparation to meet the problems of his day. The Prophet Joseph Smith laid the enduring foundations. The Prophet Brigham Young preserved the Church in isolation and built a great religious commonwealth in the Rocky Mountain wilderness. The Prophet John Taylor led a defense of this commonwealth against a nation bent on its destruction or modification. The Prophet Wilford Woodruff preserved the Church from political and economic disaster when defense was no longer feasible. The Prophet Lorenzo Snow redefined and redirected the program and goals of the Church to make possible its survival and in doing so ushered in a new era of Church history. The Prophet Joseph F. Smith implemented this new program and by his patience and kindliness began the process by which the Church has come to a position of respectability before a critical world. These great prophets belonged to the first century of the Church. All had known the Prophet Joseph. All but Joseph F. Smith had been his close associates.

The next president and prophet of the Church, President Heber J. Grant, stood astride the first and second centuries of the Church's existence. During his twenty-seven years as the living prophet of God he cemented together the achievements of the past and initiated temporal and spiritual growth in preparation for the great progress of the future.

Heber J. Grant became president of the Church on November 23, 1918, four days after the death of President Joseph F. Smith. Several things marked the period of his leadership: the steady growth of the Church, the attaining of financial stability that survived the long depression of the thirties, the building of temples and many other church buildings, and the development of the Church welfare program.

Membership between 1918 and 1945 grew from 600,000 to 900,000. The number of stakes grew from 75 to 150. During the years following World War I the people became prosperous, the tithes increased, and the activities of the Church, especially in providing temples and other buildings, expanded. The inspiration with which President Grant prepared for the depression years, which he felt would surely come, saved the Church from seriously curtailing its program. From 1918 to 1930 part of the tithes of the Church were placed in reserves, invested largely in real estate close to the Church center. When the great depression struck and the tithes of the Church dwindled, the Church reserves enabled the Church to maintain its missionary program, its temples, and its schools. Out of these years came the realization that the Church had a responsibility to help its members by organizing them to provide for themselves. While the nation turned to the national capital for help, the Church resisted the idea of a government dole and organized the members to provide jobs, food, and clothing for themselves. Out of the experience came the Church welfare program, not merely to meet one crisis, but to meet continuing needs on an individual and Church basis. It became a permanent program in the Church, the agency for promoting extraordinary cooperation in meeting material needs, as well as building bonds of love and concern among the members.

President George Albert Smith

On May 21, 1945, following the death of President Grant a week earlier, George Albert Smith became president of the Church. During the six years that followed, the Church continued its remarkable growth. It was a period when goodwill prevailed. President Smith won the love of his own people and the respect and goodwill of the non-Mormons he encountered. Membership in the Church grew from slightly over 900,000 to more than one million.

President David O. McKay

It was said in 1970 that more than half the members of the Church had known no other president than David O. McKay. So fast did the Church grow during his leadership from 1951 to 1970 that the membership more than doubled, increasing from 1,111,000 to nearly three million. The number of stakes increased from 180 to 400. When he became the prophet of God, he had been uniquely trained to provide effective leadership for a rapidly expanding worldwide Church membership which necessitated a more cosmopolitan outlook on the part of the Church. In that day God timely raised up a prophet adaptable to the revolutionary change that could provide many nations of the earth with wards, stakes and temples, visits of the prophet and other General Authorities and the full Church program.

President Joseph Fielding Smith

President of the Church for a shorter period of time than any of his predecessors, this prophet of the Lord left a remarkable record of achievement.[10] His hands upheld by two very able counselors, Harold B. Lee and N. Eldon Tanner, this great prophet, who had also been uniquely trained, brought

[10] See *Ensign*, Aug. 1972, pp. 40-41.

about a revolutionary extension of Church services to its members. Health, social, literary, educational, and many other charitable services are being innovatively reorganized and/or expanded. He dedicated two temples and inaugurated the first regional conference of the Church, in Manchester, England. This probably was the first of what will prove to be a lasting practice of holding regional general conferences throughout the world and could well be an additional important step in internationalizing the Church. Programs started by his predecessor, President David O. McKay, such as the correlation program, family home evening, and home teaching, were pushed with vigor. He initiated a reorganization of the Church educational program. A Church commissioner of education was chosen and all Church schools were brought under his leadership.

President Harold B. Lee

The Church in the 1970s faced its greatest challenge—to reach and amalgamate into one great brotherhood the many races and cultures accepting the word of God. The task was a staggering one, for it involved the development of unity in separation. No longer were the converts being gathered from many lands into one central area which could become the melting pot of nationality that prevailed in the early days of the Church. But the Church was being set up in separate lands, in the midst of cultures and customs differing from one another and often antagonistic to Church standards. The problems of language barriers and the dearth of translated materials intensified the problem. To meet these problems the Lord called another prophet of vision—a prophet attuned to the voice of the Master. On October 6, 1972, the Priest-

GRAPHIC MAP SHOWING THE EXODUS OF THE MORMON PIONEERS IN 1847, WITH DAILY STOPPING PLACES OF BRIGHAM YOUNG'S COMPANY

hood and general membership of the Church in solemn assembly in Salt Lake City, Utah, unanimously sustained their new prophet. The Church was again under the leadership of a man who had been tempered and trained by long experience to lead it toward its increasingly remarkable destiny. Characteristic of all of these men was the fact that they denied that they had been able to do anything worthwhile apart of the sustaining influence and power of God. Their greatness was the greatness of God and they denied that it could be otherwise.

The Church Moves Onto the International Scene

". . . God had a work for me to do; and that my name should be had for good and evil among all nations, kindreds, and tongues, or that it should be both good and evil spoken of among all people."[11]

The above prophecy from the Angel Moroni to a young man of eighteen, Joseph Smith, in the year 1823 must have seemed sobering and the vision of the future of the Church quite astounding. Even in the depths of despair over the plight of his people, as he lay in prison in Missouri in the bitter winter of 1838-39, the Lord reminded him:

"How long can rolling waters remain impure? What power shall stay the heavens? As well might man stretch forth his puny arm to stop the Missouri river in its decreed course, or to turn it up stream, as to hinder the Almighty from pouring down knowledge from heaven upon the heads of the Latter-day Saints."[12]

The events which transpired in the second century of the Church's existence mark the literal fulfullment of the original prophecy and vision referred to above. The progress of the Church has erased most artificial barriers so that it can embrace all peoples and cultures.

As the Church in its second century emerged as a world church, thoughtful men began to recognize its great force. A non-Mormon student of history observed:

"The story of the changing image of the Mormons is one . . . of the literal triumphs of education over prejudice . . . yet they have survived a library of abuse and are today not only an accepted but an admired and respected people."[13]

Two conditions were important in bringing the Church to its new position in the world. These were the developments in communication and in transportation. After centuries during which communication by voice was limited to a few hundred feet, almost instantaneously a voice could be heard around the world. The development of the telephone, the radio, television—the speed with which happenings in the world could be brought to man's attention in a matter of hours or even minutes—made it possible for ideas to be quickly disseminated, for ignorance and misunderstanding gradually to give way to an enlightenment. The exploration of outer space and the use of satellites opened a new era of communication. Conference addresses and images of the speakers were now transmitted by satellite and by radio and television to the ends of the earth. The voice of the Lord through his servants was being heard from the air. Iron and bamboo curtains, long a barrier to communication, were being broken down as inef-

---

[11]Joseph Smith 2:33.
[12]D&C 121:33.

[13]L. H. Kirkpatrick, "Utah in the Eyes of the Nation", *Utah Educational Review*, January 1, 1962.

fectual in preventing communication between peoples. One man could now speak to millions at one time. A few could teach the world.

The change during the latter part of the twentieth century was not to be limited to the speedy dissemination of ideas and images. Men could now travel at high speeds to all parts of the earth. General Authorities of the Church and heads of auxiliary organizations could in the matter of a few hours be meeting with the Saints in a distant land and in an equally short time be back at Church headquarters in conference with their respective quorums or boards. It was no longer necessary for a General Authority, in order to preside over the missions and stakes in a distant area of the earth, to reside there. He could now preside from Church headquarters and be in continual touch with the First Presidency and with his own quorum.

Members of the Church all over the world now found themselves acquainted with the voice and the person of the living prophet, other prophets, seers and revelators, and other General Authorities, and a unity was created never before possible.

Missionary work accelerated. Missionaries no longer found it nesessary to spend months in reaching or returning from their fields of labor but within a matter of hours could reach any mission on earth. Further, within the mission itself, the use of automobiles and other forms of transportation doubled and redoubled the number of contacts.

Changes Brought About by Church Growth

The test of an organization is often its ability to adjust to growth. In the case of The Church of Jesus Christ of Latter-day Saints the adjustment has been made smoothly and effectively.

Without losing or altering the basic organization given by revelation in the beginning of the Church, the organization and functions of the Priesthood and its auxiliaries have proved flexible enough to respond to the needs of a Church with many millions of members, and the pattern followed seems adequate for the future. The secret lies in the nature of the Holy Priesthood wherein under the direction of a living prophet, men holding the Melchizedek Priesthood may be called and given the authority to function in any needed capacity as directed, as assistants to the General Authorities of the Church. Thus in 1941 President Heber J. Grant called five high priests to be Assistants to the Twelve. This group of men has been maintained and enlarged under succeeding presidents. In 1967 President David O. McKay called sixty-nine high priests to be Regional Representatives of the Twelve. Traveling throughout the world these men have brought uniformity into Church practices by becoming teachers of local authorities, and their duties and authority are enlarged as needed to keep the Church in order.

On June 28, 1972, twenty-nine high priests were called as Mission Representatives of the Twelve to give aid and assistance to mission presidents. With tens of thousands of elders, seventies, and high priests in the Church there is a vast reservoir of leaders available on call to extend the arm of the Church over the world, and this without change to the basic organization.

Assistants to the quorum of the First Presidency were called in the past by Joseph Smith, Jr., and by Brigham Young to meet the needs of their times. In 1965 David O. McKay called two men, Joseph Fielding Smith and Thorpe B. Isaacson, as assistants to the First

Presidency. In 1968 Elder Isaacson was replaced by Alvin R. Dyer. Joseph Fielding Smith did not call any assistants to the First Presidency, and President Harold B. Lee and his counselors, N. Eldon Tanner and Marion G. Romney, have called no assistants to this date (1972).

The Correlation Program

To keep all the lines of Church activity under the direction and authority of the Priesthood and to avoid useless duplication of efforts, the Church organized a correlation committee of the General Authorities with subcommittees as needed. The Priesthood Executive Committee, established in 1967 with Harold B. Lee of the Council of Twelve as chairman, showed a vigor and vision that had a profound effect upon every aspect of the Church program. Correlation of Church activities under the Priesthood proved to be a continuing need and with changes in personnel as circumstances required, the committee gradually assumed an important and perhaps permanent function in the Church.

Changes Brought About by Social Conditions

The Lord is concerned with the temporal as well as the spiritual welfare of all his children; and the Church, which is the arm of the Lord in the earth must reflect that concern.

The obligation of the church of Jesus Christ was made plain by the Prophet Joseph Smith, who inaugurated plans for consecration of property for the welfare of the whole and the development of cooperatives for production and distribution. It was manifest in his concern for the health of his people; in his promulgation of the Lord's word on foods, cleanliness, recreation; in his organization of the Women's Relief Society; in his plans for cities of Zion.

Nor has the Church ever lost sight of this obligation to its people.

In the latter part of the twentieth century there occurred a reawakened concern for the welfare of Church members. This revival of interest was heightened as the Church reached out to its underprivileged members in various parts of the world and came to acknowledge changing social conditions in all lands.

In February, 1970, the Department of Social Welfare was reorganized, uniting under one head the activities of the Church which were intended to cope with economic and social problems of the members.

In April, 1970, the establishment of the Department of Inservice Training for those in military assignments was effected.

On June 6, 1970, Church magazines were changed in both name and structure and correlated with other Church activities, and the changes went into effect in January, 1971.

In July, 1970, the Department of Health was organized to extend professional help to Church members throughout the world.

Management of the fourteen Church-operated hospitals was consolidated in 1972 into a single cohesive and smoothly functioning unit under the Health Services Corporation. This corporation, functioning under the Presiding Bishopric, is managed by the Church Commissioner of Health with three associate commissioners and administrators the health program of the Church throughout the world.

On August 6, 1972, the Department of Physical Facilities was established.

In 1972 the Department of Internal Communications and the Department of External Communications were established.

On July 24, 1972, the first technical and professional missionaries were called to train members of the Church in underprivileged societies in matters of health. economics, etc.

The picture of the world in the latter part of the twentieth century was one of tremendous Church activity, but by contrast also a period of moral decay over much of the world. Crime, abuse of drugs, atheism, breakup of homes, and wars in many lands presented a challenge to the Church such as it had not faced before in this dispensation. To meet this challenge the Church launched a program to strengthen the home by instituting a revitalized home-teaching program and by promoting a Family Home Evening throughout the Church. These programs combat the above evils by promoting unity in the home and love and understanding of the gospel of Jesus Christ.

The First Presidency and Quorum of the Twelve were freed from many detailed administrative responsibilities, so as to allow more time for the consideration of overall Church policies and for giving direction to the Priesthood leadership of the Church at all levels.

The Expansion of the Church in
Latin America

The growth of the Church in Central and South America in the 1960s and 1970s was little less than phenomenal. Missionary work in South America dates back to 1851 when Elder Parley P. Pratt, his wife and Elder Rufus Allen disembarked in Valparaiso, Chile, where they remained for seven months, but owing to a revolution then in progress and the restrictive laws pertaining to religious freedom, little could be accomplished, and they returned to California in May 1852.

The next attempt to open missionary work in Latin America was in 1875 when the Mexican Mission was opened under the presidency of Anthony W. Ivins in the state of Chihuahua. They experienced limited success. In 1877 a mission was sent to Mexico City under the direction of Elder Moses Thatcher. A small branch was organized. In 1880 a Mormon colony was established in Colonia Juarez and the nearby valley in the state of Chihuahua, but little missionary work was done at that time.

The missions in Mexico continued during the period of internal political strife beginning in 1921. In 1926 the Mexican government decided to enforce an old constitutional amendment barring foreigners from active ministerial work. Church missionaries had to be withdrawn. The Catholic Church resisted the law, and civil war resulted. The government won. The only missionary work which could be carried on by the Church would depend on members who had been born in Mexico, chiefly from the Juarez Stake.

In 1940 missionaries were again sent from the stakes under an agreement with Mexican officials that they enter as tourists and stay for only six-month periods.

The growth in Church membership began slowly at first, then accelerated during the 1960s and early 1970s. By 1972 there were nearly 90,000 members in Mexico and more than 120,000 in Mexico and Central America combined. In August, 1972, the General Authorities held an area general conference in Mexico City attended by over 16,000 members. Members from eight stakes and seven missions in Mexico and Central America received the word of the Lord for the first time directly from a living Prophet. The future of the Church in Mexico and Central America is bright.

In 1925 Elder Rey L. Pratt was called to assist Elder Melvin J. Ballard and Rulon S. Wells in opening a mission in Buenos Aires, Argentina. The mission lasted only eleven months. Elder Ballard said of the work:

"The work will go slowly for a time just as an oak grows slowly from an acorn—not shoot up in a day as does the sunflower that grows quickly and thus dies. But thousands will join the church here. It will be divided into more than one mission, and will be one of the strongest in the Church. The work here is the smallest it will ever be. The day will come when the Lamanites here will get their chance. The South American Mission is to be a power in the Church."[14]

This prophecy was remarkable considering the discouragements facing those early missions. Its fulfillment has been even more remarkable. In 1947 the Uruguayan Mission was opened with Frederick S. Williams as president. Then in 1961 the South American Mission was opened in Argentina by President A. Theodore Tuttle. By that year there were five missions operating in South America, which were soon increased to seven; the Brazilian, South Brazilian, Uruguayan, Andean, Chilean, Argentine, and South Argentine. In Mexico the mission started in Mexico City grew to five missions, with two more, the Guatamala–El Salvador and the Central-American to the south of Mexico.

By 1973 (see *Ensign* Sept., 1972) the membership of the Church in Mexico and Central and South America had increased to 250,000. With the astonishing growth of the Church in the Latin American countries, some were predicting that by the end of the century more than half the members of the Church might well be Spanish-speaking.

Education Follows the Church in Latin America

The missionary leads the investigator to hear or read the message and pray to the Lord for the confirmation of the Spirit. This confirmation of the Spirit leads to baptism. At this point the missionary leaves him, and it remains for the Church to give further guidance and lead him into activity. In the early days of the Church this necessary instruction and Church activity could be had only by gathering the scattered converts to a central Zion. With the spread of the Gospel throughout the world and the rapid conversion in many lands, the gathering of the Saints to one central Zion became impractical if not impossible. Consequently the Church with all its functions had to be taken to them. This is being done. In many lands wards and stakes are being organized which form, as it were, gathering places to strengthen and hold the Church members. In many of the lands where the mission's success is greatest, especially in the Latin American countries, educational opportunities for Church members is being made available and requests to the General Authorities to set up Church schools are numerous. The needs have been for both secular and religious training. The Church is making a vigorous response. In the 1960s and 1970s private Church schools were organized in many lands.

In Mexico thirty-four private elementary schools, six high schools, and one school on the higher level, Benemerito at Mexico City, were established. By 1972, 8,000 students were receiving secular schooling in Church schools. But this was only part of the program. Seminaries and institutes of religion were established separate from the secular training but paralleling and supplementing it. By 1972 there were more than 15,000 seminary students in Mexico and Central America.

In South America secular education

---

[14] Conference Report, A. Theodore Tuttle, April 1962, p. 121.

was started by the Church in Chile with four schools, and the movement promised to spread to other countries where the Church is being firmly established.

The reason for establishing secular schools lies in the fact that the awakening countries south of the United States cannot supply enough schools for an expanding population, and numerous children have no school opportunities at all.

The policy of the Church has been to provide secular education where the state cannot supply it and to withdraw from secular education whenever and wherever public schools become adequate. In the matter of religious education the Church policy is to establish seminaries and institutes of religion wherever the Church members are found. The development of home-study seminaries and institutes of religion in addition to the regular seminary classes has enabled the Church Department of Seminaries and Institutes to encircle the globe. Starting in 1964 in Mexico and extending into Central and South America in 1969-70 seminaries were established in all wards and stakes and in some missions. By 1972 there were seminaries in Mexico, Guatemala, El Salvador, Costa Rica, Panama, Ecuador, Argentina, Brazil, Chile, and Uruguay. In 1972 seminaries were extended to Bermuda, Bolivia, Canada, Paraguay, Peru, Venezuela and Colombia.

The total number of seminary students by the end of the 1971-72 school year had reached some 7,000 in countries of South America.

The Church in Asia

The story of the expansion of the Church in Asia would fill volumes, but they would be concentrated in depicting what has happened in the 1960s and 1970s, for in those years what had for-

merly seemed improbable, if not impossible, took place.

In August, 1852, only five years after the first Mormon pioneers arrived in Utah, President Brigham Young called the first Latter-day Saint missionaries to labor in Asia. Of the missionaries assigned to Asia, nine were called to Calcutta, India, four to Siam (presently Thailand), and four to China.

Heber C. Kimball of the First Presidency instructed missionaries called at the special conference:

"I say to those who are elected to go on missions, go, if you never return, and commit what you have into the hands of God— your wives, your children, your brethren and your property.

"The missions we will call for during this conference are generally not to be very long ones; probably three to seven years will be as long as any man will be absent from his family.

"If any of the Elders refuse to go, they may expect that their wives will not live with a man a day, who would refuse to go on a mission."[15]

Despite the spirit in which the missionaries assigned to Asiatic countries set forth on their long and tedious journey, all of these missions ended in failure. It is not known whether the missionaries made a single convert in China during this mission, and the other missions failed to set up a single branch.

Early in the morning of August 12, 1901, three men and a boy sailed into Tokyo Bay aboard the *Empress of India*. Heber J. Grant, the leader, had been assigned to open a mission in Japan. With him were Elders Horace S. Ensign, Louis A. Kelsch, and Alma O. Taylor, a young man of nineteen. Thus began the first established mission in Asia, but there was little initial success. Closed by order of President Heber J. Grant in 1924, the mission had

[15]Heber C. Kimball, Tabernacle Address of August 28, 1852.

had seven presidents, a total of eighty-eight missionaries, and only 166 baptisms.

In the winter of 1921, David O. McKay of the Council of the Twelve, in company with Elder Hugh Cannon, traveled through eastern Asia on a special mission for the Church. These elders traveled in Japan, Korea, and China and dedicated China for the preaching of the Gospel.

As early as 1902 Elder Charles W. Penrose of the Council of Twelve predicted:

"We shall find, I believe with all my heart, that the opening of the Japanese mission will prove the key to the entrance of the Gospel in the Orient. We will find that an influence will go out from Japan into other oriental nations. The ice has been broken, and the barriers will be removed from the way, and the Gospel will spread into other eastern nations."[16]

In 1937 the Japanese Mission was reopened with headquarters in Honolulu, Hawaii, but it was not until after the great shakeup of World War II that real success began in the Far East.

As related by Dr. Spencer Palmer, a former missionary in the Far East and a president of the Korean Mission, in a summary made in 1970:

Japan now has over twelve thousand members of the Church. There are four thousand in Korea, nearly six thousand in the Philippines, some four thousand in Hong Kong, and more than that in Taiwan. Beginnings have been made in Thailand, Singapore, and Indonesia. There are strong Latter-day Saint congregations in Okinawa, and a nucleus of Vietnamese have come into the Church. Mormon servicemen in Korea laid the foundation for the Church there, and it is hoped that when peace comes to Vietnam the gospel may be spread among that people. In Vietnam, the servicemen are helping construct chapels and making friends and converts for the Church. There are three districts of Latter-day Saint servicemen in

Vietnam, and some Vietnamese converts have already been ordained to the Melchizedek Priesthood. Latter-day Saint military personnel are also in Thailand, where more than a score full-time missionaries are laboring.

On October 29, 1969, the islands of Indonesia, with 130 million people, were dedicated for the preaching of the gospel, and the work has started with a few missionaries in Djakarta.

Singapore, dedicated for missionary work in May of 1969, has two branches with over three hundred average attendance. A new Southeast Asian mission has been established with headquarters in Singapore.[17]

Kazuo Imai—Asia's First Bishop

At 1:30 p.m., March 15, 1970, a new era opened as, under the hands of Elder Gordon B. Hinckley of the Council of the Twelve, Kazuo Imai, 40, was ordained Asia's first bishop and set apart as bishop of the newly created Tokyo Ward. He was followed in order by Yasuhiro Matsushita, Tokyo Second Ward; Ryuichi Inouye, Tokyo Third; Kiyoshi Sakai, Tokyo Fourth; Noboru Kamizo, Tokyo Fifth; and Genya Asama, Yokohama Ward.

Bishop Imai is typical of a generation of Japanese that saw a world and a religion turned upside down. As a teenager he lived eight months in and out of bomb shelters watching Tokyo leveled and burned. He learned to hate America.

Then came the occupation and an understanding that Americans were not evil, that the Japanese militarists had been wrong, that the emperor was not divine, that Shinto was not a true religion.

"War was horrible," he recalled, "But through it the Lord prepared Japan for the Gospel. I have found the

[16]Penrose, Conference Report, April 6, 1902, p. 52.

[17]Spencer J. Palmer, The Church Encounters Asia, (Salt Lake City, Utah: Deseret Book Co., 1970) p. 4.

true purpose of life. I pray I can help others find and live it."[18]

The work of the Lord is moving forth in Asia. The Church is passing through an era of unprecedented growth in that part of the world. The number of baptisms doubles each year.

In 1970 the Church set up a pavilion in Expo 70, the world fair in Japan, and some seven million people passed through the Latter-day Saints' exhibit area. Hundreds of thousands left names and addresses inviting further contacts from the missionaries.

In early 1970 two new missions were formed in Japan. A new Tokyo Stake of Zion, the first in Asia was established March 15, 1970. A stake was organized in Manila in 1972.

Christianity as taught by Catholic and Protestant churches is not new in Asia, and Latter-day Saint missionaries profit from the fact that many families have a knowledge of the Bible —but it is the restored Church of Jesus Christ which is destined to touch most deeply the lives of the teeming millions.

The seminary and institute program is following the Church into Asia. Although seminary classes were held for some years for English-speaking youth at U.S. military bases, it was not until the 1971-72 school year that seminaries were opened for Japanese members in the Japanese language. In that school year seminary enrollments rose to 950 in Japan, and this increased to some three thousand in the fall of 1972. Institute students were enrolled in Japan by 1972 numbering 1,430 with another 623 institute students in Korea. In 1971-72 seminary students numbered twenty-nine in Okinawa, and forty in Hong Kong. In the fall of 1972

[18]*Church News*, April 25, 1970, p. 10.

seminaries were begun in the Philippines.

The Strength of Mormonism

The Church of Jesus Christ of Latter-day Saints has shown to the world fruits worthy of its existence and by their fruits shall all institutions upon the earth be judged. A Church worthy of perpetuation must lead its members into a finer development and a happier way of living; it must possess a heaven-sent message for mankind and a vitality sufficient to carry that message to the world.

Three things attest the strength of Mormonism as it enters its second century. First, there is great missionary zeal. Never at any time in the history of the Church has the gospel been preached to more people than in the present era. Missionary methods have changed. The missionary uses visual methods of presentation as well as dialogue. Modern methods of communication — radio, television, filmstrip projectors, movies, etc. — have aided in conveying the message of the Church. Church information centers, the Tabernacle Choir, singing groups in various centers of the Church, displays in world fairs, world tours of entertainers and athletes from Church colleges have all aided in attracting the attention of people to the Church and have served to open doors to the missionary and his message.

As the Church has rapidly developed into a worldwide institution, it has attracted men and women of influence. Many of its members have come to be recognized as business leaders, educators, scientists, statesmen, artists, musicians, and craftsmen, all of whom become missionaries by example and by bearing testimony to their fellowmen.

An institution possessed of such a missionary spirit has a strength greater than mere numbers. In an age of doubt where members of many churches seem to lose the faith, The Church of Jesus Christ of Latter-day Saints has shown increased vigor in proclaiming the divinity of Jesus Christ and the place of his gospel in an enlightened world.

Second, the members of the Church continue to pay their tithes. A tithe-paying people are a great people. The Lord God said unto his people in ancient times:

"Bring ye all the tithes into the storehouse, that there may be meat in mine house, and prove me now herewith, saith the Lord of hosts, if I will not open to you the windows of heaven, and pour you out a blessing, that there shall not be room enough to receive it.[19]

That promise has had a modern-day fulfillment.

One does not part easily with one-tenth of his income unless prompted by a testimony that God lives and that the Church is his divinely established institution. So the payments of tithes becomes a measuring-stick for the deep, underlying strength of the Church, which lies in the testimony of its people. It must not be supposed from the above that all the Mormon people pay their tithes—far from it. Such an ideal has never been achieved in the history of the doctrine. The lack of belief by some in this principle of voluntary cooperation in God's work, is one of the disturbing factors in the Church. But the facts are—and these are important—the number of honest tithepayers within the Church runs into the hundreds of thousands—a greater number than at any previous period of the Church. This barometer of faith is rising, not falling.

Third, the work of the Church is being done by volunteers. Out of a membership of 3,200,000 in 1972, nearly 450,000 are either officers or teachers in the Church. For their work they receive but one form of remuneration, the joy of service. Multitudinous as these offices and duties in the Church have become, there still remains an overabundance of Church members willing to volunteer their services.

A church which can ask and receive the services of four hundred thousand members to carry on its functions without cost; a church which can keep from fifteen to twenty thousand missionaries in the field at their own expense or that of their families; a church which, in this day, can continue to collect millions in voluntary tithes from its people is a church which the whole world must acknowledge as a mighty institution. Such is the strength of The Church of Jesus Christ of Latter-day Saints.

All three of these evidences of strength are but an index to a vital living faith. Mere figures and numbers do not indicate the greatness of a church. Its greatness lies in individual testimony. The apostle Paul, possessed of a mighty faith, could, singlehanded, change the religion of the Mediterranean world. And it is the same faith which prompts the members of the Church today, with Paul of old, to say, "I am not ashamed of the gospel of Jesus Christ, for it is the power of God unto salvation."

Supplementary Readings

1. *Conference Report*, Apr. 1930 "Centennial Address of the First Presidency of the Church to All the World."

2. Roberts, *A Comprehensive History of the Church*, vol. 6, pp. 559-573. ("Address of the First Presidency at the Centennial Conference of the Church, April 6th, 1930.")

[19]Malachi 3:10.

3. *Ensign*, Aug. 1972. Entire issue is devoted to life and accomplishments of President Joseph Fielding Smith.

4. *Ensign*, Sept. 1972. Entire issue is devoted to growth of the Church in Mexico and Central America.

5. Spencer J. Palmer, *The Church Encounters Asia* (Salt Lake City, Utah: Deseret Book Co., 1970).

CHAPTER 40

TEMPLES OF GOD

A Visit to an L. D. S. Temple

"In the elder days of art
  Builders wrought with greatest care
Each minute and unseen part;
  For the Gods see everywhere."

One who visits the Temple Block at Salt Lake City sees the embodiment of the above sentiment wrought in imperishable stone. The great grey Temple of God, which dominates that historic inclosure, is one of the finest structures in the world, and as a monument of sacrifice and devotion it has no equal.

The visitor who views the Temple from the outside is impressed by its massive appearance and magnificent proportions. His eyes invariably are raised to the three great spires surmounting either end of the building, and his gaze lingers upon the gold figure of the Angel whose feet rest lightly upon the highest stone of the Temple, and who has a trumpet raised to his lips as if to blow a mighty signal to the people of the world. The representation is of the Angel Moroni, announcing to mankind the restoration of the gospel of Jesus Christ. It is the work of a Utah son, C. E. Dallin, whose fame as a sculptor has been widely heralded.

There is a great story connected with the building of those granite walls, which never grows old in the telling. It covers many years of time, involves the account of many lives, and the toil of many hands. And inside those walls is told the most beautiful story in all the world, for it is God's story of love for his children which has its beginning before the earth was formed and has no ending.

Could we have stood upon that plot of ground in July of 1847, we would have witnessed a patch of grey sage, intersected by a sparkling stream, the hazy purple of the mountains in the west and the blue vault of sky overhead. Perhaps that is all we would have seen. But one man stood upon that spot in that very month and year who saw more than sage and stream and mountain and sky. That man was a Prophet of God, the leader of the Mormon people, who upon that occasion saw through a Prophet's eyes the vision of the future. On April 6, 1853, Brigham Young says of that vision:

"I scarcely ever say much about revelations, or visions, but suffice it to say, five years ago last July I was here and saw in the spirit the Temple not ten feet from where we have laid the chief cornerstone. I have not inquired what kind of a Temple we shall build. Why? Because it was presented before me. I never looked upon the ground, but the vision of it was there. I see it as plainly as if it was in reality before me. Wait until it is done, I will say, however, that it will have six towers, to begin with, instead of one. Now do not any of you apostatize because it will have six towers and Joseph built only one. It is easier for us to build sixteen, than it was for him to build one. The time will come when there will be one in the center of Temples we shall build, and, on the top, groves and fish ponds. But we shall not see them here at present."[1]

The occasion for the above remarks was the laying of the cornerstone of the Salt Lake Temple. What a heroic enterprise—a four million dollar structure commenced in a desert, while the

[1]Brigham Young, *Millennial Star*, Vol. 15, p. 488.

terrific struggle for existence was being waged, and by an impoverished people who, in the whole territory, numbered less than twenty thousand.

It took forty years of sacrifice and toil to complete the Temple. By the time of its final dedication April 6, 1893, three successive presidents of the Church had had a hand in its building, and the Church population in the territory had grown to hundreds of thousands.

Twice during that forty years the work came to a standstill. In 1857 the entire excavation was filled in and the mason work; which had not then risen above the ground, was completely covered up, the ground was plowed and the whole plot presented the appearance of a cultivated field. Johnston's army was approaching Utah, and the entire population was preparing to destroy their homes and move to the south.

Once again, with peace and understanding restored, the Saints removed the soil from the foundations of the temple and set to work again, only to have a second interruption. The foundations were found insufficiently solid for the massive weight which was to rest upon them. Brigham Young ordered the entire foundation reset, announcing to the people, "this Temple must stand through the millennium." And well might it stand for a thousand years, for the walls are built of solid granite blocks, and are sixteen feet thick at the foundation, tapering to six feet thick at the top.

During the days of construction the Temple Block, which had been inclosed by a massive twelve foot wall,[2] became a great workshop. The water of City Creek was converted into power, and air blast equipment, an iron foundry,

[2]Completed May 23, 1857.

and machine shops for metal and wood were operated.

Picture of Granite quarry in Little Cottonwood Canyon showing workmen cutting the giant slabs used in the construction of the Salt Lake Temple.

The granite for the building was obtained at the mouth of Little Cottonwood Canyon, twenty miles to the Southeast. There the elements of an earlier epoch had loosened huge blocks from the massive granite walls and deposited them at the mouth of the canyon. It was not necessary to quarry into the granite mountain mass. These boulders often weighed many tons and had to be divided by the use of hand drills, wedges, and low explosives. Even the broken stones often weighed several tons. These were hauled to Salt Lake City by ox teams, four or five yoke of oxen to a single stone. The round trip took three or four days.

The slowness with which the work progressed caused the Saints to look for easier means of transportation. It was finally decided to construct a canal from the mouth of Little Cottonwood Canyon to Salt Lake City, and to float the great stones to the Temple on barges rather than to haul them with ox teams. The canal was begun but, before many miles were constructed, the Saints received assurance that a transcontinental railway would be built through Salt Lake City. As the railway promised a better solution to their problem the Church contracted to construct a section of the road line through Salt Lake City. In that they were disappointed, but when the railroad was completed to Ogden, a branch line was soon run to Salt Lake City and then extended to the mouth of Little Cottonwood Canyon. The building of the Temple proceeded at a faster rate. Even then, when Brigham Young died in 1877, the great temple was only twenty feet above ground. The building continued during the troubled administration of President Taylor and was vigorously pushed to completion during the administration of President Woodruff.

Foundation of the Salt Lake Temple with view of the old and new Tabernacle in the background.
Used by permission, Utah State Historical Society

proposed roadbed, and work on the Temple during 1868-1869 almost ceased, as Mormon laborers worked feverishly to complete the railway. The Saints had urged the construction of the main rail-

Other Temples Erected

Before the Temple at Salt Lake City had been dedicated, three other temples had been completed. At St. George,

Picture showing the construction of the great Salt Lake Tabernacle.

Utah, a temple site was dedicated November 9, 1871. The Temple was completed in 1877, and the final dedication was held in connection with the forty-seventh annual conference of the Church held in the Temple April 6, 1877. The Temple was built of red sandstone.[3]

In the same year that the St. George Temple was completed, two other temple sites were dedicated.

The site for the Logan Temple was dedicated May 17, 1877, and the completed Temple dedicated May 17, 1884.

The site for the Manti Temple was dedicated April 25, 1877, and the completed structure dedicated May 21, 1888. The Temple built of cream colored oolite was erected upon a barren slope of rock. The beauty of the present

grounds attests the industry of the Mormon people in transporting soil for lawns and flowers. The cost was one million dollars.

All of these Temples were built in the days of poverty and represent the sacrifice and cooperation of a whole people. The spirit with which the work was carried on at each Temple is displayed in the words of Brigham Young at the dedication of the site for the Manti Temple:

"We intend building this temple for ourselves, and we are abundantly able to do it; therefore, no man need come here to work expecting wages for his services. The neighboring settlements will send their men, and they can be changed whenever, and as often as desirable; and they can get credit on labor tithing or on donation account for their services, and we expect them to work until this temple is completed without asking for wages. It is not in keeping with the character of Saints to make the building of temples a matter of merchandise.

"We want to rear this temple with clean

---

[3]The St. George temple is now painted white, making it conspicuous against the red sandstone of its surroundings.

hands and pure hearts, that we with our children, may enter into it to receive our washings and anointings, the keys and ordinances of our holy Priesthood, and also to officiate in the name of our fathers and mothers and our forefathers who lived and died without the gospel, that they with us may be made partakers of the fruits of the tree of life, and live and rejoice in our Father's kingdom. The gospel is free, its ordinances are free, and we are at liberty to rear this temple to the name of the Lord without charging anybody for our services.

"We call upon the sisters also to render what assistance they can in this matter. They can do a great deal by way of encouraging their husbands and sons, and also by making clothing of various kinds for them, and in otherwise providing for them while they are working here."[4]

During the administration of President Heber J. Grant, three new temples were completed. The Hawaiian Temple, commenced under the administration of President Joseph F. Smith in 1916, was dedicated November 27, 1919. This temple is one of the attractions of the Hawaiian Islands.

A temple at Cardston, Alberta, Canada, was begun September 15, 1915, and dedicated August 26, 1923.

On November 23, 1923, work was begun on a temple at Mesa, Arizona. The completed structure was dedicated October 23, 1927, the dedicatory services being broadcast over the entire countryside.

In the year 1939 work was begun on a temple at Idaho Falls, Idaho. By 1944 the temple had reached completion and was dedicated September 23, 1945.

On September 22, 1951, work was begun on a temple at Los Angeles, California. This magnificent temple was completed in 1955 and dedicated March 11, 1956. On August 5, 1953 ground was broken for a temple in Bern, Swit-

zerland. The temple construction was begun in December, 1953 and the temple finished and dedicated September 11, 1955.

On December 21, 1955, work was begun on a temple at Hamilton, New Zealand, and the temple was finished and dedicated on April 20, 1958.

On August 25, 1955, work was begun on a temple at New Chapel, England, and the temple was finished and dedicated on September 7, 1958.

On May 26, 1962, construction work was begun on a temple at Oakland, California, and the temple was completed and dedicated November 17, 1964.

Construction on the Ogden and Provo Temples was begun in September-November of 1969 and they were dedicated January 18-20, and February 9, 1972 respectively. A temple being built in Washington, D.C., is scheduled for completion in 1974.

Temple building by The Church of Jesus Christ of Latter-day Saints is just in its infancy. It is the belief of the Saints that temples will some day be numbered by the hundreds, and that a mighty work during the Millennium will be wrought in them.

In 1967 temple sites were chosen at Ogden and Provo, Utah and at Silver Springs, Maryland. The Ogden Temple was completed in 1971, and was dedicated on January 18, 1972. The Provo Temple was also completed in 1971 and was dedicated on February 9, 1972.

These new temples revolutionize ordinance work in regards to the time it takes companies to complete the endowment. The compactness of the new temples allow six companies of eighty to go through for their endowments at any one time. It is estimated that a session

---

[4]*Millennial Star*, Vol. 39, No. 24, June 11, 1877, p. 373.

ST. GEORGE TEMPLE, dedicated by Daniel H. Wells, April 6, 1877.

LOGAN TEMPLE, dedicated by President John Taylor, May 17, 1884.

SALT LAKE TEMPLE, dedicated by President Wilford Woodruff, April 6, 1893.

can be completed each hour and a half, thus 480 endowments may be given in this period of time. Approximately 3000 endowments can be given in these new temples each day. Some 700 temple workers are called to labor in each of these new temples which were constructed at a cost of four million dollars each.

The temple at Silver Springs, adjacent to the Capitol of the United States is larger than the other new temples. It is designed for the use of Latter-day Saints in the fast-growing stakes and missions east of the Mississippi. This temple will accommodate many thousands of temple workers each day. It will be ready for dedication during 1974.

Within the Temples of God

When we leave the interesting account of the building of temples we come to the most beautiful story of all—the story of what transpires inside the Temple walls. In that story lies the reasons for the mighty sacrifice of millions of dollars and millions of hours of toil which have gone toward the erection and maintenance of those Houses of God.

Every member of the Church in good standing may, on reaching adulthood, enter the temple and receive his or her endowments.

"The endowments given to members of the Church in the temples are, essentially, courses of instruction relative to man's existence before he came on this earth, the history of the creation of the earth, the story of our first earthly parents, the history of the various dispensations of the gospel, the meaning of the sacrifice of Jesus Christ, the story of the restoration of the gospel, and the means and methods whereby joy on this earth and exaltation in heaven may be obtained. To make this large story clear and impressive to all who partake of it every educational device, so far known to man is employed; and it is possible that nowhere outside of the temple, is a more correct pedagogy employed.

Every sense of man is appealed to, in order to make the meaning of the gospel clear, from beginning to end."[5]

Perhaps nothing in the Church is so little understood or appreciated by the general membership as the ritual and symbols connected with ordinance work in the Temple. The reasons for this lie in the lack of understanding of the gospel on the part of those entering the temple for ordinance work and the speed with which it has become necessary to officiate in those ordinances in order to accommodate the great numbers seeking to do temple work for the dead.

Several fundamentals must be grasped if the beauty of temples and temple work is to be fully appreciated. In the first place, a distinction must be kept in mind between the end sought—salvation, and the means used to help attain that end—ritual and symbols.

Salvation is sometimes termed a gift of God, but it is nonetheless an attainment of man. While man cannot reach salvation without God, God cannot extend salvation except as it is obtained by the growth of the individual. Man cannot attain salvation except through obedience to all law, for salvation means freedom from all pain, and the breaking of a law is always accompanied by a penalty. Hence the path to freedom is the path of obedience to the laws of progress, which are the laws of God. The law of human progress is the Gospel of Jesus Christ. Those who are brought to realize what that law is have a better opportunity to abide that law than others. Further, those who have taken solemn covenants to abide the laws of God are more apt to follow those laws than those who do not so covenant, or

---

[5]John A. Widtsoe, *A Rational Theology*, pp. 124-127.

if they transgress the laws are more anxious to repent of that transgression.

Further, those who by some device or symbol are constantly reminded of their covenants with God are more apt to keep those covenants than those who are not thus reminded.

These are fundamental principles of psychology and God, the Master of the science of psychology, has not overlooked them in his desire to bring to pass the immortality and eternal life of man.

So, in the temples of God, members of the Church may be instructed more fully in the eternal laws of God and enter into a solemn covenant with Him to keep His commandments, while receiving, at the hands of His ordained servants, a promise of the great blessings which will follow obedience to those covenants. This ordinance of entering into covenant with the Lord in His holy house is called the receiving of "endowments," that is, the recipient is endowed with blessings from God according to his obedience to the covenants. Here, again, a great psychological principle is used. A high jumper invariably jumps higher when a pole is placed for him to jump over than when he has no mark at which to aim. Similarly, people drift through life making less than their best efforts in righteousness because they have no understanding of the eternal and lasting joy which righteousness results in. God has decreed that His people build temples to His name and in them become acquainted with the blessings in store for the righteous, that, realizing them, they will strive to attain them.

In order to lead the person to be "endowed" into a realization of the laws of God, symbolism has been instituted by the great Master Teacher. From the time the recipient of the endowment

enters the temple until he emerges, every stage of his progress should, if he has a good preliminary knowledge of the gospel, impress upon him God's great plan for the salvation of men.

"The letters on the written page are but symbols of mighty thoughts that are easily transferred from mind to mind by these symbols. Man lives under a great system of symbolism. Clearly, the mighty, eternal truths encompassing all that man is, or may be, cannot be expressed literally, nor is there in the temple any attempt to do this. On the contrary, the great and wonderful temple service is one of mighty symbolism. By the use of symbols of speech, of action, of color, or form, the great truths connected with the story of man are made evident to the mind."[6]

The Lord has decreed that His House is the proper place for the revealing of His great promises unto men. In early days the Savior warned His disciples, "Give not that which is holy unto the dogs, neither cast ye your pearls before swine, lest they trample them under their feet and turn again and rend you."[7]

To a world not yet conversant with the complete gospel of Jesus Christ and to those who term themselves members of the Church but are equally ignorant of the plan of salvation, the symbolism used in the House of the Lord might appear mere foolishness. Just so the symbols of fraternal organizations appear ludicrous to the uninitiated who have not looked beyond the symbol to the principle represented.

As Church members grasp the beauty and harmony of the temple ordinances they resolve deep in their hearts to live truer and finer lives, that the rewards of righteousness might come to them.

Three great principles underlie the ordinances of God. *First*—God is no respecter of persons. The poor and the rich, the humble and the proud, who en-

[6]*Ibid.*, p. 126.
[7]*Matthew* 7:6.

ter the precincts of the Temple, don a uniform apparel that they might learn the first great principle—all men will be judged by the same law and all who attain salvation must present the same qualities worthy of salvation unto a just God.

Second—A man can be saved only so fast as he gains knowledge of the laws of God. This law of eternal progression is symbolized by a learning process during the endowment and without a mastery of which the recipient cannot advance.

Third—Salvation is obtained by obedience to the laws upon which such blessings are predicated. So the results of obedience and disobedience are symbolized that the recipient might never forget the importance of the great principle once stated by the great Prophet Samuel, "Behold, to obey is better than sacrifice and to hearken than the fat of rams."[8]

Temple work for the living and for the dead will be discussed in detail in a later chapter.

The story of temple work is a story of love—the love of God for man—and of men for each other.

"A life without love in it is like a heap of ashes upon a deserted hearth—with the fire dead, the laughter still, and the light extinguished. It is like a winter landscape—with the sun hidden, the flowers frozen, and the wind whispering through the withered leaves."[9]

Supplementary Readings

1. *Doctrine and Covenants*, Section 2 (Elijah to come).

2. *Ibid.*, Section 124:25-145. (Commanded to Build Temple. Ordinances.)

[8] *I Samuel* 15:22.
[9] *Improvement Era*, Vol. 32, p. 971. (Article by Frank P. Tibbetts.)

3. *Ibid.*, Section 110. (Vision in Kirtland Temple. Keys of Temple Work.)

4. *Ibid.*, Section 127:6-12; Section 126. (Baptism for the Dead.) *Ibid.*, Section 131, 132. (Marriage.)

5. *Book of Mormon*, I Nephi 5:16.

6. *Bible*, Mal. 4:5-6. (Elijah to come.)

7. *Ibid.*, I Cor. 15:29.

8. *Ibid.*, John 13:4-13.

9. Widtsoe, *Discourses of Brigham Young*, Chapter 36.

10. Widtsoe, *A Rational Theology*, Chapter 23. (Temple Ordinances.)

11. Joseph F. Smith, *Gospel Doctrine*, pp. 469-472. ("Work for the Dead." "Temple Ordinances Unchanged." "Care and Need of Temples." "Preaching the Gospel in the Spirit World.")

12. *Ibid.*, pp. 472-476. ("Vision of the Redemption of the Dead.")

13. Joseph Fielding Smith, *The Way to Perfection*. pp. 39-40. (Relief Prepared for the Dead.)

14. *Ibid.*, pp. 260-271. (The New Jerusalem and its Temple.)

15. *Ibid.*, pp. 322-327. ("Temple work in the Millennium.")

16. Roberts, *A Comprehensive History of the Church*, Vol. 2, pp. 133-136. (Temple Ritual Endowment Ceremonies.)

17. *Ibid.*, Vol. 6, pp. 230-236. ("Dedication of Manti and Salt Lake Temples." "Spiritual Manifestations During the Dedication of Manti Temple.")

18. James E. Talmage, *Articles of Faith*, pp. 153-156. (Temples, Ancient and Modern.)

19. James E. Talmage, *The House of the Lord*. (An entire book devoted to Temples and Temple work. Pictures of our temples all that were built when it was published are in this book.)

20. Evans, *Heart of Mormonism*, pp. 146; 325; 435; 406; 454; 479; 488; 500; 505. (On these pages are pictures of nine temples. See illustrations XI-XII.)

21. *Ibid.*, pp. 146-151. ("The House of God.")

22. *Ibid.*, pp. 406-410. ("A Four-Million-Dollar Temple in the Sage Brush.")

23. Smith, *Essentials in Church History*. See index for histories, facts and comments on Temple Work.

24. Harris and Butt, *Fruits of Mormonism*, pp. 105-115. (Marriage and Divorce. A Comparative Study.)

CHAPTER 41

A VITAL PROGRAM
FOR HAPPINESS

The Care of the Body

When the Savior announced to the world, "I am come that they might have life, and that they might have it more abundantly,"[1] He laid down the fundamental basis of true religion. Later, the Apostle James in defining religion for the churches in Asia, said:

"Pure religion and undefiled before God and the Father is this, To visit the fatherless and widows in their affliction, and to keep himself unspotted from the world."[2]

That religion which does not bring happiness to those who profess it is not worthy of the name. The Heavenly Father is not desirous of curtailing the pleasures of his earthly children or of denying them the good things of the earth. It may seem at times that the commandments and admonitions of the Father do restrict our actions and we chafe at these restrictions. But the wise and benevolent Father, like an earthly father, is interested in the welfare and progress of his children. His laws and commandments are the outcome of the experiences of the eternities. They are not new and experimental. They have governed the progress of human beings throughout eternity. The Patriarch Moses, through the goodness of God and in recognition of his great faith was allowed to get a glimpse of the magnitude of the universe and the universality of God's laws. The Lord said to him:

"And worlds without number have I created; and I also created them for mine own purpose; and by the Son I created them, which is mine Only Begotten.

"And the first man of all men have I called Adam, which is many.

"But only an account of this earth, and the inhabitants thereof, give I unto you. For behold, there are many worlds that have passed away by the word of my power. And there are many that now stand, and innumerable are they unto man; but all things are numbered unto me, for they are mine and I know them.

"And it came to pass that Moses spake unto the Lord, saying: Be merciful unto thy servant, O God, and tell me concerning this earth, and the inhabitants thereof, and also the heavens, and then thy servant will be content.

"And the Lord spake unto Moses, saying: The heavens, they are many, and they cannot be numbered unto man, but they are numbered unto me, for they are mine.

"And as one earth shall pass away, and the heavens thereof even so shall another come, and there is no end to my works, neither to my words.

"For behold, this is my work and my glory —to bring to pass the immortality and eternal life of man."[3]

Man, in his finite understanding, may not comprehend all of the commandments of the Father. He is like the child who would eagerly eat an entire dollar's worth of candy and think himself in a seventh heaven, but for the loving mother, who, in her wisdom, perceives the sure suffering which would follow the present apparent happiness.

As one comes to understand the laws of God he perceives them to be the laws of life all about him. Obedience to those laws brings freedom and happiness. In the words of Harry Emerson Fosdick:

"Many young people are brought up to think that goodness means repression. All

---

[1] *John* 10:10.
[2] *James* 1:27.

[3] *Pearl of Great Price*, Moses, 1:33-39.

through their maturing youth they keep
coming upon new powers, new passions, new
ambitions, and they are told that these must
be repressed. At first they docilely accept
that negative idea. They try to be good by
saying 'no' to their surging life. Then, some
day, they grow so utterly weary of this tame,
negative, repressive goodness that they can
tolerate it no longer, and they start out to be
free in wild self-indulgence, only to find it
the road not to freedom, but to slavery, with
habits that bind them and diseases that curse
them and blasted reputations that ruin them.

"Would not Jesus say to them some such
thing as this: 'You have made a bad mistake.
Goodness is not mainly repression. It is
finding your real self and then having it set
free. It is positively living for those things
which alone are worth living for. It is expression, the effulgence of life into its full
power and its abundant fruitage. I came
that ye might have life, and that ye might
have it more abundantly'."[4]

Believing that its mission is to bring
real happiness to mankind, The Church
of Jesus Christ of Latter-day Saints has
accepted its duty of guiding its members in the road which leads to happiness and to help young people find
themselves socially through the proper
exercise of their budding powers.

In guiding its members to happiness
the Church is first of all vitally interested in the health of its people. Healthy
people are generally happy people, and
sick people, even when they maintain a
cheerful attitude, are not happy.

"The Latter-day Saints, consequently,
teach moderation and wisdom in eating,
drinking, sleep, work and play; they set forth
the foods best adapted to promote physical
well-being; they discourage the use of alcohol, tobacco, or any drink or substance that
injures or unnaturally stimulates the body.
This code of health laws, known as the Word
of Wisdom, explains the high average health
and longevity of the Mormons. The birth-
rate (300 per 10,000) among them is one of
the highest, if not the highest, for a group of
similar size in the civilized world, and the
death-rate (75 per 10,000) is less than one-

half of the most favorable elsewhere in the
world."[5]

The basis of the teachings of the
Church on the care of the body is the
"Word of Wisdom." (See *Doctrine and
Covenants*, Section 89.)

This simple, effective method of
maintaining good health has been tested
for one hundred years by the Mormon
people. Even a partial observance of
this great law has brought remarkable
results.

Detailed health statistics are given
by the International Health Yearbook.
The average of six nations—Germany,
France, Netherlands, Sweden, Great
Britain, and the United States, may be
compared with the corresponding data
of the Latter-day Saints.

Deaths per 10,000 from the following diseases (in 1926-1927):

	Six Nations	Latter-day Saint
Tuberculosis	120	9
Cancer	119	47
Disease of the Nervous System	123	52
Disease of the Circulatory System	196	115
Disease of the Respiratory System	167	105
Disease of the Digestive System	73	56
Kidney and Kindred Diseases (Nephritis)	44	23
Maternity (per 1,000 births)	45	10

The Word of Wisdom was revealed
to Joseph Smith in answer to prayer.
The slow, laborious methods of science
have at last uncovered the truth of that
fundamental law and the world is bene-

---

[4]Guy C. Wilson, *Religion and Life*, p. 53.

[5]John A. Widtsoe, *Missionary Pamphlet, Centennial Series*, No. 8.

fiting by that knowledge. True religion is ever in advance of science, which necessarily walks by sight and not by faith. The resurrected Christ said unto the Apostle Thomas, who had to see and feel before he would believe, "Thomas, because thou hast seen me, thou hast believed: blessed are they that have not seen, and yet have believed."[6]

Blessed indeed have been those Latter-day Saints who have believed, for they have found it a true guide to health and happiness.

Action shot from the MIA All-Church Basketball Tournament, the largest in the world.

Used by permission, Deseret News

[6]*John* 20:29.

Recreation and Happiness

The strength of the Church lies in its guidance and not in its repression of the normal appetites and instincts of man. An entire catalog of "dont's" is not nearly so effective in getting results as a few "do's." A boy who has drifted into the pool halls in his leisure hours resents being lectured for his bad habits. The same boy, encouraged to join in wholesome recreation, finds himself too busy for lesser pastimes. The bad habit is unconsciously replaced by a good one.

In the Mormon philosophy there is no time for idleness, but there is ample time for wholesome play. The Prophet Joseph in his extraordinarily busy life found time to engage in sports, dance, and attend theatricals. As we have seen, the recreation in the pioneer camps on the plains produced a mental health which changed the face of the earth from sorrow to gladness.

In the conquering of the desert, recreation played a unique part. It brought the peace of forgetfulness to tired minds and aching bodies.

Today there has been built in connection with practically every chapel in the Church a recreation hall. These halls are fast becoming places of beauty and attraction, and scarcely an evening of the week finds them unused. Recreation leaders are being developed and schooled for the all-important task of directing the leisure-time activities of the communities.

The burden of the recreational program, as previously stated, has been placed upon the Mutual Improvement Association. Through that Association tens of thousands of young men and women are experiencing the joy and development which comes from proper recreation. Thousands of amateurs are performing on the stage, others are reading, speaking, dancing, or participating in athletic events.

In this day of increased leisure time and often vulgar commercial entertainment, the Church faces a momentous task. "As a man thinketh so is he"; hence the Church must ever be alert to direct the social life of its people.

Oscar A. Kirkham, late L.D.S. Scout Leader, relates an experience which illustrates the far-reaching nature of the Church program for happiness:

"Last year I had an interesting experience. At Kansas City, I resided at the headquarters of one of our largest youth movements in America; in New York I met with a number of other national movements; in Berlin I heard the story of Hitler's Youth Movement; in Italy leaders of Mussolini's, Ballila's and the Fascist Youth Movements. They were very gracious and gave me the details of their program. But on my way home in London, searching still further to get in touch with the subject, I was quite startled and interested to hear an international representative of the Y.M.C.A. say, that if I wanted to get the best program that he had ever heard of for young men and young women, I should by all means visit, on my return to America, Salt Lake City, and get in touch with the Mormon program for its young people."[7]

The Church and Scouting

In 1935, on the twenty-fifth anniversary of the Boy Scout movement in America, Dr. James E. West, Chief Scout Executive, Boy Scouts of America, wrote:

"Among no church which has sponsored Scouting have we met with more whole-hearted and effective cooperation and generous support than in the Church of Jesus Christ of Latter-day Saints, or finer, more enthusiastic leaders of unusually high calibre. The State of Utah has a larger percentage of Scouts in its boy population, I am told, than any other state in the Union and a larger per capita Scout membership in the Mormon

faith than that of any other religious body on record.

"All of this seems to me deeply significant, proves not only that we are offering a boy program which meets the needs of the great Church of Jesus Christ, but also that the ideals for which that Church stands are substantially the ideals of Scouting itself, the 'recognition of God as the ruling and leading power of the Universe' as a fundamental requisite for good citizenship and that correlative faith that only by living, clean, generous, fine lives, serving others before remembering oneself, can we, either as boy or man, serve God properly."[8]

When the oath taken by Scouts is considered, the reason becomes apparent for the interest of the Church in the growth of Scouting.

"On my honor I will do my best: To do my duty to God and my country, and to obey the Scout Law. (2) To help other people at all times. (3) To keep myself physically strong, mentally awake, and morally straight."

There is a close connection between the keeping of that pledge and the living of true religion as defined by the Apostle James, "to visit the fatherless and widows in their affliction, and to keep himself unspotted from the world."[9] The Church has been eager to sponsor a movement which leads their youth to be "doers of the word of God" and not merely "hearers of it." The Church has made Scouting an activity of priesthood.

The Boy Scout movement was first organized in England by Lieutenant-General Robert S. S. Baden-Powell, who is rightly called the "Father of Scouting." General Powell became interested in the organization of boys during the Boer War in South Africa. Late in 1907 Powell brought together the first organization of Boy Scouts. In 1908 the Boy Scouts of England were officially organized and in 1910 were granted a Royal Charter.

---

[7]June, 1934.

[8]*Improvement Era*, Vol. 38, No. 2, p. 72.
[9]*James* 1:27.

Scouting is promoted in the Church through the MIA.

Meanwhile in America two movements, which later joined with Scouting, had commenced. Daniel Carter Beard organized the "Sons of Daniel Boone," for the purpose of interesting boys in outdoor life and activities, and Ernest Thompson Seton organized the "Woodcraft Indians," for similar purposes.

In 1910 the "Boy Scouts of America" came into existence. In the same year The Church of Jesus Christ of Latter-day Saints sent Y.M.M.I.A. leaders to investigate the movement and enterprising boy leaders in various parts of the Church organized troops upon the lines recommended by the national organization. In 1911 Scouting was officially recognized by the Church and officially organized under the M.I.A. Dr. John H. Taylor was assigned the task of promoting Scout work in the stakes and wards under the direction of the M.I.A. athletic committee, composed of Lyman R. Martineau, Hyrum M. Smith, Oscar A. Kirkham, B. F. Grant, B. S. Hinckley and John H. Taylor.

During the June Conference in 1913 the first general Scout gathering in the Church was held at Wandamere, Salt Lake City, June 7. In the same year the M.I.A. Scouts became a part of "The Boy Scouts of America."

The growth of Scouting in the Church has been very rapid and its results in solving many of the problems of Youth has been very gratifying. Scouting continued with the Y.M.M.I.A. its sole sponsor until 1928, when it was named as the activity program of the Lesser Priesthood of the Church.

In 1973 the Y.M.M.I.A. and the Y.W.M.I.A. were replaced by Aaronic Priesthood M.I.A. A program for the girls, which is an intensive course in mental, spiritual, and physical activity, is a companion program to Scouting for the boys.

Supplementary Readings

1. *Doctrine and Covenants*, Section 89. ("Word of Wisdom.")

2. Joseph F. Smith, *Gospel Doctrine*, pp. 365-367. (Missionaries and the Word of Wisdom.)

3. Joseph F. Merrill, *Is Faith Reasonable?* Radio Addresses.

4. James E. Talmage, *Sunday Night Talks*, pp. 447-451.

5. John A. Widtsoe. (A missionary pamphlet on a study and some experiment on the Word of Wisdom.)

6. Evans, *Joseph Smith, An American Prophet*, pp. 232-235. (Interesting approach, and comments.)

7. Evans, *Heart of Mormonism*, pp. 194-199. (On Running Without Weariness.)

8. Frederick J. Pack, *Breadth of Mormonism*, Address No. 16, pp. 1-7. (Radio Address, bound in a book.)

9. Pack, *Tobacco and Human Efficiency*. (The entire book is a study of tobacco and human efficiency.)

10. Fisher and Fiske, *How to Live*, pp. 199-281; 333-382; 383-413. (Chapters on food, alcohol, and tobacco are cited here.)

11. Fisher and Fiske, *How to Live*. (A pamphlet based on or taken from book cited in No. 10 above. Published by the Y. M. and Y.W.M.I. Association General Boards.)

12. Gates and Widtsoe, *Life Story of Brigham Young*, p. 333.

13. Roberts, *A Comprehensive History of the Church*. Vol. 1, pp. 43. note 12; 305-306.

CHAPTER 42

MORMONISM TOMORROW

An Enduring Faith

As Mormonism forges ahead well into its second century, one may ask how long its vitality and growth will continue. What will the Church be tomorrow? Has it reached the zenith of its influence? Will it become the dominant religion of the age or will it eventually decline until it has passed out of the religious picture? What changes may come within the Church itself? What are the present Church trends which may help to foresee its destiny?

These are questions best understood in the light of the past century and a half of Church history, and in the light of the history of all great religions. The same questions have been asked repeatedly over the years by observers of the Mormon faith. Most of the answers given have been proved erroneous by the march of time. Only those observers who have lived among the Mormon people have made any intelligent forecasts. The more accurate statements have come from the Mormons themselves. In the early days of the Church some of the non-Mormon observers predicted an early end to Mormonism and based their predictions upon the assumption that the Church was built around a personality who, either because of charm or fraud or psychic powers, was able to attract a sizeable following. Hence their conclusion, that upon the death of that leader the Church would decline. Time has shown the assumption wrong. The Church survives the death of even the greatest of its leaders and seems to have suffered no serious results therefrom. On the other hand, the Church produces leaders by the score capable of carrying on its work. From the standpoint of leadership the Church can well expect to continue its phenomenal growth and influence.

Other early observers saw the growth of the Church as the result of a stupendous fraud on the part of Joseph Smith and his close associates. These predicted its downfall as soon as the fraud should be discovered. But time and inquiry revealed no such fraud but on the other hand tended more and more to substantiate the honesty and sincerity of the Church founders. The Church strengthened and grew where it was expected to decline.

Still other observers contended that the Prophet was honest and sincere but was mistaken. These considered the visions of the Prophet as hallucinations of the mind which caused him actually to believe that he had seen heavenly personages and received heavenly messages. We need not here consider the difficulties these same critics had in explaining the reality of the *Book of Mormon* as coming from an hallucination or the profound wisdom displayed in the revelations to the Prophet. All of those, however, who did not doubt the sincerity of the Prophet Joseph but labeled his visions and revelations as tricks of the mental processes looked for an early decline of Mormonism. Indeed, if such had been its origin, Mormonism could not have survived and flourished for a long period of time in a scientific age.

We face the fact that the testimony and zeal of one man, however received and however strong, gradually loses its potency and reality with passing generations unless it is vitally renewed in the hearts of his followers, and if the testimony and zeal thus declines the church declines. But if the testimony of its founder is continually renewed in the hearts of his followers so that they have the same zeal as the founder, there can be no end to such a church. That is what the most careful critics are observing today. The zeal of The Church of Jesus Christ of Latter-day Saints shows no sign of abating. The missionary spirit was never stronger than now. Converts to the Church continue to send their sons and daughters into the mission field to convert others. Men and women by the tens of thousands still bear testimony to the world of the restoration of the power of God with all of its attendant gifts. This mighty faith is not confined to the mind—it is a living faith manifesting itself in voluntary service for others, in the payment of tithes and offerings, in increased temple work, and in the individual lives of its members.

The Look Ahead

We can look with genuine assurance for the Church to continue in its strength for we can perceive in it the vital elements necessary to a world religion. *First*, it is a religion of certainty. The existence of God the Father as a personal Being, the resurrection of His Son Jesus Christ, the certainty of revelation, the power of the priesthood, are realities in the minds of Latter-day Saints. *Second*, Mormonism is a religion with a goal. The program of the Church—to carry the Gospel to every kindred, nation, tongue and people, to establish Zion, and to do ordinance work for the living and the dead—is specific and real. This program transcends that of any Church in the history of religions. There is no danger that the cause of the Church will stagnate for want of a goal, and the very magnitude of its aims augurs well for its future.

It is not likely that the goals of the Church will change, for there is no dispute or uncertainty within the Church concerning them which might result in modification. The means, however, by which these goals may be reached will likely undergo changes as new circumstances enter into the picture.

So long as the gift of the Holy Ghost continues with the Church members, missionary activity will continue. As this gift can only be enjoyed by a righteous people, the missionary activity of the Church will show periods of intense activity and decline in keeping with conditions within the Church. Further, while the missionary aim will remain the same, the methods by which missionaries work will perhaps undergo, as it is already doing, certain changes. The use of the radio, motion picture film, and sound devices has greatly altered missionary techniques. There is a growing tendency to demonstrate Mormonism rather than to preach it. From the success missionaries are obtaining by this method we may expect this change to become increasingly pronounced. The exemplary life lived by the missionary has always been a vital factor in conversions. Now the tendency is to organize Church auxiliaries, the Relief Society, Sunday School, Primary, M.I.A., and the Church Welfare Program and to invite non-Mormons to see the Church in action. Where formerly these activities followed the organization of a branch, now many even precede such organization. Sunday Schools and Primaries, for example, are being set up with the nucleus of a single Mormon family. To these organizations non-Mormons, who may never have heard a Latter-day Saint sermon, are invited. Thus activity in the Church may precede membership and become a most vital factor toward conversion.

A Great Objective

The aim of establishing "Zion" upon the earth may be further defined as the aim to make the ideal of Jesus prevail in the world. In his book *The Heart of Mormonism*, John Henry Evans writes concerning this objective.

Three things interfere with the realization of this ideal of the abundant life in man as we know him in this world of the flesh.

"The first of these is war. War defeats the purpose of the abundant life in three ways: First, it destroys life, cuts off a career in its first strivings for the ideal, before it has acquired any of the habits of attainment. Second, it maims life, cripples it in some of its functions so as to make self-realization in its fulness impossible. And, third, it brutalizes life, coarsens it immeasurably, snatches it from the plane of idealism and flings it back into the slime of primitive life, out of which it has come with effort and pain.

"The second of these is ignorance. Ignorance prevents one from making a choice that will preserve life. At least, it makes it impossible for one to be sure beforehand that one is making the right choice. Unless one knows the difference between the poisonous weed and the wholesome plant, the chances are fifty-fifty that he will live or die. And the same thing is true of the higher life of the spirit. Ignorance, therefore, becomes a deadly enemy to man so far as concerns his realization of the abundant life.

"And the third of the hindrances to the abundant life is poverty. Poverty is an interference because, although one may see the necessary differences clearly enough, yet one cannot make the choice if one lacks the means to do so. Food, clothing, shelter—these cost money. But, if one has no money or too little of it, one has to go without some of the things that are necessary to the abundant life. Also education, books, pictures, what not in the higher life, require money. In a world of "plenty and to spare," as God himself puts it, men, women, and little children go hungry, naked, and shelterless, not to mention their lack of the higher necessities.

"War, ignorance, and poverty, moreover, combine to bring on what is perhaps the greatest blight of the modern world—external motivation. From the cradle to the grave we are dominated by the desire to "get by" with something or other. In our schools we work for credits; in our vocations we strive for advancement, so that we may get more money. If we are in the government service, our main object is to retain our seat; if in business, to make profits and obtain power in the world. The social aspirant wants to be known as having made the grade. Everywhere the motivation comes from without, not from within. No greater curse can overtake a nation or an individual than that. And no greater departure from the Christian ideal is possible.

"The grand objective of Mormonism therefore, in the coming century and thereafter will be to take such steps, and to take them aggressively, as will tend to make the abundant life prevail in the world. It will insist upon this as a human right. It will endeavor to take off from every son and daughter of God the clamp of ignorance and poverty, so as to make it possible for him to develop his personality under conditions of peace and universal good will.

"And it will endeavor to do this by the creation of a state of mind in the individual. Not only will it oppose all war, foster education, and work for a better economic system, but it will change the source of motivation from the outside to the inside.

"The student will then ask about what he is getting out of the course, instead of the marks on the report card. The politician will inquire, not as to his re-election, but as to whether or not his constituents are benefited by what he is doing. The employer of labor will not, under the new circumstance, be so much concerned with what he can get out of life. Society will not be so greatly interested in the punishment of the criminal as with finding out how he became a criminal and how he may be changed into a self-respecting citizen.

"That is what Mormonism will attempt more and more to do in the years to come, and that is in general the method by which the Church will go about this task. The center of interest all the time will be the human personality."[1]

The aim of the Church to perform ordinance work for the living and the dead, like its other general aims is certain to continue. Neither will the ordinances be changed. Changes, however, may be expected in the organization fostering the gathering of genealogy, in temple architecture, and in the efforts used to create a consciousness of this Church aim. The increased interest in temple work for the living and the dead in the past two decades promises well for the future. One may logically expect to see many additional temples erected in widely scattered areas of Church population and an intensified

effort made to teach the youth of Zion the importance of temple ordinances.

The success of Mormonism now and in the future depends in the last analysis upon the conviction of the individual member that the Church was divinely established by the resurrected Lord and Savior Jesus Christ and that His power is in the Church by those holding His holy priesthood. As individual testimony shows no signs of disappearing but is manifest on an ever-more-broadening base the future of the Church seems well assured.

Supplementary Readings

Evans, *Heart of Mormonism*, pp. 510-517. (The Church program for the future.)

James E. Barker, "The Church Worth Having," *Deseret News*, Church Section, September 22, 1940.

Thomas Nixon Carver, "A Positive Religion," *The Westerner*, April 1930.

---

[1]Evans, *The Heart of Mormonism*, pp. 511-513.

PREVIEW OF UNIT IV

THE MORMON PHILOSOPHY

While a study of the Mormon story gives a deep insight into the beliefs of the Mormon people, and vividly illustrates the effects of those beliefs upon the lives of men and women, a finer appreciation of the restored Church and its message to mankind can be obtained only from a study of the deep underlying philosophy and beliefs of the Latter-day Saints. In this unit we shall discuss some of the fundamentals of Mormon philosophy and come to realize in some degree the contributions the Church offers to the religious knowledge of the world.

CHAPTER 43

THE LATTER-DAY SAINT
UNDERSTANDING OF GOD

The Nature of God

Take God out of the story of Mormonism and the story would sink into insignificance. The Latter-day Saints' concept of God, the intimacy of their relationship to Him, and the glorious revelations received by their Prophet concerning Him, constitute the heart and core upon which Mormonism has been built. Hence, to understand the religion re-established upon the earth by Joseph Smith we must begin with a study of God and the light which latter-day revelation has thrown upon the subject.

The perfection of God has been proclaimed by all the prophets. His Son, Jesus Christ, exemplified it while in the flesh and declared it by revelation before and after that time. Also, God Himself has proclaimed it. To Moses the Lord said, "Behold, I am the Lord God Almighty, and Endless is my name; for I am without beginning of days or end of years; and is not this endless? ... my works are without end, and also my words, for they never cease . . . all things are present with me, for I know them all."[1]

Unto Abraham the Lord declared:

"These two facts do exist, that there are two spirits, one being more intelligent than the other; there shall be another more intelligent than they; I am the Lord thy God, I am more intelligent than they all."[2]

In light of this announcement the Prophet Joseph Smith declared, "The glory of God is Intelligence."[3]

During one of the Prophet's discourses in Nauvoo he said:

"God himself was once as we are now, and is an exalted man, and sits enthroned in yonder heavens! That is the great secret. If the veil were rent today, and the great God who holds this world in its orbit, and who upholds all worlds and all things by his power, was to make himself visible—I say, if you were to see him today, you would see him like a man in form—like yourselves in all the person, image, and very form as a man; for Adam was created in the very fashion, image and likeness of God and received instruction from, and walked, talked, conversed with him, as one man talks and communes with another. . . .

"It is the first principle of the Gospel to know for a certainty the character of God, and to know that we may converse with him as one man converses with another, and that he was once a man like us; yea, that God himself, the Father of us all dwelt on an earth, the same as Jesus Christ himself did; and I will show it from the Bible."[4]

"Jesus declared unto men, 'Be ye therefore perfect, even as your Father which is in heaven is perfect.'"[5]

The Nephite Prophet Mormon perceived God as embodying all that is good:

"Wherefore, all things which are good cometh of God; and that which is evil cometh of the devil; for the devil is an enemy unto God, and fighteth against him continually, and inviteth and enticeth to sin, and to do that which is evil continually.

"But behold, that which is of God inviteth and enticeth to do good continually; wherefore, every thing which inviteth and enticeth to do good, and to love God, and to serve him, is inspired of God.

"Wherefore take heed, my beloved brethren, that ye do not judge that which is evil

---

[1]*Pearl of Great Price*, Moses 1:3-4, 6.
[2]*Ibid.*, Abraham, 3:19.
[3]*Doctrine and Covenants*, 93:36.
[4]King Follett Discourse, *Times and Seasons*, August 15, 1844. For a reprint see *Teachings of the Prophet Joseph Smith*, p. 345.
[5]Matthew 5:48.

to be of God, or that which is good and of God to be of the devil."[6]

Work and Attributes of Jesus Christ, His Son

As Revealing of the Perfection of God Unto Man

The greatest revelation of God unto man is the revelation of His attributes and powers through the person of His Son, Jesus, the Christ. So revealing are the words and actions of Jesus that it is strange that any who really acquaint themselves with Him should fail to understand their Father, who is in heaven. Repeatedly during His ministry the Master made clear to His closest associates the oneness that existed between Father and Son.

In explanation of His good works upon the Sabbath day, the Savior said,

"My Father worketh hitherto, and I work. . . .

"Verily, verily, I say unto you, The Son can do nothing of himself, but what he seeth the Father do: for what things soever he doeth, these also doeth the Son likewise.

"For the Father loveth the Son, and showeth him all things that himself doeth; and he will show him greater works than these, that ye may marvel.

"For as the Father raiseth up the dead, and quickeneth them; even so the Son quickeneth whom he will. . . .

"For as the Father hath life in himself, so hath he given to the Son to have life in himself."[7]

To those enemies who asked of Jesus, "Where is thy Father?" Jesus answered.

"Ye neither know me, nor my Father: if ye had known me, ye should have known my Father also."[8]

When they lifted up their hands to stone him, Jesus said unto them, "Many good works have I shewed you from my Father; for which of those works do ye stone me?"[9]

Jesus further clarified the picture of the Father when in a later response to Philip's request, "Show us the Father," Jesus replied:

"Have I been so long time with you, and yet hast thou not known me, Philip? he that hath seen me, hath seen the Father; and how sayest thou then, Shew us the Father?

"Believest thou not that I am in the Father, and the Father in me? the words that I speak unto you I speak not of myself: but the Father that dwelleth in me, he doeth the works."[10]

From the above statements it is clear that the attributes of the Father are revealed through the life of the Son. The experiences of man with the Son of God have caused a revision of many ideas concerning God which prevailed everywhere before that time.

First: Jesus revealed the all-embracing love of God for all mankind, a love so deep that few have even attempted to emulate it in perfection. The love of Christ embraced rich and poor, bond and free, the saint and the sinner, friend and enemy. His words represent a new order of life:

"But I say unto you, Love your enemies, bless them that curse you, do good to them that hate you, and pray for them which despitefully use you, and persecute you;

"That ye may be the children of your Father which is in heaven: for he maketh his sun to rise on the evil and on the good, and sendeth rain on the just and on the unjust.

"For if ye love them which love you, what reward have ye? do not even the publicans the same?"

"And if ye salute your brethren only, what do ye more than others? do not even the publicans so?

"Be ye therefore perfect, even as your Father which is in heaven is perfect."[11]

---

[6]Moroni 7:12-14.
[7]John 5:17, 19-21, 26.
[8]John 8:19.

[9]John 10:32.
[10]John 14:8-10.
[11]Matthew 5:44-48.

All viewpoints of men concerning God and His dealings with mankind at variance with the perfect love Christ taught and lived must be revised in the light of the greater truth.

Second: Jesus revealed God as having compassion upon sinners and as being desirous of bringing them again to a condition of happiness. Jesus never found an individual so low in spirit, so broken in body, or steeped in degradation and sin that He did not see a possibility of saving him if he would but believe and follow the Master's teachings. Perhaps nothing so portrays this compassion of the Father for His children as these lines,

"For God so loved the world, that he gave his only begotten Son, that whosoever believeth in him should not perish, but have everlasting life."[12]

Third: Jesus reveals God's compassion and impartiality. He threw wide the gates and beckoned all mankind to follow the way of life, admonishing them: "And whosoever will be chief among you, let him be your servant."[12a] Men were to be judged by their fruits. Neither race, money, position, nor creed would alter that judgment.

God's compassion for His children is further portrayed in the following outpouring of the soul of Christ:

"O Jerusalem, Jerusalem, thou that killest the prophets, and stonest them which are sent unto thee, how often would I have gathered thy children together, even as a hen gathereth her chickens under her wings, and ye would not!"[13]

Fourth: The Father hears and answers the righteous petitions of His children. Even His Son constantly sought guidance of Him and implicitly lent Himself to the Father's will.

"Ask, and it shall be given you; seek, and ye shall find; knock, and it shall be opened unto you."[14]

Fifth: The life of Christ portrays how God works in obedience to law. For Jesus submitted Himself to both physical and spiritual laws, suffering all the pains of the body, and embracing all spiritual laws, allowing Himself though sinless to be baptized, and showing forth in all His life a perfect obedience unto the Father.

Sixth: The life of Jesus portrays the tolerance of God. When the people of a Samaritan village refused Him food and lodging, He rebuked the anger of His disciples who would have called down fire from heaven to consume the village by these words,

"Ye know not what manner of spirit ye are of. For the Son of man is not come to destroy men's lives, but to save them."[15]

Again when His disciples complained that one not a follower of Christ was doing works in His name He rebuked their intolerance by saying:

"Forbid him not: for there is no man which shall do a miracle in my name, that can lightly speak evil of me. For he that is not against us is on our part."[16]

In all His life Christ portrays the Father unto man, and in all of God's attributes thus portrayed, man has reason to rejoice. For the goodness of God becomes as a stream of cooling water in a thirsty land and His perfect example as the beckoning rays of the rising sun. To the believer fear of God is replaced with love and confidence and the gloom of uncertainty is forever dispelled.

[12]John 3:16.
[12a]Matthew 20:27.
[13]*Ibid.*, 23:37.

[14]*Ibid.*, 7:7.
[15]Luke 9:55-56.
[16]Mark 9:39-40.

Latter-day Saint Contributions to an Understanding of Jesus Christ

The Latter-day Saint Concept of Jesus Christ

The Latter-day Saints accept the Bible account of Jesus as found in the gospels, letters and other writings of the New Testament. These represent Him as the literal Son of God in the flesh, as having taught the perfect gospel, as being in frequent communion with His Father during His ministry, of performing mighty miracles, of dying upon the cross to save mankind, and of arising from the dead with His actual body of flesh and bones which He showed to many of His disciples. The Latter-day Saints, through the goodness of God, have come into possession of a great deal of evidence supporting the Bible accounts as well as much additional knowledge concerning Jesus and His teachings. This additional knowledge is found in two channels, ancient records brought to light and translated by the gift and power of God, and additional revelations to the Prophet Joseph Smith.

Book of Mormon Contributions

The principal ancient scriptures brought to light are the *Book of Mormon* and the *Book of Abraham*. The entire *Book of Mormon* throws light upon the relationship of Christ to men and was written especially to convince all of the generations now upon the earth "the JESUS is the CHRIST, the ETERNAL GOD, manifesting himself unto all nations."[17]

The birth of Jesus as the literal Son of God in the flesh was foretold to Nephi nearly six centuries before it occurred

as recorded so beautifully in Nephi's writings:

"And it came to pass that I looked and beheld the great city of Jerusalem, and also other cities. And I beheld the city of Nazareth; and in the city of Nazareth I beheld a virgin, and she was exceedingly fair and white.

"And it came to pass that I saw the heavens open; and an angel came down and stood before me; and said unto me: Nephi, what beholdest thou?

"And I said unto him; a virgin, most beautiful and fair above all other virgins.

"And he said unto me: Behold, the virgin whom thou seest is the mother of the Son of God, after the manner of the flesh.

"And it came to pass that I beheld that she was carried away in the Spirit; and after she had been carried away in the Spirit for the space of a time the angel spake unto me, saying: Look!

"And I looked and beheld the virgin again, bearing a child in her arms.

"And the angel said unto me: Behold the Lamb of God, yea, even the Son of the Eternal Father!"[18]

Nephi was also shown in vision the twelve apostles of the Savior in Palestine, and the Savior's crucifixion and resurrection.[19] This ancient account found on the American continent thus confirms the Bible story.

The *Book of Mormon* makes clear the work of Jesus Christ as a Creator,[20] as God unto the inhabitants of the earth, according to the will of the Father,[21] as the Redeemer of mankind[22] and as our great Advocate and Judge.[23]

Above all other things the *Book of Mormon* testifies to the actual resurrection of Jesus; that He appeared as a resurrected Being on the American continent teaching His gospel in great

---

17See *Book of Mormon*, title page.

181 Nephi 11:13-15, 18-21.
191 Nephi 11:24-34.
20See Mosiah 3:8; 4:2; 3 Nephi 9:15, Ether 3:15-16.
21See 3 Nephi 18:19-30; 19:6-8; Mosiah 15:2-3; Alma 5:50; 11:38-40, 15:2-5.
221 Nephi 22:12; Enos 1:27; Alma 7:7; Moroni 8:8.
23Alma 11:44; 1 Nephi 12:9-10; Mormon 3:18-22.

plainness to the people.[24] The recorded words of Jesus spoken in America fill thirty-three pages of the *Book of Mormon* and nearly equal in number the recorded words of Jesus in the Bible.

Book of Abraham Contributions

The Book of Abraham, now published in the *Pearl of Great Price*, adds remarkable information concerning Jesus Christ. It reveals the part which He played in the council of the heavens before the world was, His selection and appointment as the Redeemer, and the acceptance of Him as such by those who were to come into earth life.[25]

Thus the *Book of Mormon* and the *Book of Abraham* reveal the godhood of Jesus and in the light of the words found in these records we may follow His teachings without question or doubt.

Contributions of Latter-day Revelation

Much additional knowledge of Christ has come to the Church through revelation to the Prophet Joseph Smith. These are found in the *Doctrine and Covenants*, *Book of Moses*, and in his journal writings. The first great vision of the Father and the Son made clear that they were separate personages with bodies like unto that of man. It further established the actual resurrection of the Savior, that He still lives and reigns. Joseph testifies that during the appearance of the Father and the Son, the Father spoke first pointing to the Son and saying, "This is My Beloved Son, Hear Him!"[25a] Afterwards it was the Son who instructed Joseph and gave unto him subsequent revelations, thus showing unto men the relationship of the Father to His Son. From this event and subsequent revelations it appears that Jesus Christ has been given charge of this world and represents the Father in all that He does or says.

The book of *Doctrine and Covenants*, which contains a collection of revelations received subsequent to the first great vision is full of information regarding the mission of Jesus Christ and His relationship to men. For example we read:

"For, behold, I, God, have suffered these things for all, that they might not suffer if they would repent.
"But if they would not repent they must suffer even as I;
"Which suffering caused myself, even God, the greatest of all, to tremble because of pain, and to bleed at every pore, and to suffer both body and spirit—and would that I might not drink the bitter cup, and shrink—
"Nevertheless, glory be to the Father, and I partook and finished my preparations unto the children of men."[26]

And again,

"Wherefore, the Almighty God gave His Only Begotten Son, as it is written in those scriptures which have been given of him.
"He suffered temptations but gave no heed to them.
"He was crucified, died, and rose again on the third day;
"And ascended into heaven, to sit down on the right hand of the Father, to reign with almighty power according to the will of the Father;
"That as many as would believe and be baptized in his holy name, and endure in faith to the end, should be saved—"[27]

The whole mission of Jesus and His relationship to the Father and to man is portrayed in the following:

"Verily, thus saith the Lord: It shall come to pass that every soul who forsaketh his sins and cometh unto me, and calleth on my name, and obeyeth my voice, and keepeth my commandments, shall see my face and know that I am;

---

[24]Students should read carefully the entire book of 3 Nephi.
[25]See *Pearl of Great Price*, Abraham 3:22-28.
[25a]*Ibid.*, Joseph Smith 2:17.

[26]*Doctrine and Covenants* 19:16-19.
[27]*Ibid.*, 20:21-25.

"And that I am the true light that lighteth every man that cometh into the world;

"And that I am in the Father, and the Father in me, and the Father and I are one—

"The Father because he gave me of his fulness, and the Son because I was in the world and made flesh my tabernacle, and dwelt among the sons of men.

"I was in the world and received of my Father, and the works of him were plainly manifest.

"And John saw and bore record of the fulness of my glory, and the fulness of John's record is hereafter to be revealed.

"And he bore record, saying: I saw his glory, that he was in the beginning, before the world was;

"Therefore, in the beginning the Word was, for he was the Word, even the messenger of salvation—

"The light and the Redeemer of the world; the Spirit of truth, who came into the world, because the world was made by him, and in him was the life of men and the light of men.

"The words were made by him; men were made by him; all things were made by him, and through him, and of him.

"And I, John, bear record that I beheld his glory, as the glory of the Only Begotten of the Father, full of grace and truth, even the Spirith of truth, which came and dwelt in the flesh, and dwelt among us.

"And I, John, saw that he received not of the fulness at the first, but received grace for grace;

"And he received not of the fulness at first, but continued from grace to grace, until he received a fulness;

"And thus he was called the Son of God, because he received not of the fulness at the first.

"And I, John, bear record, and lo, the heavens were opened, and the Holy Ghost descended upon him in the form of a dove, and sat upon him, and there came a voice out of heaven saying: This is my beloved Son.

"And I, John, bear record that he received a fulness of the glory of the Father;

"And he received all power, both in heaven and on earth, and the glory of the Father was with him, for he dwelt in him.

"And it shall come to pass, that if you are faithful you shall receive the fulness of the record of John.

"I give unto you these sayings that you may understand and know how to worship, and know what you worship, that you may come unto the Father in my name, and in due time receive of his fulness.

"For if you keep my commandments you shall receive of his fulness, and be glorified in me as I am in the Father; therefore, I say unto you, you shall receive grace for grace.

"And now, verily I say unto you, I was in the beginning with the Father, and am the Firstborn.

"And all those who are begotten through me are partakers of the glory of the same and are the church of the Firstborn.

"Ye were also in the beginning with the Father; that which is Spirit, even the Spirit of truth;"[28]

Having come to an understanding of the Lord and Savior Jesus Christ through a remarkable vision of the heavens, Joseph Smith and Sidney Rigdon bore witness in these words:

"And while we meditated upon these things, the Lord touched the eyes of our understandings and they were opened, and the glory of the Lord shone round about.

"And we beheld the glory of the Son, on the right hand of the Father, and received of his fulness;

"And saw the holy angels, and them who are sanctified before his throne, worshiping God, and the Lamb, who worship him forever and ever.

"And now, after the many testimonies which have been given of him, this is the testimony last of all, which we give of him, that he lives!

"For we saw him, even on the right hand of God; and we heard the voice bearing record that he is the Only Begotten of the Father—

"That by him, and through him, and of him, the worlds are and were created, and the inhabitants thereof are begotten sons and daughters unto God."[29]

The Term "Father" as Applied to Jesus Christ

Because the work of Christ and His Father is the same, for they are One in all they do, it is easy to confuse their personages. The titles God, God the Eternal Father, the Everlasting Father and others, apply to both the Father and the Son and need some explanation. The

---

[28]*Ibid.*, 93:1-23.
[29]*Ibid.*, 76:19-24.

many passages of scripture in which Jesus speaks as the Father are numerous but are easily understood when we consider the oneness in purpose and procedure of the Father and Son.

The term "Father" as applied to Deity occurs in sacred literature with plainly different meanings. The term is used to designate either God, the Father, or Christ, the Son, as are other titles. In the Latter-day Saint Temples the name "Elohim" for the Father, and "Jehovah" for the Son are consistently used and all confusion and misunderstanding is thus avoided. Both Elohim and Jehovah are frequently referred to in scriptures as God, as Father, as God the Eternal Father, as God the Everlasting Father, etc. In present usage, Elohim is the only title of Deity which is not applied to Jesus Christ, the Son, as well as to the Father. Because various titles involving the term "Father" are thus applied to Jesus Christ, it is important that we understand wherein He may properly be designated as our "Father."

When we use the term "Father" in referring to Elohim, we have in mind that Being who is the literal parent of our Spirit bodies. Scriptures embodying this idea of literal parent are very numerous. The purport of them is to the effect that Elohim is the Literal Parent of our Lord and Savior Jesus Christ and of the Spirits of the human race.[30] We are taught by Jesus to pray, "Our Father which art in heaven, hallowed be thy name."

Jesus Christ applies to Himself both titles, "Son and Father." In appearing unto the brother of Jared He said, "Behold I am Jesus Christ. I am the Father and the Son."[31] He is not using the

term "Father" here in the sense of literal parent, for manifestly we cannot have two literal Fathers of our spirits. There are, however, other scriptural meanings of the term.

"Father" as Creator

An important scriptural meaning of "Father" is that of Creator.

"God is not the Father of the earth as one of the worlds in space, nor of the heavenly bodies in whole or in part, nor of the inanimate objects, and the plants, and the animals upon the earth, in the literal sense in which He is the Father of the spirits of mankind. Therefore, scriptures that refer to God in any way as the Father of the heavens and the earth are to be understood as signifying that God is the Maker, the Organizer, the Creator of the heavens and the earth."[32]

With the above meaning Jesus Christ, who under the direction of Elohim organized the heavens and the earth, is referred to in numerous scriptural passages as "The Father," "The Everlasting Father," and even the "very eternal Father of heaven and of earth."[33] In the *Book of Mormon* we read: "Now Zeezrom saith again unto him: Is the Son of God the very Eternal Father?

"And Amulek said unto him: Yea, he is the very Eternal Father of heaven and of earth, and all things which in them are. . . ."[34]

Thus Jesus Christ, being the Creator, is properly referred to as the "Father." Since His creations are of an eternal character, He is very properly called the "Eternal Father of heaven and earth."[35]

Jesus Christ the "Father" of Those Who Abide in His Gospel

A second sense in which Jesus Christ

[30]See Hebrews 12:9.
[31]Ether 3:14.

[32]Statement of the First Presidency and the Council of the Twelve Apostles of The Church of Jesus Christ of Latter-day Saints, June 30, 1916. *Articles of Faith*, Talmage (Appendix).
[33]See Mosiah 15:4; 16:15; Ether 4:7.
[34]Alma 11:38-39.
[35]See Talmage, *Jesus the Christ*, Chap. IV; Isaiah 9:6. Compare 2 Nephi 19:6.

is regarded as the "Father" has reference to the relationship between Him and those who accept His Gospel and thereby become heirs of eternal life.

This meaning is made clear by examining a few scriptural passages.

At the Last Supper with His apostles just prior to His entrance into the Garden of Gethsemane, Jesus Christ prayed unto His Father in behalf of those His Father had given unto Him:

"I have manifested thy name unto the men which thou gavest me out of the world: thine they were, and thou gavest them to me; and they have kept thy word.

"Now they have known that all things whatsoever thou hast given me are of thee.

"For I have given unto them the words which thou gavest me; and they have received them, and have known surely that I came out from thee, and they have believed that thou didst send me.

"I pray for them: I pray not for the world; but for them which thou hast given me; for they are thine.

"And all mine are thine, and thine are mine; and I am glorified in them.

"And now I am no more in the world, but these are in the world, and I come to thee. Holy Father, keep through thine own name those whom thou hast given me, that they may be one as we are.

"While I was with them in the world, I kept them in thy name; those that thou gavest me I have kept, and none of them is lost, but the son of perdition: that the scripture might be fulfilled."[36]

And further:

"Neither pray I for these alone, but for them also which shall believe on me through their word;

"That they all may be one; as thou, Father, art in me, and I in thee, that they also may be one in us: that the world may believe that thou hast sent me.

"And the glory which thou gavest me I have given them; that they may be one, even as we are one:

"I in them, and thou in me, that they may be made perfect in one; and that the world may know that thou has sent me, and hast loved them, as thou hast loved me.

[36]John 17:6-12.

"Father, I will that they also, whom thou hast given me, be with me where I am; that they may behold my glory, which thou hast given me: for thou lovedst me before the foundation of the world."[37]

In a revelation to the Latter-day Saints given through the Prophet Joseph Smith, the Savior said:

"Fear not, little children, for you are mine, and I have overcome the world, and you are of them that my Father hath given me."[38]

Repeatedly the Savior has spoken unto His followers as his sons. In a revelation addressed to Hyrum Smith in 1829 we read:

"Behold, I am Jesus Christ, the Son of God. I am the life and the light of the world.

I am the same who came unto my own and mine own received me not;

"But verily, verily, I say unto you, that as many as receive me, to them will I give power to become the sons of God, even to them that believe on my name. Amen."[39]

In a revelation addressed to Orson Pratt in 1830 we read:

"My son Orson, hearken and hear and behold what I, the Lord God, shall say unto you, even Jesus Christ your Redeemer;

"The light and the life of the world, a light which shineth in darkness and the darkness comprehendeth it not.

"Who so loved the world that he gave his own life, that as many as would believe might become the sons of God. Wherefore you are my son."[40]

Men may become children of Jesus Christ by being born anew—born of His spirit. When an individual believes in Christ and is properly baptized into a new spiritual life, and confirmed, he is born of the water and the spirit into a new spiritual life, wherein Jesus is His Father.[41] Thus John wrote to the members of the early Christian Church:

[37]John 17:20-24.
[38]Doctrine and Covenants 50:41.
[39]Doctrine and Covenants 11:28-30.
[40]Doctrine and Covenants 34:1-3; for additional passages, see 9:1; 25:1; 121:7.
[41]See I Peter 1:23; I John 3:9; 5:1-5; John 1:1-14.

"And this is the record, that God hath given to us eternal life, and this life is in his Son.

"He that hath the Son hath life; and he that hath not the Son of God hath not life."[42]

Those who have been born unto God through obedience to the Gospel may, by valiant devotion to righteousness, obtain great honors in the Kingdom of Heaven and may even reach the status of Gods. Of such we read:

"Wherefore, as it is written, they are gods, even the sons of God."[43]

They remain, however, subject to Jesus Christ as their Father and so we read, "And they are Christ's and Christ is God's."[44]

Thus by the new birth—that of water and the Spirit we may become "begotten sons and daughters unto God."[45] The great truth is emphasized by the words of the Savior through Joseph Smith in 1833:

"And now, verily I say unto you, I was in the beginning with the Father, and am the Firstborn; And all those who are begotten through me are partakers of the glory of the same, and are the church of the First-born."[46]

It is hence proper for those thus born into Christ's Kingdom to speak and write of Him as "Father."

Jesus Christ the "Father" by Divine Investure of Authority

A third reason for applying the title "Father" to Jesus Christ is found in the fact that in all His dealings with the human family, Jesus, the Son, has represented and yet represents Elohim, His Father, in power and authority. In His premortal state in which He was known

to man as Jehovah, during His embodiment in the flesh, during His labors as a disembodied spirit in the realm of the dead, and since that period in His resurrected state, Jesus Christ has represented His Father and has been unto man as the Father and has spoken unto man as the Father.

In a similar manner heavenly messengers sent by Christ to the earth often speak unto man in the first person, as if they were Christ. John the Revelator records that he was visited by an angel who ministered unto him and spoke in the name of Jesus Christ. In his account of the event we read:

"The Revelation of Jesus Christ, which God gave unto him, to shew unto his servants things which must shortly come to pass; and he sent and signified it by his angel unto his servant John."[47]

John was about to worship the angelic being who spoke in the name of the Lord Jesus Christ but was forbidden:

"And I John saw these things, and heard them. And when I had heard and seen, I fell down to worship before the feet of the angel which shewed me these things.

"Then saith he unto me, See thou do it not: for I am thy fellow servant, and of thy brethren the prophets, and of them which keep the sayings of this book: worship God."[48]

And then the angel continued to speak as though he were the Lord Himself:

"And, behold, I come quickly; and my reward is with me, to give every man according as his work shall be.

"I am Alpha and Omega, the beginning and the end, the first and the last."[49]

The resurrected Lord, Jesus Christ, had placed His name upon the angel sent to John and the angel spoke in the first person, saying, "I come quickly," "I am Alpha and Omega," though he

---

[42] I John 5:11-12.
[43] Doctrine and Covenants 76:58.
[44] Doctrine and Covenants 76:59.
[45] Doctrine and Covenants 76:24.
[46] Doctrine and Covenants 93:21-22. Compare also I Cor. 4:15; Doctrine and Covenants 84:33-34.

[47] Revelation 1:1.
[48] Revelation 22:8-9.
[49] Revelation 22:12-13.

meant that Jesus Christ would come, and that Jesus Christ was Alpha and Omega. Just so Jesus Christ represents the Father.

Thus we see that in three separate ways we may consider Christ as the "Father." These considerations do not, however, alter in the least degree the literal relationship of Father and Son between Elohim and Jesus Christ. And while we call the Savior our "Father" it is also proper to call Him our "Elder Brother," for He is literally our Elder Brother and is of the same order of spirit being to which we belong.[50]

He is essentially greater than His brethren by reason of (1) "His seniority as the oldest or first born; (2) His unique status in the flesh as the offspring of a mortal mother and of an immortal or resurrected and glorified Father; (3) His selection and foreordination as the one and only Redeemer and Savior of the race; and (4) His transcendent sinlessness.

"Jesus Christ is not the Father of the spirits who have taken or yet shall take bodies upon this earth, for He is one of them, He is the Son, as they are the sons or daughters of Elohim. So far as the stages of eternal progression and attainment have been made known through divine revelation, we are to understand that only resurrected and glorified beings can become parents of spirit offspring."[51]

The Spirit of God

The terms, "Spirit of God," "Holy Spirit," "Holy Ghost," and "light of Christ," are often used synonymously in our scriptures and in our sermons. The terms, however, have distinct meanings and these must not be forgotten. The Spirit of God, although not entirely comprehensive unto man, can be understood at least in part.

Manifestly, since God is a perfected person, having a body with definite form and size, He cannot, in body, at least, be present in more than one place at one time. The questions then arise: How can God from one place govern the immensity of the universe? How can He even be aware of each of His many sons and daughters? We are human beings, limited greatly in our knowledge of the universe in which we live, and quite unable to comprehend anything outside the realm of our limited experience. It must have taken unusual faith in and understanding of the Lord to have prompted the Psalmist to write these lines:

"The Lord looketh from heaven; he beholdeth all the sons of men.

"From the place of his habitation he looketh upon all the inhabitants of the earth.

"He fashioneth their hearts alike; he considereth all their works."[52]

Since the mind of man has been opened by experiences with radio and television and the universality of electricity as a medium for the transmission of vibrations that produce sound, sight, color, etc., it is not difficult to believe in the power of God as a personage to keep in constant touch with all of His universe and the inhabitants therein.

The medium through which God controls the universe and by which He may inspire and direct His children is called by the Scriptures the Spirit of God. While it has been likened to the light of the sun, to electricity, or to the electrons of which all matter and life are composed, it has not been identified with any one of them, and may be a substance unknown to man aside from his

---

[50]See Hebrews 2:17.
[51]Statement of the First Presidency and the Council of the Twelve, June 30, 1916. See Talmage, *Articles of Faith*, Appendix.

[52]Psalms 33:13-15.

spiritual experience with it. Some things, however, we know concerning it.

"The Spirit giveth light to every man that cometh into the world; and the Spirit enlighteneth every man through the world, that hearkeneth to the voice of the Spirit."[53]

". . . which is the same light that quickeneth your understandings; Which light proceedeth forth from the presence of God to fill the immensity of space—The light which is in all things; which giveth life to all things, which is the law by which all things are governed. . . ."[54]

The Holy Ghost

The Holy Ghost is not to be confused with the Spirit of God though the terms are often used synonymously. The Holy Ghost is a person. Unlike the Father and the Son who have bodies of flesh and bone, the Holy Ghost has no body of flesh and bone (that is, of the elements as we know them) but is a personage of spirit.[55] While we do not know of a certainty what a spirit body is like, considerable light is thrown upon the subject by the statement of Christ to Moriancumr, the brother of Jared, when he saw the Lord upon a high mountain centuries before He appeared on the earth in the flesh:

"Behold, I am he who was prepared from the foundation of the world to redeem my people. . . . And never have I showed myself unto man whom I have created, for never has man believed in me as thou hast. Seest thou that ye are created after mine own image [likeness]? Yea, even all men were created in the beginning after mine own image. Behold, this body which ye now behold, is the body of my spirit; and man have I created after the body of my spirit; and even as I appear unto thee to be in the spirit will I appear unto my people in the flesh."[56]

As an individual the Holy Ghost can be in only one place at one time. His in-

fluence, however, may reach unto the uttermost bounds of the universe by operation through that same medium, the Spirit of God, by which all things are governed and controlled. Because the Holy Ghost functions by and through the Spirit of God this influence is often termed the Spirit of God. This influence of the Holy Ghost emanates, however, from the person of the Holy Ghost and is not to be confused with the Spirit of God which is the medium through which the Holy Ghost acts. Neither should the person of the Holy Ghost be confused with the message which comes from Him and which is often designated as the Holy Spirit.[57]

"The Holy Ghost is a personage of Spirit, he constitutes the third person in the Godhead. The gift or presentation of the Holy Ghost is the authoritative act of conferring him upon man. The Holy Ghost in person may visit men and will visit those who are worthy and bear witness to their spirit of God and Christ, but may not tarry with them. The Spirit of God which emanates from Deity may be likened to electricity, * * * which fills the earth and the air, and is everywhere present. It is the power of God, the influence that He exerts throughout all His works by which He can effect His purposes and execute His will in consonance with the laws of free agency which He has conferred upon man. By means of this Spirit every man is enlightened, the wicked as well as the good, the intelligent and the ignorant, the high and the low, each in accordance with his capacity to receive the light; and this Spirit or influence which emanates from God may be said to constitute man's consciousness, and will never cease to strive with man, until man is brought to the possession of the higher intelligence which can only come through faith, repentance, baptism for the remisson of sins, and the gift or the presentation of the Holy Ghost by one having authority."[58]

The Prophet Joseph said: "There is a difference between the Holy Ghost and the gift of the Holy Ghost.

---

[53]*Doctrine and Covenants* 84:46.
[54]*Ibid.*, 88:11-13. See also *Ibid.*, 50:27; 12:9; 29:30; 84:45; 88:7; 66:67.
[55]*Ibid.*, 130:22.
[56]Ether 3:14-16.

[57]See Talmage, *Articles of Faith*, pp. 157-170.
[58]Joseph F. Smith, *Improvement Era*, Vol. 12. p. 389 (March 1909).

Cornelius (New Testament character) received the Holy Ghost before he was baptized, which was the convincing power of God unto him of the truth of the Gospel, but he could not receive the gift of the Holy Ghost until after he was baptized. Had he not taken this sign or ordinance upon him, the Holy Ghost which convinced him of the truth of God would have left him. Until he obeyed these ordinances and received the gift of the Holy Ghost by the laying on of hands, according to the order of God, he could not have healed the sick or commanded an evil spirit to come out of a man and it obey him."[59]

The Holy Ghost is the messenger of God the Father and of the Son Jesus Christ unto those who have entered into the Kingdom or Church of God. The bestowal of the Holy Ghost or gift of the Holy Ghost follows baptism, and is bestowed by the laying on of hands by those having authority of Christ so to do. For Christ has said: "He that is baptized in my name, to him will the Father give the Holy Ghost, like unto me; wherefore, follow me, and do the things which ye have seen me do."[60]

And again:

"Verily, verily, I say unto you, that this is my doctrine, and I bear record of it from the Father; and whoso believeth in me believeth in the Father also; and unto him will the Father bear record of me, for he will visit him with fire and with the Holy Ghost.

"And thus will the Father bear record of me, and the Holy Ghost will bear record unto him of the Father and me; for the Father, and I, and the Holy Ghost are one.

"And again I say unto you, ye must repent, and be baptized in my name, and become as a little child, or ye can in nowise inherit the kingdom of God."[61]

Concerning the personal powers and attributes of the Holy Ghost we know little. He must, however, be perfect in these things for He is as one with the Father and the Son. From the scriptures we learn that He teaches and guides,[62] speaks, commands, and commissions,[63] reproves for sin,[64] makes intercession for sinners,[65] is grieved,[66] searches and investigates,[67] entices,[68] testifies of the Father and the Son,[69] and knows all things.[70]

The Holy Ghost, or the right to be instructed of Him is a gift of God to the worthy who have obeyed the commandments and complied with the ordinances. The instructions of the Holy Ghost are a prerequisite to knowledge that God is, and that Jesus Christ is His Son. Without the Holy Ghost men might believe and from the many evidences develop faith, but as the Apostle Paul declared, "No man can say that Jesus is the Lord [that is, with certainty], but by the Holy Ghost."[71] Thus, the Holy Ghost is a revelator and no one receives him without being the recipient of a revelation.[72]

Supplementary Readings

On Specific Topics:

  How We May Come To Know God
    Talmage, *Sunday Night Talks*, pp. 7-28.

  Work and Attributes of God, the Father
    Talmage, *Sunday Night Talks*, pp. 29-50.

    Doctrine and Covenants, Section 20:16-36.

  Work and Attributes of Jesus Christ
    Talmage, *Sunday Night Talks*, pp. 510-519.

---

[59]*History of the Church*, Vol. IV, p. 555.
[60]2 Nephi 31:12.
[61]3 Nephi 11:35-36, 38.
[62]John 14:26; 16:13.
[63]Acts 10:19; 13:2; Rev. 2:7; 1 Nephi 4:6, 11:2-12.
[64]John 16:8.
[65]Rom. 8:26.
[66]Eph. 4:30.
[67]I Cor. 2:4-10.
[68]Mosiah 3:19.
[69]John 15:26.
[70]Alma 7:13.
[71]I Cor. 12:3.
[72]See Joseph Smith, *History of the Church*, Vol. VI, p. 58.

Talmage, James E., "Our Lord, the Christ," *Improvement Era*, Vol. 35 (Dec., 1932).
Doctrine and Covenants, Section 93:1-29.

The Holy Ghost
Talmage, *Sunday Night Talks*, pp. 195-206.
Smith, *Gospel Doctrine*, pp. 218-224.

Communication Between God and Man
Talmage, *Sunday Night Talks*, pp. 308-318.
Smith, *Gospel Doctrine*, pp. 215, 218, 219. (Prayer.)
Roberts, *Defense of the Faith*, Vol. I, pp. 501-532.
("Revelation and Inspiration.")

General Readings:
Widtsoe, *A Rational Theology*, pp. 24-29, 65-82.

Doctrine and Covenants, Section 93:1-40.

Smith, *Gospel Doctrine*, pp. 42-57, 72-79, 274-279.

Talmage, *Articles of Faith*, pp. 29-51.

Talmage, *Sunday Night Talks*, pp. 7-50, 195-206, 308-318, 442-451, 510-519.

Book of Mormon, Ether 3; 3 Nephi 11.

Doctrine and Covenants 76:19-24; 110:1-4.

Pearl of Great Price, Moses 1; Abraham 3.

Roberts, B. H., "The Revelation of God," *Deseret News*, Church Section, February 11, 1933.

Talmage, *Vitality of Mormonism*, pp. 42-45, 51-54.

CHAPTER 44

THE GOSPEL PLAN OF LIFE

What a Belief in God as Our Father Involves

Once we have come to look upon God as our Father, our whole attitude toward Him changes. He seems no longer distant, no longer remote and unapproachable. We begin to turn to Him with that same ease with which we turn to our earthly parents, confident of being heard and confident that our requests worthily made will be granted if they are for our good and the good of all. Jesus said to His wondering followers:

"Ask, and it shall be given you; seek, and ye shall find; knock, and it shall be opened unto you: For every one that asketh receiveth; and he that seeketh, findeth; and to him that knocketh, it shall be opened. Or what man is there of you, whom if his son ask bread, will give him a stone? Or if he ask a fish, will he give him a serpent? If ye then, being evil, know how to give good gifts unto your children. how much more shall your Father which is in heaven give good things unto them that ask him!"[1]

For since we are His children, God, as our Father, must be interested in us. He must desire us to be happy, not one or a few of us, but all His children. Hence all that he does pertaining unto man must be for the good of man. Mormon had this relationship in mind when he wrote:

". . . All things which are good cometh of God. . . . that which is of God inviteth and enticeth to do good continually; wherefore everything which inviteth and enticeth to do good, and to love God and to serve him is inspired of God."[2]

It is logical also that God, as our Father, should have laid plans for us, His children, whereby we could progress toward the perfection which He has attained, and that having formulated those plans He works continuously for their completion and success. The belief in a personal God, the literal Father of our spirits, gives purpose to creation and to life. To understand that purpose is to establish a premise around which our whole philosophy of life may safely rest.

It would be manifestly impossible for an infant to understand much of his earthly father's plans for him unless his father should choose to explain them in simple words or by simple illustrations. As the child grows and develops he becomes capable of grasping more and more of his father's plans for his education, travel, and business preparation. He will eventually come to appreciate such plans and may cooperate in their accomplishment.

We are like infants when we attempt to understand God's eternal purposes. Some of His plans for us we can grasp; part of them may be beyond our present understanding. Our learning becomes a process of adding truth to truth! Of the Lord's plans for us we could know but little had He not seen fit to declare them unto some of His children who have appealed directly to Him for light and understanding.

As we come to view God as our Father and come to understand His eternal purpose to bring to pass the immortality and eternal life of His children, our hearts naturally turn to-

---

[1] Matt. 7:7-11.
[2] Moroni 7:12-13.

ward Him in appreciation, and there arises within us a desire to aid Him and to please Him. It is the same feeling with which we seek to aid our earthly parents in a worthy project designed for our happiness and with which we hope to win words of encouragement and praise.

Happily for us God has revealed unto those who are prepared to read and believe as much of His plans as we can comprehend and follow.[3]

The Gospel Plan of Life
Man's Pre-Earth Life

Before this world was organized we existed as spiritual children of our Father. The full nature of this existence is unknown to us. Except for some revelations on the subject we would know nothing at all. The important facts so far as we can profit by them in this existence have perhaps been received. We learn that all individuals who are on the earth today, or have ever lived here, or are to come to this earth were in a spiritual stage of existence before this world began.[4]

In that pre-earth life, man exercised his own will or free agency, was subject to laws of progression, and did progress in varying degrees of capacity and intelligence. The ancient Patriarch Abraham records that the Lord revealed unto him, by Urim and Thummim, a vision of the pre-earth life. After showing unto Abraham the varied orders of created worlds, some greater than others, the Lord said:

"If there be two spirits, and one shall be more intelligent than the other, yet these two spirits, notwithstanding one is more intelligent than the other, have no beginning; they existed before, they shall have no end, they shall exist after, for they are gnolaum, or eternal. And the Lord said unto me: These two facts do exist, that there are two spirits, one being more intelligent than the other; there shall be another more intelligent than they; I am the Lord thy God, I am more intelligent than they all . . . I dwell in the midst of them all; I now, therefore, have come down unto thee to deliver unto thee the works which my hands have made, wherein my wisdom excelleth them all, for I rule in the heavens above and in the earth beneath, in all wisdom and prudence, over all the intelligences thine eyes have seen from the beginning; I came down in the beginning [that is the beginning of the earth] in the midst of all the intelligences thou hast seen."[5]

The spirits thus referred to were without bodies of flesh and bone such as we now possess but were in form like unto present man, definite in size, shape, and substance.[6] They could converse one with another,[7] exercise their will in the matter of making choices,[8] could experience anger,[9] and joy,[10] in short, except for the limitations which lack of physical bodies entail, and the limitations of environment, they must have enjoyed the association of one another and listened to the teachings of one another like unto man as we know him on the earth.

In that existence men and Jesus were the same order of beings, of the same race, nature and essence. Jesus is literally our Elder Brother, the Firstborn of the Father.[11]

Hence, while very far removed from us in the development which He had attained and in His intellectual and spiritual powers, a study of Jesus reveals much concerning the nature of

---

[3]See Alma 29.
[4]*Pearl of Great Price*, Abraham 3:22-24.
[5]*Pearl of Great Price*, Abraham 3:18-19, 21.
[6]See Ether 3 (in which a personage of spirit is revealed).
[7]*Pearl of Great Price*, Moses 4:1-2; Abraham 3:27.
[8]*Pearl of Great Price*, Moses 4:3-4.
[9]*Pearl of Great Price*, Abraham 3:28.
[10]Job 38:4-7.
[11]Hebrews 2:10-11; *Doctrine and Covenants* 93.

man and his possible achievements. Jesus said to His followers:

"And now, verily, I say unto you, I was in the beginning with the Father, and am the Firstborn. . . . Man [meaning the race] was also in the beginning with God. Intelligence, or the light of truth, was not created, or made neither indeed can be. All truth is independent in that sphere in which God has placed it, to act for itself, as all intelligence also; otherwise there is no existence. Behold here is the agency of man, and here is the condemnation of man, because that which was from the beginning is plainly manifest unto them and they receive not the light. And every man who receiveth not the light is under condemnation, for man is spirit."[12]

God, the Father of us all, is interested in the advancement of His children and revealed this interest unto us in these words:

"For, behold, this is my work and my glory—to bring to pass the immortality and eternal life of man."[13]

The accomplishment of the work cannot be attained by God alone. Each intelligence is an entity, independent of other intelligences, free to act and possessing a will to act. In that spirit world as in the physical world about us wrong choices were often made and progress retarded. That existence, as this one, is governed by laws. These laws must have been taught by the Father to His children. Some observed them and made progress while others must have disobeyed them.

Fore-ordination

It appears that so well were the characters of His children known to Him, that God made some selections, even during that pre-earth life for specific missions in carrying forward His plans when they should live upon the earth in the flesh.

[12]*Doctrine and Covenants* 93:21, 29-33.
[13]*Pearl of Great Price*, Moses 1:39.

Abraham records:

"Now the Lord had shown unto me, Abraham, the intelligences that were organized before the world was; and among all these were many of the noble and great ones;

"And God saw these souls that they were good, and he stood in the midst of them, and he said: These I will make my rulers; for he stood among those that were spirits, and he saw that they were good; and he said unto me: Abraham, thou art one of them; thou wast chosen before thou wast born."[14]

The appointment by God of His spirit children to do specified tasks upon the earth is called "fore-ordination." How many were thus called beforehand is not revealed, but it may not be that all of us were called to specific missions. This belief in fore-ordination must not be confused with the doctrine of predestination, which is contrary to the gospel plan.[15] Those called to certain labors did not lose their free agency. They could at any time reject the work to which they had been called.[16] They could even reject the Lord who called them. But their call was based upon an understanding better than our own and made from among those who had proved themselves noble and great.

Planning for an Earth Life

While happiness and joy were to be had in the spirit world there were evidently many limitations to growth, which could only be removed by the acquirement of a physical body or the union of the spirit with the elements. From the scriptures we learn:

"For man is spirit. The elements are eternal, and spirit and element, inseparably connected, receive a fulness of joy;

"And when separated man cannot receive a fulness of joy."[17]

[14]*Pearl of Great Price, Abraham* 3:22-23.
[15]Talmage, *Articles of Faith*, pp. 189-192.
[16]See God's instruction to Joseph Smith, *Doctrine and Covenants* 3:4, 9-11.
[17]*Doctrine and Covenants* 93:33-34.

The Lord as a Father, interested in the welfare of His children, sought to bring about an eternal union of the spirit with the elements. That ultimate state would require experience and knowledge of physical things, so the Lord planned an earth where a spirit might dwell in the flesh and obtain, if he were obedient, the knowledge necessary to the final and lasting union of spirit and body. Abraham was shown the plan of the Lord in these matters and wrote:

"And there stood one among them that was like unto God, and he said unto those who were with him: We will go down, for there is space there, and we will take of these materials, and we will make an earth whereon these may dwell;

"And we will prove them herewith, to see if they will do all things whatsoever the Lord their God shall command them.

"And they who keep their first estate shall be added upon; and they who keep not their first estate shall not have glory in the same kingdom with those who keep their first estate, and they who keep their second estate shall have glory added upon their heads for ever and ever.

"And the Lord said: Whom shall I send? And one answered, like unto the son of man: Here am I, send me. And another answered and said: Here am I, send me. And the Lord said: I will send the first.

"And the second was angry, and kept not his first estate; and, at that day, many followed after him."[18]

An explanation of the acceptance of the Firstborn and the rejection of Lucifer, Son of the Morning, was made by the Lord unto the Prophet Moses and was also revealed unto Joseph Smith in the year 1830.

"And I, the Lord God, spake unto Moses, saying: That Satan, whom thou hast commanded in the name of mine Only Begotten, is the same which was from the beginning, and he came before me, saying—Behold, here am I, send me, I will be thy son, and I will redeem all mankind, that one soul shall not

be lost, and surely I will do it; wherefore give me thine honor.

"But, behold, my Beloved Son, which was my Beloved and Chosen from the beginning, said unto me—Father, thy will be done, and the glory be thine forever.

"Wherefore, because that Satan rebelled against me, and sought to destroy the agency of man, which I, the Lord God, had given him, and also, that I should give unto him mine own power; by the power of mine Only Begotten, I caused that he should be cast down;

"And he became Satan, yea, even the devil, the father of all lies, to deceive and to blind men, and to lead them captive at his will, even as many as would not hearken unto my voice."[19]

The plan of Satan to compel obedience so as to bring all God's children back into God's presence without sin appealed to many in the Spirit World so that about one-third of the host of heaven followed after him. The plan, however, would have robbed man of his free agency, his right and power to make choices. Without such right there can be no growth and hence no reward. The Lord made this clear in modern revelation.

"For behold, it is not meet that I should command in all things; for he that is compelled in all things, the same is a slothful and not a wise servant; wherefore he receiveth no reward.

"Verily I say, men should be anxiously engaged in a good cause, and do many things of their own free will, and bring to pass much righteousness;

"For the power is in them, wherein they are agents unto themselves. And inasmuch as men do good they shall in no wise lose their reward."[20]

The gospel plan of Jesus Christ, acceptable to the Father, was presented to a great council of spirits in the heavens that they might, in the exercise of their free agency, accept or reject it. It appears that the great majority accepted it and entered into an everlast-

---

[18]*Pearl of Great Price*, Abraham 3:24-28.

[19]*Pearl of Great Price*, Moses 4:1-4.
[20]*Doctrine and Covenants* 58:26-28.

ing covenant that they would abide by it. The followers of Lucifer refused to come to earth under the plan.

The General Nature of the Plan

The essence of the plan was that spirits, forgetting temporarily their spiritual home, should enter into tabernacles or bodies of grosser materials. The home of these embodied spirits was to be a new earth or material world. Upon this new earth men were to continue their existence, shut off from the immediate presence of their Father. They were not, however, to be left wholly ignorant of Him, but knowledge of Him and the entire gospel plan was to be revealed by the Father unto His children. Further, upon obedience to certain principles and the performance of certain ordinances by those who should receive power to officiate in them, men should receive the Holy Ghost who would bear witness in their hearts of the existence and goodness of God and be a messenger from the Father and the Son unto them.

In such a strange world, man in the exercise of his free agency would naturally fail to conform to many laws upon which the maintenance of physical bodies depends, and bring about a condition where the body would no longer be a fit abode for the spirit. When such a state should be reached, the plan of God provided for the release of the spirit from the body, which release should be known as the death of the body. At the time of death the spirit of man would go into the spirit world while his body would return to the elements from whence it had come. Not only would man by his actions bring death to his body but by his sins he would shut himself off from the pres-

ence of God. From this condition he must be redeemed. The gospel plan provided for this redemption. The Only Begotten Son, whose plan had been accepted by the Father and by His brethren in the heavens, was to come to earth in the flesh and by virtue of His Godhood and by living a life free from sin was to gain such mastery over the body as to have power to lay it down and power to take it up again, thereby robbing the grave of its victory and gaining the power by which He can draw all others unto Him.

The story of the creation of the earth by the Only Begotten and His helpers under the direction of the Father is told in the old Hebrew Genesis,[21] in the *Book of Moses*,[22] and in the *Book of Abraham*.[23] It is a story of matchless beauty and simplicity. From it we learn several great truths. The earth did not come into existence by accident but was a planned event, the work of an intelligent Being. The creation of the earth had a specific purpose—to provide a home where the spirits might dwell in tabernacles of flesh. The creation was brought about in various stages according to the preconceived plan. The details of that plan and the time involved in bringing it about are unknown to us but are relatively unimportant to our understanding of the gospel plan.

The Type of World Necessary for the Development of Man.

The Capacities of the Human Being for Joy

Many of the problems of life are clarified by keeping constantly in mind the purposes for which the earth was

[21]Genesis 1 and 2.
[22]*Pearl of Great Price*, Moses 1 to 4.
[23]*Pearl of Great Price*, Abraham 4; 5.

created. The earth was made as a fit abode for man's development and growth that he might gain eternal joy.

The human being has many inherent capacities for joy. *First* of all, he has the capacity for a wide range of physical enjoyments and achievements. In addition to eating, sleeping and keeping warm, he has the capacity of obtaining joy from the exertion of the muscles in running, jumping, dancing, skating, in games, and a thousand and one activities of the physical man. The world, then, to be a suitable place for the development of physical man must be a physical world—a world of mountains and plains, of rivers and oceans, of ice and snow, of sunshine and rain, of plant and animal life, all of which he might learn to use and enjoy.

Second, a man has the capacity for mental joy growing out of the activities of the mind. The abode of man, then, must be a world where the intelligence or mind of man might be developed. Hence it must be a challenging world— a world that rewards efforts and punishes stupidity and slothfulness. It must be a world where emotions might find expression in art and music. To develop an appreciation of music and harmony it must contain disharmonies. To develop an appreciation of the beautiful it must contain that which is ugly. To develop an appreciation of love it must contain hatred and greed.

Third, man has a capacity for spiritual joy obtained by unselfish service which sets him apart from all of the earth's other creatures. Spiritual joy is the product of unity of the mind of one person with that of another so that one mind catches and partakes of the joys of another. The greatest of such union of souls is the oneness achieved by Jesus the Christ with His Father, and which is possible for all men. The Savior could think of no greater joy and achievement for His twelve than to pray that they might be one: "Holy Father, keep through thine own name those whom thou hast given me, that they may be one, as we are."[24]

"Neither pray I for these alone, but for them also which shall believe on me through their word;

"That they may all be one; as thou, Father, art in me, and I in thee, that they may be one in us: that the world may believe that thou hast sent me.

"And the glory which thou gavest me, I have given them; that they may be one even as we are one:

"I in them, and thou in me, that they may. be made perfect in one; and that the world may know that thou hast sent me, and hast loved them, as thou hast loved me."[25]

This joy which comes from being "at one" with another person is experienced to a certain degree in friendships, in marriage relationships, in parent and child relationships. Such spiritual joy finds expression in form of worship, acts of love and kindness, devotion, gratitude, and rejoicing. It follows that spiritual joy cannot be had apart from God and man, and can only be complete when it embraces both.

A world for the development of spiritual joy must, then, be a world of human relationships where interdependence links mind to mind and offers opportunity for unselfish service.[26]

A World of Law Needed

A world which will be productive in growth in human beings must be a reliable world—a world of law.

There could be no progress without constant and eternal values. Cause and

24John 17:11.
25John 17:20-23.
26Matthew 25:37-40.

effect must ever remain the same. If water were good for the body today and poisonous tomorrow, if the law of gravitational pull should suddenly be reversed, in short, if in any particular this world should prove unreliable the whole purpose of life would be frustrated.

An existence suitable for the development of man must leave man to exercise his own will power or free agency. One who has no opportunity to turn to the right or the left does not develop strength of character. Character grows as a result of right choices.

Hence, although the free agency of man may lead him to destroy himself or his neighbors, a world without individual freedom would be useless.

The plan of Lucifer, Son of the Morning, involved compulsion upon the souls of men, robbing them of their free agency.[27] Even though Lucifer could promise that by forcing all mankind to obey the laws and commandments of God not one soul would be lost, yet the plan was rejected because it could not be productive of growth. At the end of such an existence man would be no further advanced in character and intelligence than at the beginning. The free agency of intelligences is an eternal law, and could not be taken from man at any stage of his existence without violating such eternal law.

An environment suitable for human growth must contain the possibilities of pain and evil as well as the possibilities of joy. Pain results from the sensitiveness of the body to conditions unfavorable to cell life. There must be a sensitiveness of body and mind or there could be no existence at all. If it were not possible to feel cold it would not be

possible to feel warmth, and if it were not possible to feel either cold or warmth man could not survive for he could not avoid such degrees of heat and cold as are destructive to the cells of the body. This is true of all the sensations of physical pain. If man were not sensitive to harmful physical circumstances he would have no warning to enable him to remedy the situation. Hence, pain is a safeguard and corollary of life and there can be no existence without it. Physical sensitiveness to pain is necessary to physical preservation and the attainment of physical joy.

Likewise, mental sensitiveness, though it might lead to anguish and sorrow, is a necessity to mental and spiritual development. There could be no joy without the possibility of pain. The great Prophet Lehi taught this to his people in plain words:

"For it must needs be, that there is an opposition in all things. If not so, my firstborn in the wilderness, righteousness could not be brought to pass, neither wickedness, neither holiness nor misery, neither good nor bad. Wherefore, all things must needs be a compound in one; wherefore, if it should be one body it must needs remain as dead, having no life neither death, nor corruption nor incorruption, happiness nor misery, neither sense nor insensibility.

"Wherefore, it must needs have been created for a thing of naught; wherefore there would have been no purpose in the end of its creation. Wherefore, this thing must needs destroy the wisdom of God and his eternal purposes, and also the power, and the mercy, and the justice of God.

"And if ye shall say there is no law, ye shall also say there is no sin. If ye shall say there is no sin, ye shall also say there is no righteousness. And if there be no righteousness there be no happiness. And if there be no righteousness nor happiness there be no punishment nor misery. And if these things are not there is no God. And if there is no God we are not, neither the earth; for there could have been no creation of things, neither

---

[27]*Pearl of Great Price*, Moses 4:1-4.

OGDEN TEMPLE, dedicated by President Joseph Fielding Smith, January 18, 1972.

PROVO TEMPLE, dedicated by President Joseph Fielding Smith, February 9, 1972.

Architect's rendering of the new WASHINGTON, D.C. TEMPLE.

to act nor to be acted upon; wherefore, all things must have vanished away."[28]

To build character requires that individuals shall live together. After many contacts with one's fellows, solitude may be productive of deep thinking, but it would be unproductive if no contacts with other personalities had ever occurred. The higher attributes of man— love, kindness, charity, forgiveness, mercy, helpfulness — are attributes which require fellowship with others for their development. Further, as stated above, spiritual joy, the joy of sharing another's thoughts, emotions, and achievements, requires knowledge of and association with others.

The evil in the world is the result of the above-mentioned factors. People exercising their free agency in a universe of law surrounded by their fellows, all of whom are sensitive to pain, cannot in their imperfections escape evil. Laws will sometimes be broken, wrong choices will sometimes be made, conditions unfavorable to cell life will be experienced and people in the exercise of their free agency will injure one another.

But who would change the nature of the world in which we live? For to change the universe in any of these particulars is to deny ourselves the possibilities of joy and growth.

When we observe individuals enduring physical suffering, when we see them in mental torment, when man's inhumanity to man reaches tremendous proportions on the wings of war, we often wonder where and if God can be. But these ills cannot be wholly removed without changing the basic laws on which human progress depends, and although the heavens may weep over man's stupidity and sin God will not alter His eternal decrees.

In viewing the whole picture we are too prone to see the evil and overlook the good which life in the flesh has produced. The greatest wonder in the universe is not the evil of God's children but their inherent goodness. Under the laws of existence on this earth joy is much more prevalent than pain, and the accomplishments of man even in ancient times led the Psalmist to explain:

"What is man, that thou art mindful of him? and the son of man, that thou visitest him?
"For thou hast made him a little lower than the angels, and hast crowned him with glory and honour.
"Thou madest him to have dominion over the works of thy hands; thou hast put all things under his feet."[29]

When one weighs the willingness of most individuals to sacrifice goods and comfort and even give their lives for others; their willingness to serve; their interest in the welfare of their neighbors; when we sense the deep love that develops in most homes; the abiding friendships we have witnessed; the ability of people to live together in large numbers in relative peace and harmony; and above all, when one contemplates some of the outstanding products this world has produced—the perfection of the Christ, the love of a mother and the devotion of a father—all the evil of the universe fades into insignificance in the eternal scheme, and the wisdom of God in creating such a world reveals itself like the light of day.

The Fall and Atonement

The Fall

Before the earth was formed and man placed upon it in the flesh, God the

---

[28]2 Nephi 2:11-13.

[29]Psalms 8:4-6.

Father in His eternal wisdom knew the nature of the joy and pain that awaited His children. Only in perfection could they obey all the physical and spiritual laws of their new existence and that perfection had not been reached. It was, in fact, to give His children an acquaintance with bodies of flesh and bone, about which they knew nothing, that the earth was formed. Hence, it was foreseen that all of His children in greater or lesser degree would violate the laws under which they were to live and would reap the consequences of so doing. Even though God should command His children not to violate the laws of their new existence and should warn them of the consequences of breaking them, it would be inevitable in their inexperience that laws would be broken.

To help man overcome evil, the principles of progress known as the Gospel were taught to him. To aid him in keeping the commandments of God and to test his readiness to keep the spiritual laws of God so as to obtain the blessings which follow, God instituted ordinances and gave, unto those of His sons who were worthy, the power to act in His stead and to officiate therein.

By obedience to the principles of the Gospel, man could constantly correct the errors committed and overcome the state of unhappiness which would otherwise follow.

From the consequences of breaking some of these laws man could not free himself. The first of these was the breaking of those laws of immortality whereby man became subject unto death in the flesh. The first parents, Adam and Eve, having become subject unto death, subjected all of their descendants to death in the flesh. The changes which took place in their bodies, as the result of the breaking of certain laws, were inherited by their offspring. Thus, without any apparent fault of their own the offspring of Adam became subject to the conditions brought about by the fall of their ancestors.

These descendants of Adam and Eve should not, however, entertain any feeling of condemnation toward their first parents for the condition in which they find themselves, for none of them is sinless, save one, Christ, and each in his own turn would have fallen from his immortal state could he have inherited one. Indeed, but for the "fall" of Adam he never could have become a mortal being, subject to the laws of mortality and thus able to distinguish good and evil in a physical world. Nor without inheriting from our ancestors such a changed condition of body could any of us experience mortality and come to know the joys which the union of body and spirit may bring.

The breaking of the law of immortality by which our first parents became mortals, subject to death in the flesh, is called "The Fall." The story of the fall is one of the most persistent stories of the human race. In various forms the story has been found in the literature of most of the peoples of the earth, but the account which has reached us from the writings of Abraham and Moses surpasses them all in perfection and literary beauty. Abraham's account of "The Fall" is to be found in the *Pearl of Great Price*, Book of Abraham. Moses' account may be found in the *Pearl of Great Price*, Book of Moses, and in an imperfect form in the Holy Bible, Book of Genesis. These three accounts are witnesses of the reality of the events. There is little known of the nature of the laws involved in "The Fall" and probably little could be understood by man. Endless dispute concerning the literalness of the story has done little to solve the perplexities. The great cardinal truths, however, have endured in their simplicity; man was first formed in the image of God and placed upon the earth. A mortal condition wherein the body became subject to death followed the acts of our first parents and was inherited by their descendants. From this death, man is powerless to redeem himself and could never rise therefrom without aid. In His goodness and wisdom God permitted death to come to the human family but provided a way whereby man could both profit by his experiences in mortality and also be redeemed from his fallen state.

Thus, we read that after the Fall,

"And in that day the Holy Ghost fell upon Adam, which beareth record of the Father and the Son, saying: I am the Only Begotten of the Father from the beginning, henceforth and forever, that as thou hast fallen thou mayest be redeemed, and all mankind, even as many as will.

"And in that day Adam blessed God and was filled, and began to prophesy concerning all the families of the earth, saying: Blessed be the name of God, for because of my transgression my eyes are opened, and in this life I shall have joy, and again in the flesh I shall see God.

"And Eve, his wife, heard all these things and was glad, saying: Were it not for our transgression we never should have had seed, and never should have known good and evil, and the joy of our redemption, and the eternal life which God giveth unto all the obedient."[30]

In September, 1830, Joseph Smith inquired of the Lord through prayer concerning the subject and received the following:

[30]*Pearl of Great Price*, Moses 5:9-11.

"Wherefore, it came to pass that the devil tempted Adam, and he partook of the forbidden fruit and transgressed the commandment, wherein he became subject to the will of the devil, because he yielded unto temptation.

"Wherefore, I, the Lord God, caused that he should be cast out from the Garden of Eden, from my presence, because of his transgression, wherein he became spiritually dead, which is the first death, even that same death which is the last death, which is spiritual, which shall be pronounced upon the wicked when I shall say: Depart, ye cursed.

"But behold, I say unto you that I, the Lord God, gave unto Adam and unto his seed, that they should not die as to the temporal death, until I, the Lord God, should send forth angels to declare unto them repentance and redemption, through faith on the name of mine Only Begotten Son.

"And thus did I, the Lord God, appoint unto man the days of his probation—that by his natural death he might be raised in immortality unto eternal life, even as many as would believe;

"But, behold, I say unto you, that little children are redeemed from the foundation of the world through mine Only Begotten;

"Wherefore, they cannot sin, for power is not given unto Satan to tempt little children, until they begin to become accountable before me;

"For it is given unto them even as I will, according to mine own pleasure, that great things may be required at the hand of their fathers."[31]

As a result of the added knowledge which thus came to Joseph Smith he voiced the doctrine unto the world:

"We believe that men will be punished for their own sins, and not for Adam's transgression."[32]

The Prophet Lehi summed up the doctrine in these memorable words: "Adam fell that men might be; and men are, that they might have joy."[33]

While man inherits a body subject to death and enters this world shut off from God's presence, he nevertheless is under no condemnation of God. He is

[31]*Doctrine and Covenants* 29:40-43; 46-48.
[32]*Pearl of Great Price*, Articles of Faith, No. Two.
[33]2 Nephi 2:25.

innocent and if he dies in his infancy would return without condemnation unto his Father.[34] But individuals come under condemnation of God when they consciously disobey His commandments or violate their covenants with Him. This, too, constitutes a "fall," a fall from a state of innocence, a state of fellowship with the Father.

Just as a man, conscious of having injured his neighbor, cannot be comfortable in his neighbor's presence, so a man conscious of having broken the laws of God cannot endure His presence.[35] As all mankind are guilty of sin in some degree, none could return to the presence of God, and joy in that presence, save a way should be provided whereby this consciousness of sin should be removed. That was provided for in the gospel plan. The Son of God was commissioned of the Father to reveal Himself to man, to urge man to have faith in the Father, and eventually to win man's love by giving His life in man's behalf. Having awakened in man a knowledge of God and a consciousness of sin, man was called upon to repent, with the promise that upon sincere repentance God will forgive man his sins and man can stand unashamed in the Father's presence. Not only was the Son commissioned to reveal the Father unto man, acquaint man with His laws and urge man to repent of his sins, but Christ was commissioned to judge all mankind as to the sincerity of their repentance and their worthiness to receive the forgiveness of the Father.[36]

[34]*History of the Church*, Vol. II, p. 380-381; *Doctrine and Covenants* 74:7; 93:38.

[35]*Mormon* 9:4-5.

[36]*Doctrine and Covenants* 19:3; 76:111; *John* 5:24.

The Atonement

It must be apparent to all who have thought deeply about it that man, in and of himself, could never have entered upon this mortal stage of existence. Except as individuals already here undergo sacrifices and pain, other spirits could not enter into earth life. Neither could a spirit, having entered a tabernacle of flesh prepared for it, hope to retain such a body without the loving care and sacrifice of others.

In the beginning God formed tabernacles of flesh for the first man and woman and named them Adam and Eve. How those bodies were formed has not been revealed, the single sentence being found in scripture, "And the Lord God formed man of the dust of the ground, and breathed into his nostrils the breath of life."[37] Not only were the bodies of Adam and Eve thus formed of the "dust of the ground," but the bodies of all men have been, and are being, formed of the dust of the earth. The process by which the elements are transformed into living tissue is so wonderful and remarkable as to cause the wisest of men to stand in awe, and none has come to understand. But one cardinal truth must not be forgotten, our spirits did not have power to acquire bodies of flesh and bone, and, but for the act of God, must have remained forever in the spirit world.

When man dies he is unable to repossess his body and must remain forever in a spiritual condition but for the act of God again in his behalf. As we cannot, in our weaknesses and limitations, fully understand the process by which man became mortal, so we cannot fully understand the process by which it again is made possible for man

[37]*Genesis* 2:7.

to acquire an immortal body of flesh and bone. This we can know, that as God called Adam in the beginning to the mission of leading the procession of spirits into bodies of flesh, so God called His Son, Jesus Christ, to lead all spirits into a reuniting with the flesh, which constitutes the resurrection. As the scriptures say, "For as in Adam all die, so in Christ shall all be made alive."[38]

Wherein Jesus acquired His power to again take up His body, after death had separated Him from it, is not fully understood, but the accomplishment of it is the greatest fact in Christian history and constitutes the cornerstone of Christian doctrine. The Savior's own explanation of it was given in simple terms:

"Therefore doth my Father love me, because I lay down my life, that I might take it again.

"No man taketh it from me, but I lay it down of myself. I have power to lay it down, and I have power to take it again. This commandment have I received of my Father."[39]

Not only did the Savior have power over His own body but also over all flesh. In His great prayer to the Father on the occasion of the Last Supper He said, "As thou hast given him power over all flesh, that he should give eternal life to as many as thou hast given him."[40]

As none could enter this mortal existence save through Adam, so none can enter the resurrected state of existence save through Christ. Hence He is the "door,"[41] "the way,"[42] the "resurrection and the life."[43]

To bring about the resurrection it

seems that it was necessary for Christ Himself to pass through mortality and suffer death as to His body. As all worthwhile attainments require a price, the attainment to the position of "Savior" called for a sacrifice and a struggle. Hence Paul could write to the Corinthians: "Ye are bought with a price."[44] And in referring to the Church of God, Paul adds: "Which he hath purchased with his own blood."[45]

The leadership of mankind is not an easy position to acquire, and the price of winning the love of all men is infinitely beyond our understanding. When one contemplates the amount of self-sacrifice, devotion and service, life requires as the price of cementing by love a little family of children to their parents, one is appalled at the amount of sacrifice required to win the love of all mankind.

To win the love of all mankind required that Christ should do a service of such a nature that every son and daughter of Adam would be benefited thereby. This service must extend to all those who had ever lived upon the earth or were yet to live upon it. It must be such a service as would give Christ a claim upon them, and such a service as would be acceptable unto the Father and glorify His name. All mankind needed just such a service—someone who had the power to lay down his life and the power to take it up again— to break the bonds of death and make resurrection a reality for all men. Christ was chosen, before the world was, to render this service and by conquering death became the *Redeemer of all mankind*. As all of the descendants of Adam must die, regardless of

[38]I Cor. 15:22.
[39]John 10:17-18.
[40]John 17:2.
[41]John 10:7, 9.
[42]John 14:6.
[43]John 11:25.

[44]1 Cor. 7:23.
[45]Acts 20:28.

whether or not they keep the commandments of God, so all through Christ shall be made alive, the just and the unjust.[46]

But man needs more than redemption from temporal death or the death of the body. He must also be redeemed from his fallen spiritual condition which has arisen as the result of his own sins. He must, if he would achieve eternal happiness, be restored to a "oneness" with God, the Eternal Father, from whom his disobedience has estranged him. For even with a resurrected body man cannot be happy in his sins. To emphasize this fact Moroni in an address to unbelievers said:

"Behold, I say unto you that ye would be more miserable to dwell with a holy and just God, under a consciousness of your filthiness before him, than ye would to dwell with the damned souls in hell.

"For behold, when ye shall be brought to see your nakedness before God, and also the glory of God, and the holiness of Jesus Christ, it will kindle a flame of unquenchable fire upon you."[47]

Man cannot be redeemed from this spiritual death by an act of Christ alone. Neither can it be accomplished by man alone. Man cannot free himself from the consequences of sin except he repents and receives forgiveness of God. The Savior, however, by His sinless life, by His revelation of the goodness of the Father, by His unparalleled love for mankind, and by His assurance unto man of eternal life, became the greatest factor and incentive for the repentance of all mankind. By his obedience unto the Father He became one with Him in purpose and in goodness. Being one with the Father, whatsoever the Son advocates that will the Father do. And if Christ advocates

that the Father forgive a man his sins that will the Father do because Christ and the Father are one. Hence Christ becomes our "advocate"* with the Father. In a revelation to the Church through Joseph Smith, March 7, 1831, the Savior said:

"Listen to him who is the advocate with the Father, who is pleading your cause before him,

"Saying: Father, behold the sufferings and death of him who did no sin, in whom thou wast well pleased; behold the blood of thy Son which was shed, the blood of him whom thou gavest that thyself might be glorified;

"Wherefore, Father, spare these my brethren that believe on my name, that they may come unto me and have everlasting life."[48]

In order for Jesus to plead for us, to become our mediator and advocate at the eternal bar of God, we must accept Him as our Savior and Redeemer. An acceptance of the Savior involves faith in Him, a willingness to forsake our sins, and the entrance by baptism into a covenant with Him that we will keep His commandments. Thus, when we comply with the requirements of the gospel of Jesus Christ we receive His sure promise that our sins will be remitted. For His perfect obedience to the Father, even to the suffering of death on the cross, Jesus earned the right to adopt as His children and receive blameless into His kingdom all who would believe in His name.

The Spirit World

As we contemplate the mistakes we make in caring for our bodies and all the accumulated bodily weaknesses of our ancestors which we inherit, we begin to realize that eternal life in the

---

[46]2 Nephi 9:22.
[47]Mormon 9:4-5.

*advocate—one who pleads the cause of another, an intercessor.
[48]Doctrine and Covenants 45:3-5. Read Sec. 45:1-15.

body we now possess might be far from joyous. We see about us some tabernacles of flesh which have become poor homes for the spirit, tabernacles which have fallen into decay—men and women no longer able to run and jump, to dance, to skate, to climb mountains; men and women, and even children, whose bodies will no longer respond to their will, bodies hurt and crushed and ravaged by disease until they have become habitations of pain and anguish to the spirit.

As we observe life in all its aspects we begin to see the wisdom of the Almighty in releasing spirits from their earthly tabernacles when habitation within them becomes too painful to endure. This release of the spirit from the earthly body, which we call death, has been provided for by a loving Father. No one who thinks deeply upon the matter would want life in these bodies to continue beyond the time when habitation in them may serve some purpose. We want to care for our bodies so that life in them will be full and joyous for many years. We would continue as long as possible our sojourn in this remarkable world of physical things.

Many look forward to the death of the body with dread, for to the casual observer it seems the end of the individual. Such an end is not desired for either ourselves or our loved ones. Nor has all the intelligence and ingenuity of man enabled him, of himself, to look beyond death and to fathom its mystery. But God, our Father, in His goodness and wisdom, sought to remove the dark shadow that death would otherwise cast over the earth. Unto Adam, the first man, God taught the gospel plan of life. From Adam unto now

prophets of God have proclaimed unto mankind certain great truths which, if believed, bring understanding and comfort. The death of the body is no more the end of the individual than the acquirement of the body was his beginning. As the spirit of man existed before entrance into a mortal tabernacle, so it will continue to exist when the cloak of earthly elements has been lost. Concerning the state of the individual after the death of the body the Nephite prophet, Alma, said:

"And now I would inquire what becometh of the souls of men from this time of death to the time appointed for the resurrection?

"Now whether there is more than one time appointed for men to rise it mattereth not; for all do not die at once, and this mattereth not; all is as one day with God, and time only is measured unto men.

"Therefore, there is a time appointed unto men that they shall rise from the dead; and there is a space between the time of death and the resurrection. And now, concerning this space of time, what becometh of the souls of men is the thing which I have inquired diligently of the Lord to know; and this is the thing of which I do know.

"And when the time cometh when all shall rise, then shall they know that God knoweth all the times which are appointed unto man.

"Now concerning the state of the soul between death and the resurrection—Behold, it has been made known unto me by an angel, that the spirits of all men, as soon as they are departed from this mortal body, yea, the spirits of all men, whether they be good or evil, are taken home to that God who gave them life.

"And then shall it come to pass, that the spirits of those who are righteous are received into a state of happiness, which is called paradise, a state of rest, a state of peace, where they shall rest from all their troubles and from all care, and sorrow.

"And then shall it come to pass, that the spirits of the wicked, yea, who are evil—for behold, they have no part nor portion of the Spirit of the Lord; for behold, they chose evil works rather than good; therefore the spirit of the devil did enter into them, and take possession of their house—and these shall be cast out into outer darkness; there shall be weeping, and wailing, and gnashing of teeth, and this because of their own iniquity, being led captive by the will of the devil.

"Now this is the state of the souls of the wicked, yea, in darkness, and a state of awful, fearful looking for the fiery indignation of the wrath of God upon them; thus they remain in this state, as well as the righteous in paradise, until the time of their resurrection."[49]

The fundamental truths concerning the spirit world which we now know might be summed up as follows:

1. Upon death, all spirits enter the spirit world, both the good and the evil.

2. The state of mind of the individual in the spirit world will be determined largely by his conduct while upon the earth in the flesh. If he is full of remorse of conscience for lost opportunities, for wrongs done to God and man, or if he has failed to cultivate the joys of the mind, his condition will not be a happy one. The condition of remorse and regret in which one may find himself, even in this world, we call "hell." If man has lived a life of usefulness and righteousness his condition in the spirit world will be one of joy. In a joyful state or condition of mind the spirit world is a "paradise" to him. If he is in a state or condition of remorse the spirit world is a "hell." No two individuals may be in quite the same condition of happiness or unhappiness, for no two lives may have run exactly the same course.

3. Remorse in the spirit world for our sins might be avoided by repentance of them so that we remember them no more. Repentance is more difficult the longer it is delayed and may be especially difficult in the spirit world. Hence God urges His children to repent while in mortality. This is easily understood when we realize that habits acquired in the body can hardly be overcome when out of the body. A simple example from life will illustrate. A boy has acquired the bad habit of taking too many steps, called "progressing," with the ball while on the basketball court. In a crucial contest this habit costs his team the game. In his dressing room the boy is full of gloom; nor can the gloom be easily thrust aside, for he cannot return to the basketball floor and play the game over and so rectify himself in the eyes of his teammates. Nor can he overcome his fault off the floor. All he can do is practice and wait for another game, perhaps in a later season, in the hope of so playing the game as to win the approval of coach and players.

4. The Gospel of Jesus Christ will be taught to all who enter the spirit world and sinners may there learn the principles of truth and embrace them. The truth will cause them to forsake evil, to repent insofar as they are able to seek the forgiveness of God for their sins so that they may live in His presence without remorse and shame. But the conditions upon which Christ has promised that He will plead unto the Father for such forgiveness calls for the entrance into the covenant of baptism by immersion in water. Water is a physical substance and the ordinance of baptism pertains to mortality and cannot be performed in the spirit world. Hence, regardless of his acceptance of the principles of the gospel in the spirit world, man cannot there enter into the covenant with God whereby his sins can be remitted and his remorse and mental torment come to an end. Wherefore, man must remain in his state of hell or paradise during

---

[49]Alma 40:7-14.

all his sojourn in the spirit world save some provision is made for him to fill the requirements of the gospel in regard to earthly ordinances. This provision has been made by an all-just Father who has virtually said unto such of His children: "If another upon the earth shall out of the goodness of his heart and his love for you, his kindred dead, stand in your stead and enter into covenants in your name and you are willing to accept of these covenants, the desires of your heart and the work of your brother shall constitute a claim upon me, and I will recognize the covenant which has been made and the blessings thereof will flow unto you."

5. In the spirit world we shall know one another and converse with one an-another. Within limitations which necessarily exist without a physical body, we shall progress or retrogress, teach and be taught.

6. The Prophet Joseph taught us that the spirit world is all about us, nearer than we suppose, but of substances beyond our physical powers to perceive.

7. The period of time during which we remain in the spirit world is probationary, a time to repent and learn to obey God.[50] If man should immediately take up his body of flesh after leaving it, without having first been given a chance to learn and understand the laws of God, he would be liable to the same mistakes by which mankind has brought death to these bodies, and having again committed those mistakes suffers a second death.[51] Indeed, there will be some who even having remained in the spirit world unto the last great resurrection because of disobedience will still prove disobedient unto God and will, though resurrected, bring upon themselves a second death both spiritually and physically.[52]

The Resurrection

No matter how righteous man might be and how well prepared to enjoy an existence in the spirit world, there cannot be a fulness of joy for him apart from a body of flesh and bones. The Lord has explained this in revelation: "For man is spirit. The elements are eternal, and spirit and element, inseparably connected, receive a fulness of joy; and when separated, man cannot receive a fulness of joy."[53]

Individuals in the spirit world look forward to the day of resurrection when the spirit shall again be united with the body. The reality of this resurrection was made known unto man in the beginning as part of the gospel plan. Centuries before the resurrection of anyone who had dwelt upon this earth prophets of God spoke of the resurrection as a certainty. This they could do because God had revealed unto them the gospel plan which included the coming of Christ to break the bands of death and begin the resurrection of the dead.[54]

That to which the ancient prophets looked confidently forward became an accomplished reality with the resurrection of Jesus Christ. His resurrection is well attested by witnesses in Jerusalem and the regions of Galilee and

---

[50]Alma 12:26; 42.
[51]In *Doctrine and Covenants* 63:50-51 we learn that during the Millennium some who are old shall die, but shall be changed to a resurrected state "in the twinkling of an eye." This will be possible only where obedience to God has been learned and followed, hence no waiting period will be necessary.

[52]Alma 12:16-18; *Doctrine and Covenants* 63:17; 76:31-37, 40-44.
[53]*Doctrine and Covenants* 93:33-34.
[54]For a treatment of the ability of man to foretell future events in the plans of God see "Prophecy," pp. 646 ff.

their testimony is recorded in the writings of the New Testament. Strong and convincing as these accounts are, some scepticism concerning the truth of their claims has arisen among many in the Christian world. The coming forth of an American record which also bears witness to the resurrection of Christ and His appearance as a resurrected Being on the American continent drives doubt from the hearts of those who accept the *Book of Mormon*. Added to this are the testimonies of Joseph Smith, Oliver Cowdery, and Sidney Rigdon that Jesus Christ appeared to them. These testimonies give the same assurance of the resurrection of Jesus as prompted the ancient Apostle Paul to devote his life to preaching Christ, resurrected.[55]

Not only is the resurrection of Christ a fact established by evidence, but the resurrection of others who once lived upon the earth is equally well established. Since the accounts of the resurrection of the Master are true, then equally true must be the statements of the respective witnesses that following the resurrection of Christ many others arose from the grave and appeared unto many. In the New Testament account we read:

"And the graves were opened; and many bodies of the saints which slept, arose,

"And came out of the graves after his resurrection, and went into the holy city, and appeared unto many."[56]

The above testimony is verified by the *Book of Mormon* account. Speaking unto His disciples on the American continent the Savior said:

"Verily I say unto you, I command my servant Samuel, the Lamanite, that he should testify unto this people, that at the day that the Father should glorify his name in me that there were many saints who should arise from the dead, and should appear unto many, and should minister unto them. And he said unto them: Was it not so?

"And his disciples answered him and said: Yea, Lord, Samuel did prophesy according to thy words, and they were all fulfilled.

"And Jesus said unto them: How be it that ye have not written this thing, that many saints did arise and appear unto many and did minister unto them.?"[57]

Concerning the question, Who of all the dead were resurrected at, or following, the time of Christ? the scriptures contain a partial answer:

"Yea, and Enoch also, and they who were with him; the prophets who were before him; and Noah also, and they who were before him, and Moses also, and they who were before him;

"And from Moses to Elijah, and from Elijah to John, who were with Christ in his resurrection. . . ."[58]

The above quotation is in keeping with the understanding of the Nephites on the doctrine of the resurrection. The Prophet Alma is recorded to have said unto his son:

"And behold, again it hath been spoken, that there is a first resurrection, a resurrection of all those who have been, or who are, or who shall be, down to the resurrection of Christ from the dead.

"Now, my son, I do not say that their resurrection cometh at the resurrection of Christ; but behold, I give it as my opinion, that the souls and the bodies are reunited, of the righteous, at the resurrection of Christ, and his ascension into heaven."[59]

The appearance to Joseph Smith of the Angel Moroni, whom the Prophet

---

[55]Note: For careful study of this subject read the gospels of Mattthew, Mark, Luke, and John where they relate the events of the resurrection; the Book of Acts; *Book of Mormon,* 3 Nephi 8; *Doctrine and Covenants* 110:76; *Pearl of Great Price,* Writings of Joseph Smith (account of the first vision).

[56]Matthew 27:52-53.

[57]3 Nephi 23:9-11.

[58]*Doctrine and Covenants* 133:54-55.

[59]Alma 40:16, 20.

describes as a resurrected Being,[60] indicates that the resurrection did not stop at the time of the resurrection of Christ, for Moroni died as late as 421 A.D.[61] We have little information concerning the numbers of those who have been resurrected since the resurrection of Christ and must be satisfied with the knowledge that such resurrections have occurred.

The term "first resurrection" has appeared in sacred literature with various meanings. The promise is made in many patriarchal blessings that the recipient* of the blessing will come forth in the "first resurrection." A similar promise is made to those who enter into the covenant of marriage for time and eternity. What, then, is the "first resurrection"? In answering the question we need to bear in mind this truth. Not all who have entered the spirit world remain there for the same length of time and all are not resurrected at the same time or to the same glory.[62] Those who, because of the knowledge of God which they have obtained and their obedience unto His commandments, have entered into the necessary covenants with the Father, may be resurrected first, and hence are a "first resurrection." That is, they will not have to wait in the spirit world until the end of the Millennium for their resurrection. But even those worthy of an earlier or "first" resurrection do not come forth at the same time. Christ was the firstfruits of the resurrection, appearing as a resurrected being the third day after His spirit had entered the spirit world. As

none could be resurrected until Christ broke the bands of death so none of the righteous who had lived upon the earth prior to the coming of Christ had been resurrected before the Savior arose from the dead. But following his resurrection many of the Saints arose from the grave as previously indicated, and appeared unto many. In the *Book of Mormon* the words of the Prophet Abinadi are found on this subject:

"But behold, the bands of death shall be broken, and the Son reigneth, and hath power over the dead; therefore, he bringeth to pass the resurrection of the dead.

"And there cometh a resurrection, even a a first resurrection; yea, even a resurrection of those that have been, and who are, and who shall be, even until the resurrection of Christ—for so shall he be called.

"And now, the resurrection of all the prophets, and all those that have believed in their words, or all those that have kept the commandments of God, shall come forth in the first resurrection; therefore, they are the first resurrection.

"They are raised to dwell with God who has redeemed them; thus they have eternal life through Christ, who has broken the bands of death.

"And these are those who have part in the first resurrection; and these are they that have died before Christ came, in their ignorance, not having salvation declared unto them. And thus the Lord bringeth about the restoration of these; and they have a part in the first resurrection, or have eternal life, being redeemed by the Lord.

"And little children also have eternal life.

"But behold, and fear, and tremble before God, for ye ought to tremble; for the Lord redeemeth none such that rebel against him and die in their sins; yea, even all those that have perished in their sins ever since the world began, that have wilfully rebelled against God, that have known the commandments of God, and would not keep them; these are they that have not part in the first resurrection."[63]

This "first resurrection" of Christ and of the righteous who died before His coming is not, however, all that is

---

[60] Smith, *Teachings of the Prophet Joseph Smith*, p. 119; *History of the Church* 3:28-30.
[61] This approximate date is generally agreed upon by *Book of Mormon* students.
*recipient—the one who receives.
[62] *Doctrine and Covenants* 88:15-24; 27-32.

[63] Mosiah 15:20-26. See also Mosiah 18:8-9; Alma 40:16-21.

meant by the "first resurrection" as indicated by the promises which are yet being made to the living. Moroni, who lived long after the time of Christ, was nevertheless of the "first resurrection."

The problem is somewhat clarified if we use the terms "resurrection of the just" and "resurrection of the unjust." The resurrection of the just, whenever it may occur, precedes the resurrection of the unjust and is hence a "first resurrection." So resurrections of the righteous, yet to take place, are a "first resurrection," as contrasted with the last resurrection which shall take place at the end of the Millennium.

The promise is repeatedly found in scripture that, at the second coming of Christ, the righteous dead who have not previously been resurrected, will arise from their graves and dwell on the earth during the Millennium. This resurrection, being definitely a resurrection of the "just," is also a "first resurrection," and it is the promise of this resurrection which is used in temple ordinances[64] and patriarchal blessings in our day. Concerning the resurrection of the "just" at the second coming of Christ we read:

"And again we bear record—for we saw and heard, and this is the testimony of the gospel of Christ concerning them who shall come forth in the resurrection of the just—

"They are they who received the testimony of Jesus, and believed on his name and were baptized after the manner of his burial, being buried in the water in his name, and this according to the commandment which he has given—

"That by keeping the commandments they might be washed and cleansed from all their sins, and receive the Holy Spirit by the laying on of the hands of him who is ordained and sealed unto this power;

"And who overcome by faith, and are sealed by the Holy Spirit of promise, which

the Father sheds forth upon all those who are just and true.

"They are they who are the church of the Firstborn.

"They are they into whose hands the Father has given all things—

"They are they who are priests and kings, who have received of his fulness, and of his glory;

"And are priests of the Most High, after the order of Melchizedek, which was after the order of Enoch, which was after the order of the Only Begotten Son.

"Wherefore, as it is written, they are gods, even the sons of God—

"Wherefore, all things are theirs, whether life or death, or things present, or things to come, all are theirs and they are Christ's and Christ is God's.

"And they shall overcome all things.

"Wherefore, let no man glory in man, but rather let him glory in God, who shall subdue all enemies under his feet.

"These shall dwell in the presence of God and his Christ forever and ever.

"These are they whom he shall bring with him, when he shall come in the clouds of heaven to reign on the earth over his people.

"These are they who shall have part in the first resurrection.

"These are they who shall come forth in the resurrection of the just.

"These are they who come unto Mount Zion, and unto the city of the living God, the heavenly place, the holiest of all.

"These are they who have come to an innumerable company of angels, to the general assembly and Church of Enoch, and of the Firstborn.

"These are they whose names are written in heaven, where God and Christ are the judge of all.

"These are they who are just men made perfect through Jesus the mediator of the new covenant, who wrought out this perfect atonement through the shedding of his own blood.

"These are they whose bodies are celestial, whose glory is that of the sun, even the glory of God, the highest of all, whose glory the sun of the firmament is written of as being typical."[65]

From the above statement it is evident that while the resurrection has been in process from the time Christ arose from the grave an unusual resur-

---

[64]See *Doctrine and Covenants* 132:19.

[65]*Doctrine and Covenants* 76:50-70.

rection shall take place at the time of the second coming of the Redeemer. The resurrection of others shall also continue during the Millennium. The Lord has also revealed that at the end of the thousand years there will be a general resurrection of all not previously resurrected, the wicked as well as the righteous, wherein the words of the scriptures will be fulfilled, "as in Adam all die, even so in Christ shall all be made alive."[66]

There are many questions in regard to the manner by which the resurrection is accomplished which cannot be answered by man. The process by which God first clothed His spirit children with the elements about us is beyond our comprehension, so likewise the process by which a reclothing of the spirit with the elements shall be accomplished. The important truth to mankind is simply this: "God in His goodness clothed our spirits once with the eternal elements, of which we are evidence. Having done so once He must have the power to do so again." Of this we also have evidence, for a resurrected being has visited mankind and invited examination of his resurrected body.[67]

The Great Judgment Day

John, the Revelator, in his great vision on the Isle of Patmos witnessed the coming of the Millennial reign upon the earth and the last great resurrection of the dead. Then he records:

"And I saw the dead, small and great, stand before God; and the books were opened: and another book was opened, which is the book of life: and the dead were judged out of those things which were written in the books, according to their works.

"And the sea gave up the dead which were in it; and death and hell delivered up the dead which were in them: and they were judged every man according to their works."[68]

That which John saw in vision has been called by various prophets as the "last great judgment day." Not all of the inhabitants of the earth shall be judged on that last great judgment day, however, for those who have been resurrected in the resurrection of the "just" will have been already judged and will have already received the glory for which they have prepared themselves. Joseph Smith and Sidney Rigdon beheld in vision the judgment of the righteous and the celestial glory which becomes their lot.[69] It appears that all men are judged when they leave the spirit world and enter into the resurrected state. The last great day of judgment must follow the last great resurrection of the dead. In using the term "final judgment" we must then bear in mind that we are referring only to the final day of judgment for those who have lived on this earth, and not the last judgment which might be passed upon the individual in the endless eternity which stretches beyond the resurrection. The free agency of man is eternal and being so man will forever be judged of God for his actions. But just as there is a judgment time at the end of each race, at the end of each school year, at the end of every course of instruction, so there is a judgment time at the close of each phase of man's existence.

In speaking of the great judgment day for each of us we must not lose sight of the fact that every day is in a sense a judgment day, for each day we

---

[66] I Cor. 15:22.
[67] Luke 24:36-43; John 20:24-29; 3 Nephi 10:18-19, 11:12-15; *Doctrine and Covenants* 27:5-13; 129:1; *Book of Mormon* 3 Nephi 23:9-11.

[68] Rev. 20:12-13.
[69] *Doctrine and Covenants* 76:50-70.

reap the consequences of our acts "whether they be good or whether they be evil." The growth or retrogression of character is its own reward or punishment. There are, however, definite times in our lives when we see ourselves more clearly than at others, when the consciousness of our weaknesses comes upon us and in the judgment of ourselves we reap remorse. There are in addition occasions when we are judged by others, when our fate hangs in the balance—our job, our social or economic position, perhaps our life.

The "great judgment day" is that day when we shall meet God face to face and be judged of Him; it is that day when the record of our lives shall be as clear before us and our Heavenly Father as are the written records in a book; it is that day, when entering anew into an existence with bodies of flesh and bones, we shall receive exactly what we are worthy of receiving.

The actual judgment of man has been given unto Jesus Christ as indicated by the following:

"He [God] hath appointed a day, in which he will judge the world in righteousness by that man whom he hath ordained; whereof he hath given assurance unto all men, in that he hath raised him from the dead."[70]

"For the Father judgeth no man, but hath committed all judgment unto the Son."[71]

The Son shall be aided in His judgment by His Holy Priesthood as indicated by His own words:

"The Twelve which were with me in my ministry at Jerusalem shall . . . judge the whole house of Israel, even as many as have loved me and kept my commandments, and none else."[72]

In speaking of the judgment of his own people Mormon said:

"This people . . . shall also be judged by the twelve whom Jesus chose in this land; and they shall be judged by the other twelve whom Jesus chose in the land of Jerusalem."[73]

The Lord revealed unto His Church through Joseph Smith and Sidney Rigdon the condition in which individuals will find themselves after the resurrection. All mankind save the sons of perdition were shown to obtain some degree of the glory of God. There were within this group three great classifications, or degrees of glory. These are designated as the celestial, or highest, the terrestrial, and the telestial. The difference between these conditions has been likened to the difference in brilliance of the sun, moon, and stars as viewed from this planet. Within each glory there are again numerous divisions or gradations according to the worthiness of the individuals who enter therein. Concerning the celestial glory, for example, the Prophet said:

"In the celestial glory there are three heavens or degrees;

"And in order to obtain the highest, a man must enter into this order of the priesthood [meaning the new and everlasting covenant of marriage];

"And if he does not, he cannot obtain it.

"He may enter into the other, but that is the end of his kingdom; he cannot have an increase."[74]

The conditions for entrance into the celestial kingdom have been clearly set forth, but the conditions necessary for entrance into the lesser kingdoms have not been made known with the same degree of clarity.

All who have faith in Jesus Christ, have fully repented of their sins, have been baptized by water in His name,

[70]Acts 17:31; Eccl. 3:17.
[71]John 5:22; see also *Doctrine and Covenants* 19:2, 3; II Cor. 5:10, Romans 14:10, Mormon 3:20, 3 Nephi 26:4-5.
[72]*Doctrine and Covenants* 29:12; Matt. 19:28; Luke 22:29-30.

[73]Mormon 3:19.
[74]*Doctrine and Covenants* 131:1-4.

and have received the baptism by fire and the Holy Ghost, are candidates for the celestial world. Without filling these requirements man would be unable to endure the presence of God. As many of God's children have lived and died upon the earth without an opportunity of hearing the gospel or being baptized into Christ's Kingdom the provision is made whereby the gospel shall be preached to them in the spirit world while the earthly ordinances may be performed for them by those still in the flesh.

The great vision of the degrees of glory was had jointly by Joseph Smith and Sidney Rigdon on February 16, 1832. The vision makes clear certain fundamentals of the gospel plan concerning resurrected beings.

First, it establishes the fact of eternal progression where the laws of progression are obeyed.

Second, it establishes the fact that in the Father's house there are many mansions or glories, each individual inheriting that condition or existence for which he has fitted himself.

Third, it establishes the fact that all of the children of God except the sons of perdition,[75] those who deliberately have chosen to follow Satan rather than Christ, after having received the witness of the Holy Ghost, will eventually progress far enough to receive some glory in the resurrection. This eventual salvation of the vast majority of mankind shows the wisdom of God in His plans for His children and should cause mankind to rejoice.

Fourth, the vision shows the celestial or higher glory as containing joys beyond our power in the flesh to comprehend and should awaken desire in the heart of man to seek to attain such an existence. In fact, even the telestial kingdom is described as glorious beyond human comprehension.

Supplementary Readings

On Specific Topics:
   The Gospel Plan of Life
      Smith, *Gospel Doctrine*, pp. 16-28.
      Talmage, *Sunday Night Talks*, pp 359-368.
      Ibid., pp. 230-239 (Pre-earth Life).
   The Fall and the Atonement
      Talmage, *Sunday Night Talks*, pp. 51-94
   The Spirit World
      Book of Mormon, Alma 40:7-14.
   The Resurrection
      Doctrine and Covenants, Section 76.
      Smith, *The Way to Perfection*, pp. 290-307.
      Talmage, *Articles of Faith*, pp. 381-392.
      Smith, *Gospel Doctrine*, pp. 559-574.
   Eternal Increase
      Doctrine and Covenants, Section 131: 1-4.
      Smith, *Teachings of the Prophet Joseph Smith*, pp. 300-301.
   The Millennial Reign
      Smith, *The Way to Perfection*, pp. 308-314.
General Readings:
   Talmage, *Sunday Night Talks*, pp. 51-94, 230-239, 440-538.
   Book of Mormon, II Nephi 2:14-28; 9:3-27; III Nephi 27:1-22; Ether 3:15-16.
   Doctrine and Covenants, Section 93.
   Smith, *The Way to Perfection*, pp. 24-32
   Widtsoe, *A Rational Theology*, Chapters IV, VII, IX.
   Widtsoe, John A., "What Is Man?" *Deseret News*, Church Section, October 10, 1936.
   Hale, Heber Q., "Man's Quest for Joy," *Improvement Era*, Vol. 37, October, 1934.

---

[75]"Perdition" is one of the names given to Satan. In the *Doctrine and Covenants* 76:25-29, we read:

"And this we saw also, and bear record, that an angel of God who was in authority in the presence of God, who rebelled against the Only Begotten Son whom the Father loved and who was in the bosom of the Father, was thrust down from the presence of God and the Son.

"And was called Perdition, for the heavens wept over him—he was Lucifer a son of the morning.

"And we beheld, and lo, he is fallen! is fallen, even a son of the morning!

"And while we were yet in the Spirit, the Lord commanded us that we should write the vision; for we beheld Satan, that old serpent, even the devil, who rebelled against God, and sought to take the kingdom of God and his Christ—

"Wherefore, he maketh war with the saints of God, and encompasseth them round about."

PRESIDENTS

Of The Church

Since

JOSEPH SMITH

the

Prophet

Brigham Young

John Taylor

Wilford Woodruff

Lorenzo Snow

Heber J. Grant

Joseph F. Smith

David O. McKay

George Albert Smith

Joseph Fielding Smith

Harold B. Lee

CHAPTER 45

PRIESTHOOD AND THE CHURCH

The Nature and Necessity for Authority in Social Institutions[1]

Imagine what would happen if a man without any authorization whatever should enter a city, profess to set up a branch of some great business concern, and commence to transact business in its name. Certainly the transactions entered into would be denied and discredited by the business he professed to represent, and the individual guilty of misrepresentation would face serious civil and criminal charges. Society cannot permit the act of one individual to be binding upon another unless authority for such act actually exists. If any other rule should prevail, society would be plunged into hopeless confusion.

Much of the business of the world is, however, transacted by individuals acting for others in accordance with the authority extended to them. This authority may be almost without limitation or may extend only to the performance of the simplest tasks and responsibilities. The manager of a store has an almost unlimited authority as far as business is concerned to act in the name of its owners. In turn, the cashier has authority from the manager to act within a more limited field. He has authority to handle the cash receipts, make deposits, keep accounts, issue drafts in accordance to demands, etc., and his acts within that limited area are as binding upon the owners of the establishment as if they themselves did the several acts. The clerk in the same store also has authority, but it is very limited. He may recommend and sell goods to customers. He may or may not be authorized to receive money for the same, or to make change. However, within his limited field his actions are as binding upon his employers as are those of the manager or the acts of the owners themselves.

This system of authority in business, government, and society is recognized by mankind as essential and necessary for the maintenance of order in the world and for the general welfare of mankind. Violations of authority come under severe legal and social condemnation.[2]

The Authority to Act in the Name of God

When one considers God as an individual, a person, ruling over the universe with its billions of individuals as the head of a government rules over a nation, one quickly senses the need of God to call others to aid in His work. The scriptures inform us that God called His Son, Jesus Christ, to oversee the affairs of this world and its inhabitants. The call was accepted by the Son and recognized by those who were to come into mortality upon this earth.[2] But Jesus Christ, generally known aside from His life in the flesh as Jehovah, needed help in the immense task assigned to Him. Accordingly, He called others and gave unto them

---

[1]For another treatment of authority see Talmage, *Sunday Night Talks*, pp. 222-224.

[2]*Pearl of Great Price*, Moses 4:1-4; 5:4-12; Abraham 3:22-28.

authority to act in His name, saying unto them: "And I will give unto you the keys of the kingdom of heaven: and whatsoever thou shalt bind on earth shall be bound in heaven: and whatsoever thou shalt loose on earth shall be loosed in heaven."[3] This authority and call to act in the name of Christ is known as the Holy Priesthood after the order of the Son of God.

As in the case of agency in business or other common examples of acting in the name of another, so in the matter of priesthood there must be first, a *call* to the position of authority; second, an *acceptance of the call;* and third, some outward *ceremony or symbol by which others may know of the appointment.* Any other system would result in chaos and confusion. To expect God to be bound by the acts of any individual, even if performed in His name, where no actual and specific authority to perform that act has been given, is wrong. Such a view would ascribe to God less intelligence than that possessed by His children and would infer that the truths we come to know in this life do not apply to His Universe.

Kindness and acts of service may be extended by one individual to another without any authority. These acts may win the love of others and also the love of the Father of us all. But acts which are performed in God's name cannot be binding upon Him, except where actual authority has been given by definite call, acceptance, and public acknowledgment.

Callings Within the Priesthood

While there is only one Priesthood of God, which is the Priesthood of Jesus Christ, there are many offices and callings within the priesthood. An analogous situation may be found in studying the government of a nation. In a particular country there is but one general government and all authority to act in the name of that country must come through a direct line from the governing powers. But there is a wide difference in callings. One man may be called and given authority to direct internal affairs, another foreign affairs, another to judge civil disputes, another to carry on investigations, etc. So in the government of God, authority may be given to act in God's name in different capacities and powers. There are two great divisions of those powers:

"The power and authority of the higher, or Melchizedek Priesthood, is to hold the keys of all the spiritual blessings of the church—

"To have the privilege of receiving the mysteries of the kingdom of heaven, to have the heavens opened unto them, to commune with the general assembly and church of the Firstborn, and to enjoy the communion and presence of God the Father, and Jesus the mediator of the new covenant.

"The power and authority of the lesser, or Aaronic Priesthood, is to hold the keys of the ministering of angels, and to administer in outward ordinances, the letter of the gospel, the baptism of repentance for the remission of sins, agreeable to the covenants and commandments."[4]

The Aaronic Priesthood is sometimes called the Levitical or Lesser Priesthood. It is called Aaronic because Aaron, the brother of Moses, was called to preside over those holding the Lesser Priesthood in his day, and his name came to be applied to it. It is referred to as the Levitical Priesthood because during Aaron's day and for centuries following only members of the tribe of Levi (one of the twelve tribes of Israel) were called to serve in it or were ordained to this office. It is called the Lesser Priesthood because the Higher, or Melchizedek Priesthood, when upon

---

[3] Matthew 16:19.

[4] *Doctrine and Covenants* 107:18-20.

the earth, has authority or directing power over it.[5] Within the Aaronic Priesthood are three callings, that of deacon, teacher, and priest, and each calling has its separate duties and powers. These duties and powers were explained by revelation to Joseph Smith shortly before the organization of the Church:

"The priest's duty is to preach, teach, expound, exhort, and baptize, and administer the sacrament,

"And visit the house of each member, and exhort them to pray vocally and in secret and attend to all family duties.

"And he may also ordain other priests, teachers, and deacons.

"And he is to take the lead of meetings when there is no elder present;

"But when there is an elder present, he is only to preach, teach, expound, exhort, and baptize,

"And visit the house of each member, exhorting them to pray vocally and in secret and attend to all family duties. . . .

"In all these duties the priest is to assist the elder if occasion requires.

"The teacher's duty is to watch over the church always, and be with and strengthen them;

"And see that there is no iniquity in the church, neither hardness with each other, neither lying, backbiting, nor evil speaking;

"And see that the church meet together often and also see that all the members do their duty.

"And he is to take the lead of meetings in the absence of the elder or priest—

"And is to be assisted always, in all his duties in the Church, by the deacons, if occasion requires.

"But neither teachers nor deacons have authority to baptize, administer the sacrament, or lay on hands;

"They are, however, to warn, expound, exhort, and teach, and invite all to come unto Christ.

"Every elder, priest, teacher, or deacon is to be ordained according to the gifts and callings of God unto him; and he is to be ordained by the power of the Holy Ghost, which is in the one who ordains him."[6]

The Higher Priesthood has come to be known as the "Melchizedek Priesthood," although it has been called by various names during the history of mankind. Its true name is "The Holy Priesthood after the order of the Son of God," but to avoid the too frequent use of the name of deity this authority of God on the earth is referred to as that authority held by Adam, Enoch, Noah, Melchizedek, etc., which is after the order of the Son of God.[7]

Melchizedek was a great High Priest, king of Salem, who lived in the days of Abraham and from whom Abraham received the Priesthood.[8]

There are three offices within the Melchizedek Priesthood, the office of an elder, a seventy, and a high priest.

It is the duty and calling of an elder, "to baptize."

"And to ordain other elders, priests, teachers, and deacons.

"And to administer bread and wine—the emblems of the flesh and blood of Christ—

"And to confirm those who are baptized into the church . . .;

"And to teach, expound, exhort, baptize, and watch over the church;

"And to confirm the church by the laying on of the hands, and the giving of the Holy Ghost."[9]

It is the duty and calling of a Seventy "to act in the name of the Lord, under the direction of the Twelve, or the traveling High Council, in building up the Church and regulating all the affairs of the same in all nations."[10]

The calling of the High Priest is the call to preside.

"The Presidency of the High Priesthood, after the order of Melchizedek, have a right to officiate in all the offices in the Church.

"High priests after the order of the Melchizedek Priesthood have a right to officiate in their own standing, under the direction

[5]*Doctrine and Covenants* 107:14.
[6]*Doctrine and Covenants* 20:46-60.
[7]*Doctrine and Covenants* 76:57; 107:1-6; *Pearl of Great Price*, Moses 6:67.
[8]*Doctrine and Covenants* 84:14.
[9]*Ibid.*, 20:38-43.
[10]*Ibid.*, 107:34.

of the presidency, in administering spiritual things. . . ."[11]

There are many callings growing out of the various offices of the Priesthood.

"Of necessity there are presidents, or presiding officers growing out of, or appointed of or from among those who are ordained to the several offices in these two priesthoods.

"Of the Melchizedek Priesthood, three Presiding High Priests, chosen by the body, appointed and ordained to that office, and upheld by the confidence, faith, and prayer of the church, form a quorum of the Presidency of the Church.

"The twelve traveling councilors are called to be the Twelve Apostles, or special witnesses of the name of Christ in all the world —thus differing from other officers in the church in the duties of their calling.

"And they form a quorum, equal in authority and power to the three presidents previously mentioned."[12]

We must remember that the priesthood is greater than any of its offices. It is from the priesthood that the office derives its authority and power. One who holds the priesthood after the order of Melchizedek holds all the priesthood. An elder, seventy and high priest all hold the same priesthood. One is no greater than another.[13] However, the offices of elder, seventy, and high priest involve the call to labor in particular capacities in the service of Christ. The Apostle Paul likened these different duties to functions of different parts of a human body, all essential to its perfect functioning: "And the eye cannot say unto the hand, I have no need of thee: nor again the head to the feet, I have no need of you. Nay, much more those members of the body, which seem to be more feeble, are necessary."[14]

The fact that offices and callings within the Melchizedek Priesthood do not require additional priesthood or power one over the other is well-stated by the late President Joseph F. Smith:

"Today, the question is, which is the greater—the high priest or the seventy— the seventy or the high priest? I tell you that neither of them is the greater, and neither of them is the lesser. Their callings are in different directions, but they are from the same priesthood. If it were necessary, the seventy, holding the Melchizedek Priesthood as he does, I say *if it were necessary* he could ordain a high priest, and if it were necessary for a high priest to ordain a seventy, he could do that. Why? Because both of them hold the Melchizedek Priesthood. Then again, if it were necessary, though I do not expect that the necessity will ever arise, and there was no man left on earth holding the Melchizedek Priesthood, except an elder, that elder, by the inspiration of the Spirit of God and by the direction of the Almighty, could proceed, and should proceed, to organize the Church of Jesus Christ in all its perfection, because he holds the Melchizedek Priesthood. But the house of God is a house of order, and while the other officers remain in the Church, we must observe the order of the priesthood, and we must perform ordinances and ordinations strictly in accordance with that order, as it has been established in the Church through the instrumentality of the Prophet Joseph Smith and his successors."[15] [16]

Keys of the Priesthood

We must constantly bear in mind during our study of the priesthood the difference between holding an office in the priesthood and having authority to use that office or power as we see fit. In other words, we must determine carefully between what is termed "priesthood" and "keys of priesthood." While a man may be given power to act in the name of Christ by bestowing upon him the Priesthood of God, nevertheless he may not exercise that power save as

---

[11]*Ibid.*, 107:9-10.

[12]*Ibid.*, 107:21-24.

[13](Note) In the Aaronic Priesthood the deacon, teacher, and priest are not equal in authority but each holds a restricted authority given by the Higher Priesthood. The teacher holds more authority than a deacon and a priest more than a teacher.

[14]I Cor. 12:21-22. (Read entire twelfth chapter).

[15]Joseph F. Smith, *October Conference Report*, 1903, p. 87.

[16]For other readings on "Calling within the Priesthood," see: Widtsoe, *Priesthood and Church Government*, pp. 78 ff; *In the Realm of Quorum Activity*, Supplement to Second Series, 1932, pp. 19-20.

he be given authority by those who hold the keys of that authority. A person holding the office of priest has the necessary power to baptize another into the Church but may not do so until the bishop or mission president or individual holding the keys of his particular church area so calls and appoints him. Even one holding the holy Melchizedek Priesthood may not baptize an individual desiring it unless he is called to do so by his bishop, stake president, branch president, etc. In the mission fields elders may be given authority to baptize all who come unto them for baptism, such authority lasting only as long as their mission. Upon the missionary's release that specific authority vested in him to baptize is curtailed and he may exercise this power only as directed by the bishop of his ward or the president of his stake.

As this is the Priesthood after the Order of the Son of God, all of the keys of authority rest in Him and authority to act in different capacities upon the earth may be had only from Christ or from those to whom He has given such authority. Authority to do certain work has at times been withdrawn while authority to carry out other functions of the priesthood continued.[17]

While Joseph Smith and Oliver Cowdery received the Melchizedek Priesthood from the hands of Peter, James and John they received the keys of authority upon the earth to baptize, to confer the Holy Ghost, to organize a Church, to ordain others to the priesthood, to administer to the sacrament, etc. Some keys of priesthood were not given them at that time. The keys of authority necessary to perform ordinances in the temple for the living and for the dead were withheld until the completion of the Kirtland Temple in 1836. There may be many functions of the priesthood to which God has not as yet called man. To perform further functions would not require additional priesthood, but only the call and authorization to use that priesthood in particular ways.

All the keys of authority which have been given to the Church of Christ in these latter days rest in the Priesthood of the Church and no man in the Church may exercise any authority or power of the priesthood save only as authority is delegated to him from the President. If, for example, the President of the Church, while being sustained by its members, should issue a proclamation to all those holding the priesthood within the Church that no baptisms should be solemnized during the first three months of a particular year or for any length of time, no one in the Church, regardless of the office of priesthood he might hold or the position he might occupy, would have authority to solemnize a baptism, and any baptism performed contrary to this established order would be unacceptable unto God. Without such established authority the Church might easily reach a point of disorder and chaos.

Church Democracy

On April 6, 1830, in the house of Peter Whitmer, at Fayette, New York State, a small group of individuals met for the purpose of formally establishing a Church. Six of those affixed their signatures to the Articles of Incorporation, as required by the State of New York for the organization of a church or benevolent society. None of these six had had previous experience

[17](Note) This was true during the history of Israel after Moses. Authority to perform certain ordinances of the Church was withdrawn, though the Priesthood continued.

Pres. Harold B. Lee

Pres. N. Eldon Tanner   Pres. Marion G. Romney
The First Presidency of The Church of Jesus Christ of Latter-day Saints (1973)

in the organization of religious bodies. None had been instructed by learned men on the principles necessary to an organization's success, nor was any guidance sought through the ordinary channels. Yet there was pronounced on that day the basic principles of a spiritual democracy which sacrificed neither the efficiency of central authority nor the personal growth which feeds upon democracy.

Joseph Smith on that day pronounced two fundamentals of church government which have proved monumental. First, the authority (priesthood) in the Church of Jesus Christ comes only from Jesus Christ and none may hold any office or authority save as they are called by Him directly or by those previously called by authority to act in His stead. Secondly, no man, though he be called of God, may preside over his brethren, except with the consent of his brethren, and no decision shall be binding upon the people of the Church except with their common consent.[18] These two concepts of church government have guaranteed both efficiency and democracy in the Church. Without the first, authority from God to officiate and act in His name could not be preserved, and without the second, man's free agency would be destroyed.

If men, by aspiring to church office and securing the support of their friends, were elected to office they would hold position by virtue of that election and not by virtue of being called of God to serve Him. They would be, in fact, forcing their services upon God and would be expecting recognition of their acts by a Being who never called them to act. By such an arrangement the whole theory of agency upon which priesthood rests

would be destroyed. If the officers of the Church are to have their acts done in the name of the Lord, binding upon Him, they must hold authority or agency from the Lord to perform those acts. But authority in one person to act in the name of another cannot be presumed; it can only come from the person represented and hence by his call or appointment.

In the true Church of Christ no man may aspire to office. There can be no candidates. All who occupy positions are called to them by those who hold authority of Jesus Christ.

The second fundamental of church government is equally important to the welfare of the church members—the common consent of the members of the Church in all matters pertaining to them. No person called to office whether the highest or lowest in the Church, may officiate or function in that office save those under him vote to sustain and support him in that position. Even after he has been once sustained the democratic principle continues. At regular intervals his name is presented to the people in order that they may express by vote their desires to sustain or reject him. If the majority reject him he may not officiate or act further in the capacities of his office, though retaining the office until those who called him release him and call another in his stead.

This democratic principle preserves the God-given right of free agency, preserves harmony in the Church, and prevents any long continuation in office by those who have proved unworthy.

In announcing these great principles to his people Joseph Smith placed in their hands the power to strip him of office whenever, in their eyes, his exercise of authority ceased to be in righteousness. Thus, from the highest to the

[18]*Doctrine and Covenants* 20:63; 65-66.

least, no person may govern in The Church of Jesus Christ of Latter-day Saints except he be called of God and sustained by the people over whom he is called to preside.

In the Church there is no fixed tenure of office, nor any particular class entitled to office. Any person in the Church may be called to a position of responsibility and authority. Joseph Smith brushed aside all class lines, declaring in words of soberness that God is no respecter of persons. Rich or poor, bond and free, learned and unlearned, male and female, meet and worship in common brotherhood and are judged by a common standard. While men and women are called to labor in different positions according to their several capacities and circumstances, neither birth nor social prominence nor money become a criterion for selection.

An individual in the Church who prepares himself for service and desires to serve will not wait long before being called to some specific duty and responsibility. Of the membership of the Church more than ten per cent are constantly active in various duties and offices. Further, this vast service is largely a free service. It is a labor of love, and love of fellowmen is essential to democracy.

To those holding the priesthood the Lord has said:

"That the rights of the priesthood are inseparably connected with the powers of heaven, and . . . the powers of heaven cannot be controlled nor handled only upon the principles of righteousness.

"That they may be conferred upon us, it is true; but when we undertake to cover our sins, or to gratify our pride, our vain ambition, or to exercise control or dominion or compulsion upon the souls of the children of men, in any degree of unrighteousness, behold, the heavens withdraw themselves; the Spirit of the Lord is grieved; and when

it is withdrawn, Amen to the priesthood, or the authority of that man.

"No power or influence can or ought to be maintained by virtue of the priesthood, only by persuasion, by long-suffering, by gentleness and meekness, and by love unfeigned;

"By kindness, and pure knowledge, which shall greatly enlarge the soul without hypocrisy, and without guile,

"Reproving betimes with sharpness, when moved upon by the Holy Ghost; and then showing forth afterwards an increase of love toward him whom thou hast reproved, lest he esteem thee to be his enemy;

"That he may know that thy faithfulness is stronger than the cords of death;

"Let thy bowels also be full of charity towards all men, and to the household of faith, and let virtue garnish thy thoughts unceasingly; then shall thy confidence wax strong in the presence of God; and the doctrine of the priesthood shall distill upon thy soul as the dews from heaven.

"The Holy Ghost shall be thy constant companion, and thy scepter an unchanging scepter of righteousness and truth, and thy dominion shall be an everlasting dominion and without compulsory means it shall flow unto thee forever and ever.[19]

It is significant that the principles of priesthood and church government enunciated by Joseph Smith as coming from the Lord have worked successfully without alteration throughout all the changes which the past century has produced. They function as well in a church of three million members as in a church of a dozen members. They will be as applicable to millions. They are as workable in a widely scattered church as in a geographically compact one. They find successful application in any country, and among the people of any nationality or mixture of nationalities. This has been true because the principles have been tested in the crucible of eternity and were revealed unto Joseph Smith by the Lord and Savior Jesus Christ.

---

[19]*Doctrine and Covenants* 121:36, 37, 41-46.

Supplementary Readings

On Specific Topics:

The Nature and Necessity of Authority
Smith, Gospel Doctrine, pp 174-175.
"The Need and Nature of Authority,"
Improvement Era, Vol. 39 (Sept., 1936).

The Authority to Act in the Name of God
Talmage, *Sunday Night Talks*, pp. 220-229.

The Giving of Authority to Joseph Smith
Doctrine and Covenants, Section 13.
Joseph Smith, *History of the Church*,
Vol. I, pp. 39-42, 175-176; Vol. III, pp. 383-389.

Church Organization
Talmage, *Articles of Faith*, pp. 198-216, 492-493.
Widtsoe, *A Rational Theology*, pp. 104-110.

Callings within the Priesthood
Widtsoe, *Priesthood and Church Government*, pp. 78-79.
In the Realm of Quorum Activity, Supplement to Second Series, 1932, pp. 19-20.

Keys of the Priesthood
Joseph F. Smith, *Gospel Doctrine*, pp. 163-169.

Limitations of the Call
Widtsoe, *Program of the Church*, p. 81
(Women and the Priesthood).
Smith, *The Way to Perfection*, pp 43, 103-111 (Negroes and the Priesthood).

Church Democracy and Church Leadership
Joseph F. Smith, *Gospel Doctrine*, pp. 196-199.

How the Priesthood Functions Through
the Church
Doctrine and Covenants, Section 20.
Evans, *One Hundred Years of Mormonism*, pp. 107-111.
Joseph Smith, *History of the Church*,
Vol. I, pp. 75-80.

General References:
Talmage, *Articles of Faith*. pp. 179-197.
Keeler, *Church Government*.
Joseph F. Smith, *Gospel Doctrine*, pp. 136-200.
Doctrine and Covenants, Section 20; 84; 107.
Widtsoe, *Priesthood and Church Government*.
Smith, *The Way to Perfection*, pp. 210-224.

CHAPTER 46

PRINCIPLES AND ORDINANCES
OF THE GOSPEL

The Principle of Faith

The term "Gospel of Jesus Christ," embraces so much as to be somewhat confusing when we attempt to tell others what it is. In order to appreciate and understand the Gospel one must begin with the simple foundation principles just as one who would learn mathematics must start with simple numbers and not with trigonometry or calculus.

In a letter written to John Wentworth, editor of the *Chicago Democrat*, in 1840, Joseph Smith summarized the beliefs of the Church in thirteen crisp statements which have been adopted by the Church and called the "Articles of Faith."[1] In the fourth Article he declared: "We believe that the first principles and ordinances of the Gospel are: first, Faith in the Lord Jesus Christ, second, Repentance; third, Baptism by immersion for the remission of sins; and fourth, Laying on of hands for the gift of the Holy Ghost."[2]

It is significant that Joseph Smith considered each of the above as principles of true religion, for they are also principles of life and ordinances built upon such principles attain thereby new meaning and importance. Certainly, in seeking to understand the gospel we must begin with the first principles.

Why is faith the first principle of the Gospel? Simply because it is the first principle of all human progress. As the Gospel is concerned with the progress of man the first principle of the Gospel and the first principle of human progress must be the same.

What is the principle of faith and how is it a principle of life? Let us consider a few examples where faith functions. A farmer sees the snow melt from his fields in the spring leaving the ground brown and barren. Moved by some inward feeling he plows the land, harrows and levels it, and seeds it down to grain. In accomplishing this he has expended both money and effort. That state of mind which prompted his efforts we call by the name "faith." Faith is less than knowledge[3] because the farmer does not know that he will reap where he has planted. Frost, flood, drought, rot, hail, or fire may cause his efforts to come to nought and destroy his expected harvest. Faith, however, is more than mere belief. The farmer might believe that his soil would grow crops but still sleep quietly on the front porch.

The same condition of mind prompts the merchant to stock the shelves of his store with goods. He has faith that he can sell the goods he has purchased for a profit. Without that essential state of mind he would not buy but would retain his money or his credit.

The scientist who sets up his elaborate equipment for an experiment does so because of faith that his venture

---

[1]See Appendix. For the complete text of the Wentworth letter, see Joseph Smith, *History of the Church*, IV, pp. 536-541.

[2]Joseph Smith, *History of the Church*, IV, p. 541.

[3]Faith is based on some knowledge and leads to greater knowledge but is less than knowledge of the thing hoped for. See Mosiah 5:4; Alma 26:21-22. For a splendid treatment of the growth of faith to perfect knowledge read Alma 32:21-43.

will bring certain results. Without such faith experiments would end and all invention would cease.

Years ago many men expressed the belief that airplanes could be flown across the Atlantic but mere belief did not result in any attempts. It remained for one Charles A. Lindbergh to attain that state of mind called faith, which is more than belief, before an attempt was made. The faith of Lindbergh in the possibility of the journey led to action.

From these illustrations of faith in common walks of life we may now construct a definition. If faith causes the farmer to plant, the merchant to buy, the scientist to experiment, and the aviator to fly, then faith must be the moving cause of all human action. Thus faith is certainly the foundation principle of all progress, for manifestly there can be no progress if we do nothing.

But, we may ask, how does one obtain this state of mind called faith? If we should ask the farmer why he expects to reap this year he would undoubtedly inform us that he reaped last year, and the year before, and the years before that, and so he expects to reap again. His faith, then, is built upon evidences of what soil, the elements, and the efforts of man can accomplish. The greater the number of unbroken successes in planting and reaping the firmer his faith. A series of crop failures may cause a loss of faith and eventually result in no effort on the part of the farmer to plant.

The same is true with the merchant. His faith, which prompts him to buy, is built upon the evidences of previous purchases, sales, and profits. The scientist has the evidence of previous experiments with the nature of chemi-

cals, their reactions, etc., and on that evidence rests the faith for new experiments.

Charles A. Lindbergh flew his plane, "The Spirit of St. Louis," above the city of St. Louis for a longer period than would be required to cross the Atlantic if all went well and this evidence of what his ship would do gave him faith for his venture.

From such reasoning the Apostle Paul, many centuries ago, came to the conclusion, "Now faith is the substance of things hoped for, the evidence of things not seen."[4] Without evidence faith cannot exist and the greater the evidence the greater the faith.

The Prophet Joseph Smith, while recognizing faith as a general principle of all life, was especially interested in faith in Jesus Christ. As a farmer without faith in a harvest will not plant, so without faith in Jesus Christ he will not follow Christ's teachings. If the following of Christ's teachings is the road to happiness and eternal life, then faith in the Lord and Savior Jesus Christ is the first principle of the Gospel. A farmer might have faith in a coming harvest and plant his crops, a merchant might have faith to buy merchandise, but neither planting nor buying are important when compared with the growth and salvation of the soul. "For what shall it profit a man, if he shall gain the whole world, and lose his own soul?"[5]

If faith is built upon evidence, how can those who have never seen God have faith in Him? How did Joseph Smith as a boy have sufficient faith to pray as earnestly as he did on that spring morning in 1820? Evidences are of two kinds, those we experience ourselves,

[4]Heb. 11:1.
[5]Mark 8:36.

and those we acquire from other peoples' experiences. The boy Joseph was a reader and believer of the Bible. The Bible gives evidence that God is and that He hears and answers prayers. Joseph Smith accepted that evidence, together with the statements of his parents and others concerning prayer, and on the basis of that evidence developed the faith which pierced the heavens and brought an answer to his problems.

Not only is faith necessary to prayer, but it is also necessary before effort is made by an individual to change his personality and character. One who is selfish will never be otherwise until he acquires that state of mind (faith) which prompts him to change his manner of thought and action. The evidence upon which his faith is based— hence his assurance that he can change his character—consists in his observations of individuals about him, in his own experiences and especially in the supreme example of the unselfish Christ. In fact, the knowledge of the Master becomes the highest evidence of what character might become and the faith in one's own possibilities engendered by it has been the greatest force for good in the world.

Faith in the Lord Jesus Christ is the moving cause of many actions of man. If we have faith that Christ still lives— that because of Him all will rise from the dead and be judged according to their works "whether they be good, or whether they be evil," then that faith motivates us to good deeds, becomes the moving cause of our attitudes and actions in life and hence molds our character. It is the first law of all spiritual growth.

Not only is faith the first principle of life upon the earth; it is the first principle by which God operates. It is the moving cause of the activities of God. We read in the scriptures, "Through faith we understand that the worlds were framed by the word of God. . . ." God also operated by faith, for without faith that worlds could be organized none would have been attempted. Hence, by faith the farmer plants. By faith the merchant buys. By faith man is led to pray; and by faith God framed the worlds.[5a]

Repentance
A Universal Law of Progress

If the actions of an individual have taken him in the wrong direction, the farther he goes the worse he becomes. For example, Richard Roe sets out on a journey from Los Angeles to San Francisco. He has faith that his car will take him to his destination. A paved but narrow highway leads to his objective, but it is intersected at many places by other highways. At one of these intersections he takes a road which in time leads him directly away from San Francisco and eventually into a swamp. How can Richard Roe reach San Francisco? Until he recognizes his error he will, of course, continue blithely on his way, so that the first requirement will certainly be a recognition that he is on the wrong road. But even knowing that he is on the wrong road may not cause him to alter his course. He may conceivably be glad that he took it and so continue his course. A mere recognition of wrong does not cause one to do right. Men who know that tobacco and drugs harm their bodies still persist in using them. The thief who knows it is wrong to steal nevertheless continues in his wrong-doing and even rejoices in his ill-gotten gains.

Recognition by Richard Roe that he has taken the wrong road must be followed by regret, regret that he has

[5a] Hebrews 11:3.

wasted time and money, that night will find him far from his destination and that the friends he was to meet will be gone.

But even regret does not alter the momentum of his car which is ever carrying him farther and farther from his desired destination. He must resolve to stop his car, to turn it around, and to retrace his journey to the place where the error began. But resolutions have no value in themselves. Despite Richard Roe's recognition that he is on the wrong road, his regret that he has taken such a course and his resolve to go back to the intersection, he is at that point still in the swamp, and no supposition can make him otherwise.[6]

The fourth step becomes then an important and necessary one. He must do the thing which he has resolved to do, stop the car, turn it around, and retrace his steps back to the straight and narrow way which leads to the desired destination.

Richard Roe has now repented of his error and may continue his progress to his destination. But even his repentance does not replace the time and money and perhaps opportunity lost.

This repentance is a law of life. It is applicable to the progress of man in every line of endeavor. The farmer whose faith prompts him to plant his fields to grain may find a poor harvest. Wrong methods of irrigation, improper soil fertilization, or the diseases of rust and smut might seriously cut his yield.

How can he make progress as a farmer? Only as he recognizes what he has done wrong, or failed to do at all, regrets his failure, resolves to correct the faults and actually does so can he hope to make any progress as a farmer.

The merchant whose faith to buy is followed by disappointing sales may face bankruptcy if he does not soon recognize what is wrong; regret it; resolve to change his merchandise or his methods; and change them. The chemist in his laboratory who sets up his elaborate equipment for an experiment only to find that the expected results are not forthcoming may sit by his instruments until doomsday and accomplish nothing unless he recognizes what is wrong, regrets his error, resolves to make changes and actually makes them.

Many years ago Thomas A. Edison[6a] learned that when electricity was forced through a very fine wire the wire became hot—white hot—producing light. Edison realized that here was a possible means of replacing the oil burner for the lighting of homes. But there was one serious drawback—the wire thus subjected to an overload of electricity burned off, or as we would say today, oxidized, in a few minutes' time. The good housewife would hardly put up with the inconvenience of constantly replacing this wire. Edison was convinced that an incandescent light could be perfected and he set about the task of experimenting until he had found it.

During the course of his experiments a neighbor said to him, "Mr. Edison, have you found out how to work it yet?" With a twinkle in his kindly eyes, Edison replied, "No, but I have found five thousand ways that won't work."

The answer Edison gave is significant. Time after time the faith of that

---

[6]This illustrates the fallacy of the doctrine of death-bed repentance which prevails in a number of Christian churches. A sinner on his deathbed may be brought to a recognition of the miserable path of life that he has taken and may sincerely regret the course he has followed. He may even resolve to change his manner of living and correct his errors, to go back and begin again, but the sands of life are running fast and life ends before he can retrace his steps or change his character. No theological fiction can change his status as he enters the world of spirits. He is, literally speaking, in the swamp when he dies and from the swamp he must extract himself.

[6a]Edison, Thomas Alva (1847-1931), American inventor of the incandescent lamp, phonograph, etc.

man caused him to set up an experiment, and time after time he corrected his error, until by continual application of faith and correction he achieved results that have blessed the whole world.

But greater in importance than the improvement in farming, or the success of business or even the harnessing of the forces of nature is the development of character and personality which brings everlasting joy to the soul. For example, selfishness in a human being seriously hampers his happiness because it creates a barrier between himself and those who would be his friends, creates distrust and suspicion, and destroys the possibility of joy that comes from giving. Such an individual can improve his character and personality only by conforming to the law of growth and progress. He must have faith in his own ability to change. He must recognize his personality defect, regret that trait in his makeup, resolve to change it, and actually change it by constant self-discipline over a considerable period of time before he can be said to succeed in this particular. This same law applies to all character growth.

The recognition of one's defects of character comes partially from a comparison of one's self with those who live about us, but more especially by seeing ourselves in the light of the character of Jesus and in the light of His admonitions and commandments unto men. No individual can compare his own character with that of Jesus of Nazareth without suffering by the comparison. Whether we consider the virtue of love, kindness, tolerance, understanding, or any of the qualities of character which we have come to admire, the Master infinitely surpasses his fellows in them all.

A study of the life and example of Jesus brings wayward man to an inward shame and has a remarkable effect upon him. If one is brought to desire to emulate the character of Jesus he is by the same token brought to follow His way of life—the gospel.

Above all other things, the Master taught the eternal nature of man and demonstrated His power over death by allowing His fellowmen to kill His body in such a manner that none could dispute the fact of His death; to lay that body away in a sealed tomb for three days; and then to arise among them and allow His followers to see and feel His resurrected body.

The realization that man will live forever and will be brought to an accounting before God and man is the most potent force for character growth in the whole world.

Faith in Jesus Christ as the Son of God is forever the incentive for character change toward the pattern He set so that repentance in our human relationships logically follows faith in Christ.

It must early become apparent that there is but one road to progress, one road to salvation, and we begin to grasp what Jesus meant when He said:

"Enter ye in at the strait gate: for wide is the gate, and broad is the way, that leadeth to destruction, and many there be which go in thereat:

"Because strait is the gate, and narrow is the way, which leadeth unto life, and few there be that find it."[7]

Damnation

He who will not follow the exacting law of progress is stopped. It is as if he had run his head against a wall—a barrier, and being unwilling to remove the barrier stone by stone must forever remain obstructed by it. We say of such

[7]Matthew 7:13-14.

an individual that he is damned or stopped in his progress because he will not obey the laws of progress which are the laws of God. Thus disobedience to the laws of God brings damnation to the souls of men. The farmer who will not repent in his farming methods will remain as inefficient as he begins. He is damned so far as progress in farming is concerned. And so in all fields of life the person who fails to obey these laws of life is damned—at least so far as his particular field of endeavor is concerned, not by God, but by himself while exercising his own free agency. But while people all about us damn their progress in material accomplishments, the greater and more serious damnation is that of the eternal soul of man which results from rejection of and disobedience to the spiritual laws of God.

It is inconceivable that man, given his free agency in a universe of law, should do all things perfectly. It is equally inconceivable that having broken law man can achieve progress and eternal joy without repentance. Laws are broken in two ways, through ignorance or mistake and through deliberate or willful action. Both bear their inevitable results. In the physical world it makes little difference as to whether or not one is aware of running in front of an automobile. The result is the same in both instances—a bruised body, broken limbs, or possibly death.

Knowledge and Condemnation

Ignorance of the physical laws about us is seemingly no excuse for our breaking them as the penalty follows regardless of our lack of knowledge in the matter. To a certain degree that is true of the man-made laws with which society strives to regulate the relationship of its individuals. The maxim is frequently heard "ignorance is no excuse in the law."

Even in the realm of personality and character development, ignorance of the laws involved does not change the effects of those laws upon us. One of the laws of personality, however, is that only the conscious doing of a wrong seriously affects the serenity of mind or disturbs that which we have come to call our conscience. For example, John Doe, who has never been taught that it is wrong to take his neighbor's goods, picks fruit from his neighbor's farm and consumes it. His mind remains at ease despite his act. In fact, he may for the time being be more content and happy than before because of the satisfying food. On the other hand, if John Doe has been taught that it is contrary to the laws of God and man to take his neighbor's goods, he is conscious of doing wrong. The effect of his action now is to cause him to fear detection and punishment and produces a feeling of uneasiness and shame when in the presence of his neighbor which can only be eliminated by repentance and forgiveness.

It is the conscious doing of a wrong, that which produces regret and remorse, which is called a "sin." Little children cannot sin. That is, not knowing right from wrong they cannot commit acts which bring remorse of conscience. Neither can adults commit sins, or acts which may be followed by remorse of conscience, if they are ignorant of the law, either because they are not intelligent enough to understand the law, or because they have never been taught the law. Having no remorse of conscience, they have no need for repentance, or, in other words, cannot repent.

The Nephite Prophet, Mormon, wrote a letter to his son, Moroni, concerning this and other problems upon which there had been considerable disputation in his day. In the course of his letter he said: "Little children are whole, for they are not capable of committing sin . . . and their little children need no repentance, neither baptism."—Moroni 8:8, 11.

We also find a statement concerning those who have lived without knowledge of the law. "For the power of redemption cometh on all them that have no law; wherefore, he that is not condemned, or he that is under no condemnation, cannot repent."

Thus, while the physical effects of the breaking of law cannot be avoided but must inevitably follow the violation, the condemnation of our associates and of our Father in Heaven follows only when we consciously do that which is wrong.

Baptism

A Third Great Principle of Progress

There is a third great principle of progress discernible in all avenues of life, the constant burial of the mistakes and sins of the past and the rebirth into a new life. This is a fundamental law of happiness. Man is a creature of mistakes and the consequences of them as they accumulate might well rob life of its pleasures and joys. But the great Lord of the universe has instituted a wise law. The withered and torn leaves fall from the tree in the fall of the year and the tree has a rebirth in the spring. In all nature there are periods of rebirth. The past, with its mistakes and ugly scars, is buried and new life covers the earth. Except the rebirth occurs death and desolation prevail.

The principle of burial and rebirth is also observable in the various phases of the life of man. This may be illustrated in the business field. A business man who does not put his losses and failures out of his mind and live constantly in the hope of the present and future soon looses his courage and faith. The memory of past failures destroys his faith. His business ceases to expand and may gradually cease to exist.

During business depressions when some individuals lose fortunes almost overnight one may observe this principle at work. Those who have never learned to bury the past and live afresh allow the memory of their losses to rob them of appetite and sleep until their health is broken and a bitter hell on earth becomes their lot.

Only that business man succeeds who is forever burying the mistakes and failures of the past and lives in the hope of tomorrow. During the business depression of the nineteen-thirties a newspaper reporter asked Henry Ford of the Ford Motor Company this question, "Mr. Ford, what would you do if you should suddenly lose all of the holdings you have built up, every factory, mine and railway, every dollar and every bond?" Of course the question was a hypothetical one. Mr. Ford had not lost his holdings. But the reporter testified that he would never forget Mr. Ford's reply. With a gleam in his eye and his fist tightened in determination, the business magnate replied, "Give me ten years and I would build it all back again." This statement contains the spirit of the Gospel of Jesus Christ. How often the words of the Master rang over the cobbled streets of Jerusalem, "Go thy way and sin no more." Bury the past with all its vice and sin. Build a new life.

The burial of the mistakes, vices and hatreds of the past is one of the crying needs of the world. It is a cardinal principle of the happiness of individuals and nations.

In the great spiritual Kingdom of God every day is a new era of opportunity. He who will not bury the past and live in the future has already invited oblivion. We need to catch the spirit of that grand old man, Edwin Markham, who, on his eightieth birthday, wrote:

The Look Ahead

I am done with the years that were; I am
    quits:
    I am done with the dead and old.
They are mines worked out: I delved in their
    pits
    I have saved their grains of gold
Now I turn to the future for wine and bread:
    I have bidden the past adieu—
I laugh and lift hands to the years ahead:
    "Come on: I am ready for you!"

So in order to reach the Kingdom of God one must accept the third great principle of progress, and without it there can be no entrance, worlds without end.

The Nephite Prophet Moroni wrote:

"Behold, I say unto you that ye would be more miserable to dwell with a holy and just God, under a consciousness of your filthiness before him, than ye would to dwell with the damned souls in hell.

"For behold, when ye shall be brought to see your nakedness before God, and also the glory of God, and the holiness of Jesus Christ, it will kindle a flame of unquenchable fire upon you."[8]

Not only must man repent of his sins but they must be removed from his consciousness before he can enter God's presence. The Lord has promised forgiveness upon repentance to all those who have complied with the ordinance

[8]Mormon 9:4-5.

Baptismal font in the Salt Lake Tabernacle.

of baptism and have been spiritually reborn.

The Ordinance of Baptism

When we come to understand the principle of baptism as one of the basic laws upon which progress of the individual depends we begin to realize the impossibility of achieving salvation (freedom from the evil effects of wrong-doing) except the individual complies with this basic law. There is, indeed, no other road back to God.

In the light of our understanding of this principle it becomes logical for God, who is interested in the welfare of His children, to require of them an outward token or symbol which shall indicate the acceptance of this basic law and a covenant to obey it. This ordinance to be useful and meaningful should symbolize and help to preserve the principle involved. All forms of baptism which fail to do this have no relationship to life. Because the acceptance of the principle which underlies baptism is a requirement for entrance into the kingdom of God, the ordinance becomes an initiatory ceremony for entrance into that kingdom. It should therefore exemplify the greatest idea of the Gospel, the burial and resurrection of the Christ, and should become a test of the candidate's fitness for the Kingdom. Further, the ordinance must be available without price to rich and poor in all parts of the world. To say that there should be no ordinance or formality required for entrance into the Church or Kingdom of God is to say that no requirements are necessary for the enjoyment of or full participation in that Kingdom, and if that were true the Kingdom becomes valueless and entrance into it would not be sought at all. Surely no earthly institution without requirements, small or large, for entrance on its membership roll is worth our joining, nor would we be any different or better for joining.

If the Church of Jesus Christ made no requirements of those who seek admission how could it serve to change the lives of individuals or bring them one whit nearer salvation. And if an organization is for the purpose of bringing its members to salvation, of bringing them into an observance of the basic principles of human growth, how can it test the willingness of the candidate to accept and live those principles without requiring of him some outward act which would signify and serve as a covenant or solemn promise that he will obey?

It is conceivable that God, our Father, might have devised other tests than baptism as an initiatory rite, but the human mind cannot conceive a more fitting and beautiful ceremony than the ordinance of baptism, or one which so well accomplishes its purpose when properly performed. God in His wisdom has chosen the only form of baptism that can possibly meet all the requirements— baptism by immersion in water. As we examine this ordinance we appreciate more and more its appropriateness. First, the immersion in water is a complete burial. It signifies a complete death and burial of the old self, a complete turning away from sin, and a complete rebirth of the soul. A sprinkling could not signify that; a pouring would not suggest it. A partial burial of our old faults will not let us forget them. A partial turning away from wrong-doing will not save. The break with error must be complete if we would reach salvation. So there must be a complete burial in the water and a complete rebirth from the water.

Secondly, such baptism best tests the heart and soul of the candidate. Just as death humbles the mightiest of men and the grave removes all vestige of power and pride, so the symbolic death and burial in baptism at the hands of a servant of God has a humbling effect on an individual's mind. To seemingly die and be buried, as one before his time, and that, too, before the eyes of his fellows, humbles the human heart as perhaps nothing else could do.

Men enter into covenants with one another by affixing their signatures to written documents or solemnly pledging themselves by the uplifted hand, but none of these outward symbols carries the beauty and impressiveness of the token of the covenant with God which a person enters into at baptism.

Baptism a New Birth

"Baptism in water for the remission of sins, and the laying on of hands for the gift of the Holy Ghost," constitute the birth of the water and of the Spirit. This is essential to salvation. It is more than a symbol; it is a reality, a birth in very deed. How could a man get unto this mortal world without being born as other men are born? Has anyone ever done so? It has never been done because there is a law controlling mortal birth. No man can obtain the second birth except by complying with the law of that birth, which is to be born of the water and of the Spirit in the way the Lord has prescribed. No man can come unto God without repentance. Unforgiven sinners could not dwell in His presence. To gain entrance there we must be sanctified, or cleansed from sin, and the law governing this matter has been unalterably fixed. We may rebel; we may protest and think this method a very foolish one; a very unnecessary one; but it is in the wisdom of One who knows all things, that this commandment has been given. Who is man that he should question God? 'Shall the ax boast itself against him that heweth therewith? or shall the saw magnify itself against him that shaketh it? as if the rod should shake itself against them that lift it up, or as if the staff should lift itself, as if it were no wood.'—Isaiah 10:15.

Effect of the First or Spiritual Death

"We have all been taught that baptism is for the remission of sins, but the Lord has given us further explanation as to the purpose and efficacy of this ordinance. Baptism dates from the fall of man. Adam was cast out of the presence of the Lord because of his transgression, and thus was banished from the presence of the Father. This banishment is called the "first" or "spiritual" death. All who are unrepentant, who have not accepted the gospel, are spiritually dead. That is, they are subject to the "first" death which is banishment from the presence of the Lord.

"Death is banishment. Explaining this matter the Lord said to Joseph Smith:

"'Wherefore, it came to pass that the devil tempted Adam, and he partook of the forbidden fruit and transgressed the commandment, wherein he became subject to the will of the devil, because he yielded unto temptation.

"'Wherefore, I, the Lord God, caused that he should be cast out from the Garden of Eden, from my presence, because of his transgression, wherein he became spiritually dead, which is the first death, even that same death which is the last death, which is spiritual, which shall be pronounced upon the wicked when I shall say: Depart, ye cursed.'"—Doc. & Cov. 29:40-41.

"This same banishment has been pronounced on all those who do not repent and accept the ordinances of the Gospel, 'For they cannot be redeemed,' saith the Lord, 'from their spiritual fall because they repent not.'"

Being Born Again into the Kingdom of God

"Now, how can we overcome this death? How can we get back from that banishment? By being born again of the water and of the Spirit. To be brought back we must comply with certain laws which have been eternally fixed and which are as immutable as the heavens. These laws are those of the water burial, or birth, and the birth of the Spirit of God by receiving the gift of the Holy Ghost by the laying on of hands.

"So we see baptism is the means by which we come back into the presence of the Lord after being shut out of His presence. For this reason it is a burial in the water and symbolizes both a death and a birth into a new life, and is in the similitude of the death of Jesus Christ as well as of birth into this world. John understood this and has said:

" 'Who is he that overcometh the world, but he that believeth that Jesus is the Son of God?

" 'This is he that came by water and blood, even Jesus Christ; not by water only, but by water and blood. And it is the Spirit that beareth witness, because the Spirit is truth.

" 'For there are three that bear record in heaven, the Father, the Word, and the Holy Ghost; and these three are one.

" 'And there are three that bear witness in earth, the Spirit, and the water, and the blood: and these three agree in one.'—I John 5:5-7.

" 'This doctrine was not introduced by John; evidently he was taught it from earlier prophets, for we read in the Book of Moses:

" 'That by reason of transgression cometh the fall, which fall bringeth death, and inasmuch as ye were born into the world by water, and blood, and the spirit, which I have made, and also became of dust a living soul, even so ye must be born again into the kingdom of heaven, of water, and of the Spirit, and be cleansed by blood, even the blood of mine Only Begotten; that ye might be sanctified from all sin, and enjoy the words of eternal life in this world, and eternal life in the world to come, even immortal glory;

" 'For by the water ye keep the commandment; by the Spirit ye are justified, and by the blood ye are sanctified.'—Moses 6:59-60.

"The significant likeness between birth and baptism, and between death and baptism, with the symbolism found in the expression of the witnesses in heaven and on earth, is very apparent to those who understand the order of heaven in relation to the second birth."[9]

Authority to Baptize

As in all the affairs of life where entrance into organizations of any kind is effected, authority is necessary on the part of someone to grant the admittance, so to admit another into the Kingdom of God requires authority in the one officiating.[10] Only Christ can

[9]Joseph Fielding Smith, *The Way to Perfection*, pp. 190-193.
[10]The necessity for authority to act for another is discussed more fully in the previous chapter.

truly admit another into fellowship with Him. If Christ cannot personally be present and some other must act in His stead, surely that other must have direct authority from Christ before the action in His name shall be binding upon Him. For while any group of individuals might organize a church and authorize one or more of their number to initiate new members, and might even make the same requirement of applicants as does the Christ, yet the church so set up is still the church of man, founded by man, and the initiate is a member of that church and not a member of the Church of Christ. This might be perfectly satisfactory to all concerned if such a church could offer its members the same blessings Christ might offer. If, however, there is any additional power in Christ or any blessings which He can bestow beyond the power of ordinary man, then membership in the church of men becomes a poor substitute for the Church of Christ, and the authority which goes no further than the members of that earthly organization becomes rather hollow and meaningless.

That individual who does not have even the delegated authority of the membership of a church as a basis upon which to act, but who relies only upon his own desires to serve the Christ as a basis of authority to act in Christ's name is in even a worse predicament. The person baptized or initiated by him is as a matter of fact no better off after baptism than before, for he can claim blessings from neither an organization of men nor from Christ. It would seem a paradox that men should deem it necessary for a candidate to the Kingdom of God to be admitted by a definite method and ordinance requiring fixed forms and activities and yet consider that actual authority of God to so officiate could be obtained without corresponding formalities.

What are the benefits which accrue to worthy members of the Church of Jesus Christ admitted by proper authorization which are not available in any church organization effected by man? The best spokesman on the subject is Jesus Christ Himself. To the Nephites on the American continent nineteen hundred years ago He said:

"Blessed are ye if ye shall give heed unto the words of these twelve whom I have chosen from among you to minister unto you, and to be your servants; and unto them I have given power that they may baptize you with water; and after that ye are baptized with water, behold I will baptize you with fire and with the Holy Ghost; therefore blessed are ye if ye shall believe in me and be baptized, after that ye have seen me and know that I am.

"And again, more blessed are they who shall believe in your words because that ye shall testify that ye have seen me, and that ye know that I am. *Yea, blessed are they who shall believe in your words, and come down into the depths of humility and be baptized, for they shall be visited with fire and with the Holy Ghost, and shall receive a remission of their sins.*[11]

We notice here two distinct blessings which may accrue to those properly baptized. *First*, Christ promises a baptism by fire and the Holy Ghost. *Second*, He promises a remission of sins. While both promises are conditional upon the performance of the initiate in keeping his promise to live up to the laws of the kingdom, both may be attained. Neither of these blessings can be bestowed by man nor by an organization of men, for while man can baptize with water, the action is a purely mechanical one and does not in and of itself alter the character of the recipient. The outward ordinance does not reach the heart or bring testimony to the mind. But when Christ sends the Holy Ghost and His comforting influence touches the heart, man is baptized from within. The testimony of the truth of Christ's words entering into his soul transforms him. He is now truly reborn and his testimony acting as a mainspring to righteous living prompts him to a course in life which leads toward salvation. Right at this point it becomes apparent that baptism improperly performed avails nothing, for while man can perform the outward ordinance, that ordinance in and of itself has no power of salvation. Without the authority to bestow the Holy Ghost the inner baptism of the soul cannot take place and the whole ordinance becomes an empty form.

Similarly with the second promise: the Savior has said that those who are baptized by fire and with the Holy Ghost "shall receive a remission of sins." This blessing cannot be given by men. It comes only from God. The mechanical act of baptism does not cause a remission of sins but it is the inward cleansing of the heart which follows the reception of the Holy Spirit which really enables an individual to thrust aside his former manner of living and stand clean before his Maker. Thus, the physical act of baptism does not wash away sins, but is the token of a promise unto God that man will abide by the principles of human progress with which the Gospel has acquainted him, that he will exercise faith, practice repentance, and be willing to bury constantly the old self and live afresh. This physical act brings a promise from God in return that if these principles are lived all sin will be remitted. As Mormon states in the *Book of Mormon* record:

"Behold, baptism is unto repentance to

___
[11]3 Nephi 12:1-2.

the fulfilling the commandments unto the remission of sins."[12] And again:

"And the first fruits of repentance is baptism; and baptism cometh by faith unto the fulfilling the commandments; *and the fulfilling the commandments bringeth remission of sins.*"[13]

No man may take upon himself the right and power to bind Christ to a promise. If Christ is not bound the promise of man is of no avail. Hence, if baptism is to bring the blessings of God it must be performed as God has commanded, by virtue of authority which has been obtained from Him in a manner as fixed and definite as is the ordinance of baptism itself.

Who, Then, Should Be Baptized?

If the real value of baptism follows the outward mechanical ordinance and consists in the transformation of the soul, baptism is useless where for any reason this transformation of the heart cannot follow. Thus, the ordinance of baptism avails the imbecile nothing for he cannot comprehend it or alter his way of life one whit because of it. And if his way of life is not altered he is not any closer to salvation. So the Lord does not require that the outward act, being useless, be done at all. This applies to all those who are "without the law," that is, all those who, because of their lack of understanding of the Gospel, cannot comprehend the laws and principles of the Gospel. Not understanding the laws they are not brought any closer to observing them by an ordinance that has no meaning to them. The same is true in regard to little children. Not yet having developed their minds to a point where the principles of the Gospel might be taught to them, the ordinance of baptism can have no meaning to them and will in no wise alter their

[12]Moroni 8:11.
[13]Moroni 8:25.

course of life. But in the case of infants a further factor also enters. The child has not sinned and need not repent and hence does not immediately need the Holy Ghost to turn him from his sins or bring remission of them. Hence, the baptism of infants is without value or meaning and is not required by the Lord. In this connection the Latter-day scriptures speak with much plainness. Consider the words of the Prophet Mormon:

"Listen to the words of Christ, your Redeemer, your Lord and your God. Behold, I came into the world not to call the righteous but sinners to repentance; the whole need no physician, but they that are sick; wherefore, little children are whole, for they are not capable of committing sin. . . .

"And their little children need no repentance, neither baptism. Behold, baptism is unto repentance to the fulfilling the commandments unto the remission of sins.

"For behold that all little children are alive in Christ, and also all they that are without the law. For the power of redemption cometh on all them that have no law; wherefore, he that is not condemned, or he that is under no condemnation, cannot repent; and unto such baptism availeth nothing.

"But it is mockery before God, denying the mercies of Christ, and the power of His Holy Spirit, and putting trust in dead works."[14]

[14]Moroni 8:8, 11, 22-23.
Note: Many so-called Christians consider that infants need baptism because of the original sin of Adam in the Garden of Eden. The concept developed in early Christendom that because of this original sin all children were conceived in sin, and could not be members of the Kingdom of God unless they were baptized and this condemnation removed. In the light of the additional words of Christ and the prophets, which were restored through Joseph Smith, this concept is shown to be wrong. This is revealed in the following words: "And our father Adam spake unto the Lord, and said: Why is it that men must repent and be baptized in water? And the Lord said unto Adam: Behold I have forgiven thee thy transgression in the Garden of Eden. Hence came the saying abroad among the people, that the Son of God hath atoned for original guilt, wherein the sins of the parents cannot be answered upon the heads of the children, for they are whole from the foundation of the world."—*Pearl of Great Price,* Moses 6:53-54.
Also the following:
"Wherefore, little children are whole, for they are not capable of committing sin; wherefore the curse of Adam is taken from them in me, that it hath no power over them. . . ."—Moroni 8:8.

The Laying of on Hands for the Gift of the Holy Ghost

A Fourth Principle of Progress

It must be universally recognized that inasmuch as man enters this life devoid of knowledge of either the world or the basic laws which govern it, that progress would be extremely slow and painful without contact with other individuals. In fact, the dependence of one individual upon others for his learning permeates all of life and his willingness to thus learn greatly conditions his rate of progress. For example, our entire educational system is based upon the assumption that one person can learn from others or with others faster than he can learn by himself. All our books and. literature have come into being because of the same basic law of progress. When the invention of printing enabled man to preserve and to extend the knowledge he possessed to others, and those others became able and willing to read and accept such knowledge, the progress of man received a powerful impetus.

The babe would be lost and destroyed by the physical world in which he finds himself except for the advice, council, and care of those who have already traveled at least a part of the road of life. If all mankind should cease to be taught by one another a single generation would reduce us to barbarism.

That individual who adds to his own experiences the experiences and findings of others multiplies by many times the knowledge he would otherwise possess. The boy who wishes to be a chemist will make infinitely greater progress by acquiring the knowledge others have learned conquering chemistry and by sitting at the feet of those who are already acquainted with chemi-cal laws than by ignoring all the knowledge of chemistry which man has gained and shutting himself away from those who might help him.

The young man who sits at the gates of a university, saying in his heart, "I am as good, as intelligent, as eager for knowledge as are these who are entering the university. But why should I enter such an institution? Why should I register and attend classes?" is ignoring a law of life. Granted that what the young man thinks about himself is true, the results of the two possible courses of action are quite apparent. The young man might sit at the gates till doomsday and still know little or nothing of chemistry, history, geology, or other subjects taught at the university; while the young man who satisfies the entrance requirements and eagerly seeks aid from those who are trained to aid him makes marked progress and in a few short years may acquire the learning that generations of men and long years of patient experiment have accumulated.

This illustrates a basic law of life. Progress is most rapid where man acquires the right to be taught and actually is taught by those who know. The right to be taught by parents is acquired by birth or entrance into the family unit; the right to be taught in a school is acquired by fulfilling the entrance requirements, paying fees, registering, etc. Likewise, the right to be taught of God is acquired by entrance into the Kingdom of God. This entrance is obtained by being baptized and by receiving the right to the instructions of the Holy Ghost through the laying on of hands.

Searching for Knowledge of God

In ancient times the writer of the

Book of Job quoted Job in these words, "Canst thou by searching find out God?" And the answer, from that day to this, has been very much in the negative. Yet many have continued such a search. Like the boy who takes the clock apart wheel by wheel, and spring by spring, seeking to understand the secret of its power, so men have delved deep into the workings of the universe to discover the nature of its creator; and just as the wheels of the clock become dead bits of steel in the boy's hands and the intelligence that fashioned them remains as remote as ever, so he who would find God in nature falls forever short of his objective and must fashion from his own imagination the God he cannot see. Thus, his god is a creation of his own mind and cannot rise above it in intelligence or coherence.

How then can man come to know God? Only as man searches for God and God reveals Himself unto him and only as he who has thus received knowledge of God teaches that knowledge to others.

The Holy Ghost

The Kingdom of God may be likened unto a school. All who can fulfill the entrance requirements may enter. In the case of the school the entrance requirements are the payment of fees and the evidence of certain basic knowledge. Without such basic preparation the student could not hope to profit from membership in the school.

The entrance requirements for the Kingdom of God are likewise essential to the enjoyment and benefit of the Kingdom. Except one has faith in God and in His Son, Jesus Christ, has repented of his sins, and is willing to enter into a covenant with God to lead a new life as evidenced by the burial and re-

birth of baptism, he cannot hope to be taught by the Holy Ghost or be influenced by Him. However, just as a student may have membership in the school class and fail to receive instruction, so one might have membership in the Kingdom of God and fail to receive the influence of the Holy Ghost.

The right to instruction has been bestowed in both cases by those having authority to bestow such right—in the case of the school by a duly appointed official who represents the state or people, and in the case of the Kingdom of God by one holding authority of God.[15] But the student may sleep through the class period and the member of God's Kingdom may never seek the influence of the Holy Ghost.

This is the straight and narrow way which leads into life. It is not the end of the road. One who has become a member of Christ's Church has not attained a final goal—he has but entered the gate. Concerning such individuals the first Prophet Nephi said:

"And now, my beloved brethren, after ye have gotten into this straight and narrow path, I would ask if all is done? Behold I say unto you, Nay; for ye have not come thus far save it were by the word of Christ with unshaken faith in him, relying wholly upon the merits of him who is mighty to save.

"Wherefore, ye must press forward with a steadfastness in Christ, having a perfect brightness of hope, and a love of God and of all men. Wherefore, if ye shall press forward, feasting upon the word of Christ, and endure to the end, behold, thus saith the Father: Ye shall have eternal life.

"And now, behold, my beloved brethren, this is the way; and there is none other way nor name given under heaven whereby man can be saved in the kingdom of God."[16]

It is related that an infidel once said to the great Pascal,[16a] who was a devout

---

[15]Note: For a discussion of the nature and calling of the Holy Ghost, see the earlier treatment.
[16]*Book of Mormon*, 2 Nephi 31:19-21.
[16a]Pascal, Blaise (1623-1662), French mathematician, physicist, philosopher and writer.

Christian, "If you will prove your religion to me I will try it."

Pascal replied, "If you will try the religion, it will prove itself."

No person ever fully lived the Gospel of Jesus Christ who did not find happiness. No person ever fully kept the Word of Wisdom who did not receive a testimony of its truth.

It has been the history of the Church that those who have entered into the Kingdom of God and received the Holy Ghost have new objectives in their lives. Men who have entered into this kingdom have willingly traversed the earth, enduring privations, sacrificed their wealth and the association of their loved ones, in order that others of mankind might learn of the Kingdom, and entering, have the same fulness of joy.

So powerful is the effect of the Holy Ghost upon those who have entered the Kingdom of God that the ancient Nephite prophet, Jacob, warned his people who were acquiring great wealth:

"But before ye seek for riches, seek ye the Kingdom of God.

"And after ye have obtained a hope in Christ [i.e., a testimony of Him] ye shall obtain riches, if ye seek them; and ye will seek them for the intent to do good—to clothe the naked, and to feed the hungry, and to liberate the captive, and administer relief to the sick and the afflicted."[17]

To the Jews who expected the Kingdom of God to have armies and boundaries, the Savior said:

"The Kingdom of God cometh not with observation.

"Neither shall they say, Lo here! or, Lo, there! for, behold, the kingdom of God is within you."[18]

It is a development from within which is the product of conformity to the laws of God. It is a union of the soul with the soul of God, being fed by His Holy Spirit and acting according to His Holy will.

The Lord has said of such:

"And blessed are they who shall seek to bring forth my Zion at that day, for they shall have the gift and the power of the Holy Ghost; and if they endure unto the end they shall be lifted up at the last day, and shall be saved in the everlasting kingdom of the Lamb; and whoso shall publish peace, yea, tidings of great joy, how beautiful upon the mountains shall they be."[19]

Supplementary Readings

On Specific Topics:

Faith

Talmage, *Sunday Night Talks*, pp. 500-509.

Nephi Jensen "Faith, a Moral Strength," *Deseret News*, Church Section, September 2, 1933.

Book of Mormon, Alma 56 (Faith of Helaman and his 2,000 young warriors); 1 Nephi 2:16-19; 7:6-20 (Incidents of great faith in God.)

Bible, I Kings 18:17-39 (Faith of Elijah); Genesis 41 (Faith of Joseph in Egypt); Daniel 2 (Faith of Daniel in Babylon); Hebrews 11 (Nature of Faith with examples.)

Repentance

Talmage, *Jesus the Christ*, pp. 392-395.

Baptism

Talmage, *Sunday Night Talks*, pp. 160-171.

Book of Mormon, Alma 32:17-43; Helaman 5:10-51; III Nephi 11; Moroni 8; Mosiah 26-17-31.

Laying on of Hands for the Gift of the Holy Ghost

Talmage, *Sunday Night Talks*, pp. 195-206.

General Readings:

Joseph F. Smith, *Gospel Doctrine*, pp. 91-99.

Talmage, *Articles of Faith*, pp. 96-170.

Widtsoe, *A Rational Theology*, Chapter 16.

Widtsoe, "The Certain Steps in Progress," *Improvement Era*, Vol. 38. (November, 1935.)

---

[17] *Book of Mormon, Jacob* 2:18-19.
[18] *Luke* 17:20-21.

---

[19] *Book of Mormon,* 1 Nephi 13:37.

CHAPTER 47

THE BLESSINGS OF THE
HOLY SPIRIT

The Gift of Faith

The Savior promised certain special blessings to those who believed and were baptized in His name. These are usually referred to as the blessings of the Holy Spirit. The various types of blessings are enumerated by the ancient Apostle Paul in his famous letter to the Corinthian Saints:

"Now concerning spiritual gifts, brethren, I would not have you ignorant.

Ye know that ye were Gentiles, carried away unto these dumb idols, even as ye were led.

"Wherefore I give you to understand, that no man speaking by the Spirit of God calleth Jesus accursed; and that no man can say that Jesus is the Lord, but by the Holy Ghost.

"Now there are diversities of gifts, but the same Spirit.

"And there are differences of administrations, but the same Lord.

"And there are diversities of operations, but it is the same God which worketh all in all.

"But the manifestation of the Spirit is given to every man to profit withal.

"For to one is given by the Spirit the word of wisdom; to another the word of knowledge by the same Spirit;

"To another faith by the same Spirit; to another the gifts of healing by the same Spirit;

"To another the working of miracles; to another prophecy; to another discerning of spirits; to another divers kinds of tongues; to another the interpretation of tongues:

"But all these worketh that one and the self-same Spirit; dividing to every man severally as he will."[1]

All the above blessings have been continually manifest within the Church from the time of the restoration of the Priesthood until the present day.

Faith in God can be stronger than the evidences on which it is based. The influence of the Holy Spirit upon the heart of man bears undeniable evidence of God's existence and goodness. Faith in God may be found among men where this direct evidence of the Holy Spirit is lacking, for there are many and diverse evidences of the Lord. But such faith cannot be so strong as where this additional evidence is had, and usually attains to little more than a hope or belief. So sure was the Apostle Paul of this that he solemnly stated, "No man can say that Jesus is the Lord, but by the Holy Ghost."[2] That is, faith in Jesus Christ cannot reach a certainty without evidence beyond that which flesh and blood can reveal. The Savior taught this to Peter when in response to Peter's answer to him, "Thou art the Christ, the Son of the Living God." Jesus asserted, "Blessed art thou, Simon Barjona: for flesh and blood hath not revealed it unto thee, but my Father which is in heaven."[3]

The effect of this blessing of faith among the Latter-day Saints is most noticeable in their payment of tithing, in the spirit of missionary work, in the intense devotion to the Church which has enabled them to endure privations, and in the vast voluntary service which the majority of members render.

Healing

While Jesus lived in the flesh among men His great heart was touched by the

---

[1] Cor. 12:1-11. Read also *Doctrine and Covenants* 76:5-10.

[2] Cor. 12:3b.
[3] Matthew 16:16-17.

human suffering He witnessed. Some of those suffering ones He healed, some He did not. One of the saddest lines of the New Testament concerns His second visit to His home town of Nazareth, "and he did not many mighty works there because of their unbelief."[4] The amazing thing, however, is not the number of people Jesus did not heal but the wide extent of His healings, for they included the most virulent diseases and the most difficult physical handicaps. Two things seem necessary for such a healing, actual power of God in the individual administering to another, and faith on the part of that other that the healing will be effected.

The administration of the sick by the authority and with the power of God and the healings which may follow must not be confused with those healings which are effected among men by the application of purely psychological principles. The power of the mind over the body is so great that some forms of illness are produced, or at least the healing delayed, by the depressed condition of the mind. In such instances remarkable healings are effected by restoring confidence and faith to the mind which then reacts favorably upon the functioning of the body. Such healings may occur independently of Priesthood, in fact independently of religion, although religious beliefs seem most potent in producing the required mental changes. The types of physical ailments thus cured seem to have definite limitations and apparently do not extend to the cure of virulent diseases, the restoration of sight, or the correction of deformities of the body, although a healthy state of mind undoubtedly is an essential aid to the cure of such ailments by any means whatsoever.

The great healings by Jesus Christ during His earthly ministry cannot be explained by purely psychological principles. They remain forever a puzzle save we recognize a healing power in God which can be administered and controlled by those of His Holy Priesthood.

Mankind is unable to understand or master all the physical and mental conditions which disrupt bodily functions. Startling discoveries of healing agencies in recent years have opened to the mind the possibilities of many other healing agencies hitherto unknown and unadministered by man. The most important discoveries concern the healing power of certain light rays, both those generated by the sun and those generated by such substances as radium or produced electrically. Just as there are healing properties in the light from the sun, when properly administered, so there is a healing power in the Spirit of God, which, properly used, restores health in a most remarkable fashion. The power to control this healing influence rests in God. As the power of God is delegated unto men who are directly called of Him and ordained to the Holy Priesthood, so these may administer this healing influence unto the sick and if they are receptive to it they may be healed. The Apostles of Jesus, having been given authority from Him, exercised this healing power to the astonishment of many observers.[5] Wherever and whenever the true Priesthood of God has been found in the world the power to heal the sick has accompanied it.

The gift of healing spoken of by the Apostle Paul in the first letter to the Corinthian Saints must be distinguished from the power of the Holy

---

[4]Matthew 13:58.

[5]Read Acts 3:1-16; 4:1-22; 4:12-16.

Priesthood. While this gift cannot be enjoyed apart from the Priesthood, it may not always be present in those who hold the Priesthood.

We have already spoken of the two requirements for healing through the ordinance of administration, actual authority from God, and faith on the part of the person to be healed.

This faith of the individual who is ill may be increased by the very presence of one who has his complete confidence. Not all who hold the power of the Priesthood to administer to the sick will have equal success in healing them, not because of any difference in power, but because of the difference in faith engendered in the sick by the personalities of the different men who do the administering. Some men are so sure of the healing power of God, because of the influence of His Spirit upon them, that the sick feel that spirit in the clasp of the hand, the look in the face, or the quiet assurance in the voice. That evidence of the presence of the Spirit of God increases their faith sufficiently to allow them to be healed. This gift of the Holy Spirit is called the gift of healing. Thus, all who hold the Priesthood may not possess the spirit of healing, but nevertheless, may administer to the sick and the power of God which they exercise may raise the sick whose faith is sufficiently strong.

Prophecy

The gift of prophecy is one of the greatest of the gifts of the Spirit and one of the most important to mankind. Prophecy as a principle is used by both God and man. As practiced among men it does not always go under that name. Two types of prophecy, however, are current in our daily life.

As an example of the first, occasionally one sees in a conspicuous place on some city corner a great placard upon which may be written words such as these: "Blank and Company will open a new department store on this site on blank day of blank month of blank year." Generally, at the time the announcement is made, old and decrepit buildings occupy the site and to the casual observer there would be no thought of a new structure's appearing. One of the distinguishing characteristics, however, of man is his ability to project himself into the future, to plan events which will occur in the future, and then laboriously work to have these plans fulfilled. Thus, the forecast or prediction that a new building will be erected upon a certain site will ordinarily be brought to pass. If one were to inquire further into the matter of such projected new building he would possibly discover many pertinent facts relating to it—its height, its floor space, the number of doors and windows, almost the number of bricks and the number of nails which the building would contain. But there is a limitation to the prophetic power of those who plan buildings. The architect, for example, could not tell that on such and such a day John Doe would hit his thumb with a hammer, or Richard Roe would fall off a beam and break his leg, for those are actions involving human agency and cannot be accurately predicted; but one thing is sure in the minds of those who plan the construction of the building—that if for any reason one workman may be forced to quit, another will be hired to take his place, the building will be completed, and the prophecy fulfilled.

Likewise, man plans in advance for

most of his activities and predicts the happening long before it occurs. No one, for example, would think of starting to build a home until he had in advance determined the size of the home, the number of rooms, and scores of details. Nations now plan national enterprises on five- and ten-year programs. Company projects are planned far into the future. Individuals plan for the future education of sons and daughters and guarantee the fulfillment of their predictions by insurance policies and trust funds.

It is strange that individuals, who thus practice planning themselves, deny God sufficient intelligence to plan ahead for His children, for if God is as intelligent as man He cannot ignore the value of working according to a preconceived plan. To the degree that His intelligence surpasses that of man his plans will project themselves farther into the future. As man plans a house before he starts to build, so God planned the earth before He started to create, and so He planned for the peopling of the earth before the creation began. It is as reasonable to suppose that God planned to send His Son Jesus Christ into the world before the world was created and that He could make that portion of His plan known unto men on the earth long before the event occurred as it is to suppose that a man may plan to have his son occupy a dwelling long before that dwelling has been erected. This form of prophecy is found in Holy Scriptures when at various times men of faith have inquired of God concerning His plans for the future. God has revealed portions of that plan unto man. When any man who has thus been instructed communicates that portion of the plan of God unto his fellowmen, his

fellowmen term him a prophet. The words of the prophet concerning the future plans of God are more certain to come true than are the plans of man for the future. Prophesying is, of course, only a part of a prophet's work and many great prophets have done little of it.

Some of the most remarkable prophecies of the Old Testament and of the *Book of Mormon* concern the coming of the Son of God upon the earth. Men have marveled and some have doubted that Isaiah could foresee that momentous event sufficiently to cause him to write these words:

"Who hath believed our report? and to whom is the arm of the Lord revealed?

"For he shall grow up before him as a tender plant, and as a root out of a dry ground: he hath no form nor comeliness; and when we shall see him, there is no beauty that we should desire him.

"He is despised and rejected of men; a man of sorrows, and acquainted with grief: and we hid as it were our faces from him; he was despised, and we esteemed him not.

"Surely he hath borne our griefs, and carried our sorrows: yet we did esteem him stricken, smitten of God, and afflicted.

"But he was wounded for our transgressions, he was bruised for our iniquities: the chastisement of our peace was upon him; and with his stripes we are healed.

"All we like sheep have gone astray; we have turned every one to his own way; and the Lord hath laid on him the iniquity of us all.

"He was oppressed, and he was afflicted, yet he opened not his mouth: he is brought as a lamb to the slaughter, and as a sheep before her shearers is dumb, so he openeth not his mouth.

"He was taken from prison and from judgment: and who shall declare his generation? for he was cut off out of the land of the living; for the transgressions of my people was he stricken.

"And he made his grave with the wicked, and with the rich in his death; because he had done no violence, neither was any deceit in his mouth.

"Yet it pleased the Lord to bruise him; he hath put him to grief: when thou shalt make his soul an offering for sin, he shall see his seed, he shall prolong his days, and the pleasure of the Lord shall prosper in his hand.

"He shall see of the travail of his soul, and shall be satisfied: by his knowledge shall my righteous servant justify many; for he shall bear their iniquities.

"Therefore will I divide him a portion with the great, and he shall divide the spoil with the strong; because he hath poured out his soul unto death: and he was numbered with the transgressors; and he bare the sin of many, and made intercession for the transgressors."[6]

The *Book of Mormon* records that when Nephi inquired of the Lord by prayer concerning the Messiah who was to come that God gave him a remarkable vision of that future event, enabling Nephi to write:

"And I looked and beheld the Redeemer of the world, of whom my father had spoken; and I also beheld the prophet who should prepare the way before him. And the Lamb of God went forth and was baptized of him; and after he was baptized, I beheld the heavens open, and the Holy Ghost came down out of heaven and abide upon him in the form of a dove.

"And I beheld that he went forth ministering unto the people, in power and great glory; and the multitudes were gathered together to hear him; and I beheld that they cast him out from among them.

"And I also beheld twelve others following him. And it came to pass that they were carried away in the Spirit from before my face, and I saw them not.

"And it came to pass that the angel spake unto me again, saying: Look! And I looked, and I beheld the heavens open again, and I saw angels descending upon the children of men; and they did minister unto them.

"And he spake unto me again, saying: Look! And I looked and I beheld the Lamb of God going forth among the children of men. And I beheld multitudes of people who were sick, and who were afflicted with all manner of diseases, and with devils and unclean spirits; and the angel spake and showed all these things unto me. And they were healed by the power of the Lamb of God; and the devils and the unclean spirits were cast out.

"And it came to pass that the angel spake unto me again, saying: Look! And I looked and beheld the Lamb of God, that He was taken by the people; yea, the Son of the everlasting God was judged of the world; and I saw and bear record."[7]

The belief in the power of God to make known this part of His plan is no more difficult than the belief in the power of man to give to his neighbor a sketch of the house or the building that is to be erected.

It is to be noticed in such prophecies that just as man cannot predict what individuals may do in regard to a building, so God in revealing His plans unto man seldom refers to individuals and then only to those principal characters who are to come into the same, which might be comparable to the builder's revealing the architect and the chief contractor to his neighbor. The entire plan of God for this world and for the inhabitants thereof is not known among men. If it has ever been revealed the record of it is not now to be had. There are, however, certain fundamental elements of the plan of God that have been made known, for example, the coming of Christ in the Meridian of Time and the restoration of the Gospel in the last days. Concerning the latter, the Lord made known unto Joseph Smith that he was called as an instrument to effect the Lord's plan, but the Lord warned him that if he failed to carry out the commandments of God another would be chosen in his stead because the work of God would be completed as planned. In the *Doctrine and Covenants*, Section Three, we read these words:

"The works, and the designs, and the purposes of God cannot be frustrated, neither can they come to naught.

---

[6]Isaiah 53:1-12.

[7]1 Nephi 11:27-32.

"For God doth not walk in crooked paths, neither doth he turn to the right hand nor to the left, neither doth he vary from that which he hath said, therefore his paths are straight, and his course is one eternal round.

"Remember, remember that it is not the work of God that is frustrated, but the work of men;

"For although a man may have many revelations, and have power to do many mighty works, yet if he boasts in his own strength, and sets at naught the counsels of God, and follows after the dictates of his own will and carnal desires, he must fall and incur the vengeance of a God upon him.

"Behold, thou art Joseph, and thou wast chosen to do the work of the Lord, but because of transgression, if thou art not aware thou wilt fall.

"Nevertheless, my work shall go forth, for inasmuch as the knowledge of a Savior has come unto the world, through the testimony of the Jews, even so shall the knowledge of a Savior come unto my people."[8]

In order, however, to understand prophecy in all its phases we must consider the second known type of prophecy. Two great universities are scheduled to play a football game. Days before the game takes place sports writers predict the results. Perhaps even the man on the street will make his own prophecy concerning the coming game. The prophecy may prove true or false. That individual who has had the best opportunity for knowing both teams, who has made the closest observations, and who perhaps has witnessed them in other games, is best qualified to become a true prophet of the coming event. Similarly, a man observing the life of a neighbor's boy and finding him reckless, disobedient to authority, irreligious, given to drinking and licentious habits, may, on the basis of his observations, predict for him a prison cell, and if his observations have been accurate the prophecy is likely to be fulfilled.

It is doubtful if there is any type of prophecy more indulged in by human

beings than the forecasting of events based upon past and present observations. Similarly, if God has intelligence surpassing that of man, He can foresee the possible results of man's course of action and predict the calamities or blessings that will come upon man. To take a concrete example: long before it occurred, the Lord foresaw a civil war for this nation. In His position as God He must be an infinitely more keen observer than man of the events transpiring upon the earth, and perceiving the bitterness between the North and the South and the trend that the thinking people were taking, could foresee an eventual bloody war. When the Prophet Joseph Smith, disturbed by the violent articles in the press in his own day concerning slavery, prayed unto the Lord on the matter, the Lord revealed unto him that the course which men had taken in this nation would cause a great civil war that would break out in South Carolina. As historians today look back upon events it is not difficult to realize and to believe that God could thus foresee that mighty calamity and that He could thus reveal this information unto His servant, Joseph Smith.

It must, however, be kept in mind that because the Lord foresaw the war does not indicate that He desired the war. On the other hand, He must have been greatly grieved that His sons and daughters should bring themselves to such a pitiable state. Often when God has thus revealed unto men the dark calamity that awaits them under their course of action men have changed and repented and the calamity has been averted. One can only suppose the great joy of the Father in such an outcome. Thus, in ancient times it is recorded that the Prophet Jonah went

[8]*Doctrine and Covenants* 3:1-4, 9, 16.

into the city of Nineveh and because of its excessive wickedness predicted its overthrow and destruction. But it is recorded that so vigorous were Jonah's words, so deep did they sink into the hearts of the people of Nineveh that the inhabitants repented and dressed in sackcloth and ashes. Because of their repentance the dire destruction was averted. One recalls that Jonah was disappointed, for having predicted the destruction, he felt that it should come to pass and that God had made him out a liar. Thus it was, that to teach Jonah a lesson, the Lord caused a gourd to grow and offer him shade as he sat upon the hillside. Jonah was grateful. But a worm ate its roots so that it withered and died and Jonah was sorry for the gourd. Then the Spirit of the Lord came upon him and the message of God sank deep in his heart. The Lord said in effect: You have been sorry for the gourd which thou didst not plant. How much more shall I the Lord be sorry for my children who are my own creation.

And Jonah perceived a lesson that should come to all mankind: that God is the Father of us all and that never at any time does He delight in the destruction of His children, but in His great wisdom and His eternal experience can and does foresee where the course of men may lead and makes known that fact unto men. It must ever be His hope that they will repent and avoid the calamity.

This great lesson was taught unto the ancient prophet, Enoch. In vision he beheld the flood that was so soon to engulf the earth, the dying cries and anguish of its inhabitants. Then he perceived the heavens weeping and said unto God: "How is it that the heavens weep?" and then the Lord said unto him:

"Behold these thy brethren; they are the workmanship of mine own hands, and I gave them their knowledge in the day that I created them; and in the Garden of Eden, gave I unto man his agency;

"And unto my brethren have I said, and also given commandments, that they should love one another, and that they should choose me, their Father; but behold they are without affection, and they hate their own blood ..

"But behold, their sins shall be upon the heads of their fathers; Satan shall be their father, and misery shall be their doom, and the whole heavens shall weep over them ... ; wherefore should not the heavens weep seeing these shall suffer?"[9]

This great message to Enoch is borne out by the realization that God, foreseeing the calamity of the flood, sought to save all His children from it and one hundred twenty years before the catastrophe occurred called Noah, who through his faith had caught the message of God, to warn the people of its coming that all might escape.

In like manner, a father seeing his own son following a downward course will urge him with all his power to turn back and avoid the pitfalls that inevitably lie ahead. Not only did the heavens weep when that early generation turned deaf ears to the warnings of their Father, but so must all righteous men and women feel sorrow whenever they perceive the calamities which men bring upon themselves.

From the above it must become apparent that two types of prophecy have existed from the beginning of time and these must be carefully distinguished if man is to understand God and his relationship to Him. In many periods of time and even in the present, individuals who fail to make this distinction, impugn God, giving Him a

---

[9]*Pearl of Great Price*, Moses 7:32-33, 37.

character which is harsh and cruel, making Him responsible for all the wars and calamities among His children and making it appear that it is His desire that these calamities come, all of which is contrary to the life and words of the Lord Jesus wherein He said: "It is not the will of your Father which is in heaven, that one of these little ones should perish,"[10] and also contrary to the teachings of the *Book of Mormon* wherein we read these beautiful words:

"Wherefore, all things which are good cometh of God; and that which is evil cometh of the devil; for the devil is an enemy unto God, and fighteth against Him continually, and inviteth and enticeth to sin, and to do that which is evil continually.

"But behold, that which is of God inviteth and enticeth to do good continually; wherefore, every thing which inviteth and enticeth to do good, and to love God, and to serve him, is inspired of God.

"Wherefore, take heed, my beloved brethren, that ye do not judge that which is evil to be of God, or that which is good and of God to be of the devil.

"For behold, my brethren, it is given unto you to judge, that ye may know good from evil; and the way to judge is as plain, that ye may know with a perfect knowledge, as the daylight is from the dark night.

"For behold, the Spirit of Christ is given to every man, that he may know good from evil; wherefore, I show unto you the way to judge; for everything which inviteth to do good, and to persuade to believe in Christ, is sent forth by the power and gift of Christ; wherefore ye may know with a perfect knowledge it is of God.

"But whatsoever thing persuadeth men to do evil, and believe not in Christ and deny him, and serve not God, then ye may know with a perfect knowledge it is of the devil; for after this manner doth the devil work, for he persuadeth no man to do good, no, not one; neither do his angels; neither do they who subject themselves unto him."[11]

There is nothing so disastrous to a faith in God as a failure to perceive that a God of intelligence may reveal unto man in advance both His plans for His children and the inevitable results where men persist in wickedness.

The Gift of Tongues

One of the most astonishing and misunderstood of the gifts of the Spirit is known as the gift of tongues. This gift rested upon the Apostles of the Lord Jesus on the day of Pentecost following the resurrection of their Master. Attending the feast at Jerusalem were Jews from various parts of the Mediterranean world. Some of these had no knowledge of Hebrew but spoke the tongue of the respective countries from whence they had come. Then the Apostles of Jesus began to preach with great vigor and these "multitudes came together, and were confounded, because that every man heard them speak in his own language.

"And they were all amazed, and marvelled, saying one to another, Behold are not all these which speak Galileans?

"And how hear we every man in our own tongue, wherein we were born?

"Parthians, and Medes, and Elamites, and the dwellers in Mesopotamia, and in Judea, and Cappadocia, in Pontus, and Asia,

"Phrygia, and Pamphylia, in Egypt, and in the parts of Libya about Cyrene, and strangers of Rome, Jews and proselytes,

"Cretes, and Arabians, we do hear them speak in our tongues the wonderful works of God."[12]

This gift was manifest in all the early church. Some in their ignorance overrated its importance or misunderstood its purpose. On that first day of Pentecost it had enabled the Apostles to carry the message burning in their own hearts into the hearts of others who could not have understood them in their native tongue. In aiding one

[10]Matthew 18:14.
[11]Moroni 7:12-17.
[12]Acts 2:7-11.

person to thus carry the Gospel to those of another tongue the gift is of paramount value. Many of Paul's contemporaries in the Church must have expected the Holy Ghost to manifest his power to them by the frequent manifestations of this gift. To the saints at Corinth Paul wrote:

"Now, brethren, if I come unto you speaking with tongues, what shall I profit you, except I shall speak to you either by revelation, or by knowledge, or by prophesying, or by doctrine?

"And even things without life giving sound, whether pipe or harp, except they give a distinction in the sounds, how shall it be known what is piped or harped?

"For if the trumpet give an uncertain sound, who shall prepare himself to the battle?

"So likewise ye, except ye utter by the tongue words easy to be understood, how shall it be known what is spoken? for ye shall speak into the air.

"There are, it may be, so many kinds of voices in the world, and none of them is without signification.

"Therefore if I know not the meaning of the voice, I shall be unto him that speaketh a barbarian, and he that speaketh shall be a barbarian unto me.

"Even so ye, forasmuch as ye are zealous of spiritual gifts, seek that ye may excel to the edifying of the church.

"Wherefore let him that speaketh in an unknown tongue pray that he may interpret.

"For if I pray in an unknown tongue, my spirit prayeth, but my understanding is unfruitful.

"What is it then? I will pray with the spirit, and I will pray with the understanding also; I will sing with the spirit, and I will sing with the understanding also.

"Else when thou shalt bless with the spirit, how shall he that occupieth the room of the unlearned say Amen at thy giving of thanks, seeing he understandeth not what thou sayest?

"For thou verily givest thanks well, but the other is not edified.

"I thank my God, I speak with tongues more than ye all:

"Yet in the church I had rather speak five words with my understanding, that by my voice I might teach others also, than ten thousand words in an unknown tongue."[13]

Just when the gift of speaking in tongues ceased in the early church is not our immediate problem. This gift was not found upon the earth when Joseph Smith went into the woods to pray. That the gift became manifest after the restoration of the priesthood and has continuously since been found to some degree in the Church is an evidence of the divine origin of the Church and a continuation of divine guidance.

This sudden and temporary ability to speak the tongue of those with whom we would converse is exemplified in our Church by the experience of Joseph F. Smith, a President of the Church who related:

"I believe in the gifts of the Holy Spirit unto men, but I do not want the gift of tongues, except when I need it. I needed the gift of tongues once, and the Lord gave it to me. I was in a foreign land, sent to preach the gospel to a people whose language I could not understand. Then I sought earnestly for the gift of tongues, and by this gift and by study, in a hundred days after landing upon those islands I could talk to the people in their language, as I now talk to you in my native tongue. This was the gift that was worthy of the gospel. There was a purpose in it. There was something in it to strengthen my faith, to encourage me and to help me in my ministry."[14]

The experience of Joseph F. Smith is one of hundreds of like nature and there is scarcely a Mormon community of any size in which some witnesses of this gift cannot be found, either to testify to their own exercise of the gift or to their having been present when the gift was manifest. This gift must not be confused with the meaningless babblings of individuals worked up to a religious frenzy or the outcrys so often heard in various denominational revival meetings. These latter have no value

---

[13]I Cor. 14:6-19.

[14]Joseph F. Smith, *Gospel Doctrine*, p. 201.

and convey no intelligence. In short, they lack all the earmarks of the true gift as found in the primitive church.

The true gift of tongues involves: First, the use of a definite language which is either well known by some of the inhabitants of the world today, or was well known at some period of man's history. Second, the language and words used will ordinarily be well known to the listeners, or at least one of them will have full understanding and can convey the meaning to the others. Third, the whole manifestation will be for a definite purpose. Usually, it is a means, and the only means, of a missionary's conveying his message to one of another tongue. It may, however, be a witness to a group who speak the same language of the presence of the Spirit of God. In both instances there is an intelligent message and in both the audience comes to full understanding. Further, the gift will be manifest without frenzy or excitement or physical contortions on the part of anyone, and in the broad light of day.

The Gift of Interpreting Tongues

A kindred gift to that of speaking in an unknown language is the gift or power which may come to one through the Spirit to understand the individual who speaks in an unknown tongue. This gift is spoken of as the "gift of interpretation of tongues."

In this latter-day dispensation of the Gospel it is well exemplified by the experience of Dr. Karl G. Maeser, second president of Brigham Young Academy.[15] Dr. Maeser was the first German

convert to the Church to be baptized in Saxony. He could not at the time speak English and President Franklin D. Richards, who had gone to Germany to be present at the first baptisms in Saxony, could speak no German. Dr. Maeser relates the following:

"On coming out of the water, I lifted both my hands to heaven and said, 'Father, if what I have done just now is pleasing unto Thee, give me a testimony, and what ever Thou shouldst require of my hands I shall do, even to the laying down of my life for this cause.

"There seemed to be no response to my fervent appeal, and we walked home together, President Richards and Elder Budge at the right and left of me, while the other men walked some distance behind us as not to attract attention. Our conversation was on the subject of the authority of the priesthood. Suddenly I stopped Elder Budge from interpreting the President's remarks to me as I understood them perfectly. I replied to him in German, and again the interpretation was not necessary, as I was also understood by the President. Thus we kept on conversing until we arrived at the point of separation, when the manifestation as suddenly ceased as it had come. It did not appear to be strange at all, while it lasted, but as soon as it stopped, I asked Brother Budge what that all meant, and received the answer that God had given me a testimony. For some time thereafter, whenever I conversed with President Richards in English, we could understand each other more readily than when I was conversing with others, or rather trying to converse, until my progress in the English language made the need of an interpreter unnecessary.

"This is the plain statement of the power of the Holy Spirit, manifested to me by the mercy of my Heavenly Father; the first of many manifestations I have had that have corroborated the sincere convictions of my soul that the Church of Jesus Christ of Latter-day Saints is of God and not of man."[16]

In the case of the interpretation of tongues, the Holy Ghost may be said to be the intermediary or interpreter, understanding what is said by the

---

[15] Warren W. Dusenberry, the first Principal, served from January, 1876, to April 15, 1876, when he resigned to engage in the practice of law. The Academy later became the Brigham Young University. See Bennion's *Mormonism and Education*, p. 148.

[16] Reinhard Maeser, *Karl G. Maeser*, pp. 24-25.

speaker and conveying that meaning into the heart of the listener.

Other Gifts of the Spirit

Besides the gifts treated above there are many gifts of God which may come to man. All true inspiration is a gift of the Spirit, and all revelation and knowledge which comes from God may be termed gifts of the Spirit. As the Apostle Paul stated, "the things of God knoweth no man, but the Spirit of God."[17]

The Nephite prophet, Moroni, wrote an enlightening message concerning the gifts of the Spirit:

"And when ye shall receive these things, I would exhort you that ye would ask God, the Eternal Father, in the name of Christ, if these things are not true; and if ye shall ask with a sincere heart, with real intent, having faith in Christ, he will manifest the truth of it unto you, by the power of the Holy Ghost.

"And by the power of the Holy Ghost ye may know the truth of all things.

"And whatsoever thing is good is just and true; wherefore, nothing that is good denieth the Christ, but acknowledgeth that he is.

"And ye may know that he is, by the power of the Holy Ghost; wherefore I would exhort you that ye deny not the power of God; for he worketh by power, according to the faith of the children of men, the same today and tomorrow, and forever.

"And again, I exhort you, my brethren, that ye deny not the gifts of God, for they are many; and they come from the same God. And there are different ways that these gifts are administered; but it is the same God who worketh all in all; and they are given by the manifestations of the Spirit of God unto men, to profit them.

"For behold, to one is given by the Spirit of God, that he may teach the word of wisdom;

"And to another, that he may teach the word of knowledge by the same Spirit;

"And to another exceeding great faith; and to another, the gifts of healing by the same Spirit;

"And again, to another, that he may work mighty miracles;

"And again, to another, that he may prophesy concerning all things;

"And again, to another, the beholding of angels and ministering spirits;

"And again, to another, all kinds of tongues;

"And again, to another, the interpretation of languages and of divers kinds of tongues.

"And all these gifts come by the Spirit of Christ; and they come unto every man severally, according as he will.

"And I would exhort you, my beloved brethren, that ye remember that every good gift cometh of Christ.

"And I would exhort you, my beloved brethren, that ye remember that he is the same yesterday, today, and forever, and that all these gifts of which I have spoken, which are spiritual, never will be done away, even as long as the world shall stand, only according to the unbelief of the children of men."[18]

Most of the greater gifts of the Spirit would be unknown to an observer but are quietly enjoyed by those who have believed and accepted the Gospel. Their enjoyment is the basis of true testimony. Indeed, we may say such testimony will continue so long and just so long as the gifts of the Spirit are enjoyed by Church members.

The various gifts of the Spirit are not usually manifest at the time of the laying on of hands for the gift of the Holy Ghost and will become manifest during the life of the individual only as the occasion arises and the proper faith is exercised. The Prophet Joseph said:

"There are several gifts mentioned here, yet which of them all could be known by an observer at the imposition of hands? The word of wisdom, and the word of knowledge, are as much gifts as any other, yet if a person possessed both of these gifts, or received them by the imposition of hands, who would know it? Another might receive the gift of faith, and they would be as ignorant of it. Or suppose a man had the gift of healing or power to work miracles, that would not then be known; it would require time and circumstances to call these gifts into operation. Suppose a man had the discerning of spirits, who would be the wiser for it? Or if he had the interpretation of tongues, unless someone spoke in an unknown tongue, he of course

---

[17]I Cor. 2:11.

[18]Moroni 10:4-19.

would have to be silent; there are only two gifts that could be made visible—the gift of tongues and the gift of prophecy. These are things that are the most talked about, and yet if a person spoke in an unknown tongue, according to Paul's testimony, he would be a barbarian to those present. They would say that it was gibberish; and if he prophesied they would call it nonsense. The gift of tongues is the smallest gift perhaps of the whole, and yet it is one that is the most sought after. . . . The greatest, the best, and the most useful gifts would be known nothing about by an observer."[19]

The manner in which the Holy Ghost may aid a member of Christ's Church depends upon the individual, his faith and his desires. All members should desire true knowledge of God, a testimony concerning the mission of His Son, Jesus Christ, comfort in times of sorrow, and guidance in meeting the great problems of life. Inasmuch as these gifts are sought in humility and righteousness they may be had in abundance.

Supplementary Readings

The Blessings of the Holy Spirit
Bible, I Corinthians 12:1-12.
Doctrine and Covenants 42:43-52; 84:65-72.
Book of Mormon, Moroni 10:3-19.
Karl G. Maeser, "My Conversion," *Improvement Era,* Vol. III, p. 25.
Cowley, *Wilford Woodruff,* pp. 103-107 (healing the sick).
Heber J. Grant, "Faith Promoting Incidents," *Improvement Era,* Vol. 30, p. 9 (Nov., 1926).
Joseph Smith, *History of the Church,* Vol. I, pp. 108-109.
Widtsoe, Osborne J. P., *The Restoration of the Gospel,* pp. 103-104. (Healings)
Pratt, Parley P., *Autobiography,* pp. 73 ff. (Healings)

---

[19]Joseph Fielding Smith, *Teachings of the Prophet Joseph Smith,* p. 246.

CHAPTER 48

MARRIAGE AND THE FAMILY

The Purpose of Earth Life

The Prophet himself taught that the most important and precious thing in the whole universe is the human soul. The development of personality, or the soul of man, is the chief purpose of life upon the earth. The Gospel of Jesus Christ as restored by the Prophet centers all values in life around man. The earth was created as a home for him, the Gospel was revealed for his benefit, the Son of God was sent to redeem him from death, and provisions were made for his continued existence beyond the grave.

This concept of the individual man, as being more important than physical things or political or social organizations, colors all the history of the Church. The growth of the individual soul has been an important subject of all the prophets. The Savior of mankind, while upon the earth, devoted His time to individuals rather than to political, social, or economic groups. This was done to the end that man might live more abundantly here and hereafter. The Prophet Lehi was thinking in terms of the individual and the eternal purpose of life when he said, "Men are that they might have joy." When we consider man as eternal, the spiritual offspring of Almighty God, we place him far above all other creations.

Once we adopt this view of man we have a basis from which to judge the value of social institutions and political and economic structures. Any institution which is conducive to the growth and progress of the individual is good. That which inhibits the development of the soul is evil. Even mechanical efficiency, if obtained at the price of individual growth, may, in the eternal scheme of things, be detrimental to man. The organization of the Church for lay leadership and the practice of calling all of the membership into some service results in much mediocre performance, but is conducive to the growth of all individuals, and this is the purpose of life.

The Family as a Suitable Environment for Personality Development

The proper development of personality requires an environment which will stimulate the exercise of the human will and which will prove a testing ground for human relationships. The family provides a remarkable environment for this purpose.

When we consider such attributes of our Father as love, kindness, patience, tolerance, forbearance, willingness to forgive, mercy, justice, and others, and desire to emulate them so as to taste in some measure the joy He must have, we find that we are dealing with qualities of the individual which cannot be given one to another, not even by God to man. They are qualities we must develop for ourselves. God has, however, placed us in an environment suitable to that development and has set before us both example and precept.

An individual enters this life utterly dependent upon other individuals for a continuation of life, and for subsequent guidance. Love grows with sacrifice. The sacrifice of a mother for her offspring in order to bring a soul into the world, painful as that sacrifice may be, is productive of good. It results in a burning mother love for the infant which links the two inseparably together. This is one of the roots of family life. But there is another. God has so created man and women that they have mutual need for each other, and normal men and women are never quite content without a mate. The union of man and woman and the union of parents and children link them all together in sacrifice and love. Because the roots of family life are basic to human existence, the institution of the family has continued wherever man has lived, and can never be fully eliminated from society.

Marriage is considered by a great many people as merely a civil contract or agreement between a man and a woman that they will live together in the marriage relation. It is, in fact, an eternal principle upon which the very existence of mankind depends. The Lord gave this law to man in the very beginning of the world as a part of the Gospel law, and the first marriage was to endure forever. According to the law of the Lord every marriage should endure forever. If all mankind would marry in strict obedience to the Gospel and in that love which is begotten by the Spirit of the Lord, all marriages would be eternal; divorce would be unknown.

Divorce is not a part of the Gospel plan and has been introduced because of the hardness of heart and unbelief of the people. When the Pharisees tempted Christ, saying: "Is it lawful for a man to put away his wife for every cause?" He answered them: "Have ye not read, that he which made them at the beginning made them male and female, And said, For this cause shall a man leave father and mother, and shall cleave to his wife: and they twain shall be one flesh? Wherefore they are no more twain, but one flesh. What therefore God has joined together, let not man put asunder." Then when they asked why Moses permitted divorce, the answer of the Lord was: "Moses because of the hardness of your hearts suffered you to put away your wives: but from the beginning it was not so."[1]

The Church of Jesus Christ of Latter-day Saints, being concerned with the growth of its members, fosters and encourages marriage, teaching that all individuals who are mentally and physically able to beget sound bodies should enter into the marriage state and become parents. Concerning this the Prophet Joseph received by revelation in March, 1831, the following:

"And again, verily I say unto you, that who so forbiddeth to marry is not ordained of God, for marriage is ordained of God unto man.

"Wherefore, it is lawful that he should have one wife, and they twain shall be one flesh, and all this that the earth might answer the end of its creation."[2]

The sanctity of the home and the values of parenthood can only be preserved where marriage laws are upheld and enforced by society and the improper relationships of the sexes aside from the marriage vow censured and punished. Immoral acts on the part of man or woman destroy the mutual bonds of love and respect which are possible eternal values of family life.

The Church of Jesus Christ of Latter-day Saints recognizes as legally and

---

[1]Matt. 19:3-8; see also Smith, Joseph Fielding, *The Way to Perfection*, pp. 240-41.
[2]*Doctrine and Covenants* 49:15-16.

lawfully wedded any couple who have in sincerity of heart complied with the marriage requirements of the state or country or tribe where the union of individuals has taken place. For wherever marriage is entered into by two individuals with full honesty of purpose, with a desire to cleave unto each other and none else, and those desires continue, the development of the soul will take place. Love and affection will grow and flourish, and the happiness intended by God for His children will be at least partially achieved.

Not all marriages result in a growth of the soul. Sometimes there are marriages without a mating. That is, the man and woman may have little or nothing in common. Their religion, their tastes, and their standards may be entirely different and friction results. The union which should have produced a growth of personality through the development of love, kindness, patience, sacrifice, and kindred virtues produces instead disgust, suspicion, and bitter disillusionment. Drunkenness, cruelty, desertion, and unfaithfulness to marriage vows destroy the chances for a happy home life and the growth of character that should result. Sometimes the coming of children to the home partially heals these breaches and a measure of love and devotion within the family unit may result.

Where the purposes of marriage are being wholly defeated by the faults of the two individuals involved and misery rather than happiness has become their incurable lot, a divorce is allowed by the Church. The Church recognizes the validity of divorces obtained according to the law of the land and the validity of subsequent marriages if any, but looks with disfavor upon the growing frequency of divorce as an indication of an unhealthy state of society and as contrary to the conditions which must prevail in the Kingdom of God. Especially does the Church decry the growing prevalence of divorce without real cause other than the attraction of one of the married couple for some other member of society or an unwillingness to face the responsibilities of establishing a home.

Unhappy home life can be avoided by Church members who marry in accordance with the desires of the Lord and in the manner which He has provided.

The Latter-day Saints look upon children as gifts from God committed to our parental care, and for whom we will be held strictly accountable.

"The family institution comprises more than the wedded union of husband and wife with its moral obligations and responsibilities, for the status of parenthood is the flower of family existence, while marriage was but the bud. Under the revealed law parents are as truly answerable to God for the adequate discharge of duty to their children as for the faithful performance of the marriage covenant respecting themselves. Within the family established and maintained according to the word of God, man and woman find their holiest and most ennobling happiness. Individual development —the education of the soul for which earth life has been provided—is incomplete without the impelling and restraining influences incident to the responsibility of the wedded and parental state."[3]

Temple Marriages

Marriage Ordained of God

The Lord has declared that marriage is a sacred institution and while marriages performed according to the law of the land are recognized for this life

---

[3] James E. Talmage, *Sunday Night Talks*, pp. 456-457.

and are productive of good, it is God's desire that His children should seek His holy blessing upon their union. This blessing of our Father in Heaven is given in His stead by men holding power and authority from Him for this purpose and is performed in a holy house or temple. When the conditions and requirements of marriage decreed by our Father in Heaven are complied with, our marriage is recognized in His Kingdom. As His Kingdom endureth forever, even in the life beyond this, so the marriage is recognized forever and the covenant entered into becomes an eternal and everlasting covenant. This is a reasonable doctrine. A marriage in a political state must conform to the laws of the state, or it is not recognized, and the attempted union is punishable. If a marriage is to be recognized in the Kingdom of God it must conform to the requirements of that Kingdom. The Lord made this law clear unto His people in the following words:

". . . If a man marry a wife, and make a covenant with her for time and for all eternity, if that covenant is not by me or by my word, which is my law, and is not sealed by the Holy Spirit of promise, through him whom I have anointed and appointed unto this power, then it is not valid neither of force when they are out of this world, because they are not joined by me, saith the Lord, neither by my word; when they are out of the world it cannot be received there, because the angels and the gods are appointed there, by whom they cannot pass; they cannot therefore inherit my glory; for my house is a house of order, saith the Lord God."[4]

Requirements for Marriage in God's Kingdom

What are the requirements for marriage in the Kingdom of God? *First,* faithful membership in the Church so that the man and woman may be recommended to the house of the Lord by those in authority over them. *Second,* the young man must have fitted himself and accepted the call to service in the Holy Melchizedek Priesthood. *Third,* the young man and woman must have both previously entered into the covenants of the endowment ordinance. This ordinance acquaints individuals with the purposes of God in His dealing with His children, with His plan for their development and happiness, with the eternity of life and the great blessings which await those who prepare for them. Above all, so far as preparation for marriage is concerned, the ordinance acquaints the individuals with the sacredness of the marriage relationship, the possible permanence of family ties beyond this life, and the possibility of Godhood which awaits those whose marriage is recognized by the Lord in His Kingdom.[5]

The endowment, while required of those who wish marriage in the temple, is not a part of the marriage ceremony and may be entered into long before marriage or even by those who do not at the time contemplate marriage.

Those who are married by God, through His Holy Priesthood, in accordance with the requirements of His Kingdom, must also comply with the requirements of the civil state wherein the couple live. This is necessary for a legal marriage and the protection of property rights. In most states, this requirement consists of the obtaining of a marriage license and the performance of a wedding ceremony by one authorized by the state. In practically all states and nations a ceremony performed by an administrative officer of

---

[4]*Doctrine and Covenants* 132:18.

[5]See *Doctrine and Covenants,* Section 132:19-21.

the Church such as a bishop, stake president, or one of the general authorities fulfills the civil requirements in this regard.

The Values of Temple Marriage

The values of temple marriage are many. Part of them are realized during this life; part in the existence yet to come.

Considered from the light of the results in this life alone temple marriages prove a blessing to the Church membership. The result of such marriages is happier home life. Perhaps the best index to happy home life, in a church which allows divorces, is the low percentage of divorces which occur. Every divorce means an unhappy home. Hence a low percentage of divorces is indicative of a happy home conditions.[6]

Among Latter-day Saints the divorce rate among those married in the temple is practically negligible (one out of 55), while the divorce rate of those married outside the temple is many times higher (one out of twelve), but less than the prevailing rate among non-Mormons in the same area, (one out of seven).

The low divorce rate among those married in Latter-day Saints temples may be attributed to several factors: *First*, marriage becomes a significant

[6]Note: It must be remembered, however, that the difficulty of obtaining a divorce has a deterrent effect upon the number of people seeking them, even where unhappy home life exists. In some states divorces are almost impossible to obtain, and in such states the divorce rate is hardly an indication of happy or unhappy home life.

Marriage for eternity, a blessing to be obtained only in the temples of The Church of Jesus Christ of Latter-day Saints.

covenant held sacred by God, our Father. *Second*, the holiness of the house in which the marriage takes place gives force to the covenants entered into and creates a deep desire to keep them. *Third*, the blessings promised concerning the hereafter to those who abide by the marriage covenant causes man and wife to overlook petty quarrels and minor differences and consciously seek to promote happy family life so that the eternal blessings might be obtained. *Fourth*, the approval of God for the marriage and His blessing through His authorized servants upon the married couple has a steadying effect throughout their lives. *Fifth*, the requirements before people may enter the temple for marriage and the recommend of character which they must present to the temple authorities prevent hasty and ill-considered marriages, guarantee equal moral and religious standards, and bring about a mutual respect of the man and woman rarely attained elsewhere.

The values of a temple marriage are high when we consider the future existence of man. The first value is a continuation of the married state in that future existence and the possibility of having children there. Concerning this the Prophet Joseph Smith said:

"Except a man and his wife enter into an everlasting covenant and be married for eternity, while in this probation, by the power and authority of the Holy Priesthood, they will cease to increase when they die; that is, they will not have any children after the resurrection. But those who are married by the power and authority of the Priesthood in this life, and continue without committing the sin against the Holy Ghost, will continue to increase and have children in the celestial glory. The unpardonable sin is to shed innocent blood, or be accessory thereto. All other sins will be visited with judgement in the flesh, and the spirit being delivered to the buffetings of Satan until the day of the Lord Jesus. . . . In the celestial glory there are three heavens or degrees; And in order to obtain the highest, a man must enter into this order of priesthood [meaning the new and everlasting covenant of marriage]; And if he does not, he cannot obtain it. He may enter into the other, but that is the end of his kingdom; he cannot have an increase."[7]

A second blessing is the promise of a resurrection, man and wife together, in the resurrection of the just. From the revelations we read:

"And again, verily I say unto you, if a man marry a wife by my word, which is my law, and by the new and everlasting covenant, and it is sealed unto them by the Holy Spirit of promise, by him who is anointed, unto whom I have appointed this power, and the keys of this priesthood; and it shall be said unto them—Ye shall came forth in the first resurrection; and if it be after the first resurrection, in the next resurrection; and shall inherit thrones, kingdoms, principalities, and powers, dominions, all heights and depths—then shall it be written in the Lamb's Book of Life that he shall commit no murder whereby to shed innocent blood, and if ye abide in my covenant, and commit no murder whereby to shed innocent blood, it shall be done unto them in all things whatsoever my servant hath put upon them, in time, and through all eternity, and shall be of full force when they are out of the world; and they shall pass by the angels, and the gods, which are set there, to their exaltation and glory in all things, as hath been sealed upon their heads, which glory shall be a fulness and a continuation of the seeds forever and ever.

"Then shall they be gods, because they have no end; therefore they shall be from everlasting to everlasting, because they continue; then shall they be above all, because all things are subject unto them. Then shall they be gods, because they have all power, and the angels are subject unto them."[8]

One could hardly ask a greater promise of God for those who obey His law of marriage. Although we cannot in this life realize in full the significance of these possible blessings, we can grasp

[7]*History of the Church*, Vol. V, pp. 391-392; *Doctrine and Covenants* 131.
[8]*Doctrine and Covenants* 132:19-20.

enough to cause us to have an earnest desire so to live that we may merit them.

When we consider the advantages of a temple marriage both in this life and in the life to come we become grateful unto our Father in Heaven for the restoration of His power and authority in the earth and the privilege of entering temples erected in His name.

Heirs of the Covenant

Not only does the covenant of marriage in the temple bring blessings to the husband and wife, but many of these blessings are had by their children born after such marriage. We say of such children that they are "born under the covenant" and are hence "covenant children" or "heirs of the covenant." As children born under the covenant of marriage in the civil state become heirs of the property and contracts rights of their parents, so children born of parents having a covenant with God become heirs of that covenant and are entitled to their share of the blessings which flow from it.

Sealing Children Born Before a Temple Marriage

Unfortunately, many marriages of Church members take place outside the temple. This may be because of a failure to understand and appreciate the advantages of a temple marriage, or because the great distance a couple lives from a temple renders it financially impossible for them to be married there. Whether the reason is a valid one or not, the temple is always open to them when they wish to comply or have opportunity to comply with the law of the Lord. Many parents converted to the Church desire marriage according

to God's laws, though they have been married for years under the civil law. Such parents may have children born of their civil marriage, who are legal children so far as this world is concerned, but whose relationship to their parents are not recognized in the Kingdom of God after this life.

To bring such children within the covenant with the Lord requires a sealing of such children to their parents. This sealing is done in the temple following the marriage ceremony. Through authority from the Father, men holding the Holy Priesthood seal these children to their father and mother so that they will be known as members of that family group throughout all eternity.[9]

The Permanence of Family Relations

As a family increases in size the love of its members reaches out to the new individuals, and the former members are in turn loved by the later arrivals. This love usually extends beyond the immediate generation. A father and mother not only love their sons or daughters but also the children of their sons and daughters. The original love of parenthood which produced the son or daughter likewise made possible the grandchild. And the grandchild, coming to sense the love of his mother and father for their parents, develops a love for his grandparents. This love grows as the result of service and sacrifices for one another within this enlarged family group.

The love within a family group, the members of which are bound together by kindred ties, is limited by the fact

[9]Children over eight years must be baptized before being sealed to parents. Children 21 years of age or over must have their own endowment before they can be sealed to their parents.

that only two or three generations may be living upon the earth at any given time. There are no immediate bonds with the generations that have gone and the generations yet to be. If all of the ancestors of a family, all of the present members, and all of the descendants of those now living could be brought together in one group, bound by common bonds of service and affection, the joy of the members of that family would be great indeed.

Do family ties continue beyond this life? Is there any way by which the present generation can win the love of generations long since dead and generations yet to be? The answer to both of these questions is in the affirmative. Where the laws of God are complied with the family will be preserved. But to preserve a family in name only is an empty shell. The members of the family, all of them, though they extend over the centuries in mortality, must be bound together in love for the greatest value to the family unit. As love develops with sacrifice, some such sacrifice and service for those who are gone and those who are yet to come must be made.

Salvation for the Dead

How can the living do a service for the dead? Very frequently we have an opportunity to do a service at our place of residence for a person who is in another city and cannot do the particular task himself. The result is a lasting bond between us and the person benefiting from the service. A bond can develop in this manner between two people who have never seen each other.

By the design of the Almighty we have been placed in a world where service to one another is necessary and easy, otherwise no ties of fellowship would ever develop. If, then, there is some service which we can render to our kindred dead for which they will be grateful, we can establish a lasting fellowship with them. The possibility of service to our kindred dead is a part of God's plan.

We are all aware that billions of individuals have died without hearing the Gospel of Jesus Christ and hundreds of millions more have heard it only in part but have had no opportunity of accepting its ordinances administered by individuals holding actual authority from God. Concerning such individuals the Prophet Joseph said,

"To say that the heathens would be damned because they did not believe the gospel would be preposterous, and to say that the Jews would all be damned that do not believe in Jesus would be equally absurd; for 'how can they believe on Him of whom they have not heard, and how can they hear without a preacher, and how can he preach except he be sent;' consequently neither Jew nor heathen can be culpable* for rejecting the conflicting opinions of sectarianism, nor for rejecting any testimony but that which is sent of God, for as the preacher cannot preach except he be sent, so the hearer cannot believe without he hear a 'sent' preacher and cannot be condemned for what he has not heard, and being without law, will be judged without law.

"When speaking about the blessings pertaining to the Gospel, and the consequences connected with disobedience to the requirements, we are frequently asked the question, What has become of our fathers? Will they all be damned for not obeying the gospel, when they never heard it? Certainly not. But they will possess the same privilege that we here enjoy, through the medium of the everlasting priesthood, which not only administers on earth, but also in heaven, and the wise dispensations of the Great Jehovah."[10]

President Joseph F. Smith, a short time before his death, while pondering

---

*culpable—blameworthy.
[10]*History of the Church*, Vol. IV, p. 598.

over the mission of Jesus to the Spirits in prison during the time His body lay in the tomb, saw in vision the redemption of the dead. In recording the vision President Smith wrote,

"And as I wondered, my eyes were opened and my understanding quickened, and I perceived that the Lord [Jesus Christ] went not in person among the wicked and disobedient who had rejected the truth, to teach them; but behold from among the righteous he organized his forces and appointed messengers, clothed with power and authority, and commissioned them to go forth and carry the light of the gospel to them that were in darkness, *even to all the spirits of men. And thus was the gospel preached to the dead.* And the chosen messengers went forth to declare the acceptable day of the Lord, and proclaim liberty to the captives who were bound; even unto all who would repent of their sins and receive the gospel. Thus was the gospel preached to those who had died in their sins, without a knowledge of the truth, or in transgression, having rejected the prophets. These were taught faith in God, repentance from sin, vicarious baptism for the remission of sins, the gift of the Holy Ghost by the laying on of hands, and all other principles of the gospel that were necessary for them to know in order to qualify themselves that they might be judged according to men in the flesh, but live according to God in the spirit.

"And so it was made known among the dead, both small and great, the unrighteous as well as the faithful, that redemption had been wrought through the sacrifice of the Son of God upon the cross. Thus it was made known that our Redeemer spent His time during His sojourn in the world of spirits, instructing and preparing the faithful spirits of the prophets who had testified of Him in the flesh, that they might carry the message of redemption unto all the dead unto whom He could not go personally because of their rebellion and transgression, t h a t t h e y through the ministration of His servants might also hear His words."[11]

In the spirit world are many who are in bondage to their sins. That is, a consciousness of sins committed during earth life has come to them in the spirit world. The teaching of the Gospel to them there causes them to be unhappy in the presence of those whom they have wronged and shuts them out from the presence of God and His holy angels.[12] This consciousness of guilt is like unto a chain or bond which holds them in a state of unhappiness. Hence they are in bondage to their sins. These may hear and accept the Gospel in the spirit world, but how, we ask, may they rid themselves of the consciousness of their sins? How may they be redeemed? By exactly the same process by which we may be healed from such spiritual discomfiture in mortality and which has been previously discussed.[13] In short, they must repent and receive the full forgiveness of those who have been wronged and comply with all the requirements of the Gospel. But as we have previously seen, although an individual may come to recognize the wrong that he has committed, regrets his former actions, resolves to change his ways of living, and does so, and even though he asks the forgiveness of those who have been wronged, the breach is not healed, and the wrong cannot be forgotten until the forgiveness sought is received. All that the sinner can do by himself in this life, or any life, is not sufficient to restore him to a fellowship with those wronged. The law is as certain as the law of gravity, that except for the act of another there could never be a redemption from sin.

Laws of the Gospel Universal

God our Father has commissioned His Son, Jesus Christ, to teach His laws and commandments to the inhabitants of this earth. He has appointed His Beloved Son to judge the acts of His chil-

---

[11]Joseph F. Smith, "Vision of the Redemption of the Dead," *Gospel Doctrine*, p. 474.

[12]See Chapter 46 for previous discussion of sin and its effect upon our relationship with those wronged.

[13]See Chapter 46.

dren and their worthiness to inherit His eternal glories. Whom will the Son recommend unto the Father? Jesus Christ has answered this question from the beginning—those who obey the laws of the Gospel. What are the laws of the Gospel concerning the forgiveness of God? One seeking such forgiveness must have faith in the Lord and Savior Jesus Christ, repent of his sins, and be reborn of water, a son or daughter of Christ, as a token of a solemn covenant with God to keep His commandments. Having conformed to this law, the individual is ready to receive the Holy Ghost by the laying on of hands, nor can the Holy Ghost bring unto the individual that complete change of heart spoken of as the "baptism of fire" until these conditions have been met.

Those who have entered the spirit world without conforming to all of these requirements cannot hope to have the law changed in their behalf. Neither could the law be changed, for it is an eternal one.[14] Moreover these requirements open the way for eternal progress. To say that baptism by water is necessary for people in mortality, but should not be required of those who have entered the spirit world without it, would be to put a premium on delaying the time of repentance. Such a variance would make God a changeable God, a partial God, and a respecter of persons, and it would set at naught the Gospel for the redemption of man.

Although a person in the spirit world might come to have faith in the Lord and Savior Jesus Christ and might repent of his sins, yet he cannot be born of water there, for water belongs to the physical world from which he has

[14] (Note) Review Chapter 46 on the First Principles of the Gospel.

departed. Without the baptism in which he cannot participate, the Holy Ghost cannot be bestowed or the remission of his sins received. He must, therefore, remain forever in a consciousness of guilt, being unable to win the forgiveness of God. But God in His mercy prepared a way to satisfy the law and yet bring joy to His wayward children. Where the individual in the spirit world has done all that he can do to win the forgiveness of the Father and has shown himself desirous of being baptized by water and of receiving the Holy Ghost, God is willing to accept the actual physical baptism performed by one upon the earth for, and in behalf of, the individual who is in the spirit world.

It may seem strange, at first thought, that an act required of one person might be accepted when performed by another in his behalf and with his consent, but the practice of accepting work done by proxy is a very prevalent practice in society. For example, in nearly all stockholders' meetings of a corporation, a part of the voting is done by absentee stockholders by having a "proxy" vote in their stead. Yet no one questions the effectiveness of the vote. Taxes are paid to the state by "proxies" and automobile licenses may thus be obtained. Even marriage in some states can be performed by "proxy," as also the casting of votes at an election. In none of these instances would anyone say that because the various acts could not be performed by the individual directly affected that no act would be required at all, that the stockholders at the meeting could consider the particular stock voted without being voted, that the state would consider the taxes paid without actually being paid, or that the couple would be considered married without the ceremony, or that the vote could be counted without actually being cast.

God requires the physical performance of certain ordinances to be done in this mortal life, but will accept the mechanical part of the act for the dead when performed by a "proxy" upon the earth.

When we consider how the physical act of being baptized in the temple for one who is dead may complete the requirements of God for the forgiveness of that individual in the spirit world and release him from the bonds of sin which have prevented him from enjoying God's presence, we begin to realize his joy over our act of sacrifice. We begin also to appreciate something of the bond of love that has been developed, not only between us and the individual directly benefited, but also with those of his kindred who have taught him in the spirit world but have been unable to perform for him the necessary ordinances. We have further won the love of our Father in Heaven because we have kept His great commandment: "Thou shalt love the Lord, thy God, with all thy mind, might, and strength, and thy neighbor as thyself."

The natures of individuals do not change when they enter the spirit world. Those who have known and rejected the Gospel in earth life do not about-face in the spirit world and accept it. Concerning such individuals the Nephite Prophet Jacob said:

"But wo unto him that has the law given, yea, that has all the commandments of God, like unto us, and that transgresseth them, and that wasteth the days of his probation, for awful is his state!"[15]

The Prophet Alma, speaking to those

who had rejected the gospel after having known it, said:

"Yea, I would that ye would come forth and harden not your hearts any longer; for behold, now is the time and the day of your salvation; and therefore, if ye will repent and harden not your hearts, immediately shall the great plan of redemption be brought about unto you.

"For behold, this life is the time for men to prepare to meet God; yea, behold the day of this life is the day for men to perform their labors.

". . . For after this day of life, which is given us to prepare for eternity, behold, if we do not improve our time while in this life, then cometh the night of darkness wherein there can be no labor performed.

"Ye cannot say, when ye are brought to that awful crisis, that I will repent, that I will return to my God. Nay, ye cannot say this; for that same spirit which doth possess your bodies at the time that ye go out of this life, that same spirit will have power to possess your body in that eternal world.

"For behold, if ye have procrastinated the day of your repentance even until death, behold, ye have become subjected to the spirit of the devil, and he doth seal you his: therefore, the Spirit of the Lord hath withdrawn from you, and hath no place in you, and the devil hath all power over you; and this is the final state of the wicked."[16]

Endowment Work for the Dead

Baptism for the dead, as for the living, prepares the way for a release from the bondage of sin. It prepares the individual for entrance unashamed into God's Kingdom. For all such the Savior has won salvation from the consequences of their sins. The eternal joy, however, which the Lord has prepared for those who love Him comes as a result of growth within the kingdom and this growth follows obedience to the laws of the Kingdom. To bring an understanding of the Gospel plan to His children and to help them to keep His commandments, the Lord has established an ordinance in His holy temples

---

[15] 2 Nephi 9:27.

[16] Alma 34:31-35.

Baptistry of the Salt Lake Temple, where baptisms for the dead are performed.
Used by permission, First Presidency of the Church of Jesus Christ of Latter-day Saints

called the "endowment." The endowment ordinance exemplifies great Gospel principles, teaches the story of man and his relationship to God, instructs the recipient concerning the order and symbols of the Holy Priesthood, and makes known the great honor and glory which await those who faithfully keep their covenants with God. The endowment takes the individual through a symbolic growth into the Celestial Kingdom, binding him by covenant to keep the laws upon which such growth might be actually realized. To enter into these higher covenants with God, the man must hold the Holy Melchizedek Priesthood.

The dead as well as the living can profit by such covenants with the Lord. If the endowment was not done before death, it may be done by proxy in the temple by people still in the flesh. There must also be a baptism either by the dead for themselves while they were living upon the earth, or by the living for them after they have died.

In entering the endowment on behalf of one who is dead, the man or woman assumes the name of the member of his or her own sex for whom the work is being done during the entire ordinance, and the work is recorded. The educational value of the endowment cannot of course be transferred to the individual in the spirit world for whom the work is being done, but he can there receive instruction in these things from those in the spirit world who already have knowledge of them. The ordinance, however, like baptism, is an ordinance to be performed in mortality and cannot be performed in the spirit world. If the man who is dead did not hold the Holy Melchizedek Priesthood while upon the earth, it must be bestowed upon him by proxy in the temple before entrance into the regular endowment procedure.

As the number of our ancestors who have died without the Gospel greatly exceeds the number of living members in our families upon the earth, the work to be done in the temples is largely a work for our dead.

Sealings for the Dead

There remains one other important work which may be done in the temples for those who are dead—to seal family groups together so that the family relations will continue in the resurrection. This consists of a sealing, by proxy, of couples who were married under the civil law only, and the sealing of their children to them by proxies. This opens the way for eternal increase and growth toward Godhood.

It must be remembered that the law of free agency prevails throughout eternity, and work done in the temple for individuals in the spirit world does not deprive them of their agency. The dead may or may not accept the work done on earth in their behalf. If the work is rejected, it is as if the work had not been done at all, except for the personal growth which has come to the individual on earth through his sacrificial efforts and his contact with the environment of the temple. It is the hope of the Church that eventually the vast majority of mankind will desire to follow the principles and enter into the ordinances of the Gospel.

Supplementary Readings

Smith, Joseph Fielding, *The Way to Perfection*, pp. 155-162 (The Coming of Elijah).
Ibid., pp. 163-178 (Work for our dead and why).
Ibid., pp. 240-259 (The family in eternity).
Ibid., pp. 322-327 (Temple work in the Millennium).
Smith, Joseph F., *Gospel Doctrine*, pp. 272-281 (Marriage) ; 437-452 (Redemption of the dead) ; 469-476 (Work for the dead—vision of the redemption of the dead).
Talmage, James E., *Articles of Faith*, pp. 145-155 (Temple work for the dead).
Widtsoe, John A., *A Rational Theology*, pp. 125-129 (Temple work and marriage).
Doctrine and Covenants, Sections 131; 132.

APPENDIX

The Articles of Faith of The Church of Jesus Christ of Latter-day Saints[1]

1

We believe in God, the Eternal Father, and in His Son, Jesus Christ, and in the Holy Ghost.

2

We believe that men will be punished for their own sins, and not for Adam's transgression.

3

We believe that through the Atonement of Christ, all mankind may be saved, by obedience to the laws and ordinances of the Gospel.

4

We believe that the first principles and ordinances of the Gospel are: first, Faith in the Lord Jesus Christ; second, Repentance; third, Baptism by immersion for the remission of sins; fourth, Laying on of hands for the gift of the Holy Ghost.

5

We believe that a man must be called of God, by prophecy, and by the laying on of hands, by those who are in authority to preach the Gospel and administer in the ordinances thereof.

6

We believe in the same organization that existed in the Primitive Church, viz., apostles, prophets, pastors, teachers, evangelists, etc.

7

We believe in the gift of tongues, prophecy, revelation, visions, healing, interpretation of tongues, etc.

8

We believe the Bible to be the word of God as far as it is translated correctly; we also believe the Book of Mormon to be the word of God.

9

We believe all that God has revealed, all that He does now reveal, and we believe that He will yet reveal many great and important things pertaining to the Kingdom of God.

10

We believe in the literal gathering of Israel and in the restoration of the Ten Tribes; that Zion will be built upon this [the American] continent; that Christ will reign personally upon the earth; and, that the earth will be renewed and receive its paradisiacal glory.

11

We claim the privilege of worshiping Almighty God according to the dictates of our own conscience, and allow all men the same privilege, let them worship how, where, or what they may.

12

We believe in being subject to kings, presidents, rulers, and magistrates, in obeying, honoring, and sustaining the law.

13

We believe in being honest, true, chaste, benevolent, virtuous, and in doing good to all men; indeed, we may say that we follow the admonition of Paul—We believe all things, we hope all things, we have endured many things, and hope to be able to endure all things. If there is anything virtuous, lovely, or of good report or praiseworthy, we seek after these things. Joseph Smith.

The Kingdom of the Evil One[2]

If there is progression, there may also be retrogression; if there is good, there may be evil. Everything has its opposite.

Descending Beings

In a universe containing eternal, intelligent personalities possessing free agency, there may be beings who are in opposition to the general laws of progress. In fact, such opposing intelli-

---

[1] *Pearl of Great Price.* Writings of Joseph Smith, p. 60.

[2] From Widtsoe, *A Rational Theology*, pp. 83-86.

gent spirits or men have always and everywhere been found. Naturally, those who devote themselves to the opposition of law are waging a hopeless battle, and lose their strength as time goes on. Nevertheless, since many of them acquired great knowledge before they turned against the truth, they may long continue active in their opposition to righteousness. The final end of such beings is not known. As they are eternal, it is doubtful if they can ever fully destroy themselves. Nevertheless, as they oppose law, they will at last shrivel up and become as if they were not. Beings who would stand in the way of progress, also use the forces of the universe, as best they can, and must be considered, in the ordering of life, whether in or out of the earth.

The Devil

The number of descending spirits in the universe is not known. In fact, little is known about the whole matter which probably is for the good of man. The scant knowledge that we have comes largely from the account of the Great Council. One of the great spirits there present proposed to save men without the use of their free agency. When he and his numerous followers failed to secure the adoption of this plan, they left the Council, and set themselves thenceforth against the plan adopted by the majority. The leader in this rebellion was Lucifer, said to be a prince of the morning, who, undoubtedly, through much diligence, had acquired a high position among the spirits. Even those of high degree may fall. No man is sure of himself, unless from day to day he can keep the germ of opposition from settling within his breast.

Lucifer and his followers, who fell from the Great Council, are the devil and his angels, possessing definite wills and free agencies, who are still continuing the battle that originated in the heavens. The fundamental conception of eternalism, including eternal beings, make reasonable the existence of a personal devil, with personal agents, whose indestructible wills are used to oppose the Great Plan through adherence to which man entered upon his earth career.

Man and the Devil

If man wills not to be helped by God, he fails to receive the benefit of any divine assistance that may be tendered him. Even so, if the will of man is opposed to evil the devil has little or no power. It is only when man so wills that he may hear fully the voice of God; and it is only when man so wills that he listens to the message of the devil. There must be a surrender to God or to the devil, to participate in good or evil. The Lord sends His messages throughout the universe; so does the devil as far as his knowledge permits. However, the messages of the evil one need not be heard unless man so desires, and tunes his spirit to evil. In reality, therefore, a man who has command of himself does not need to fear the evil one. He is not a force that can work harm, unless man places himself under the subjection of evil; but, if the devil be allowed a hearing, he may become the master of the man, and lead him downward on the road to retrogression.

The Devil Subject to God

Though the free agency of man is

supreme with respect to himself, it must not interfere with the free agencies of others. This law provided by the Lord, the perfected intelligence, holds for all ascending or descending intelligent beings. Therefore, the devil, subject to God, is allowed to operate only within well-defined limits. He may suggest ways of iniquity, but he cannot force men to obey his evil designs. A man who sincerely desires to walk in righteousness need have no fear that the devil may force him into evil. That is not permitted.

By the knowledge of opposites, man may draw conclusions of far-reaching importance in his course of progression. The observation of the operations of the devil and his powers may, therefore, serve some good in setting up contrasts for man's guidance. This does not mean that it is necessary for man to commit evil to know truth. On the contrary, every rational impulse resents the thought that a man must know sin to know righteousness better. The will for righteousness is strengthened when temptation is overcome. Unfortunately, the works of the evil one may be plentifully observed in the world, among those who have forsaken the Great Plan and the path of progression.—[Chapter 15.]

Zion[3]

ARTICLE 10—We believe . . . that Zion will be built upon this [the American] continent; . . .

Two Gathering Places

Some of the passages quoted in connection with the dispersion and the subsequent gathering of Israel make reference to Jerusalem, which is to be re-established, and Zion, which is to be built. True, the latter name is in many cases used as a synonym of the first, owing to the fact that a certain hill within the Jerusalem of old was known specifically as Zion, or Mount Zion; and the name of a part is often used figuratively to designate the whole; but in other passages the separate and distinctive meaning of the terms is clear. The prophet Micah, "full of power by the Spirit of the Lord, and of judgment, and of might"[4] predicted the destruction of Jerusalem and its associated Zion, the former to "become heaps," and the latter to be "plowed as a field";[5] and then announced a new condition that is to exist in the last days, when another "mountain of the house of the Lord" is to be established, and this is to be called Zion.[6] The two places are mentioned separately in the prophecy: "For the law shall go forth of Zion, and the word of the Lord from Jerusalem."[7]

Joel adds this testimony regarding the two places from which the Lord shall rule over His people: "The Lord also shall roar out of Zion, and utter His voice from Jerusalem."[8] Zephaniah breaks forth into song, with the triumph of Israel as his theme, and apostrophizes the daughters of both cities: "Sing, O daughter of Zion; shout, O Israel; be glad and rejoice with all the heart, O daughter of Jerusalem." Then the prophet predicts separately of each place: "In that day it shall be said to Jerusalem, Fear thou not: and to Zion, Let not thine hands be slack."[9] Furthermore, Zechariah records the revealed will in this way: "And the

---

[3]Talmage, *Articles of Faith*, pp. 345-347.

[4]Micah 3:8.
[5]*Ibid.*, 3:12.
[6]*Ibid.*, 4:1.
[7]*Ibid.*, 4:2; Isa. 2:2-3.
[8]Joel 3:16.
[9]Zeph. 3:14-16.

Lord shall yet comfort Zion, and shall yet choose Jerusalem."[10]

When the people of the house of Jacob are prepared to receive the Redeemer as their rightful king, when the scattered sheep of Israel have been sufficiently humbled through suffering and sorrow to know and to follow their Shepherd, then, indeed, will He come to reign among them. Then a literal kingdom will be established, wide as the world, with the King of kings on the throne; and the two capitals of this mighty empire will be Jerusalem in the east and Zion in the west. Isaiah speaks of the glory of Christ's kingdom in the latter days, and ascribes separately to Zion and to Jerusalem the blessings of triumph:[11] "O Zion, that bringest good tidings, get thee up into the high mountain; O Jerusalem, that bringest good tidings, lift up thy voice with strength; lift it up, be not afraid; say unto the cities of Judah, Behold your God!"[12]

The Name "Zion" is used in several distinct senses. By derivation *Zion*, or as written by the Greeks, Sion, probably meant bright, or sunny; but this commonplace signification is lost in the deeper and more effecting meaning that the word as a name and title came to acquire. As stated, a particular hill within the site of the city of Jerusalem was called Zion. When David gained his victory over the Jebusites he captured and occupied the "stronghold of Zion," and named it the city of David.[13] "Zion" then is the name of a place; and it has been applied as follows:

1. To the hill itself, or Mount Zion, and, by extension of meaning, to Jerusalem.

2. To the location of the "mountain of the house of the Lord," which Micah predicts shall be established in the last days, distinct from Jerusalem. To these we may add another application of the name as made known through modern revelation, viz.:

3. To the City of Holiness, founded by Enoch, the seventh patriarch in descent from Adam, and called by him Zion.[14]

4. Yet another use of the term is to be noted—a metaphorical one—by which the Church of God is called Zion, comprising, according to the Lord's own definition, the pure in heart.[15]

The Millennium[16]

In connection with scriptural mention of Christ's reign on earth, a duration of a thousand years is frequently specified. While we cannot regard this as indicating a time limit to the Kingdoms' existence, or a measure of the Savior's administration of power, we are justified in the belief that the thousand years immediately following the establishment of the Kingdom are to be specially characterized, and so be different from both preceding and succeeding time. The gathering of Israel and the establishment of an earthly Zion are to be effected preparatory to His coming. His advent is to be marked by a destruction of the wicked, and by the inauguration of an era of peace. The Revelator saw the souls of the martyrs, and of other righteous men, in power, living and reigning with Christ a thousand years.[17] At the beginning of this period Satan is to be bound, "that he should deceive the na-

---

[10]Zech. 1:17; see also 2:7-12.
[11]Isa. 4:3, 4.
[12]Isa. 40:9.
[13]See 2 Sam. 5:6-7; see also 1 Kings 2:10, and 8:1.

[14]See *Pearl of Great Price*, Moses 7:18-21.
[15]See *Doctrine and Covenants* 97:21.
[16]Talmage, *Articles of Faith*, pp. 368-371.
[17]See Rev. 20:4; see also verse 6.

tions no more, till the thousand years should be fulfilled.[18] Certain of the dead are not to live again until the thousand years are past;[19] while the righteous "shall be priests of God and of Christ, and shall reign with him a thousand years."[20] Among the most ancient of revelations regarding the Millennium is that given to Enoch: "And it came to pass that Enoch saw the day of the coming of the Son of Man, in the last days, to dwell on the earth in righteousness for the space of a thousand years."[21]

It is evident, then, that in speaking of the Millennium we have to consider a definite period, with important events marking its beginning and its close, and conditions of unusual blessedness extending throughout. It will be a sabbatical era[22]—a thousand years of peace. Enmity between man and beast shall cease; the fierceness and venom of the brute creation shall be done away,[23] and love shall rule.[24] A new condition of affairs will prevail later, as was declared in the word of the Lord to Isaiah: "For, behold, I create new heavens and a new earth: and the former shall not be remembered, nor come into mind."[25]

Concerning the state of peace, prosperity, and duration of human life, characteristic of that period, we read: "There shall be no more thence an infant of days, nor an old man that hath not filled his days: for the child shall die an hundred years old; but the sinner being an hundred years old shall be accursed. And they shall build houses, and inhabit them; and they shall plant vineyards, and eat the fruit of them.

They shall not build, and another inhabit; they shall not plant, and another eat: for as the days of a tree are the days of my people, and mine elect shall long enjoy the work of their hands. They shall not labor in vain, nor bring forth for trouble; for they are the seed of the blessed of the Lord, and their offspring with them. And it shall come to pass, that before they call, I will answer; and while they are yet speaking, I will hear. The wolf and the lamb shall feed together, and the lion shall eat straw like the bullock; and dust shall be the serpent's meat. They shall not hurt nor destroy in all my holy mountain, saith the Lord."[26]

The Lord's voice is heard today declaring the same prophetic truths, as shown in the revelations touching the Millennium given in the present dispensation of the Church.[27] In 1831, He thus addressed the elders of His Church: "For the great Millennium, of which I have spoken by the mouth of my servants, shall come. For Satan shall be bound, and when he is loosed again he shall only reign for a little season, and then cometh the end of the earth."[28] On another occasion these words were spoken: "For I will reveal myself from heaven with power and great glory, with all the hosts thereof, and dwell in righteousness with men on earth a thousand years, and the wicked shall not stand. . . . And again, verily, verily, I say unto you that when the thousand years are ended, and men again begin to deny their God, then will I spare the earth but for a little season; And the end shall come."[29]

During the millennial period conditions will be propitious for righteous-

[18]Rev. 20:2, 3.
[19]*Ibid.*, 20:5.
[20]*Ibid.* 20:6.
[21]*Pearl of Great Price*, Moses 7:65.
[22]See *Doctrine and Covenants*, 77:12.
[23]See Isaiah 11:6-9; 65:25.
[24]Talmage, *Articles of Faith*, Appendix 20:2, 3.
[25]Isa. 65:17.

[26]Isa. 65:20-25.
[27]See *Doctrine and Covenants* 63:49-51.
[28]*Ibid.*, 43:30, 31.
[29]*Ibid.*, 29:11, 22, 23.

ness; Satan's power will be restrained; and men, relieved to some degree from temptation, will be mostly zealous in the service of their reigning Lord. Nevertheless, sin will not be wholly abolished, nor will death be banished; though children will live to reach maturity in the flesh, and then may be changed to a condition of immortality in the "twinkling of an eye."[30] Both mortal and immortal beings will tenant the earth, and communion with heavenly powers will be common. The Latter-day Saints believe that during the millennial era they will be privileged to continue the vicarious work for the dead, which constitutes so important and so characteristic a feature of their duty,[31] and that the facilities for direct communication with the heavens will enable them to carry on their labor of love without hindrance. When the thousand years are passed Satan will again be permitted to assert his power, and those who are not then numbered among the pure in heart will yield to his influence. But the liberty thus recovered by "the prince of the power of the air,"[32] will be of short duration; his final doom will speedily follow, and with him will go to the punishment that is everlasting, all who are his. Then the earth will pass to its celestial condition and become a fit abode for the glorified sons and daughters of our God.[33]

Christ's Second Coming Predicted and Signs Described: Biblical Prophecies[34]

The prophets of the Old Testament and those of *Book of Mormon* record

who lived and wrote before the era of Christ, had little to say regarding the second coming of the Lord, little indeed in comparison with their numerous and explicit predictions concerning His first advent. As they looked into the sky of futurity their vision was dazzled with the brilliancy of the meridian sun, and saw little of the glorious luminary beyond, whose proportions and radiance were reduced by distance. A few of them saw and so testified as the following passages show. The Psalmist sang:

"Our God shall come, and shall not keep silence: a fire shall devour before him, and it shall be very tempestuous round about him."[35]

These conditions did not attend the coming of the Babe of Bethlehem, and are yet future.

Isaiah cried:

"Say to them that are of a fearful heart, Be strong, fear not: behold, your God will come with vengeance, even God with a recompense; he will come and save you."[36]

Aside from the evident fact that these conditions were not characteristic of the first coming of Christ, the context of the prophet's words shows that he applied them to the last days, the time of restitution, the day of the "ransomed of the Lord," and of the triumph of Zion.[37] Again Isaiah spake:

"Behold, the Lord God will come with strong hand, and his arm shall rule for him: behold, his reward is with him, and his work before him."[38]

The prophet Enoch, who lived twenty centuries before the first of those words are given above, spoke with vigor on the subject. His teachings do not appear

---

[30]*Ibid.*, 63:50-51.
[31]Talmage, *Articles of Faith*, "Baptism for the Dead," Chap. 7.
[32]Eph. 2:2.
[33]See Talmage, *Jesus the Christ*, concluding part of Chapter 42, pp. 368-371.
[34]Talmage, *Articles of Faith*, pp. 357-363.

[35]Psalms 50:3.
[36]Isaiah 35:4.
[37]*Ibid.*, 35:5-10.
[38]*Ibid.*, 40:10.

under his own name in the Bible, though Jude, a New Testament writer, cites them.[39] From the writings of Moses we learn concerning the revelation given to Enoch:

"And the Lord said unto Enoch: As I live, even so will I come in the last days, in the days of wickedness and vengeance, to fulfil the oath which I have made unto you concerning the children of Noah."[40]

Jesus taught the disciples that His mission in the flesh was to be of short duration, and that He would come again to earth, for we find them inquiring in this wise:

"Tell us, when shall these things be? And what shall be the sign of thy coming, and of the end of the world?"[41]

In reply, our Lord detailed many of the signs of the latter times, the last and greatest of which He thus stated:

"And this gospel of the kingdom shall be preached in all the world for a witness unto all nations; and then shall the end come."[42]

With great clearness, Jesus spoke of the worldliness in which the children of men had continued to indulge, even to the eve of the deluge, and on the day of the fiery destruction which befell the Cities of the Plains, and added:

"Even thus shall it be in the day when the Son of Man is revealed."[43]

Another of our Lord's predictions concerning His second coming is as follows:

"And they [the disciples] asked him, saying, Master, but when shall these things be? and what sign will there be when these things shall come to pass? And he said, Take heed that ye be not deceived: for many shall come in my name, saying, I am Christ; and

the time draweth near: go ye not therefore after them. But when ye shall hear of wars and commotions, be not terrified: for these things must first come to pass; but the end is not by and by. Then said he unto them, Nations shall rise against nation, and kingdom against kingdom: And great earthquakes shall be in divers places, and famines, and pestilences; and fearful sights and great signs shall there be from heaven. But before all these, they shall lay their hands on you, and persecute you, delivering you up to the synagogues, and into prisons, being brought before kings and rulers for my name's sake. And it shall turn to you for a testimony. Settle it therefore in your hearts, not to meditate before what ye shall answer: For I will give you a mouth and wisdom, which all your adversaries shall not be able to gainsay nor resist. And ye shall be betrayed both by parents and brethren, and kinsfolks, and friends; and some of you shall they cause to be put to death. And ye shall be hated of all men for my name's sake. . . . And there shall be signs in the sun, and in the moon, and in the stars; and upon the earth distress of nations, with perplexity; the sea and the waves roaring; Men's hearts failing them for fear, and for looking after those things which are coming on earth: for the powers of heaven shall be shaken. And then shall they see the Son of Man coming in a cloud with power and great glory. And when these things begin to come to pass, then look up, and lift up your heads; for your redemption draweth nigh."[44]

Many of these dire predictions were realized at the destruction of Jerusalem; and the oft-quoted twenty-fourth chapter of Matthew undoubtedly has a double application—to the judgment brought upon Israel in the complete overthrow of the Jewish autonomy, and in the events now current immediately preceding the Lord's coming, when He shall take His rightful place as Ruler.

Again, by way of warning, the Lord said:

"Whosoever therefore shall be ashamed of me and of my words in this adulterous and sinful generation; of him also shall the

---

[39]See Jude 14; 15.
[40]*Pearl of Great Price*, Moses 7:60.
[41]Matt. 24:3. See *Jesus the Christ*, Chap. 32.
[42]*Ibid.*, 24:14.
[43]Luke 17:26-30. For exposition of "The Son of Man" see *Jesus the Christ*, p. 142; see also Chap. 32.

[44]Luke 21:7-28; see also Mark 13:14-26; Rev. 6:12-17; *Pearl of Great Price*, "Writings of Joseph Smith," Chap. 1. For more detailed treatment see *Jesus the Christ*, p. 32.

Son of man be ashamed, when he cometh in the glory of his Father with the holy angels."[45]

At the time of the ascension, as the apostles stood gazing into the firmament where a cloud had hidden the resurrected Lord from sight, they became aware of the presence of two visitants in white apparel, who said:

"Ye men of Galilee, why stand ye gazing up into heaven? this same Jesus, which is taken up from you into heaven, shall so come in like manner as ye have seen him go into heaven."[46]

Paul instructed the churches in the doctrines of Christ's second advent, and decribed the glory of His coming.[47] So also did others of the apostles.[48]

Among *Book of Mormon* prophecies concerning our present subject, it is sufficient to consider here the personal assurances of Christ at the time of His ministrations to the Nephites in His resurrected state. To the multitude He explained many matters, "even from the beginning until the time that he should come in his glory."[49] In promising the three disciples the desire of their hearts, which was that they might be spared in the flesh to continue the work of the ministry, the Lord said to them:

"Ye shall live to behold all the doings of the Father unto the children of men, even until all things be fulfilled according to the will of the Father, when I shall come in my glory with the powers of heaven."[50]

The word of modern revelation is no less sure regarding the appointed advent of the Redeemer. To servants, specially commissioned, instructions were given to this effect:

"Wherefore, be faithful, praying always, having your lamps trimmed and burning, and oil with you,[51] that you may be ready at the coming of the Bridegroom—For behold, verily, verily, I say unto you, that I come quickly."[52]

And further:

"Cry repentance unto a crooked and perverse generation, preparing the way of the Lord for his second coming. For behold, verily, I say unto you, the time is soon at hand that I shall come in a cloud with power and great glory."[53]

In a revelation to the people of the Church, March 7, 1831, the Lord speaks of the signs of His coming, and counsels diligence:

"Ye look and behold the fig-trees, and ye see them with your eyes, and ye say when they begin to shoot forth, and their leaves are yet tender, that summer is now nigh at hand; Even so it shall be in that day when they shall see all these things, then shall they know that the hour is nigh. And it shall come to pass that he that feareth me shall be looking forth for the great day of the Lord to come, even for the signs of the coming of the Son of Man. And they shall see signs and wonders, for they shall be shown forth in the heavens above, and in the earth beneath. And they shall behold blood, and fire, and vapors of smoke. And before the day of the Lord shall come, the sun shall be darkened, and the moon be turned into blood, and the stars fall from heaven. And the remnant shall be gathered unto this place; And then they shall look for me, and, behold, I will come; and they shall see me in the clouds of heaven, clothed with power and great glory, with all the holy angels; and he that watches not for me shall be cut off."[54]

A distinctive characteristic of the revelations given in the present dispensation, regarding the second coming of our Lord, is the emphatic and oft-

[45]Mark 8:38.
[46]Acts 1:11; see *Jesus the Christ*, p. 695.
[47]See I Thess. 4:16; II Thess. 1:7, 8; Heb. 9:28.
[48]See I Peter 4:13; I John 2:28, 3:2.
[49]3 Nephi 26:3; see also 25:5.
[50]*Ibid.*, 28:7; see also verse 8; see *Jesus the Christ*, Chap. 39.

[51]An allusion to the parable of the Ten Virgins; see Matt. 25:1-13.
[52]*Doctrine and Covenants* 33:17-18.
[53]*Ibid.*, 34:6-7.
[54]*Ibid.*, 45:37-44; see also verses 74, 75.

repeated declaration that the event is near at hand.[55] The call is, "Prepare ye, prepare ye, for that which is to come; for the Lord is nigh." Instead of the cry of one man in the wilderness of Judea, the voice of thousands is heard authoritatively warning the nations and inviting them to repent and flee to Zion for safety. The fig-tree is rapidly putting forth its leaves; the signs in heaven and earth are increasing; the great and dreadful day of the Lord is near.

The precise time of Christ's coming has not been known to man. By learning to comprehend the signs of the times, by watching the development of the work of God among the nations, and by noting the rapid fulfilment of significant prophecies, we may perceive the progressive evidence of the approaching event:

"But the hour and the day no man knoweth, neither the angels in heaven, nor shall they know until he comes."[56]

His coming will be a surprise to those who have ignored His warnings, and who have failed to watch. "As a thief in the night,"[57] will be the coming of the day of the Lord unto the wicked.

"Watch therefore, for ye know neither the day nor the hour wherein the Son of Man cometh."[58]—*The Articles of Faith*, pp. 357-363.

---

[55]See the numerous references in connection with *Doctrine and Covenants* 1:12; see *Jesus the Christ*, Chap. 42.

[56]*Doctrine and Covenants* 49:7.
[57]II Peter 3:10; I Thess. 5:2.
[58]Matt. 25:13. See also 24:42, 44; Mark 13:33; Luke 12:40; see *Jesus the Christ*, Chap. 42.

BIBLIOGRAPHY
(of works referred to in the text))

Basic References

Bible
Book of Mormon
Doctrine and Covenants
Pearl of Great Price

DOCTRINAL TREATISES

In the Realm of Quorum Activities. Supplement to Second Series, 1932.

Keeler, Joseph B., *Church Government*, Salt Lake City: Deseret News Press, 3rd edition, 1929.

Morris, Nephi L., *Prophecies of Joseph Smith and Their Fulfillment*, Salt Lake City: Deseret News Press, 1920.

Nelson, N. L., *Scientific Aspects of Mormonism.* New York: Knickerbocker Press, 1904.

Pratt, Parley P., *A Voice of Warning*, Salt Lake City: Deseret News Press, Reprint, 1920.

Reynolds, George, *Book of Abraham.* Salt Lake City: Deseret News, 1879.

Roberts, Brigham H., *Defense of the Faith.* Vol. I, Salt Lake City: Deseret News Press 1907.

...............*New Witness for God. Vols. I, II, III*; Salt Lake City: Deseret News Press, 1927.

...............*Mormon Doctrine of Deity.*

...............*The Seventy's Year Book, Deseret* News Press, 1908.

Smith, Joseph F., *Gospel Doctrine*, Salt Lake City: Deseret Book Company, 1939.

Smith, Joseph Fielding, *Teachings of the Prophet Joseph Smith.* Salt Lake City: Deseret Book Company, 1939.

...............*The Way to Perfection.* Salt Lake City: Deseret Book Co., 1936.

Stewart, Walker and McGavin, *Priesthood and Church Welfare.* Salt Lake City: Deseret News Press, 1938.

Talmage, James E., *Articles of Faith.* Salt Lake City: The Church of Jesus Christ of Latter-day Saints, 1968.

...............*Sunday Night Talks.* Salt Lake City: Deseret News Press, 1930.

...............*The House of the Lord.* Salt Lake City: Deseret Book Company, 1968.

...............*Vitality of Mormonism.* Boston: Gorham Press, 1919.

Widtsoe, John A., *A Rational Theology.* Salt Lake City: Deseret Book Co., 7th Ed., 1966.

...............*Priesthood and Church Government* Salt Lake City: Deseret Book Company, 1964.

...............*The Program of the Church.* L.D.S. Dept. of Education. Salt Lake City: Deseret News Press, 1936.

...............*Discourses of Brigham Young.* Salt Lake City: Deseret Book Company, 1954.

HISTORIES, CHRONOLOGIES, AND BIOGRAPHIES

A Brief History of the Church. Church Radio and Publicity Committee. Salt Lake City: Deseret News Press, 1936.

Alter, Cecil, *The History of Utah.* New York The American Historical Society, 1932.

Anderson, Edward H., *Young People's History of the Church.* Independence, Missouri: Zion's Printing and Publishing Co., 1925 Edition.

Anderson, Nephi, *A Young Folks History of the Church.* Salt Lake City: George Q. Cannon & Sons, 1900.

Bancroft, Hubert Howe, *History of Utah.* San Francisco: A. S. Bancroft & Co., 1889.

Bennion, M. Lynn, *Mormonism and Education.* Salt Lake City:Deseret News Press, 1939.

Berrett, William E., *The Restored Church*, Salt Lake City: Deseret News Press, Rev. Ed., 1940.

Brown, James, *Autobiography.* Salt Lake City: Deseret News

Cannon, George Q., *Life of Joseph Smith, the Prophet.* Salt Lake City: Deseret News Press, 1907.

Cowley, Matthias F., *Wilford Woodruff.* Salt Lake City: Deseret News Press, 1909.

Egan, Howard R., *Pioneering the West.* Salt Lake City: Skelton Publishing Company, 1917.

Evans, John Henry, *Charles Coulson Rich.* New York: MacMillan Co., 1936.

...............*Joseph Smith, An American Prophet.* New York: MacMillan Co., 1936.

...............*One Hundred Years of Mormonism,* Salt Lake City: Deseret News Press, 1905.

...............*The Heart of Mormonism.* Salt Lake City: Deseret News Press, 1930.

...............*The Message and Characters of the Book of Mormon.* Salt Lake City: Deseret News Press, 1929.

Gates, Susa Young, *Life of Brigham Young.* New York: MacMillan Co., 1930.

Gates, Susa Young, and Widtsoe, Leah B., *Life Story of Brigham Young.* New York: MacMillan Co., 1930.

Golder, Frank Alfred, *The Mormon Battalion*. New York: Century Press, 1928.

Hunter, Milton R., *Brigham Young, the Colonizer*. Salt Lake City: Deseret News Press, 1940.

...............*The Mormon and the American Frontier*, Salt Lake City: L. D. S. Dept. of Education, 1940.

L. D. S. Biographical Encyclopedia. Vols. I to IV. Salt Lake City: Deseret News Press 1901 ff.

Linford, James, *Liverpool Route*. Liverpool-London, 1855.

Little, James, *Jacob Hamblin*, Salt Lake City: Deseret News Press, 1909.

Merrill, Melvin Clarence, *Marriner Wood Merrill*, Salt Lake City: Deseret News Press, 1937.

McClintock, James H., *Mormon Settlements in Arizona*, Phoenix, Arizona: The Manufacturing Stationers, Inc., 1921.

Nibley, Preston, *Brigham Young, the Man and His Works*. Salt Lake City: Deseret News Press, 1936.

Olsen, Joseph William, *Biography of Erastus Snow*. Master's Thesis, MS. Salt Lake City: Church Historian's Library.

Pratt, Parley P., *Autobiography of Parley P. Pratt*, Salt Lake City: Deseret Book Company, Eighth Printing, 1970.

Richards, Claude, *J. Golden Kimball*. Salt Lake City: Deseret News Press. 1934.

Roberts, Brigham H., *A Comprehensive History of the Church*. 6 vols. Salt Lake City: The Church of Jesus Christ of Latter-day Saints, 1930.

...............*Life of John Taylor*. Salt Lake City: George Q. Cannon and Sons, 1892.

...............*Outlines of Ecclesiastical History*. Salt Lake City: Deseret News Press. 5th Ed., 1924.

...............*The Falling Away*. Salt Lake City: Deseret Book Company, 1931.

...............*The Mormon Battalion*. Salt Lake City: Deseret News Press, 1909.

Smith, Joseph Fielding, *Essentials in Church History*. Salt Lake City: Deseret News Press, 1922. 25th Edition (enlarged) 1972.

...............*Life of Joseph F. Smith*. Salt Lake City: Deseret News Press, 1938.

Smith, Lucy Mack, *History of Joseph Smith by His Mother Lucy Mack Smith*. Bookcraft, 1958.

Smith, Joseph Jr., *History of the Church*, Period I, Vols. I to VI, Salt Lake City: The Church of Jesus Christ of Latter-day Saints. 1966. (Documentary History of the Church.)

Snow, Eliza R., *Biography and Family Record of Lorenzo Snow*. Salt Lake City: Deseret Book Company, 1884.

Spencer, Clarissa Young, and Harmer, Mabel *One Who Was Valiant*. Caldwell, Idaho: The Caxton Printers, 1940.

Sweet, William Warren, *The Story of Religions in America*. New York City: Harper & Son, 1950.

Talmage, James E., *The Great Apostasy*. Salt Lake City: Deseret News Press, 1909.

...............*The Great Salt Lake, Past and Present*. Salt Lake City: 1900.

...............*Jesus the Christ*, Salt Lake City: The Church of Jesus Christ of Latter-day Saints, 35th Edition, 1963.

Tullidge, Edward W., *Women in Mormonism* New York: 1877.

...............*Life of Brigham Young*. New York: 1876.

Tyler, Daniel, *History of the Mormon Battalion*. Salt Lake City: Juvenile Instructor Press, 1885.

West, Franklin L., *Franklin Dewey Richards* Salt Lake City: Deseret News Press, 1924.

Widtsoe, Osborne J. P., *The Restoration of the Gospel*. Salt Lake City: Deseret News Press, 1912.

Whitney, Orson F., *History of Utah*. 4 vols. Salt Lake City: George Q. Cannon and Sons, 1892.

...............*Life of Heber C. Kimball*. Salt Lake City: Juvenile Instructor Press, 1888.

...............*Popular History of Utah*. Salt Lake City: Deseret News Press, 1916.

Woodruff, Wilford, *Leaves From My Journal*. Salt Lake City: Juvenile Instructor, 1881.

Young, Brigham, *History of Brigham Young*. Ms. 1858. (1844-1877.) Church Historian's Library, Salt Lake City.

...............*History of the Church*, Period 2, Apostolic Interregnum, Vol. VII, Salt Lake City: The Church of Jesus Christ of Latter-day Saints, 1966.

Young, John R., *Memoirs*. Salt Lake City: Deseret News Press, 1920.

JOURNALS AND RECORDS

Clayton, William, *Journal*. Salt Lake City: Deseret News Press, 1921.

Journal of Discourses. Liverpool, England: 1853.

Journal of History. (Published by Reorganized Church of Jesus Christ of Latter Day Saints, Independence, Missouri).

Conference Reports.

Far West Record.

Manuscript History of Brigham Young. Salt Lake City: Files of Church Historian's Office.

Woodruff, Wilford, *Journal*.

Documents, Published by the Missouri Legislature.

Little's Report to Brigham Young; Executive Document Number 60.

COMMENTARIES, DICTIONARIES, READY REFERENCES

Ready References, (Authors not given). Salt Lake City: 1887.

Reynolds, George, *Concordance of the Book of Mormon.* Salt Lake City: 1900.

................*Dictionary of the Book of Mormon.* Salt Lake City: 1891.

Richards, Franklin D., and Little, James A., *The Compendium.* Salt Lake City: 1882.

Rolapp, Henry H., *Two Thousand Gospel Quotations.* Salt Lake City: Deseret News Press, 1918.

Smith, Hyrum M., and Sjodahl, J. M., *Doctrine and Covenants Commentary.* Salt Lake City: Deseret News Press, 1923.

Widtsoe, John A., *Concordance of the Doctrine and Covenants.* Salt Lake City: Deseret News Press, 1906.

PERIODICALS AND PAMPHLETS

Clark, J. Reuben, Jr., *Church Welfare Plan.* Salt Lake City: 1939.

Deseret News (Church Section) Salt Lake City.

Improvement Era, The, Salt Lake City.

Messenger and Advocate, 1834.

Millennial Star, Vol. 14.

Pamphlets on *Church Welfare.* Issued by Church Welfare Committee.

Times and Seasons. 1844

Wayne Sentinel, March 18 and 26, 1930. (Original copies in the New York State Library, Albany, New York).

Westerner, The, Salt Lake City.

What Is the Church Welfare Plan? Salt Lake City: General Church Welfare Committee, 1939.

MISCELLANEOUS WRITINGS

Pratt, Parley P., *Millennium and Other Poems.* New York: 1839.

Pyper, George D., *Romance of An Old Playhouse,* Salt Lake City: Seagull Press, 1928.

Rich, Ben E., *Mr. Durant of Salt Lake City.* Chattanooga, Tenn., 1899.

Sjodahl, J. M., *An Introduction to the Study of the Book of Mormon.* Salt Lake City: Deseret News Press, 1927.

Spencer, Orson, *Letters.* Liverpool, England, 1866.

Scrapbook of Mormon Literature, Vols. I and II.

General Index

(All References are to Pages)

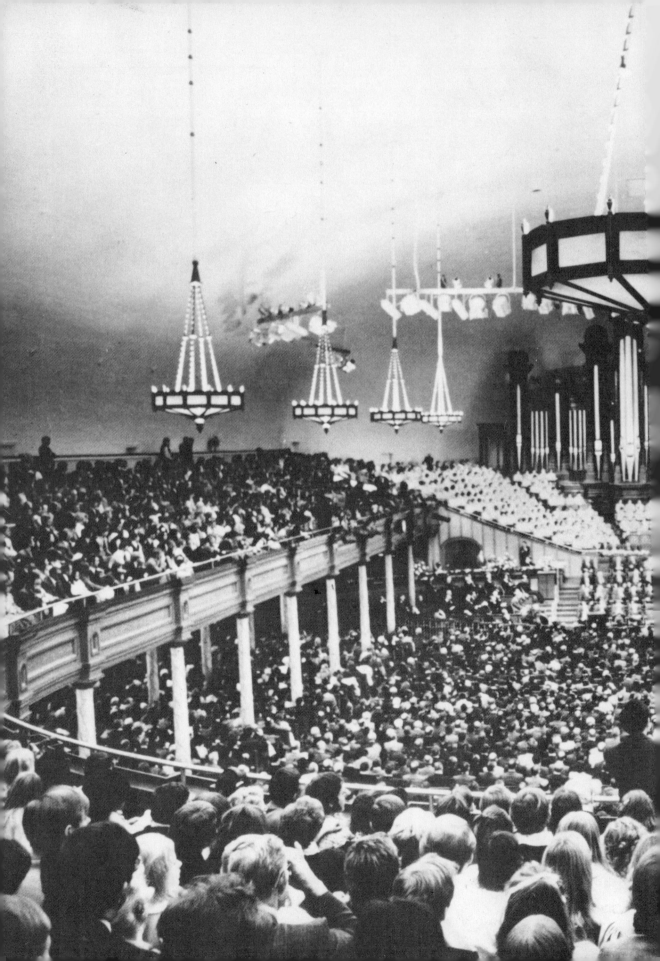